recounting minnesota

To David!
Just Shalom!
Wingler

recounting minnesota

blogging the al franken election saga

by

carl "winerev" eeman

edited by

J.B. Chimene, Jeff Cook, Kimberley Debus, Susan Hageness,
Pam Hystad, and Laura Tennen

with

Caroline Parks, John Tehans, Robert Pohl, Mike Blatt, Nancy Winningham,
and Irene Michelitsch

Mélange press
Round Lake, NY

Published by
Mélange Press
a division of Word Alchemy, Inc.
5 Albany Avenue
PO Box 696
Round Lake, NY 12151

Printed by Boyd Printing

Library of Congress Control Number: 2009931102

ISBN 978-0-9824337-1-3

Printed in Canada

Book design by Kimberley Debus
Cover design by Jeremey Bingham

Dedication

Dedicated to the author of the Constitution of the United States,

James Madison,

the defender of government of the People, by the People and for the People

Abraham Lincoln,

the 2,887,337 voters of Minnesota who voted for US Senator in 2008

and the thousands of poll workers across 87 counties, in 4,131 precincts,

who counted the ballots of the People

and re-counted the ballots

and challenged the ballots

and ruled on the ballots

and sued over the ballots

and opened the ballots of the absentees

so the People would rule themselves.

Supporters

The following people took a chance on a book that was not yet finished.
Thank you for your support.

Martin Aavik	Patrick Dodge	James Knockleby	Barb Ruehl
Christopher Allen	John Doty	Jack Knorst	Sharon Salzberg
Bil Alverson	James Dotzler	Julie Koehnen	Larry Seiler
Robert Anderson	J. Fenn Duncan	Mary Kolencik	Warren Senders
Anonymous in Alabama	Thomas Ebel	Kevin Kooiker	David Shannon
Lawrence Anthony	JK Eichenberger	Jim Wooten and Kris Prasad	Patricia Sheller
Tracy Bell	Rebecca Falkenberg	Lloyd Lachow	Alex Sherbuck
Wendy Berninger	Richard Fall	Jeremy Lamberth	Shirley Sherman
Greta Bickford	Mickiel Fedde	Cynthia Leichter	Sigma Plastronics, Inc
Jeremey Bingham	Bill Fersch	Ann Loper	Blaze Skinner
Michael Blatt	Andrew Fico	Mary Lundeen	Bonnie Sloane
Robert Blees	Linda Finder	Steven Maass	Joshua Slone
Charles Blocker	C David Fischer, Jr.	Donald Markham	David Smith
Adam Blomeke	Jonathon Fish	Diane Markin	Lee Spencer
DJ Bolger	Terri Foster	James Massar	Jared Stein
Devon Bond	Gadgets-Gizmos-n-More	Luke Maurer	Dave Steinheider
Alyce Bowers	Edward Garratt	Ryan McCleary	Christie Stoermer
Paul Brannigan	Robin Gates	Martha McIntosh	Craig Stone
Randy Bright	Charles Gaunce	William McLauchlan	Janet Stonecipher
David Brown	Mark Gebert	Laura McNerney	Rawson Stovall
Elizabeth Brown	John Gladden	Suzanne Melton	Andrew Teitelman
Pat Brown	Rick Goheen	David Minter	Kathleen Tibbetts
Karen Bunting	Maureen Goodyear	Tom Montag	Margaret Trehub
Alan Cameron	David Gormin	Brendan Montgomery	James Tunis
Matthew Campbell	Laura Graf	Jeremy Morgan	Larry Vanden Berg
Faith Chaplick	Scott Graupner	Amy Myrbo	Communitarian Visions
DT Clapp	Denise Grimshaw	Jeffrey Nelson	Steven Wagenseil
Ari Colin	Susan Hageness	Jeffrey Nibert	David Wagoner
Dave Comstock	Shelley Hamilton	Christina Nowacki	John Walden
Bill Conwell	Bonnie Harner	Michael Orban	Aaron Walker
Michael Conwell	William Harnsberger	Joy Osterberg	James Wamsley
Stephen Corrick	Donovan Hart	Theresa Ouellette	Clare Ward-Jenkins
Peter Coschigano	David Hearn	Anthony Pantuso	Cindy Ware
Andrew Cotton	John Hobbs	Craig Parker	Namon Washington
Mary Cowan	Lukas Hoffland	Adam Perryman	Frances Weightman
Lorna Crosby	Anne Hoffman	Dale Pfeiffer	Belinda West Burnore
Nora Daly	Christopher Holm	Richard Pierce	Bruce White
Roger Dalziel	Kirk Howe	Carla Purdy	Leslie Witterschein
John D'Ausilio	Jennifer Jorissen	Jason Reed	Leslie Wolfe
Shawn DeFrance	Robert Justin II	Kirstin Replogle	Gayla Wynn
Thomas DeStasio	Lynne Kelly	John Richardson	Yoomaki, GbR
Terri Diamantoukos	Roberta Kelm	Barbara Rikeu	Tracy Zullo
Greg Diamond	Anders Kierulf	Cathy Ritacco	

Foreword

It was a story for the ages: the closest Senate election contest in decades in a charged political environment, replete with lawyers, spinners, political hacks, clueless pundits, and enraged (and engaged) partisans. Kind of like Florida 2000.

But unlike Florida, technology had empowered a new generation of political enthusiasts to participate in the process, taking advantage of Minnesota's unparalleled openness and transparency to get cameras and reporters into chambers previously the domain of the elite. And via the web, countless others watched the proceedings evolve, step by step.

I remember my wife coming into the living room as I avidly stared at the computer and asking me what I was watching. "They're counting challenged ballots!" I might as well have answered, "Paint is drying!" as she rolled her eyes. But at TheUptake.org, they weren't just showing government officials reviewing the ballots, but also showing us the ballots so we could play along at home. Sure, it might the most bizarre game I ever played, but I was sucked in.

And I wasn't alone. Carl "WineRev" Eeman was also playing along at home, but rather than remain a spectator, he decided to chronicle the historic saga. The whole darn thing. Day in, day out. And while the Associated Press and local media ran their predictably dull copy, reducing the election contest into a boring bureaucratic process, Eeman infused his reports with so much personality and life they seemed to burst at the seams. Who said news reporting had to be dry? Impersonal? Devoid of life? With Eeman's reports, you got the facts, you laughed, you groaned. You might even learn a bit about post-war Baltic history and myriad other seemingly unrelated topics, yet his detours had a point — to entertain as he informed. At a time when the traditional news media is panicking over declining audiences, Eeman underscored why sites like Daily Kos are picking up much of that slack.

What Eeman did was true journalism, no matter what traditional media naysayers might derisively say about online citizen reporting. He offered first-hand reporting from the proceedings, quickly distilling the important points and cutting through the legal (and rhetorical) clutter to inform his quickly growing audience. He cited original documents and sources (ballots, administrative and judicial rulings, county demographics, etc) while other media outlets depended heavily on the political spin of the two parties.

But for Eeman, reporting the facts was just the foundation. Thousands of users provided additional insight, corrected errors, worked through difficult concepts, and, quite appropriately for a race involving a former comedian, cracked lots of jokes. What seemed like chaotic chatter was really a vibrant, organic working example of open source journalism, with the back-and-forth interplay between the various writers and commenters helping build the narratives that succinctly distilled an incredibly complex process into something understandable to the lay reader. I have no doubt that by the end of the whole saga, Daily Kos readers had a far better understanding of what went on in those Minnesota government buildings than readers of any traditional media outlet, and certainly readers of conservative news outlets that were too quick to revert to a "Franken is stealing the election" storyline in defiance of reality.

For all their strengths, sites like Daily Kos, with their massive flow of information, have one particular weakness – they aren't efficient repositories of archived information. Readers tend to live in the moment, and the sheer volume of information inadvertently fosters short-term memory. News cycles, once measured in days, are now measured in hours. Yesterday's news isn't just obsolete, it's forgotten, buried deep beneath subsequent events. So while WineRev could write the most brilliant overview of a particular day's events, that triumph was transitory at best.

That's why this book – yet another community-built and fueled project – is so important. Rather than let his work swirl down that memory hole, the finest has been captured in a medium that can best preserve it. And yes, even in these digital times, it's the analog book. Within these pages, you'll come to understand how a community, with WineRev leading the way, educated itself on the complex saga of the fiercely fought Minnesota Senate seat while, at the same time, clearly having a blast.

Markos Moulitsas
Publisher
Daily Kos

Acknowledgments

I never meant to write this book, just post a few stories of local color about a quick recount here in Minnesota... but things got a little out of hand.

Markos Moulitsas, founder and driving force behind DailyKos, kindly provided enough bandwidth to allow this endless stream of diaries grow to 300,000 words in raw form. He also added enough mainframes to reproduce the 400,000 words thousands of readers and commenters produced.

I am grateful to so many people who provided raw material for diaries: recount officials, the members of the State Canvassing Board, traditional and on-line reporters, and their websites. The Minneapolis StarTribune arrived faithfully every morning and reporters like von Sternberg, Lopez, Duchschere, Doyle, and Kaszuba struck me by turns lazy, informative, infuriating, silly and sharp, but as you can see, always stimulating. Rachel Stassen-Berger of the St. Paul Pioneer Press showed journalism still lives in traditional media. The MinnPost, the Minnesota Independent, the MN Progressive Project and MNPublius are all excellent New Media examples of where journalism might be headed in the new century. The merry band of citizen journalists at The UpTake, along with the insightfully side-splitting writers on their Live Blog, were a constant source of information, insight, analysis and creative good humor. Many of their words are included in these pages.

I offer special thanks to the campaigns of both Norm Coleman and Al Franken, particularly their attorneys. Beginning in January when the Recount moved to the courts Trimble, Knaak, Friedberg, Langdon, and even Ginsberg for Coleman, and Elias, Pentelovitch, Hamilton, and Lillehaug for Franken were a steady stream of words, maneuvers, motions, and legalities that provided more to write about.

I also offer my salute to Judges Hayden, Reilly and Marben who had to listen to both sets of attorneys with excruciating fairness and inexhaustible patience for seven weeks. They did so with magnificent aplomb and set a high example for judicial equanimity. The Justices of the Minnesota Supreme Court similarly showed brilliance, incisiveness and vigor and the attorneys before them strained themselves to their limits in arguing for their positions. Justice is a combination of law, mercy and wisdom and every member of the judiciary in this Recount showed the People how much they deserved to be on the bench.

The true heroes in this Recount are the thousands of ordinary citizens who spread out across the state on November 4 to open the polls and conduct the vote. The Secretary of State Mark Ritchie, the Deputy Secretary Jim Gelbmann and the elections director Gary Poser and those working for them insisted the election (and subsequent Recount) be fair, transparent to the public and meticulous in following the laws. Because of this focus and training and determination, Minnesotans can say to the Secretary's office, "Well done, good and faithful servants," and be confident in the results.

All these from the election and judicial systems provided their share of quotes, drama and opinion which made this book possible. But there were others, all volunteers mind you, who made this book readable: a crew of editors (nicknamed "the Amazons"): Caroline Parks, Pam Hystad and Laura Tennen, who pulled diaries off the Internet and cut them down carefully to a manageable 215,000 words. Other members of the DailyKos community stepped up to do copy editing: Jeffrey Cook, J.B. Chimene, and Sue Hageness, with an assist from Nancy Winningham and Barbara Ching. J.B. and Mike Blatt assembled a timeline out of the stream of writing. John Tehans made connections with the Franken campaign and gently prodded people to order early and order often. Jeremey Bingham offered his artistic talents for the front cover. Robert Pohl was the source and mind behind the work on the back jacket.

To all these people I owe great thanks and deep gratitude, and I will salute them in a moment, once I mention one more.

Riding herd on a project like this that by turns seemed impossible, unending, tedious... and then breakneck, exhausting, frustrating and gratifying, I cannot thank enough the people at Mélange Press, and publisher Kimberley Debus. Kim's patience, focus, dedication and gentle chiding and goading us all drove this effort through. While the judges in the Recount showed superb poise and patience, Kim lapped them all like Paavo Nurmi trotting home with the gold medal in the 5,000-meter to save his strength for the 10,000. Her unfailing good humor, her warm-hearted patience, unfailing vigor and utter dedication to seeing this mass of verbiage cut and polished into the book you hold was remarkable and inspiring. The words seem small but the heart is full: Thank you, Kim.

And to all of you who helped: who stopped by DailyKos and tipped, recommended, commented in these diaries, those who simply read them, those who helped in some way, small or large, to make this book possible:

WineRev rises and doffs (DOFFS!) his hat to all of you.

Note to Readers

When people started asking WineRev to turn this diary series into a book, way back in March of 2009, none of us had any idea the saga would draw out so long (245 days), with so many words (over 300,000 in the diaries alone, with another 400,000 in reader comments). In those hundreds of thousands of words are not only the content of the story but also the context: a state, a party, a country— frustrated and anxious, and yet highly amused.

Turning the Manhattan Yellow Pages-sized manuscript into the book you hold in your hands required a great deal of handwringing; how do we portray the immediate, raw feel of these near-daily diaries and still present an engaging page-turner? We think we came up with a suitable solution – some of which requires additional explanation.

1. We excluded most of the reader comments, short of the truly significant and those WineRev himself quoted in diaries. We agonized over this decision, since the interplay among Daily Kos members is a vital part of the online blogging experience. However, we believe you still get some of that experience without having to wade through pages of "this is great!" and "when will this be over?!?" We do, however, indicate comments from Daily Kos readers, also known as "Kossacks", with the initials DK next to them.

2. You will note that each entry begins with a tally of comments, recs, and tips:

   Comments are self-explanatory – you can see how some diaries generated more discussion than others (even if the discussion was about the proper way to speak Yoda or the best way to cook lutefisk).

   Recs – or Recommendations – are marks of approbation given to diaries by members of the site; it is an honor to have enough people recommend a diary that it appears on the "Rec List" – an honor that the WineRev diaries achieved quickly and consistently.

   Tips are a recognition of informative, profound, or humorous comments. We include these totals as a nod to the many members who commented, rec'd, and tipped; thanks for your support.

3. Some diaries have not been included; these diaries, by and large, were during times of waiting for courts to act. These diaries largely consisted of recaps, reviews, and conjecture – which, while interesting in the immediate, and certainly reminding us of the interminable sense of waiting, were, for the purposes of this book, repetitive. Others were deleted for Seinfeldian reasons: Simply put, they were about nothing, and we chose to delete them for the sake of narrative.

4. All of the quoted material is taken from various online sources, including both traditional and "new" media. Items quoted generally appeared in that morning's or the previous day's posts/ issues. Because of the transient nature of online architecture, web addresses for news articles are not included. Often, article-specific URLs change frequently or are deleted wholesale. To accomplish sufficient credit to the sources, we do note the source in general (aka "Star Tribune"). If you wish to read the specific articles in their entirety, we refer you to the list of our sources in Appendix B.

5. We are grateful to the fine folks at DailyKos, The UpTake, the MN Progressive Project, and the MN Independent for their support of this book and the content contained herein. We apologize in advance for any oversights or misattributions, which are purely accidental.

6. All court documents quoted in this book are located in PDF format at the Minnesota Judicial Branch website, mncourts.gov.

7. The nature of blogging also leads to quirks in language – abbreviations and shorthand that make the typing go faster. As much as possible, we have replaced abbreviations with actual words; however, you may run into some of the following:

BTW	by the way
DK, dKos	Daily Kos
ECC	Election Contest Court
FWIW	for what it's worth
IMO, IMHO	in my opinion, in my humble opinion
LOL	laughing out loud
MNSC, SC	Minnesota Supreme Court
MSM	Mainstream media
ROFL	rolling on the floor laughing
Strib, StarTrib	Star Tribune
TPM	Talking Points Memo

8. You will note that there is no index; we humbly submit a timeline instead, detailing events, non-events, and significant information.

Finally, we fully acknowledge the snarkiness of the writing; this book is unapologetically biased toward Senator Al Franken and a reality-based belief in the democratic process. Nicknames, criticisms, and out-and-out parodies are meant to expose the emperor's nakedness. And to make you laugh.

Kimberley Debus
Publisher
Mélange Press

Introduction

At 8:00pm on November 4, 2008, the polls closed in Minnesota, and election workers began counting the first of 2,887,337 ballots cast in the race for the United State Senate. The last votes of the election were officially counted 156 days later on April 7, 2009. In the closest Senate race in Minnesota history Democrat Al Franken edged Republican incumbent Norm Coleman by 312 votes, a margin of 0.014%. How firm is that 312 number? As firm, accurate, and legal as humanly possible.

No one imagined a statewide race could be this close – except for the Minnesota legislature of 1963, who had just seen a race for governor be decided by 91 votes. Having endured a six-month nightmare of court battles to determine the outcome, the legislature crafted a model law for settling close elections. At the end of 2008, their 45-year old handiwork was sorely tested for 156 days... and found to be strong, sturdy, and equal to the load with only a few minor flaws.

The race itself generated intense interest both in-state and nationwide. It attracted nearly $50 million around the country, which produced an immense barrage of media advertising. The tone, harshness, and bluntness of these ads were well beyond anything Minnesotans had ever seen. Some voters stayed home in disgust. Others voted for Independence Party candidate Dean Barkley (who scored 15% of the total votes cast) as a way of saying, "a pox on both your houses." Incessant polling showed Coleman and Franken swinging within the margin of error, both pivoting around 42% of the vote, both hoping they would be swinging up on election day. On November 4th, the voters proved the pollsters accurate – it was too close to call.

This story of what happened in those 156 days between the first and last ballot counted, as well as the 89 days that followed to the end of court proceedings, is from an Internet perspective called "blogging." In the early '00s internet fees fell to virtually zero, and people began putting up their own web sites and keeping public journals in electronic form. These were called "web logs," like a ship's log of events on board. Soon after the "web logs" in many cases became "diaries" – electronic, public diaries. Web logging a diary became "Blogging" (web log).

DailyKos is a web site for progressive politics, started by Markos Moulitsas in 2002. Over two-hundred thousand users are registered at DailyKos (the "o" is long if you want to be savvy) and daily traffic often tops a million views per day. It has become a model, a clearinghouse, a springboard, a meeting place, an electronic "Speaker's Corner" transposed from London to online. It has also become a force in American politics for everyone to the left of Rush Limbaugh, so about 91% of the country.

Stories, often political, often moderate or liberal, are posted as they break, think pieces emerge and online arguments occasionally erupt – all in the "diaries." As it occurs on Daily Kos, blogging is not journalism but it is often first with breaking news in raw form, a form of pre-journalism or citizen journalism. It is not lecturing but it is often immensely informative, as diaries cover a wide spectrum of thought and ideas. It is not a columnist's piece on the op-ed page but it is often opinionated. A diary may have a point of view (usually does in fact) but there is little attempt to hide that viewpoint so you'll know pretty quickly where a blogger stands on just about anything.

Again these are public diaries, open to comment, and here's where the fun and information begin. Imagine your last big, extended family get together – Thanksgiving dinner with ALL the relatives and then some. You look around the table and some of these people you love dearly and some you love because you have to. Some you haven't thought once about since last year's feed. Out in the kitchen where the teens and little people eat there may be a flat out stranger or two, someone's new boyfriend or girlfriend. And (unfortunately) there may be one or two people you can't stand.

After the blessings and the carving people are talking in all kind of parallel conversations. If you'd swing secret microphone over the table you'd pick up snatches: "...then Edna says to me, she says..." "...the Raider's linebackers are lousy, but better than the Cowboys' today..." "I love the way you make these beans..."

When you click "publish diary" it's for public consumption and comment. If you have something to say and say it well, a Thanksgiving Day dinner table-type conversation can ignite. Someone will comment, "By the way, correct spelling for 'a naturil" is actually "au naturelle." Someone else might comment "I was in Tulsa too in May of '93 (because the diary noted that) but the gas main in front of my house was at 2146 not 2136." A third person drops in: "I have to disagree with you about Lithuanian beekeeping. I have two Masters' in Lithuanian beekeeping and I've always found..."

Then this last comment might bring its own comment: "But the Polish beekeeping standards that hold in Lithuania clearly say that..." and they go off back and forth. Everyone else sort of stands back, like you did when your uncle Herman and your grandfather went at it between bites of mashed potatoes on the best fly-tying rigs for rainbow trout.

At its best, DailyKos is like that, often tuned to politics and also religion (you know, the two things not allowed at a lot of family dinners). Everyone across the political line is welcome BUT you need to be able to state your case and keep your cool. Name calling is out because then you get ignored. Being flat wrong about something can get you corrected or ignored. (At Thanksgiving dinner your aunt Gussie may still refer to black men of her age as "boy" or cousin Bill will seriously believe the "X Files" was a documentary. You can't call them on it and you can't walk out because you're staying in Gussie's guest bedroom. On line you CAN challenge and you CAN walk out.) Of course, when its a really big gathering you might find people eating in the kitchen, the family room or the den, and they have their own conversations rocking along. You'll notice in this book many quotes from the table marked "The UpTake" – a citizen journalism group that posts news online and has their own blogging strings.

It's this "Thanksgiving dinner" quality that makes blogging freewheeling, informative, immediate, and provocative all at once. Now fortunately for all the relatives in town, Thanksgiving dinner is only one day, one meal. You can put up with them that long. But it would be... daunting to even consider staying with these people for 7 solid months.

The Minnesota Senate Recount was like that. The only way to survive for 156 days with the same relatives was to keep talking and keep it light, and that's what the diaries were in this story. To get a sense of who came to dinner and stayed, allow me introduce you to the three guests and the host and then we'll move to the table for pie, whipped cream and the story.

Candidate Norman Bertram Coleman, b. August, 1949 Raised on Long Island and still carries the accent to prove it. Norm moved to Minnesota in the mid-1970s to work in the Minnesota Attorney General's office. He was first elected Mayor of St. Paul in 1993 as a Democrat, and in 1996 he managed Paul Wellstone's senate reelection campaign but left the Democratic Party and became a Republican. He was reelected mayor and served until 2002. He was the Republican nominee for governor in 1998, a race won by Reform Party candidate Jesse Ventura (the former wrestler). In 2002 Coleman was nominated to run for US Senate against Paul Wellstone who was seeking a third term. It was close down through October but Wellstone showed a small, consistent lead.

On Oct. 25, 2002, Wellstone and his wife Sheila were killed when their campaign plane crashed near Eveleth, MN. The Minnesota Democratic party leadership chose former senator and Vice President Walter Mondale to fill Wellstone's slot on the ballot. Wellstone's public memorial service a few days later turned political when Democrats were tarred with seeming to exploit the occasion for political gain. In this swirl of emotions on Election Day, Coleman defeated Mondale by 49,000 votes out of 2,250,000 cast.

(Between the Election Day announced totals and the final certified count several weeks later Coleman's total vote fell by 9,000. Mondale's rose by 16,000, a net swing of 25,000 but it was of no significance then. Coleman still won by almost 50,000. Six years later the irony of this swing would be deep.)

Coleman served on several committees: Foreign Relations, Agriculture, Small Business and Homeland Security. In June of 2006 as chair of the Senate Permanent subcommittee on Investigations he called George Galloway, a British Member of Parliament, as a witness to testify on the Food-for-Oil abuses by Saddam Hussein. Galloway turned the tables on Coleman and dismantled his questioning so vividly the Senator gained an unwanted reputation as ineffective.

On March 26, 2008 Coleman announced he would run for reelection.

Candidate Alan Stuart Franken, b. May, 1951 in New York but raised in St. Louis Park, a Minneapolis suburb. Franken could make people laugh and he was talented enough after graduating from Harvard to become a writer for NBC's Saturday Night Live for 15 years on and off starting in 1975. He had enough stage presence to gain a following as an entertainer with his trademark curly hair, glasses and gravely voice and then became an author. Through the 1990s he turned his humor to politics, aiming at the rising Republican right. (2 best sellers: Rush Limbaugh is a Big Fat Idiot, and Lies and the Lying Liars who Tell Them: A Fair and Balanced Look at the Right). Vocal conservative and FoxNews host Bill O'Reilly was so incensed by Lies he and Fox filed a libel suit against him. The judge declared the case "wholly without merit" and laughed Fox and O'Reilly out of court.

Franken moved into radio, Air America radio, a progressive answer to various conservative media empires (Clear Channel, Murdoch Group – Fox News, Scaife, etc.) Franken continued critiquing conservatives in the days of the Bush Ascendancy and articulating alternatives to conservative dogma.

In 2005 Franken moved back to Minnesota. On Feb. 14, 2007 Franken resigned from Air America and announced his candidacy for US senate from Minnesota, his first effort for elective office.

Candidate Dean Malcom Barkley, b. August, 1950, in Annandale, MN. Graduated U. MN in '68 and UMN Law school in '76. McGovern campaign worker, '72. Practiced law and worked for Dayton's Furniture. Founder & chair of MN Reform party (1992, Ross Perot's effort at the state level; later re-named the Independence Party). Ran for Congress ('92) and US Senate ('94 & '96) all as Reform party candidate. Campaign manager for Jesse Ventura's winning governor's race in '98. Appointed director of MN Strategic & Long Range Planning in MN government. Appointed by Ventura to serve out last 2 months of Wellstone's term in 2002.

MN Democrats in the summer of '07 approached Barkley to possibly run for Congress against incumbent Michele Bachmann (R), MN-6 on both the Independence and Democratic tickets. Instead, he entered the Senate race with Coleman and Franken in July of '08. One poll put him as high as 19% Oct. 1. He was part of the 5 debates held in the fall between the candidates. He raised $170,000 total (1% of either Franken or Coleman) and received 435,00 votes (15%). Its anybody's guess where Barkley's votes would have gone if he had not run; polling on this matter is contradictory.

Host and MN Secretary of State Mark Ritchie, b. 1951 in Georgia but grew up in Iowa, graduating from Iowa State in '71. From 1986 to 2006 he was president of the Institute for Agricultural and Trade Policy in Minneapolis, an advocacy group for rural communities. In 2006 Ritchie ousted incumbent Mary Kiffmeyer from her position as MN Secretary of State by a margin of over 100,000 votes. The post is the chief elections officer for the state. MN's long-standing reputation as a state with clean, transparent, fair elections, had eroded under Kiffmeyer. A capable, careful man Ritchie set about to restore Minnesota's reputation through careful training of election officials and stressing transparency in the process.

Now if you'd all take your seats and dig into your pie, here's how it began:

Minnesotans voted between Coleman, Franken and Barkley on November 4th. Mailed in absentee ballots numbered over 280,000, doubling the old record. Many were still being delivered from county seats to precincts far into the night on Nov. 4.

Despite thousands of votes yet unreported on Wednesday morning Nov. 5 Senator Coleman met the press. Unofficial news reports showed him leading state wide by 725 votes over Franken.

MN law requires an automatic hand recount of all ballots if the difference between candidates is under 0.5% of the total votes in a race. In this case that would be 14,000, so a recount would happen, with one legal exception, which Coleman proposed:

> "I recognize that because of my margin of victory, Mr. Franken has the right to pursue an official review of the election results," the Republican Senator said. "It is up to him whether such a step is worth the tax dollars it will take to conduct."
>
> If I were trailing, "I would step back," he added. "I just think the need for a healing process is so important [and] the possibility that any change magnitude is so remote." *(Minnesota Public Radio)*

Al Franken appeared to the press later in the morning:

> "We won't know for a little while who won the race, but at the end of the day we will know the voice of the electorate is clearly heard," Franken said. "This has been a long campaign, but it is going to be a little longer before we have a winner."
>
> "This is the closest Senate race in Minnesota history. This is just part of the process to make sure that every vote is counted fairly." If the recount confirms that he has come up short Franken said, "I'll be the first to congratulate Senator Coleman." (*Minnesota Public Radio*)

It would be Franken's last public statement until January 5, 2009. By the evening of November 5th Ritchie's office was reporting the margin between Coleman and Franken was down to 477.

On November 12, Al Franken's attorney David Lillehaug filed a motion in Ramsey county court for the county to release the names of voters who had cast their ballots absentee. (Required by law, but Ramsey was balking.)

The next morning in a third floor apartment St. Louis Park, I got up early and read the Minneapolis Star Tribune over coffee. They had a story about this court filing, and the shrinking margin, so I put them in summary form on my computer. I went to DailyKos, put in the summary and put a title on it, "MN-Sen Events v. 1.0" A count is usually not done but I figured this could go a few more days. I made it "point 0" so if something happened during the day that rated a sharp change or addition to my summary instead of posting a title of "Updated" I could just change it to 1.1.

And I clicked "publish diary."

...this one...

November 2008

Gearing Up for the Recount
November 13, 2008

Comments: 261   Recs: 473   Tips: 168

The Coleman-Franken recount state machinery is gearing up. Both sides are lining up lawyers for each of the 100+ recount sites (87 counties + multiple sites in larger cities).

Secretary of State is Mark Ritchie, a Democrat elected in 2006. He's taking heat from the usual suspects (the Katherine Harris/Ken Blackwell branch of American politics) but seems to be doing everything possible to be even-handed. The Coleman camp is miffed by this while the Frankenites (now there's a moniker!) are mostly keeping a Zen-like quiet.

Precincts and counties have been "certifying" their votes since Nov. 4: adding in absentee ballots, checking & correcting for math errors. During each day both candidates' numbers have moved up and down but the net has drifted toward Al Franken, from a Coleman lead of 775 to this morning's 206.

This morning's Minneapolis *Star Tribune* has a story by Patricia Lopez for upcoming events:

1. On Nov. 19 Sec. of State Ritchie will "certify" the results from across the state (that the count is as corrected as can be so far) This will certify that the difference between Coleman & Franken is less than 0.5% of the total votes cast, triggering an automatic, state-paid recount of all ballots. (Cost estimated = $86,000.)

2. County election boards, watched by observers & lawyers from each campaign, will recount each paper ballot (and they are all paper) by hand, including absentees.

3. Any ballot in dispute where there is some question of the voter's intent will be set aside and sent to the State Canvassing Board.

> By Dec. 16, Ritchie said, the Canvassing Board—which also includes Supreme Court Justice G. Barry Anderson, Ramsey County District Chief Judge Kathleen Gearin and Ramsey Assistant Chief Judge Edward Cleary—will start ruling on challenged ballots one by one, in favor of either Republican Sen. Norm Coleman or Democratic challenger Al Franken. Votes for other candidates will not be included in the recount, and ballots where no voter intent can be determined will be set aside. (*Star Tribune*)

Ritchie said that, however long it takes, the recount will not be rushed. Whatever is produced, he said, has to be "absolutely, exactly correct."

4. State Canvassing Board, named by Ritchie:

Mark Ritchie, Secretary of State, Minnesota. Chief elections officer.

Mark Ritchie

Eric Magnuson, Chief Justice, Minnesota Supreme Court. Appointed June 2008 by Governor Tim Pawlenty (R). Former head of Pawlenty's judicial appointment advisory board.

Eric Magnusun

Edward Cleary, Assistant Chief Judge, Ramsey County. Appointed 2002 by Gov. Ventura (Indep.—very independent). Prior: director, 5 years, state Office of Lawyers Profesional Responsibility. Public defender and private practice for 20 years.

Edward Cleary

G. Barry Anderson, Associate Justice, Minnesota Supreme Court. Appointed October 2004 by Pawlenty. Prior: Minnesota Court of Appeals [appointed 1998 by Gov. Arne Carlson (R-normal]. In 2006, state GOP endorsed him for election to bench and Anderson rejected the honor, saying "partisan political endorsements are neither appropriate nor helpful in maintaining an impartial judiciary."

G Barry Anderson

Kathleen Gearin, Chief Judge, Ramsey County. (Ramsey County is city of St. Paul, state capitol.) First elected 1986. Prior: 11 years as a county prosecutor, 4 years social studies teacher. *[Coleman campaign filed suit in her court on Saturday to block counting of 32 absentee ballots in Hennepin County (Minneapolis). Gearin dismissed suit in 6 hours, stating she did not have jurisdiction. Oddly enough, Coleman campaign has NOT re-filed in a Hennepin County court so far this week.]*

Kathleen Gearin

Standard will be "voter intent": Voter should fill in the dot (so machine can read). Instead, did voter put an X on the dot? Circle the candidate's name? Cross out candidate they did NOT want? If intent can be determined (at county level or by State Board), vote will be counted. Otherwise it will be set aside.

4. Finally: absentee ballots.

> One thing that won't change the Minnesota recount is any dispute over *rejected absentee ballots. (Emphasis added)* Ritchie said Wednesday that the Franken campaign's request last week to have 461 such ballots counted in Hennepin County can be resolved only in court, not by recount officials. *(Star Tribune)*

Sooo.......there still might be lawsuits (unless the trailing candidate chooses to "step back" – right, Norm?)

Some comments from readers:

DK First AK swings - next MN? I don't feel like I can get closure on the election until these recounts are completed - so thank you for helping feed my electoral addiction! I'm really hoping we pull it out in both AK and MN! *(awkward007)*

DK And that's what really pisses of Coleman and his like: Ritchie said that, however long it takes, the recount will not be rushed. Whatever is produced, he said, has to be "absolutely, exactly correct." Given the choice between "winning" and "correct", I'm sure a Republican would choose winning every time. *(frsbdg)*

DK Al's gone to court over the 461. Apparently he does know what's good for him, he's filed in court to get the voter lists for the rejected absentee ballots. *(puppethead)*

DK

I've met Ritchie a few times. He's as smart as they come, and a cool customer. They're not tangling with some Katherine Harris-like buffoon here.Of course the GOP has already started whining about how he's partisan and / or corrupt, but they have NO evidence to back it up except their usual lies.

P.S. Ritchie WILL certify a Norm Coleman win in a second, if and when the recount shows that result. There should be no doubt about that.But Coleman, Pawlenty, and the usual GOP smear artists started gaming this from the very start, painting anything other than a victory for Coleman as somehow illegitimate. They're shameless. *(chumley)*

DK

That's a bunch of crap. I'm on an elections board here in MN (getting ready to count like mad next week), and I can tell you without question there are no "missing truckloads" of ballots. This is a surprisingly secure and reliable process from my vantage point, but one thing I know for sure is that they know where the ballots are, and that the totals are going to match. They can gripe all they want, but I have a very good feeling about this process, and that it will be very difficult to poke holes in it, whichever way it turns out. I still believe Franken lost (gut - no other basis), but we'll see how it goes. It's just nice knowing that there is a secure and reliable vote trail that will reliably tell us what really happened one way or another. *(AmericanIdeal)*

Wait & see everybody, but this is the latest.

Shalom.

Recount Moves in the Counties
November 14, 2008

Comments; 12   Recs: 18   Tips: 27

Couldn't sleep, so up to help crack the dawn (should take about an hour) with some STRONG morning Joe (coffee, not Biden). The *Star Tribune* has landed outside the apartment door with Patricia Lopez's latest word on the Senate race.

At the secretary of state's office, preparations for the recount continued Thursday. The office provided an online training session for election officials across the state that covered issues ranging from how to organize the recount room to how to sort the ballots. After the session, [Secretary of State Mark] Ritchie told a reporter that his office was completely focused on the recount but that he was not surprised to see the fight already taken to court. *(Star Tribune)*

About 120 recount sites across the state (87 in each county seat + multiple locales in larger cities) have received instructions about transparency, disputes, and I imagine, security.

[The Coleman/Pawlenty camp has raised issues about "ballots riding in the back seat of a car." Ah, guys, those ballots have to be physically taken from the precinct to the county seat—in most cases—and how are they physically supposed to do that? Pony Express bag? Kangaroo pouch? Armored truck? Oh, and if the last, would you like to hire (and who would pay?) over 4000 armored trucks and their armed guards? Just asking.]

Myself, I would like to know if Ritchie told county election officials to think nasty about security. After all, suppose the recount is happening in downtown Bemidji at an unused storefront where anyone can look in through the plate-glass front window...public transparency. What's to stop a member of some "Army of God" (real American/fundy/Bachmann-lovin' dittohead Palinista) from aiming the old 1966 Ford pick-up with lots of gasoline cans in the bed at the front window, gunning the engine and bailing out on the sidewalk while the thing ignites—and burns up the ballots? Just asking.

And speaking of Bemidji, in a moment we come to the Beltrami County seat, to note the impact of a Twin Cities court ruling...

The Franken campaign filed suit yesterday over those 461 absentee ballots in Hennepin County (Minneapolis) rejected by the county. State law says ALL names of those who voted absentee can be released after the polls close on election day (although counties do not break these down into whose absentee was accepted and whose was rejected.) Hennepin and Ramsey (St. Paul) officials did not release the absentee names so Franken went to court to force it. Pending.

BUT the Franken campaign had apparently asked in Beltrami County and the folks there said, "Here you go." From there came the story of the 84-year-old woman, stroke victim, whose signatures did not match between registration and absentee.

Beltrami County Auditor Kay Mack disputed the story, sounding both upset and a bit hacked off. She did say they had in fact rejected the absentee of an 87-year-old woman in assisted living since her ballot had no signature or mark at all....one of 69 rejected absentee ballots out of the county total of 1918. ("No mark"! Just a stray line? Or leftover law from illiterate days when you either signed your name or made your mark?)

Franken campaign is backing off the 84-year-old story, still "digging for facts," and that this does not affect the Hennepin/Ramsey lawsuit.

Unclear why Hennepin & Ramsey are holding out.

Sec. of State Ritchie has no opinion on lawsuit since it concerns rejected absentee ballots, which by law are not in his jurisdiction but a court matter.

If court orders release of names, both campaigns will get them (and presumably go contact all the absentees to check stories). Coleman campaign has "grave concerns" such contact could lead to "harassment of said voters." Touching concern.

That's the news from yust southeast of Lake Wobegon.

Shalom.

Recount Moves & How we got here
November 15, 2008

Comments: 32   *Recs:* 26   *Tips:* 40

Nothing today on the *Star Tribune* front page... a complete and utter shock to political addicts and a sign that *some people* have lives outside of their parents' basement and actually change out of their pajamas from time to time.

Below is the executive summary of Brunswick and von Sternberg's long *Star Tribune* article:

1. Sec. of State Ritchie continues to get the state ready for the recount. The 5-member State Canvassing Board will meet as a body for the first time on Tuesday the 18th, review the county-by-county totals and brace themselves when Wednesday the 19th Ritchie certifies the results. As he will certify a less than 0.5% difference in the Senate race, the Recount machinery can officially start up.

2. Franken campaign's lawsuit to get Hennepin & Ramsey Counties to release names & addresses of rejected absentee ballots: filed, but no news from the court.

3. Gary Poser, chief election official in Ritchie's office, goes on record as advising *other counties* (i.e., the 85 remaining) to make such names & addresses public so anyone could have them. Coleman campaign sent Ritchie a letter raising "serious concerns" about Poser's stance (calling it: "identical to the Franken campaign").

4. A voter in Beltrami County admits he didn't sign the outer envelope of his absentee ballot (and county has rightly rejected it). Franken campaign has approached him to sign an affidavit that he wants his vote counted. Beltrami County officials are standing pat—and I think rightly so. The Frankenites should move on.

5. Pawlenty earlier in the week made some growls about ballot security (the now-debunked "ballots in the back seat of a car" story). Ritchie refused to badger back but thanks Pawlenty for his concerns and gave the gov. his personal cell phone number for any further issues. Pawlenty spokesman says gov. was "raising concerns" and appreciated Ritchie's "clarifications."

The op-ed page carries a retro story about the 1962 governor's race that ended election night with a difference of 133 between the 2 candidates. After 6 months the final diff. was settled at 91 votes and the new governor was sworn in. That fiasco led to creation of the current recount process that is gearing up now.

And what was it like in '62? A couple of bits:

> Some paper ballots had all sorts of markings, some had been used by election judges to keep score of various card games, others had coffee cup rings and various notes.
>
> Votes were being counted in the backwoods of northern Minnesota where there were no telephones. A snowstorm struck, delaying the reporting of the handful of ballots. A bush pilot flew the ballots out 3 days after the election. *(Star Tribune)*

And of course it wouldn't be politics without this sort of thing:

> There were charges of voting irregularities. Republicans claimed they knew of places in northern Minnesota where Canadians had voted. And (Democrats) charged possible irregularities at St. James, where ballots were removed from a sealed jail cell and almost hauled away to the dump. *(Star Tribune)*

(Nothing proved on either side.)

So that's the update from southeast of Lake Wobegon. I'll just put my Cleveland Browns coffee mug down here on this 8 x 11 coaster with the funny markings, "Minnesota Official Ballot..."

Shalom.

People of the Recount
November 16, 2008

Comments: 23	*Recs:* 30	*Tips:* 41

Well, this is turning into a little series, isn't it? But it's you, people, YOU. Some of my first diaries I agonized over word choices and struggled with embedding pix—and got some recommends and up to 30 comments. But a little 20-minute summary of Franken-Coleman: *Bam!* Rec list (!) and 200+ comments! All part of your collective plot to get me to start a series and keep writing. Alright—so be it. (And as the old wine cooler ads used to say, "Thank you for your support.")

Minneapolis *Star Tribune* puts Coleman-Franken "The Rematch" front page, top right, about 1/2 the page, and a full-page continuation on A18. Well if they can do it so can I.

Executive Highlights

Most of the main story is lots of little vignettes on the people volunteering across Minnesota to be part of the recount. What is incredibly heartwarming is how *determined* these people are to ensure a fair count and PROUD to volunteer to do their bit for the election process! One guy has worked 18-hour days for 10 months for Franken. He's going to help with the recount and is white-hot dedicated this count will be *clean*. These sons and daughters of Scandinavia may be a little stunted on the emotional side (I think its climate) but they are down the middle fair on all sorts of public/ civic matters. And all the immigrants that have come since (our local high school lists over 30 different languages spoken at students' homes) think clean government, fairness, and transparent elections are how things ought to be... and they're RIGHT!

DK

> I love my (former) big blue state. This exemplfies what is Minnesotan to me. No matter where I live, I'll always be a Minnesotan. *(Cecile)*

This interior decorator is a to-the-bitter-end Coleman backer and she feels the same way when it comes to a clean count.

> "We're really going to be in the nuts and bolts of an amazing process," said (Renee) Golinvaux, 43, the decorator and an ardent Coleman backer. She already knows some Franken observers on a first-name basis after recent post-election random precinct audits in Scott County, a dry run of what's to come.
>
> "We might want a different person in the end," Golinvaux said. "But we all have the same goal in mind: We want this to come to an end and be fair." *(Star Tribune)*

Lorraine Cecil, 79 going on 80, retired English teacher in Bemidji,

> said it's hard for some of her older friends to get out and vote, as well as for younger folks juggling school and work. So days of tedious ballot watching are the least she can do.
>
> "I'm not sure boring is a term that will even be remotely applicable," she said. "To me, it's a fascinating process and I think everybody has to bend over backwards to make sure all the votes are counted." *(Star Tribune)*

Nutsy-boltsy

- Recount will start Wednesday morning the 19th, but counties (87) can set their own schedules. All counting must be done by Dec. 5.

- 45 counts are known to start Wednesday, another 26 Thursday.

- EACH ballot (over 2 million) will be examined by hand by election officials, looking for voter intent. Each campaign will have a rep on hand and can challenge any ballot. Disputed ballots go to State Canvassing Board.

- Recount will be open to the public for observation and public can attend Canvassing Board meetings as well, as they settle things after Dec. 5 in St. Paul.

- Final report of Canvassing Board (including final totals) is December 19th but are willing to take longer. (As Ritchie said earlier last week, we will not be rushed.)

Lawyering Up

There are now two heavy-hitter lawyers for each candidate:

Coleman:

- Fritz Knaak, former state senator, $ contributor to MN GOP. In 2002 represented a losing candidate in a state senate race that was recounted. His client lost.....by 5 votes. *(He's local, but his name is from Berlin!)*

- Tony Trimble, $$ contributor to GOP. Joined Coleman campaign election night when it looked this close. Had defended Gov. Pawlenty on ethics issues. Also Congressman Mark Kennedy (R) in 2000 when Kennedy won election through a recount. *(So Coleman has a buddy in the legal biz named Tony...."music: Sopranos")*

Franken:

- David Lillehaug, former aide to Mondale (as VEEP under Carter; yeah he's older). Was big wheel in 2002 Wellstone campaign and switched to Mondale at end in final battle with Coleman. *(Think David would like to beat Coleman in this rematch?)*

- Marc Elias, former general counsel to 2004 Kerry campaign, 2008 Chris Dodd prez campaign. *(Marc, no Ohio wimp-out, okay?)*

It wouldn't politics unless...

According to an online, *Star Tribune* sidebar, Knaak is already attacking Secretary of State Ritchie, questioning his fairness. Ritchie is keeping quiet while he is being publicly defended by... wait for it...

Governor Tim Pawlenty (R). Once again displaying the caliber of staff Coleman chooses.

Funny pages

1. Jay Leno's take on the recount: "Everyone's watching the recount coming up in Minnesota. 'Minnesota' is an old Indian word that means 'Florida.' "

   Folks laughed, Jay, but it ain't that funny up Nord here. (WineRev channels the ghost of George Jefferson and his maid.) Florida! Listen up and pay attention. This will be recount done RIGHT. Take notes. Copy if you need to. Some Bushista good ol' boy WILL give you a test in the near future, so be ready.

2. Training session for overflow crowd of 400 poll workers/watchers/recounters/volunteers at Macalester College in St. Paul. Al Franken unleashed his sense of humor by leading them in a warm-up cheer: "What do we want? Patience. When do we want it? NOW!"

Time to refill the Cleveland Browns coffee mug, resting on the ballot coaster. Hope you liked this update from yust southeast of Lake Wobegon.

Shalom.

A Full Quiet
November 17, 2008

Comments: 20   Recs: 22   Tips: 35

A quiet Monday morning in the north country, sunny and chilly. The political news is likewise chilly with thin sunshine.

I suspect this is the calm before the storm starting Wednesday, although tomorrow's 1st official Canvassing Board meeting at 1:00 may stir up some news.

The *Star Tribune* is here and they have a life beyond computers in basements. Some Obama/Cabinet/economic news but nothing on the MN senate race (The Single Most Important News Story *ON THE FACE OF THE PLANET!!!*...according to some) in the entire first section.

Only thing worth noting is this: Al Franken will fly tomorrow to Washington DC to brief Harry Reid and other Democrats about the recount situation. Reid and the others want to fill in Franken on upcoming legislation so he can hit the ground running in January if he is elected. (Nota Bene: this is a separate event from the orientation session for newly elected senators coming up later this week, which Al is *not* attending.)

Franken will also do some fund-raising in DC to help pay for the recount expenses (the lawyer brigade in particular I'd imagine).

The Coleman campaign sent out their "communications director" to denounce Franken's trip as "highly presumptuous" "partisan" (obviously for meeting with Harry Reid) and to accuse him of... fund-raising,,, from non-Minnesotans.

No doubt Al will concede this afternoon after being called to task by such a scintillating demonstration of logic and moral culpability.

Well, the Cleveland Browns mug resting on the ballot coaster needs a refill so here's the latest from yust southeast of Lake Wobegon.

Shalom.

Sorting out some Rules of the Recount
November 18, 2008

Comments: 19   Recs: 8   Tips: 21

So the Cleveland Browns mug resting on the ballot coaster tastes especially good this morning after last night's nailbiter. *(Go Browns!)* And today the State Canvassing Board has its first official meeting to hear Sec. of State Mark Ritchie certify election results, including certifying the Senate race is officially ‹0.5% apart and thereby invoking a state-required (and publicly paid for) recount.

And let's see what the *Star Tribune* brings?

Duchschere, Kaszuba, and Brunswick (OBVIOUSLY all good Scandinavians!) get the front-page story just under the masthead . High, low, and side lights:

1. Norm Coleman's lead in the race is now 215, up from 200 yesterday, a result of some of the audits being completed in random precincts as part of the canvassing process.

2. Franken campaign filed a brief with Sec. of State Ritchie asking *rejected absentee ballots* be included in today's certified vote totals. Asked Canvassing Board to so rule. Ritchie took request to MN State Assistant Attorney General Kenneth Raschke Jr. The AG issued 3-page opinion to the Sec. of State & Canvassing Board (citing prior court rulings) that such ballots "are not cast in an election" so No, Al. However, the eligibility of such ballots CAN be challenged in court.

    So Franken does not get these rejected absentee ballots included in today's certified totals. *(To be fair, there may well be similar ballots the Coleman campaign knows of and they might have ideas of court challenges on those. But they won't be included today either.)*

    To be clear, these ballots are NOT what the recount is meant to catch (X on the bubble instead of fill in the circle, circled name, etc.) but rather *absentee* ballots that local officials had cause to reject. Per Raschke's letter, both sides will be able to file court cases about them, where such matters have been settled in the past.

    [I wonder if AG Ken Raschke is related to the "Baron von Raschke" of Saturday afternoon wrestling fame? The "Baron" lives here in Minnesota with his family and his Iron Claw. :-)]

3. Sec. of State Ritchie released the final list of 107 recount location sites.

    The Sec. of State's website will show unofficial running tally of votes each for Coleman & Franken, number of challenged ballots during recount, ballots cast for other candidates (mostly Barkley). Updates will be 8:00 p.m. every day and broken down by counties and their precincts. *("Yucatan Precinct, Houston County! I gotta know the numbers!! And WHY didn't Al do better in Funkley Township, Beltrami?? He shoulda had a rally there!!")*

Typical Republican Sleaze Tricks Dept.

Al flies to DC Wednesday for meetings with Harry Reid and other leaders to get a fill-in on upcoming legislation. The Coleman campaign already groused about this but other Repubs can't resist.

> [Minnesota] GOP chairman Ron Carey on Monday said the trip suggested a "presumptuousness" about victory, even though Franken had already announced he would skip an orientation program for new senators. Carey said he objected to attempts by Senate Democrats to intervene in the race but said he had no evidence that might happen. *(Star Tribune)*

Just makin' stuff up as you go along, eh Carey? What a worthless fool!

OK, time to refill the Browns mug. Hope this helps you keep up on the news yust southeast of Lake Wobegon.

Shalom.

Touching off the Recount (with sparks)
November 19, 2008

Comments: 37   *Recs:* 23   *Tips:* 34

From Thief River Falls to Pipestone to New Caledonia to Grand Marais, let the Great Minnesota Recount begin!

Coffee is brewing (this is required; for hard-core Minnesotans, brewed with a raw egg in the grounds), ballots are being stacked in groups of 25 for easy counting, Jello salad with shaved carrots or marshmallows is jiggling in the fridge, and (if you're lucky) someone will bring some lefse to pass around at lunch time. (If you are unlucky, someone will bring lutefisk to pass around. Lutefisk is horrid but biblically sanctioned as "the piece of cod that passes all understanding.")

Lopez and Kaszuba (good Scandinavians both, obviously) have the front-page story at the fold, reporting that the 5-member **State Canvassing Board** convened Tuesday at 1:00pm in front of a packed house. The Franken legal team filed a brief (to the Board) claiming 49 of Minnesota's 87 counties:

> "have failed, in violation of the unambiguous requirements of state law, to canvass fully the results of the election." As a result, they said, the board could not certify the accuracy of the vote totals reported by the counties. They asked the board to reconsider the rejected ballots in the recount, which could add hundreds, perhaps thousands, of ballots to a contest in which Republican Sen. Norm Coleman leads by 215 votes. *(Star Tribune)*

Franken's team claims county auditors botched the canvassing by rejecting ballots (I expect mostly absentee) that should have been counted and included in the *certified* result. (Sort of the baseline for the recount.) The Board met him partway by NOT certifying the result of the Senate race (but declaring it to be within 0.5%, and ordering the recount to go ahead). They wanted time to study the "blizzard of paperwork" they were handed on Tuesday morning (Franken's stuff, and probably from Coleman's side too, although nothing was mentioned).

KSTP-TV did a fast survey of 37 counties (not including the 2 biggest: Hennepin & Ramsey) and found 2,072 absentee ballots had been rejected.

Franken's lawsuit in Ramsey County to get the names of absentee voters in that county will be heard today.

1. **The PR game.** Franken attorney Mark Elias said the recount in some ways resets the scoreboard to 0-0. He claimed since the Canvassing Board had not rejected their brief out of hand, the rejected absentee ballots "remain a live issue."

    Coleman's campaign sent out their legal heavyweight Fritz Knaak to say basically, we were ahead on election night, we're still ahead after the canvass so we still lead and we're winning. He thought the Franken brief was "horseplay" and that Franken's REAL aim is to get this race into such a mess that it would be decided by the Democratically-controlled Senate. Elias replied they just want the whole process to work out.

2. **From DC.** Harry Reid found time to praise the recount process in Minnesota, calling for every vote to be counted. Norm Coleman said he was "looking forward" to the recount done "in the Minnesota way." To me, both Knaak's and Norm's comments sound pretty generic, rather Minnesota-nice in tone. Maybe they've figured out they've been too over the top. Maybe they really think they could lose this thing (although the Knaak scenario on the Senate floor seems rather outré). Franken is pushing hard to defend his side (as he should) but there might be a slight whiff of desperation in here too.

3. Also **in Hennepin County Court** a 19-year-old student in Washington state voted absentee. She got a notice that her ballot had been rejected because she wasn't registered to vote. But on Oct. 30 she'd gotten a Board of Elections postcard telling her she WAS registered. This looks open-and-shut (a clerical error sort of thing; 1st and only suit of its kind out of 2.9 million voters), but it's in court.

Ok, gotta refill the Cleveland Browns mug and get to work. That's the latest from yust southeast of Lake Wobegon.

Shalom.

Recount First Reports
November 20, 2008

Comments:	41	Recs:	42	Tips:	42

Whooo boy! Coffee mug don't fail me now! Recount Day was off and running, so I'll put up highlights and links from yesterday, and as much updating as will stay updated.

From Wednesday evening.

Recounted Ballots

Secretary of State's Office 8:00pm Nov. 19

Total % of Ballots Recounted: 9%

	Coleman	Franken
Recounted ballots	195,638	180,923
Change from election day	-70	-27
Apparent difference		+43
Start of Recount difference	+215	

Both the "change from election day" and "apparent difference" lines INCLUDE the challenged ballots noted next, so don't read too much into these numbers.

Challenged Ballots

- Franken has challenged 106 "Coleman & other" ballots statewide.
- Coleman has challenged 115 "Franken & other" ballots statewide.

Those 106 + 115 = 221 ballots will go to the State Canvassing Board for final decisions.

1. Beyond the *Star Tribune* (and their cool online map) we also have 2 new-media outlets for more current and running info at The UpTake and the MinnPost. Big tip of the chapeau to Kossack chumley for the info!

   AND for you fans of the nefarious: The Coleman campaign continually bars The UpTake from its press conferences because (wait for it!)...... "you're funded by George Soros!" (OH NO! We've been discovered.) Also shows the quality of journalism they are practicing, as in, "if a Republican doesn't like your reporting, you must be doing something right!"

   > **DK**
   >
   > I live in Zimmerman, MN (6th district, home to our fav vilianness, Bachmann), and I read every diary about this recount. I know they are trying to redo the Florida recount...and whoever said they are trying to challenge everything and keep the count in Coleman's favor and then at the end stop the counting of the challenged votes, that person is absolutely right IMO. I, too, am glad we have someone like mansky who is doing the thing right, no matter whose court the ball falls in.
   >
   > And I have mentioned before I used to work with David Lillehaug, Frankin's lead attorney I believe, and there is no attorney smarter, more assertive, more pure aggressive and who hates to lose more than David. he is a great pick. *(GrandmaJ)*

2. Ramsey County (St. Paul) court ruled in favor of Al Franken in a lawsuit to get access to the names of voters who voted absentee in Ramsey County. Such names are supposed to be available "for

public inspection" after the polls close on election day in each county. For some reason Ramsey County has been holding back, not just from Franken but from everybody (including the Coleman and Barkley campaigns, for that matter) for reasons unclear. Judge ordered release by 5:00 p.m. Wednesday.

Hennepin County (Minneapolis) has likewise not released their absentee names either. No word on a similar lawsuit by anyone. No word Hennepin County was going to release their names (as of 9:00 p.m. Wednesday).

> Read the ruling, important to note ruling does not order the state to count absentee ballots, only to grant Franken campaign access to rejected absentee ballots and the written reasons for their rejection. *(unknown blogger at The UpTake)*

3. Also from Ramsey County, a brief set-to at the recount. Everyone is being very careful (apparently state law does not permit anyone except an election official to even **touch** a ballot during the recount; *I'll bet that's probably called "tampering with an election," which sounds REALLY serious)* but things reached this point:

> One dustup came when Coleman observer Bob Murray questioned Ramsey County elections manager Joe Mansky on all the people jamming in the room as well as how ballot stacks were being counted. When Murray challenged a handful of ballots in which voters appeared to mark Franken clearly, Mansky said they were frivolous challenges, something state law prohibits.
>
> "If you want to deal with it, take me to court," Mansky said. *(Star Tribune)*

"State law prohibits frivolous challenges."

WOW! Now I realize there's ground for argument here but I'll bet serious money there are also precedents here (since the 1960s when the law was written). Sooo...how much do you want to risk raising a "frivolous challenge"? Mr. Murray, can you enumerate all forms of a frivolous challenge and are you sure you are on the right side of frivolity? Sounds to me like Mansky is running a pretty tight ship in Ramsey County.

> Someone needs to photocopy that Mansky guy and send him to every county.
>
> I suspect that the current Coleman tactic is to challenge enough Franken votes so that Coleman stays ahead in the recount and then Franken gets given the lead at the state canvassing board (when all the Franken votes that Coleman challenged get reinstated) and then try to delegitimize the state canvassing board.
>
> Mansky seems to be successfully stopping these shenanigans in Ramsey. *(Anarchofascist)*

5. AHA! Further fact-checking *(journalism students, watch closely)* provides further background, foreground, and sideground on the above Murray-Mansky to-do:

> Grace Kelly, who was there all day, said that Murray got louder and louder each time he didn't get his way. Mansky stayed calm the entire time. McIntee commented that Murray later apologized. Noah Kunin had this comment on the [*Star Tribune*]'s article:
>
> 'The quote from Mansky is slightly inaccurate as posted here. Consultation of video from the incident produces the following exact quote:
>
>> MANSKY: If you want to deal with them, you can take my determination to court.
>
> Slightly more politic, I'd say...' *(MNBlue)*

Funny pages

1. The webmeister of The UpTake, Mike McIntee, reports the following:

> Snark from the Minnesota Democratic Party today: CNN reported today that Senator Norm Coleman met with embattled, and recently defeated, Senator Ted Stevens (R-AK) behind closed doors in the Capitol.

> Minnesota Democratic Party spokesperson Frank Benenati released this statement:
>
> "Norm Coleman and Ted Stevens' meeting today makes many wonder what the two senators were discussing behind closed doors. Was Stevens offering advice on the best way to fight allegations of illegally-funneled money and unreported gifts from donors? Were they planning another fishing trip to Alaska with high-powered lobbyists and oil executives? Or were they merely discussing what lobbying firms on K Street are hiring next year?" *(The UpTake)*

"Makes many wonder"? Mr. Benenati, you may have just invented the reply to Faux Noise's "some people say." Good job!

2. Want to play election judge? Minnesota Public Radio has pictures of challenged ballots on their website.

    To me some are pretty obvious, but there's at least a couple where I want another sip from my Cleveland Browns mug before I make a call. In NE Minneapolis, one challenged ballot was marked with an X, between Coleman and Franken's names... sigh.

Now for Thursday morning.

1. Lopez & Brown write the story for the top half of the front page of the *Star Tribune*, which lists Coleman's lead at 174, total challenged ballots at 269, and 18% counted (unclear if ballots or precincts). Franken gained a net of 23 votes in St. Louis County (Duluth, although in this case not in the city of Duluth itself but from the outlying areas that stretch to Canada) because some precincts were using an older-model optical scanner that couldn't read some of the ballots.

2. **Lawyers swing lightsabers.** Mark Elias (Franken) was pleased by Ramsey County court decision to allow access to names of absentee voters. Has impact across state in other counties. Fritz Knaak (Coleman) complained voter privacy should prevail. Elias said, "We'll decide what to do with the data once we get it. I promise you I will not knock on Mr. Knaak's door, in order to avoid frightening him."

3. Lots of interest, lots of help, and some heat. Franken campaign says they have "deployed 2100 trained volunteers across the state, bolstered by an array of national and local legal talent." One of those deployed 2,100 was Kossack ImpeccableLiberalCredentials, who got out of his parents' basement, changed out of pajamas, drove his Volvo with the snow-machine engine into Bemidji in Beltrami County in order to park himself, his latte and his Birkenstocks 7 feet from the county recount table for all the drama.

    Knaak (Coleman) said his side has about 200 lawyers monitoring the process, along with "hundreds of volunteers."

> Ramsey County Elections Manager Joe Mansky took another strong stand on Wednesday afternoon, insisting that in disputed ballots where voter intent was clear, he should make the call.
>
> Coleman recount attorney Knaak told reporters that Mansky "just can't do that," and had to be made to understand that once challenged, ballots had to be set aside for the state Canvassing Board to make a determination.
>
> But Mansky, a longtime elections expert who logged years at the Secretary of State's office, instead called Franken and Coleman lawyers aside at the end of the day to review the 13 challenged ballots. "I'm going to win all those challenges, I guarantee 100 percent," Mansky said. "We have some folks who are new to this and feel they have to challenge something."
>
> When the informal meeting was over, only a single ballot remained in dispute, out of 30,000 votes counted that day. *(Star Tribune)*

So there's a fair news round-up from yust southeast of Lake Wobegon.

Shalom.

Recount Crunching
November 21, 2008

Comments: 181   Recs: 272   Tips: 228

Thursday Night Updates
Recounted Ballots

Secretary of State's Office 8:00pm Nov. 20

Total % of Ballots Recounted: 42.3%, Whoa! BIG day counting; better than 25% of the total votes cast. (Way to go, you egg coffee addicts! Have another lefse!)

	Coleman	Franken
Recounted ballots	534,475	494,800
Change from election day	-212	-126
Apparent difference		+86
Start of Recount difference	+215	

Both the "change from election day" and "apparent difference" lines INCLUDE the challenged ballots noted next, so don't read too much into these numbers.

Challenged Ballots

- Franken has challenged 374 "Coleman & other" ballots statewide.
- Coleman has challenged 360 "Franken & other" ballots statewide.

Those 374 + 360 = 734 ballots will go to the State Canvassing Board for final decisions.

1. Everyone recounting is being very careful, but also trying to keep things moving. But for speed of counting nobody's going to touch these two precincts from St. Louis County. (Duluth, but the county stretches north LONG to the Canadian border. The town of Embarrass makes the national news from time to time, as in "the cold spot in the lower 48 states last night at MINUS 47 was Embarrass, MN."). Larry Oakes writes for the *Star Tribune* Online:

   > You might call them "ballots from the boonies."
   >
   > Recount workers in St. Louis County this morning dispensed quickly with two precincts—one with one ballot to count; the other with two.
   >
   > Unorganized Precinct 6's single vote was cast for Republican Sen. Norm Coleman. The 48-square-mile precinct is in a heavily forested area just south of Hoyt Lakes. The two voters in Unorganized Precinct 20—a 36-square-mile tract of similarly sparse wilderness between Embarass and Babbitt—both cast their ballots for Democratic challenger Al Franken.
   >
   > "These are wilderness areas where they might have to drive 50 miles to vote, so we arrange for them to vote by mail," said Paul Tynjala, the county's director of elections. Trouble is, the county's ballot vendor has a 50-ballot minimum, and each precinct must have its own ballots. "So we order 50 ballots so that one guy can vote," Tynjala said.
   >
   > For the record: The results in both precincts are unchanged from Election Day. And there were no challenges. *(Star Tribune)*

   It literally chokes me up with pride reading that son of Finland Tynjala matter-of-factly saying they are willing to throw away 49 blank ballots for the sake of one voter. It's ordinary....and amazing, both at once. Edasi Tynjala!! WAY TO GO!!

2. I'm sure Franken partisans on this site (and upholders of the Constitution and common sense everywhere) remember **Ramsey County (St. Paul) elections manager Joe Mansky** laying the lumber to a particularly obstreperous Coleman recount watcher. *(Be careful Coleman! Democrats have JOE POWER this year! Joe Biden and now Joe Mansky. All the Joe YOU'VE got is a plumber NOT named Joe, and the south end of a northbound Connecticut horse and Senator named Joe.)*

Well there's this little tidbit from Wednesday with Joe Mansky in action, as reported by cgseife over at The UpTake:

> I absolutely agree that individual personalities of the challengers are important. Yesterday AM, Ramsey County, one table got a little out of hand. A Coleman observer challenged 5 ballots that were bubbled in properly and had no obvious flaws—but the challenger complained that Franken bubble was a wee bit lighter than the other bubbles. To his credit, Joe Mansky immediately dismissed the challenges as frivolous. *(The UpTake)*

Go JOE!!

3. **Point of Information.** County Recount boards can count as long as they want on a given day. If they want results to be included in the SoS update every night at 8:00 p.m. (CT) they need to fax in their tallies by 6:00 p.m.

(Wednesday, Olmsted County—Rochester, home of the Mayo Clinic—went until 10 p.m. in a *14-hour marathon* so they could recount all 76,000 county ballots in one effort! Now that is SERIOUS Recount power!)

> **DK** Whoever wins the recount will do so in a fair process. I was an election Judge (in St. Louis Co) and I was impressed (the process, the two poll watchers (DFL/REP) where positively chatty with each other, all the poll Judges, who are suppose to be partisan, worked well with one another... I can only imagine the recount process being an extension of that in general, sure there is going to be some over-zealous lawyers, that is what they are paid for, but the mechanisms seem to be working well and transparently. FL 2000 this ain't. *(edgeways)*

Friday morning

MN Sec. of State's Office will hold a **news conference** today at 3:30 p.m. Some local press are hoping to get a closer look at some of the disputed/challenged ballots. *(I think they're looking for more Lizard People[1] votes.)* The UpTake sounds like they will cover it in video, possibly streaming at their site.

> **DK** Can you imagine being the "Lizard People" voter? And having your stupid little joke talked about around the country? 15 minutes of fame, indeed. *(AlyoshaKaramazov)*

> **DK** Sadly, the name of said voter will never be given. But it is funny... in a sad... sad way. If your going to waste a vote... *(RElland)*

> **DK** He obviously didn't like either guy.
> My best friend lives in Sydney, Australia and she says its a law you have to vote there so some young people will write in stuff like that or Mikey Mouse. I have a feeling lizard people guy wanted to vote for Obama but not the rest. *(marlakay)*

> **DK** Lizard People is not a wasted vote! Lizard People will go to the Senate and EAT all the wimpy Dems. *(recontext)*

Lopez & Von Sternberg *(surely a couple of Swedes)* get front and center on the headline story today in the *Star Tribune*, leading with a Roseville voter who **voted absentee** whose ballot was rejected in Ramsey County, the sort of goof-up Franken seems he's getting ready to use just in case. *(Star Tribune* scoreboard numbers are: Margin +136, Coleman; total ballots challenged 823; 46% counted—all higher than the Sec. of State's numbers from 8:00 p.m. last night.)

Three pages inside, Franken press guy Andy Barr reports they've received lists of names of **rejected absentee ballots** from about 36 counties so far. Coleman legal honcho Knaak thinks it's all to set up a post-recount court challenge. *(Ya think?)*....

Minneapolis elections director **Cindy Reichert** has added four more tables of counters at a warehouse location to keep things moving in the recount of 131 city precincts. A Coleman monitor on location, Pat

---

1 *The "Lizard People" ballot is displayed on the cover of this book.*

Shortridge, says Reichert and her staffers have made it "an open and fair process... It's easy to be nonpartisan when the stakes aren't so high and the results aren't so close. This is the real test." *(Right on, Pat; and thanks for the kudos to Reichert for her fairness.)*

This whole thing might well come down to the **challenged ballots** sent to the State Canvassing Board for final disposition after Dec. 5. You've seen pictures at the Minn. Public Radio website of what some voters do to their ballot *(apparently these are a new set of pix from Thursday's recount, not just the ones from Wednesday).* But what about ruling on them? What are the odds? The *Star Tribune* quotes our rising star from **Ramsey County, Joe Mansky,** in his Joe Power!

> The number of challenged ballots continued to increase Thursday, reaching 823. Mansky—who worked from 1984 to 1999 in the secretary of state's office and is widely considered the state's foremost elections expert—said that people shouldn't expect many of those challenges to bear fruit.
>
> "I can only remember two ballot challenges in all those years that were sustained," he said, meaning that the campaign lawyers' views prevailed over the opinion of election judges. He said he wouldn't be surprised if campaign lawyers negotiate a reduction in the number of challenged ballots before the Canvassing Board meets next month to go through them.
>
> The same issues come up regularly, Mansky said—one filled-in oval with a faint dot in another (typically voters tapping their pens on the ballot as they read it), two ovals filled in with one crossed out, which "comes up every election."
>
> The third most common challenge, Mansky said, involves stray marks on the ballot. State law prohibits identifying marks, such as initials, because they can signal vote fraud. "If they don't jump out as an attempt to identify the ballot, they should be counted," Mansky said. *(This cites the Star Tribune count of challenged ballots, which differs right now from the Sec. of State count from last night.)*

I can see how both sides might meet to cut down the number of challenges with some horse trading, just to make it easier on the Canvassing Board. And I find it sort of reassuring to hear Mansky saying basically, "Here's 3 routine things we see every election, every canvass, every recount. No big deal. Here's how we handled them before..."

Cool. I can buy this. No drama. No hysterics. Just another day at the office. And for me that stolid "ordinariness" seems like a strong defense against any sort of "Brooks Brothers" riot, Florida-style, from happening here. *(Channels the ghost of Hunter Thompson; tones down language)* I can just see Mansky or Judge Gearin of the Board looking at some pesky bunch of "operatives" chanting "Stop the count" and saying in a flat monotone that could freeze a Minnesota lake in July, "Touch one ballot or try to break up this meeting and I'll bite your arm off and use it to beat the snot out of the rest of those scum behind you."

Testimonial Moment

OK, I gotta say this. Stepping back from the nuts & bolts of the counting, speculation, and anecdotes, I'm finding myself choked up with tears brimming for no apparent reason about every 15 minutes of writing this series and maybe I've figured out why.

Little old ladies in Bemidji coming out to count. Hawk-eyed lawyers who have faced each other at the courthouse in St. Cloud verbally sparring across a citizen's ballot. An unemployed pipe-fitter in Redwood Falls solemnly counting ballots into a group of 25 while his neighbors, a welder, a cashier, and a church secretary, count with him under their breath.

"Minnesota, hats off to thee..." (from the University fight song); the words are right but this is far more dignified and far bigger than Minnesota. This is Norman Rockwell come to life. This is "government OF the *people*, BY the *people*, FOR the *people*" in the flesh. This IS *the people*, securing "the blessings of liberty for ourselves and our posterity" before our very eyes.

This is my schoolboy patriotism and righteous civic pride welling up, throwing into tawdry relief the political carnival-barking, spin, and fraudsters of the past years as just false, putrid, petty, and blaring venality.

I say this before God and all of you: whoever goes to the Senate, whether I voted for him or not, whether I support him or work to unseat him, goes to the Senate by a fair, clean, democratic **process** that produced the correct result, as accurate as humanly possible. Unlike Florida 2000, unlike Ohio 2004, this will be CASE CLOSED.

I need to find a flag to salute, and a hand to shake. *(Sniff!)*

OK, I can see the bottom of my Cleveland Browns coffee mug, so I'll set it down on my ballot coaster and leave you with the news yust southeast of Lake Wobegon.

Shalom.

Recount Nuggets
November 22, 2008

Comments:	17	Recs:	30	Tips:	34

Thank you so much for your comments, tips, links, and thoughts for the last nine entries in this (accidental) series. I'm also grateful for the personal support and that you like my writing. *[There really ARE people who don't love the Cleveland Browns. Some must be from Pittsburgh—understandable.... but the rest??.... must just be Cincinnati Bungles fans :-)]*

Recounted Ballots

Secretary of State's Office 8:00pm Nov. 21

Total % of Ballots Recounted: 60.86%

	Coleman	Franken
Recounted ballots	751,898	723,378
Change from election day	-540	-440
Apparent difference		+100
Start of Recount difference	+215	

Both the "change from election day" and "apparent difference" lines INCLUDE the challenged ballots noted next, so don't read too much into these numbers.

Challenged Ballots

- Franken has challenged 778 "Coleman & other" ballots statewide.
- Coleman has challenged 747 "Franken & other" ballots statewide.

Those 778 + 747 = 1,525 ballots will go to the State Canvassing Board for final decisions.

According to yesterday's slick little chart from Kossack jmknapp, Franken ought to be trailing by 87 instead of his current 115 with 60% recounted. His trend is good, but not enough to catch. Of course the little red line is a fancy *straight* line *("not that there's anything **wrong** with that! I have friends who are straight lines!")* and it's something of an average.

(My late Dad, the engineer, always wanted the actual measurement. "Never trust an average," he said. "Put one foot in an oven and the other in the freezer. On average you're comfortable.")

Life rarely moves in straight lines, so I still have hope. *("There may be more turns along the way, but I still have hope. I have hope for all Frankenites to laugh with their senator, not at their senator, because I still have hope..." turns off conference phone-call with Obama speech-writing team and goes back to diary.)*

From the WingNuts are Nuts Dept.

Don't like the recount process in MN? With all these challenges, canvassing and lizard people, do you think something is rotten in Denmark? *("so stop standing downwind from the lutefisk")*

Well, you guys are rank amateurs compared to the Reichwingers warming up in the bullpen to attack the recount in general and Secretary of State Mark Ritchie (D) in particular. According to Aaron Landry at

MNPublius and Media Matters, a Faux Noisemaker, Andrew Napolitano, is suspicious of Ritchie because he's a "secret Communist"! No, really! Since Mark Ritchie once made a $250 contribution to the Center for Cuban Studies at cubaupdate.com, and since this group believes in "normalizing relations between the US and Cuba," Ritchie is a secret Communist. Leave it to the FoxNews/RedStaters to find a Red... or invent one if necessary.

Lawyers Swinging Lightsabers II

> Lawyers from both campaigns said Thursday it was too early to assess the signifi-cance of the challenge pile. Both questioned whether the other had gone too far in some cases.
>
> "We have seen examples of challenges that clearly are non-meritorious and will not be upheld by the canvassing board. Where that winds up going, we'll see," said Franken's legal chief, Marc Elias. "Maybe the Coleman campaign was a little overexuberant on Day One."
>
> Coleman's top lawyer, Fritz Knaak, said he expected the number of challenges to be greater. Still, he's on the lookout for "no-brainer Coleman votes" that are wind-ing up in the disputed stack. "We see some of their challenges and shrug and say 'Where did that come from?' " Knaak said.
>
> The campaigns get copies of the challenged ballots and they can lift their hold on a ballot being counted if they have second thoughts. *(Star Tribune)*

Both sides sound nervous with everyone feeling the closeness of the vote. On the other hand, maybe they realize their turn as lawyers is coming and not yet.

The last line is interesting: Each campaign can look over its cards in this poker game and say at any time, "Naah, this one isn't worth it." It lets a very interested party (the campaign) take a private, "let cooler heads prevail," second look at the acts of its own observers and challengers. A campaign can quietly back down without having to publicly either lose face in retreat or defend the ludicrous (a major infection of the last 8 years). It trims away the challenged ballot pile the Canvassing Board ultimately has to look at, making their job a bit easier.

I like it. It's fair. Another shiny little cog in the recount machinery I wouldn't have thought of but is a really GOOD THING.

More JOE Power

Remember how "many wondered" if new immigrants/elderly/occasional voters might be more inclined to both vote Democratic (as in Franken) and vote in a more messed-up way (X instead of fill in the oval, etc.)? And that those votes might not be read by the optical scanners but *would* be picked up by human be-ings in a recount? We might have a case of that in this *Star Tribune* story (and needless to say the Coleman campaign ain't happy. But then they are facing off against JOE Mansky, wielding his JOE power.)

> Mike Roman, Coleman's lead representative in Ramsey County, says he remains unsatisfied with the apparent emergence of 12 new ballots in a St. Paul precinct, but that the campaign's only recourse might be to take the issue to court—a step that would be made by campaign officials superior to him.
>
> The issue could be important because, as of Thursday afternoon, Franken had picked up at least 13 more votes than he did Election Day.
>
> The concern arose late yesterday when the total number of ballots sorted in Ward 3, Precinct 9 was discovered to be 1,759—12 more than the 1,747 that Roman said was tallied on Election Day. The precinct was recounted this morning (Friday) with the same results.
>
> But, unlike the process being done in other counties, Ramsey County Elections Manager Joe Mansky is not attempting to reconcile such differences in total bal-lots cast.
>
> "I'm confident that these numbers are accurate," Mansky said of today's results. He had no explanation for the discrepancy in total ballots. Roman said, "We're not satisfied at all. It's very difficult to challenge this situation because they're limiting this to voter intent on each ballot." *(Star Tribune)*

Ahhh,, Mike? JOE and the election judges are "limiting this to voter intent on each ballot" because the recount LAW says, and the Secretary of State says, election directors and judges are limited to determining the voter intent on each ballot for the recount. I don't think JOE Mansky was even breathing hard after this one, presumably in sharp contrast to Mike Roman. *GO JOE!*

Saturday Morning Fresh News (with coffee)

As Hunter S. Thompson would say, "Cazart!" The first snowfall, about one inch. For me, the prettiest snow of the year. Go to bed and wake up with the entire view transformed. Beautiful!

(Oh yeah, the political stuff.) Several counties will be recounting today, although in many cases for limited hours. Hennepin for instance will go 9 a.m. to 1 p.m. today. Most everybody will take Sunday off, but apparently a few places around the state may have a Sunday session in order to finish.

The *Star Tribune* front page scoreboard: Coleman lead = 120; challenged ballots combined = 1,669; 64% counted. (*Star Tribune* includes numbers later than 6:00pm cut-off for Sec. of State's numbers.)

Reporter Kevin Duchschere *(must be one of them infiltrating French-Canadians!)* reports a Coleman sighting in Wright County (NW of Minneapolis, exurban ring county). Reporters got to ask questions (this being Bachmann's MN-6, they were of course anti-American questions and trapping questions which deserve nothing but urban myth answers), among which was YOUR question (paraphrase): "Say Norm, like you said the morning after the election, since Franken was behind he should step back and concede. If you are trailing after the recount, you gonna step back and concede?"

Norm with the polished politician's reply:

> However, (Coleman) expressed second thoughts about his comments that morning. He noted that his lead at the time was substantially larger, more than 700 votes, and also that he hadn't slept in 36 hours. Now, he said, "I don't think I'd have made the same statement." *(Star Tribune)*

Sec. of State Mark Ritchie said he expects about 75% of the ballots to be recounted by tonight and stated the Canvassing Board will meet Wednesday to discuss "what to do about the Franken campaign's request to consider rejected absentee ballots and count them if they were improperly turned aside."

In Anoka County (N of Twin Cities exurban), Coon Rapids recounters found one precinct 3 ballots fewer than the machine total. In St. Louis County (Duluth) 4 ballots were missing with a search under way, according to Paul Tynjala (from yesterday's posting. FINLAND!). Neither county reports finding them by press time.

Also in Duluth city one precinct came in 74 ballots off, which were found after a nervous search locked inside one of the precinct scanning machines. Both Coleman and Franken camps agreed this was an honest mistake and called "no harm, no foul."

Mutual sniping department

Coleman campaign at a press conference hung copies of 51 Franken Frivolous Follies (challenged ballots) on a wall for reporters to see. Several had an X instead of a filled-in oval. Coleman spokesperson Sheehan said the Franken campaign has increased its number of challenges to artificially close the gap between the vote totals.

Franken campaign claimed their internal numbers showed it a "double-digit" race (under 100) but they include some challenged ballots to get there. They also showed off copies of challenged ballots, including several that the Colemans had challenged because...the presidential vote was for McCain (remember him?) and the Senate vote was for Franken. Apparently in the Coleman/Bachmann world such an event is a mathematical impossibility.

Funny Pages

Pioneer Press offers some sidelights to the recount. The St. Paul Saints are a minor-league baseball team with a wacky sense of marketing and organizational humor. So naturally, even though baseball season is months away, they have jumped into the recount situation to get the fans out:

The latest Saints invention: A figurine named "Re"Count, with a head that has Norm Coleman's face on one side and Al Franken's face on another. With a body modeled on Count von Count from "Sesame Street." (Count von Count—get it?)

The first 2,500 fans that enter the gates on Saturday, May 23, 2009 are scheduled to receive a "Re"Count, but that number may change daily leading up to the event. For example, the Saints may only have 2,400 dolls to give away if an employee accidentally leaves a box of the dolls sitting in their vehicle overnight.

There will be a coloring competition where the winner will be the person who can correctly color inside of an oval shaped object. Following the third inning of their game against the Sioux Falls Canaries, no matter the score, the Saints will claim victory, "a victory for all Minnesotans."

While fans choose whether to spin the doll to the side of Coleman or Franken, lawyers will be on hand to help determine their intent and challenges may be submitted to the Saints Fan Services Booth in written or oral form. All fans will participate in various counting exercises during the course of the game, including the popular exercise: "What's the difference between 24 and 124?" *(Pioneer Press)*

And although I've never watched the show, somebody was wondering if the State Canvassing Board had a different set of judges:

AMERICAN IDOL STYLE!!

SCENE: Minnesota Canvassing Board, Dec. 16. (A ballot is held up for examination.)

Randy: "I don't know, dog. A little scribbly for me. I kind of see what you were trying to do, but you just missed the lines sometimes with your marks. A little scribbly. But it was all right...."

Paula: "I loved it. I think you knew what you wanted to do going into the voting booth, and you did it. I think you're going to be a voting superstar one day."

Simon: "I've got to be honest with you. I just thought that was a horrible effort. If you want to get your candidate elected, you're going to have to do much, much better than that. That was atrocious. There are marks all over the ballot. I don't even know what you were trying to do there. You could be in jeopardy of being rejected, but we'll have to see. It's really too bad, because I know you could be a good voter. But this ballot was just terrible. Truly awful." *(Rachel Stassen-Berger, from her blog at Pioneer Press)*

OK I've got time to refill the Not-Cincinnati-Bungles mug for a second cup, get dressed and head off for the wine sale. I'll try to check in between orders for Maso Canali Pinot Grigio and cases of Rutherford Hill Merlot. Prosit! I'll leave you with this comment...

DK   Whatever the result is this will end up in court and eventually will end up in the supreme court. Most likely they will refuse to hear this case and whatever the supreme court of MN says will probably be the final result. *(JOEL1954)*

...and the latest news from yust southeast of Lake Wobegon.

Shalom.

Recount Cracks and Comments
November 23, 2008

Comments: 18   Recs: 32   Tips: 33

Recounted Ballots

Secretary of State's Office 8:00pm Nov. 22

Total % of Ballots Recounted: 65.65%

	Coleman	Franken
Recounted ballots	808,785	783,401
Change from election day	-669	-621
Apparent difference		+48
Start of Recount difference	+215	

Both the "change from election day" and "apparent difference" lines INCLUDE the challenged ballots noted next, so don't read too much into these numbers.

Challenged Ballots

Franken has challenged 945 "Coleman & other" ballots statewide.

Coleman has challenged 948 "Franken & other" ballots statewide.

Those 945 + 948 = 1,893 ballots will go to the State Canvassing Board for final decisions.

The challenged ballots continue to pile up for the canvassing board. Apparently either camp can UN-challenge a ballot (apparently just by notifying somebody; could be Sec. of State Ritchie, or could be the county auditor of the ballot in question, but they do NOT need to notify the press/public about it). So the 1,893 would best be thought of as "best case" scenarios for each camp; it also means some of the more "obvious" or even "frivolous" challenges (e.g. Lizard people, stray pencil mark on the *back* of a ballot) may well be withdrawn before the Board ever has to take a look at it.

1. Duchschere of the *Star Tribune* (in a Saturday evening story) notes with Saturday's limited counting nonetheless 53 counties (out of 87 total) have completed their recounts. Some of the Coleman observers around the Twin Cities metro had comments, but the Franken campaign seems to have taken a leaf from Obama for some message discipline:

    > Corlyss Affeldt, of Eden Prairie (new money SW Minneapolis suburb), is a Coleman volunteer who worked for 9 hours on Thursday in Bloomington and Richfield (middle-class, S Minneapolis suburbs). "I'm doing it because I want to make sure it's right ...that seems to be the prevailing motivation right now: I just want it right," she said. Another Coleman volunteer, Lynda Bodin, a dental hygienist from Wayzata (small city due W of Mpls, engulfed by suburbs), said: "If you stayed home (on election day) thinking your vote doesn't count, this proves it does."
    >
    > Nick Heille, of Minneapolis, who has served as an election judge, also volunteered for Coleman and praised the recount.
    >
    > "The process is extraordinarily honest," said Heille, a retired tech specialist for Hennepin County. "I continue to marvel at it. It's a very strong system and people don't abuse it."
    >
    > Franken observers said they were instructed to direct media inquiries to the campaign spokesmen. *(Star Tribune)*

2. JOE power leashed.

    Rising star JOE Mansky has been running a very tight ship, vigorously applying the "frivolous challenges prohibited" rule. At the end of the 1st day's count on Wednesday Ramsey County had 13 ballots challenged. Mansky called a huddle with Coleman and Franken attorneys and between them whittled that total down to ONE.

Now it appears the Ramsey County Attorney's office has told Mansky to kick the challenged ballots "upstairs" to the canvassing board. Duchschere again:

> Challenged ballots spiked in Ramsey County, where the county attorney's office squelched negotiations that had limited challenged ballots the first two days of the recount and observers from both campaigns questioned voters' intentions far more broadly than before.
>
> Ramsey County Election Manager Joe Mansky, who had negotiated down challenged ballots Wednesday and Thursday with the campaigns, was told by Assistant County Attorney Darwin Lookingbill to "punt all the disputed ballots to the Canvassing Board. So that's what we will do," Mansky said.
>
> Mansky said he thought both campaigns have instructed observers to issue challenges more widely. *(Star Tribune)*

Mansky's last observation fits the facts (with their well-known liberal bias). As of Friday night's Sec. of State report, almost 61% of the votes recounted had generated 1,525 challenges between the 2 sides. Yesterday less than 5% of ballots were recounted statewide, but 368 challenged ballots were added to the State Canvassing Board's pile.

DK It's looking tough for Franken. *(Murchadha)*

DK Win or lose, Al has conducted himself in a totally classy manner. I'm proud of him, either way! *(Julie Gulden)*

DK Then it all comes down to what types of challenges. If most of those were Franken challenging Franken votes and Coleman challenging Franken votes Franken might not be in that bad of shape. Of course, all of this might be overly optimistic and even simplistic thinking. *(Frozen Democrat)*

Brief tidbits from here and there

From The UpTake, a report there are 167 rejected absentee ballots in Hennepin County (Minneapolis and many suburbs) out of 80,000 total recounted. State Canvassing Board meets Wednesday to "discuss" (and who knows? Maybe to *decide* what to do with such rejected ballots around the state, which by some reports total more than 1,000).

Hopeful thoughts: Hibbing and Virginia (2 towns in the northern counties bordering Canada) have been recounting their respective rural votes, not yet the town votes. Franken won heavily in both (13K and 4K votes in each town, respectively). Also, same approach in St. Louis County where non-Duluth city votes have been mostly recounted up to now...through some complicated math and informed speculation [*ALWAYS the best approach to take on Daily KOS :-)*] some of the commenters at UpTake figure about 900 new votes have been counted in this recount compared to election night (i.e. votes machines couldn't read but humans can), but these don't show much because of the number of challenged ballots...

And NOW, having convinced all of you that clean elections are the result of cold weather, Scandinavian genes, egg coffee, and staying upwind from lutefisk, that Minnesotans are paragons of political virtue who would NEVER pull a hanging chad fiasco, Florida-style, and who would consider it UNTHINKABLE to have a "Landslide" Lyndon Johnson finagle (where several days after the election a very late reporting precinct reported in over 200 votes for Lyndon, with the names in the voter registration sign-in book in the exact order of the names on the property tax rolls)...

YES WE CAN pull election tricks in Minnesota! How about this from the *Pioneer Press* in a background story on other recounts we have known and loved:

> The race: 2002 Minnesota **State Senate** election
>
> The candidates: Republican state Sen. Grace Schwab and DFL (Minnesotan for "Democrat") challenger Dan Sparks.

> The 2002 Austin (Southern central MN along the Iowa line) state Senate race was hot during the campaigning and got hotter after Election Day results showed a 33-vote difference between Schwab and Sparks. A three-day recount ensued, the candidates challenged 32 ballots, and after a state canvassing board settled those ballots, Sparks (D) led by 11 votes. Schwab (R), represented by **Fritz Knaak**—now Norm Coleman's lead recount attorney—decided to contest the canvassing board's decision.
>
> That was in part because of the little problem of the burned ballots. On the evening of the election, according to a Mower County Court opinion, the tally of voters who signed in and the number of ballots didn't sync. There were *17 ballots too many*. So, a DFL election judge chose 17 ballots and "removed them, obtained a brown plastic bag, and drove them to her home." Then she did as she told a Republican election judge she was going to do: "The DFL election judge intentionally destroyed the ballots by burning them in her fireplace," according to the opinion. Despite arguments about how those ballots should be counted, a Mower County judge decided on Jan. 6, 2003, that they should not be counted at all. The next day, Schwab conceded the election and Sparks was sworn in. *(Pioneer Press)*

OK, gotta get out to sing in the choir. Lutheran coffee awaits. I'll leave you with the latest from yust southeast of Lake Wobegon.

Shalom.

Recount Fill-Ins and a Rant
November 24, 2008

Comments: 36 *Recs:* 35 *Tips:* 32

The wine sale is over and my shoulders from restocking the bins are at John McCain half-mast. Thank you for your interest and support of things Minnesotan.

FightingRegister brought news from the Holy Odin (as we say in Minnesota) of Number Crunchers, Nate Silver[2], who guesses with a fair margin for error that Al Franken could indeed pull out the recount by a 27-vote margin (including challenged ballots but NOT rejected absentees). So that's a nice shiny straw to grasp at. Vote for America had another set of statistics, regressions, and graphs that only a Nate Silver could even read, let alone love.

Sunday Night Update
UN-challenging a ballot

Apparently both campaigns, having challenged a ballot (for, say, lizard scales stuck on the back as an "identifying mark"), can back off, and privately.

> Those (*1,893 challenged*) ballots are scheduled next month to head to the state canvassing board, which will rule on them, do a final tally and declare a winner.
>
> The number of challenged ballots could fall, however. Officials with both campaigns and Secretary of State Mark Ritchie have noted the possibility of bilateral disarmaments, with each campaign agreeing to withdraw large batches of challenges before the canvassing board gets them.
>
> But Saturday, anecdotal evidence suggested the challenged-ballot arms race might be only escalating. *(Pioneer Press)*

That last line sounds like each side is piling up some extras so they can show how generous, reasonable, and fair-minded they are when they go to "ballot disarmament."

---

2 Nate's site is FiveThirtyEight.com

> Washington County (Stillwater, E of St. Paul, up against the Wisconsin border) had 30 challenges in four precincts counted Saturday. The county has 90 precincts, and its total number of challenges stands at 111, (election supervisor Carol) Peterson said. *(Pioneer Press)*

Saturday was Washington County's last day recounting.

> Anoka County (exurban, N of both Minneapolis & St. Paul) elections manager Rachel Smith said her county expects to finish Monday. On Saturday, 28 ballots had been challenged by late afternoon, compared with 20 on Friday and a total of 22 for the first two days of the recount. *(Pioneer Press)*

Personal Rant

(Vaguely political; non-recount-related. Skip if you like.)

Thank you for indulging me a few days ago on a Testimonial Moment praising democracy in action. I just have to get something off my chest as word has come that *Samuel Joseph Wurzelbacher* AKA "Joe the Plumber" looks like he's getting a book deal, cashing in on his newfound celebrity (one report has it a ghost writer is already at work on it, with a target date of December 1! No turkey dinner for that guy, but I'll bet Joe himself gets his turkey and football on Thursday.)

WHAT THE HELL??

Not-Joe Joe the Not-Plumber gets 30 sec. airtime with Obama on a rope line. John "Never Mention POW" McCain mentions him 20 times during a debate in between off-camera drools. And now this hack has a book deal? A literary agent?? A publisher??? A ghost writer????

WHAT A CROCK!! Well crap, just crap!! Yeah I'm hacked off and YES I'm jealous!!

My novel took 7 years to write. 5 full rewrites and endless revisions. Historical fiction on race, reconciliation, and national healing in America. Hard-nosed, honest friends who've read it still quote it to me. Every man who has read it has told me it made them cry (and not because of the writing style). Two years of contacting literary agents. 18 months of contacting small publishers who don't require an agent. One ASS of a publisher who, because of an e-mail glitch, didn't get my manuscript but just the index and turned me down because he didn't like the index! Still got it here and can't get a break, or even a read from someone!

And now this Toledo ASS (I'm from Toledo; I can say it) is going to get into print???!!!

By all that is holy...by Plato's pen...by Grabthar's Hammer ...

WHERE IS JUSTICE?

I am SO READY for change.

I want change.

I need change.

I am the need that change needs to change.

(Stomps off fuming toward liquor cabinet...sound of liquid being poured and a shot glass slammed down...soft clank of bottles draw near for...)

Kossack Sommelier Moment

For those of you getting ready for the typical Thanksgiving meal, or traveling to one and needing a gift, how about some wine?

Turkey has a very mild flavor *(everything around it on your plate has lots more)* and the meal is heavy *(as in the post–pumpkin pie organ recital: "Oh my stomach! Oh my liver! Oh my gallstones!")*

(All about $15 or less. From Blue States or some places where any junior senator from Illinois can draw 250K for a speech, or are at least anti-Bush.)

A light riesling is a great counterpoint; Starling Castle, slightly sweet, Chateau St. Michelle, Fess Parker or Polka Dot average sweet, anything "late harvest" (Hogue for instance) rather sweet—although still much less than a white zinfandel.

Gewurztraminer is likewise a light white, often quite aromatic, with a ginger/nutmeg zing on the tongue. Same names as above.

On the red side the light ones work best: Beaujolais *(villages or the nouveau that was released Thursday)* like DeBoeuf or Jadot or Drouhin. Also Pinot Noir: Mark West, Echelon, even Smoking Loon and Blackstone on the American side, and a beautiful Bouchard & Fils on the French side. Someone noted the national difference is when you get an American pinot noir in your mouth it wants to make a statement; a French one in your mouth wants to have a conversation—less fruity or forward, more nuanced and a longer finish. (Excellent Oregon Pinots start around $20 or so: Erath, Brandborg, Cloudline, Willamette, Adlesheim.)

Bon appetit!

Monday Morning Latest

Non-Cincinnati Bungles coffee mug resting on the "Minnesota Official Ballot" 8x10 coaster, the Star Tribune is here and...

(((***Crickets shivering in the cold*** *)))*

Nothing. No really. No RECOUNT news on the front page, jump page, 2nd section. No letters to the editor. No updates online for the Star Tribune, the Pioneer Press, or anywhere around the state. Just some stuff about a global economic crisis, Obama's transition team/cabinet choices, a Detroit bailout, a Citibank bailout...in other words, filler...fluff...trivia...nothing on the *most important political story on the planet:* the Coleman/Franken ballot challenges in Koochiching County, Minnesota!

NO RECOUNT News.

3. I mean c'mon, *Star Tribune*! Just because no one counted any votes or didn't file in court or didn't hold a press conference shouldn't mean there's no recount news. Swallow your pride and look how broadcast media does it... Dig deep baby!

Maybe a blond white woman (plenty of them in Minnesota) was driving to the recount in Tofte and took a wrong turn because of road construction and is possibly missing... so Nancy Grace from Faux Noise can breathlessly tell us she knows what the woman must be feeling right now... held captive by the lizard people... (but enough about Matt Drudge and Cindy McCain...)

But look! The Kossacks respond to fill the vacuum! Analysis. Ranting. Hoping. Speculation. Who knows? Maybe even pie fights in the comments (one can only hope!) Kossack Tomtech is valiantly on the diary list with a look at recount "undervotes." Gandharva has an actual rant about...the recount strategies. *(In a foxhole; panting, dirt on the face: "Thank you, thank you my friends. We held on as long as we could Did you bring any wine?")*

OK, well then here's the latest from yust southeast of Lake Wobegon.

Shalom.

Recount Throws off "Issues"
November 25, 2008

Comments: 84   Recs: 220   Tips: 187

As we might expect, some dirt and dust is getting into the recount machinery (or judging from a couple stories, somebody may have dropped in a piece of lutefisk) as we come up on the 3/4 pole. Light-fingered shenanigans! Shouting and tears in the recount room!

Monday While I Was at Work Updates
Trouble in Recount Paradise Part I

A small story catching on a bit in the MN blogs is from Dakota County (exurban sprawl, S of St. Paul). Procedure is count the ballots and then stack them in groups of 25. (Since the ballots are 8x10, you then stack them in groups of 25 at right angles to each other.) At the end of the recounting you can visually tally totals by going 25-50-75 etc.

On Saturday a woman working at the recount was found putting 26 Franken ballots into a group (which of course later would be tallied at 25). Franken observer caught it and called foul...twice. Attorneys from both sides went into a huddle with the election officials, who then recounted several Franken stacks—and caught 6 stacks of 26. No word on consequences for the woman in question.

Kudos to the Franken observer! And, ugly as something like this is, it was caught, dealt with, and fixed. (I'll bet the attorneys on both sides might feel pretty good about what they did actually serving justice.) Whew!

Trouble in Recount Paradise Part II

First day recounting in Mower County (Austin, home of Hormel Meats, including SPAM!, S of Twin cities on the Iowa line) and all is **NOT WELL**.

On Monday morning:

> (About 9:30 a.m.) We have a report from Mower County that the election official is "publically (sic) humiliating" a Franken challenger for making what appears to be a legitimate challenge...The person who contacted us, who is an observer with a labor union says she has a video camera... Apparently when the Franken representative makes a challenge, the head election person stops everyone in the room and makes her state to everyone why she is challenging. He then publicly scolds her for making the challenge.
>
> (About 12:30 p.m.) The Mower County election official has over ruled the only two ballot challenges. They have both come from the Franken campaign. The election official reportedly started screaming and made the Franken representative cry. According to eyewitnesses the ballots in question were not clear on voter intent and the challenge was legitimate. *(The UpTake)*

The UpTake was ALL over this story all day. Official in question is Doug Groh the Mower County Auditor, so he is THE election recount official... *UpTake* also say they have video of said screaming.... (Mid-afternoon) Mike McIntee, webmeister at The UpTake calls Sec. of State's office, asks if Ritchie aware of boil-over in Mower County. Negative, but thanks for tip, will check on it and call Mike back... Asst. Sec. of State Aiken calls back, says he called Mower County re: issue and matter was "resolved" (no further comment)... Later reports from Mower County report challenges happen again but Groh much calmer, apparently having had a phone call sometime mid-afternoon.

And...in case you're wondering just how much leeway an election director/county auditor HAS in a matter like this, the LAW says:

> The candidate's representative authorized to challenge ballots at a Table may challenge the decision of which of the three piles the Table Official place [sic] a ballot. He or she must state a reason for the challenge pursuant to M.S.(2008) Section 204C.22. Challenges may not be automatic or frivolous.
>
> The Table Official will reexamine the ballot to determine into which pile it should be placed. If either candidate's representative who is authorized to challenge ballots does not agree with the Table Officials' final determination, the ballot will be placed in one of two new piles of challenged ballots. One pile of challenged ballots will be for all ballots challenged by Coleman's representative; the second pile of challenged ballots will be for all ballots challenged by Franken's representative. Challenges may be withdrawn at any time. *(The UpTake)*

Uhhhhh, Mr. Groh, Mower County Auditor, sir? What part of "the ballot will be placed in one of two new piles of challenged ballots" **don't you understand**, when a "candidate's representative...does not agree with the Table Officials' final determination"? You DO get to ask for a reason for the challenge. You DO have to write down the reason. But after that, sir, you don't get to say ANYTHING! Shut up and put the vote in the right pile and MOVE ON! *(ACORN to you too, buddy!)*

Cheers to The UpTake, a new-media, shoestring operation. (They are thinking of taking to the air, not with a helicopter, but maybe with a helmet cam and a jet pack! If you'd like to throw them a few bucks they'd appreciate it.)

Lawyers swinging lightsabers II?
NO! Judges swinging light lances!

Knaak and Elias have taken a few swings, but according to Jay Weiner at *MinnPost*, the State Canvassing Board is warming up in the legal bullpen.

> Last week, when he arrived for his meeting at the State Canvassing Board, Minnesota Supreme Court Chief Justice Eric Magnuson carried two historic legal cases with him.
>
> Give His Honor credit for dusting off the law books in his library.
>
> One case—O'Ferrall vs. Colby—was decided in December 1858, barely seven months after Minnesota became a state. The other—Taylor vs. Taylor—hearkens to 1865, when another cool guy from Illinois was president. *(MinnPost)*

There you go, legal eagles of a Minnesota feather! A 143-year-old Minn. Supreme Court decision as possible precedent... and a 150-year-old one that might invoke *"territorial legislative law"* (Betcha haven't touched territorial law in a while :-). Magnuson gave copies to the other board members, 3 of whom are also judges (a Supreme Court associate justice, and 2 Ramsey County court judges, along with Sec. of State Ritchie).

Also, the Canvassing Board is scheduled to meet Dec. 16 to rule on the (in)famous challenged ballots. The total of these stands at nearly 3,000 today, although there are "ballot disarmament" talks under way between the camps and Ritchie's office to see if some of them can be taken down by either camp withdrawing some of their challenges against the other side. Hope so, because Weiner also writes:

> Here's the challenged vote problem: If it takes three minutes per ballot for a thorough examination and there are 3,000 challenged ballots, that's 9,000 minutes or 150 hours or more than six straight days of ballot counting . . . without sleep. Won't work. *(MinnPost)*

Speaking of the State Canvassing Board

They are all going to "cleanse the palate" for Thursday by having an official meeting on Wednesday with both camps. First word (again from Weiner) is this is no court case or hearing with lawyers doing a lot of blah, blah. Instead...

> ...the State Canvassing Board has told both campaigns to prepare for a two-hour meeting Wednesday and that there will be no oral arguments from the lawyers; they should only be there to answer inquiries from the judges. *(MinnPost)*

Just me, but why do I think judges might ENJOY the chance to ask nosy, uncomfortable questions and do the talking while lawyers squirm?

Campaign posturings

As you know,the Coleman campaign has challenged some ballots that had a McCain vote for president and a Franken vote for senate. Nothing wrong with the ballot physically, but Norm and his people apparently can't comprehend this combination is possible.

Now we have a report of a challenged ballot that has a McCain vote for president and no vote at all for senate. OK, so? Your classic "undervote." So? Coleman campaign has challenged, holding that a McCain + blank ballot *should be counted for* COLEMAN! S'truth! WAY! And as they say in Brooklyn (home of Norm's accent), "Da noive!"

Franken campaign held a press conference this afternoon. A press release had the following for lovers of numbers.

> Each night, the Secretary of State will update its count at 8 p.m. Central Time. But because we have observers in every precinct (many of which counted into the night), our internal data is more up-to-date. In addition, whereas the Secretary of State removes all challenged ballots from his tally, we are able to report the election judge's actual calls from the table. Thus, we believe that Norm Coleman's margin has been cut down into double digits, below 100 votes, and that it has narrowed further since dipping into double digits late last week.

(As of Saturday night:)

We believe that 68% of the ballots have been counted. Among the ballots that have been counted, Al Franken won 49.3% of the two-way vote on Election Day. Among the ballots that have not yet been counted, Al Franken won 51.6% of the two-way vote on Election Day.

In Hennepin County: 67.3% of the ballots have been counted. In the precincts counted, Al Franken got 52.9% of the two-way vote on Election Day. In the precincts not yet counted, Al Franken got 68.8% of the two-way vote on Election Day.

In Ramsey County: 43.2% of the ballots have been counted. In the precincts counted, Al Franken got 70.6% of the two-way vote on Election Day. In the precincts not yet counted, Al Franken got 52.8% of the two-way vote on Election Day.

In St. Louis County: 78.6% of the ballots have been counted. In the precincts counted, Al Franken got 62.3% of the two-way vote on Election Day. In the precincts not yet counted, Al Franken got 64.3% of the two-way vote on Election Day.
(Press release from Al Franken, reported in MNPlubius)

Nota Bene: Also in press release Franken campaign has asked Sec. of State's office *"to find missing ballots that have been reported across the state. Press reports indicate that ballots are missing in Saint Paul, Duluth, Coon Rapids, Hermantown, Crystal, Hopkins, Berlin, Apple Valley, and Chisago, among other places."*

Missing ballots? This IS news, but very little else to go on. How many? Why? How did the Franken campaign find out they were missing, apart from press reports?

Oh, and for out-of-staters: St. Paul you know. Coon Rapids is in Anoka County, WNW of St. Paul, exurb. Chisago is the county seat of Chisago, N & a bit east of St. Paul. Apple Valley is in Dakota County S of St. Paul. Crystal & Hopkins are both suburbs W of Minneapolis in Hennepin Co. Hermantown is a suburb of Duluth in St. Louis County. Berlin is in Steele County—no further information received since 1971...from anyone.

Coleman challenged over a hundred more than Franken in Saint Louis County, and he lost that county. The challenge ratio is over twice the rest of the state. I wouldn't be at all surprised to see Franken net 100 votes from that county alone.
(Scarce)

Recounted Ballots

Secretary of State's Office 8:00pm Nov. 24

Total % of Ballots Recounted: 74.18%

	Coleman	Franken
Recounted ballots	908,063	899,891
Change from election day	-1,051	-1,008
Apparent difference		+43
Start of Recount difference	+215	

Both the "change from election day" and "apparent difference" lines INCLUDE the challenged ballots noted next, so don't read too much into these numbers.

Challenged Ballots

Franken has challenged 1,401 "Coleman & other" ballots statewide.

Coleman has challenged 1,400 "Franken & other" ballots statewide.

Those 1,401+ 1,400 = 2,801 ballots will go to the State Canvassing Board for final decisions.

DK

I will tell you for a fact that Coleman people are, indeed, making these kinds of challenges. One Coleman challenger said he didn't like a ballot (Franken vote) because "the dots were extra big," and challenged it. The ballot was very cleanly and clearly filled out.

In another precinct, a Coleman lawyer was asked by a Coleman rep whether or not a ballot was a legitimate challenge. The Coleman lawyer said: "Well, that is a Franken vote. But if you want to challenge it tit for tat, go ahead!" *(KuanShiYin)*

Whew! Heavy day, Monday! Ok, now we'll add the AM report and head off to work.

Tuesday Morning Updates

Republican Projection and Strategy Dept.

(With a hat tip to Karl Rove) if you want to know what a modern Republican's strategy is on a given issue, look at what they are accusing their opponent of. Then you know for 100% what the Republican plan is. ("Democrats ruin the economy by overspending" = "We will ruin the economy by overspending." "Liberals are perverts" = "My name is Mark Foley/Larry Craig/Ted Haggard" OR "Democrats hate America/small business/capitalism" = "We are destroying the Constitution, supporting Wal-mart, bailing out Wall Street.")

See how that works?

So keep those glasses on and read this quote from Fritz Knaak, Norm Coleman's legal eagle:

Knaak, meanwhile, said the Coleman camp's analysis of the challenged ballots, as of mid-afternoon Monday, gave Coleman a five-vote lead among them, but he acknowledged it was an ever-changing number.

He added that the Coleman campaign was suspicious that Franken's campaign was increasing its ballot challenges in an attempt to "artificially deflate" Coleman's lead before a Canvassing Board meeting Wednesday. Knaak said it was "a pitch to appearances as opposed to reality." *(Star Tribune)*

This is EXCELLENT news for the Franken campaign! This means the Coleman campaign believes

a. Franken is leading;

b. it's a rather big lead, probably flirting with 3 digits;

c. The Coleman campaign is increasing its ballot challenges in order to "artificially deflate" Franken's lead, and

d. Coleman's side is playing up "appearances as opposed to reality." GO AL! GO AL!

DK Just wondering if anyone knows what happens in an exact tie. I know it's improbable, but I'm curious. *(khassani)*

DK MN law "shall be decided by lot." Coin flip. Cut the cards. *(WineRev)*

DK Arm wrestle for it? *(elwior)*

DK Stormin' Norm and Smilin' Al in a Texas Steel Cage Death match. Special guest referee: former Minnesota governor Jesse "the body" Ventura.
Pay per view could be off the scale. *(WineRev)*

OK, The Not–Cincinnati Bungles coffee mug resting on the "Minnesota Official Ballot" needs a refill, so here's the latest from yust southeast of Lake Wobegon.

Shalom.

Recount Round-up of You Name it
November 26, 2008

Comments: 14   *Recs:* 24   *Tips:* 26

A full day Tuesday on the recount front. Wednesday will be a big send-off for the Thanksgiving break: The State Canvassing Board has scheduled a 2-hour meeting w/ both campaigns' lawyers, and mostly the Board is going to do the asking and the lawyers the answering.

Recounted Ballots

Secretary of State's Office 8:00pm Nov. 25

Total % of Ballots Recounted: 80.62%

	Coleman	Franken
Recounted ballots	978,751	976,187
Change from election day	-1,370	-1,393
Apparent difference	+23	
Start of Recount difference	+215	
Both the "change from election day" and "apparent difference" lines INCLUDE the challenged ballots noted next, so don't read too much into these numbers.		

Challenged Ballots

Franken has challenged 1,758 "Coleman & other" ballots statewide.

Coleman has challenged 1836 "Franken & other" ballots statewide.

Those 1,758 + 1,836 = 3,594 ballots will go to the State Canvassing Board for final decisions.

Obviously the **headline tomorrow** will be Coleman's lead, starting at 215 and swinging as low as 113 last Thursday, has rebounded and added votes to lead by 238. This will be a big PR, 24-hour news cycle win for the Coleman campaign. Incoming! for Frankenites.

Silver linings

1. Today the Franken precincts came in strongly and will perhaps show in tomorrow's numbers.

2. *Rejected absentee* ballots the Franken campaign knows of are over 6,400. (More below, and more of these coming.)

3. *Challenged* ballots are still climbing, 800 more today combined from the 2 camps. If they are starting to climb down on their number of challenges, it doesn't show yet in these numbers. (More below)

Still, a tough day for the Franken camp on at least the PR front. Tomorrow could be a hunker-down day, but the Canvassing Board meeting may well provide some fireworks.

Some of my own thoughts on Ballots
Rejected Absentee Ballots

(These ballots sound like they're small puppies accidentally locked in the garage overnight: 'rejected,' sniff...'absentee' yip, yip, eeeeoooo "whimper, whimper"; poor ballots!)

A good 280,000 of the 2.9 million votes cast were by absentee ballot. MN doesn't have early voting, but absentees functioned as a form of that. So, roughly 10% of all ballots came in by mail.

Now the Franken campaign said today they have received information on rejected absentee ballots (names, addresses, and written reason for rejection) from 66 of the 87 counties, and that the list is over 6,400. (6,400/280,000 = 2.29% of absentees; 0.22% of all ballots in election.) If some decent fraction of these ballots were improperly rejected and can be "reinstated as votes" the election will definitely... *take a new turn!*

But what are the standards, and what are chances?

The *Star Tribune* editorial board this morning on its own op-ed page listed the 4 state requirements for an absentee ballot to be accepted and counted:

> a. name/address on return envelope matches absentee ballot application info
>
> b. voter signature on envelope matches sig on app. (w/ certain narrow exceptions)
>
> c. voter must be registered OR register with absentee ballot (included with return envelope)
>
> d. voter may not have voted in person at polls. *(Star Tribune)*

These look like pretty straightforward requirements for voting absentee, preventing fraud *and laying out grounds for rejecting such a ballot.*

Point a) is obvious to me (If it reads "Wine Rev, 123 Lutefisk Lane, Norsky, MN" the response should be: "Looky darr, Sven. Dis return envelop-en has the same name and address from da VineRev as his application.") This just has to match.

Point d) is a matching operation that's simple but effective. ("Vell, Ol-lie, after twenty-too hundert names in da VineRev's precinct voter sign-in book-en, he vasn't dere. So I guess dis absentee is his vote.") Franken, Coleman, or anybody else trying to get absentee ballots counted that don't meet these 3 points is DOA. Nope. No way. Zip.

I think the case has to be made on b) or c). Taking **c)**—registered to vote—first, if an absentee ballot arrives with a proper registration card (included when it's sent out) and THAT registration passes muster, then the ballot is 3 for 3 so far.

A bit tougher is "registered to vote". Mostly it's another matching operation like d) but looking at a different record. Where a petitioner *can* make a case, it seems, is where a voter is actually properly registered but there's some slip-up between ballot and registration (I think middle initial might be a common one). Franken campaign has said at least a few of its rejected absentee ballots are like this and should be counted. May be true, but it will be 1 by 1 and rather slow.

On this front, reporter chuckumentary at The UpTake states: "Minneapolis had a number of rejected ballots due to administrative error including registration—Secretary of State's own database shows voter was registered." If this is a clue to the rest of the counties, Franken might find fertile ground here.

In the same line, same source, "Itasca County rejected an absentee because 'we screwed up' and put in reject pile." But it's been caught—again the recount process doing what it's supposed to do.

Point b) may be the hardest without graphologists at every recount station or advising the Canvassing Board. In other words, lots of room for lawyers to argue...and yet, even here, perhaps less than meets the eye. Variations, yes, as when you lay out a bunch of your cancelled checks like a deck of cards, with all your signatures above each other for 25 or 30 times. Different? Yes, a bit here and there...but the same person? Nearly everybody would say, "Yep, dat's how Lena Anderson Peterson signs her name down here at da Larson, Carlson & Swenson dry goods store."

> The other reason for rejecting an absentee ballot is if the voter died before the morning of the election.
>
> There are several dozen of these, probably fewer than 100.
>
> These could be counted if the voter was rejected but wasn't actually dead (Insert Monty Python reference here). *(zymurgist)*

Ballots lost and found

From around the state: Elias is miffed ballots are missing (recount total does not match election night machine tapes when accounting for challenged and corrections). Several dozen(!) may be missing in Becker County (*NW Minnesota, about 50 miles E of Fargo ND—home of losing vice-presidential accents*)...

And now, more on Becker County from the big Minneapolis TV & Radio complex WCCO, Sue Turner writes in part:

> 61 as-yet-uncounted election ballots have been located in Becker County, which could have a significant role in deciding a very close Senate recount...

> The discovered ballots were absentee and mail-in votes. They were found in a secured cubicle late last week and were not counted in the original total. As per the canvassing board rules, those ballots are eligible for inclusion in the recount numbers.
>
> According to Secretary of State Mark Ritchie, both Coleman and Franken's campaigns have acquiesced to the inclusion of those ballots. He added that their inclusion points to the importance of recounts in close races...
>
> (AND STILL MORE) Also in Becker County, 15 ballots have gone missing. Workers there believe it's due to a sorting issue between Spruce Grove Township and Wolf Lake, which vote together. *(WCCO)*

City officials in Crystal (West Minneapolis first-ring suburb) on Friday night found 8 absentee ballots, still sealed, among the opened ones. Now have recounted them. (I know you want to know: Franken 7, Coleman 1.)

(Reichwingers who are gearing up to rant about "manufacturing votes" or "stupid counters"—SHUT UP! This is how it's supposed to work, to catch stuff just like this. WineRev straightens hat. Does the Obama brush-off on shoulders. Resumes diary)

Republican Projection and Strategy Dept. II

As I mentioned yesterday, if you want to know what a modern Republican's strategy is on a given issue, look at what they are accusing their opponent of. Today's installment from Mike McIntee at The UpTake:

> The Coleman campaign and its surragates (sic) were complaining of Franken aides challenging "Obama-Coleman" or "Obama-nobody" ballots before the recount began. Since then, we've seen no challenges like that, and ironically the Coleman campaign has used that same tactic as documented in our video.

Lawyers Wielding Lightsabers IV, Bigfoot, and Star Trek

Re: Rejected Absentee Ballots (will be big tomorrow at State Canvassing Board Meeting).

Elias (Franken). Obviously not all 6,432 rejected ballots were wrongly rejected, and we don't know who those voters chose.

Knaak (Coleman): The affidavit (filed by DFL guy here in MN) for this is a knock on the hard-working election officials of MN.

Re: How close is the count?

Elias: As close as 84, using "Frankenmath" in guessing how Canvassing Board might rule on certain challenged ballots.

Knaak: Coleman camp doesn't buy the "artificial numbers" of the Franken vote count. "We hope you'll treat these numbers with the same credibility that we would treat sightings of Bigfoot."

Re: Lost & Found Ballots

Elias: Still increasingly concerned about 100s of missing ballots or those officials won't count for some reason. (Cited Becker County, Crystal, other locations noted above.)

Knaak: When ballots go missing "Immediately the alarms will go off, shields up, here come the Klingons, that kind of thing. Then, you realize you have to be patient ... Generally [the ballots] do surface." (And the Crystal and Becker reports came in later in the day.)

Re: Canvassing Board deciding on rejected absentee ballots

Elias: Of course the Board has authority to decide the question.

Knaak: Of course the Board doesn't have authority to decide the question, only the courts do.

I don't know...on balance I'd give the day's duel to Knaak. He sounded a bit calmer, Elias a touch strained. I mean, how can you not like a lawyer who cites Bigfoot and Klingons? Stay tuned.

Wednesday Morning News

The State Canvassing Board meets TODAY, 2 hours, starting at 9:30 a.m. CT with the 2 campaigns' lawyers, and judges (and Sec. of State Ritchie) get to ask the questions. Rejected absentee ballots sure to come up. Probably less than 50-50 that the Board will rule on any of them. *(Do you want a recount on those odds? Maybe 48-48? That's less than 50-50.)*

Mower County Follow-up/JOE Power

Elias, Franken's legal front man, was asked at press conference yesterday re: screaming incident in Mower County by County Auditor, bringing Franken representative to tears. ANS: "Election officials apologized for how worker was treated, and we accept that apology."...The UpTake still waiting for video of Mower County Meltdown and will post when they have it...

Itasca County (N Central, WAY N, and NW of Duluth) Auditor Jeff Walker said one(!) absentee ballot that was *properly filled out* was put in the rejected pile by mistake of the officials. So even though Itasca County has finished recounting, Walker is going to call in some volunteers and observers and REOPEN the recount (for this one, and 2 more absentees that have come to light!)

OK, so he's a Jeff, not a Joe—as in Mansky, or Biden *(although he's got that first letter)*, so GO JEFF! Way to show that JOE POWER! [Since ya gotta know, the one mis-piled (?) absentee vote was for Barkley. But damn it, now it's counted!]

So Civic-minded everywhere? All you who think even ONE ballot deserves respect and proper counting? Atten-hut! Dress the line! *(Jeff Walker nervously steps up to the Mansky-Tynjala Podium, looking out over the vast Orange throng, star-spangled flags luffing softly over the scene.)* Those in the service, Salute! Civilians, un-cover! *(WineRev doffs hat.)*

Tidbit from the Star Tribune

David Lillehaug, Franken's legal heavy, gets a guest column on the op-ed page...cites case of voter in Pennington County (WAY NW MN, North and a bit east of Fargo...*you know, not the end of the world, but you can see it from there?*) who went to County courthouse to fill in absentee ballot paperwork, but county official who witnessed this forgot to sign, so vote rejected...not voter's fault... cites Itasca County...argues Board should decide such cases, not courts (Coleman position)...calls on Board to side with enfranchisement and count every proper vote...

Yipes, with this much news I need stronger coffee in the Non-Cincinnati Bungles coffee mug over here on the "Minnesota Official Ballot" Coaster. I'll head off to work soon, leaving you with the latest from yust southeast of Lake Wobegon.

Shalom.

December 2008

Leftovers: Thanksgiving & Recount
December 1, 2008

Comments: 36 *Recs:* 43 *Tips:* 39

Welcome back from your Thanksgiving adventures. The WineRev also had a nice thanksgiving with the WineRevER and older-sister-home-from-college WineRevette, along with their mom.

Minnesota recounters took a few days away as well but swing back into it today. We'll be counting 11/4 ballots, challenging ballots, un-challenging ballots, daring other campaigns to un-challenge ballots, rejecting absentee ballots, dis-un-rejecting absentee ballots to make them present ballots maybe sort of, all while talking things over in front of the State Canvassing Board, bruiting (what a word!) court cases and solemnly mentioning the United States Senate.

Recounting Ballots

Although the Sec. of State's office has posted daily updates, there have been no new numbers. Things will spring to life this week. The following counties (according to the Sec. of State's website; *Star Tribune* and other sources may have later, more recent numbers. I'm using the Ritchie numbers since they will be the final ones eventually) have NOT begun counting but will do so this week. Some start today, others later.

	Total Vote 11/4	11/4. Coleman or Franken?		Total Vote 11/4	11/4: Coleman or Franken?
Brown	10K	C	Sherburne	35K	C
Dodge	8,100+	C	Stevens	4,700+	C
Jackson	4,500+	C	Winona	24K	F
Rock	4,400+	C	Wright	51K	C
Scott	54K	C			

Obviously the big numbers will come from Scott, Sherburne, Winona, and Wright counties. Scott is S of Twin Cities, exurban. Sherburne is NW of Minneapolis, exurban sprawl. Winona is SE MN along the Mississippi. Wright is NW of Minneapolis, exurban sprawl. Just because Coleman won all but one of these counties has had little to do with the recount. Franken has been breaking even or better in the recount.

Then there are 4 counties that are partially recounted:

	Total Vote 11/4	11/4: Coleman or Franken?	Percent Counted
Beltrami	19K	F	99.97
Blue Earth	28K	F	77.31
Hennepin	567K	F	87.13
Ramsey	234K	F	91.19

Apparently Beltrami (Bemidji) has one precinct incomplete. Blue Earth is SE of Twin Cities toward Iowa. Hennepin is Metro Minneapolis and Ramsey is Metro St. Paul. From earlier counties Franken showed recount gains in counties he won on the 4th; not a lot, but then at 282 votes a few dozen here and there add up fast.

So, by Saturday morning these ballots should be nearly 100% recounted, allowing for an odd glitch like Beltrami, or some precincts asking Sec. of State Ritchie for an extension for some reason. So, wait and see.

Challenged Ballots: Total: 4,740

Franken has challenged 2,292 "Coleman and other" ballots.

Coleman has challenged 2,448 "Franken and other" ballots.

Wednesday the 26th the State Canvassing Board met in public session. Challenged ballots figured in the meeting. Both camps have publicly said they are willing to stand down and un-challenge some of their ballots, but neither seems to have done so in any numbers. (Either or both might have dropped a few here and there, but these were lost in the 300–400 new challenges added each of the past few days.)

It seems to me someone could score some good PR and some goodwill by announcing, "We've reviewed the challenges our observers have filed and we thank them for their work. Upon further review we are dropping X number (say, oh, 350) from our pile. We call upon our opponent to follow through on their promises to do likewise, in order to spare the Canvassing Board any additional work."

Psychologically, too, I think the Board would at least look unconsciously in favor of the camp that did this. *("Man, this is a pile to rule on one by one, but at least it's 350 fewer than it could have been.")*

The conventional wisdom at the moment is most of the challenges will be dismissed, so a bunch of ballots will go back into their original piles. Our hero Joe Mansky, Ramsey County elections director and former state elections director, offered some cold-water realism: "Based upon the kinds of challenges I've been looking at in the last two weeks, I think that's just not going to happen." (i.e., Franken will close the gap on challenges won.)

If they are indeed rejected at exactly the same rate, and as Coleman has at the moment challenged 156 more ballots than Franken, that *could* mean 156 more votes going back for Franken—which helps, but is still not enough. To pull even, and starting from down 282, Franken would need to "win" the challenged ballots by 53-47%. (Ignoring for a moment challenged Barkley ballots, the ballot with an X not in the oval but exactly between both names of Coleman and Franken; both sides challenged that one, etc.)

The key question, of course, is will the challenges be rejected at the same rate? Franken's campaign has made noises their challenges are "better" and not as frivolous. Coleman's side has been very quiet about their side, and at least some of the anecdotal news has been that Coleman observers have been "aggressive" and going after the least little thing. Again, a thread, but it would tend to fit the Repug "take no prisoners/ we are the righteous/anything to win" mindset, and if they are cumulatively about 6% like that...

The Canvassing Board will take up these challenged ballots on **Dec. 16**, one by one. They hope to finish by Dec. 19 but Board Chair Mark Ritchie, Sec. of State, has said repeatedly that the Board will NOT be rushed, and they will take as long as they need to get an accurate final count.

Rejected Absentee Ballots

The Frankenites won a court ruling a couple weeks ago binding on the counties, that they (and anyone else) could obtain the name, address of absentee voters whose ballots *were rejected at the county level and not counted on 11/4.* Just before Thanksgiving the Frankenites said they had received about 6,400 of these, from 66 of the 87 counties. The Coleman side has been also very quiet about any such ballots.

Last Wednesday the Franken side asked the Canvassing Board to take up these ballots and rule on them one by one as well. The Coleman side argued the State Board did not have jurisdiction over these ballots nor the authority to examine the reasons for rejection. After discussion the Board ruled (5-0) for Coleman's side. (Coleman further argued only courts have jurisdiction, but the Board did not exactly go there.)

However, 2 other events say this is not over for the Franken side. First, having made this judgment of their jurisdiction, the State Canvassing Board asked for a further ruling from the Minnesota Attorney General (Lori Swenson, D). No word from the AG as of this morning, but this is still a live issue.

Second, The Board also said (although not in an actual vote) that while they did not have jurisdiction, that the county election boards certainly did (and even the Coleman side was silent at this) and rather broadly hinted that the county boards could revisit this. [Itasca County is reopening their recount Monday in order to reexamine 3(!) rejected absentee ballots, one of which the County Auditor has already admitted they goofed on. Story in yesterday's diary.]

They suggested the creation of a "Fifth Pile" of rejected absentee ballots. County boards (apparently on instructions from the Sec. of State's office) have created 4 groups of absentee ballots they have rejected (and NOT counted) based on the 4 reasons such a ballot can be rejected.

Two of the five Board members liked this 5th pile:

> Two judges, Gearin and Cleary, indicated they'd want to see the fifth pile of ballots opened up and counted. However, the board did not vote on this but asked the state attorney general's office for an opinion. (*Pioneer Press*)

This famous 5th Pile is supposed to be for reasons other than the 4 official reasons. The Franken side believes there may be several 100 votes here (although obviously not all for them) that ought to be counted but have not been. The Coleman side is pretty quiet about counting the votes but loud about saying (again) that such ballots should be ruled on by a court. The Colemaniks also have been rather quiet about the county boards revisiting these ballots; to me this says they are nervous about these.

But maybe I'm biased: Here is Fritz Knaak after the Board meeting on rejected absentee ballots, sounding rather reasonable:

> Knaak said the Coleman campaign was pleased with the ruling and supports the idea of counting votes from ballots that have no legal basis for being rejected.
>
> For example, Knaak said he supports the decision by Itasca County Auditor-Treasurer Jeff Walker to reopen his county's recount to reconsider three ballots, including one rejected absentee ballot whose official reason for rejection by election judges begins, "We messed up."
>
> In essence, Knaak said, the Fifth Piles already are being created. (*Star Tribune*)

Secretary of State Ritchie said after the Wednesday meeting that as far as he could see, the only way a rejected absentee voter who believes their vote was rejected/not counted for no good reason would be to go to court. Hat tip to the *Minnesota Independent*:

> "At the moment, they have to go to court," (Ritchie) said. "We can discuss whether that's a good thing or not."
>
> I asked the secretary of state what he thought of allowing the responsibility for resolving the problem of wrongly rejected absentee ballots fall to individual voters. "If there's a thousand people having to go to court?" Ritchie let his voice drop to a stage whisper. "It's a bad thing. ... If there are 500 to 1,000 [cases], that would be crushing to the judicial system." (*Chris Steller, MN Independent*)

The Board said they expected court cases. Joe Mansky feels the Franken side's best chance may be in the courts.

Republicans Telegraphing Own Strategy Dept. III

Mark Elias outlined possible steps where he could see things going. He mentioned the courts and also noted the US Senate can make a determination on seating a member.

US Senate Majority Leader Harry Reid (D-Nevada) came out with a statement that the Senate could indeed determine its own membership and if needed would be willing to do so in the Minnesota case. Stated he wanted to see the votes counted. (Democratic mantra—but a good one; see Fl, 2000; OH 2004)

Colemaniks had a series of reactions (scattered across the past few days):

> The Coleman campaign called on Franken to denounce Elias' comments. And the campaign had an equally strong reaction when, shortly after the canvassing board met, Senate Majority Leader Harry Reid, D-Nev., weighed in.
>
> "Today's decision by the Minnesota Canvassing Board not to count certain absentee ballots is cause for great concern," Reid said in a statement.

> Coleman campaign manager Cullen Sheehan accused the Franken campaign of being ready to take the case to the Senate if Franken's side doesn't emerge the winner in the recount, which ends Dec. 5.
>
> "This is a stunning admission by the Franken campaign that they are willing to take this process away from Minnesotans if they fail to win the recount," Sheehan said. "It is even more stunning that the Democratic Senate leader would inject himself into the Minnesota election process." *(Star Tribune Online)*

Well, Cullen Sheehan, have some smelling salts. You are double stunned (stunned! yea even shocked! to find out there is gambling going on here at Rick's Cafe in Casablanca...sorry...back to Minnesota). Well, Cullen, you have a low stun level.

"Take this process away from Minnesotans..."

AHA! Stand BY! Headline:

The Coleman campaign is looking for ways to remove the recount process from Minnesota!

"Democratic (Cullen missed the "democrat" memo) Senate leader would inject himself into the Minnesota election process." (you know, by pointing out what possible outcomes might finally come to.)

AHA! Stand By! Headline:

The Coleman campaign readies plans for US Senate/Congress/Supreme Court to crush Minnesota election process!

Coleman campaign overlapped some of this (but bristled at the US Senate possibility) when they released this:

> Coleman's campaign issued a statement Friday (11/28) saying the outcome of the dispute "isn't about matrices, lawsuits or U.S. Senate intervention. This is about the recounting of ballots legally cast by Minnesotans, and we are confident Senator Coleman will be reelected."

How bad could it get?

Pretty bad. Paul Demko had an article last Tuesday in the *Minnesota Independent*, at points citing David Schultz, professor of law and political science at Hamline Univ. in St. Paul. Dr. Schultz had expected lawsuits to be filed on Wednesday after the State Canvassing Board meeting, but neither side did. However, at the end of the article Demko raises this (first time I've seen this in the media).

> If the contest drags on into January with no resolution, the opportunity to fill the seat would likely fall to Gov. Tim Pawlenty. That undoubtedly would result in Coleman being re-appointed to his post. But it would only be, at best, a temporary solution. If there's no resolution, a new election would need to be held next November to determine who would fill the final five years of the term. "We'd have to run through the whole damn thing all over again," says Schultz.
>
> That's a prospect that should be terrifying to Minnesotans of all political stripes. *(Minnesota Independent)*

Monday Morning with the Star Tribune

Ah, coffee mit schlag in the Not–Cincinnati Bungles mug resting on the Minnesota Official Ballot coaster!

Well, with no real recount news to report over the weekend the Star Tribune this morning takes a typical, liberal media tack: *they report no news.* SOOOOooo different from a fair and balanced real American newspaper that would, you know, just make stuff up (that would be Faux Noise in print—the ultimate in birdcage liner fishwrap).

A couple of letters to the editor, striking while the iron is hot in favor of instant-runoff voting. Hennepin County Auditor Jill Alverson writes to defend her office's work in sending out an absentee ballot, saying they sent it out in September to a resident stationed in Iraq and that they are subject to the vagaries of the postal service like everybody else. One letter snarking people who can't fill in a circle with a dot; they have to use an X or check mark, comparing them to folks who can't turn on their headlights during a rainstorm while driving.

And then, saving the best for last:

JOE POWER!

In the second section of the *Star Tribune*, Curt Brown gives us a half-page bio on Joe Mansky.

Joe's recount site is the largest single site in the state. He's watching over 278,000 ballots.

The first two days of the recount, Joe would meet at the end of the day with lawyers from both sides over challenged ballots. Both camps averaged 5/day by this process. The Ramsey County attorney then weighed in and said Joe should stick to auditing and recounting and lay off being an arbiter. So since then challenges have averaged 50/day.

You KNEW you liked this guy: Age 55.... Rides his bicycle to work almost every day (yes, in the winter; yes, wearing a suit & tie) 12 miles one way...graduate degree in hydrology (water stuff) from U. Wisconsin–Green Bay and Univ. of Nebraska...moved from Nebraska to MN because he likes cross-country skiing...has run the Twin Cities marathon twice...and he's got a great sense of the job, mixed with humor:

> Mansky said the escalating tensions that have been observed from both campaigns are to be expected, given the high stakes that have everyone "on a knife's edge."
>
> At one of his recount meetings, he told the various campaign observers: "You have nothing to apologize for. If you weren't being a pain in the butt, you wouldn't be earning your pay."
>
> To which an observer said: "Joe, we're volunteers."
>
> "Then," Mansky quipped, "you've got some get-a-life issues." (*Star Tribune*)

OK that's the post-Thanksgiving update of the events happening yust southeast of Lake Wobegon. Shalom.

Recount Wind-Down
December 2, 2008

Comments: 46   *Recs:* 61   *Tips:* 60

The Big Minnesota Recount is winding to a close, but challenges, absentees, court fights, PR moves, and other matters loom ever larger.

Recounting Ballots
Recounted Ballots

Secretary of State's Office 8:00pm Dec. 1

Total % of Ballots Recounted: 91.13%

	Coleman	Franken
Recounted ballots	1,100,922	1,105,030
Change from election day	-2,369	-2,468
Apparent difference	+129	
Start of Recount difference	+215	
Both the "change from election day" and "apparent difference" lines INCLUDE the challenged ballots noted next, so don't read too much into these numbers.		

Challenged Ballots

Franken has challenged 2,876 "Coleman & other" ballots statewide.

Coleman has challenged 3,067 "Franken & other" ballots statewide.

Those 2,876 + 3,067 = 5,943 ballots will go to the State Canvassing Board for final decisions.

Utter Snark Moment, based on the top line numbers here

Now class, if you are playing "Republican Election," what is your next move? Anyone?

Yes, Pat in the third row? Yes, that's right!! Everyone go to your closets and get out your tassel loafers and other preppie gear from Brooks Brothers and head down to the Secretary of State's Office in St. Paul and START A RIOT!

Your Chant: "Stop the count! STOP THE COUNT!! **STOP THE COUNT!!!**"

And you know why of course? *AL FRANKEN LEADS SENATE RECOUNT!* See the numbers above? For the very first time since Nov. 4, by the number of votes now (un)officially recounted under Minnesota Law, Al Franken LEADS Norm Coleman by 4,108 votes. So cancel all that other stuff about "count every vote," "fairness," "democracy" and "democratic elections." Tell Harry Reid to shut up.

(*Ahem-snark*) In the interest of bipartisanship,
in the need to move on from equality under the law,
since the American people in the last election voted for *change*,
and yet since we are still a center-right nation,
and so a great change would be "center-right" tactics applied to a Democratic candidate recount,
therefore we on the left side of the political street *need* a "republican election" right now in Minnesota!

So stop the Count! Franken is Elected!

Challenged Ballots II

Guess what? Recounting resumed today and so did challenging ballots. Kaszuba and Brown (or as we say in Minnesot-ese, "Kaszubanen and Brownson") at the *Star Tribune* report both camps again are talking about reducing their challenged ballots before the State Canvassing Board starts ruling on them one by one on Dec. 16. Mark Elias said they are ready to drop "more than dozens" of their challenges this week.

Coleman campaign replied they are willing to sit down and talk with Franken campaign to reduce number of frivolous challenges. Frankenites sound like they are ready to do this unilaterally, apart from any conversations with the Coleman side.

> Coleman spokesman Mark Drake downplayed the significance of Elias' announcement, saying that simply dropping dozens of challenges "doesn't seem like too much of a dent." Drake said he did not know whether the Coleman campaign would likewise independently withdraw challenges as early as this week. *(Star Tribune)*

Nice, Mr. Drake. If it's 10 dozen (120) then the Frankenites have taken down 4% of their challenges— and that's a dent larger than Coleman has made. Any comment, Mr. Drake, on the 600+ challenges (that's 50 dozen by the way) your side ADDED today? I thought so.

Then there was this:

> Drake also said the Franken campaign seemed to be moving closer to asking the U.S. Senate to decide the ultimate outcome, and said it was another sign Franken intended to "ignore the results of the recount." *(Star Tribune)*

No, Mr. Drake. Elias was asked to describe the whole range of options available to them *(you know? The SAME range of options available to YOU and to the sitting, senior senator of Minnesota, Mr. Norm Coleman?)*. YOU are latching on to the last, final-resort option in order to... what? Hoo boy!

So we will continue piling up challenged ballots for the next 4 days... like in Sherburne County (NW of Minneapolis, halfway to St. Cloud). They finished counting last Wednesday and reported to the Sec. of State today. *"Sherburne County Deputy Administrator Luci Botzek said the Franken campaign picked up the list of rejected absentee ballots Monday. That county, which finished its recount Wednesday, had its process slowed by 874 challenges, the highest percentage of total ballots cast."* 874 challenges over 51,000 votes? Wow. Stay tuned for more laughs.

Rejected Absentee Ballots

The Franken side said they have now received names, addresses, and reasons for rejection of absentee ballots from 78 of 87 counties, numbering over 9,000. Elias did say these ballots *as a last resort* could end up in the US Senate, but only after the local election board, State Canvassing Board and the courts have been exhausted. Also, that the vast majority of these ballots were properly rejected but Frankenites think maybe 500–1,000 merit a second look at the reasons. Sec. of State Ritchie (from different sources I would suppose) also mentioned a figure of 500, give or take, that might be questionable.

> **DK**
>
> The absentee ballot issue is an issue for the court to decide, the canvassing board simply stated it did not have the authority to determine the legitimacy of those ballots. If this is as close as it seems to be then the absentee ballot issue will go to court to determine whether or not they are legitimate, if so they will be counted.
> *(edgeways)*

Scraps and Pieces

Wright County (NW of Minneapolis) starts counting Wednesday and hopes to go through 51,000+ ballots by Friday. Since this is one of the last counties counting, CNN is rumored to be sending a team for "live coverage."

Both Hennepin & Ramsey Counties (Minneapolis and St. Paul metros, respectively) are both about 93% recounted and may finish on Tuesday.

The Senate Race and Recount has reached the level of Fear and Loathing; that is, our little recount has become a major story, "The Last Recount," in *Rolling Stone* by Matt Taibbi.

From *MinnPost*, a small item on "missing ballots" that might be nothing or...

> Also, Elias said, according to the Franken campaign's examination, as many as 700 ballots from the original count seem to be missing. Some missing ballots could simply be a case of election machines jamming on Nov. 4 and, so, an incorrect vote count on Election Day. That is, a voter puts her ballot in the machine to be counted; the machine spits it back once; and, then, on a second try, grabs it for a count.
>
> But in some precincts double digits of votes are missing.
>
> "That's a lot of jamming," Elias said.
>
> The Coleman campaign last week wondered about such discrepancies, too.
> *(MinnPost)*

Off to get that second cup of coffee, so I'll leave you with the latest from yust southeast of Lake Wobegon.

Shalom.

Absentee Ballots Becoming Present
December 3, 2008

Comments: 108   Recs: 134   Tips: 147

Yesterday, Kossack Sardonyx posted an excellent piece of hard news in *Franken's favor:* Talking Points Memo (TPM) reports Franken side for 1st time claims a tentative lead.

Grouping the recount into 3 types of ballots—recount, challenged, and rejected absentee—here's the latest.

Recount ballots - last counties
Recounted Ballots

Secretary of State's Office 8:00pm Dec. 2

Total % of Ballots Recounted: 92.69%

	Coleman	Franken
Recounted ballots	1,119,878	1,112,413
Change from election day	-2,339	-2,427
Apparent difference	+88	
Start of Recount difference	+215	

Both the "change from election day" and "apparent difference" lines INCLUDE the challenged ballots noted next, so don't read too much into these numbers.

Challenged Ballots

Franken has challenged 2,910 "Coleman & other" ballots statewide.

Coleman has challenged 3,093 "Franken & other" ballots statewide.

Those 2,910 + 3,093 = 6,003 ballots will go to the State Canvassing Board for final decisions.

CAUTION: Finding difference between C & F recount numbers (today yielding Franken +2,623) is an unusable number. While it is the second day Franken's number is larger (as opposed to the first 15 days when Coleman's number was larger) both camps have not mentioned this number AT ALL. Both consider it bogus & misleading until: end of recounting, Dec. 5 AND end of rulings on challenged ballots by State Canvassing Board (begins Dec. 16) AND final disposition of rejected absentee ballots (major examination of these runs Dec. 8–18—see below—but MAY end up in court). Given that, this difference should only be noted in a salt cave after 30 minutes of licking.)

In a midday press conference Mark Elias for the Franken camp said their "Frankenmath" says they are still down, but only by 50 votes. [They are taking into account new votes being added for both sides and making an educated guess (probably sprinkled with hope) on how the challenged ballots will break.] With over 200,000 votes left to recount, this is getting squeaky tight.

Just after Franken presser ended comes word from Maplewood (Ramsey County, suburb of St. Paul; precinct 6): Minn. Public Radio reports **171 uncounted ballots** have turned up. Apparently on Nov. 4 a scanning machine broke down and was replaced by another, but the first 171 votes fed into the first machine before the malfunction were never counted.

After a flurry of excited counting, no doubt watched over in eagle-eyed fashion by every spare person in the room *(including the Ramsey County election director JOE MANSKY! JOE POWER was in the room!)* those 171 votes broke (no word if any, or how many were for Barkley) by +37 for Franken.

As this news came in AFTER the Franken presser, doing the math 50 − 37 = 13 votes might be the difference (by "Frankenmath"), albeit still in Coleman's favor. But a great piece of news for the Frankenites.

UPDATE 1: More JOE POWER, but on a critical matter. *The Star Tribune is saying that there are now 31 ballots more in that precinct than the total number of voters (!). Elections Director Mansky is looking into it to try and figure out if that is a tabulation error or what...* Bears watching. Will try to update more if something comes in...

UPDATE 2: could be 31 more than people who signed in, not 31 more than total registered voters in precinct—which might be accounted for by a missing page from sign-in log...

UPDATE 3: Some Reichwingers are already claiming fraud, saying a +37 break is statistically way out of bounds. Unfortunately for the Reichwing, the reality-based wing knows how to do math (and statistics). I don't quite get it (I was good at math but hated "sadistics" class) but apparently the +37 is not an unreasonable statistical variation. So there! (I guess.)

UPDATE 4: AHA! the 31-vote discrepancy solved!

The Star-Trib story has been updated with an explanation for the 31-ballot gap. It was indeed from forgetting to log cards of those who voted absentee. When those cards are included, the numbers match exactly—and this exact match is a check against fraud. *(KWRegan)*

Yep, the system is working again (took from 2:05 to 3:14 by The UpTake time markers for Ramsey County's Joe POWER to settle this. Another hat tip to Joe Mansky and crew!)

Noah Kunin *(Lithuanian power! WineRev is Estonian, so we East Baltics hang tough together. Edasi!)* of The UpTake with detail on the machine breakdown *(slightly edited to eliminate repetitions)*:

"Here's how it went down—the ballot counter is a small device that sits on top of the ballot box. When elections judges determined the counter was defective they replaced it. However, the new counter was not run after its replacement... So, these 171 ballots remained securely in their box until today, when the box was reopened to conduct the hand recount. Workers quickly determined that there were more ballots in the box then on the machine tape from election night." *(The Uptake)*

Challenged Ballots

Seems like this would have been a good day for either camp to whittle down their stack, but so far it's been all talk, no walk.

Franken side keeps saying they will "un-challenge" "dozens" of ballots in challenge limbo *(sounds Caribbean and competitive, with lots of rum, Mon!)* later this week, so we'll see.

Coleman side keeps saying they are willing to talk to Franken side about climbing down on some of the challenged ballots but want a meeting first so both do it together. I don't exactly get why but that's their position so far for several days. (One wag has suggested if such a meeting comes to pass, Ritchie & the Canvassing Board may have to first help both sides settle on the shape of the table, height of the chairs, etc.)

Rejected Absentee Ballots

Elias for the Franken campaign now reports 9,267 absentee ballots were rejected across the state, with information from all but 4 counties [and partial information from St. Louis County (Duluth)].

Admits heavy majority were properly rejected, but still believe 500–1,000 may have been improperly excluded.

Elias at the presser said that Sec. of State Ritchie and the Canvassing Board *(potent pair there)* have now directed county (and in heavily populated areas, city) election boards to sort absentee ballots into these 4 rejection piles and that **any ballot that does not fit one of these 4 (in effect the famous "5th pile") should be counted.** If this is so, then perhaps 500 (according to Sec. of State) to as many as 1,000 (range of 500–1,000 according to Franken side) ballots might *(might!)* be added to the 11/4 vote totals. No one is hazarding a guess on how those ballots might break between Coleman and Franken.

Sec. of State Mark Ritchie sent out a directive to all county election boards to search for and report any "missing ballots" (sometime Monday) and instruction re: absentee ballots. The email is exported here:

From: Elections Dept
Sent: Monday, December 01, 2008 4:31 PM
Subject: Rejected Absentee Counts
Dear County Auditors and County and City Election Officials:
Once again I would like to thank you for helping the Secretary of State's Office conduct a hand recount of the ballots cast in the U.S. Senate contest. I know this task has required much more work than anyone originally anticipated, and we are very grateful for your assistance.

....

The purpose of this e-mail is to once again ask for your assistance. We need your help in reviewing all previously-rejected absentee ballots and determining the number of ballots that were rejected for each of the following four statutory reasons:

1. The ballot was rejected because the voter's name and address on the return envelope are not the same as the information provided on the absentee ballot application.

2. The voter's signature on the return envelope is not the genuine signature of the individual who made the application for the ballot and the signature is required under applicable Minnesota law, or the certificate has not been completed as prescribed in the directions for casting an absentee ballot.

3. The voter was not registered and eligible to vote in the precinct or has not included a properly completed voter registration application. Elections personnel shall use available voter rosters to determine whether the voter was registered.

4. The voter had already voted at the election, either in person or by absentee ballot. Elections personnel shall use available voter rosters to determine whether the voter had already voted.

In addition, please create a fifth category of rejected absentee ballots as described below:

5. If the rejected absentee ballot does not meet one of these four reasons, or if the reason used to reject the absentee ballot is not based on factual information (e.g. the voter was initially determined not to be registered to vote at the address given, but a subsequent review determines the voter was registered at that address), that ballot should be counted as part of a fifth category of previously-rejected absentee ballots—absentee ballots that were mistakenly rejected on or before election day.

If the election judges do not agree into which of the first four categories the ballot should be placed (e.g. because it was appropriately rejected for more than one reason), simply assign the ballot to one of the appropriate categories at random. If the election judges disagree as to whether the ballot was appropriately or inappropriately rejected, please assign the ballot to the fifth category. Please note the disagreement on a sticky note and attach it onto white space on the envelope

The State Canvassing Board is primarily interested in determining how many ballots throughout the state would be included in this fifth category of rejected absentee ballots. At this time we are not asking you to open or count the votes contained in any of the five categories of rejected absentee ballots, nor are we asking you to compile a list of names and addresses of the absentee voters who have their ballots placed in any of these five categories. We simply are looking for the number of rejected absentee ballots that were legitimately rejected for one of the four statutory reasons and the number of rejected absentee ballots that were mistakenly rejected by a County Absentee Ballot Board and/or election judges at the individual precincts.

We understand that this will require a significant amount of work on your part. This review should be done with the assistance of two election judges of different parties and you or a member of your staff. It must be done in a public setting where the public and representatives of the two campaigns would be allowed to observe, but not participate in the review nor question the election judges' decision into which category each previously-rejected absentee ballot is placed. In other words, candidates are not to be given the opportunity to challenge the decisions relative to the category into which each previously-rejected absentee ballot is placed.

....

If you are willing to participate in this process, please identify a date, time and location when you would begin sorting the rejected absentee ballots. Please forward this email to any municipal clerks in your county if they maintain possession of the rejected absentee ballots.

Please do not begin any earlier than Monday, December 8 and plan to complete the review and submit the numbers of rejected absentee ballots for each of the five categories forwarded to the Secretary of State's Office by 5:00 p.m., Thursday, December 18.

Date When We Will Begin Sorting Rejected Absentee Ballots:

Time When We Will Begin Sorting Rejected Absentee Ballots:

Location Where We Will Begin Sorting Rejected Absentee Ballots:

My best regards!!!

So consider:

 a. The recount for nearly all ballots comes FIRST, and is expected to be completed by Fri. Dec. 5.

b. Starting Monday, Dec. 8 county and city election officials will concentrate on ONLY the absentee ballots, and do so for up to 10 days.

c. These will be public meetings, open to the people of the county/city.

d. Coleman and Franken camps should send an observer to watch over this reexamination of absentee ballots, but they have to stay quiet. They MAY NOT CHALLENGE which pile the election board reaches on any absentee ballot.

e. Ritchie wants the boards to sort and segregate these rejected absentees BUT NOT OPEN OR COUNT THEM. He is waiting for an opinion/ruling from the State Attorney General Lori Swanson (Dfir) on whether or not such "5th Pile" votes should be counted. He has said before this process will NOT be rushed and if taking time helps ensure the integrity of the process, so be it.

Is this open enough? Transparent enough? Deliberate enough? Covering as many legal bases as possible? Sure feels like it to me (*swelling civic pride at democracy at work...sniff*).

Lawyers Dueling with Lightsabers V

Knaak (Coleman) noted in nearly 2,600 precincts (out of 4,193) there had been no challenges at all... and of those precincts Coleman had picked up 1 net vote. [And also noting today his Franken counterpart, Elias, was in DC—to literally spend time with his family :-), since his wife and children live in their house in northern VA and he hasn't seen them in 2 weeks—and phoned in his noontime presser from the DSSC press room in the Capitol]:

> The implication: The recount will look like the first count, with the incumbent winning, if only by a hair—and a margin "not below three digits," Knaak said.
>
> "The math isn't working for the Franken campaign, and that may explain the move of their recount headquarters to Washington, D.C., at least for now," Knaak said, with a twinkle in his eye and a poke in his words. (*MinnPost*)

Elias, never shy about playing to the press or throwing chaff (or stronger) at the other side:

> But, hey, no problem. Elias, who has led other victorious recounts, keeps on ticking.
>
> "I think we're going to win this recount," he said, with nary an if, and or but. "I have no doubt in my mind that Al Franken got more votes in this election than Norm Coleman, and the only question is whether or not Norm Coleman is going to continue to have his lawyers fight" and not have all the votes counted, Elias said. (*MinnPost*)

Wednesday Morning Star Tribune

Kaszuba and Brown (or as you learned yesterday, "Kaszubanen and Brownson") get the front-page headline which is a heartening, "Volatile pendulum swings to Franken." While not as good as "Franken gains lead" or "Senator-elect Franken praises Coleman for concession speech," at this point it's nice to read,

Joe POWER quote:

> "Joe Mansky said the discovery of 171 ballots at the end of the county's 278,000-ballot recount proves the system works—even when recounting 40,000 ballots a day as they did in Ramsey County. "Our object here is to make sure every ballot gets counted as it was cast by the voter," Mansky said. "If we pick up some ballots that are not properly counted on Election Night, so much the better. That's a good thing. I don't see any downside." (*Star Tribune*)

Neither do we, Joe, and would say this in all seriousness if the 171 had swung +37 to Coleman; this is how it's supposed to work. Today it fell Franken's way. Notable that after Coleman camp's skepticism and concern that nothing further was heard from them; mute evidence of the force of Joe POWER and the transparency and accountability this recount continues to show.

Absentee Ballots

Coleman's chief briefcase swinger Fritz Knaak said he was satisfied with the instruction letter because it called for sorting out the rejected absentee ballots into the 5 piles. Since the Board had encouraged as much and such sorting was already happening last week Knaak simply shrugged it off. He also pointed out that none of those ballots being sorted were being counted (which sounds like a whole different issue to him, and I agree).

Scraps and Leftovers

Of course, having sounded reasonable and decent, Knaak then went on to sound like every lawyer every non-lawyer likes to hate. *(Couldn't keep it up, could you?)*

You'll remember Knaak's counterpart on the Franken side is DC lawyer Marc Elias. Elias went to see his family for a few days and has been staying in touch with Minnesota electronically (and flew back to MN last night). But Knaak has to read something ominous into it:

> Marc Elias, Franken's lead recount attorney, also said there was no significance to the campaign's decision to hold its daily briefings this week for reporters in Washington, D.C., a move Knaak described as further evidence that Franken's overall strategy was to have the U.S. Senate ultimately decide the race.
>
> "I'm presuming he's strategizing with Democrats about his Senate floor strategy to ignore the will of Minnesota voters," said Knaak. *(Star Tribune)*

Yeesh.

You're the Cream in my Lutefisk

DK If we ship some lutefisk to the counters, will this go faster? *(mspicata)*

DK Lutefisk, NO. Coffee, yes. *(WineRev)*

DK Just the mention of Lutefisk could bring on a donut in my book!! Just kidding, of course. *(Fiddlegirl)*

DK Mmmmm.... Donuts and lutefisk. And black coffee, of course. Just the thing to get a body moving. *(mspicata)*

DK Quite a combination there! My stomach is in knots just thinking about it! *(Fiddlegirl)*

DK Pardon the elitist East Coast ignorance, but WTF are lutefisk and egg coffee? Some kind of Norwegian Bachelor Farmer thing? What Marge Gunderson has for breakfast every day? *(Upper West)*

We turn to the expert, Garrison Keillor, to answer this question:

> Lutefisk is cod that has been dried in a lye solution. It looks like the desiccated cadavers of squirrels run over by trucks, but after it is soaked and reconstituted and the lye is washed out and it's cooked, it looks more fish-related, though with lutefisk, the window of success is small. It can be tasty, but the statistics aren't on your side. It is the hereditary delicacy of Swedes and Norwegians who serve it around the holidays, in memory of their ancestors, who ate it because they were poor. *(from* Pontoon *by Garrison Keillor)*

Hope this gives you enough to go on today. I'm gonna need extra coffee today in the Non–Cincinnati Bungles mug if today's action is anything like Tuesday's. I'll be able to sip for a little while this morning with you as I've got the late shift. So that's the latest from yust southeast of Lake Wobegon.

Shalom.

Recount Notes, News & Witnesses
December 4, 2008

Comments: 16   Recs: 35   Tips: 31

The Frozen Tundra Network welcomes fans from the Georgia Bowl Martin-Chambliss tournament. There's plenty of seating for you next to the Begich-Stevens fans from the Juneau Glacier Bowl. Choose an entry gate, whether the aquavit-plastered Norwegians over at Fjord Gate-son 3 bawling out Leif Ericsson's favorite hymn, "Skol, Vikings, let's get that ball..."; Smorgasbord Gate-son 4 with acres of tiny sandwiches, pickled herring, and a shot of Absolut between each bite; or Dansk Gate-sEn 5 with all the spare, sleek 1962 modern furniture done in blond wood with endless bottles of Carlsberg resting on endless teak coasters (spare and sleek as well).

Recounting Ballots
Recounted Ballots

Secretary of State's Office 8:00pm Dec. 3

Total % of Ballots Recounted: 97.58%

	Coleman	Franken
Recounted ballots	1,174,964	1,186,134
Change from election day	-2,501	-2,602
Apparent difference	+101	
Start of Recount difference	+215	

Both the "change from election day" and "apparent difference" lines INCLUDE the challenged ballots noted next, so don't read too much into these numbers

Challenged Ballots

Franken has challenged 3,085 "Coleman & other" ballots statewide.

Coleman has challenged 3,241 "Franken & other" ballots statewide.

Those 3,085 + 3,241 = 6,326 ballots will go to the State Canvassing Board for final decisions

TWO big pieces of Recount Ballot News Wednesday (The Lord Giveth and the Lord Taketh Away)

1. Franken campaign in their midday presser advanced the claim that using their recount numbers and their approach to the challenged ballots, "Frankenmath", they believe for the first time in the recount process that they have a lead—of about 22 votes. This was obviously helped along by Tuesday's discovery in St. Paul suburb Maplewood of 171 votes not counted 11/4 but added Tuesday to the total count... and those 171 broke +37 net for Franken. But...

2. Wednesday afternoon came word 133 (or 131, or 129; various reports) votes in Hennepin County (Minneapolis metro) were not showing up in one precinct's recount. First reports were these votes may have been write-in ballots (proper ones) that by human error were run through the optical scanning counter *twice* and so double-counted. This being a heavily Democratic precinct, they broke for Franken net +88. But if they were double-counted, and now corrected, then Franken goes down 88. Later report says no to 88, but perhaps Franken net −46.

Now from McIntee at The UpTake with hard numbers:

> From Minneapolis Ward 3 Precinct 1
>
> 1,047 voters signed in on the roster.
>
> 932 additional voters registered in person on Election Day.
>
> 35 absentee ballots were accepted in this precinct by the city.
>
> 15 absentee ballots were accepted in this precinct by the county.

TOTAL: 2,029 voters cast legal ballots (2,028 votes are recorded on the machine tape).
TODAY: 1,896 ballots were included in the recount.

That means there were 133 more voters (not just votes) on election day than there were ballots available for the recount.

That would seem to call into question the explanation of running 133 ballots through the machine twice.

(By the way, that is one awesome set of same-day registration numbers!)

Campaign Contrast

Tuesday in Maplewood the Colemaniks sent a legal team to find out what had happened in the 171 case, and were "skeptical" going in (and quiet coming out). The Frankenites were of course pleased by the +37 swing their way but were quiet about the Colemaniks.

Wednesday in Minneapolis the Frankenites sent a legal team to find out what had happened in the 133 case and were concerned that number of ballots might be missing, asking Director Reichert and staff to search for the ballots. The Colemaniks were of course pleased by the possible +46 swing their way and sent out Mark Drake to say:

> In a statement, Coleman campaign spokesman Mark Drake said, "The Minneapolis officials appeared to be quite thorough in their search today, and it is disappointing that the Franken campaign, once again, is attacking local election officials and blaming them for simply doing their jobs." *(Star Tribune)*

If things stay this way, Franken's +37 from Tuesday could well be canceled out by a −46 on Wednesday. Also this whole thing unfolded AFTER the Franken Presser and their claim to a 22-vote possible lead, so this will throw those calculations out the window. Situation unresolved as of last night. Check in morning for developments.

> I was an election judge in the recount). I can tell you that the Franken methodology is likely a good one, and that the Director of Elections in our county was discussing this very same thing with me after our last precinct was counted before Thanksgiving.
>
> Both of us noted that of the hundreds of challenges entertained during the six days of counting, each of the teams of judges already had a very good grasp of challenges that would likely be warranted versus those that were frivolous. I remember sorting through one where I literally could not have guessed myself what the voter's intent was (Coleman oval filled in, and a circle around Franken's oval, but not in it at all). But that was the only one the entire six days (I processed over 23,000 ballots at our table during that time). My guess is that Coleman ballot may get overturned but will likely stand - what do you think? *(AmericanIdeal)*

DK

Challenged Ballots

Total challenged ballots: 6,326 (up 323 from Tuesday)

Big news Wednesday was the Franken campaign followed through on Monday's promise [how quaint! how anti-political! what a change!... *(fade in voice:)* "and this is the change we need. We all need change *(voice fades away amid cheering)*..."] and announced they are dropping 633 ballots they have challenged so far. So far more than the "several dozen" Elias announced Monday (about 52 dozen plus) and more than 1/5 of Franken's total as of Wednesday night. So first move to Franken.

Coleman campaign has been pushing for a meeting with the Frankenites to hash out a mutual standdown on challenged ballots. Franken campaign said they've heard this for a week from Colemaniks—via the press, **but not once** by letter, e-mail, or phone call from Norm's nabobs. In other words, all talk, no walk. BUT the Colemaniks DID have a theory about the Franken stand-down on 633 challenged ballots.

> Fritz Knaak, Coleman's lead recount attorney, while acknowledging the Franken campaign's challenge withdrawals, suggested the announcement may have been an attempt to "create news" and keep momentum to help with political fundraising. Knaak said the announcement also may have been timed to deflect the effect

of the reelection Tuesday of U.S. Sen. Saxby Chambliss, a Georgia Republican, a result that prevents Democrats from gaining a 60-vote, filibuster-proof Senate majority.

Chambliss' victory, said Knaak, had dealt "a serious blow" to Franken's attempt to show his race is critical to Democrats nationally. Franken's people said Chamblis' reelection will have no effect on strategy for the Minnesota race. *(Star Tribune)*

Rejected Absentee Ballots

At last count these numbered 9,200+ and yesterday we posted a letter sent from the Sec. of State's office to county and city auditors across the state directing the county boards to sort the rejected absentee ballots into 5 piles, 4 for each of the 4 mandatory reasons for rejecting in state law and a "5th pile" of those rejected for something else. (Statewide those 5th piles could add 500–1,000 votes across the state.) But no one is allowed to count these yet until we find out if we can legally.

Now comes word the State Canvassing Board will meet December 12 (Friday) to **consider the rejected absentee ballots**. Back on Nov. 26th at their last meeting the Board agreed with Coleman (by 5-0) they did not have jurisdiction to rule on these. But they also held the county boards *did* have jurisdiction (which the Colemaniks conceded) AND they asked the State Attorney General Lori Swanson (D) for an opinion or ruling. Now they are going to meet on the matter (and just before Tues. Dec. 16 when they meet to start ruling on each of the challenged ballots one by one).

Stay tuned, this area is getting interesting!

Hats Off Dept.

Remember that scene in *To Kill a Mockingbird* where Atticus Finch has been defending Tom against a rape charge? He's packing up to leave court, and a woman in the "colored" gallery rouses Scout, saying, "Stand up, Miss Finch." Scout does, sees everyone else in the gallery rising as Atticus walks toward the rear. "Why?" she asks, still sleepy. "Because your father's passing."

Well for all the reporting, wondering, and hair-pulling over the MN recount, there have been several Kossacks who have been actually *doing democracy*. Two of them, Sharpner and MNLatteLiberal, pass by here and answer why a "stray mark" can disqualify a ballot.

But first, for all of us in the gallery: "Stand up, Kossacks." "Why?" "Because two patriots are passing." *(Doffs hat)*

DK   **Having looked at about 9,000 ballots myself** in the last few days, I can say that almost nobody gets it wrong. Maybe 3 of those 9,000 (or 0.03%) appear to have been filled in by someone who didn't get the "fill in the oval" concept.

From my slim experience, it appears that a significant majority of challenges arise from the "identifying mark" criterion (e.g., someone signed or initialed or otherwise identified the ballot uniquely) rather than the "voter intent" criterion (where we couldn't tell which oval as indicated).

Also from my experience, the vast majority of challenges on both sides will not be upheld.

I come away from this with a great respect for the optical scan system, and for the Minnesotans who so carefully filled them out. (Sharpner)

DK   Why does an identifying mark make a ballot invalid? Why does that matter? *(bear83)*

DK   *Per Minnesota Statutes 204C.22 Subd. 13. Identifying ballot. If a ballot is marked by distinguishing characteristics in a manner making it evident that the voter intended to identify the ballot, the entire ballot is defective.*

I'm told this is to prevent a form of corruption more common in earlier times when political machines would pay people for voting a particular way and would use the signed or marked ballot to substantiate that the vote occurred and payment was due to that particular person. (Sharpner)

> I looked at close to **10,000 myself** here in Washington County. And while the Franken training was very good overall, and based on the Coleman challenges at my tables WAY better than the other side's, the limits/boundaries of what constitutes an id'ed ballot were left rather vague. Intentionally vague, I'd say.
>
> Having said that, I've challenged two ballots for intent, where next to a filled in Coleman oval there was a marking in Al's slot, and two for identifying marks. One of those was a partial fingerprint. I sincerely hope that Elias does not give up "my" fingerprint among those 633 today. I also picked up a Franken vote that wasn't registered by the scanner because the voter chose to create his/her own ovals to the right of the names, refusing an easier and more traditional path :).
>
> As to the frequency of voter inability to fill in the oval (once the oval is found), in Washington County I'd put that frequency at 1 per every 200 ballots. Typically it's a check mark or an "x", but those were still picked up by the optical scanner. Some folks lightly crossed the oval, as if to make a mathematical null set sign or the old computer font zero. But surprisingly many, imho, simply refuse to color within the lines!
>
> These are not physically impaired or mentally challenged voters en masse. These are just the "creative" types who cannot be bothered to read instructions. *(MN Latte Liberal)*

Funny Pages

Laughs from Nevada. No, not Harry Reid promising to kick Joe Liebermann in the pants on national TV. And not Harry being fitted for a crown in the Obama-Reid co-monarchy a Reichwinger was warning about Monday.

No, this is from the OTHER side of Senators from Nevada, the one with the good golf game, great tan and scrub-brush for brains, Sen. John Ensign (R-NV). The NRSC ran a ton of attack ads against Franken in MN, with Ensign saying, "It's pretty clear that Norm Coleman is going to win this race in the recount, just like he did on election day.""

Gotta get a 2nd cup in the Not–Cincinnati Bungles mug and then off to work. Here's the latest from yust southeast of Lake Wobegon.

Shalom.

Missing Ballots = Flaring Tempers
December 5, 2008

Comments: 26 *Recs:* 20 *Tips:* 20

Just Friday left to go in the big phase of the Recount. About 56,000 votes left to recount statewide. Only one more diary in this series *(before the weekend when the WineRev no doubt has MORE time for bigger diaries!.... dream on; we'll keep it shorter)*.

Big news? 133 ballots in Minneapolis are MIA.

Recounting Ballots
Recounted Ballots

Secretary of State's Office 8:00pm Dec. 4

Total % of Ballots Recounted: 99.88%

	Coleman	Franken
Recounted ballots	1,193,307	1,197,965
Change from election day	-2,578	-2,568
Apparent difference		+10
Start of Recount difference	+215	

Both the "change from election day" and "apparent difference" lines INCLUDE the challenged ballots noted next, so don't read too much into these numbers.

Challenged Ballots

Franken has challenged 3,197 "Coleman & other" ballots statewide.

Coleman has challenged 3,311 "Franken & other" ballots statewide.

Those 3,197 + 3,311 = 6,508 ballots will go to the State Canvassing Board for final decisions

Al Franken is back on the right side of this but it's paper thin. Some of the last votes are coming in from Wright County which went for Coleman decisively (but it's the changes in the margin which are more significant).

Ballots MIA

The Minneapolis precinct where 133 ballots seem to be missing is not far from the University of Minnesota in an area with a lot of student housing...,Minneapolis Mayor R.T. Rybak (D) went public with a request for time for his city to find the 132 missing ballots from Ward 3, Precinct 1. Sec. of State Ritchie publicly said basically "Take as long as you need." Minneapolis Election Director Reichert said they would keep the precinct numbers open and unreported to the Sec. of State's office until they can resolve the situation. Otherwise ALL of Hennepin County (567,000 votes, largest in the state) has been officially reported.

Franken presser midday Thursday: By their "Frankenmath" they still believe they have a 10-vote lead (down from yesterday's 22, apparently NOT taking into account the 133/132 "missing ballots" in Minneapolis) overall with about 56,000 votes left to recount.

Late Press Release from Franken side (about 5:45 p.m. CT):

> Tonight, Minneapolis elections director Cindy Reichert revealed new information about a missing envelope, marked "1/5," which contains the 133 ballots lost from Minneapolis Ward 3, Precinct 1. Meanwhile, the Secretary of State's office has agreed to keep the recount open in that precinct in order to allow officials to find that envelope. *(Al Franken press release, quoted in Star Tribune)*

Franken Communications director Andy Barr:

> "We're glad that Minneapolis elections officials now acknowledge that these ballots are missing, and that they are committed to finding them. To fail to do so would disenfranchise 133 Minnesota voters and call into serious question the integrity of this election. The Secretary of State's office has rightly recognized the importance of this matter by giving Minneapolis officials the time they need to locate this envelope. Simply put, these ballots must be found." *(Al Franken press release, quoted in Star Tribune)*

Challenged Ballots

Total challenged ballots: 6,508 (up 182 from Tuesday)

Colemaniks matched Wednesday's Franken challenged-ballot stand-down of 633 and announced they are taking 650 off their own pile. N.B. The Sec. of State's numbers do NOT reflect these challenges being removed by both camps in the last couple days.

Rejected Absentee Ballots

Just 2 bits to recap:

1. County boards begin Monday 12/8 to revisit their rejected absentee ballots and sort them into 4

statute-mandated reasons for rejecting and a fifth "other" pile. They will NOT open and count any of these (the first four because they are invalid ballots; the 5th pile because...)

2. The State Canvassing Board meets Friday 12/12 to hear a ruling/decision by State Attorney General on these ballots and make a decision on whether to count them and under what conditions. Losing side of these decisions will likely immediately file suit.

Dueling Campaigns

Well, the fur is flying now *(and in Minnesota in December if you lose your fur outdoors it's VERY serious)* over the missing 133 ballots in Ward 3 Precinct 1 in Minneapolis. The hard facts that everyone agrees on is that 2,029 people signed in to vote and did on 11/4; as of Thursday night the Minneapolis Election board recounters can only point to 1,896 ballots. One oversize envelope that holds such ballots is missing.

Coleman campaign apparently likes Reichert's initial "double count" theory even though she has discarded it. *[Even the Holy Odin of Numbers, Nate Silver, threw cold water over this by pointing out you can't produce an odd number (like 133) by double counting anything of whole numbers. Double any whole number is ALWAYS an even number.]* But Coleman PR guyMark Drake came out Thursday saying all the concern over the allegedly missing ballots was "imaginary outrage over an imaginary problem."

Marc Elias for the Frankenites was all over this at the presser with real fury. He noted the precinct is heavily U. Minn. student populated and that based on surrounding precincts it went pretty heavily for Franken, but that there were certainly Coleman votes in there too. "For the Coleman campaign to tell these people who actually came to vote, who took time out from their schedules, who signed in, who were registered, who got their 'I voted' sticker, who were really there, and some of whom voted for their candidate Norm Coleman, that their votes are imaginary and that their outrage is imaginary is insulting... These ballots must be found."

Dueling Campaigns Part II

The voting in the precinct with the missing 133 ballots took place at University Church of Hope, a big, social justice, grand Lutheran place with a longtime mission of connecting the student body with the surrounding community. The Franken side sent Minneapolis Election director Reichert a letter spelling out what they wanted Reichert to do to find the missing ballots. In part:

> Interview every person who worked at the precinct on Election Day, every person who had a role in setting up or cleaning up at the church that served as a polling place, and every person who touched or transported the ballots either on Election Day or at any point between then and now.
>
> Conduct a systematic forensic search of the church that served as a polling place, any vehicle used to transport ballots or other elections materials, the warehouse where the ballots were stored. *(letter quoted in Star Tribune)*

That's pretty strong, harsh even, and a sign of the weight they are putting on this. *(A great example of how a Democrat can fight, for those of you wondering if a comedian will throw a punch.)*

The Colemaniks were miffed they had to read the letter online along with everybody else and didn't like the mayor getting involved either. But they really came down on the Frankenite call for a "systematic forensic search of the church."*(And that does seem rather over the top to me too.)* The Colemaniks said the Frankenites want to have the authorities "raid" the church for the forensic examination and solemnly declared it would set a bad precedent for the state to interfere with religion this way. Whew!!

(As they say in Brooklyn, "Da NOIVE!" Raiding the church?? While the Repubs declare the sanctity of separation of church and state?? I'm sure this is just the opening shot of our Muslim-elect president to shut down Christianity and make us into an Islamic state......yeeeessshh, even for snark!)

OK that's the lastest from yust southeast of Lake Wobegon.

Shalom.

How to UN-Challenge a Ballot and Other Stuff
December 6, 2008

Comments: 34 *Recs:* 19 *Tips:* 26

Recounting Ballots
Recounted Ballots

Secretary of State's Office 8:00pm Dec. 5

Total % of Ballots Recounted: 99.93%

	Coleman	Franken
Recounted ballots	1,208,344	1,207,657
Change from election day	-2,651	-2628
Apparent difference		+23
Start of Recount difference	+215	

Both the "change from election day" and "apparent difference" lines INCLUDE the challenged ballots noted next, so don't read too much into these numbers.

Challenged Ballots

Franken has challenged 3,280 "Coleman & other" ballots statewide.

Coleman has challenged 3,375 "Franken & other" ballots statewide.

Those 3,280 + 3,375 = 6,655 ballots will go to the State Canvassing Board for final decisions.

So where are we at? In many places: All the votes have been recounted

EXCEPT: 133 ballots still missing in Minneapolis (which if found, would add a net of +46 to Franken's number, which would then = -146);

EXCEPT: 6,655 challenged ballots (3,280 by Franken, 3,375 by Coleman).

EXCEPT: An estimated 12,000 rejected absentee ballots.

Needless to say, Coleman bloggers want to stop the count (Florida Playbook, chapter 4, "Dressing for a Riot, Brooks Brothers"). Frankenites are reaching for that third cup of coffee this morning and hunkering down for at least 2 more weeks. Sales of Kahlua, Bailey's, and Starbucks coffee liqueur are up sharply.

ITEM: The search for the missing 133 ballots at the Minneapolis Recount Warehouse has not found them. BUT they did uncover an envelope from the same precinct containing 20 absentee ballots NOT counted 11/4 and NOT included in the recount. These 20 are reported to be overseas ballots or military ballots.

No one is counting them yet *(pay attention knuckle-draggers!)* because Director Reichert, watched over by Deputy Sec. of State Gelbmann, wants to know more about these ballots, where they came from and where they've been and how they got lost and now found (chain of custody). *(You know, Reichert and Gelbmann are treating these ballots like parents having had to pick up their teenagers from the local precinct(!) station; no charges filed BUT some serious questions.)*

ITEM: Officials are satisfied the missing 133 are NOT in the Minneapolis Recount Warehouse, having searched top to bottom. 'The search continues' is the vague term. (I would think this has to include the church that was the polling station, but after the flap about "forensic searching" and "raiding" the church everyone is being VERY quiet about this. May have more as the weekend goes on.)

What if the 133 missing ballots from Ward 3, Precinct 1 in Minneapolis are not found? They are net swing to Franken of +46 so with the race this tight you can bet they want them counted. The Coleman camp continues to say there are no Ward 3, Precinct 1 ballots missing at all; if you listen carefully you can count them saying this 46 different ways.

The votes were actually cast and recorded on the voting machines, which have tapes of who each ballot showed for the Senate race. So could we use the machine tapes to produce the final numbers rather than the actual ballots?

The idea is under consideration (while continuing the search of course) and has a **precedent** (check that word out, lawyer types! a precedent, a parallel situation in a similar legal environment and circumstance) set in a Minnesota State Senate race:

> Beth Fraser, the director of governmental affairs for the (MN) Secretary of State's office, said that there's actually a recent precedent for such a move, going back to a 2002 recount of a state legislative race that also had ballots missing from the recounted data set. "In that case, the state canvassing board gave each of the candidates the higher number of votes," said Fraser. *(Star Tribune)*

Dang! Another good idea thought of and already road-tested. And why wasn't this brought up before? There was no need... BUT somebody compiled a "What if?" database of stuff at the Sec. of State's office and now Ms. Fraser just punched it up and said with an almost Obama-esque calm, "Chill out. We got this covered. Nothin' but net... *swwwiiishhhhhh*"

Absentee Ballots (Rejected etc.)

ITEM: Also starting Monday the recount boards, per a letter sent Dec. 1, and under the eyes of an official observer from each camp, will sit down to sort out their rejected absentee ballots into 5 piles, 4 for statutory reasons and the fifth for "other."

The Boards are NOT to open or count "UNrejected ballots" (5th pile; get used to this term. You'll be hearing it a lot) but just sort them.

ITEM: State Canvassing Board on Wed. Nov. 26th declined to rule on rejected absentee ballots, agreeing (5-0) with Coleman side they did not have jurisdiction. Directed local boards to sort these (which Coleman side agrees DO have jurisdiction) AND sought an opinion/ruling from State Attorney General Swanson (D).

Board will meet THIS FRIDAY, Dec. 12 to receive AG opinion and make a ruling on these 5th pile ballots.

The math here is: total ballots cast for Senate = about 2.9 million.

Total absentee ballots = about 288,000 (about 10%, a new record)

Total absentee ballots rejected = (from Franken campaign) = about 12,000

Best guess as to how many of these were NOT rejected for 4 statutory reasons? (Sec. of State Ritchie) 500; (Franken) 500–1,000; (Coleman) flossing his teeth.

Soooo... IF, say, 750 of these ballots were wrongly rejected and are then opened and added back to the recount pile, and IF the absentees voted a bit more Democratic this year (pure guess), then AL needs a 51-vote edge to take the lead by 1. (Like 401-350.) Can this happen? That's this week's excitement.

That's the lastest from yust southeast of Lake Wobegon.

Shalom.

Recount Breather
December 8, 2008

Comments: 22 *Recs:* 31 *Tips:* 21

Oval-shaped dots swimming in front of the eyes. Tongue turning green at the sight of polka dots or really nasty case of acne. Even chessboards prompting the phrase, "Franken to bishop-5, check, not filled in..."

Hundreds of election judges across the state took an insanely deserved break this weekend, as did reporters, lawyers and even the WineRev. But as Monday dawns under 20 Fahrenheit there's a bit of news that can be scraped off the windshield.

Recounted Ballots

The dust has settled on phase 1 of the recount. In this phase Coleman leads by 192 (down from the 215 at the start of this phase). ONE precinct (Minneapolis Ward 3, Pct. 1) in the state has not reported (the one where the 133 ballots are missing; 20 overseas ballots found). As of 7:00am Monday no one has any news (like they've been found.)... Sec. of State Ritchie is holding open the state results until Monday, 12/16 to allow this precinct to come in...

IDIOT REPORT: At last report (Friday), the Coleman campaign was sticking to its position that there are NO votes missing in the precinct (as though this is a Reichwing fantasy to manufacture more Franken votes) even though the scanning machines AND the sign-in voter logs BOTH report not 1,896 but 2,029 votes cast.

Challenged Ballots

County and city election boards will work through this week UN-challenging the 633 (Franken) and 650 (Coleman) ballots across the state in their turfs and adjusting their vote totals accordingly. Expect UN-challenges to rise through the week as both camps saw away at the pile headed to the State Canvassing Board starting Dec. 16.

Rejected Absentee Ballots

Between UNchallenges those same election boards will while away the time by sorting through their rejected absentee ballots, sorting them by the 4 statutory reasons for rejection, and into a "5th pile" for "other reasons." Those 5th pile absentees (estimated to number between 500-1000 statewide) will take center stage this FRIDAY, Dec. 12 at a State Canvassing Board Meeting, live-streamed on The UpTake. The State Attorney General is expected to send over an opinion/ruling re: these ballots for the Board to consider.

Funny Pages

Many Minnesota sports fans recall the "ahem" **legendary** trade by the Vikings that ranks with the Red Sox trading Babe Ruth to the Yankees. A *Star Tribune* letter to the editor today takes note of the fact that in the 2010 census Minnesota might well lose one congressional seat, and that Texas (among others) will gain at least one.

> If Minnesota really does lose one of its representatives to Texas, can we send them Michele Bachmann? After the Herschel Walker trade and the theft of the North Stars, Texas is due for a little payback. *(Star Tribune)*

So it's a slow Monday. I'm going to write out a Christmas letter and see how many cards I can get down today, maybe even buy a tree. So that's the latest from yust southeast of Lake Wobegon.

Shalom.

Concerning
December 9, 2008

Comments: 16   Recs: 25   Tips: 35

Con-cern. Middle English, from Middle French & Medieval Latin; Middle French concerner, from Medieval Latin *concernere*, from Late Latin, *to sift together, mingle*, from Latin com- + cernere *to sift*.

In Minnesota's senate election everyone has become *concerned*. Some are sifting, some are mingling and of course some are just being *concern* Trolls (e.g. Republicans/pundits trying to keep their jobs/press flacks in general/ who have been caught by facts, logic, reason or by a vote that leaves them on the far side of humanity who then express their *concern* about moves made by winners).

You too can *com+cernere* through the latest news.

Recounted Ballots

The Big news here is the city of Minneapolis has decided to give up looking for the missing 133 ballots. The original machine counts and the tapes in those machines prove said ballots were cast and how they were cast. BUT (according to Brunswick & Von Sternberg in their 2nd section story in the Star Tribune) the Coleman campaign is *concerned* the search is suspended, is *concerned* the Sec. of State's office and the State Canvassing Board have a precedent for still counting these ballots, and is *concerned* the Sec. of State's office is simply buying into the Franken campaign spin about these 133 ballots.

> The Coleman campaign questioned suspending the search and expressed worry that the Franken campaign may have influenced a suggestion by Secretary of State Mark Ritchie that there is precedent for counting vote totals from Election Day when similar mistakes have occurred. *(Star Tribune)*

What else is a Rethug to do in a case like this? Why threaten to sue of course, while throwing up (!) plausible scenarios about what could have *really happened*:

> (Coleman spokesman) Friedrich declined to speculate about whether the campaign might take legal action to force the search to continue. Among the possible other explanations for the discrepancy, Friedrich said, were ballots being counted twice on Election Day and people signing in but leaving without voting. *(Star Tribune)*

Mr. Friedrich? You're saying 133 people lined up to vote, signed in, had a ballot in their hot little hand and were waiting for a little booth to open up or for their turn to slide the ballot into the machine and decided, "This isn't really a concern of mine, I'm leaving." THAT's the scenario!? Yep, Kossacks, I'm concerned as much as you that Friedrich is off his meds and is allowed to talk into a microphone.

Challenged Ballots

The news here is the Franken campaign decided to UNchallenge another 425 ballots, bringing their total of UNchallenges to 1,063 and the total the State Canvassing Board will need to consider next week to under 5,000.

The Coleman side is hinting strongly they will also announce another stand down today, no doubt out of *concern* the Frankenites get ahead of them and out of *concern* for the Board's workload.

Rejected Absentee Ballots

Here there is *actual concern* from the Franken side. The Sec. of State's office directed the counties and cities to make 5 piles of rejected absentee ballots and several counties are refusing to do so. Their reasoning is not clear, so in my book this is a *concern*.

> "Let me be clear, an absentee ballot that was not rejected for one of the four legal reasons is nothing more than an uncounted ballot," Elias said at a news conference. "It is deeply concerning that some counties are refusing to determine whether they have uncounted ballots among their previously rejected absentee ballots."

> While Elias refused to name the counties, John Aiken, a spokesman for the secretary of state's office, said at least five – Ramsey, Washington, Itasca, Freeborn and Sherburne – have declined to separate their rejected absentee ballots, several on the advice of their attorneys. *(Star Tribune)*

Why is this? I'm *concerned*, *concerned* about what might be going on, *concerned* enough to invite rampant speculation, *concerned* enough to invite coolly reasoned counter claims. *Concern!* Spell it for me, Aretha: C-o-n-c-e-r-n, find out what it means to me!

DK
> I'm also concerned about rejected absentees. It seems like Franken needs those to be counted, but more important than that is the principle. If an absentee ballot is rejected because of a clerical error, the voter should not be disenfranchised. *(desmoinesdem)*

DK
> I don't get it. Last week the Coleman camp was complaining because the Franken camp wanted to search the church for the 133 missing ballots. This week they are complaining because they stopped the search? *(lenzy1000)*

OK here it is, the latest concerns from yust southeast of Lake Wobegon.
Shalom

Little Nothings Making a Something
December 10, 2008

Comments: 71 Recs: 113 Tips: 145

So? Wednesday morning and we have...?

Nothing big but lots of littles that add up to yet another diary in this series, keeping you current.

Recounted Ballots

No changes from yesterday. No ballots found or lost. Oddly enough, no change in the Sec. of State's numbers at the website. Odd because both campaigns have been UNchallenging ballots, which are then returned to their original precincts *for counting*. And once counted doesn't the precinct/county then alter its total reported to the Sec. of State? But no movement so far, so we'll keep watch.

Challenged Ballots

The Colemaniks stood down on 475 challenged ballots Tuesday, continuing their pathetic little game of "anything you can do we can do better" (Ballot UNchallenges: Round 1: Franken 633, Coleman 650; Tuesday: Round 2: Franken 425, Coleman 475.) Makes the overall total withdrawn 2,183, from a starting total of 6,500+. So the Canvassing Board is still facing about 4,400 challenges, but Tuesday's actions mean about 1/3 of the challenges have been withdrawn... and that HAS to be seen as good news by the Board.

From the Tuesday Franken presser, The UpTake reports:

> Recapping: Franken campaign says its lead remains at 4 votes and then offered rhetoric to counter Coleman campaigns suggestion that the 133 ballots missing from a Minneapolis precinct should not be counted. Only new twist to anything was a question from the Star Tribune about *challenged ballots that are no longer challenged*. The Star Tribune reporter apparently has seen some ballots where the challenge has been withdrawn that does not indicate the judge's original ruling on who got that vote. Franken lawyer Marc Elias said the Franken campaign would look into it. *(Mike McIntee, The UpTake)*

Hmmmm, now that IS an interesting issue: a recount election judge picks up a ballot and is about to declare it for Coleman or Franken and one of the 2 camps issues a challenge (stray mark, etc.), so the election judge puts it in the challenged pile with notation as to why, but NOT how the ballot was going to be counted. Understandable, but does it favor one or another candidate? Ponder away Kossacks, that's a nice one!

For what it's worth, Kossack Tom Tech waded through 2,700 images of challenged ballots and came to the conclusion....112 ballots may swing this.

The *Star Tribune*'s main story Wednesday morning from Pat Doyle (an Irishman in New Scandinavia?) from the front page to A16 fills in some background on the challenged ballots.:

- each campaign gets to be present/represented at the Canvassing Board while they work through the challenges but its a bit vague how much they'll get to say on each ballot.

- both camps can continue withdrawing challenged ballots while the Board is working on other ones (starting next Tuesday, 12/16).

- the Sec. of State's office will "award the withdrawn challenges to candidates before the Canvassing Board meets Tuesday" (answering the issue in part 1, above).

Important nugget!

> The board is made up of two state Supreme Court justices, two district court justices and Ritchie, who chairs the panel. It was unclear Tuesday whether a split board vote on a ballot would be decided by majority opinion, or whether the ballot would be rejected for lack of an unanimous vote.
>
> Initially, Ritchie said he thought a split vote would be resolved in favor of the majority, but later said, "I think we don't know. Because we haven't as a group discussed any aspect of how this part will proceed. ... We have to figure how we handle those. Do we put them aside and come back to them?" *(Star Tribune)*

For fans of politics and everyone who is a Perry Mason/Arnie Becker/Boston Legal wannabe those arguments should be crucial–and entertaining!

Rejected Absentee Ballots

Elias in today's Franken presser was asked about MN Attorney General's opinion on the rejected absentee ballots. Elias said he expects AG Swanson's opinion to be issued BEFORE Friday, which is new speculation...

Most counties & cities ARE sorting their rejected absentees into 5 piles but NO ONE is opening or counting them yet, which I think is fair. Duchschere of the *Star Tribune* reports:

> Sixty-eight counties, along with 14 cities in Hennepin County, have volunteered to sort the ballots.
>
> Few of the ballots were found to have been rejected in error. In Clay County, 21 of 166 rejected absentee ballots were improperly turned down; in Beltrami County (Far N, Bemidji) it was six out of 100, and in Lyon County (SW, Marshall) it was two out of 52.
>
> County officials said they refused to open and count the rejected ballots, as the Franken campaign asked them to do last week. "We have no authority to do that," said Lori Johnson, Clay County auditor-treasurer in Moorhead. "If the Canvassing Board told us to do it, or a court order, we'll do it." *(Star Tribune)*

Hmmmm....21 of 166, 6 of 100, 2 of 52? I don't know; in a race this close those 21s, 6s & 2s could well amount to something (part of the 500-1000 that is becoming the CW). I think the case for counting them (and let's remember Coleman and Barkley will get a good share of them) is self-evident: someone needs/wants to vote absentee. They get the forms, fill them in to the letter, cross every T, dot every I, enclose a lizard scale as ordered, make sure they sign it ending in "son" or "sen" and send it in on time. And THEN there is a clerical error and through *no fault of their own* this voter is disenfranchised? I think those calling for a NOT vote have a very hard case to make.

The *Pioneer-Press* in St. Paul adds a bit more on these:

> Houston County (Far SE corner, Caledonia) mistakenly rejected two out of 15 – about 13 percent of their total rejected absentees.

> Minneapolis mistakenly rejected 171 out of 610 rejected absentees, while that's about 1 percent of the total absentees cast in the city it's about 28 percent of total rejected.
>
> Anoka County (just N of Twin Cities) mistakenly rejected 25 absentees.
>
> *(Pioneer Press)*

Aaron Landry ties together 2 hot stories at *MNPublius* and asks:

> Illinois Gov. Blagojevich Arrested; What About Coleman?
>
> Gov. Rod Blagojevich and his chief of staff, John Harris, were arrested by FBI agents on federal corruption charges Tuesday morning.
>
> Blagojevich and Harris were arrested simultaneously at their homes at about 6:15 a.m., according to Frank Bochte of the FBI. Both were awakened in their residences and transported to FBI headquarters in Chicago.
>
> Why? Pay-for-play politics and taking illegal money.
>
> Two people under oath, under penalty of perjury, have accused Norm Coleman of doing exactly that. Blagojevich had a three-year federal corruption investigation. How long do we have to wait to find out about Coleman? *(MNPlubius)*

OK time for coffee, lefse, NO lutefisk, a shower and off to work. That's the latest from yust southeast of Lake Wobegon.

Shalom.

Grinding Forward
December 11, 2008

Comments: 7   *Recs:* 20   *Tips:* 31

Recounted Ballots and Challenged Ballots Together for Thursday

Once again as of Wednesday night there was no change in the Sec. of State's recount numbers. Yesterday I wondered why, if ballots are being UNchallenged by both camps, why the SoS numbers haven't changed a bit for both sides (as those unchallenged ballots are now clear to be added to county totals.)

Well like any good reality based progressive, liberal, fact-seeking reader of this website, Kossack Laura Stein *(a doff of the hat to you!)* took matters into her own phone yesterday and posted the following comment:

> **DK**
> I spoke to the Election Office in MN and the official who answered the phone (full of MN "nice") told me that the reason the unchallenged ballots hadn't been added to the official SOS total was that there's a bit of a drawn out process that has to take place after the campaign states it wants to withdraw a challenge, before the withdrawal is official. Paperwork has to be legally filed in a couple of places, etc.
>
> He said that in a few days those "unchallenged" ballots will start showing up in the tally. (Laura Stein)

What this will mean is that both candidates' numbers will go up but that the all important *difference* between them will stay quite close to the 192 we are currently at.

Rejected Absentee Ballots

Franken Wed. Midday Presser: Elias getting pushy about having the "5th pile" ballots counted; says Minneapolis alone is sitting on 171 of them... Elias also (in a muted way) called out the Coleman camp for not joining in calling for the same thing since *there are Coleman voters being disenfranchised* if the 5th pile votes idle in neutral. Kind of a "you owe it to your own voters, Norm" sort of thing (pretty effective I think)...

The State Canvassing Board will meet TOMORROW (Friday) to discuss the rejected absentee ballots. It will be an open, public meeting.

Yep, there they go AGAIN: an open, above-board, public meeting on a matter of public significance. No closed doors. No smoke-filled room. No foul-languaged governor of the state. No bundles of cash being asked for or offered. No Brooks Brothers rioters chanting "Stop the vote." (Well, as far as we know. Who knows what madness the Rovians are cooking up in their lutefisk?) Yes it's slow and messy... or you could call it careful, deliberate and even-handed. AND... we all get the right to chafe, complain, wonder, and chew over what they do... you know, like in a democracy?

(Oh and by the way, you Brooks Brothers' Florida wannabes? I wouldn't try it... I haven't seen him in action, but I get the feeling Board Member and Chief Justice of the MN Supreme Court Magnuson would probably not only have a BB mob arrested on the spot, he'd have the cops book them outdoors... on the front lawn (and its going to be about +22 Friday with a stiff wind)... with no coats...and then he'd get them in his courtroom and get mad.)

Capsule Summary

Total votes cast in Senate race: about 2.9 million. Total of these cast absentee: about 290,000 (10%, a new state record). Total of these correctly filled out and counted on Election Day (and lately recounted as well): about 278,000. Total rejected for cause: about 12,000. Total rejected for solid, legal reasons: about 11,000 to 11,500. *(Attention FAUX NOISE, per a comment yesterday; Al Franken wants NONE of these 11,000-11,500 rejected ballots counted. None. Zip. Zero. Nada...even nada one! You vote absentee, then show up to vote because you plans changed, BINGO—the absentee is gone; so saith the Law.)* But those last 500-1,000 that may have been rejected for no good reason or no legal reason, those 500-1,000 ballots for Coleman and Barkley and Franken,,,THIS is what we're talking about here.

The Franken campaign's ultimate aim on these rejected absentee ballots (total of about 12,000) is to

1. get them sorted into the famous 5 piles (4 rejected for statutory reasons) and

2. have the 5th pile ballots (total about 500-1000) be counted like any other absentee ballot.

The Sec. of State's office (with an assist from the Canvassing Board) asked the county and city election boards to do that sorting this week (as Franken asked) BUT not to open or count any of the "5th pile" ballots (as Coleman asked.)

The Coleman camp argued the State Canvassing Board did not have jurisdiction to actually sort out these ballots and the Board (by 5-0) agreed. The Board did do 2 other things: they kicked the sorting back to the local level (which even the Coleman side admits DO have jurisdiction) AND asked for an opinion from state Attorney General Lori Swanson *(back to Scandinavian names!)*

The Coleman camp (reluctantly) wants the absentees sorted but only wants the "5th pile" ballots opened under the eyes of a court. To me while this opens things up to lawyers arguing every ballot this doesn't seem too far out of line (unless they want ONE judge to rule on each of these 500-1,000; to me THAT would indeed be out of line.)

With 87 counties (and in the larger cities multiple judges) I can see a case being made to take, say, the 2 "5th pile" ballots in Houston County (bottom right corner of the state) to the county court in Caledonia and in the presence of a Coleman and a Franken lawyer (and the public) rule on those 2 ballots, open them, count them and send the total to Ritchie's office. Gavel to gavel you could be done in 10 minutes.

Even in Hennepin County (Minneapolis), currently sporting 171 of these ballots, their website[3] says the county has 62 judges. While some of them might be tied up in trials if even half are available that's 6 ballots/ judge.

There may be trap doors here I'm not aware of and I invite your thinking on this *(especially Kossacks of the legal persuasion, known as "at the bar"; the rest of us will continue at the bar as well—but with better things to drink :-D)*. Maybe it sets precedents, or opens the door to "differing standards", or long appeals—which would then swing the thing back to the Canvassing Board and/or Sec. of State's Office making the call. But what do you think?

And by the way, on the PR front the Franken campaign has a Web ad[4] up called "Count my Vote" for rejected absentee ballots. It MUST be good because the Coleman camp has come out and denounced this YouTube as "a new low" and an attack on local election officials.

---

3   *Hennepin County website: http://www.co.hennepin.mn.us/*
4   *As of this printing, the video is available at youtube.com.*

Thursday Morning with the Star Tribune

The 133 missing ballots in Minneapolis provided a chance for Lawyers Swinging Light Sabers V. Mike Kaszuba's *(that is one ODD name for a Norwegian.....maybe its Lapp? And by the way, what nationality is someone who can't stand up on a moving bus? A Lap-lander! :-D)* article from Thursday morning shows us all the action:

> In a letter to Minneapolis' top election official *(by inference that would be Cindy Reichert –WineRev)*, the Coleman campaign argued that only the precinct's recounted total should be given to the state Canvassing Board, even though it does not include the 133 missing votes, and results in a net loss of dozens of votes for Franken.
>
> If Minneapolis submits the "conflicting" election night and recount totals, stated Fritz Knaak, Coleman's lead recount attorney, "we will request the [board] to follow the clear directives under Minnesota law and certify only the administrative recount results."
>
> Franken's campaign, in a legal brief filed Wednesday with the board, said "well-established law and common sense dictate" the election night results are the "proper tally." *(Star Tribune)*

You can all choose up sides and start throwing things after reading that!

More background on the Norm Coleman shady money stuff: This morning Tony Kennedy and David Shaffer *(a new set of names, still lacking a certain Nordic air to them, alas)* get the front page story. You know, if the local press, while waiting for bigger recount news, is going to fill time and column inches with stories and background on Norm Coleman's smarmy financial life.....I *really don't mind* them doing that. One way or the other...

Got the early shift again down at the shop so I need breakfast, coffee and a drive; I'll try to check in during the morning and over lunch. That's the latest from yust southeast of Lake Wobegon.

Shalom.

Get Your Ballots Here! All Flavors!
December 12, 2008

Comments: 12   *Recs:* 24   *Tips:* 25

Hands down the BIG news today will be the State Canvassing Board meeting at 9:30amCT. The hot topic, counting rejected absentee ballots– the famous "5th pile" in each county and city voting site. Opinions offered, points argued, motions filed or bruited *(what a word!)*, lawsuits darkly hinted at– and that will just be you Kossacks before 9:30! Wait until the Board and the campaign lawyers strut *their* stuff.

(If you want to watch the meeting on your computer the place to go is TheUpTake. This is a great "New Media" outfit billing themselves as a half dozen folks with a video camera, a computer, and a van. They are contemplating offering aerial shots of their work, not via helicopter, but via the video camera duct-taped to a helmet (a "helmetcam") and then getting airborne either via a jet pack, or base-jumping from the State Capitol Dome or the Minneapolis IDS tower. They ARE intrepid–but a shoestring operation– that does fine work. Salute!)

Recounted Ballots

No changes in the recount numbers posted at the Sec. of State's website for the 4th day in a row. At some point we'll see change ("and we all need change") as UNchallenged ballots are added back in to county totals, but nothing so far.

In the case of the missing 133 ballots in Minneapolis, Marc Elias at today's Franken presser continued to call for them to be counted on the basis of the machine tapes, coupled with the 133 voters in question actually signing in to vote. According to TheUpTake Elias offered the Canvassing Board *100 years of examples (whoa! Good homework, Marc!)* of this sort of issue being addressed this way (and you know how lawyers and judges love a precedent!)

Challenged Ballots

The Coleman campaign today took down another 225 of their challenges of Franken (and other) ballots. This brings the statewide total under 4,200. About 37% of the challenged ballots (of the peak of 6,655) have now been taken down. It is still quite a pile for the State Canvassing Board to take up on Tuesday the 16th, but the trend line is nice for everybody.

Rejected Absentee Ballots

At the Franken midday presser Thursday campaign spokesman Andy Barr restated the Franken side's desire to see all the lawful absentee ballots counted and again called out the Coleman side for not joining in this: "Are you willing to look people (including Coleman campaign workers and voters) in this video in the eye and tell them their vote shouldn't count?"...NOT a question the Coleman side probably wants to answer...

I think this puts the Frankenites on the "good government" side with a lot of the Minnesota public. It shows Franken taking this seriously yet trying very hard to be fair, which undercuts both the Coleman side's rhetoric AND offsets the typical public lament: "politicians are all alike." If the Rethugs are trying to paint a "steal the vote" narrative, then I think this "count every legal vote", (even if cast by the lame, the halt or the blind, and even if cast for my opponent,) is a pretty good antidote for those only paying passing attention to the whole recount business. I'm not alone thinking this. (From the *Star Tribune*'s Mike Kaszuba (still gotta be some name dug out of fjord cave; even Kaszuba-son sounds like a student of Mr. Miaggi in *The Karate Kid*):

> The League of Women Voters, Common Cause Minnesota and Citizens for Election Integrity Minnesota this week called on board members to count the mistakenly rejected ballots.
>
> "If they were properly cast by voters, they must be counted," said League executive director Keesha Gaskins. "It's not a political issue. If you, the voter, do everything you're supposed to, an administrative failure shouldn't disenfranchise you." (*Star Tribune*)

Beyond the PR side of things the Franken campaign Thursday also sent **62 affidavits** to the Canvassing Board of voters who voted absentee who have been informed their vote was not counted (and are presumably in a "5th pile" somewhere between Pipestone and Grand Marais.) This sounds like a serious move.

Significant: According to the *Pioneer Press*, Minnesota Attorney General Swanson has issued an opinion on the rejected absentee ballots matter to the State Canvassing Board.

> The state law on recounts says that the scope of a recount is limited to the "determination of the number of votes validly cast" for the office in question. The rejected absentee ballots were never counted in the Senate race, so were they cast?
>
> The state canvassing board received some advice on that subject and others related to the rejected absentee ballots from the state attorney general's office Wednesday.
>
> Citing attorney-client privilege, neither the attorney general's office nor the secretary of state's office would share the opinion. Only the complete canvassing board, the client in this case, can release it," officials said. The board may decide to share it Friday. (*Pioneer Press*)

It is also not clear whether attorneys for both camps have received copies of the opinion from either the AG or the Board. (Elias for Franken had mentioned Tuesday he *hoped* the AG would issue an opinion before Friday's meeting and *implied* he hoped both sides would get a copy before Friday, but no word on this.) Soooo... the Board might have shown the opinion to both camps Thursday OR the Board might just hang onto it for their own use for now and enjoy watching attorneys for both sides do their song and dance today! Could go either way I think.

How Many Rejected Absentee Ballots?

Remember the margin between Coleman & Franken rests at 192 in Coleman's favor with 4,400 challenged ballots still outstanding? The other pool of outstanding ballots is those improperly rejected absentee ballots. And how many rejected absentee ballots are there (the "5th pile" ballots)?

- Sec. of State Ritchie last week he thought it might be 500 ballots.
- The Franken side has long held to a range of 500-1,000.
- The *Pioneer Press* calculates:

> According to a *Pioneer Press* analysis of information from 12 counties, which have made progress in sorting their absentees and told the newspaper their results, 358 absentee ballots were improperly rejected out of 2,216. That's a wrongful rejection rate of 16 percent.
>
> If there were 12,000 rejected absentee ballots statewide and 16 percent were improperly rejected, that would mean about 2,000 ballots should have been counted on Election Day but weren't.

SO maybe 2,000? Hmmmm..... curiouser and curiouser. Stay tuned for more developments.

The Star Tribune doesn't do the math (*that's minus 5 for not showing your work, and minus 5 more for not actually coming up with an answer and making the WineRev do it instead*) but they looked at 29 counties and 3,484 ballots, with 512 of the "5th pile" sort. This yields= 14.69%, applied to the earlier statewide rejected absentee ballot figure we get 1,763–rather closer to the *Pioneer Press*'s number and again far stronger than the top of the Franken 500-1,000 range. So we'll see.

Friday Morning with the MinnPost

You want a GREAT capsule summary of today's State Canvassing Board meeting? Not only does *TheUpTake* live stream it, but in written form Jay Weiner at the *MinnPost* does it with REAL style along with substance. (He includes a link to a PDF of the Franken filing with the Board, complete with all those legal precedent citations (like from 1887!), David Lillehaug's signature (the BIG queen piece on Franken's legal chessboard) and a table summarizing the 62 affidavits– sadly not a one from a Lizard person or the FSM.)

Ya gotta love an article that

1. uses the word "ginormously" *(and correctly I might add)*
2. brings in just-about-former Idaho Senator Larry (The Men's Room Footsie Man) Craig
3. wants to have not just recounted, challenged and rejected absentee ballots, but also *vaporized* ballots. Thanks Jay!

Clashing Campaigns!

Another example of Republican projection and telegraphing their own strategy by accusing the other side of their own approach. Kaszuba-son writes on this morning:

> Franken attorney Elias says any improperly rejected absentee ballots "could yield votes for Coleman as well as Franken. 'We have never argued that the only votes that ought to be counted are improperly rejected absentee votes for Al Franken.'
>
> Luke Friedrich, a Coleman spokesman, said the Franken campaign 'could care less about the outcome of the recount and are instead focusing their energies on building a legal challenge to the Board's action–or making their case before the US Senate.'" *(Star Tribune)*

Bleech!

OK I've got the late shift today, so I'll get a 2nd cup of coffee in the not-Cincinnati-Bungles mug and stay here for a bit while you read the latest from yust southeast of Lake Wobegon.

Shalom.

Franken Rises Edition
December 13, 2008

Comments: 159   Recs: 406   Tips: 289

With this note, this diary was put on the "Front Page" of DailyKos, a rare & singular honor.

DK From the diaries. Anyone would be hard pressed to come up with a better recap of the state of the Minnesota recount – kos

Yumpin' yimminy, uffda! By the beard of St. Olaf EVERYTHING happened yesterday in the great Minnesota Recount: Canvassing Board, ballots of every species, attorneys, an attorney general, people coming out in 20 degree weather to cram the hearing room carrying signs and buttons "Count every vote"! New and old media acting like journalists, Kossacks putting up diaries on the front page *(that skinny Kos kid did one again; man does George Soros like him or what?)*, bloggers blogging AND:

Al Franken's prospects for Senate took such a definite turn for the better that the Coleman campaign has gone to court (a sure sign a Repub. is losing? Batting average the past 8 years says YES.)

Cast members for this episode

State Canvassing Board: Eric Magnuson, Chief Justice, Minnesota Supreme Court; G. Barry Anderson, Associate Justice, Minnesota Supreme Court; Kathleen Gearin, Chief Judge, Ramsey County; Edward Cleary, Assistant Chief Judge, Ramsey County; Mark Ritchie, Secretary of State, Minnesota, chief elections officer.

Recounting Ballots

The Board heard from Minneapolis Elections Director Cindy Reichert about the missing 133 ballots. She ran down everything they could think of to find them and described their ballot and recount process, winding up with: "We determined definitively the ballots were missing." While that sounds obvious it is in *flat opposition* to the Coleman camp's contention that these 133 ballots never existed in the first place (the germ of the idea behind the Reich-wing ranting about "creating votes.")

The Board talked it over and then voted **5-0** that the 133 ballots are IN, thanks to the sign-in voter books and the machine tapes that recorded them. Most reports say this means a net gain to FRANKEN of +46. Starting from the 192 margin Coleman was holding last Friday, this would mean the difference is now 146.

5-0 huh? Man in Minnesota, the State of Hockey, 5-0 is a *major* shellacking, and it is also by this Board. Sure Coleman can take it to court (likely) but I seriously doubt a Minnesota court (or even a Federal Court) is going to overturn a 5-0 decision by a Board that includes 2 MN Supreme Court justices and has the sole task and total focus on finishing this election right. In defense the Franken side would have the Board's unanimous decision, precedent from other Minnesota elections, strong evidence (the sign-in logs and machine tapes) if not "best evidence" (which, if we would have the 133 ballots NONE of this would be in court), and the "voter intent" standard on its side. No way. These 133 votes are in, counted, and broke +46 for Franken. Over and out.

Recounted Ballots

Secretary of State's Office 8:00pm Dec. 12

Total % of Ballots Recounted: 100.0%

	Coleman	Franken
Recounted ballots	1,208,935	1,208,747
Change from election day	-2,655	-2,688
Apparent difference		+27
Start of Recount difference	+215	

Both the "change from election day" and "apparent difference" lines INCLUDE the challenged ballots noted next, so don't read too much into these numbers.

SO the simple math is Coleman's lead at the start 215-27= **188**

This 188 number does NOT include the net +46 swing to Franken from the famous 133 missing ballots.

Oh and remember when Reichert and Team were looking for the missing 133 and they found another ballot envelope of 20 absentee ballots? (Or maybe 12...maybe military ballots...maybe overseas; still a bit murky on how this has shaken out.) Well it would seem likely those 12 will be added to the Minneapolis total but not right away. The Board amended its motion on the 133 and also said (perforce 5-0) that these 12 should be added to the Minneapolis "5th pile"...which is not too bad a move.

The Coleman side will definitely want to hear the whole story of just how these 12 were lost and found. *I don't blame them one bit for that.* I think Reichert should be called to task over them as well. If she comes out of this election and recount with a black mark about anything in my book its not the lost 133 but these badly handled 12...really seems sloppy in my book. By sheer dumb luck they were recovered and look like they'll get counted but it shouldn't hinge on luck. Something went badly wrong and Reichert and her people (with maybe an assist from Ritchie's office) need to figure it out and take steps to prevent a repeat (and maybe add a procedure or 2 for statewide use so other places won't go through the same slip-ups.)

Challenged Ballots

As of the Board meeting this morning 4,472 challenged ballots are still facing the Board starting Tuesday. (That's down from 6,655 but a long way to go.) Gearin spoke for the Board, warning both campaigns that challenges need to be serious and that neither side should be playing games; "I hope both sides are respecting every single ballot that they see."

(What a great way to phrase that: "respecting every ballot"—as in respecting the voter who voted it, and respecting the will of the people who are in charge of this here democracy.

Hear, hear, Judge Gearin! Doffs hat in salute.)

DK I think I'm developing a crush on Minnesota. "Respecting every ballot".....it gives me a thrill up my leg. *(FrozeAgain)*

The Sec. of State mentioned the challenged ballots rather pointedly:

> The board encouraged the campaigns to further withdraw frivolous challenges. Ritchie, in particular, had harsh words for both camps, saying they should spend less time filing legal briefs with the board and more time reducing frivolous challenges.
>
> "I'm not happy about this," Ritchie said. *(Pioneer Press)*

("spend less time filing legal briefs...and more time reducing frivolous challenges"–Oh yeah! Just what anybody has wanted to say publicly to a lawyer at least once in life! Thank you Mr. Ritchie for laying on the smack for all of us.)

AND...maybe already planned but maybe not, in the afternoon the Franken side is dropping 750 more challenged ballots bringing their total down to about 1100. Board total (also accounting for Coleman's 225 reduction yesterday) is now 3,497.

Board plans to start in on challenged ballots Tues. 12/16 and hopes to finish by Friday 12/19...Ritchie says they are willing to go longer for accuracy's sake but this is the goal.

For those of you utterly condemned to their parents' basements, The UpTake says they will **live stream (!)** the Board ruling on the challenged ballots one by one starting on the 16th. *Paint Drying Channel? Fireplace Log Burning Network? You've got competition!*

Rejected Absentee Ballots

After its opening salvo on challenged ballots the Board waived attorney-client privilege and released the opinion they had received from Attorney General Lori Swanson and passed out copies in the hearing room.

In brief, county and city election boards/ Canvassing Board should count the "5th pile" ballots IF both campaigns sign off on it in writing. (MN Atty General Swanson: "There is no doubt that voters who have complied with all legal requirements, but whose ballots were improperly rejected, should have their votes counted.")

Obviously either campaign can refuse to sign off (any guesses who might NOT want every vote counted?) but as WCCO (TV/Radio-Minneapolis) adds in their story:

> The (Atty. Gen.) opinion laid out several options for getting the ballots into the count, some involving court action and others through administrative means. It says that the campaigns are free to seek court orders to compel counties to take part. *(WCCO)*

So its sounds like Attorney General Swanson would LIKE both camps to play nice, but also thinks if they don't, either campaign (like one who WANTS every vote counted) could go to court on their own to get a court order to force it.

Ritchie informed the Board the Sec. of State's office is aware of 638 improperly rejected absentee ballots out of over 4,000 such ballots examined so far across the state. By extrapolation at the moment this goes over 1,500 statewide.

Deputy Sec. of State Gelbmann gives Board a report from city of Duluth: 127 absentees rejected because officials said the signatures did not have a date with them as well. As everyone started reviewing these ballots last week those same officials had a "read the freaking manual" moment and looked it up in their election board guidebooks and also checked Minnesota election Law. Result: *no such requirement,* so according to Gelbmann those 127 absentee ballots should be counted. *(Good news for Franken! Duluth is very strongly Democratic. Between the Democratic drive to have voters vote absentee this year (10% did in MN, a new record) and the natural Democratic advantage in Duluth, Franken could very easily and realistically carry those 127 by 90-25-12 (F, C, & Barkley) for a pickup of +75. We'll see.)*

Board votes **5-0** to urge county boards to sort their rejected absentees into the 5 piles, 4 rejected for each of 4 statutory reasons and the 5th for "other." They did NOT order/compel/require the county & city boards to do so, since in the AG's opinion they do not have that authority. However this vote backs up Ritchie's Dec. 1 letter to the boards to do likewise and opens the door to filing for court orders (which WOULD order/compel/require the boards to sort.)

To facilitate the review of challenged ballots, the State Recount Official is directed to open the challenged ballot envelopes to remove those challenged ballots which have been withdrawn by each of the two candidates or their representatives. The State Recount Official shall report to the Board the allocation of votes resulting from the withdrawal of these challenges.

The withdrawn challenged ballots shall be sealed into separately labeled envelopes for return to the jurisdiction from whence they were received.

The State Recount Official will arrange for this process to occur in an appropriate room and at an appropriate time and shall inform the candidates and the public of the time and location so that they may observe if they so desire. The State Recount Official may designate any member of the staff of the Office of the Secretary of State to assist in this task.

The remaining challenged ballots shall be sealed into separately labeled envelopes by jurisdiction from whence they were received and be kept secure for review by the Board.

Passed, 5-0.

Sec. of State Mark Ritchie held a presser right after the Board meeting broke up. Asked if county boards would continue to NOT sort since he can't order them and the Board can't either. Ritchie: Most of the county boards he's spoken to are "eager to get it right"...So far Ramsey, Washington, Freeborn, Sherburne and Itasca counties have not been sorting per Ritchie's letter (and others may have been holding back too) all waiting on today's Board meeting. Having heard it they may move on it...

Both Camps' Reaction to Board Meeting

Andy Barr of the Al Franken campaign:

> We are pleased that the state canvassing board has affirmed what we always believed to be true: Minnesota is not a state that disenfranchises its voters.
>
> Today's decisions represent positive and productive steps towards ensuring that this election is decided fairly and accurately, as well as a complete rejection of the Coleman campaign's effort to throw out lawful votes from Minnesotans. *(quoted in Star Tribune)*

From Mike McIntee at The UpTake:

> Noah reports that the Coleman campaign representative Mark Drake was generally unavailable to the media to day. He gave some statements to a few reporters and left.

Saturday Morning Fallout
Lawyers Dueling with Light Sabers VI

(Hat tip to *Minnesota Independent* for offering their ship for the duel)

Knaak for Coleman, going to MN Supreme Court to stop 87 counties + cities from sorting & counting rejected absentees (*2 hand, overhead swing*):

> "Complaining in a statement this afternoon that "[A]dvocates for the Franken campaign stood outside [the meeting] with signs reminiscent of Florida in 2000," Coleman attorney Fritz Knaak asserted:
>
> [T]here is *[sic]* no longer any uniform, statutory levels or standards by which legally rejected absentee ballots are being considered and reviewed in Minnesota."
> *(Minnesota Independent)*

Elias for Franken (*shower of sparks*) in a conference call with reporters:

> "There is a uniform counting standard in Minnesota: It is the election code of Minnesota. ... They are hoping to run out the clock. ... I don't know what the Supreme Court or the state would say except, 'Read the election code.'"
> *(Minnesota Independent)*

Knaak (*crossed light beams inches from his face, heard in his 1st 5 words*)

> Although Minnesota law is clear on the grounds upon which absentee ballots may be rejected, a strong likelihood exists that these standards will be interpreted differently by each county that engages in this process ... *(Minnesota Independent)*

Elias: (*spin move, straight arm gesture and the "Force" sends Knaak skidding across the floor*)

> The move represented a "change in perspective" for Knaak, pointing to Knaak's reported Nov. 26 statements that the number of wrongly rejected ballots (now estimated by Secretary of State Mark Ritchie to be between 1,000–2,000 statewide) would be "miniscule" and break both ways, and that such ballots should be counted. *(Minnesota Independent)*

Scary Thought Department

At several sites the bloggers have brought up the following, perfectly reasonable yet a political junkie's dream come true:

The county & city boards start publicly opening their "5th pile" ballots to count them...in the presence of observers from both camps...who can then CHALLENGE (un-frivolously of course) ballots that have a stray/identifying mark, lack a lizard scale, etc.

That's right. The 1,500+ rejected absentee ballots that are being UN-rejected are subject to challenge just like any other ballots...fortunately most of them will be over and done with, but still...thats the Law.

Whew!

> DK You know, after Florida 2000, however this turns out, it is just such a pleasure to see this recount being done right! *(Seneca Doane)*

Well this morning's *Star Tribune* hasn't arrived yet but I think this may cover it anyway. MUST have coffee X 2 so I'll put it up with the latest from yust southeast of Lake Wobegon.

Shalom.

The Final Week
December 14, 2008

Comments: 25   Recs: 26   Tips: 33

After yesterday's diary made the Kos Front Page (*"Thank you, thank you very much"*), some commenters thought it was Too Much Information. So...here is an ultra brief summary for those wanting fast-food, without braking at the drive thru window, with many abbreviations (abbr.):

Norm lead: 188.

NO new recounted ballots.

Challenged ballots (CB): Down to 3,497; physical separation withdrawn CBs from other CBs by SoS Office Monday, 12/15. Rulings on remaining challenged ballots, Tues.-Fri. by Canv. Bd.

Rejected Absentee Ballots (RAB): About 12,000 statewide, with nearly all counties sorting them into 5 piles for WHY rejected. Between 1,500 & 2,000 in the "5th pile": OTHER reasons. Legal maneuvers brewing about the RABs.

(70 wds. & abbrs.—will try 4 smaller Mon. Sound of shrieking tires as ultra brief summaries (UBSs) are thrown through open windows of passing readers' vehicles.)

Smell of burning rubber dissipates as we continue below.

Recounted Ballots

Still no changes here at the Sec. of State website, but of course ALL the ballots are going to end up here at the end. That could be as soon as *this Friday, Dec. 19.*

IF (big IF) the State Canvassing Board a) finishes ruling on all the challenged ballots, and b) all the rejected absentee ballots are opened and counted for their respective candidates, THEN all these ballots, along with the first 2.8 million, will end up recounted and the Board I believe will formally inform the Sec. of State of the final numbers of the recount.

Secretary of State Ritchie will then be in a position to issue a Certificate of Election—which is the key to the kingdom, or at least a seat in the Senate of the United States for the people of the State of Minnesota.

This happy scenario assumes nothing goes wrong, there are no hitches, and no court intervenes with an injunction or order of some sort. I judge the odds of THAT happening by dusk on Friday the 19th at something less than 10%, but sooner or later that is the end of this frozen road.

And as achingly close as this might end up (even the Holy Odin of Numbers, Nate Silver, took a stab at a final Franken win by 27 votes—out of 2.8million?? Whew! Whisker close)

DK   I know that the odds are getting longer ...but I still hope that Lizard People can pull it off. *(RoIn)*

Challenged Ballots

Two pieces to this section.

First, on Monday, Dec. 15 the Sec. of State's office will be pulling hundreds of the withdrawn challenged ballots from the stacks the Board will face and the numbers on the website will begin to reflect this. From SoS Office:

> STATE RECOUNT OFFICIAL WILL SEPARATE WITHDRAWN
> CHALLENGES FROM OTHER CHALLENGED BALLOTS
> WHAT: In accordance with a resolution passed by the State Canvassing Board, staff of the Office of the Secretary of State will open the envelopes of original challenged ballots and remove the withdrawn challenges.

Total challenged has gone from 6,655 to 3,497, so the Sec. of State staff will have to pull at least 3,158 ballots (and the right ones) – although hopefully they've been at it for several days. *(AHA. A new Franken withdrawal, so the total left for Board is about 2,900.)*

Both candidates can continue withdrawing challenges all the way through Friday so the staff will have something to do this coming week, and it won't be Christmas shopping. (Given the rather testy mood of the Board over "frivolous" challenges and "respecting every ballot" (from Gearin & Ritchie in particular) both camps will be busy as well.)

Second, beginning Tuesday, Dec. 16 the Canvassing Board begins a one-by-one examination of each challenged ballot and votes to accept or reject each challenge. Ritchie is hoping for unanimous votes as often as possible but apparently a simple majority will do it. Sooooo...no more than -3,497-/2,900 ballots will be added to the Recount totals. Ritchie still hopes to finish by Friday but is insisting on accuracy and said often, "We will not be rushed."

Rejected Absentee Ballots

About 290,000 Minnesotans voted by absentee ballot on Nov. 4. About 278,000 of those ballots are already in the totals and were also recounted.

About 12,000 absentee ballots were rejected by local boards, not opened, and not counted.

Fellow East Baltic Noah Kunin (*only a Lithuanian not Estonian like WineRev,] but on the right shore of the Baltic*) has THE text from the statutory code over at TheUpTake:

> The election judges shall mark the return envelope "Accepted" and initial or sign the return envelope below the word "Accepted" if the election judges or a majority of them are satisfied that:
>
> 1. the voter's name and address on the return envelope are the same as the information provided on the absentee ballot application;
> 2. the voter's signature on the return envelope is the genuine signature of the individual who made the application for ballots and the certificate has been completed as prescribed in the directions for casting an absentee ballot, except that if a person other than the voter applied for the absentee ballot under applicable Minnesota Rules, the signature is not required to match;
> 3. the voter is registered and eligible to vote in the precinct or has included a properly completed voter registration application in the return envelope;
> 4. the voter has not already voted at that election, either in person or by absentee ballot.
>
> There is no other reason for rejecting an absentee ballot. In particular, failure to place the envelope within the security envelope before placing it in the outer white envelope is not a reason to reject an absentee ballot.
>
> The return envelope from accepted ballots must be preserved and returned to the county auditor.
>
> If all or a majority of the election judges examining return envelopes find that an absent voter has failed to meet one of the requirements prescribed in clauses (1) to (4), they shall mark the return envelope "Rejected," initial or sign it below the word "Rejected," and return it to the county auditor.

These are the first "4 piles" of absentee ballots each election board is asked to create. Somewhere between 10,000 and 11,500 ballots were so rejected. Anything else goes into the famed "5th pile."

Attention has been focused on the "5th pile" and should these be counted BUT, dear readers, I've become convinced that MAYBE the first 4 piles aren't as cut and dried as I would like them to be. I think it was Wright County that had rejected some 36 such ballots because the voter wasn't registered (#3 reason & pile). BUT somebody last week at the county board responded to the Sec. of State's letter of Dec. 1 to revisit and re-sort the ballots found these 36 actually contained a voter registration card in the returned ballot packet. Sooo... those 36 presumably now pass muster and can be/should be counted although it is unclear whether the county board has done so and adjusted its vote totals accordingly.

On a positive note this shows the value of Ritchie's letter in a close election. Mistakes happen and they can be caught and corrected. Kudos to the system for this.

But more negatively this means those first 4 piles may not be as settled as many hoped.

Does this mean we're talking John Q. Public vs Johnny Public? Or 123 Main Street vs. 123 Main St.? Or let's say you have an, apartment building: 25 units in one building located at street address 1234 Elm St.

Ole Gunderson sorts the daily mail into the 25 resident boxes and knows Lena Anderson Peterson-Olsen lives in #215 for the last 20 years. Because of this Lena rarely writes "215" on the 2nd line of her address because she always gets her mail.

So, is her legal address merely 1234 Elm? (Ambiguous by 25 units?). Or, since there is no other Lena Anderson Peterson-Olsen at 1234 Elm, and she does indeed reside there, she is the only one who could possibly be the voter in question? I hate this, but I think it's a lawyer's field day.

Ouch! You can see *either Franken or Coleman* could ask a court to decide these are the SAME or they are DIFFERENT...and hence the grounds for the Coleman filing with the MN Supreme Court asking for "uniform standards" in each county and city election board. You can see the difficulty in writing such standards that would take into account every possible circumstance. But if you let human beings use "common sense" (which is often in uncommonly rare supply) how do you avoid abuse and arbitrary decision-making?

(After all, a distinguished member of the United States House of Representatives who was just re-elected has asserted that other members of the House and Senate may be anti-American and seditious. What if some of them were elected by absentee ballots cast by anti-American voters? A Bachmann-ist election judge (or county judge) could be a nightmare.)

I don't know a good way out of this but it sure seems a lawyer's delight. It's why I'm only going with 10% by Friday.

Legal Maneuvers

Some readers have wondered if this might end up in Federal Court. (It is telling to me that both Franken and Coleman's court appearances have all been in Minnesota State or county courts so far.) While this is possible it may not be all that likely as noted in a terrific comment from Kossack Sara in yesterday's diary:

> Two reasons this will not get into Federal Court:
>
> First, they went to Federal Court in 1962 in the Elmer Anderson - Karl Rolvaag race, first District Court in St. Paul, then the 8th Circuit Court of Appeals in St. Louis, and then to the Supreme Court. Ruling was that since the election in question was a State Election, it was Minnesota State Law that governed. The 8th Circuit wrote that ruling, and the Supreme Court affirmed it.
>
> Unlike Bush v Gore, a Senate Race is all within one state, and each state sets the law, rules and procedure for itself. So long as the Canvass Board and the Minnesota Courts stay away from an equal protection matter, the Federal Courts will not take this case, given Rolvaag v. Anderson.
>
> Second, The Constitution gives the full Senate jurisdiction over seating its own members. That was not the case with Bush v. Gore. *(Sara)*

Sunday Morning with the Star Tribune and other Places

Great bit in a *Star Tribune* story from Dr. Charles Seife, NY University and recount observer. High praise for the process but points out that in a close election every little thing is magnified. Uses a wonderful example:

> With the margin between winner and loser in the thousandths of 1 percent, Seife said "there's not a system in existence right now capable of doing something this large with such a level of precision."
>
> He likened it to trying to eyeball which of two 6-foot guys is taller.
>
> "They're within a width of a hair, so you'd have to shave their heads, remove their socks and shoes and measure them at the same time in the morning so their spines are equally stretched," he said. "Even the tiniest thing will screw up your measurement."
>
> That's why elections officials always hope for blowouts. *(Star Tribune)*

Soooo...yay! I think Al will win because he has better hair! :-).

And speaking of our next (cross my fingers) Senator-elect, the Franken side says they will reduce their challenged ballots (currently at about 1,100):

> Two days after members of the state canvassing board issued an urgent plea for campaigns to withdraw additional challenges in order to allow them to finish their work in a timely fashion, the Franken campaign today announced that it would have fewer than 500 challenges remaining for the board to consider on a ballot-by-ballot basis when it meets on Tuesday. *(Al Franken press release)*

Legal Maneuvers II

In a sidebar in the *Star Tribune*, Mark Brunswick reports on the sound of Lawyer Light Sabers humming off stage. Coleman had announced Friday they will file with the MN Supreme Court for "uniform standards" not 87 different ones (like in 87 counties) for the rejected absentee ballots. This apparently will be filed formally on Monday.

"It asks that the Court order county elections officials to take no further action related to the rejected ballots until the court approves."

Andy Barr, Franken campaign spokesman, went into outrage mode. He said the actual motion is NOT a request for clarification or guidance, but is asking the Court to overturn the Canvassing Board Friday decisions (both by 5-0) and to STOP THE COUNT. (Florida Playbook, copyright 2000). No word from Knaak (Coleman) or Elias (Franken) but stand by for the next duel on the Death Star, this time maybe in court chambers.

Sorry there's not more substance today but I couldn't find a kidnapped blond white woman *(and you'd think in Minnesota that wouldn't be so hard, right Faux Noise?)* to fill this out. So that's the latest from yust southeast of Lake Wobegon.

Shalom.

5 Days to Go
December 15, 2008

Comments: 16   Recs: 30   Tips: 31

The final week of recounting (officially) although Sec. of State Ritchie has been vocal about leaving himself and the State Canvassing Board more time by insisting, "We will take all the time we need to be accurate."

Of course that's just the State of Minnesota. The courts may prolong this, but Ritchie, the Canvassing Board and the whole Recount Process are taking their last bows this week.

Recounted Ballots

No change in the SoS website numbers, and no updates since 12/12. This will change TONIGHT as the Secretary Ritchie's staff does major work today and physically pulls the withdrawn challenged ballots from both camps and begins posting them on the website to Franken, Coleman and others. They need to pull 3,600+ challenges, and pull the right ones.

Challenged Ballots

The Challenged Ballots are being withdrawn almost as fast as they piled up during the recount. Franken peaked at just under 3,300 but has been withdrawing challenges all week. Sunday afternoon they said they will pull another 600 or so, bringing their total to under 500. The Colemaniks topped out at just about 3,400 and have shaved away at their pile, but they are still sitting on about 2,300. You can imagine how the Canvassing Board might feel about looking at almost 5X more crap challenges from one camp than the other (which presumably, many here hope, look at least plausible.)

Late Sunday the Colemaniks caved to the perception and sent out chief mouthpiece Fritz Knaak with the word:

> "We continue to have concerns that the Secretary of State's Office has not provided to the Canvassing Board either a clear description as to what types of ballot challenges should be 'board worthy' or a uniform set of standards under which the board should count ballots. Nonetheless, we are committed to a process that is efficient and reasonable. With that in mind, it is our intent to reduce our challenges to somewhere south of 1,000 ballot challenges by the time the board meets on Tuesday. It is our hope that prior to the Canvassing Board meeting the board and the Secretary of State will have a credible process that is both uniform and consistent for reviewing challenged ballots." *(quoted in the Star Tribune)*

Well Fritz your team trained and sent out several hundred official observers from Harmony to Thief River Falls with instructions on what to challenge and how, based on what you got from a) Minnesota Law, b) the Sec. of State's Office, and c) your own esteemed counsel and interpretation. If a challenge isn't "board worthy" then MAYBE it shouldn't have been challenged at all, eh? So whose fault IS that pile of 3400 your trained and esteem-ably advised compiled? Turkey.

But Fritz? You are doing the right thing and cutting it down–playing catch-up, but its the right move. Thank you. As a Minnesota resident who is pro-Canvassing Board (and whose salaries I am paying at rather less than your "customary and reasonable" rate that you are socking to Norm and his friend Nasser), thank you for taking it easy on MY public servants.

The State Canvassing Board meets Tuesday to start ruling on the challenged ballots. TheUpTake, the Star Tribune and the MNSenate public access channel all plan to **live stream** the process for all 4 days. You want democracy in action? Want to see "your tax dollars at work"? Have no other life, are a hopeless political junkie, have a spare pair of pajamas there in your parents' basement?

Well tune in!

What to watch for?

1. Secretary Ritchie estimated the other week that maybe 75% of the challenges will be "no-brainers" that won't take 60 seconds apiece. He guessed (and it is only that) maybe 250 or more will be "real head-scratchers" where the Board will really have some honest doubts about a voter's intent (which is THE standard for this process.)

2. Joe Mansky (Ramsey Cty. election chief and former state election director) said in his 15 years experience on the state election board that sustained challenges were rare, about 2/1,000. (As in, "this ballot looks like Barkley but really is Coleman. Challenged by Coleman. Awarded to Coleman.") With under 1500 challenges that would mean about 3 might see this happen (should make for a safe drinking game!).

3. Both camps can continue withdrawing challenges until Friday, so as the Sec. of State's office works through the withdrawals, the stacks for the Board may shrink even as they are ruling.

4. Will some sort of trend develop for either side? Of course around here we would like to hear "Franken challenge sustained" on a thin but steady basis. (Matched of course by, "Coleman challenge denied" in mind-numbing repetition.)

5. Secretary Ritchie has expressed the hope that the Board rulings will be unanimous as often as possible (5-0) but holds that a majority will suffice. So how will the 4-1s break? The 3-2s? Do blocs or coalitions appear as rulings go by? Is Anderson mostly lining up with Franken? Is Magnuson siding more with Coleman? Is Cleary being feisty? Is Gearin the comic relief? Is Ritchie voting last and on the spot breaking those 2-2s?

My swipe at a few numbers: Total votes cast in Senate race: 2.9 million. Total challenged votes that will be ruled on by Canvassing Board (as of Sunday night): about 1500. This means (apart from the 12,000 rejected absentees, below) 0.0517% of the voter's intent will be decided by the Board. Or 99.9483% of the voters have already expressed their intent–so the Board really is working out at the 1/10,000th margins. Not necessary as a rule, EXCEPT with a margin of 188, the difference is 0.0064827% (expressed in 1/millionths).

Should you write a law to deal with millionths of a percent...or is that a "waste of taxpayer's money" and a "one in a million" scenario just isn't worth it? Bless their hearts, the 1960's Minnesota legislature (albeit having just gone through a 4 month nightmare WITHOUT such a law) said, "Yeah, (or Yah) its vorth it Sven. Lets write a good von." I think they did.

Rejected Absentee Ballots

As noted yesterday the rejected absentee ballots (total statewide about 12,000) are mostly sorted into the famous "5 piles", and the real focus is on that "5th pile" of ballots rejected for "other reasons" apart from the statutory 4.

But now it's developing that the 1st 4 piles may not be as steady as I've thought. Kossack Jeff in CA has reported in a diary Friday that absentee ballots are rejected for reason #3 (voter is not registered to vote), but that the absentee ballot packet includes a voter registration card, so you can fill it out and return it with the ballot. You're now registered and so your ballot can be counted (if it passes muster on the other reasons). Now one county has found about 40 ballots rejected for reason #3 that look like they HAVE said registration card and so are eligible to be counted (and even challenged for that matter.)

So more drama looms apart from the "5th pile" ballots.

At Friday's Board meeting Deputy Sec. of State Jim Gelbmann gave a report about some erroneously rejected absentee ballots from St. Louis County (Duluth). Sunday night the *Pioneer Press* gave a few more examples (and its nice to see one from the Coleman side; this issue affects both camps, even though many here are pulling for Franken.)

> In Golden Valley (*Hennepin County, 1st ring Minneapolis suburb*), 12 absentee ballots were rejected because the voters were not properly registered. But the city reported it looks like those voters mistakenly included a voter registration application inside their ballots. Other areas reported 10 similar ballots. Those ballots have not been included on the error pile, but that matter might have to be litigated.
>
> Coleman campaign lawyer Fritz Knaak said Scott County (*exurban, S of Twin Cities*) rejected some ballots "for lack of only the city in the witness line" and left them rejected. But Dakota County placed such ballots in its mistakenly rejected pile.
>
> Washington County (*E of St. Paul, jammed up against Wisconsin*) elections director Kevin Corbid said that 22 witnesses of absentee ballots gave out-of-state addresses, which initially led elections officials to assume the witnesses were not registered in Minnesota. But upon checking, county officials found registered voters with the same names in Minnesota. Since many of those ballots came from places near universities, it could be that Minnesota students simply gave their school addresses when they witnessed, not their home addresses. (*Pioneer Press*)

Legal Maneuvers III

There seems to be a divergence between Coleman's PR and Coleman's legal team. Friday the Canvassing Board voted 5-0 to count the 133 ballots from Minneapolis that are missing, based on their machine totals, and voted 5-0 to strongly request (the MN Attorney General Swanson said they don't have authority to flat order it) the county Boards sort the absentees into the 5 piles.

The Colemaniks said *Friday* they would file suit with the MN Supreme Court (today, Monday) for the Court to provide "clarification/ guidance" to the 87 county boards about this sorting process (instead of having "87 different standards".) They mean it because the word came from attorney Tony Trimble. Trimble is the *queen piece* on Coleman's side of the chessboard. (*Cue Darth Vader March music*)

> Without Supreme Court guidance, Coleman attorney Tony Trimble said, Minnesota could end up in a "Florida situation," where in the 2000 presidential race voters in different areas got treated differently. (*Pioneer Press*)

Now *Sunday* they announce they will be asking the Court to order the boards take "no further actions" about these ballots until the Court rules.

The Frankenites sent out PR guy Andy Barr to howl "Foul." He went to the heart of the Coleman move by flat out declaring the Colemaniks "want to overturn the decision of the State Canvassing Board" and have the Court "stop the count." (*That is SO Florida 2000!*) No sign of the lawyers(either Knaak/Trimble or

Elias/Lillehuag–Franken's queen piece) on Sunday night, so they are probably tuning up their Lightsabers for tomorrow's filing at the Supreme Court, followed by a trip to the microphones.

Supreme Court spokesman John Kostouros *(must have been a Greek visiting Copenhagen when the ship sailed for Minnesota)* said the Court would move quickly. "They tend to handle election matters pretty expeditiously," he said.

I'll leave you with the latest from yust southeast of Lake Wobegon. (Browns play tonight! *Raises mug in salute!*)

Shalom.

Events, Dad, and Ludwig
December 16, 2008

Comments: 104   Recs: 168   Tips: 139

Four days left. The State Canvassing Board begins ruling on challenged ballots. The MN Supreme Court chooses from 3 options on Norm Coleman's suit (the legal one, not one of the ones Nasser bought him.)

Recounted Ballots

Much to my surprise, no changes as of Monday night at the SoS website, with Norm's lead unchanged at 188. BUT these numbers will change, perhaps as soon as today for 3 reasons:

    a. UN-challenged ballots from both camps (numbering about 5,000) will be going back into the Franken and Coleman piles.

    b. Challenged ballots will also be added.

    c. Perhaps some of the previously rejected absentee ballots will be counted and posted.

WARNING: ANY numbers you read about "who's ahead" or "who's gaining" should be taken with doses of salt large enough to feed a herd of cattle. This includes MY numbers. To take just one example: Franken has UNchallenged about 2,800 ballots. Assume for a moment they ALL end up on Coleman's pile. "Coleman increases lead to 2,988!" RedState will scream (188 current lead+ 2,800).

Of course Coleman has UNchallenged about 2,400 ballots. If they ALL go onto Franken's pile even Faux Noise would run a crawler: "Franken surges from almost 3,000 back to only down 588" (2,988-2,400=588). But the Canvassing Board is still ruling on 1,500 challenges...and there are the absentees.

So those of you on blood pressure medication and with certain heart conditions–WARNING! LOTS of salt in use in MN-Sen race this week.

Challenged Ballots

Marc Elias for Franken at Monday's presser summed it up nicely: "This is a dead even race heading into the challenges."

And the Coleman side is rather quiet on this point–their silence is telling.

What will you be seeing at the Canvassing Board Meeting today?

You know how folks around here say reading DailyKos is like getting the newspaper a few days early? How about almost a MONTH early?? Back on Nov. 21 Kossack Anarchofascist explained what will happen with the challenged ballots and *their effect on the vote totals:*

DK

> Challenges can be either to move a vote from the other side to the discard (or other) pile, or to move a vote from the discard (or other) pile to your candidate.
>
> Assuming most challenges get tossed and a higher proportion of Coleman challenges are to strike Franken votes, then Franken is going to pick up big when the canvassing board meets.

DK In Hennepin (county) in particular, looking city by city, it seems to me almost all of Coleman's challenges are to strike Franken votes, and a fair portion of Franken's are to add Franken votes.

(Note that if a challenge to strike a vote for your opponent fails, they net a vote. If a challenge to add a vote for your candidate fails, there is no net change in votes. So once again, if Coleman's challenges are disproportionately to strike Franken votes compared to Franken's challenges, then Franken stands to pick up a lot at the Canvassing Board.) (*Anarchofascist*)

The People Speak (and agree with YOU)

You know all those 6,000 challenged ballots? You can view ALL of them for yourself at the *Star Tribune* website like Kossack Federalist did over the weekend.

DK Well about 26,000 people did likewise (acc. to *Star Tribune*) and left their opinions (emph. added): "There appeared to be widespread consensus that Franken won slightly more disputes than Coleman, *enough to theoretically erase the incumbent's narrow lead by late Monday.*" (*Federalist*)

26,000 sets of eyeballs! Whoo-Hooooo for your dedication...and for (ahem) seeing it the right way!

A bit more hope folks! But now all eyes on the Canvassing Board.

Rejected Absentee Ballots/ Legal Maneuvers

Coleman's filing with the Supreme Court is for a Temporary Restraining Order to halt counting of rejected absentee ballots that have been UNrejected.

Franken has filed "Motion to Intervene" so they have an interest (ya think?) in the Coleman petition.

Coleman side filed suit Monday with the MN Supreme Court. The Court's options?

What we were told is that EITHER (the Court) will:
1. Reject the request outright.
2. Issue a ruling without a hearing.
3. Have a hearing. (*Noah Kunin at The UpTake*)

Late Monday: Court has opted: They will hold **hearing Wednesday, 1:00pm**. Wants oral arguments from both sides.

The *Star Tribune reports that* two Justices ordered the hearing. "The order does NOT *(WR emphasis)* block county officials from sorting or counting absentee ballots before the hearing"...As if in confirmation:

Hennepin County (largest in state) is not waiting for Court moves and is going ahead and sorting absentee ballots and **opening and counting "5th pile" ballots** as valid and sending Sec. of State their adjusted totals. Hope to finish Wednesday. Whoa! Could be a big finish!

The Al Franken for Senate campaign today commended Hennepin County for its decision to correct errors related to the improper rejection of absentee ballots. The county today instructed localities within its jurisdiction to immediately sort rejected absentee ballots and report the results to the county canvassing board so that so-called "fifth pile" ballots may be included in a revised count. Hennepin County set a deadline of tomorrow *(Tuesday)* for the sorting to be completed. (*Star Tribune*)

A Personal Moment

It's a hard few days right now. Today was Dad's birthday, the 15th. He would have been 85 today, but he passed away last year on the 23rd, making for a very dark Christmas. Ludwig von Beethoven's birthday was the 16th. Dad always liked having his day right next to Ludwig's and Ludwig's music was one of only three things he was passionate about.

He told of when he was a refugee in the Displaced Persons' camp near Munich. Somehow a bunch of musicians in the spring of 1945 found each other, found instruments, sheet music, a conductor and time and place to practice. They went to the American Military Governor to get permission to hold a public concert. After a thorough check of all the musicians and the pieces permission was granted. They drew a good crowd, mostly locals, but my Dad also managed to trade some Lucky Strike cigarettes (currency of the day) for a ticket.

The last piece was Beethoven's Fifth Symphony, the one that opens with three quick eighth notes and down in a minor sound to a dotted half: "Fate knocking on the Door" is the nickname. Now a symphony is in 4 movements, with a break between each, tied together with common musical elements. Ludwig's Fifth is a famous exception: he runs the 3rd movement right into the 4th without a break, with a big key change. (Hey, he's Beethoven. He can do that.)

The 3rd movement features a plaintive oboe above sad but moving strings. Then the low strings and low winds set up a brooding, insistent lamentation, and soon the middle voiced reeds and strings join the building sorrow and hurt. But the oboe and first violins scurry nervously and negotiate furiously with the high brass and percussion until the trumpets ignite the 4th movement with three rising notes in MAJOR that covert the whole movement into what somebody called, "fierce rejoicing."

When the concert ended not only was there applause and a standing O, but the audience wept, then stormed the stage (Germans performing anarchy!), mobbed the musicians and carried the conductor around the hall on their shoulders. Later in the year the "orchestra" held other concerts, massively attended, but regardless of what was played, at the end of each program the chant went up, "The Fifth, the Fifth!" People blocked the doors and would not let the musicians leave until once again they would play "The Fifth." They had survived the War.....and that was worth noting.

Well Dad, I'm still in my 3rd movement. You know Mrs. WineRev is no longer Mrs. and I'm not a Rev. anymore. But grand-daughter WineRevette loves college and the WineRever grandson could look you in the eye now, he's that tall. It's hard this season, but not as hard as last year. And if I can get that book of mine published this coming year, the one we talked through and even cried over once in awhile, well, Dad, then I think I'll see the trumpeters blowing out their spit-valves and the tympanist stepping back slightly to give herself more room to swing her arms down for the fortissimo. Hope so. Miss you.

PS. Dad? Now that Ludwig has his hearing back, what do you think of his Tenth Symphony?

> **DK**
>
> Thanks for the story about your Dad, and mojo for Beethoven.
>
> My neighbor, a cellist, tells of one of her cello teachers, who survived a concentration camp. Still had the tattoo on his arm. Once, a trainload of something arrived at the camp and her teacher and a few other campers were told they had one hour to unload it all or they would be killed. They had learned to pace themselves so as not to work to exhaustion, but they of course had no watches or clocks. The teacher knew of a particular cello concerto which lasted just under 20 minutes. He hummed the concerto three times for him and his coworkers so that they'd know it was an hour. *(classico)*

That's the latest (and it may be out of date; things are moving THAT fast) for now from yust southeast of Lake Wobegon.

Shalom.

Final Three Days
December 17, 2008

Comments: 33   *Recs:* 59   *Tips:* 62

Today features an afternoon legal thriller: The MN Supreme Court at 1:00pmCT will hear oral arguments on Coleman's request for a) uniform standards for rejected absentee ballots, and b) a Temporary Restraining Order to halt inclusion of such ballots.

We'll wrap up Tuesday and try to give you a heads up for Wednesday.

Your WineRev is really feeling under the gun on this one. Yesterday we had someone miss their shift at the shop so yours truly pulled a 12 hour day and got in about 11:00pm. It's back off to work for the EARLY shift this morning (leaving by 7:00am) so this diary is done under the inspiration of the ghost of Hunter S. Thompson. You're getting almost straight Gonzo journalism, hashed together in a desperate effort around midnight. There are heavy cups of morning coffee and "Crouse is downstairs yelling at those bastards at the Rolling Stone, 'Sure. He's up there right now. We'll start sending in about 10 minutes. It won't make a lot of sense but there'll be lots of it.' Still he won't be able to hold them off much longer. Now if the damn seals would stop barking on the rocks..."

Recounted Ballots

No changes yet AGAIN at the SoS website in the numbers. At some point Ritchie has got to crack and put up something new but not yet. Maybe it's his Deputy Gelbmann *(pours shot of Wild Turkey)* that's gumming it all up. Or maybe neither one has the time because they are all running around like kangaroo rats in heat trying pull those damn challenged ballots while taking phone calls from scared election judges in Park Rapids or Detroit Lakes (which should be in Michigan...)

Challenged Ballots w/ Lightsabers VI

The Canvassing Board dug into the challenges Tuesday but not before both sides took a few minutes to address the board. Coleman main man Tony Trimble *(music: Darth Vader March)* unleashed his double-ended Lightsaber Quarterstaff *(from Acme Co.- Sith Lord page: Creates authentic low humming sound when swung!)* and wanted *(Hummm!)* the Board to consider 137 precincts where original and duplicate ballots may have been double counted. (When an absentee ballot arrives folded in its envelope county election officials create a duplicate ballot that is then run through the optical scanner. Helps eliminate jammed machines, like avoiding running wrinkled stuff through a copier auto-feed.)

Brave Franken Front man Marc Elias *(swings single blade into parry position with a ch-ch-ch-cheeyoooo)* to protect Board members:

> (Elias) suggested that the Republicans are now trying to change the rules of the recount. "Those were the rules that we were given, and neither party objected to those rules that we were given," he said. "It seems to me that today ... is a bit late in the process for us to now say these rules which the Secretary of State set forth need to now be the subject of a intensive audited review." *(Star Tribune)*

Both Trimble and Elias then closed down their saber and quarterstaff and left the room scowling darkly as we await their next encounter.

Canvassing Board started in on Franken's 436 challenges and has about 230 to go, so they nailed off about half in a half day.

Tally: Coleman +94 Franken +21. As expected when the Franken challenges are ruled down, Coleman's numbers will go up, since these ballots are no longer challenged but are now countable.

The fact that Franken picked up 21 is nice to see and may be a straw in the wind for how things might turn tomorrow.

> In it's counting, the Franken campaign has assumed it would win none of the challenges and still be up by 4 votes. Today they won about 20. *(Michael McIntee, The UpTake)*

So this is REALLY GOOD NEWS!

Wait! Even better.

> About 20 of the Franken votes were reversals of the original decision. There were about 7 of the "other votes" that were originally in the Coleman side... so a net of about 27 for Franken today. *(Michael McIntee, The UpTake)*

And from the Republican Dumb/ Nasty Dept

At the end of challenges Tuesday evening the Colemaniks had STILL not delivered their list of challenges being withdrawn to Sec. of State's office. Deputy Sec. Gelbmann said workers are looking at a 1 a.m. Wednesday finish as it is to physically separate the withdrawn ballots from the ones in the Canvassing Board room...Way to get everyone's warm fuzzies, Norm.

Part II...As today's count was ending word came the Colemaniks, already sitting on about 1,000 challenges, may ADD to their pile. They saw how the Board was ruling on certain challenges and may *put some back in.* The Board was major league upset with THAT prospect and weren't shy about saying so...Way to get everyone on your side, Norm.

Still, there is no rule about candidates withdrawing or adding challenges before they are ruled on.

From the Democratic Fight the Good Fight Dept.

(So UN-Democrat-like; no wonder lots of folks around here like AL Franken!)

In view of how the Board is ruling Marc Elias said at the close of Tuesday that the Frankenites may *also add back in* 200 or so challenges they had withdrawn. Hooo boy!

This sort of thing may have blown the Board's chances of finishing by Friday, or even finishing by year end (they ARE going to take some time off for the holidays). Ritchie joked that he personally has until Nov. 2010 to get it done (election for him).

Reading Tea Leaves Dept

Some of the Tuesday challenges were settled by 4-1 votes. Anybody see any patterns developing there? Eric Black at *MinnPost* thought he did:

> (T)here were several split votes, all of them by a 4-1 tally... And on every one of them, it was either Ramsey County Judge Edward Cleary voting by himself for a ruling that would have favored Franken, or it was Associate Supreme Court Justice G. Barry Anderson voting by himself for a ruling that would have favored Norm Coleman. The Cleary protest votes outnumbered the Anderson cases. *(MinnPost)*

Rejected Absentee Ballots

Several reports from around the state to Secretary of State Ritchie's office sound like a lot of counties are slow walking or even halting their sorting of Rejected Absentee Ballots (as strongly requested by the Canvassing Board on Friday, as allowed by the Court when it took the case Monday, and as requested by Ritchie's office 12/1) pending the outcome of today's Supreme Court hearing.

To that extent Coleman's suit has had some of the effect he is asking for formally from the Court.

On a related line, Frankenites filed suit in **County Court** in Olmsted County (SE MN, Rochester– home of the Mayo Clinic). It's not directly related to the Supreme Court case but that case hangs over it.

> While Republican U.S. Sen. Norm Coleman has asked the Minnesota Supreme Court to clarify how counties should tabulate absentee votes that may have been mistakenly rejected prior to the Nov. 4 vote, the Franken campaign said the new suit is over a unique situation where election officials in Olmsted County accepted 27 absentee ballots, but then mistakenly placed them in the rejection pile.
>
> "They just physically put them in the wrong place by accident," Franken campaign spokesman Andy Barr said. Barr said the county delayed including the ballots in its totals and was going to forward the ballots to the state for a decision. *(Pioneer Press)*

To me this is a classic "chilling effect" in action (and may in part lie behind Coleman filing what he did.) With no suit pending before the highest court in the state, Olmsted County could look at Ritchie's letter from Dec. 1, look at Friday's Canvassing Board letter and say, "Oops. Our bad. These 27 should have been over here next to Sven, but Ole dropped them off by Heikinenennen's table instead. Lena! Put those 27 back over by Sven."

NOW they are sending the 27 "to the state for a decision." Piffle! Absurd piffle! *(Would Hunter Thompson use the word piffle?)* BUT this hyper-cautious effect (not all bad, considering the opposite) is part of the lawsuit effect. (Of course if the Alan Page and the Supremes–look out Diana Ross– toss out Coleman's stuff like an ice chunk off your snow shovel on the driveway, well Sven is going to get back that 27 high coffee mug coaster right quick.)

Legal Maneuvers IV

Coleman has filed his case with the Minnesota Supreme Court.

First pass at who the players will be (Magnuson and Barry Anderson have recused themselves from the Court in dealing with this case...as they should, but in a Rethug state would probably be trying to disband the Canvassing Board...) :

Minnesota Supreme Court: (not including Canvassing Board members Magnuson & Anderson)

Alan Page, 63, Notre Dame '67, JD U Minn. School of Law '78, Asst. Atty Gen. State of MN 1985-1993. Appointed 1993 (Gov. Carlson R-Normal/Moderate). (Got his JD while employed full time by the NFL)

Paul Anderson (NOT Barry), BA Macalester Collge '65, JD U. Minn. Law '68.

Private practice 71-92. Chief Judge MN Court of Appeals, '92-94. Appointed in '94 (Carlson).

Helen Meyer BA & JD from U. Minn. Founded her own law firm. 3 years Gov. Ventura's chief Judicial appointment advisor. Appointed by Ventura in '02.

Lorie Skjerven Gildea (NOT a typo), BA '83, U. Minn.-Morris; JD, magna cum laude, order of Coif, Gerogtown Univ. '86. Private practice 86-93; Univ. Minn.General Counsel '93-'04; Hennepin County Judge '04-'06. Appointed '06 (Pawlenty)

Christopher Dietzen, 61, BA '69 and Law degree '73 both Gonzaga Univ.. Private practice '73-'04 in Washington state & Minnesota; Judge, MN Court of Appeals '04-'08. Appointed in '08 (Pawlenty).

I'm guessing the hearing will feature two rather new faces: it may well be not only Knaak vs. Elias but Trimble (Coleman) vs. Lillehaug (Franken's main man), two heavy hitters swinging those super lightsabers, the double ended ones (like that Sith Lord), hereby dubbed **Lightsaber Quarterstaffs (LSQ).**

OK its Wednesday morning. The Star Tribune just re-hashed all this stuff and downstairs the Rolling Stone people are yelling at Crouse for feeding in the last 2 pages upside down and now the damn machine light is blinking for more...so OK.

That's all I can manage for this morning. Here's the latest from yust southeast of Lake Wobegon.

Shalom.

2 Days to go?
December 18, 2008

Comments: 86   Recs: 138   Tips: 131

Another great day Wednesday, filled with challenged ballots, the new duplicate ballots, and the Minnesota Supreme Court.

Franken is doing OK on several fronts. Is today the day, FINALLY, when some semi-official numbers start to swing hard to Al and he finally takes a lead? Maybe...or it may be Friday (or even slop into the weekend, even though a whole lot of tired people don't want it to go there; but it might.)

The Colemaniks have *senate recount* lawyers tripping over their FBI investigation *defense* lawyers, (even though Norm "welcomes" the investigation) who are running into the federal *election* lawyers who are asking if Norm can use campaign funds for legal defense expenses.

Recounted Ballots

Still NO Change at the Sec. of State's website (none since Dec. 12.) There have been little stories running around that Ritchie isn't going to try to update things as they go along this week (too dizzying) but wait till the dust settles and then make a big post all at once. Seems to be what he's doing.

Challenged Ballots

The Canvassing Board had a better (and longer) day than Tuesday. They have just about finished the Franken challenges (those Franken challenged vs. Coleman, other, or vs. no-vote.)

Now the "Frankenmath" (salt shaker close by) has been that after every ballot gets counted (challenged, absentee, duplicate, etc.) Franken would be +4 (that's 4 votes, not 4% or something like that.) It's even more pessimistic that the Holy Odin of Numbers, Nate Silver, who early in the recount took a shot and said (with a fairly broad margin for error) that Franken could win by +27.

One of the working assumptions (and it IS a pessimistic one, but also realistic) has been that ALL the challenges from both sides would be rejected and those ballots returned to their "original piles" as it were and simply counted for C, F or Barkley. And on THIS basis the Franken side has been saying +4.

So after the 415 challenges addressed so far (just a few dozen Franken challenged ballots left to go) the Franken working assumption has been that these would sort out something like:

Coleman XXX

Barkley YY

Franken 0 with this "0" being the key. (Naturally, when the Board goes through the Coleman challenges, the reverse would be true, and this scoreboard would have Coleman = 0 on those ballots.)

Instead we get the following report from The UpTake:

| % DONE FRANKEN CHALLENGES 93.3% |
| COLEMAN 238 |
| FRANKEN 63 |
| OTHER 114 |

See that Franken line? That's a +63 that Franken had not figured into their calculations. Sooo...nothing solid yet, but a slowly growing reason for hope.

[And remember (unless even the Colemaniks have sense enough to withdraw them and just put them on the Franken pile) the Board might be looking at some of those idiotic challenged ballots that were challenged because they listed McCain for President and Franken for Senate.]

Rejected Absentee Ballots

All on hold pending the outcome of the Supreme Court hearing, recounted below in Legal Moves (today with CLEATS!)

NEW! Duplicate Ballots!

On the surface it's not that big a deal and perfectly legitimate: An overseas voter fulfills all righteousness with an absentee ballot form and e-mails it to their home county election board. The county prints out the e-mail on 8 1/2 by 11 paper just like you would. But you can't run that through the optical scanner: no ovals and the paper is too lightweight and would likely jam the machine. So in the presence of witnesses the county election judges create a "duplicate ballot" using a blank "in-person" ballot of heavier (almost card stock) paper and carefully fill in the ovals. Keep the original and run the "duplicate" through the reader on election day.

The Colemaniks are asking loudly if some of these duplicate ballots a) still have their originals around (they are supposed to be kept but apparently there is some slop in the system) for comparison and b) were any of these duplicates run through the scanners more than once (producing duplicate votes, which would be a serious matter)?

This is once again feeding the Reichwing frenzy about "Franken people making up new votes/new ballots, i.e. stealing the election." The Frankenites are answering this was all agreed to before the election (like under the law) and that this is a hell of time to be bringing it up.

The Canvassing Board has said they will **discuss and rule on** this matter TODAY as the challenge session gets started in the morning.

I can see the issue in theory but it does seem like trying to throw more dust in the air and working the refs. And I agree with the Franken side the timing really seems forced...and maybe a bit desperate? This seems like a reach for Team Norm, and does seem to play for more "delay, delay".

The risk to the Colemaniks is: a) they lose the ruling by the CB. b) Then they appeal to a court–dragging out the thing even longer and appearing more and more obstructionist than they already are.

The risk to the Canvassing Board is that they get so hacked off at all this they react emotionally and let Norm have it...and give him grounds to appeal to a federal court on grounds of bias and prejudice. I don't think that's all that likely: 4 of the 5 on the Board are judges after all and they know how to express displeasure ("This Court finds it unlikely/ no basis/ considers without merit..." and other fine legal ways of saying, "That is such a crock...get outta here!") and I think they'll do something like this here.

Both sides put their lightsabers and lightsaber Quarterstaffs (LSQs) in the shop for tune-ups and repairs, forcing them to play a different game today:

Legal Moves and Lawyers in Shoulder Pads

Some new names at the Supreme Court hearing this afternoon: Roger Magnuson for Coleman (NOT Chief Justice *Eric* Magnuson, Canvassing Board member who has recused himself from this matter). William Pentelovitch (sounds like an Intel processor from Eastern Europe) for Franken.

At issue:

> Coleman's campaign does not want the Canvassing Board to count any improperly rejected absentee ballots, saying it is not the proper body to settle that issue. Instead, it wants those ballots set aside and preserved in the event either campaign goes to court after the recount to try to get a judge to include them in the tally. The Franken campaign wants the recount before the Canvassing Board to include the ballots. *(Star Tribune)*

(Crowd noises from 75,000 spiked up political nerds fill the stadium. Brooding, thumping background music. The baritone, graveled voice of NFL films, John Facenda):

"Teams Coleman and Franken want to make it to the Senate Bowl but their road runs through the frozen tundra of Justice Alan Page and teammates, whose home field is the legendary 'Court Room.' Many an opponent has swallowed hard as they look up over the main entrance; there in the marble are carved words of immortal fame that are defended here: 'Where law ends, tyranny begins.'

"In a great display of focus Justice Page's Team insisted both visiting Teams focus on *Rolvaag vs. Anderson*, the 1962 governor's race that ended with less than a 100 vote difference and led directly to the creation of the current recount machinery. But one Team kept trying to bring in a more recent thriller from out of town, *Bush v. Gore*, which did not sit well with the Page-ers.

"The Colemaniks bring in a fresh-faced starter with Florida Recount experience, Roger Magnuson, acquired from *the Bush v. Gore legal team* of the year 2000. Magnuson wasted no time in opening with his Sunshine State experience from the year when he was part of Legal Team Bush in the Supreme Bowl epic 5-4 thriller.

> Magnuson argued that the state canvassing board's actions of December 12, when it recommended that all 87 counties count wrongly rejected absentee ballots, were an "an invitation to go to Florida." *(MN Independent)*

"All eyes turned to All-American, All-Pro Alan Page, the heart of the Minnesota team so respected in the state they are simply called, "Supremes." But while the wily veteran drew the attention, it let Paul Anderson from little Macalester College spring a blitz and he clotheslined Magnuson for a back field loss in the opening moments:

> But before Magnuson could begin to back up this assertion, he was interrupted by a clearly irritated Justice Paul Anderson. "This is not Florida," he stated. "I'm just not terribly receptive to you telling us this is Florida." *(MN Independent)*

(Crowd shots of waving purple pennants, icy breath rising from thousands, a married couple holding up the letter D and a picket fence, and seven bare-chested, goose-bumped college guys with N-O C-H-A-D-S in body paint above the waist.)

(Facenda continues in his deliberate style :) "Anderson was a surprise star in the Supremes' lineup. Magnuson was left reeling later on when Anderson continued his relentless play in a move called, 'Election Integrity.'"

> Justice Paul Anderson, who appeared to reserve his most pointed questions for the Coleman campaign, said he worried about the rights of an absentee voter who cast a ballot that was improperly rejected. "Why should a voter who does cast a ballot that's valid have to bring a [legal] contest [to get it counted]?" he asked. "That just doesn't seem right." *(MN Independent)*

"Magnuson was also hemmed in by local University of Minnesota star Helen Meyer. The former Gopher evoked the glory of mid-century, powerhouse Minnesota teams:

> "What did the canvassing board do that's objectionable?" she asked, noting that they merely recommended that local election officials sort rejected absentee ballots into five piles. "As I understand that's the complete sum of what they've asked them to do." *(MN Independent)*

"As they say in France, 'evidement!'"

(Fans howling as teams change line-ups on the field. Shot of skin-head fan holding sign, "Norm's normal and so am I." His friend holds a purple and white one: "Morans for Norm." On the other side of the field some pretty girls wave to the cameras and point to their sign: HI ABC spelled vertically with ABC the first letters each of "All Ballots Count!")

"Pentelovitch for Team Franken faced his own trial by fire. Justice Page came straight at him by asking:

> Why the disputed absentee ballots could not be counted afterward should a court challenge be mounted. "What's the difference?" he asked.
>
> Pentelovitch replied that once the Canvassing Board finishes the recount and issues a certificate of election to the winner in the race, "the presumption [is] the person who has the certificate is the winner." *(MN Independent)*

(Crowd shot, fans standing & cheering. Facenda: "Even these fans respected Pentelovitch fending off Page to a draw on this play.")

"But this was Paul Anderson's day as even Pentelovitch felt his force:

> Justice Paul Anderson wondered if they were facing a deadline for adjudicating the matter. "Is there a date beyond which this court cannot act?" he asked. Pentelovitch's response: "I don't think so." *(MN Independent)*

"After 70 minutes Justice Page signaled halftime and all teams left the field. On the way to the locker room (known locally as "Judges' Chambers") Justice Page was both gracious and typically determined with reporters. 'Thank you all. A decision will be forthcoming.'

"Fairness, justice and the opportunity of the Senate Bowl all now rest in the hands of Justices Page, Meyer, & Anderson, and also in the hands of unsung and unquoted Dietzen and Gildea. Millions await their return to the field..." *(fade to crowd noise.)*

> Attorney Magnuson for Coleman reverted to type and continued to display his obsession. He expressed optimism that the Coleman campaign will prevail. "I think they're very concerned about the issues we raised," he said of the Supreme Court justices, "and we're very hopeful that they'll come up with a solution that doesn't walk us into the slew of Florida. *(MN Independent)*

In the Thursday morning media, Doyle, Duchschere & von Sterberg *(Attorneys at writing? Why is it always "attorneys at law?" Can't you be an "attorney at–something else"?)* get the recount write up on the Star Tribune's page B1. The Board is going to rule on the "duplicate ballots" issue. Colemaniks are "concerned" this *may have* happened in 137 precincts. Frankenites say its "yust a theory" and also a sign of panic or desperation on the Coleman side....I have to say the Frankenites sound kinda calm about this and there is a whiff of Aqua Velva...err, nervousness from Norm's team.

Ditto yesterday's Supreme Court hearing. Could be getting close.

DK
> Yesterday, I declared my life officially over. I sat and watched the Canvassing Board live, on TheUptake, for several hours. I dare anyone to have the self-esteem to be willing to declare that their life is more boring than mine. *(dfb1968)*

DK | Lizard people ballot up right now! *(buddingactivist)*

DK | Damn...i missed it. I sooooo love that ballot. what did they say? *(Cedwyn)*

DK | It took them awhile, but they counted it as an overvote. However there was a write in for Flying Spaghetti Monster that they counted for Franken. *(buddingactivist)*

Hunker down folks; it could be the last 48 hours except for the court cases. (And we might expect a ruling from the MN Supremes at ANY time...between now and Christmas...of 2010! "We will NOT be rushed!")

So for the moment that's the latest from yust southeast of Lake Wobegon.

Shalom.

FRANKEN LEADS
December 19, 2008

Comments: 352   Recs: 420   Tips: 363

As you go to (recount) infinity and beyond, savor this: probably about 20 minutes into this morning's recount you will see, with a fair level of security (not a done deal, but there aren't many cards left in the deck), the phrase I've been wanting to post in a title for weeks (wait 'til tomorrow :-D):

FRANKEN LEADS!

Recounted Ballots

One more day with no change on the Sec. of State's website for the recount (same since 12/12). Initially I was disappointed these numbers stopped changing when the hand recount ended. But since then we've had the challenged ballots, the absentee ballots in piles and just the other day, duplicate ballots. Then there are withdrawn challenged ballots and growls about re-instated challenged ballots. And that would be a nightmare of footnotes, italics, asterisks, # signs *(and maybe even umlauts, Greek "rough breathing" marks and those Scandinavian "O"s with the slash through them that must have a multi-syllabic name in Sanskrit.)*

INSTEAD, Secretary of State Mark Ritchie has opted to leave the numbers ALONE until he has something settled to add or subtract. And I've come around to see the wisdom of that, so I've curbed my frustrations (tied them up to the "Snowplow Parking Only" sign post) and am waiting with the rest of us all. ("Maybe tonight" they yap.)

Challenged Ballots

The Canvassing Board got down to it Thursday morning, going at Coleman's 1,016 challenged ballots *(16 more than 1,000; must be the Republican definition of "South of 1,000" that Knaak offered over the weekend.)*

BUT then just to make sure everyone was awake, the Colemaniks *withdrew* 400 challenges...and then *added* 204 more (which they obviously think might have a better chance of being upheld). This means the Board is now facing about 800 (truly south of 1,000).

At the 8:47 am mark The UpTake links to a spreadsheet of ALL the Coleman challenges if you want to follow along.

NOW, watch carefully...those 204 Coleman threw in include "incident reports" about what happened to a given ballot sometime during election day that may bear on it being challenged. The Franken camp said, "OK, 2 can play that game" and are ready to drop 200 or so *(I kinda like...205)* of their own (currently withdrawn) challenged ballots with similar "incident reports".

Ritchie speaks for the Board and says those 204 from each side may well be set aside (the NEW "BLUE FOLDER" and dealt with at a separate **Board meeting on December 30**– a new date for your calendars.

At the end of the day (Thursday), 642 challenges disposed of, it's Norm leading: (not the 188 he had last Friday and still up on the SoS website) but now taking into account the challenged ballots that have been decided by the Board since Tuesday. Norm: +5…or +2 by some news accounts.

And for Friday? About 380 challenges left to go.

Absentee Ballots & Legal Moves

Thursday's Legal Moves were not BY the Lawyers, they were aimed AT the lawyers. The **Minnesota Supreme Court** came back with an answer to the Coleman suit that was heard yesterday.

Commendable speed? Check. Decisive? Rather. Lopsided? Are you kidding?? This is the MN Recount! EVERYTHING is close!

Decision: 3-2! Meyer, Dietzen & Gildea// Page & Anderson.

Coleman Request, Temporary Restraining Order ("Stop the Count, I'm a Republican who's leading"): DENIED. (1-0 for the good guys)

Stop sorting Rejected Absentee Ballots into 5 piles: **DENIED** (2-0, good gals)

Let County Election Boards decide "5th pile" ballots, open & count them (so Page & Anderson; Page called anything less than following the LAW–since counties have done this before– Stalinist! He used the "whoever counts the ballots" line in his dissent.) YES, BUT (2-0-1):

County election officials and both campaigns to create a process for accepting "5th pile ballots" that *both sides agree on.* Obstreperous lawyers from either side who come up with crap reasons subject to State Rule 11 sanctions (apparently a list of increasing penalties against lawyers who act like the south end of a north bound horse. 1st take by some lawyers on some of the blogging boards seems to be, "Gulp!", so Rule 11 sounds like a fairly serious piece of artillery.)

Sounds like the drama is going to be played out at about 120 locations across the state (*ruling favors anti-Twin Cities activists!*) and fairly quickly–decision calls on local boards and candidates to report agreed upon RAB's that are re-instated by Dec. 31 (*Oh no! 2 weeks more of these diaries: "Fist fight in Yellow Medicine County election Board; 6 krumkaake reported broken but repaired with extra frosting."*)

My take is 3 fold: the ruling is cumbersome but moves things forward; it favors whoever is leading (pay attention Norm, this will NOT be you on Friday); and it favors whichever side wants to stand for counting every vote on principle, win or lose. So that's a 2 out of 3 for Franken.

Both sides' lawyers claimed to be pleased. "We are very happy with the decision," said Knaak.

"We're happy that the Supreme Court rejected the Coleman campaign effort to stop the count," said Elias.

Funny Pages – Minnesota Nice

A ballot from Mankato (south central MN) was challenged by Coleman because the voter had filled in the oval correctly but had added to Al's name: "Franken*stin*" (Gene Wilder: "Its Frahnken-steen." Eye-gor: "They told me it was Franken-stine!") Coleman's Trimble argued voter had NOT voted for Franken but for somebody else. Franken's Elias countered the vote was still for the DFL (Minnesotan for "Democratic") candidate. Board agreed with Elias…3-2 (!).

One of the ballots Coleman had challenged (stray/identifying mark I suppose) was a Franken vote where the voter had written in the margin, "Thank you for counting my vote." The whole Canvassing Board cracked up and one of them said, "Well I guess we're going to *have* to count this one." After they voted (challenged denied, +1 Al) someone else looked at the ballot once more and said, "You're welcome."

OK, MUST have a 2nd cup of coffee, so that's a fair bit of the mostly latest (*subject to revision, updates, terms and conditions of use; performed by a professional driver on a closed course, do not attempt at home*) from yust southeast of Lake Wobegon.

Shalom.

Milestone
December 20, 2008

Comments: 94 *Recs:* 168 *Tips:* 153

OOOOhhh Momma what a day Friday! Got the tree up, the last of the cards mailed off, and almost all the presents...oh, and something happened with some ballots somewhere.

The Colemaniks have had from Nov. 5 to Dec. 18 (43 days) to get comfortable on their 215/192/188 lead. All of you have had about 22 hours...but I get the feeling progressives enjoy life a little more! (And a glass of wine helps more than a glass of whine!)

This is a milestone alright, as important as the end of the hand count across the state on the 5th. Now there are certain numbers yet to come, but one BIG number will come on **Monday, Dec. 22.** *(ONE guess who will have a live feed!)* The Canvassing Board will meet 9:00-11:00am and Sec. of State Ritchie will deliver a set of numbers of the count so far, and this should give us a first, semi-official "Frankenlead." He said at a presser Friday his office will spend the weekend checking their math.

The challenged ballots are basically done, so only 4 groups of ballots are still hanging fire:

Challenged Ballots: WITHDRAWN (Number: about 5300)

Final Numbers on the Canvassing Board's Challenged Ballots (thanks to Jennifer Wingham at *The UpTake*):

748	Franken
319	Coleman
233	Other

If we add the numbers up, the Canvassing Board dealt with 1,300 challenged ballots. (A few more may come in.)

Remember the total count of challenged ballots got up to 6,655. Then both camps started WITH-DRAWING challenges until Franken had about 415 actually undergo Board rulings. Coleman WITH-DREW a bunch as well and had about 1,016/no, 616/no, 885 up for review when the Board started (and which so many have been enjoying on the Paint Drying Channel; ;-)–actually an amazing number of people, even skinny kids in Orange from the West Coast, found democracy in action strangely riveting viewing).

NOW the 5,300+ or so WITHDRAWN Challenged ballots (6,655 - 415 -885 - 5,355) have to be re-stored to their UNchallenged piles (like the other 2.8 million), C,F, Barkley or other (as in spoiled/ no vote/ Libertarian/ FSM, etc).

THE most succinct summary of all this came yesterday in the comments. As far as I can make out, subject to analysis and correction from the many wise heads that stalk these boards, so a great tip of the hat to chuco35 and his insight here:

> **Also the mix of the challenges is important.** A withdrawn challenge returning a ballot to a 3d party candidate or the spoilt ballot pile is of no harm. However, a withdrawn challenge that returns an opponent's vote to his tally is a withdrawn challenge that allows the opponent to gain ground.
>
> So it's not as easy as looking at how many challenges each side withdrew. The mix of those challenges is still an unknown factor to us.
>
> I might add - Nate's *(Holy Odin of Numbers, Silver–WR)* calculations are based on the Franken team's math. If anyone knows the mix of these withdrawn challenges, it is the campaigns. Presumably the Franken camp took this into consideration, allo-cating all the challenged ballots to the appropriate pile, since the Franken math is based on the local election judges's original determinations. So I feel most comfort-able with Nate's plus 40 votes for Al in the end, than I do anything else. *(chuco35)*

Soooo: 2.8 million ballots voted and recounted: Coleman leads by +188.

1,500 challenged ballots decided by law –voter intent– and by a duly convened, in this case tri-partisan, State Canvassing Board. Coleman gains +319. Franken gains 748. SO Franken leads by (188+319-748) = +241

5,000 withdrawn challenged ballots left to be "re-piled"; Timeline: sometime next week. *Franken lead to fall?*...Interesting speculation: Star Tribune is calculating that after ALL these 5,300+ withdrawn challenges are put back into their respective piles, Franken will still lead...by +78. (Only 38 away from the Nate Silver latest estimate at the end of ALL ballots...or 51 away from his original +27.)

The "Blue Folder" (Number: 200-400)

As the Canvassing Board ruled on challenges both camps raised the issue of certain challenged ballots that had "incidents" attached to their being challenged. The Canvassing Board put these into the famous "blue folder". I'm sorry I'm a bit fuzzy on this set of ballots. I think it's about 200 from each camp and I think the Board put them aside to either a) look at and rule on on Monday OR b) these might end up at the Supreme Court and then get sent back to the Canvassing Board.

But I wasn't able to follow this part very closely and there's very little up on the media so this entire section is subject to much addition, correction and greater wisdom. Nate Silver seems to think these ballots will be re-instated and with an advantage to Franken in the end.

So: 200-400 "Blue Folder" Ballots. Timeline: Sounds like the next 2 weeks or less.

Soooo...Franken lead from 1): +241 to +78. If the "blue folder ballots" break Franken 55-45% that would mean Franken +20 to +40. Sooooo...running total: Franken +281 (max.) to +98 (min.)

The Duplicate/Double Count Ballots (Number: 100-150)

Wednesday the Colemaniks brought these up, that overseas and other ballots that had been duplicated to run through the scanners need to match up with their originals, or some (100-150) could be double-counted, artificially inflating the count. The Canvassing Board declined to rule, saying they did not have jurisdiction.

Fair enough. Friday the Coleman team filed suit over it in the MN Supreme Court. Canvassing Board and Franken campaign have until Monday to respond and Court will hear oral arguments **Tuesday, Dec. 23 at 2:00pm.** Justice Page will preside again as CB members Magnuson and G. Berry Anderson (NOT Paul, who will hear the case) have both recused themselves. Coleman's team filed for all the ground they could, leading off with asking the election results NOT be certified until this issue is settled. This is aggressive but fair in my book; otherwise if this goes Coleman's way but Franken is already certified the winner the task is very hard (and dammit, unfair to Coleman.)

Once again, it is THIS community that has generated the best summary of this, again from yesterday's diary comments. BIG hat tip to FischFry:

> **That's not in dispute. The issue is the recount.** The Coleman legal team is arguing the recount generated more votes because there were unmarked "duplicated" ballots counted, along with originals that the election boards could not match up to any duplicated ballots – as required by law.
>
> The duplicated ballots are supposed to be observed by judges from each party. And they're supposed to be marked "duplicate", along with the serial # from the original, so they can be matched up later to prove the duplicate is a correctly duplicated ballot.
>
> What happened in the recount, is a whole bunch of originals got pulled out of envelopes and got thrown into the pile, even though the locals hadn't been able to find duplicates with matching serial #s.
>
> Consequently, they argue that it's no coincidence that some precinct total increased during the recount, by the exact number of unmatched originals that were counted. In other words, the #s went up because the recount counted those originals and the corresponding, unmarked "duplicated" ballots.
>
> I hate to have to agree with them, but this is a pretty compelling argument, if the factual predicate is how they represent it. *(FischFry)*

The down side of being fair-minded: sometimes you have to go against your rooting interest. Coleman may have something here, subject to analysis and deeper thoughts from wiser heads. It is unclear if the 100-150 are all "pro-Coleman" votes or they just have reports from several sites that add up to this, so that these may break in something less than a shutout.

Soooo, if you're not wrapping presents or rinsing the lye off your codfish, **Tuesday afternoon at 2:00pm CT** the stadium fills again for the Minnesota Dream Team, the "Supremes." Will the voice of NFL Films make a return appearance?

So 100-150 "Double Count?/ Duplicate" ballots. Timeline: Maybe even this coming week; more likely by 12/31.

Soooo if we have Franken after part 2) at +281 to +98, and let's say these duplicates are 125 and Coleman gets the bulk of them (say 90-35), then we have Franken at +226(max.) to +43(min.)

Rejected Absentee Ballots (Number: 500-2000)

About 290,000 absentee ballots across the state. About 278,000 properly filled out and counted along with Election Day ballots. About 12,000 absentee ballots rejected for counting. Approximately 10,000 to 11,500 of these rejected for 4 legal reasons. The remaining 500-2,000 were the target of Coleman's suit on Monday ("Stop the Count"), heard Wednesday by the MN Supreme Ct., and ruled on in Thursday's decision. (Count goes on, Norm).

County election Boards and BOTH CAMPS to work out a mutually agreed process for accepting/rejecting these 500-2,000. Those accepted *(and NEITHER camp gets to "peek first"; ie, "This is a vote for Barkley that doesn't have a zip code on the outer envelope–accepted by F & C"; Both sides have to do them blind)* will then be opened and counted. Both sides have opportunity to challenge like other ballots up to now *("Stray mark!/ Lizard scale!/ Identifying mark: Voter wrote, "Election judge #4, Lyon County, U R SOOO hot! Call me")* and the State Canvassing Board will convene and RULE on them.

Then adjusted totals are due in to Sec. of State's office on or before DEC. 31.

So then 1,000-1,600 Rejected Absentee Ballots. Timeline: By 12/31–fairly hard date.

The absentees by general consensus have been Franken-friendly. While Ritchie initially thought there might be 500 ballots in this part the conventional wisdom seems to be settling in at the bottom around 1,000 and the top about 1,600.

If we take a midpoint of 1,300 and say these ballots break 55-45% for Franken then he should net about 130. (715-585). So starting with the numbers from part 3 and adding these, we get Franken +356 (max.) to +173 (min.).

AND THEN: Words I want to hear/type and/or say: *(let the Canvassing Board join in! Let the election judges say, 'Amen!')* "We have NO MORE Ballots left to recount. And the winner is..."

Legal Moves

Sure sign a latter-day Republican is losing an election?

His legal team is in court. Friday the Canvassing Board recount on challenged ballots moved Franken into the lead...and Coleman's team back to the Supreme Court for a rematch with Team Franken and the Justice Page-led "Supremes."

DK Took me awhile to read through it all. It does seem odd that the more time the Coleman camp spends in court the better Mr. Franken does. *(RustyBrown)*

Republicans Behaving Badly

David Brauer over at the *MinnPost* writes an important story on John Lott, a Reichwing tool of number cooking. As Brauer explains, by manipulating the recount numbers (and frankly this HAS been complicated) and just ignoring certain others Lott tries to provide a numerical basis for Reich-wing screaming "Franken is stealing the election." Brauer slams him, but with Lott online, he doesn't have to work alone.

You too can bring Light Epees and Light Foils to strike these Lotts, O'Reillys, et. al. (And for all you fencers who wield l'arme blanche *(like WineRev's daughter, Winerev-ette, and son, Winrev-er)* these Reich-wingers do NOT deserve "The Salute."; that is only for opponents of honor.)

Minnesota Deserves a Round of Applause

OK so WCCO IS the largest TV/Radio complex in the state, so this IS sort of patting ourselves on the back. *(Scandinavians are genetically averse to praise and often emotionally ... hmmm...limited; Know how you can spot a Norwegian extrovert? It is someone who, when you meet them for the first time, looks at YOUR shoes.)* But it's nicely said, by Esme Murphy,

> The recount process has been, as Secretary of State Mark Ritchie promised, transparent. Every single challenged ballot has been available for public viewing on numerous websites. It will be a bitter loss for whoever finishes with fewer votes. But so far the process with all its blemishes has been fair and impressive to watch as it plays out in public view. *(WCCO)*

Early shift again on the last weekend before Christmas in retail. Think we'll be busy? (It would be nice...as they said in the Old Westerns, 'Things have been quiet...too quiet.') So here's the latest from yust southeast of Lake Wobegon.

Shalom.

Eine Paus-eh
December 21, 2008

Comments: 26   *Recs:* 30   *Tips:* 40

Yes, eine pause, a breather before the run down to the 31st.

Recounted Ballots: Toward a Final Number

In yesterday's diary your WineRev did a bit of adding and subtracting with the 4 pools of votes left to go in the recount. By far the largest are the 5,300+ **challenged** ballots that both camps have **withdrawn**. And now, even as we blog, (for the Sec. of State's office is working this weekend, bless them) those withdrawn, challenged ballots are being UNchallenged and put back into their originally designated piles (F, C or Barkley/FSM/Lizard or 'no vote'-spoiled ballot).

Franken started this "re-compiling" phase leading +241. *[I've always wanted to be a computer programmer who recompiles...or is that nurse-related lingo for a patient who is re-admitted with the same hemorrhoid condition? :-)]* The *Star Tribune* made a guess-timate that recompiling the Withdrawn challenges would give him a lead of +78.

NOW, in an unusual Saturday presser, Marc Elias for Team Franken has said their internal numbers show they believe after the recompiling by this Tuesday they will still lead by +35 to +50.

> Franken's figures always "assumed those [challenged] ballots would end up in the tally of the candidate for whom each one was originally called," as a campaign statement put it. "[T]he internal count can predict the result of that work *with certainty:* a 35-50 vote lead for Franken." *(MN Independent; emphasis added)*

Remember Franken's number crunchers were saying for a couple of weeks that they believed they would lead +4 at this stage? Many of us held our breath (while staring at the Sec. of State's "forever number" of Coleman +215/192/188) and hoping they were right. I think there's a new note of confidence replacing the doggedness in the way Elias said it. And as interesting as Sherlock Holmes' "dog that did NOT bark" has been the Coleman Team's complete silence about any of their own internal numbers. They have either pointed to the SoS numbers, or have said nothing.

...Methinks the Norm-ans are worried [*as the Saxons & Celts regain their strength and move toward the field of Hastings for a rematch, perhaps leading to a reversal of the Norman influence on English! (Evictus, evictus, damnibus spottus!...Raus! Raus! Ge-damn-ische schpotten!...Ah/Ach Shakespeare done right/richtig at last!) ...or whatever ...what was I saying?...*]

Soooo......so far, so good. From the Frankenmath +4 to a range of +35 to +50.

"Blue Folder Ballots" (200-400)

No direct news, but some Excellent Kossack analysis in yesterday's comments that these ballots may include the Duplicate ballots below and Coleman's chances on both sets of these are maybe crummy:

> One point: I don't have hard evidence to back this up, but my impression is that the blue (green/yellow) folder contents are mostly original/duplicate problem ballots, with a small number of "other incidents" mixed in. So the "100-150" dupe ballots are a subset of the "200-400" blue-folder ballots, not an addition. I think it's likely that there were some instances of dupes being made but not stamped properly, and it appears that some originals have "gone missing" too; BUT the way I read that filing, the Coleman camp is basing their "proof" of double-counting on a mistaken assumption (or intentional misstatement) of what actually constitutes the official (state) calculation of "Total Voters".
>
> Coleman's filing repeatedly refers to the number produced by the machine tapes on election night as THE number used to determine "Total Voters". They claim this as a statement of fact, and it's flat wrong. The state determines the number of "Total Voters" by counting every signature in the registration books (which includes new election-day registrations) and adding the number of accepted absentee ballots. The state doesn't go by the machine counters (except as a check on the calculations – if the two tallies are different, the reg books are the official tally).
>
> To the extent that the Coleman suit relies on this false premise to PROVE that double-counting has occurred, their 'theory' fails. The ONLY way to prove that double-counting happened is to use the reg books number. If FischFry is correct that the Coleman suit does actually have evidence that more ballots were recounted than the reg-books number, then Coleman's got a valid case.
>
> Like I said, I wouldn't be at all surprised to learn that some dupes weren't properly marked and got into the main ballot 'stream' (although I think this is a pretty small number). My sole point is that what Coleman claims as his PROOF, isn't. (That's why everybody should read the PDF for yourselves and see what you think)...
> *(rincewind)*

Duplicate/Double Count Ballots (about 100-150)

These are the ones at the center of the Supreme CT hearing on Tuesday (2:00pmCT, live stream by The UpTake and other outlets). And since a court involves lawyers Saturday we had...yes!

Lawyers Swinging Lightsabers VII

(Elias' blue Lightsaber swings with a quick left-right-left, going low to cut the legs out)

As for the Coleman campaign's lawsuit about duplicate ballots... Elias called it "speculative *(huuM-Mmm!)* and hypothetical *(kissshhhh!)*"..."They simply want to create an issue *(zzzziimmm!)*."

Team Coleman disdainfully refused to send out a lawyer, just Matt Drake hacking with the red Lightsaber: *(Whack! Backward somersault roll...dodge to right, jump across hot air vent...)*

> Coleman campaign spokesman Mark Drake told *MinnPost* in an email: "This is just more bluster and hot air from a campaign that has been trailing for two years. While we can understand their need to latch onto their temporary lead, the reality is there's a long way to go in this process. We have no doubt that once this recount is fully completed, Senator Coleman will be in the lead and will be re-elected to the Senate." *(MinnPost)*

Rejected Absentee Ballots

A lot of hue and cry has been raised over the "both sides need to agree" provision. It may be fair (afterwards it's REALLY hard to argue, "they stole it" because the comeback of "then why did you agree to them stealing it?" drops the lid on the sewer.) But it also seems impractical and unworkable, even allowing for the RULE 11 sanctions the Court mentioned (apparently a nasty list of what can happen to a lawyer who gets in the way of things frivolously).

Now, once again, it is the blogging community that provides best analysis. Over at MN Progressive Project *(hat tip!)*, the delightfully named diarist Grace Kelly dances in with a story on what the Coleman Camp is facing now. In the comments, blogger "Sara" has a few razor sharp thoughts:

> After *(Dec. 31st deadline—WR)*, the SOS (who was a party to the case before the Supreme Court) can report back on failure to cooperate if necessary.
>
> If Coleman does not make a good faith effort to cooperate with Franken, the SOS, the Canvass Board, and the County Election Administrators – and do it clearly within the intent and letter of Minnesota Law and the Court Orders, you will see sanctions flying, and a new Court Order. What could the sanctions be – well big fines, loss of law license, things like that, and the vast majority of lawyers of all stripes will not jump into that thicket. *(Sara at The Uptake)*

Whew! And just to be clear, Elias/ Lillehaug/ Pentelovitch et.al. of the Franken Briefcase Set are also in the cross-hairs on this one:

> "...what we have on the table is a court order that pretty much forces the Franken and Coleman lawyers to agree to procedures that strictly follow Minnesota Law as to what criteria disqualifies or excludes an absentee ballot –and agree to count all the remaining ballots." *(quoted in Star Tribune)*

Legal Moves

We'll see how Norm does in Court on Tuesday but so far his motions and filings have produced some odd results for his side, summarized in one nugget yesterday by this Kossack:

> **DK** I've been watching for awhile now, and I can't get over how insane Coleman's challenges are. I haven't seen even one challenge go his way. What on earth was he thinking? *(Shuruq)*

I like this! So Norm, keep it up man, and keep paying Knaak, Magnuson, Trimble and the rest their daily retainers. After all Norm, you've got plenty of money. In fact, unlike Sarah Palin you OWN those suits Nasser bought you, so instead of giving them away to charity *(and have those "Sarah Suits" turned up down at the White Bear Lake, MN Goodwill store yet? Could someone check?)* you can use them as collateral for a secured loan! (Not like some auto executive come begging for a bridge loan to save 8% of the American economy... they didn't have any collateral did they?)

OK hope that will hold you till Monday. I have to go out into the minus 20 windchill after a bit this morning and sing with the choir (the WineRev has 2 solos today, the planned ones) and will be lunching with WineRev-ette and WineRev-er, but I'll check back in during The Game.

That's the latest from yust southeast of Lake Wobegon.

Shalom.

Winding Down
December 22, 2008

Comments: 109   Recs: 168   Tips: 194

Canvassing Board meeting has been moved to **TUESDAY MORNING, 9:00AM.**

(Great little vignette: at Friday evening's presser, Ritchie mentioned this meeting would not be live-streamed on the MN legislative channel and didn't know if any media would be carrying it. Either McIntee or Kunin (Lithuanian power!) was there and said, "The UpTake will have it."

Ritchie said something like, "Great. I guess that makes you our official source on Monday." NOT BAD for 6 people, a couple video cameras, cell phone audio streams, a van and some *Apple II computers* donated to THEM from a public school! ;-)) One blogger congratulated them by noting that now the Coleman campaign – different from his Senate office, who has been quite open – will have to take questions from The UpTake since they have more clout! YAY UpTake!)

Secretary of State Mark Ritchie *may* report **updated figures** for the recount (and perhaps change the website numbers too) having given each candidate their share of the withdrawn challenges. If not today, then by tomorrow.

The Board MAY also deal with the **"Blue Folder" ballots**, ballots which were challenged by one or other camp that (according to Kossack rincewind) *may* include the duplicate/ double count ballots (see yesterday's diary). The Board set these aside last week since at least some of them have "incidents" attached to them. The Board sounds like they are inclined to make a determination of "voter intent" (which is their function after all) but leave any other questions to a court.

Tomorrow, Tuesday, 12/23 at 2:00pm the Supreme Court hears arguments from Coleman re: their suit about the duplicate ballots. (This will be LIVE STREAMED by the "Official Media Source for Proceedings of the State of Minnesota" :-))

And somewhere behind the scenes some SERIOUS negotiating is going on regarding the "**rejected absentee** ballots." The Supreme Court ordered as many of these improperly rejected ones ("5th pile") counted as soon as the SoS office, county election boards and BOTH campaigns could agree on terms. This might be along 3 lines:

1. The campaigns are hammering out a process for determining which ballots should be included and (subject to input from Ritchie) this set of standards/ process communicated to the 87 county boards. Then across the state these boards in the presence of Coleman & Franken attys. will have an opening & counting party (and each side gets to challenge ballots like any other of they want to). This line addresses the "uniform standard" issue but is hard to pull off up front. It IS something of a minority opinion here at Daily Kos as to what the Supreme Court ordered.

2. The majority of comments around here has been that the Court ordered this process to be worked out *at the county level* in 87+ negotiations. This line addresses the "legal authority" issue of the local election officials to make determinations of which absentee ballots are valid. I'm not sure this is what's going on. There is also the nightmare thought of:

3. This negotiation is going to happen across the state alright, but over EACH ballot in question. ("This should be rejected since there's no zip code on the return address…But it was delivered by US mail so the Post Office affirms this is a valid address"). I don't think they are going here but I list it as seen on occasion around here.

Since after the withdrawn challenges are recompiled this is the largest remaining pool of ballots we'll watch for developments. Fortunately by all accounts the absentees seem to have favored Franken so the more of these ballots that get counted the firmer his lead. (Oh and to be clear: whatever process is designed and agreed upon NO ONE gets to look inside a ballot first and then say, "This Franken ballot should be rejected because…" They have to do them unopened just like any other absentee ballot.)

> Coleman camp says the Franken claim of a 35-50 vote lead after the allocation of withdrawn ballots is "hot air." This may be disturbing because one thing the Coleman camp knows a lot about is hot air. *(pollbuster)*

That's the latest from yust southeast of Lake Wobegon.
Shalom.

"New Numbers"?
December 23, 2008

Comments: 95   Recs: 191   Tips: 169

New Numbers.

No change at the Sec. of State's website as of 10:00pm Mon. night BUT The UpTake is reporting the Sec. of State's office has released a *preliminary* spreadsheet after adding back the UN-challenged/withdrawn challenged ballots. On Saturday the Franken camp said they would be at +35 to +50 at this point.

The report from the spreadsheet is **Franken +48.** *(Nice shootin' Tex!)*

OK it's a cliché but...this is GOOD NEWS for Franken.

1. It shows his number crunching team knows their chops...which bodes well for further guesstimates on their side. The continuing silence from the Coleman side picks up some ominous overtones *(Beethoven's 5th, 1st movement maybe? "Fate knocking on the door"?)*

2. Yes, it's down from the +241 figure from Saturday BUT the Frankenites initially expected to be at +4 at this point. More important– This was the largest remaining batch of ballots left to go. It may be +48, but it's a +48 a long step closer to the finish line, so this +48 is actually firmer than +241 before these 5,300+ ballots were recompiled to their original candidates.

3. Soooo...2 batches of ballots left: the 200-400 "blue folder" ballots that the Canvassing Board MAY rule on today and MAY include about 125 or so "duplicate/double-counted" ballots (which are at the bar in front of the Supreme Court this afternoon); AND the 1,000-1,600 rejected absentee ballots that are in "5th piles" in at least 87 locations in Minnesota (each county, + multiple sites in the larger cities).

Canvassing Board

The Board postponed its meeting to today at 9:00am. They will hear from Ritchie and get an update on where the recount stands. **Franken's number/lead MAY move around a bit; yesterday's spreadsheet was** *preliminary*. The Board MAY deal with the "Blue Folder" challenged ballots. (The Blue Folder ballots are challenged ballots from both sides, numbering about 200-400) that each camp claimed some incident or irregularity about. The Board has made some noises about ruling on the challenges on the basis of voter intent and punting the "incident/irregularity" issues *(sounds like a job for ex-lax!)* to a court. If they are going to rule we all may be treated to a follow up show of "Judge this Ballot" which was a surprise hit across the internet last week. (The UpTake thinks there will definitely be a ballot show.)

Supreme Court

A new player came in off the bench Monday: The Hennepin County Canvassing Board (HCCB). (Greater Minneapolis; most populous county). The HCC Board **filed a brief** with the Supreme Court denying facts the Coleman camp is claiming as basis for its suit.

The capsule, from Michael McIntee at The UpTake, is here:

> Hennepin County Canvassing Board files brief with MN Supreme Court saying Coleman's duplicate ballot suit should be dismissed:
>
> The Petition *(Coleman's suit–WR)* is predicated on a factual misunderstanding of the Hennepin County Respondents'*(some of whom the Coleman suit is suing–WR)* role in the recount for the United States Senate race and the role of county canvassing boards. The error alleged in the Petition relates to actions which took place only during the recount and, contrary to the factual allegations in the Petition, the HCCB did not certify any recount results or provide any summary statements in the recount to the State Canvassing Board.   Moreover, county canvassing boards have no role in correcting errors alleged to have been made in a statewide recount.   Accordingly, the Petition with respect to the Hennepin County Respondents should be dismissed. *(The UpTake)*

You think the Justices might look to pin the Coleman side with this? Action starts at **2:00pmCT!**

Oh and the Franken Legal Team will have its say this afternoon too so you'll hear from both sides. While no one can predict what angles the Justices will pursue we do have a clue into the Franken Legal Team's *attitude*.

I know an attorney is supposed to advocate for their client *(indeed in a sophisticated language like Estonian the very word for "lawyer" is actually "advokaat")* but Franken's lead man Marc Elias seemed almost feisty at a Monday presser.

> We are glad that the Coleman campaign has acknowledged that we will be ahead at the end of the challenge review process. There is no evidence that any ballot has been counted twice. None. The Coleman campaign has failed to show any legal or factual basis for their claim on this issue.

Rejected Absentee Ballots

These 1,000-1,600 votes are awaiting the SoS office and BOTH campaigns to agree on a process to open and count these mis-handled ballots.

Knaak said they are "engaged in dialogue" on the matter, which sounds like more of that desperately needed "hot air" here in the Minnesota deep freeze.

Deputy Sec. of State Jim Gelbmann said the talks about this were on but difficult:

> "We're trying," said Gelbmann, whose office is prodding the candidates to agree on a procedure. "It's like herding cats. We have not been successful as of yet." *(Star Tribune)*

Pat Doyle's article goes on to report *(HEY! Journalism! Nice to see...some new facts; pithy quotes from an informed source intelligently describing a situation. Good job Pat!)*:

> Gelbmann said there also is concern that counting mistakenly rejected absentee ballots by precinct will effectively identify voters.
>
> "You're going to take away the ability of at least dozens if not scores of individuals to have their vote private," Gelbmann said.
>
> Gelbmann said the Supreme Court may want to consider a method for tallying mistakenly rejected absentee ballots that avoids this problem.
>
> The court order calls for the counting to be done by Dec. 31. *(Star Tribune)*

Touchy little situation, this one. Kudos to Gelbmann for being on top of it...and an early warning signal to the MN Supreme Court *(who read the papers you know...although the smart ones read DailyKos :-))* they may have some work to do to bring this to an equitable close.

Republicans behaving badly (YET AGAIN!)

Yesterday afternoon, Kossack alphaaqua brought in a dripping, ugly quote from Politico[5]:

> The Coleman campaign is laying the groundwork for an "illegitimate" election of Franken based on their press release from today:
>
> *Politico story*
>
> *"If the balance of this process is handled legally and fairly, Norm Coleman will still be in the lead and will be well on his way to being elected to the US Senate," said Sheehan. But Sheehan cautioned that the secretary of state will present a misleading total tomorrow that "double-counts votes."*
>
> He (Cullen Sheehan, Coleman's campaign spokesperson) may not really be accusing Secretary of state Ritchie of being intentionally misleading, but that is an easy inference to make. Again, laying the groundwork for Coleman and Republicans to claim any final Franken win is not legitimate. Something to keep in mind as the absentees are counted and the duplicate ballot issue is resolved.
>
> *(alphaaqua)*

This kind of stuff just infuriates me and I said so:

---

5   *Original story can be found at politico.com.*

DK

> These are just shabby tactics by Camp Coleman! If Norm leads its legal and fair. If Norm **trails** its unfair and illegal!
>
> What sophistry!
>
> And NO Sheehan, Ritchie CAN'T include those "duplicate/double count" ballots because YOU have all them in your greasy little hands to lay before the Supreme Court tomorrow. They are IN DISPUTE (BY YOU) and so are not in Ritchie's coming totals...just like the "5th pile" ballots will also NOT be included in tomorrow's update because Team Norm hasn't finished being a horse's rear about agreeing to standards.
>
> What a turkey of statement! Fie on you Sheehan! *(WineRev)*

(WineRev puts on semi-bald cap in place of "years of brutal overindulgence in drugs", puts on big aviator sunglasses, fires up the mojo wire to the Rolling Stone, takes hit of ibogaine washed down by a tumbler of Wild Turkey and goes into Hunter S. Thompson screed mode:)

What a herd of unregenerate swine! Of all the obnoxious, Nixonian slimy arrogance, that little rat bastard Cullen Sheehan smells like Ron Zeigler's vomit! Here Ritchie is doing his level best to keep 87 county auditors and their local help coming back to the office to face the same Franken and Coleman jello eaters without ripping each other's lungs out to support "Their Candidate."

And now this little twerp comes whining about Ritchie about to deliver a recount update that's going to be full of double counted crap. If Ritchie would let me I'd visit that little punk with a jackhammer sap to the head and then go straight for the floating rib...where's Stedman to do a twisted drawing of that Chiclets-toothed windbag Coleman?...*(climbs into Jensen Interceptor, floors gas pedal and fishtails down the next 4 blocks. A BooHoo crossing the street behind the banshee driver picks up a set of dropped plastic press credentials, sees they have Thompson's name but no picture, grins, and heads for Coleman press conference...)*

Whew! Sorry about that but this sort of day old lutefisk just frosts my chain about Coleman and the current state of the Grand Old Party...*(fumes)*

DK

> This made my day - never thought of referring to such a set of craptastic events as "day old lutefisk!" LOVE IT!!!! *(Fiddlegirl)*

DK

> Poetry. Thompson would have been proud. *(DupageBlue)*

Hope this will hold you and YOU fill in and keep this going. Should be a full budget of news all day long and if you post it, we will come (and read it, analyze it, slam it, amplify it, serve pie with it, etc.). That's all the latest for the moment from yust southeast of Lake Wobegon.

Shalom.

Holiday Breaking Edition
December 24, 2008

Comments: 27   Recs: 44   Tips: 40

Yep the WineRev is going to post this diary, go work the wine shop and then NOT worry about any of this until MAYBE the 26th or 27th. YOU have no homework; ("Thank you for asking Mr. Gore. Yes you always asked in school and can't break the habit, I understand.") There will NOT be a quiz when we return.

Challenged Ballots

At Tuesday morning's Canvassing Board meeting Team Coleman asked for 16 challenged ballots that the Board had rejected be re-considered. They provided 24 other challenged ballots that the Board had made different rulings and basically asked "Aren't these all the same?" The Board took a bit of a recess, studied the 16 and talked things over, came back and took up all 16 ballots one by one, asking "Should we reconsider this one?"

Nope. 0 for 16, most of them the motion to reconsider not even getting a second

The Board DID find one challenged ballot it had ruled on twice and corrected its error...so now the count in **Franken +47**. (Yep, that challenged ballot went in Al's favor, but you only get it once. Ce la vie... or whatever ce la ballot/recointier should be.

The Canvassing Board will reconvene **Tues. 12/30, 9:00am**. Will move toward certifying a winner as prior Rejected absentees come in from the counties. Board looks to rule on any challenged ballots in those rejected/reinstated absentees on Jan 5 and then certify a winner Jan.6 (Opening day, 111th Congress). Ritchie stresses these are goals not deadlines.

Rejected Absentee Ballots

The "5th pile" ballots. Ritchie and the county election boards are notifying the Supreme Court they may need a bit more time to get to the end of this and may miss the 12/31 deadline (maybe until like 1/3). Reasons are vague but I strongly suspect it's partially the Court's fault in ordering the 2 campaigns to reach a mutually satisfying process with the SoS office for counting these...and those negotiations are NOT going well, smoothly or quickly.

From Kaszuba-son (reporter and karate student):

> On Tuesday, Attorney General Lori Swanson, in conjunction with several county attorneys and the campaigns, asked the court to move the deadline to Jan. 2. In addition, in the motion, the secretary of state's office sought to have until Jan. 4 to open and count ballots that all parties agreed had been improperly rejected. *(Star Tribune)*

MN Supreme Court Hearing

I don't know if I can do it justice in Gonzo journalism mode but a recap goes like this: Magnuson (Coleman) and Pentelovitch (Franken) are your 2 attorneys.

Magnuson had a rough time of it because while the Colemaniks are claiming there are these 125 or so duplicate ballots that got double counted they don't have any actual, you know, EVIDENCE! (Like, "Here's 1 original (or duplicate) ballot for Lizard people and here in Beltrami County there are 2 votes for Lizard people.") Regardless of what you think of the court system evidence is usually seen as a good thing.

Kossack JeffinCA has also made the strong point that there might be 1,200 votes double counted, not 125, *(he has crunched a terrifying pile of numbers from the PRECINCT level; Whoa, DUDE!)* and that Coleman is cherry picking these 125 (you think it might be for...gasp...political reasons?)

Pentelovitch also had to bob and weave. He clung to the fact that both sides and the SoS office had agreed to this set of Rules of Recount and that this situation was covered under Rule 9. For the Court to rule for Coleman would be overturning the Rule and that maybe the **whole recount would need to be done over**, not just in 25 precincts containing these 125 maybe duplicate ballots, but in ALL 4,130 so that it would be fair and the same rules applied statewide. The Court was **not** happy at that prospect.

You want to be a Supreme Court Justice somewhere? Here you go. The MN Supremes seemed VERY worried some ballots were maybe double counted (but that lack of evidence bugged them too). They also do NOT want a 2nd recount (but they want to be fair and equitable across the state.) They can see the situation was covered under Recount Rule 9, I think, but is the Rule out of whack/inadequate?

THAT's why they get the big bucks, to decide stuff like this. Decision: Due any time they want, and some Kossack will no doubt get a BREAKING diary up about it.

Republicans Behaving Badly
(you know, naturally)

Is Norm Coleman being this obstreperous on his own, or does he have help? Dave Orrick *(Sure this isn't a corruption of Errick-son that got mangled at Ellis Island?)* of the Pioneer Press has a short tidbit that shows Norm has help...professional help (different from *needing* professional help...or legal help...or recount help):

> ... a national heavy-hitter of recount law has been quietly sitting on the recount legal team of U.S. Sen. Norm Coleman: Washington, D.C. attorney Ben Ginsberg.
>
> "Ben Ginsberg is an advisor to our legal recount team and has been with us since the beginning," campaign spokesman Mark Drake confirmed. *(Pioneer Press)*

I know, I know; you can't place the name but the smell is familiar...here's why:

> To Democrats, Ginsberg's the prince of darkness. He was national counsel to the Bush-Cheney campaigns of 2004 and, more importantly 2000, where he played a central role in the Florida recount. Ginsberg left the Bush-Cheney campaign in 2004 after it was revealed he gave legal advice to the anti-Kerry Swift Boat Veterans for Truth. *(Pioneer Press)*

Whew! Ginsburg is All-Pro on the Why-People-Hate-Lawyers and why Kossacks start reincarnating Hunter S. Thompson.

ODD Scrap

Pawlenty's office was asked if they are working on appointing someone to the vacant seat if this isn't settled by 1/6.

> ..."spokesman Brian McClung said Pawlenty hadn't yet consulted with the state attorney general, but "our office has looked at this and it appears the governor only has the authority to appoint in the case of a permanent vacancy and this situation likely wouldn't apply." strib

Seems like a reasonable precaution for the Governor to take, and now we all know. Nice catch.

OK the brain is just mush and I've got to fire up the Jensen Interceptor so I can lash it over the ice to the shop in too few damn minutes to help out little old ladies asking for "a really GOOD white zinfandel" and gated community wannabes who chirp up "I was in Istanbul last week and had a local wine that is only produced in 7 barrels that was really good. Do you carry it?"

(Both situations closer to direct quotes than you ever want to believe. *Must NOT strangle customers; must NOT strangle customers. SMILE through iron teeth, SMILE! Keep the job!*)

The latest from yust southeast of Lake Wobegon.

A blessed Christmas, joyful Hanukkah, bawdy Festivus, rollicking Kwanzaa and general "laissez le bon temps roullez" to all Kossacks, their families, friends and friends of America.

Shalom.

Court, Centre Court
December 27, 2008

Comments: 23   Recs: 42   Tips: 52

Good to be back! Hope everyone has had a chance for a breather and maybe even a sense of relief and/or renewal.

Yes the MN Supreme Court took Centre Court (or Cent-ER for all you English readers between the Rio Grande and International Falls) the last couple days before Christmas.

On Tuesday the 22nd the Court heard arguments from the Colemaniks asking for A) a Temporary Restraining Order to keep the State Canvassing Board (and hence in sequence, Secretary of State Ritchie) from certifying the results of the election and its recount because B) about 125 ballots/ duplicate ballots may have been double counted in the election or in the recount.

Our last diary had a run down on the arguments, and it didn't seem to go well for Norm's side, but as usual those impressions were just that, impressions.

WELL, just like last week, the Court took about 24 hours and then ruled.

BUT first, Wednesday morning the Court modified part of its ruling last week on improperly rejected absentee ballots. *To take them in sequence from Wednesday:*

Supreme Court Actions Part I, Wednesday Morning

Sec. of State Ritchie and State **Attorney General** Lori Swanson asked the Supremes to allow the counties to get their final **ballots turned in** by Jan. 4 instead of Dec. 30. **Court AGREED to extension.**

ALSO, Deputy Sec. of State Gelbmann and some of the county attorneys (AG Swanson spoke for them) pointed out in some counties the number of such ballots was so small, *and* the names of such absentee voters are public information, *and* the voting totals that are public would be adjusted by such small amounts that the secrecy of these ballots would be breached.

(For instance, Houston County (SE MN, the bottom right county in the state where the toe of MN meets both WI and IA) has 2 improperly rejected absentee ballots. If they open and count them, you will know either 50/50 who voted for who (if both Coleman and Franken's county totals EACH go up +1), or you would know 100% who voted which way if the F or C totals go up by 2.)

The solution proposed is all these ballots (1,000-1,600?) across the state would be agreed to at the county level as ordered last week by the Supreme Court. Then they will be sent to the Sec. of State's office UNOPENED and UNCOUNTED. On Jan. 4 Ritchie's office will open and count all these ballots into F & C (and other, but these would be irrelevant for recount purposes), subject to challenges from either camp as with any other ballots to date*. Ritchie would add the numbers to the STATEWIDE totals for both candidates. (So Houston county's 2 would be counted, officially and legally, but those 2 would be swallowed in the, oh, say... 172 votes Coleman would pick up :-) *(hypothetically)* and in the oh, say... 1417 votes Franken would pick up :-D *(hypothetically)*, preserving the voters' secrecy. *(Presumably the county totals would NOT be adjusted by Ritchie's office.)* **Court AGREED to this plan.**

Canvassing Board will also meet Jan. 4 & 5, right across the hall from Ritchie's Office and will rule on challenges basically as they happen. If you're in MN, THIS is your chance! At Centre Court certain young people crouch by the net at the edge of the court and sprint out to collect netted balls *(which already has a kinky sound to it. Stop that!)*

That HAS to be what Ritchie's Office will need: ball boys and ball girls! You'll need good sprinting shoes in approved colors and shorts trimmed in Polar-Tec. The Sec. of State's Office will provide short-sleeved *(for native Minnesotans)* or long-sleeved *(for those from warmer climes)* polo shirts with the stylish, subtle (and HIGHLY coveted for its rarity) Secretary of State shield and logo. *(Ballots rampant on an oval field completely filled in.)*

There are 2 movements: you wait for the ripping sound of a ball(ot) being bounced, tossed in the air and then THWOCKED opened and the words, "A vote for..." Then might come either a nasal, pimply whine from above a pretentious ascot saying, "Coleman challenges for *(some freaky, Florida/Ohio "it's worked before" reason)*..." OR an elegant, modulated and mellifluous contralto with just the right amount of Barbara Jordan pepper snapping out, "Franken challenges for *(an actual, reality and law-based reason)*..."

You scurry to the table, salute Deputy Sec. of State Gelbmann sitting in the chromed referee's chair about 10 feet up *(Gelbmann very sharp in the traditional club "all whites", with the fisherman's cap in an azure pinstripe, a daring innovation and much remarked upon by members at the Club's Kos bar)*, snatch the ball(ot) in question and tear out the door, bound across the hall, and then walk!... with gravity, and, using both hands, lay the ball(ot) in question before the Canvassing Board like a business card being presented to the head of Sony Electronics, nod quietly and back away in a half bow, walking backward to join the second line.

The second section is harder in some ways. You wait in your crouch just below the table level of the Board and just out of the picture being streamed by the UpTake to the Hong Kong Ball(ot) Channel. You are close enough to overhear certain things from the Board but you MUST behave as though you don't. *The challenged ballot is examined.*

If a Coleman challenge you MUST maintain a passive face and blank look *(NO giggles or grimaces allowed)* even as you hear the soft sound of pencils being snapped in half by Judge Gearin, Justice Magnuson's whispered growl, Judge Cleary muttering, "What the hell...?" and the *sotto voce* of Justice Anderson's teeth grinding. When the call comes down from Secretary of State Ritchie in the 10 1/2 foot **Head** Referee's Chair *(chrome with polished BRASS fittings; Ritchie may be in the club "all whites", complete with the tennis sweater loosely tied by the sleeves around his neck, but his black and white herringbone pattern belt has traditionalists miffed but the ladies entranced)* he speaks with authority, "OUT, 5 nil!"

As others in the room dip into their strawberries-and-cream-mousse inside their krumkaake roll-ups, you pick up the ball(ot) with a studied casualness using both hands, walk it to the door, then spin across the threshold, again bound across the hall, and take the increasingly well worn carpet path to the Franken pile and tell the assistant, "Challenged ball(ot) from Canvassing Board." A hush falls as the assistant reads the decision from the Board to herself and then announces to a porcupine cluster of microphones (you can see a few of the call letters on the mikes: KITT- Hallock's Voice of the North/Early Canadian Invasion Warning Network Member, Kittson County; NHK- Tokyo; KPST- Pipestone, Rock County's 93-watt Rockin' Answer to Sioux Falls; RAI-Rome; BBC-London; KOS- American Patriots; Favorite Asses U eXecrate (FAUX) – "Live, Minnesota Election Steal, breaking") "Vote for Franken."

If a Franken challenge you MUST maintain a passive face and blank look (biting a lower lip to hold back a tear of pride permitted as you hear adults conducting democracy like you always thought it should be done). You may hear the soft brush of Magnuson scratching his goatee, comparing phrases from the Magna Carta between both the Latin and the Middle English, Gearin whispering "Precedent for this is in Talmud, the 4th Tractate.." while Anderson nods sagely as he whispers back, "Lao Tse's 5th Oracular also agrees, and the ball(ot) even answers the Buddha's questionings..." and Cleary riffling through the Federalist Papers to find the capping quote from Hamilton and John Jay. Ritchie beams *(with a confidence in his sartorial selection and daring, shoots a knee-melting glance and slight smile to observer and reporter Jennifer from The UpTake, who contracts a desperate case of school girl giggles,)* and then calls out, "POINT! 5 nil."

You pick up the ball(ot) with NO spring in your step, walk it *without bouncing* to the door, perform the prescribed spin across the threshold, bound, present and tell the assistant. As the assistant makes her latest call you have time to discreetly flip the bird at the FAUX pole-dancer *cum* "reporter" just before crouching down to re-join the first line of ball girls & ball boys... *(Haven't found the job application on the SoS site yet but I'm sure the ball boy/ball girl posting will be up shortly.)*

Supreme Court Actions Part II, Wednesday Afternoon

The Supreme Court came down(!) with their latest ruling Wednesday afternoon. Request for Temporary Restraining Order to prevent certification of Senate Race results: DENIED...**5-0.**

5-0! Man...tennis, hockey, even baseball, and now Supreme Court, any way you cut it 5-0 smarts. Guess that old court habit of expecting actual, you know, EVIDENCE, still has a certain power, and Coleman's side didn't offer any. Didn't want to? Or didn't have any to show? Hmmmm...

The 125 or so possible duplicate/double counted ballots (which may well break 100 or better OFF of Franken's pile, and thereby put Coleman back in the temporary lead)? We gonna hear that in the highest Court in MN? DENIED...**5-0.**

The Court ruled they are not the proper venue for hearing an "election contest." (WARNING: Lawyer talk alert! You and I talk about "the election contest" between F & C and we mean voting, recounts, GOTV, strategy, ballots, absentees, early voting, etc. When lawyers and judges talk about an "election contest" they mean a LAWSUIT involving the results of an election.) They said IF after the election is over...and certified...THEN Coleman has the right to file to "contest" the results in a court, presenting evidence, calling witnesses, getting affidavits, cross-examination ...in other words using all the apparatus of the legal system.

OF COURSE this means that if the improperly rejected absentee ballots are now reinstated and counted and the totals for the whole state then certified, and they certify Franken the winner, well then yes, Norm can file suit. BUT it's uphill big time and the term "burden of proof" weighs heavily on the one bringing the suit. It IS a civil suit and the standard for winning is a "preponderance of the evidence" (crudely put, 51% my way), significantly lower than in a criminal case (where the standard is the famous "beyond a reasonable doubt" or again crudely, "damn close to 100%").

Noah Kunin (Lithuanian power!) has a summary of rules regarding the court for an "election contest.":

> The election contest is filed with the District Court in Ramsey County (Ramsey County is where St. Paul - the state Capitol - is located) .
>
> The case must be heard and determined in Ramsey County by three judges assigned by the chief justice of the Supreme Court. If there is a division of opinion, the majority opinion prevails. *(The UpTake)*

So NOT your ordinary court...but ANOTHER provision in the MN state election law that SOMEBODY thought about and built in years ago. Rachel Stassen-Berger adds this:

> Minnesota law says that while the canvassing board can declare the result of a race, an election contest stops the governor, in this case Republican Tim Pawlenty, and the secretary of state, in this case Democrat Mark Ritchie, from signing the election certificate and sending it on to the secretary of the U.S. Senate. *(Pioneer Press)*

...can Norm afford to pursue this, given all the other claims on his money tied to his legal troubles?

My question is this: Franken currently leads by +47. Suppose there are 1,400 improperly rejected absentee ballots that end up being opened and counted by Ritchie's Office 1/4. Suppose they break (in the pair between F & C) 54-46% for Franken, same as the other absentees. So that would work out at Franken over Coleman: 766-634, a difference of +132 for AL. Add that to the current +47 and you get +179.

Now if Coleman sues in the "election contest" for these 125 "duplicate/ double counted" ballots and gets them ALL, that's 179-125= +54 Franken. End of story? If the worst case scenario (for Franken) STILL ends up with him ahead, will the court even take the case? Why should they? Oh sure, for justice and fairness and closure, but what would be the practical effect? You know, prove in court there really was a 2nd shooter on the grassy knoll in Dallas on Nov. 22, 1963? And then...?

 OK I'm gonna post this for you and get that 2nd cup of coffee. Here's the latest from yust southeast of Lake Wobegon!

Shalom.

Too Quiet
December 29, 2008

Comments: 30   Recs: 43   Tips: 47

In all the old Westerns when the wagon train would bed down for the night, some pioneer would walk up to the grizzled mountaineer who was guiding them along the Oregon Trail. "Mighty quiet," the pioneer would remark. "Yeah, too quiet," the old coot would reply, finding significance in the LACK of activity.

Well the Star Tribune had to write about the MN senator shortage looming come Jan. 6, (for weeks, *weeks I say!*, we might be represented in the upper chamber by ONLY Amy Klobuchar...and the problem is...?) The *Minn Post*, MN Independent, The UpTake and MNProgressive have all taken a well-earned breather. So yep, fellow Kossacks, it's quiet out there.

Too quiet...you may think it's because the crickets have frozen solid *(and where DO crickets go in the winter? Hibernate? Basements? Parkas?)* but it's more like the calm before the final storm in the recount.

Improperly Rejected Absentee Ballots

This is where the action will be this week. Somewhere between about 1,000 and 1,600 voters had their absentee ballots rejected by precinct and/or county officials for no good reason. Around mid month the MN Supreme Court ordered (and they CAN) BOTH campaigns and the county boards to work out a process for getting those "5th pile" ballots counted. Both camps have spent THIS WEEKEND examining spreadsheets from the counties about these mistakenly rejected ballots. (That's why things have been quiet.)

> **DK** Piles 3A and 5 make my blood boil. What the hell is so hard about letting legitimate votes count? This is not difficult, people. Coleman and the GOP have no respect for democracy. They only know propaganda and good sound bites. The process? Not at all. Ugh! *(CocoaLove)*

IMPORTANT: NOBODY GETS TO PEEK. No campaign and no county board can open one of these absentee ballots and THEN decide whether to count it, or object to its being counted. Everybody has to do them blind, like any other ballot.

ALSO, last Wednesday the Court modified its order and allowed counties until Jan. 4 to get things sorted AND accepted an idea from the Sec. of State's office (to preserve voter secrecy) that **such ballots be sent to the SoS office to be opened and counted there on Jan. 4.**

So starting today and all through the week Ritchie's office will be getting mail, UPS and FedEx.

Fun Starts Here

Now IF the campaigns and/or county board cannot agree on a given ballot Ritchie has set up 12 regional locations around the state where these are to be sent this week for further negotiation.

The FRANKENITES are leading, they have maintained a very consistent "count every vote" posture, AND absentee ballots to date have favored them, so they will push to accept as many of these as possible. I think they'll try hard at the local level to get these in as well, both for PR reasons ("we have support across the state to count every vote") and at least some legal and psychological momentum ("the county boards have the authority to make these calls like they did on all the other ballots.")

The COLEMANIKS are trailing, so they need some votes somewhere; every time they go to court they seem to fall further behind, so maybe that strategy needs to be re-thunk. They can call for "count every vote" (because its good PR), thereby totally reversing their prior position and actions, once again being total hypocrites ...and being Republicans your point is??

Their only real strategy would seem to be to somehow work to bar ballots from areas/counties/precincts that tend to break for Franken (e.g. midtown Duluth, the "Iron Range" back country along the Canadian border, etc.) but this is pretty imprecise. Then too the Frankenites' lawyers can do the same in say, the MN-6 (Bachman's district, objecting to absentees done in crayon from the JesusLovesMe precinct in St. Cloud).

How are these 2 sides going to do this across the state? Marching orders from central command (from the RNC bunker for the Coleman side)? Screenshots on iPhones (for the Franken side)?

And don't forget the COUNTY ELECTION OFFICIALS. What cross-currents affect them? Are they sick and tired of the whole thing and more than happy to bump anything to the regional meetings? Is some pride at work–"We got all ours settled and didn't have to send ANY to the regionals!"? Any personalities involved? ("Man, here comes Carol again...doesn't she ever shut up about 'her' ballots, and yammering about the 'other side's ballots'?")

Well, much more importantly than all that: *the total daylight is up to 8 hours, 50 minutes, up 2 MIN! from the bottom reached last Monday...ooohh I'm basking...)*

So for today that's all the latest from yust southeast of Lake Wobegon.

Shalom.

"Da NOIVE!"
December 30, 2008

Comments:	44	*Recs:*	60	*Tips:*	65

OK, I've been trying to be, well, if not objective, at least open about my prejudices and leanings in this race/recount: pro-democracy, pro-recount, pro-patriotism and pro-humor. But now, as we close in on the last 1,300+ ballots left to count, as various deadlines loom just days away, as lawyers swing their Lightsabers and judges duck and dodge, you know, I have to admit...I'm becoming a bit miffed at one of the campaigns!

No, really. I'm sorry my language may offend some *(and 'miffed' may well call in the diary police; I go willingly to the slammer)* and I feel sorry to have to descend to feeling almost acrimonious *(GASP! I've done it now)*, but I'm driven to say the low-tax/no-tax party is *MIGHTILY taxing* my patience with them.

Hmmm... maybe (over?)reading tea leaves here, but in going over this diary and the sources behind it I notice the Franken team has sent out a Kevin Hamilton, attorney, to do its talking. This is a new name from their side. Mostly it's been Marc Elias, in court it's been William Pentelovitch, and the *eminence gris* among the attorneys is David Lillehaug (whose name has appeared on the occasional court filing).

But on the Coleman side its been Fritz Knaak as the main man, Magnuson in court and Tony Trimble as the heavy hitter.

Maybe talks are continuing, maybe Elias, Lillehuag and the rest are just exhausted from a long weekend and longer campaign but maybe something else is happening.

Chess players? If Trimble is the queen piece why is the Franken side sending out a new knight like Hamilton? I mean for weeks we've had bishop vs. bishop or maybe rook vs. rook in Elias vs. Knaak. But now Trimble (Trimble!) vs. Hamilton?

It may be nothing, but Trimble showing up more is noteworthy I think. I'm mostly a wood-pusher in the great game, but I know when the opponent moves their queen it's always worth burning a bit of time off your own clock. Thoughts any one?

Improperly Rejected Absentee Ballots

Both camps need to work out a process to agree on how to admit these ballots to be counted (in conjunction with county/city boards.) The FRANKENITES have said, "Count 'em all."

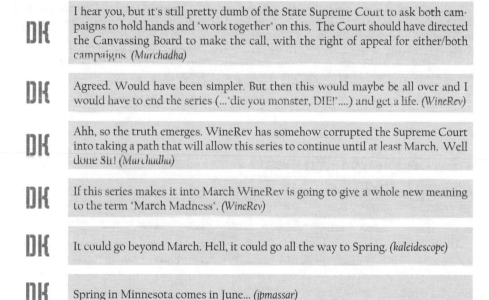

DK I hear you, but it's still pretty dumb of the State Supreme Court to ask both campaigns to hold hands and "work together" on this. The Court should have directed the Canvassing Board to make the call, with the right of appeal for either/both campaigns *(Murchadha)*

DK Agreed. Would have been simpler. But then this would maybe be all over and I would have to end the series (..."die you monster, DIE!"....) and get a life. *(WineRev)*

DK Ahh, so the truth emerges. WineRev has somehow corrupted the Supreme Court into taking a path that will allow this series to continue until at least March. Well done Sir! *(Murchadha)*

DK If this series makes it into March WineRev is going to give a whole new meaning to the term "March Madness". *(WineRev)*

DK It could go beyond March. Hell, it could go all the way to Spring. *(kaleidescope)*

DK Spring in Minnesota comes in June... *(jpmassar)*

Yesterday came word the COLEMANIKS only wanted to count 131/133/136 of these, depending on the report. Then Noah Kunin weighed in with the gory, muddy, throw-dirt-in-the-face, work-the-refs- glory:

> The Franken campaign issued a blanked *(sic; should this be blanket? Or is the statement really "blankety-blank" blanked out for children?–WR)* statement accepting the opening of 1,346 ballots local election officials listed as improperly rejected.
>
> Coleman campaign lawyers rejected a blanked *(sic)* assertion on the list. Instead, Coleman is requesting the following:
>
> - 778 absentee ballots OPENED on the basis of recommendations from local election officials.
> - 544 absentee ballots LOOKED at more closely before they are opened (or not)
> - 67 absentee ballots OPENED that are not currently on the list from local election officials
> - 587 absentee ballots LOOKED at more closely before they are opened (or not) that are not currently on the list from local election officials

> Note that 778 plus 544 does not equal the total of 1,346 absentee ballots released by local election officials. *(The UpTake)*

Those last 2 items? 67 + 587 = 654...

> According to the Associated Press, Coleman's "proposed additions skew heavily toward suburban and rural counties where he did best in the election." *(The Up-take)*

So where are those ballots coming from that Norm all of a sudden wants counted? From the 1st 4 piles.

Quickly now, on or before 11/4 about 290,000 voters voted absentee. About 278,000 passed muster and were counted that day. The remaining 12,000 were rejected for one of the 4 statutory reasons OR mistakenly so (the famed "5th pile.")

The narrowing focus of the last couple weeks has been on those last 1,000-1,600 "5th pile" ballots (now a precise 1346 according to Ritchie's office.) Coleman's team now wants to wade back into the other 12,000-1,346= 10,654 absentee ballots in the first 4 piles and mine them for votes, and naturally being a partisan, chiclet-chewing, SWINE, ALSO wants to say, "I get to do this and you don't" to the Franken side.

You CAN (if you look at it with a certain squint-eyed askance) consider this a negotiating stance... open by asking for the sun, the moon and the stars, assume your opponent will do likewise in the opposite direction, and eventually settle for just the moon.

BUT I DON'T THINK SO!...

OK that's what I've got so far from yust southeast of Lake Wobegon.

Shalom.

Desperate Norm Thread
December 31, 2008

Comments: 188   Recs: 239   Tips: 282

Main Coleman Attorney Tony Trimble opened a can of "We are really feeling the heat" yesterday morning and the smell of desperation is approaching lutefisk levels in MN. *(EPA warning for elevated levels of airborne toxins)*

State Canvassing Board Meeting

The Board met Tuesday morning at 9:00 to do what you did in school: "Do your exercises. Show all your work. Then exchange papers with a partner and grade each other's papers."

In the Board's case it was those 6,655 challenged ballots. You're right, both sides ended up pulling better than 5,300 of them off the table. But the Sec. of State's Office is in charge of getting those 5,300+ (and the other 1,300 that the Board actually ruled on) back to their proper candidates. Can anything go wrong? *Of COURSE it can.* That's why Ritchie and his office had to show all their work today.

Ritchie handed out a spreadsheet summary that showed Franken +46. The Board checked the work and found some mistakes, some trivial, and some enough to swing a vote. So NORM picked up +2 from these clerical errors, etc. That's COLEMAN +2, bringing Franken's lead down to +44. Norm picked up votes.

And why make a big deal about this? Because when I send a periscope down into the Reich-wing bunkers to look at some of those blogs somebody is always screaming about "How come ALL the recount/challenged/absentee ballots are going to Franken, huh? Ritchie/Mower County/Minnesota/democrats/liberals sux..."

Well these are NOT ALL "going to Franken." Even those famous lost 133 votes from Minneapolis? That was NOT +133 to Franken; Barkley and Coleman each got a piece of those 133 so they also GAINED votes. *(It's just Al picked up some too...ironically +46, the same as this morning's starting number from Ritchie.)*

So Tuesday Norm picked up +2 at the Canvassing Board. But to quote Paul Harvey, "And Al Franken picked up +6 at the Board meeting too to lift his lead to +50...but now you know the *rest* of the story."

Number Crunching Award

This award again goes to the unsung and unknown Franken number crew who first said they would pick up votes from Coleman's +215 apart from challenged ballots...and Coleman ended that section at +188...and that after all the dust settled Franken would lead by +4.

Then the Franken Numberteers came out and said they would pick up net on the challenged/UN-challenged/withdrawn challenged ballots and finish this section at Franken +35 to +50. The initial count was +48, adjusted to +46 and NOW, today, rests at +50.

Way to go Franken Numberteers! "All for one... *(or is that Infinity/4= 1?)* "and one for all!" *(possibly 1 4 AL?)*

Republican Desperation

Part I: Stone the Messenger

Our new friend The UpTake has been providing the raw video feed from the State Canvassing Board meeting and the Supreme Court hearing last week– sort of C-Span, MN style. Why? State holidays. State workers (including those who would otherwise run said equipment at said meetings) have the day off.

So for this public service, because ANYBODY *(TV Thailand/ RAI Milano/ WCCO Minneapolis/ Limbaugh for Lamebrains Network)* who wants the feed can have it– free, gratis and on the house– Republicans are crying bias. Bias, on a live feed with no interruptions and no comments.

> Michael Brodkorb of Minnesota Democrats Exposed *(his title says it all –WR)* writes: "'Non-partisan' Secretary of State Mark Ritchie's office has joined forces with the partisan liberal video-blog The UpTake to provide a live video feed of today's State Canvassing Board meeting." *(The Uptake)*

Who is Brodkorb? Well his latest job opportunity seems to be a paid gig as media director of the Republican Minnesota Senate Caucus. And to echo Brodkorb, a wonderful display of the MN Lockstep performed by MN Republican State Chairman Ron Carey:

> "It's amazing that a partisan, liberal blog has been made the official provider of the video for the Canvassing Board," Carey said. "To make a group with an agenda and a record of attacking one of the candidates before the Canvassing Board the purveyor of information is beyond improper, it calls into question the judgment of those who made the decision for this partisan website to be the sanctioned broadcaster of these important proceedings." *(MN Independent)*

Challenged Ballot Channel? Well, showing democracy in action is a partisan act because after all "democracy" and "democrat" share the 1st 7 letters! Yeesh!

Part II: Act Like an Ass

After the Canvassing Board meeting broke up everybody held a presser. Team Coleman REALLY started to sound desperate...there is no other word. (Desperate! As in "McCain spent another day campaigning in Cinderblock, PA, today where polls show him trailing Obama by only 4% points among unemployed dogcatchers...") Some of Tony Trimble's answers to reporters' questions:

Trimble: Secretary of State Mark Ritchie and the Franken campaign are "joined at the hip" because again the Board (led by Ritchie) refused to take up the 125 duplicate/double counted ballot issue. *(Ahhh, Tony? The Attorney General said the Board did not have jurisdiction to take that up– as in, you don't bring a parking ticket from Duluth to trial in New Ulm... Oh, and Tony? The Supreme Court told you last week THEY didn't have jurisdiction either...that it's a matter for a post-certification "election contest" trial. (The Supremes don't DO trials; they only do reviews and appeals)*

Trimble: We will sue. (Thanks Tony)

Trimble: The attorneys for the Franken side "Should be quite worried about sanctions" from the Supreme Court, since the Court threatened those against attorneys from either camp who obstructed the recount process. *(Sounds like serious projection, Tony. Or fear. One of the more common sanctions is an attorney is NOT ALLOWED to collect their fees in a case from their client, their opponent or anybody else... and attorney's insurance specifically will NOT cover lost fees due to a court sanction. As we used to say in econ classes, "When you got 'em by the wallets, the hearts and minds will follow."*)

Reporter: "Norm's 654 requested ballots he now wants included seem to be from Republican strong precincts. Is that a coincidence?"

Trimble: "It IS a coincidence. It's just our analysis happened to turn up these particular ballots..." (Said it with a straight face too...)

Quote of the Day

Norm and his 654 ballots? This says it all (comment on the Canvassing Board meeting):

> I'm thinking about renting a cherry picker and having it brought to the canvassing board meeting. A big sign that says "NORM'S" to be attached. *(Chris II at the UpTake)*

Part III: Help the Recount Process (NOT!)

At the county and regional level there has to be 3-way agreement between F, C and county election boards to send those improperly rejected absentee ballots on to SoS Ritchie's office. Ritchie called the "base universe" of votes here the 1,346 the counties have identified. Coleman has proposed some of those (first 136, lately more like 700+) and some others (like their own favorite 654). Franken proposed hard for some time the 1,346, all of them, and no more (hence Trimble's rantings about obstructing the process.)

You'll remember Team Coleman went to the Supreme Court to get "uniform statewide standards" for admitting and counting these 1,346 ballots? The one the Court ruled 3-2 instead to set up this situation we have now of the 3-way agreements? Guess what? It sounds like every county and/or regional meeting is deciding these things their own way (within the parameters of the 4 statutory reasons). Nice going, Team Norm.

The regional meetings got going yesterday around the state, with more to come today and Friday. Bits and pieces from the UpTake, *MN Independent*, MinnPost and Daily Kos:

> Carl Rosen reports from Elk River. Sherburne County *(yust NW of Minneapolis)* had 18 absentee ballots... 15 were agreed upon and sent to the Secretary of State...3 rejected for lack of a signature (Pile 1)... Mille Lac County had one absentee ballot and it was sent to the SOS office too. *(The UpTake)*

Also...Anoka County (N of Twin Cities, exurban); Coleman lawyer: we aren't going to approve any of the 1,346 statewide (including those from Anoka County) unless/until we consider the 654 too. Franken lawyer: "Let me cut to the chase. We're not going to agree to any of the 654. The 654 is from left field." Anoka County election manager Rachel Smith: "I don't want to waste anyone's time here" and shut down the meeting. *(Sent them home without supper? Way to go Rachel!)* Total breakdown in talks. Anoka County has invited both sides back for Round II today...

...Beltrami County (Bemidji) sends in 7 of 8 ballots...St. Louis County (Duluth & points north) 101 ballots sent along; one rejected ballot was from election judge Shirley Graham (!) who voted absentee in her precinct since she was judging in another precinct. Her date of signing her ballots did not match the date her witness signed her ballot. She is dumbfounded (and was a Coleman voter)...Dakota County (S of St. Paul, exurban) has 174 votes hanging fire with a 2nd day of wrangling coming up today in Hastings Regional...

OK it's a little rough around the edges but it's hard to compress all the drama into one little diary. YOUR comments will make this whole thing sing like a Norweigian Opera, fortified by a bit of schnapps (for both performers and audience; Norsk opera can only be performed or endured in an UNsober condition)."

The Terrors of Scandinavian Food

> Did someone say schnapps? No,no,no it's aquavit with lutefisk. I tried it once, the lutefisk, and thankfully they had white napkins at the legion for the "special" dinner. The aquavit I've tried a few more times. :) Another "treat" my Norwegian/Swedish husband had me try, at the nNorwegian Memorial Lutheran church basement, was rommegrot. I immediatley felt my arteries harden and had I not been young at the time would have suffered a stroke, on the spot. *(tenar)*

DK

Now I have to look up Rommegrot. Oh my god. I can just imagine lutefisk, washed down with aquavit, followed by rommegrot for dessert. Vomitorium ... *(zbob)*

DK

And above all else put it on a white plate. *(edgeways)*

DK

White Sauce is one of the many approved Norwegian Food Whitening Agents. These agents are designed to remove all traces of color from food, and if not, to make them as bland as possible.

These include, but are not exclusive to, the following foods:

- White Sauce or any Cream Sauces
- Cream of Mushroom or Cream of Celery Soup
- Miracle Whip or any white Salad Dressing
- Powdered Sugar
- Cool Whip
- White Potatoes, especially mashed
- White Bread
- Lutefisk
- White American Cheese

If not white, you should at least attempt to render the food beige or brown. Use of White Pepper is definitely contraindicated as it is a violation of the Scandinavian Spice Law, and therefore is considered Spice Abuse.

You have been warned. *(Black Brant)*

There's the latest from yust southeast of Lake Wobegon (where 9 strong, good looking, above average ballots were sent in).

Shalom.

January 2009

Hung-over Edition
January 1, 2009

Comments: 108   Recs: 168   Tips: 161

Shhhh...very gently now...*(Whispered:)* Good morning, especially to all of you in a, um, "delicate" condition (the one where the Alka-Seltzer fizzing in the glass sounds like a 16 foot roller coming over the "Pipeline" in Hawaii). Remember it's only 19 days until freedom comes in DC and even less than that until the infamous MN senate race gets called and certified. Any swearing IN will be preceded by a lot of swearing AT in the next few days.

Shoot the Messenger?
Hell, The Messenger Shoots Back!

Remember yesterday when Brodkorb of MN Democrats Exposed shot his mouth off about the UpTake video feed, and then Ron Carey, MN State Republican Chair played Little Mr. Echo?

Well, the UpTake has answered, with a restraint bordering on Obama-esque, but which in my "ethnic prose, Eubonics division via Tallinn, Estonia" reads, "Meie ei votta sitta kedagist!"

(For you poor souls who still don't speak Estonian this comes off in certain neighborhoods as "We don't take NO SH*T OFF NOBODY!"):

> ST PAUL [12/30/08] - Earlier today Ron Carey, Chair of the Minnesota GOP, called The UpTake, an online video news gathering organization, the "Official Communicator" for the office of the Minnesota Secretary of State.
>
> Mr. Carey's statement warrants a small clarification.
>
> The UpTake is not the "Official Communicator" for the Minnesota Secretary of State. The UpTake is currently providing an unedited switched video feed of Minnesota State Canvassing Board proceedings. The UpTake is also webcasting the feed live at its website, http://www.theuptake.org. The feed and webcast are free, public and available to any organization interested in obtaining it. Many press organizations have already taken advantage of our pool feed. Outlets from the Pioneer Press to Fox News have requested the code for our live webcast.
>
> The UpTake is providing this service because the Capitol staff who normally provide both the video feed and webcast were not available. The UpTake volunteered to contribute equipment and technical personnel to continue to provide both. The office of the Secretary of State accepted our offer. This conversation was transparent and also streamed live online.
>
> Jason Barnett, Executive Director of The UpTake, commented, "We are extremely pleased that the Chair of the Minnesota GOP watches The UpTake and was able to enjoy today's State Canvassing Board hearing through our live coverage."

That, my friends, is MISTER Jason Barnett from 3/4 of the court away DOWN-TOWN...and NUTHIN BUT NET!!!!!

Rejected Absentee Ballots

They are slogging through them across the state and sending them in steadily to the Secretary of State's Office.

Must See TV: Mark Ritchie and the Secretary of State's Office will open and count received ballots beginning 9:00am, Saturday, January 3.

The UpTake will provide a live, (lefty, liberal, partisan) streaming feed of the count...probably something like this:

McIntee *(breathlessly)*: "And now the wise, left-handed, in-the-tank, joined-at-the-hip-with-us, deputy SoS Gelbmann reaches into the Wadena County envelope with his RIGHT hand..."

Nate Silver *(interrupting, soft golfing commentary voice)* "That's his 14th right hand reach-in, which so far has favored Franken 59.27% of the time..."

McIntee *(rising excitement)* "...and it's...it's..a Barkley vote!"

Pat Buchanan: "This is good news for John McCain!"

Michele Bachmann: "That vote was anti-American and should be investigated, and I never said what I just said even though I was tricked into it."

Coleman Lead Attorney Mark Trimble *(enters picture from right, arms flailing, shouting)*: "This was a non-Franken vote, which was therefore clearly intended for and should be counted for Coleman. And since the Deputy Secretary used his RIGHT hand for the reach-in and since Franken is a well-known elitist, lefty, liberal, UpTake watching latte-sipper, this ballot should be counted double for Coleman. However this does not set a precedent for any future court actions the Coleman campaign may undertake at a later date..."

Should be a great show!

Close to the action

Well yeah, but, uh...there are limits, right? Michael McIntee says

> Yes. All of these meetings are to be public. We've had no problem with that. Dakota County asked that we move our cameras back so you can't see Social Security numbers and passport numbers on the ballot envelopes. We indicated we need to be close enough to hear. They are working out a way for us to do that today. *(The UpTake)*

..."so you can't see Social Security numbers and passport numbers..." A nice, respectful move by Dakota County officials saying to McIntee this is a bit TOO close but MAN, the nostril hair shots The UpTake edited out must have been FANTASTIC!

True MN praise for McIntee of UpTake from a blogger at their site. Mike said they would do their best to cover every regional meeting they could and the response came:

> neither snow nor sleet nor bad lutefisk shall stay your correspondents from the prompt coverage of recount news! Excelsior!

How to Win Friends, Influence People and Satisfy Voters

Remember the Great Anoka County Showdown on Tuesday?

Coleman Lawyer: We're not going to talk about any of the 1,346 "5th pile" ballots unless we also talk about the Coleman 654 around the state (and here in Anoka County as well.)

Franken Lawyer: We're not going to talk about ANY of the 654.

Anoka County election director Rachel: "We're not going to waste everyone's time. Meeting adjourned.")

Word on Wednesday is that the whole Tuesday meeting/trainwreck took 10 minutes! *(Whew! Like a 42 second first round: "Down goes Frazier."*

Wednesday was Round 2 in the Anoka Regional meeting. One of the other county reps present at

Anoka was Isanti County (next county north of Anoka). He/she was rather miffed at Round 1 and didn't show for Wednesday...but sent word if the 2 campaigns agree on some sort of rules for admitting absentee ballots that *they can drive up to Isanti County* and talk it over with him or her!

(I LIKE that kind of spunk! Coleman and Franken lawyers in $500 suits debating inter-planetary war, DNA sequencing strands ("On this chromosome it's CCGAT!" "No, that spells Lizard! It's CCAGT!") AND what process to devise for counting rejected absentee ballots. Some, I don't know, retired auto mechanic from Cambridge, MN AND chair of the Isanti County elections board tells them "You come to MY place, and MAYBE I'll talk to you...but only after you hand me that can of 5W-20, lick your fingers and put one each on each pole of this battery to see if there's any juice in it...")

Reports from Anoka and Dakota County Wednesday are the Coleman push for their pile of 654 ballots be looked at first (and NOT AT ALL per the Franken camp) appears to have collapsed. Both counties were looking at their share of the 1,346 "5th pile" ballots...

Process at work: Dakota county– a few absentees came in on time but near to election day and were sent to precincts BUT the new voter registration cards were sent to the county election board. Precincts rejected said ballots (pile 3) and returned them to county. Now county matched new registration cards (for new, first time voters) with these absentee ballots. BOTH campaigns AND Counties agreed these ballots are IN and have sent such to Ritchie's office... another outbreak of common sense and fair play; no wonder proto-fascists are getting antsy...

...Ramsey County (St. Paul) 133 ballots examined over 4 hours: 71 sent on to Ritchie's office, 33 rejected by Franken camp, 21 by Coleman camp...

...Wright County (1/2 way between Mpls & St. Cloud; MN-6 Bachmann district) 17 of 29 ballots sent in; Franken objected to 11 and Coleman to 1...

...Crow Wing County (North Central, Brainerd) sent in 20 of 26; Franken objected to 5 and county officials withdrew 1...

...Polk County (Waaayy NW MN, along the NDak line, Crookston) sent in 5 of 7 with Franken putting the kibosh on the other 2...

...Hennepin County sends 182 out of 231 (82 more to review on Friday), with 48 turned down by the campaigns, (24 by Franken and 24 by Coleman)...

Lawyers swing Lightsabers VIII: Back at the Supreme Court

With the last batch of ballots (most of the 1,346 "5th pile") on the brink of being counted, arriving by the score at Secretary of State's Ritchie's office for a Saturday morning grand opening and tally, the Colemaniks have moved to make sure Franken pulls further ahead! That's right, they've **filed a motion** with the MN Supreme Court! (Every time Norm, Fritz and Tony go to court Franken draws closer or moves farther ahead in the count/recount, so this is good news!)

What do they want? A DO OVER! "All these votes are coming in from all over the state and we can't stop the ones we want stopped, and we can't get our 654 super-duper coincidental ones (from piles 1-4) included at all. ("Waaahh!") So we are asking the MN Supreme Court to have all 1,346 sent in to Ritchie's office and all of them opened under one (yet to be determined) standard, which of course will be broad enough to include, oh, say, about 654 more rejected absentee ballots."

Fritz Knaak, Coleman briefcase swinger *(actions in parentheses mine)*:

> *(Overhead circle swing of Lightsaber for head cut attempt)* Coleman's aim is "bringing in ballots that were wrongly excluded," attorney Knaak said Wednesday. "I heard it a hundred times from the Franken campaign."...
>
> Knaak *(throws cluster of 87+ photon torpedoes at local election boards; a full spread!)* said in a statement that the Coleman campaign's action was prompted by concerns that a county-by-county review of the wrongly rejected ballots was resulting in the emergence of "a subtle form of political guerrilla warfare."
>
> It was inconsistent to review only those absentee ballots judged wrongly rejected by local officials, Knaak said, *("and under his mask, the words,"But the Dark Side of the Force is strong in ME")* and leave out, in some but not all cases, other ballots questioned by the campaigns. *(Star Tribune)*

Mark Elias, Franken's main public mouthpiece/attorney *(actions in parentheses mine)*:

(Forward somersault with series of 2 handed parries) Elias said the Coleman petition seeks to halt the count. "If this process can be revisited every time one candidate decides at the end of it that they're not likely to prevail, then it will never end," he said… that his campaign would fight the move and was confident it would fail.

(Wide sweeping slash at power conduit causes momentary blackout)"They are now back … asking for a do-over" even though the process ordered by the Supreme Court is nearly finished…

(Several 2 handed hacks; a desperate Knaak parrying for all he's worth; Elias lands a scoring cut) "Norm Coleman and I are both native New Yorkers, and this is the height of chutzpah," Franken attorney Marc Elias told reporters Wednesday evening. "They are trying to stop the count."

"We're simply not prepared to allow them to rewrite those rules," he said. *(Knaak dives down an escape tube, leaving behind a maze of standing, intersecting lightning bolts until the next episode) (Star Tribune, editorial comments mine –WR)*

And then… a sighting of… yes, from the Franken side: David the Lillehaug (the queen piece for the Franken legal team, the Big Kahuna, Mr. Major Mojo). There was a slight tremor as the WineRev decided to press the limits of fair use by citing one more superbly written bit (Duchschere et. al.) from the *Star Trib*… and also the earth rumbled slightly as Obi-Wan Lillehaug appeared showing the same move as seen the day before in Anoka county, but on the big stage (as befits Lillehaug):

In Hennepin County, a dramatic moment occurred when the session began. Franken recount attorney David Lillehaug objected to reviewing any of the 170 rejected absentee county ballots that Coleman's attorneys wanted to add to the 329 ballots already on the review list.

Bill McGinley, a Coleman attorney, offered to include the 30 ballots that Franken wanted to add. Lillehaug nixed that offer, too. *(Star Tribune)*

Quote of the Day

I wandered over to the *Star Tribune* online to find a LOT of complaining about Norm's changing the rules of the game as he runs to the Supremes again. I came across this gem from blogger appledumpling:

Norman, this is your appledumpling talking. Losing the senate is the price you pay for: 1. being W's lapdog; 2. fooling around on your wife and sexually harassing women while claiming to be pro-family values; 3. laundering over a hundred thousand dollars in illegal donations from rich friends through nieman marcus, hays companies, your rental and who knows what else; 4. lying about all of the above; and 5. wearing dentures that were made for somebody's horse.

Soooo, a carrot and a lump of sugar for all of you.

It's been great fun, and I suspect we have another month or so to look forward to before we bid a final adieu to Senator Horse Dentures. *(rincewind)*

Be gentle with the hangovers (lots of liquids, easy on the caffeine). Don't step on any absentee ballots you have lying around the abode…Happy New Year to all of you from yust southeast of Lake Wobegon.

Shalom.

Your Turn (Cliff)
January 2, 2009

Comments: 87 *Recs:* 143 *Tips:* 137

Late yesterday some commenters' said "be briefer." As (some of) you wish:

1. *Question:* Who won? *Answer:* No one yet. (Short enough for you? No? Oh and, uh, some of you used 16 characters to ask; I used 16 to answer. Current: Tied.)

2. *Question.:* When will we know? *Answer.:* Later. (Any more detail will drive these notes over Cliff(s)! Some of You: 21, Me: 11; Running total: I'm 10 briefer so far.)

3. *Question:* Who's ahead today? A: Franken. (Some of You: 18, Me: 10; Running: Me 18 briefer. Too wordy? Too letter-y? How about: Q: Whoz up t'day? A: Al. So some of you: 14, Me: 5; Running: Me: 19 briefer.)

4. *Inquiry:* Why is it taking so long? *Response:* Recount required by law. (Some of you: 27, Me: 30; Me still 16 briefer.)

5. *Interrogative:* How tough can a recount be? *Reply:* 3 million ballots done right ain't easy. (Some of you: 37, Me: 40; Me: still 13 briefer.)

6. *What's new today?* Invalid query. (Some of you: 15, Me: 13: Me now 15 briefer.//Query valid only for those seeking details, depth, breaking developments, and offering analysis, cracks, snark and kibbitzing (from an Israeli ~~group~~ commune?) :-D

Cliffs notes end here. What happened yesterday? The world turned, and by many calendars welcomed in a new year, and moved to within 18 days (as of this morning) of The End of an Error (trademarked by a Kossack; Jan. 20, noon, canNOT come too soon!)

In the MN Senate recount nothing happened. Zero. Zip. Nada. Courts were closed (I guess that's what they mean by "legal holiday") state government ,even county election board offices (staggering thought) were closed. Old and new media pulled a Maj. Frank Burns: "Went 100 yards in assigned direction and spotted nothing. Reporting same." Col. Sherman Potter: "A simple 'crapped out' will do, Major."

The best thing happening in the past 24 hours was a line in a letter to the editor of the Star Tribune,

"This (recount) process has been conducted with such fairness and impartiality that it may be difficult to challenge in court, quite a feat in this political environment."

[WineRev rises with op-ed page in hand, turns toward St. Paul (which means he also is facing Stillwater), Secretary of State's Office and Ritchie's collection of MN election laws...and doffs (DOFFS!) hat in salute!]

OK that's the latest and littlest from yust southeast of Lake Wobegon.

Shalom.

Political Nerd TV
January 3, 2009

Comments: 83 *Recs:* 118 *Tips:* 105

THIS is the big weekend (and please O Lord of all that is Holy and Merciful, the last weekend?) for the MN Senate recount finale. It's ALL going to be LIVE STREAMED by the (Temporarily) SemiOfficial Live-Feed Provider for State of Minnesota Stuff: The UpTake! They will have all the action, politics, speculation and left-wing, liberal, reality-based, progressive bias a live feed C-Span broadcast can have!

Canvassing board semiofficial tally: Franken +49.

Coleman campaign filed suit saying some votes counted 2 times. MN Supreme Court (12/24) said that issue needs to be filed in an "election contest" court after Canvassing Board certifies a winner.

Court ruled (12/18) counties must count improperly rejected absentee ballots (5th pile) but gave Coleman & Franken campaigns veto power over which ones. The agreed -upon absentee ballots are scheduled to be counted TODAY starting at 9 a.m.

Minnesota Supreme Court Asks...

...for responses in writing from the Franken campaign, Ritchie's Office, and several counties as to how they did or did not comply with the Dec. 18th Supreme Court Order (the 3-2 decision that set up this 3-way agreement needed between the county, the Coleman, and the Franken campaign for an improperly rejected absentee ballot to be counted).

Stop the count? NO.

Throw out Coleman's petition? NO.

A hearing? NO, but could be scheduled for later.

This latest Supreme Court Order was signed by Justice Alan Page. (You might recall the 3-2 decision was signed by Justice Helen Meyer). If I understand reading judicial tea leaves, on such a court the one who signs such a decision/order often/usually writes it with the concurrence of the others (or majority of others).

Lawyers blogging away on The UpTake see some significance that it was PAGE who signed this one, particularly since he was in dissent on the original decision on 12/18. Some believe this MAY be a sign the court is following Page's direction in resolving this, but other lawyers (being lawyers!) disagree.

... Some see the Coleman legal team REALLY treading thin ice *(a very serious crack here in MN in January!)* with their attitudes:

> I've seen judges impose sanctions (fees/costs) for far less arrogant behavior than Coleman's attorney (the late 650, wasting taxpayer time and money, a late petition to consider the 650 to distract from the prior SCT Order, delaying county meetings with the extra ballot requests – all in bad faith). *(The UpTake)*

Hennepin County has already turned in their homework (i.e., they have formally responded to the Coleman suit and Supreme Court Order, turned in what they did and did not do regarding rejected absentee ballots). Uptake's Mike McIntee found:

> Here's an interesting nugget from the Hennepin County filing: Both campaigns were required to state the reason why they wanted any "extra" ballots considered. Franken's campaign listed the reasons for its 30 ballots. Coleman campaign did not list the reasons for its 170 ballots. *(The UpTake)*

Sounds like Hennepin County reported to the Supreme Court that the Colemaniks don't do their homework. From the Hennepin Co. response about Petitioner (Coleman) :

> Nothing local election officials did in any way suggests the extraordinary relief Petitioner seeks is warranted under this Court's Order or in order to secure equal protection of the laws. *(The UpTake)*

Hennepin County also closed their filing with a Norm-berry Raspberry:

> In accordance with the foregoing, Respondent, Hennepin County Auditor, respectfully requests this Court to deny Petitioner's Motion for An Emergency Order *(The UpTake)*

Sounds like Senator Horse Dentures just got a kick in the teeth... By the way, starting soon, you can address the man as "FORMER Senator Coleman". His term OFFICIALLY EXPIRES 11:00 a.m. CT, Jan. 3, 2009 at the end of the 110th Congress.

Must -See TV for Political Junkies I

This is it: **9:00 a.m. Central Time** (on the UpTake!) the Secretary of State's Office will begin opening and counting **953 previously rejected absentee ballots.** These are 953 of the 1,346 which all 3 parties (county, Franken & Coleman) agreed should be counted.

And by the WAY: While watching, all of you can strap THIS Talking Point into your slingshot and lash out at any Reich-winger in range who has the utter gall to say something like, "Well I guess we're seeing the latest batch of Franken votes being recounted for the X-th number of times..."

NAIL the tapir- brained, single-toothed drooler RIGHT THEN with: "This is the FIRST TIME any of these ballots have been opened since the voter sealed them and the FIRST TIME they are being count-ed."

If they persist *(WineRev goes over to wall-mounted control panel, speaks several numbers, characters and letters into panel. panel makes soft glitching beep, performs retinal scan on WineRev and announces, "Authorized.")* for this occasion, I have disabled the Kos pacifist, nonviolent safety protocols. If needed, you are free to impose guilt-free, pre-forgiven, karma-free, jackbooted fury in defense of democracy and free elections. Protocols will be reinstated at the end of the The UpTake live-stream.

Personally I'd like to see Franken's lead grow from his present +49 to somewhere north of +150 to +200. (+215 would be Glow in the Dark Karma: Coleman's initial lead the "morning after" election day was 215.) That size, Coleman's pseudo-case about the 125 or so "duplicate/double counted" ballots might well be rendered legally moot. (As in dismissed, because even 125 votes all going to Coleman would leave Franken ahead with NO votes left to count.)

Ritchie says they will hand count all day until done...OR if there are other developments. And what would those developments be?

Oh, and the other 1,346 - 953 = 393, due to one of the 3 parties objecting, are NOT being counted. All 393 voters whose ballots are in such limbo are being notified by mail and can actually file suit to get their vote counted [Some rumors are about that the Franken campaign may help with filing court and legal fees for such voters. Would be worth oodles of goodwill/ democracy points if Franken did so, *regardless of who the voter voted for!*]

DK So what can the Freepers whine about? The 393 fifth pile ballots not counted? Piles 1-4? The 133 "Double counted" ballots? Can anyone explain what the 393 ballots are? *(nathguy)*

DK 393 are the rest of the 5th pile ballots that one or the other campaign objected to. 1346-953= 393.

This part stinks. The Counties made a mistake on them, admitted they should be counted, and want to count them. Either the F or C side objects/ uses their Court approved veto power to disenfranchise a voter who did NOTHING wrong.

Its just wrong. BAD result the result of the Supreme Court ruling. They should be counted and I don't care if all 393 are for Coleman or for Lizard people. Count 'em!! *(WineRev)*

Must -See TV for Political Junkies II

The MN Supreme Court gave the Franken campaign, the SoS office, the named counties, and any other county in the state *(significant? I don't know)* until...**TODAY, Saturday, 9:00 a.m. Central Time** to respond to its order from yesterday. They will apparently be meeting to review what they get... and could make a move/ issue an order at any time the Opening and Counting are going on.

The drama possibilities are so strong the The UpTake apparently will have people and camera stand-ing by at the Supreme Court for any announcements, *and will LIVE stream if it happens.*

And...it could *(longshot, but nuttier things have happened, like the Vikings winning the division)* order a halt to the Sec. of State's counting. So we'll see... and hear.

Must -See TV for Political Junkies III

Think you're tough? Got street smarts? Political moxie? Progressive chops? A second pair of pajamas in your parents' basement?

Think you are an UTTER political fanatic? Then this is your chance to prove it! Watch this!!

You know all those ballots Ritchie's office is going to start Opening and Counting today? The ones you'll be watching with every other screaming Orange fan? Blogging about in this diary's comment thread ("C'mon AL! Doggone it, you can do it!").

Well each and every one of those ballots is like any of the other almost 3 million in this race... and is **subject to challenge** by either camp. The final challenged ballot count (before withdrawals) was 6,655, but that was only an unofficial number. TODAY that one-time total could rise as the rumpled Coleman guy looks at the Traverse County ballot dated 10/31 *(you won't actually know where a ballot is from for voter privacy reasons)* and says in that pimpled, Cullen Sheehan (TM) style whine, ground through his nose like a bad country song, "Challenge by Coleman, for aroma of stale Halloween candy."

Of course you may also hear from that elegantly dressed lady with the Barbara Jordan air who sees a lizard scale and a business card from "Hitmen R US – Discount on Libruls" fall out of a ballot envelope. Her Lauren Bacall voice snaps like 50 feet of 1-inch ice breaking under a Limbaugh weigh-alike, "Challenged by Franken for statutory cause: identifying mark – the business card."

All of those challenged ballots (if any) will be reviewed and ruled on by the State Canvassing Board meeting in a **Special Sunday, January 4** Session.

Must -See TV for Political Junkies IV!

I kid you not... Part IV! **Monday, Jan. 5 at 2:30 p.m. CT**, assuming the MN Supreme Court does NOT prevent them from doing so by Order or Stay *(or Sit.. or Heel))* the State Canvassing Board will meet to check their math one more time and then sign a BIG piece of paper with ribbons and raised-ink lettering. *(WineRev would like to see Quill or Spencer Steel-Nib dipping pen used)*

Then as some LIVE -STREAM video source takes up (!) the story and focuses on the sheet you can see the wording, "This here BIG piece of paper with ribbons and raised-ink lettering and all our names signed down below, along with the Secretary of State's signet ring and hot -wax stampy thingy, says that we CERTIFY all the votes in the United State's Senate race of 2008 have been counted, recounted, counted long, counted late, but DAMMIT counted RIGHT! And the one with the biggest number of votes is..."

Aftershocks?

A candidate on the wrong end of a certified election count has 7 days to file an "election contest." Chief Justice Magnuson would appoint a 3 -judge panel to hear the con-TEST, with proceedings to begin within 20 days of filing. Full courtroom tools available to both sides. (Forensics – *WineRev whips off CSI Miami sunglasses, "I certainly hope so my friend."* – affidavits, witnesses, the whole package.)

Decision by majority vote of 3 judges. Appeals to MN court of appeals, and MN Supreme Ct. available to both sides.

US Senate has (see Mary Landrieu, D-LA) precedent for seating a certified winning candidate while legal maneuvers back home continued.

So OK that's the latest (until it's all out of date) from yust southeast of Lake Wobegon.

Shalom.

Franken +225; votes left 0
January 4, 2009

Comments: 227   Recs: 282   Tips: 266

You may have heard thunder from the North. **You heard right.**

The Sec. of State's Office Opened and Counted the 954 improperly Rejected Absentee Ballots. Franken +481, Coleman +305, (Barkley & others the rest). Net Franken +176, added to his earlier +49 = +225.

Fallout Odds & Ends

Mark Ritchie at his presser:

> "I don't think there will be a contest" *[Election lawsuit to overturn election result"-WineRev]* I've said it from the beginning. This is so accurate and done so carefully that person with the least votes is going to say, 'I'm disappointed, I'm sad, but I came in short this time.'" *(WCCO)*

He means: This was clean as breathing in at -25, open as eastern Montana, accurate as the Fonz unsnapping a bra, and fair as a Norwegian blonde...

Fritz Knaak (lightsaber at 25 watts and flickering):

> (FRIDAY: "We will definitely have an election challenge"). Saturday: "We've had better days"..."If necessary ... we are prepared to go forward to take whatever legal action necessary to remedy this artificial lead ... You always allow yourself a chance to reflect... We're still expecting to come out on top." *(MinnPost)*

Marc Elias (lightsaber NOT NEEDED):

> "It was a very important and great day. We are confident since there are no ballots left to count that the final margin will stand with Al Franken having won the election ... It is not a large margin, but a comfortable margin ... 225 votes is a real victory. One vote is a real victory, but 225 votes is a close election but it is a fairly clear victory." *(MinnPost)*

MN Supreme Court: ...**cricket teeth chattering**... People waited all day (Coleman's side in hope, Franken's in anxiety) to hear if the Court would make a ruling on Coleman's request for an emergency order...which never came. Still quiet late at night.

They have no timeline or deadline, but they could still weigh in...OR they can certainly punt by saying something like: "Since Petitioner (Coleman) has option for filing an election con-TEST where entire issue can be treated under trial conditions, request denied."

Must-See TV

For the final act (hah! I'll believe it when I see it!), tune in to you know where on **Monday, Jan. 5 at 2:30 p.m.** The State Canvassing Board will CERTIFY recounted totals of the US Senate Election between Norm Coleman, Al Franken et. al.

By MN Law, upon such certification, a candidate who believes they have evidence a certified election has produced a wrong result has 7 days to file suit in an "election con-TEST". If filed, Chief Justice of the MN Supreme Ct. (Magnuson from the Canvassing Board) appoints a 3-judge panel to hear the case. Trial begins within 20 days of filing.

This is a full-scale trial, complete with affidavits, forensics, sworn testimony, objections, overruled & sustained objections, Perry Mason lookalikes *(the WineRev is older than you think, even though he carries a certain Victor Cifuentes/ LA Law profile)*, sidebars, Jay Leno's Judge Ito Dancers from OJ I, you name it.

It is a civil action, not a criminal one, so the standard of proof is NOT "beyond a reasonable doubt" (known as "damn close to 100%") but the rather "a preponderance of the evidence" (as in "at least 51% is on this side").

Panel decides case by majority vote. Losing side has right of appeal to MN Supreme Court. (Would Magnuson & G. Barry Anderson recuse themselves if such a case came up to the High Court, since they had both been on the Canvassing Board? Maybe, maybe not.)

Soooooo...If Board certifies Monday, 1/5, some candidate like, say, Coleman *(making a BIG assumption here)* could file as late as Monday, 1/12. Trial would then start no later than 2/1.

Path A: Coleman acts like a rabid skunk and chooses to go the Full Lutefisk and files according to above procedure.

Path B: FORMER Senator Horse Teeth decides it's hopeless and concedes – formally, on paper, with Knaak, Trimble, and Magnuson (not the Chief Justice) standing by weeping softly (because they see the end of their legal fees from Norm.)

Both Paths finally lead to the Coda: A Certificate of Election is prepared (by Secretary of State? Attorney General?) and signed by Secretary of State Ritchie and Governor Pawlenty.

The US Senate

Can the Senate seat Senator Franken *(ooohh that was nice to type)* without a Certificate of Election? On the strength of the State Canvassing Board's certification, yes they can. (Precedent: Sen. Mary Landrieu of Louisiana was seated while various court actions were still pending.)

Can McConnell, Cornyn, and other Senate crazies filibuster seating someone under such circumstances? I don't know…any Senate/legal scholars/ historians out there? Could be, but it would be at least…unusual.

New Media: The UpTake

Citizen Journalism triumphant. Mike, Noah, Jennifer, Erin, Jason, and their merry band of UpTakers who all ride in the same van have delivered great coverage! And it's not just me who thought so. Part way through the afternoon The UpTake noted their feed was being picked up by the online versions of USA Today… and the *New York* frickin' *Times*! Yipes!

During yesterday's blazing recount (well, blazing after the first 7 1/2 hours of steam and smoke like a frozen, wet log) several 1,000 people and organizations were tuned in. Given the 4- minute lag in posting live comments all of them wanted to comment at the same time *(and half of them typed in "Just tuned in. How far is the count?" a minimum of 3 times per 15 minutes from 9:00 a.m. on)*.

As the comments flew by you got a sense of how far- reaching this race was and how long was the reach of the The UpTake. People said they were watching from:

> Australia
>
> Buenos Aires
>
> Boston
>
> Recife, Brazil
>
> Duluth
>
> Wales
>
> California (in brutal 78- degree conditions)
>
> "I can't sleep watching this even though it's after midnight here in" Rome, Italy
>
> Norway
>
> Sweden (who came in after Norway and noted "Norway sucks")

I mean WOW! When they're watching in Duluth you KNOW you've got reach!

As Jennifer herself put it:

> A shout-out to our team today. Behind the Scenes, on the blog: myself, Jason Barnett and Chris Dykstra. On the scene: Mike McIntee, Chuck Olsen, Tom Elko, Noah Kunin, Sarah Burt, Matt Johnson and Christian Torkelson. Thanks everyone! *(The UpTake)*

And they were on TOP of IT:

> Report from Noah says that our two volunteers - Sarah and Christian - who were doing a hand tally (hash-marks on the back of napkins sometimes!) got the most accurate count out of any outlet. Outlets were apparently asking them for the count. Rock on! *(The UpTake)*

I doff (DOFF!) my hat to you all. *(Low sweeping bow)*

> Watching the Uptake yesterday was a microcosm of the entire recount. The tedium, and the breathtaking payoff of democracy in action as legitimate votes were carefully counted. I'm completely in love with Minnesota bureaucrats right now. Good thing I'm married to one. *(underwhelm)*

Time for a cup of coffee - and even though it's Sunday, and even though it's the morning, today the coffee deserves a small zing of Bailey's, in honor of the cold, the new snow, and in celebration. I'll keep you posted on any Supreme Court news, and we HAVE to cover the Canvassing Board, but for now, that's the latest from yust southeast of Lake Wobegon.

Shalom. L'Chaim. Prosit!

MN Supreme CT: No, Norm!
January 5, 2009

Comments: 134   Recs: 181   Tips: 149

Franken Leads by +225

Just wanted to put that up all by itself.

State Canvassing Board and the Supreme Court

At 2:30 p.m. CT, the Board will meet for a semifinal session. They were going to review and settle any challenges from Saturday's Count of previously Rejected Absentee Ballots but there **were no challenges**. (I might have missed one or two; if so, they will be dealt with and rather swiftly, I think.)

Then they will check their math one more time and CERTIFY the end of the recount and the numbers. It won't be solid and final/final because: a) there is no word yet from the Supreme Court on either the 125 or so "duplicate/double counted ballots" issue, or b) the 654 rejected absentee ballots from piles 1-4 that the Colemaniks cherry picked across the state and now want included in the Count.

If the Supreme Court dismisses, the Board can go ahead (with some finality). If the Court orders hearings we wait (and will enjoy the drama). I don't think the Court would flat accept the Coleman petition and order the votes counted, so I think it's one of these two.

OR the Court might be waiting for 2:30 p.m.. (No doubt they are fans of The UpTake as well; isn't everybody?) The Court waits for the Board to go ahead and CERTIFY the Count and THEN dismiss as moot, BUT tells Team Norm that their recourse is to go the "election contest" route with the 3-judge panel and all.

MN SUPREME CT turns down Coleman's request on the 654 cherries. Go to the The UpTake for more!...No Dissents, so Justice Alan Page as lead signs off on another **5-0 decision.**

TAKE THAT NORM!!! 5-0, 5-0, 5-0!!!

Left Over Drama

The Opening and Count started at 9:00 a.m. At 9:01 Legal Heavy for Coleman, Mark Trimble, objected and said the Opening and Count should wait for a Supreme Court Ruling. Deputy Secretary of State Jim Gelbmann was miffed but kept cool. He consulted with MN Attorney General Lori Swanson and got her official opinion that they should go ahead, albeit by opening and marking both ballot and envelope just in case of legal actions later. *(This led to 6 hours of screaming boredom for a worldwide audience. Way to go Tony. No sense of showbiz.)*

So they were ready to go at 10:00 a.m. when the following happened (nice account by Rachel Stassen-Berger at *Pioneer Press*):

> Almost an hour after Trimble's Saturday morning objection, Deputy Secretary of State Jim Gelbmann said that, under the advice of the state attorney general's office, preparations and counting would begin.
>
> Trimble took to his feet to reiterate his objection.
>
> Gelbmann tried to cut him off, saying candidates' representatives already had their chance to speak.
>
> "This is a public meeting," Trimble said.
>
> "Two minutes," Gelbmann responded.
>
> "I will have my say," Trimble said.
>
> "Two minutes," Gelbmann said.
>
> "It may be 2 1/2 minutes, but I will have my say," Trimble said. He repeated his objection and said the campaign's participation in Saturday's count did nothing to nullify those objections.

With that, Secretary of State's Office staffers began the six-hour process... *(Pioneer Press)*

Well, Tony, I know you're sticking up for your client (although with Norm that IS starting from a very low base), but this was just another example why people don't like lawyers.

On the other hand, kudos to Jim Gelbmann who was going right up to the limit of accommodation and fairness and not one millimeter further. Not in the tank. Not in cahoots. Not losing his cool (though sorely provoked). And NOT backing down either. A potent combination. NICE going Gelbmann!!

Reactions from Here and There

(Hat tip to Joe Bodell over at MN Progressive Project) Waaaayyy up north in St. Louis County and Lake County (North and NorthEAST of Duluth in the "Arrowhead" region heading toward Canada), *The Timberjay Newspapers of Cook, Tower and Ely* has an editorial that is well, heartening to the anti-Coleman side. I mean, ya gotta love a lead (from the wonderfully named Marshall Helmberger) that opens fire like this:

> Norm Coleman just continues to embarrass himself. It wasn't enough that he ran one of the ugliest campaigns for the U.S. Senate in Minnesota history. He now seems intent on one of the worst displays of serial flip-flopping in the annals of election recounting. *(The Timberjay)*

In ordnance terms this is just the Enfield! The 11-inch Dahlgrens and the 128-pound Columbiads are further on. Enjoy.

(PS: A few years ago Tower, MN, set a new state record at MINUS 61 for coldest ever recorded. That's officially. Unofficially, the weather observer took that Minus 61 reading, then removed the thermometer from the overgrown birdhouse on a pole, and walked it down the hill in his/her backyard to a low, sort of marshy place and laid the thermometer at the base of a tree. Observer waited about 10 minutes and then noted the reading of -71, and then walked it back up the hill to the observation station. Even in MN people admit, "Yumpin' yimminy it gets **really** cold in Tower, MN, Ole!" Maybe Helmberger's prose is what they use to keep warm up there.)

Taking a leaf from Reich-wing pundits who ALWAYS have good "advice" for Democrats on policy, politics and elections, Zack Stephenson does the same in the other direction. Over at MN Publius he takes unemployed *(*sigh; shakes head* Norm is just another job-loss victim of the Bush Depression. Sad.)* former Senator Horse Dentures around the political map in Minnesota and what Norm's future could be (hint: Norm could find out if Jesse Ventura collected all his feather boas before leaving the Mansion)

And MN Publius doesn't stop there but rounds up pundits who add to the pile-on: Hotline, a WCCO interview and a blurb from Politico to form a Vast Left-Wing Echo Chamber *(which right now is the space under your kitchen sink when you're in there with a small flashlight in your teeth and a towel to catch the drip and you call "Hand me the wrench" and immediately a medieval barmaid is shoved in there with you – a wench.)*

The Center for Public Integrity (a much battered concept for the past 8 years, but also a Washington DC group) has a Top 10 list for 2008. Two winners are The UpTake (YAY!) and the Center for Independent Media (parent of the *Michigan Independent* and the *Minnesota Independent*) YAY! A disappointed MN voter I can respect from the *Star Tribune* blog (consolation available upon request; it's hard to lose close):

> **Unbelievable.** I am so glad this is over (almost). I am embarrassed (for the citizens of Mn) that it took so long; however the system appears to have worked, even if Franken is to be the next senator from the state of Minnesota. *(Star Tribune)*

Monday Morning Minnesota Media

There have been comments from time to time in these diaries about the Star Tribune's coverage, particularly its headline- writing slant toward endorsee Coleman. It's bugged me a bit but only a bit.

But, today I am officially annoyed. Pat Doyle gets A1 top, ABOVE the annual Viking playoff fiasco/el foldo, so good location. But the header is "Coleman's Best Hope is in Court." Bleeh. C'mon.

Four paragraphs in Doyle writes: "Barring [Supreme] court action the [Canvassing] board could certify the results of the recount this afternoon, presumably with Franken on top." Pat, who else is going to be on top? Barkley? Pat, how about "will certify Franken as the winner"?

The rest of the piece is a decent round up of news reported on these boards in the last two days...The lawyers get in shots about the 125 "duplicate/doubled- counted" ballots, Knaak for the Coleman team: "The results of entire precincts are viewed as tainted." Elias: "Double-counted ballots are a theory in search of evidence."...

DK Interesting that the procedures Coleman once called illegitimate are much like those he now demands. Probably has been said before, but it's striking. *(aimzzz)*

DK Coleman has a lot of experience in how to flip-flop. And I mean LOTS of experience. It comes naturally to him. *(Norm DePlume)*

OK, definitely time for more coffee. See you at The UpTake! That's the latest from yust southeast of Lake Wobegon everybody.

Shalom.

Norm Speaks
January 6, 2009

Comments: 111   Recs: 158   Tips: 144

Legal Maneuvers

Still not over and Norm DOES have every legal right to pursue this path. If he feels strongly enough about it (and can afford it), he can and should pursue it. It sounds like his case would come down to 3 groups of votes:

The 133 that went missing in a Minneapolis precinct (although there is strong evidence the votes actually existed and the voters actually cast them, just not the physical ballots themselves.) This batch had Franken & Coleman & other votes in it, and favored Franken over Coleman by +46. [See wingers, it's NOT +133 for Franken (and so -133 if they are disallowed). Coleman would ALSO lose votes from this batch if they are disallowed, only 46.]

The 125-150 supposedly double-counted duplicate ballots (made from originals that would otherwise jam the voting machines). These are alleged to favor Franken by +100 or so. Franken attorney Elias said it best yesterday: "It's a theory in search of evidence." Courts LIKE facts and LOVE evidence.

The 654 rightly rejected absentee ballots (twice rejected, once on election day and again during the recount). These are Norm's cherries picked from piles 1-4 of lawfully rejected absentee ballots.

[Side note: Statewide about 12,000 absentee ballots (out of a record almost 300,000) were rejected for statutory reasons (piles 1-4) or mistakenly (pile 5). SoS Ritchie was heartbroken the number was so high. He choked up at a presser pointing out there were several dozen mailed from Baghdad from the troops that arrived the DAY AFTER the Election and therefore, with deep regret, were NOT counted. That's the Law. Ouch.]

WineRev's take: The 133 are IN. There is evidence of their existence and there is precedent to support using machine tapes for the votes in a case like this. No way, Norm.

The 125-150 are OUT for lack of evidence. Subject to change what depositions and witnesses might testify to, but OUT for now.

The 654 are OUT. These are LAWFULLY rejected absentees. The address DOES NOT match, even allowing for including/excluding zip code. The name DOES NOT match. The ballots DID NOT ARRIVE IN TIME. The voter VOTED IN PERSON. Nope.

We'll know in the next 7 days whether Coleman will file or concede.

Certifiable Celebration

At approximately 2:37 p.m., CT Secretary of State Mark Ritchie turned to the rest of the Canvassing Board and asked for a motion to receive the final tabulations in the race for United States Senate as compiled in a report by MN Chief Elections Officer Gary Poser. It was moved, seconded and put to a vote. Carried, **5-0**. (*I'm going to watch hockey with a weird energy when someone is leading 4-0 "C'mon; just one more goal!"*) He passed down a certificate of the Count and everyone signed.

Franken: 1,212,431 votes

Coleman: 1.212,206 votes

Difference: Franken +225. And for now that is an OFFICIAL NUMBER.

State of Minnesota

SECRETARY OF STATE

CERTIFICATE

We, the undersigned legally constituted State Canvassing Board, as required by law, canvassed the report compiled by the State Recount Official of the summary statements submitted by the Designated Recount Officials of the recount of the votes cast for candidates for United States Senator at the State General Election held Tuesday, November 4, 2008, and the dispositions made by this Board of the ballots challenged during the recount. We have specified in the following report the names of candidates receiving votes and the number received by each.

Mark Ritchie
Secretary of State

Eric Magnuson
Chief Justice, Minnesota Supreme Court

G. Barry Anderson
Associate Justice, Minnesota Supreme Court

Kathleen R. Gearin
Chief Judge, Second Judicial District Court

Edward J. Cleary
Assistant Chief Judge, Second Judicial District Court

The 4 judicial types on the Board finally got to speak publicly and had high praise for Ritchie and election officials, and for themselves. Magnuson called it historic but noted something this big always involved some squeaks and protests, and he clearly felt they had counted every vote within "the confines of the law" – which is a very judge-y thing to say. To me, Judge Gearin faintly echoed Garrison Keillor's "women are strong, men good looking" shtick:

> Ramsey County Chief District Judge Kathleen Gearin called the recount fascinating, occasionally frustrating and always exciting.
>
> "If we have made any [mistakes] – and we probably have – our mistakes have been the mistakes of the warm-hearted, and the mistakes of the honest-hearted, and the mistakes of the good-hearted, just like the people of Minnesota," she said. *(Star Tribune)*

How Nimble is the New Media?

The Uptake was on the spot late morning from the Supreme Court and put up the PDF within minutes.

Just after noon UpTake bloggers reported the Coleman Senate offices both in DC and in Minnesota were dark and locked. Phone calls were answered by a recording noting the office was closed and asking the caller to call back later.

About 1:15 p.m., a blogger reported the website "minnesotarecount" (that had been put up by the National Republican Senatorial Committee the day after the election to watch for Democrats stealing the election) had not been updated since NOV. 30...the last time any good news came in for Norm, I guess.

At time mark 2:29 p.m., blogger Steph asked a GREAT question: "Anyone dying to watch a live Senate broadcast if Franken has to do a filibuster?" LOL! :-) :-D

Then McIntee, in his left-handed, liberal, progressive, pinko-commie way, slanted his in-the-tank coverage and **turned on the cameras for the live feed** from the Canvassing Board at 2:30 p.m. According to Jason over at the The UpTake, by 2:36 p.m. they had 1,200 viewers and were adding 1/second. At the signing CNN was in the house, not physically, *just using The Uptake's feed. CNN!*

By 3:30 p.m., the Wikipedia entry for Al Franken had been edited to say "Junior Senator" and the Norm Coleman entry now reads "Former Senator."

The UpTake headed over to Franken's HOUSE in Minneapolis for a brief presser from, **ahem,** the SENATOR-ELECT. Chuck Olson got there first and began broadcasting holding up his *iPhone and transmitting video.* (I TOLD YOU they were a shoestring operation and could use a few bucks) People said the pix were not bad but the sound was weak. Understandable since Chuck couldn't get any closer.

[What he really needs, geek engineers out there, is a new iPhone boom microphone that would extend out several feet (in a really cool, ergonomic, Apple kind of way) to pick up audio at events like this. Invent it and sell the rights to Apple. Call it maybe, iBoom! *(Note to marketing dept.: iBoom is in-house working name; need better. iBoom sounds like an Apple Suicide Bomber Kit.)]*

Al gave a gracious "Statement on the Election Results", offered empathy to the Coleman family over the strain of the past 62 days, thanked his staffers and supporters, said there is much to do, said he needed to get to work. Did not take questions.

> In Minneapolis, Al Franken says "I am proud to stand before you as the next Senator from Minnesota." Franken thanks election officials and his campaign staff while asking Norm Coleman to not file an election contest. *(Scarce)*

Blogger Dave G. was disappointed in one thing: "Franken should have come out wearing a lizard mask."

Wither Norm?

Minnesota Independent rounds up hints that Coleman may concede.

A blogger reported Norm is NOT all that popular among the Reich-wingers. You've read from time to time they call him/consider him a RINO. I hadn't realized how deep this was until someone posted a reminder from last spring. In McLeod County (WSW of Minneapolis, 2 counties over from Hennepin; Glencoe) the local Republicans refused to host a Coleman rally until he gave them assurances of his undying loyalty to...whatever their tripe is. *"Refused to host a rally"* for your own party's Senator in your own county... that is a rather serious turndown among a bunch that prizes lock-steppery above all things...Whew.

> **Coleman speaks at 3.** The more I think about it, the more I think he'll concede. If he were going to sue, he would let his mouthpieces do the dirty work (as they should). Maybe he is going to announce that he will be running the RNC. *(aslwearingen)*

Stupid Rethuglicans on Display

As word spread about the MN Supreme Court denying Coleman's last gasp before the Canvassing Board Certification of Count today, the IN THE TANK Wall Street Journal, the Joined-at-the-Hip to corrupt Republicans everywhere mouthpiece got off a **meretricious editorial** on the MN Senate race.

The opening paragraph reeks like the armpit of a defensive end in the 4th quarter:

> Thanks to the machinations of Democratic Secretary of State Mark Ritchie and a meek state Canvassing Board, Mr. Franken may emerge as an illegitimate victory. *(Wall Street Journal)*

And they LIE, as in BEAR FALSE WITNESS AGAINST THEIR NEIGHBOR, prevaricate, dissemble, **as in actionable**, LIBEL, KNOWINGLY PROPAGATING AND FOSTERING A STATEMENT KNOWN TO BE FALSE, CAUSING HARM TO REPUTATION when they print (regarding the famous "5th pile" improperly rejected absentee ballots):

> Counties were supposed to review their absentees and create a list of those they believed were mistakenly rejected. Many Franken-leaning counties did so, submitting 1,350 ballots to include in the results. But many Coleman-leaning counties have yet to complete a re-examination. *(Wall Street Journal)*

That last sentence is utterly, totally, transparently, known of common knowledge, completely, deliberately, and maliciously FALSE! [*WineRev whips off hat and flings (FLINGS!) it on the floor!*]

If you want to know what Franken Team lawyers Mark Elias, David Lillehaug, and William Pentelovitch might be doing for an encore once Al is sworn in and any election contests are finished, well, here would be something to SUE their ASSES off about! And for sheer sweet justice, bring along Fritz Knaak and Tony Trimble...after a downer like working for Coleman they deserve a better day and they could CLEAN UP.

Bless his heart the Holy Odin of Numbers, Nate Silver, refused to "endure the slings and arrows of outrageous fortune and took up arms against this (fetid and festering) sea of troubles" and refuted it line by line at fivethirtyeight.com.

Odds & Ends

What is Secretary of State Mark Ritchie going to do now that his part is (presumably) over? He wants to REFORM some of MN election laws *to make them better* and wants to capitalize on the publicity from the recount to push it through the legislature this year! (Man, this guy MEANS IT.) He's planning a statewide tour – starting NEXT WEEK – to meet with county and local election officials for two things: a) to listen to them and ask them how to improve elections in MN; b) to thank as many of them in person as he can for all their work in 2008 and on the Recount.

Do you know what democracy, transparency, and open, honest dialogue can do? Some people still say (BLEEEH) blogging is a sort of keyboard masturbation, and a way to hook up anonymously with like-minded folk. Oh yeah? Consider this testimonial from a poster over at The UpTake just at the end of yesterday's events (4:55 p.m. time mark):

> My final thoughts are this- I was Republican until 2003, and a Libertarian until this weekend. After seeing what happened to the economy, I realize that Libertarianism isn't the answer. As of today, I declare myself to be a Democrat, for the first time in my life. The openness on this site actually helped convince me a little too. Thanx. *(The UpTake)*

Back to the wine shop on the early shift today so thanks for reading. That's the latest from yust southeast of Lake Wobegon.

Shalom.

Contest!
January 7, 2009

Comments: 109   Recs: 125   Tips: 112

We were on the verge...and the verge was as close as we got. Just when we thought Norm Coleman might concede, holding his first in-person presser since the morning after the election, instead we got an announcement of his side filing an "election contest," seeking to overturn the results of the Recount.

So be it. The WineRev can take it if you can, Norm.

In brief: Franken, +225, certified count leader.

Franken NOT seated/sworn in by US Senate.

Trial to start by about the 20th.

Election Contest Timeline

Contest filed 1/6

Last Day Trial Can Start: 1/26 (20 days after filing;... there are some reports this interval is 15 days but I think it's 20...can start sooner)

Length of Trial: unknown.

Appeal from Contest Panel Decision Date to MN Supreme Court: Within 15 days or case dies.

Not a bad way to look at this whole election contest, from a blogger over at TheUpTake:

> We supporters of Al Franken should welcome an election contest... if only to tamp down somewhat the cries of illegitimacy that are rampant on the far and crazy right . *(The UpTake)*

Election Contest Court – Episode I

I'll save time and start taking bets NOW as to how far into Roman Numerals we get with this feature.

OK, Coleman's team filed Tuesday (and that's OK; they didn't take the whole 7 days, so we all saved 6 days). It is Norm Coleman's right to do this (we can debate the WISDOM of it all we want) and if the tables were turned WE would be solemnly yet eagerly insisting on Al Franken's right to do this as well.

So... Norm? Good luck, sir. Make your best case . We'll see you on the courthouse steps.

> **DK** I don't think "Nawm" is WRONG to do this. But he is a flaming hypocrite, in regards to his comments on Nov 5th (and later) that the person with fewer votes (Franken, at the time) should ask for the (state mandated) recount to be stopped (ostensibly to save the state money) and concede.
>
> I agree he has the legal right to do this, but under the circumstances (and given his earlier comments) I think he's an ass for doing so.
>
> Then again, fine. Let the MN SC make some final decisions. Every single one of them will be a nail in the coffin of Coleman's career. *(Lashe)*

> **DK** It's funny to have a political career marked by losing to a wrestler and a comedian. *(route66)*

Money Matters

YES it does. Apparently under MN Law the loser of an Election Contest is financially responsible for court costs, costs of legal "discovery" and maybe (still a swirl of stuff here) the "contestee's" (in this case Franken's) *legal fees.* This last is subject to correction but it would be sweet. (If this is so, if I were Al I would ask for a cash deposit IN ADVANCE to be held by the court until the end of the trial. It would be tacky for Norm's funds to run dry just before it came time to pay for Elias, Lillehaug, Pentelovitch, Hamilton, et. al.)

This is the first statewide election to use the "election contest" feature and end up in court since the 1962 governor's race that ended up in court for several months and was finally decided by a 91-vote margin.

That saga (*Scandinavians, esp. Icelanders, LOVE sagas*) led to the creation of the Recount Statutes we have been using since Nov. 4th for this race.

While there have been several recounts since 1962, usually for state legislative seats and the occasional US Congressional (Collin Peterson was in one in the late 1980s I believe), this apparently is the first statewide one (which would include US Senate, Governor, State Auditor, State Attorney General, and a Supreme Court appointee facing the voters) to go all the way through the recount *and still end up in court* using the "election contest" machinery. Sooo... we'll see how good that legal iron is.

In the next several days it will be up to MN Supreme Court Chief Justice Eric Magnuson (fresh from his stint on the State Canvassing Board; the large built, imposing man with the goatee, if you were watching) to appoint the 3 judge panel to hear the case (no jury). Now, while the trial will be held physically in Ramsey County apparently Magnuson can name ANY 3 MN judges (I thought he might be restricted to just Ramsey but I guess not.)

AHA: Updated from morning STar Trib: Since Magnuson served on the Canvassing Board he is Recusing himself from choosing the 3 judges. The picks will be made by...Justice Alan Page.

That's interesting and for judges across the state, I would guess, rather exciting. I mean here you are, spending 14 years in Lac Qui Parle County Courthouse (on the western border of MN, the bump that clips into S. Dak.) settling disputes over watersheds, or you've been 11 years in Koochiching County Courthouse in International Falls lowering the boom on convicted bootleggers sneaking UNTAXED Crown Royal into the States to the Hilary campaign using overnight canoes on the Vermillion River, and you get.. THE CALL.

Oh! the chance to lift a judicial finger, pause, ponder a moment and then look at Elias/Lillehaug/Pentelovitch and offer a "Sustained." What inner joy! Or the golden chance to scowl down at Tony the Trimble and snap like an overladen tree branch at 40 below, "Overruled, Mr. Trimble. Move along..." well, that's the stuff judges' dreams are made of. And to do all that for days on end while the Uptake iPhone broadcasts go out to Recife, Brazil or to the courtroom groupies squealing at the live feed in downtown Baudette at the Lake of the Woods County Courthouse... No doubt the resumes are flying into Magnuson's (**Now Page's**) in-box and favors in black robes are being called in across the state.

Echoes from the Wall Street Journal

This one isn't finished folks. Monday the WSJ editorial board got off a ROTTEN piece of writing about the MN Recount that moved the WineRev to fling (FLING!) his hat on the floor in fury. (Even that little rat bastard Cullen Sheehan from the Coleman campaign that provoked me to invoke Hunter S. Thompson didn't rate a hat fling.) Well, the Holy Odin of Numbers answered that piece of tripe line by line over at FiveThirtyEight. DailyKos' FischFry also unloaded on that bilge barge of an editorial.

Tuesday someone else publicly got into the act, and came not to praise the Journal but to bury it. Who? Ramsey County Court Judge Edward Cleary! Cleary was one of the 5-member State Canvassing Board and rendered a, well, UNdry and not-from-the-bench piece in an open letter. It is a fine, brief (and not "brief" in a lawyer's 516-page kind of way) and stringent letter that defies excerpting.

> As a subscriber of your newspaper for almost three decades, I don't expect to always agree with your editorial viewpoint. Yet I am nevertheless very disappointed when I read an editorial long on partisan tone and short on accurate reporting.
>
> As a member of the Minnesota State Canvassing Board, appointed pursuant to statute, I have attended all nine Board open meetings held the past seven weeks. I am knowledgeable about the proceedings as well as Minnesota's election laws.
>
> Our members (two Supreme Court Justices, two District Court Judges, and Secretary of State Ritchie) came from all political backgrounds, openly expressed our opinions at the meetings, and can hardly be accurately described as "meek", unless you mean "meek" by New York in-your-face standards. Your groundless attack on Secretary Ritchie reflects poorly on the author; Ritchie worked assiduously at avoiding partisanship in these proceedings.
>
> As to the Board as a whole, all of our major votes were unanimous. We consistently followed the law in limiting our involvement to a non-adjudicative role, declining

both candidates' attempts to expand our mandate. Further, we painstakingly reviewed each challenged ballot, some more than once, to confirm that we were ruling in a consistent manner.

One can only assume, based on the tone of the editorial, the numerous inaccuracies, and the over-the-top slam at Al Franken ("tainted and undeserving?") that had Norm Coleman come out on top in this recount, the members of the Board would have been praised as "strong-willed, intelligent, and perceptive."

We won't hold our breath waiting for that editorial to appear.

Edward J. Cleary

Assistant Chief Judge, Second Judicial District

Minnesota State Canvassing Board (*as quoted in MinnPost*)

The Norm Presser (Worth a few lines)

Norm came into his 3:00 presser 11 minutes early and some of his supporters set up a chant of "Norm! Norm! Norm!..".Brought his family with him (which led many to think this would be a tender concession speech with brave faces all around.) ...Claims he basically *has to* file this suit because he "won the election" on Nov. 4 and now he has to prove it (flip side of "steal the election").

Repeated WSJ editorial talking points (*MAN! Talk about singing from the same page... or gargling from the same drain.*) Does NOT take questions from the UpTake because, well...

All you need to know:

Those of you who wondering why Coleman wants to keep counting aren't paying attention to the underlying logic. As they see it: FACT: Coleman won the election. FACT: Franken is showing a higher vote total. THEREFORE: More Coleman ballots need to be counted yet. It's typical faith-first Republican logic. (*Virginia Aaron at The UpTake*)

At the presser a bit later attorneys Knaak and Trimble were in fine fettle (if you like your fettle cooked with lutefisk).

Fritz Knaak is usually better than this, but in a fit of tone deafness approaching that of the Bush family ("Message--'We care for Norm'") he managed to imply ALL the local election officials around the state LIE. We look forward to this trial so "now we can have them under oath."

Tony Trimble had a great moment regarding the missing 133 ballots in Minneapolis. This has been covered endlessly but yesterday Tony came out and said those 133 ballots *never existed*. Too bad ballots can't sue for slander.

So away we go. There's the latest from yust southeast of Lake Wobegon.

Shalom.

While Awaiting Trial
January 8, 2009

Comments: 89   *Recs:* 123   *Tips:* 122

Election Contest Court - Episode II

Waiting to Convene

Say, could I ask all you legal types out there a couple things? ("Legal types"= lawyers, judges, legal secretaries, court clerks, bailiffs, paralegals, plus anyone who's maybe had to pay a parking ticket or watched *Boston Legal* twice.)

The Election Contest court has no jury but a panel of 3 judges hearing testimony, entering evidence and all the usual "civil trial stuff" (*civicum crucibus stufficus? I told you I am not a lawyer (IANAL) and certainly no Latinist. In Latin I'm like Brian making a terrorist strike to write "Romans go home!" on the wall—nothing like conjugating at sword point!*).

But how does it work with 3 judges? Does one preside and the others just sit there and take notes? What if an attorney calls out "objection" and 2 or all 3 of them blurt out on autopilot, "Sustained" or "Overruled"? And what if they disagree? Do they go into a huddle right there? If one is presiding and says, "Sustained" and the other 2 think right away it should be "Overruled" how do they do that? And same with, "I move this ballot from the "Lizard People" be placed in evidence as Coleman exhibit #7" and one or 2 of the judges are anti-reptilian? If a lawyer doesn't like an answer can they say right on the spot (with respect) "And do you other judges concur?"

And then on the other side of the courtroom does anyone have any speculation as to who will be the trial lawyers for each side? As I understand it trial law is a kind of specialty among the legal types. Everyone studies it in law school but most don't use it regularly.

We know Trimble and Lillehaug are the main guys from Coleman & Franken, respectively. We've seen plenty from Knaak and Elias as well. In the motions before the Supreme Court it has been Roger Magnuson (C) and William Pentelovitch (F).

I suppose Magnuson and Pentelovitch might be the first expectation, but I also think making your case in front of the Supreme Court (where any of the 7—or in our cases, 5—can break in any time and ask you a question from a different angle) has some marked differences with questioning a witness in front of a 3-judge panel. Both are courtrooms, but it seems very different to (my) the untrained eye.

So, might one of the others actually try the case for their side? Does each side have, or might they bring in, a "Courtroom Courtney" trial whiz? Will each side have 3 or 4 present? Do they rotate day by day? How do they decide who opens? Examines a certain witness? Does the closing argument?

I only have my *Perry Mason* reruns, *LA Law* videotapes (told you I was old) and a well-worn copy of Paul Newman's neglected but wonderful *The Verdict* to go on, so if some real legal types can educate me I will be a willing student. Thanks in advance!

And speaking of lawyers, yes, I know it's mostly PR and posturing in ways you can't do in a courtroom, but ya gotta admit Franken main face-guy Marc Elias is doing his best to heave buckets of...cold water on the Coleman election contest. (When you heave water outdoors in January in Minnesota it's assault with a deadly splash!)

On the particulars of the 204 pages: "essentially the same thin gruel, warmed-over leftovers we've all been served over the last few weeks."

On the whole effort of the contest: "could charitably be called an uphill battle to try to overturn the will of the people."

Not quite taunting, but definitely leaning on the lever of being ahead by +225:

> "When you lose by 225 votes, you have to go mining for votes somewhere," Elias said, calling the lawsuit's renewed claims about 133 ballots missing in Minneapolis as the equivalent of believing the earth is flat. (*Minnesota Independent*)

Wall Street Journal Editorial is Dracula

That ROTTEN, hat fling-able WSJ editorial from Monday is taking on a life of its own, but not in the way the sniveling flea circus of pixel-pushing editors thought. It's like watching the tide come in on the Bay of Fundy in eastern Canada: a 22-foot difference on average, if I recall. The waves roll in much higher every minute.

First Kossack Fisch Fry gave them a drubbing and going over. Then the waves mounted as The Holy Odin of Numbers, Nate Silver dismantled them line by line at FiveThirtyEight.com. Then came word first from the MinnPost that Ramsey County Judge Edward Cleary (fresh off the State Canvassing Board) had laid the lumber to them.

But NOW!? Yes there's actually more! A rare but hence all the more welcome broadside (*aye that frigate's throw weight is a thing of beauty, me hearties!*) in defense of the Canvassing Board and the Recount process in general from the STARBOARD side of the political spectrum. The Wall Street Journal yacht o'war is taking 32-pound shot from **Power Line**, a Minnesota blog shop from the rather far right side of the fleet.

Let's just say they carry *Hinderaker as a regular*, so you get the picture.

Mr. Johnson is their webmaster and a lawyer by training.

> The Board of Canvassers that was convened to preside over the recount and rule
> on challenged ballots conducted itself honorably under difficult circumstances. ...
> I have known Chief Justice Magnuson professionally more than 25 years. Justice
> Anderson was my law school classmate and is a friend. In my view, they are two of
> the best judges serving in the Minnesota courts. Period.
>
> There was no noticeable partisan division among the board. Minnesotans are justi-
> fiably proud of the transparency and fairness of their work. I reject any imputation
> of misconduct to the board such as is implicit in the Journal editorial. *(Power Line)*

It's not quite Mitch McConnell calling for the impeachment of Dick Cheney but it's getting there!
Holy smokes... what a carronade *(as a verb)* from Mr. Johnson!! So let me add my personal thanks:

"Sir, we have never met. I believe it safe to say our respective political opinions will usually be found at
great odds. But you know well, sir, that we contend within the framework of the Constitution, of laws equal
for all so that justice be done for all. An attack on that framework, of passing off lies as truth, of selective
enforcement, these are dark markers on the way to tyranny. Your words in defense of our common heritage
and those who exercise it on our behalf are well done, sir.

Thank you, and I salute you. WineRev."

WineRev doffs (DOFFS!) hat in sweeping bow.

The Uptake and the Colemaniks

Mike McIntee has reported often that the UpTake always had fine access to the former *senator's staff*,
who were as ready to meet and talk with the UpTake as any other media outlets. BUT the Coleman reelection *campaign staff* has been doing their best to freeze out the UpTake and other New Media types. During the Recount the UpTake has had to deal with the campaigners much more than the senate staffers.

Monday's presser was held in the State Office Building, you know, a public building? At the end when
the campaign staffers were passing out copies of the 204 page filing to the "Press" the Colemaniks doing their best to make sure McIntee wasn't getting one because he *wasn't press*. Our hero Mike would
NOT back down and on camera was willing to go after both Mark Drake the press secretary...and *Tony*
Trimble(!), Coleman's main legal heavy, in order to get his copy of the filing.

(No one knew Mike was a graduate of the Helen Thomas school of "Pry it out of Them" journalism.

How Hypocritical Can You Get?

(I see it. You're smiling at this header. You KNOW its going to be about Republicans, don't you? You're RIGHT!)

The biggest number in Coleman's contest filing is the 654 absentee ballots from piles 1-4 (the absentee
ballots rejected for 1 of 4 legal, statutory, reasons) that he now wants "examined" and possibly counted.
According to his attorney, Tony Trimble, it is just "coincidence" these 654 ballots happen to come from
mostly Coleman-leaning precincts.

Now we have some word from some of the UpTake bloggers that the Coleman team thinks 67 of the
654 may be valid votes that were wrongly rejected. 67 out of 654? About 11% Norm? Well, if we do the
math one step farther and go nutso-whacko crazy and say since these are from (coincidentally) Coleman
precincts and they will (coincidentally) break big for Coleman, let's say 65-35 (which would be massive
by anyone's measure) that means the votes would split (coincidentally) FOR NORM: ...44-23...for a net
loss from the **Senator-elect's Certified Count of 225** to... 204.

Is that it? This all you've got Norm? 133 missing ballots whose votes are known that are NOT going to
change or be dismissed (I think). 125-150 maybe duplicate/maybe double counted for which evidence so
far is, generously put, between slim and none? And these (in)famous 654 which even YOU think might get
you 67, and net you 21 on a really good day?

(Clears throat) "May it please the court, the contester is going to get 0 out of 133 votes in part I, maybe 75 of 125-150 in
part 2 if he can ever find anything like paper to prove any of it, and 21 max out of part 3? Total 96. Your honors he NEEDS
226. Move to dismiss the whole 204-page bucket of lutefisk as moot." So would WineRev speak if he had the chance.

Oh and these 654/67? They are absentee ballots that have been rejected TWICE by local election officials (who have the legal authority, and in many cases, DECADES of experience to do so). But Norm wants them included now? Counted now?

WHAT could we call such a desire? Is there a **term** for such an effort to include previously un-included absentee ballots?

Lo and behold, by St. Olaf's Beard! We already have such a TERM. And wonder of wonders it is from the *Norm Coleman* Website!!

A FANTASTIC Catch over at the UpTake:

> Here's Coleman's blog post from November 10: "FRANKEN CAMPAIGN AT-
> TEMPTS TO STUFF BALLOT BOX AT THE LAST MINUTE ST. PAUL – In a
> stunning move today at the Hennepin County Canvassing Board meeting, Franken
> attorney David Lillehaug attempted to stuff the ballot box by demanding that ab-
> sentee ballots that have been rejected now be counted. This tactic was rejected by
> the canvassing board unanimously." *(Bill at The UpTake)*

So, apparently counting rejected absentee ballots is "stuffing the ballot box." Or at least it was when Coleman felt he had the upper hand.

GREAT Catch, Bill. In Minnesota terms, not only is karma sometimes a...female dog... I think after this catch Karma-nnen is a 230 lb. blue-liner from Finlandic parents who just caught Team Coleman in a tangle behind the net and has arrived on a Lonnnggg glide (no charging penalty now) 1 second after the puck has bounced in among everybody's skates. Any hard-nosed defenseman knows in this situation anyone you body check is "in possession" of the puck and therefore you can plaster them into the glass. So Norm, Quit stuffing the ballot box!! *(Whack! Thud! And the crowd in the Orange Kos sports bar bursts out with a mixed cheer, yeow, a groan, and much clapping.)*

> If Norm had any brains – or class – he'd bow out. If he were to do that, he just
> might have some shot in hell of a political future. (Run for governor, maybe?)
>
> But by fighting a certified election like this he comes across as a whiny baby. Soon,
> he'll come across as a loser, whiny baby. Nobody wants to vote for one of those.
>
> I think Norm is committing political suicide – not that I'm at all bothered by that.
> *(Snud)*

Recount News of the Weird

The Star Trib's Paul Walsh has a very odd story from up in Roseau County (Canadian line, pretty far west; Roseau--home of several great hockey players from the 1980 "Miracle on Ice" squad, including Neil Broten and brothers, and friends). A convicted felon (from another legendary hockey town of Warroad) who had lost the right to vote voted anyway, and has now been caught. Unfortunately for the Reich-wing, he is a felony sex offender who illegally voted for...Coleman!

OK, I've got the early shift today so I'll get this up now and try and get a few comments over that 2nd cup of coffee before I have to leave. That's the latest from yust southeast of Lake Wobegon.

Shalom.

Snow Falling Channel
January 9, 2009

Comments: 32   Recs: 32   Tips: 49

Waiting for Justice Alan Page

MN Chief Justice Eric Magnuson was on the State Canvassing Board. As it is that Board's decision that is being contested in the upcoming court case, Justice Magnuson has recused himself from further involvement and given a key task to the senior Associate Justice on the court. Alan Page is deciding who will be the 3 judges on the election-contest panel who will hear Norm Coleman's last gasp. According to a nice article/backgrounder from Rachel Stassen-Berger at the *Pioneer Press*, Page has broad discretion in his picks.

ANY MN judge can be asked to serve – from *any level* of the judiciary. Obviously some levels are less likely than others but still... the possibilities!

One day you swing the gavel in Alexandria Small Claims court in Douglas County: "The 18 2x4s are awarded to Sven Swenson. Menards' Lumber ordered to pay delivery charges and court costs." You might even wear the robe of office in Bagley Traffic Court in Clearwater County (and dream of the election-contest panel) as you TRY to listen to: "So during the 16-inch snowfall that night your snowmobile swung too wide on the turn onto Tarkenton Ave., spun out and went through the front window of Ivar Sonnendottir's Bakery, Bait, and Body Shop?"

And THE CALL comes... and your next time on the bench, there you are, clacking your gavel and saying, "The court has heard enough about imaginary double-counted ballots in Cottonwood County, Mr. Knaak. Sit down!" (Very heady stuff if you're a judge.)

> "We might be at the most crucial part of this process, and that's because who is on the court is so important and how they get put on the court is so important," said Edward Foley, election law professor at Ohio State University.
>
> The makeup of the panel, which by law will meet in Ramsey County court, will influence not only the decisions that are made but also the public perception of the election trial. *(Star Tribune)*

For example Page could pick one from the Supreme Court (could he pick himself?), one from Domestic Violence court in Crow Wing County, and one from the Minnesota Worker's Compensation Court of Appeals or anything in-between. (I think it unlikely he picks another Supreme. If the whole thing gets appealed to the top of the chain, Magnuson and G. Barry Anderson would already be recusing themselves. A third justice stepping aside would leave the Supreme Court rather short-handed.)

He might also take a leaf from 1963 (you know how judges LOVE precedents.) In the 1962 MN governor's race that dragged 6 months, was decided by 91 votes, and led directly to the creation of the MN recount process, Chief Justice Oscar Knutson *(now THAT's Scandinavian!)* put together a list of judges to hear final arguments in the race. He showed the list of 58(!) to both Rolvaag's and Andersen's *(I TOLD you there were Scandinavians here!)* people and let them object to any judge they didn't like. After both sides made their choices, the CJ made substitutions until both sides quit objecting. Then they went ahead with the hearing. Knutson later explained he did it this way so neither side could later claim "the judges were against us all the way." So Justice Page, it's up to you. Do us proud!

Both sides made nice public noises about Magnuson recusing himself and expressed confidence in Justice Page. It may be just boilerplate but it's still nice to hear this:

> "We have every reason to believe Justice Page will appoint a three-judge panel that will carry out its duties in a fair and impartial manner," said Mark Drake, spokesman for the Coleman campaign. *(Newsmax)*

Well, thanks for reading. Those are the latest crumbs, wood shavings, and styrofoam packing peanuts from yust southeast of Lake Wobegon.

Shalom.

Legal Maneuvers
January 11, 2009

Comments: 69   *Recs:* 79   *Tips:* 74

Election Contest Court – Episode III

The big news is still out there: who will be on the 3-judge panel for the Election Contest? When will the trial start? Meanwhile the campaigns are readying their legal cases.

First, you will recall Team Coleman on Tuesday the 6th filed their 204 page "brief" (*ya gotta love lawyer language; 204-pages of "brief"!*) and by law their opponent is the **certified count leader**, Al Franken (the "contestee.") But unlike all those motion the Colemaniks filed with the Supreme Court (one 3-2 partial victory and several 5-0 losses) in this case Franken gets to put up their own case. According to a blurb in the *St. Cloud Times*, the Franken side plans to **file their response on Tuesday the 13th**. "but had no comment on how it is preparing its case or whether it has contacted voters, said Jess McIntosh, Franken campaign spokeswoman."

Next, the lawyers are hard at work getting their lefse rolls lined up. The *Mankato Free Press* (Blue Earth County, S Central MN) has a write up of what the Coleman campaign is asking for: the Colemaniks' subpoena

> calls for copies of every absentee ballot application (there were over 2,500), all the envelopes that enclosed accepted absentee ballots, the rosters of registered voters and the Election Day registration applications (more than 9,000). (*Mankato Free Press*)

That's ONE county. Election director Patty O'Connor (whose beautiful red hair suggests she is a true daughter of the Emerald Isle) says her crew went to work on the subpoena Friday and will work Saturday, Monday, and Tuesday...because the deadline is **Wednesday the 14th**. She believes Blue Earth County is NOT being singled out, just that they were among the first to be served. She "has talked to the Coleman campaign to clarify the details of what they wanted and was assured that her county wouldn't be alone."

And who is paying for O'Connor, a staff of 4 or 6, all the copying costs and overtime? Team Coleman. The Recount up to now has been paid for by the state and local taxpayers. BUT by law in an Election Contest most of the costs are on the subpoena party (and the Franken side as of Friday had not asked anything from Blue Earth County.)

The taxpayers WILL pick up part of the cost, since by law county officials are only allowed to calculate wages and overtime on the base of the lowest-paid worker (so for instance, the difference between such a worker's wage and O'Connor's will still be charged to the county.)

O'Connor has heard of a subpoena in Ramsey County (St. Paul; this might be Team Coleman not only going after Franken but also going for a measure of satisfaction against County Election Director Joe Mansky, whose Joe POWER early in the recount left a Coleman observer irate.) Another apparently has been issued in Nobles County (far SW MN, along the Iowa line, Worthington).

> In Watonwan County, (S central MN, just W of Mankato) where Coleman edged Franken by 85 votes out of about 5,300 cast in the Senate race, auditor Don Kuhlman was hoping the county's small population might earn it a pass.
>
> "Ours was kind of a toss-up, and we wouldn't have a lot of votes down here," Kuhlman said.
>
> Watonwan County also didn't have any wrongly rejected absentee ballots and had no absentee ballots on the Coleman campaign's list of more than 600 the Republican former senator wants added to the recount. (*Mankato Free Press*)

...AND, if you LIKE the drama of someone being served a subpoena (in the case of Miers, Bolten, and Rove I would pay serious money to see a subpoena ENFORCED on these law-breaking, contemptuous, arrogant proto-fascist scumbags, complete with a team of detectives in long, black coats, flying rotten fruit and vegetables from neighbors, and jail-house video of the booking) head down to the Bloomington, MN Sheraton on Tuesday the 13th. Look for the ballroom set aside for the winter meeting of the MN Association of County Officials. O'Connor guesses both camps might use the occasion to serve papers on all sorts of county boards since they'll all be conveniently in 1 place.

Mr. Ritchie visits the Senate

That would be Mr. Mark Ritchie, the MN Secretary of State and new MN Democratic heartthrob in state politics. And that would be the MN State Senate.

The State Senate is holding some hearings to look at ways to improve MN election laws and procedures, something Mark Ritchie is also pushing hard for. They are looking at absentee voting, considering early voting, and sounds like they are going to examine instant-runoff voting. You know, good government things that our elected officials SHOULD do from time to time. Not under pressure and not on the fly, but thoughtfully, carefully, in a measured way, for the common good of all citizens who govern themselves. *(That sentence might just be the most antimatter Republican thing I've put down in 8 years.)* The Democrats have a massive majority in the Senate (almost 2-1) so they have things pretty much their way. The Republicans are reduced to snarling, whining and generally behaving badly.

Dick Day (R) from Jordan (about 25 miles S of Mpls.) whines about voters who can't seem to fill in an oval and so *should lose their right to vote!*

Mark Ritchie LAYS THE LUMBER on Day in a way that makes me choke up. Ritchie's mother takes medication that makes her hands shake so she CAN'T fill in an oval... but she should not lose her vote. His self-control I can only envy but he leaves Day a smoking crater.

I only wish Ritchie, Day, and WineRev had been born in a different age (like the WineRev's teenage years.) For this exchange in an earlier age would have provoked a further exchange after the cameras were turned off. I would want to be there... as Ritchie's second...at dawn...I would be delighted to be in charge of sharpening both rapiers to a keen edge and sparkling point. For this I would get there early and stake out the chosen ground, clearing it of every loose rock or pebble so neither man would trip or fall. (And then, when Day wouldn't show, I would hang the handbills around town decrying his lack of honor, cowardly show and unmanly conduct.) En garde!

OK, I hope that will hold you for the rest of your weekend. That's the latest from yust southeast of Lake Wobegon.

Shalom.

Barrage O' News!
January 13, 2009

Comments: 221   Recs: 268   Tips: 245

Well now! 12 Below this morning and about 4 inches new snow. We might get another 3-6 inches tomorrow...but while the weather is wintry, the politics are tropical!

Election Contest Court - Episode IV

As hoped for in these diaries, MN Supreme Court Justice Alan Page, having deliberated, talked over, phoned, e-mailed, consulted, *(and for all I know, read the entrails of a goat, or at least a Green Bay Packer :-))*, and having taken several days last week and the weekend, late Monday announced the 3-judge panel that will hear the Election Contest.

Presiding:

Elizabeth Hayden, Judge, Stearns County (St. Cloud), appointed 1986 by Governor Perpich (D). BA College of St. Benedict ('68); JD Oklahoma City University ('78); Stearns Co. Asst. County Atty. '81-'86.

Assisting:[6]

Denise Reilly, Asst. Chief Judge Hennepin County (Greater Mpls.) Appointed '97 by Governor Carlson (R-Normal). BA College of Wooster, '75. JD, Wm. Mitchell College of Law, Cum Laude '83. Law Clerk & atty, '83-89. Asst US Attorney, Narco & Firearms, '89-97.

Kurt Marben, Asst. Chief Judge, Pennington County (far NW; Thief River Falls, about 80 miles NNE of Fargo-Moorhead) Appointed '00 by Governor Ventura (I-very independent!). BS Bemidji State College, '74. JD, U. Minn. '77. Atty, private practice, '77-'00.

Let the speculations begin!

Two women and one man to hear the case—I suppose I shouldn't be surprised, but my residual sexism *does* leave me a bit surprised (and for that I apologize. Gender shouldn't enter in this at all.) Pretty progressive, Mr. Justice Alan Page!

One thing to take into account about **Judge Hayden**. She is judge in Stearns County, where being a judge could be a real balancing act. She was appointed by a Democratic Governor, but Stearns County is

---

6   *Associates? I don't know the proper titles.*

MN-06, represented in Congress by Michele Bachmann. Population is 144,000, of whom 66,000 live in the county seat of St. Cloud. According to a MN Kossack (lashe) most precincts in the city of St. Cloud went for Al Franken while the county as a whole went:

DEAN BARKLEY   15,003   19.22%

NORM COLEMAN 36,224   46.39%

AL FRANKEN   26,161   33.80%

I like this. If Judge Hayden can do a 23-year balancing act in Stearns County with all those cross currents this Election Contest court should be relatively easy.For **Judge Reilly** of Hennepin County, the Minn Post wrote a nice biography and included this quote from a former collegue of Reilly when she was a US Attorney:

> U.S. Attorney Thor Andersen, said: "Judge Reilly is all substance without puffery or pretense. She will devastate the unprepared; reach out a helping hand to the new, inexperienced and nervous lawyer; cheerfully and graciously learn from the prepared lawyer; and honor all." *(MinnPost)*

DK
> How cool is it that you actually had a US Attorney named Thor Andersen? I fully expect someone in this case to ride into court on an actual blue ox. *(dfb1968)*

DK
> No, Thor Andersen needs to arrive with a band of Vikings behind him, all fit and ready to sit at the Ting and render judgment. Babe the Blue Ox belongs to the Paul Bunyan stories, not Viking sagas. *(NonnyO)*

DK
> Got me an Uncle Thor who plays the concertina. He got lost in the woods for three days at age 83 and walked out on his own, with birch bark strapped around his shins to beat back the brambles. Sucked water off the spruce tree needles to stay hydrated. Top that. *(worldwideellen)*

Judge Marben is the mystery man so far. No news from the Moorhead or Bemidji papers. The Thief River Falls Times (weekly) hasn't updated since *(I kid you not!)* the passing of a feedlot ordinance and the possible use of a submarine to look for a missing woman and submerged car. I expect tomorrow's diary will fill in some gaps.

Franken Busts a Move on the Governor and Secretary of State

Hat tip to Kossack alswearingen who first caught news of a Team Franken move: Monday morning the **certified count leader** Al Franken sent a letter to both Sec. of State Ritchie and Governor Pawlenty **asking for a Certificate of Election**. (I kind of like this; we've been waiting for everyone else to first/ go ahead, so maybe someone just flat needed to ask.)

Well, Mark Ritchie said no...quite properly I think, and he was rather emphatic.

> "Minnesota law is very clear on when a certificate of election can be issued," Ritchie said. "Neither the governor nor I may sign a certificate of election in the U.S. Senate race until all election contests have reached a final determination. Even if the governor issues a certificate of election prior to the conclusion of the contest phase, I will not sign it." *(Minnesota Public Radio)*

Governor Pawlenty also said no *(although if he had said "yes" and Ritchie "no" the mind-bending needed to get around that combination might have used an entire bottle of Reyka Icelandic vodka (always as cool as licking a glacier) and some leftover "medications" from the Hunter Thompson Memorial Stash/ Tank Garage)* .

> "I have a duty to follow state law, and our statutes are clear on this issue. I am prohibited from issuing a certificate of election until the election contest in the courts has been resolved." *(Minnesota Public Radio)*

I suppose it was worth a shot. *(I think my bias is showing. If Coleman had done this I'd probably be ranting about the "effrontery of autocratic privilege" or something...this neutral, evenhanded stuff is hard...)* Interestingly enough David Lillehaug – Franken's main briefcase Brobdignag, but mostly behind the scenes – wrote the letter and cited MN law in issuing a Certificate *before* election contests are settled, and also contended *federal* law allows for this and applies.

Well, that was the official reply from officials. Of course the Coleman campaign just let such a letter slide like icicles cracking off the eaves? RIGHT!

Coleman campaign manager Cullen the Sheehan wound himself into a Clearasil whirlpool and issued this:

> "Al Franken knows he can't win this election contest based on the major inconsistencies and discrepancies that were part of the recount, and his attempted power play today is evidence of that. He can't and won't be seated in a seat he didn't win, so he is trying this underhanded attempt to blatantly ignore the will of Minnesotans and the laws of the state...more blah blah about how their claims will prevail in contest court." *(MinnPost)*

Underhanded? Then how did we find out as soon as the letter was sent?

Ignore the will of Minnesotans? How many pro-Bush, anti-Minnesota bills did Norm vote for? How often did Norm vote for torture, Iraq funding, Gitmo, etc. when Minnesotans were less than willing?

Laws of the state? No violations here, Cullen and no investigations...can your man say the same?

Franken Files Defense/Offense in Election Contest

(Officially the case in the Election Contest Court has been designated Sheehan & Coleman Vs. Franken –That's Cullen Sheehan, Coleman's campaign manager; I have NOT been impressed with that guy so far [see Hunter Thompson rants!]).

The grapple is underway. In the election contest it's not just Norm (and Cullen the Sheehan) putting on their case. Al Franken and his team get to mount a full-blown defense against Coleman AND add counter claims of their own. Here is a 1st look at what Elias/Lillehaug & Partners are readying.

> In addition to rebutting Coleman's petition, (the Franken countersuit) will lay out **three groups of voters** that the Franken campaign believes had their ballots wrongly rejected during the recount.
>
> The **first class consists of 35 Duluth voters** whose absentee ballots were rejected because their signatures were improperly dated — which isn't one of the four reasons laid out in state statute for why a ballot can be properly invalidated. The **second group consists of 87 ballots** for which the Franken campaign had submitted affidavits to the state Canvassing Board supporting the belief that they were wrongly rejected. Finally, there is **a group of roughly 700 ballots** that the Franken campaign has scrutinized less rigorously, but believes may have been improperly invalidated. *(from papers filed with the Minnesota Election Contest Court)*

AND...there is at least one report that the Franken campaign is/has been encouraging individual voters (like absentee voters whose ballots were rejected for improper reasons (pile 5) or by one of the campaigns using their veto (from MN Sup. Ct., 12/18)) to also contest the election and file suit (not clear if a separate action or as part of the Franken effort.)

Lawyers Swinging Lightsabers IX

Well, both sides' legal teams have gotten their weaponry thoroughly tuned up in the last few days. The Coleman side's new tranny, 1.21 gigawatt implants and "Shower of Sparks" accessory (pine-scented) were very impressive:

Fritz Knaak on the Franken request for a Certificate called it

> an "incredible and rather astonishing" power play, "an unprecedent(ed) and futile charade,"*(slash to a control panel!)* an "arrogant move" and "an insult to the process."*(flicks surprise lightning bolt from forefinger toward Team Franken)...*"Today's move by Al Franken signals his desperation ... Our voters and our laws matter too much to let politics try to influence the outcome of this election."*(Scottish brogue: "The piety readings are off the charts, captain!) (MinnPost – editorial comments mine –WR)*

While Mark Elias for Franken's side had some calm but stubborn things to say about this morning's "underhanded" open letter, he saved his real blue humming saber moves for the day's court filings:

The (204-page) Coleman petition to the Election Contest Court is *(bang! Fireball ignites and roars toward*

Team Coleman) "riddled with errors."...*(shinggg, blade skids along rail)* "an imprecise and scattershot pleading." *(Now a 2-handed, broadsword swing of great power.)* "With each passing day, the vague and open-ended litigation brought by Coleman further deprives Minnesota voters of the senator they have elected to serve them."

From the Franken filing itself:

> "Short of holding a new election ... there is no way to fashion a remedy for Coleman's challenge. In any event, because neither a new election nor throwing out ballots is among the remedies statutorily available to Coleman, the Court is powerless to provide those remedies."

Both sides sound in fine legal voice.

DK
> I wish, so very much, I could be a fly on David Lillehaug's office wall these days. I remember him so well flying around the office demanding - as only David could do - more, better, longer, more footnotes, research. I can tell you he has read and digested all the law about this topic. But as we have found so often, law and judge's personal preferences do not always align.
>
> Man, if you find out when the legal arguments for this are going to be made and if David is going to appear in court (questionable I guess since he is not the front attorney on this), I would travel to St. Paul (where I grew up) just to hear the arguments.
>
> My money is on David and his light saber. *(Grandma])*

DK
> Most of the previous Coleman filings have had multiple typos/poor syntax/mangled sentences/all-around sloppiness. I was brought up by a lawyer; nothing like that ever left his office, and that was in the days of typewriters and carbon paper (it was considered suspiciously "elitist" when he got his secretary her first Selectric!).
>
> Don't know how judges react to that kind of disrespect, but it was jarring to me reading them. *(rincewind)*

Is that rumbling sound Cavalry?

While all eyes are on the Helm's Deep of the Election Court, there may be the sound of other horses pounding across the fair fields of Rohan.

The DFL (MN-speak for MN Democratic Party) is shooting arrows from horseback into the hide of the Republican National Lawyers Assn. which is fund-raising for Norm's recount and election-contest efforts. The DFL filed a **formal complaint** with the Federal Elections Commission that the RNLA has not registered with the Fed. Elec. Comm. to do this AND they are allowing contributions up to $5,000/ individual when the limit is $2,300 AND they are taking contributions from corporations (which is a flat NO.)

Sounds like some pretty sloppy lawyering there, fellas (and Stepford gals); not at all up to the snarling bulldog level evinced by Jim (the Bush Fixer) Baker in FL in 2000. A stable stink about this could dry up some of Norm's funds. *(Thanks, MN Independent, worthy to ride with Eomer!)*

On the other hand when it comes to money, Al's team is also fund-raising among their donor base and other sources...What other sources? Well while Team Norm is under the gun for sleazing around campaign laws the Senator-elect will do some open, traditional, fund-raising at a dinner with some traditional music to help out (traditional if you're a certain kind of Boomer that is; from Tuesday's Star Tribune):

> Franken, meanwhile, is scheduled to head to Washington a few days early for the inauguration of Barack Obama so he can host a $1,000-a-plate Sunday brunch at the Willard Hotel in Washington. The event, a fundraiser for the Franken Recount Fund, promises special appearances by Grateful Dead legends Bob Weir and Mickey Hart. In a letter to supporters, Franken asked for help to "protect what we've won." *(Star Tribune)*

Deadheads for AL! A bumper sticker waiting to happen!

Whew Well, that should hold us all for much of the day and we can serve leftovers tomorrow. I'm getting some coffee while you look over the latest from yust southeast of Lake Wobegon.

Shalom.

Wind Chill Edition
January 14, 2009

Comments: 121   Recs: 127   Tips: 132

Only 6 below this morning but the windchill is a bracing minus 24. (Up north it's colder; tonight we might do 17 below in the Cities.)

Election Contest Court - Episode V

Still no word on a starting date for the Election Contest trial, Judge Hayden presiding, assisted by Judges Reilly and Marben.

Yesterday I posted some really basic bio bits *(sounds like breakfast cereal for a person-eating computer)* and asked if some of you could fill in the picture. AND YOU DID, as well as teaching me the difference between U. Minn Law School and Wm. Mitchell School of Law (2 distinct, separate schools), letting me apologize by using not one but 2 great words like "conflation" and "misprision", and also straightened me out on Justice Alan Page (U. MINN, not Wm. Mitchell).

Since there are 10 or 12 of you that really (really?) don't read through all 200+ comments (like yesterday) I thought I'd get you the best of DailyKos so far on the panel:

> Regarding **Judge Denise Reilly** (Hennepin County):
>
> I've appeared in front of Reilly. She's a fair Judge. She is a bit of a stickler for the rules, but not in a bad way. In a case like this I'd rather have a stickler than a laid back judge because Franken has the better legal argument.
>
> As for the R and D comment, you are certainly correct. I used to work for a Pawlenty appointed Judge who is very much a big R Republican, but he was one of the more liberal judges in our district. *(cafreema)*

And more:

> **Judge Reilly is fair but conservative.**
>
> She was hired as an Assistant US Attorney when Bush 41 was in office. She was a prosecutor for about 10 years. From personal knowledge I can say she is reasonably easy to talk to, but generally has a conservative bent. With that said, she is bright and competent and not prone to going off on a tangent, which is what you want when you are ahead. *(speet)*

And from Thorwald Andersen's article (1998; love his name!):

> This author knew our new judge for eight years at the U.S. Attorney's Office and everyone there was amazed at her energy, enthusiasm, and cheerful presence. It seemed that she always had a high school class under her wing touring the courthouse. Her own busy schedule never seemed to limit her ability to tackle some community or extracurricular professional task. Judge Reilly was an able and a willing teacher, leading classes over the entire state dealing with law enforcement subjects.
>
> Denise Reilly's most endearing quality is the ability to take her job and profession seriously without taking herself seriously. For example, rather than decorating her office with every diploma and award ever written in the Latin language, Judge Reilly has in her chamber her kindergarten diploma and a photograph of her sixth-grade graduating class. It is a gentle and polite put-down to those of us who wear a cowboy hat but have no cattle. *(Hennepin County Bar Association – hcba.org)*

And from the far northwest, nearing the open prairies of North Dakota, **Judge Kurt Marben** (Pennington County):

> **Judge Marben** is a very fair judge. Super nice. I'm not sure of his political leanings at all, though. Knowing what I do about him though, he would apply the law as he interprets it.

DK

> When they selected the members of the panel, I did hear that they wanted to get geographic diversity as well as judges appointed by different people.
>
> It was negative 35 degrees up in Northern Minnesota this morning. Yes, MINUS 35.
>
> Tidbit about Minnesota: There is a guy in the MN Attorney General's office named Jeffrey Lebowski. Seriously, that's his real name. ;-) *(NDakotaDem)*

Very little on presiding judge **Elizabeth Hayden** (Stearns County; no comments here at Kos) but a short blog entry in the *St. Cloud Times*:

> I was part of a jury in Judge Hayden's court room. She is an amazing judge. She is really a nice person and she is going to get this mess figured out with the other two. What a waste of tax payer dollars. Hopefully they decide it quickly. *(St. Cloud Times)*

Franken Files with MN Supreme Court

After waiting 7 days after the State Canvassing Board certified the recount for US Senate, the Franken legal team Monday sent a letter *(made public immediately, which Coleman campaign director Cullen Sheehan immediately called "underhanded")* to Governor Pawlenty and Sec. of State Ritchie asking for a Certificate of Election. Both turned him down publicly *(which Sheehan oddly did NOT characterize as "underhanded")*.

Tuesday Franken filed a petition with the MN Supreme Court asking the court order Pawlenty & Ritchie to produce such a Certificate.

In the larger scheme I think this raises the heat on Pawlenty & Ritchie to sign off on a Certificate sooner (like after the Election Contest Court rules) rather than later (like after Coleman's appeal of that ruling, and the appeal of the appeal to the MN Supreme Court). I also think the Supreme Court can sit on this and let the Election Contest Court case play out *(IOW for the Court, this is one of those situations that might actually go away if they just wait. Suppose the election contest court denies Coleman in decisive fashion and he throws in the towel. Or suppose it gets as far as the Court of Appeals and then ends. The Gov & Ritchie sign off and the Supreme Court can go back to hearing riparian-rights arguments along the Knife River estuary.)*

Oh, and for dramatic purposes if the Coleman side thought a letter to the Governor was "underhanded", how do you suppose they took a Supreme Court filing for the same purpose? After all the Coleman Camp seems to believe THEY are the only ones who get to file stuff with the MN Supreme Court (like often during the recount phase) and you think it might bug them a bit to have Team Franken run some fingernails on "their" chalkboard? YOU BET!

Attorney Fritz Knaak held a teleconference presser in the afternoon (once again pointedly excluding our new favorite The UpTake from the call list) and used phrases like "arrogance", "above the law", and "desperate." Campaign manager Cullen Sheehan worked himself into an apoplectic zit fest and sent out a fund-raising e-mail screech using such choice words as "bank robber," "running roughshod," "shenanigans," and "mischievous" (all of which he spells correctly, but oddly chooses not to capitalize "Constitution.")

Count My Vote!

Remember when (like before Jan. 5) Minnesota was actually counting votes? Recounting votes? And as the snow flakes settled, of the almost 3 million votes cast, about 290,000 were by absentee ballot? And of those 290K, something over 11,000 were rejected for cause, by law, but, as it turned out, 1,346 had been rejected for no good reason?

On Sat. Jan 5, 954 of those 1,346 were opened and counted (for the first and only time). The other 392 or so were not opened or counted: either the Coleman or Franken campaign objected, or a county board did, and so it was not counted. Those roughly 400 voters received a letter from their county noting their vote had not been counted, why, who objected, and what they could do about it.

Well, on Tuesday 64 of those voters **filed affidavits** with the MN Supreme Court: some stating their signatures between the application and the absentee ballot did INDEED match (a pile 2) or that they were INDEED registered to vote (pile 3); 12 had their votes disallowed by the Coleman side. The Court must now set up hearings for these cases and come up with remedies.

Let it be noted the Franken campaign was helping these 64 folks with the filings. This is more follow through from the Franken campaign of *(all together now!)* Count Every Vote!

The *Star Tribune* story also notes:

> Charles Nauen, the plaintiffs' attorney, said the suit was attempting to count only the 64 ballots and was not arguing that all similarly rejected ballots be counted. He said he would probably not choose to represent others who had their absentee ballots similarly rejected but voted for Coleman.
>
> "I can only speak on behalf of my clients," said Nauen, who said some voters came forward on their own and some were contacted by Franken's campaign. *(Star Tribune)*

I want to ask, since the Coleman campaign has access to the names and addresses of these same 400 voters, and they are down 225 and need every vote they can get, why hasn't the Coleman team lined up a similar lawsuit among its wrongly rejected absentee voters?

With Friends Like These Dept.

Lots of people and groups think Al Franken won the US Senate seat from Minnesota, while other folks and groups think the show is really called "The Return of Senator Horse Dentures."

Well guess who is one of the newest groups in the Franken camp? The United States Senate. Not formally yet, as in, "The Chair recognizes the junior Senator from Minnesota, Mr. Franken." but they are inching closer. And who just provided the latest inchings? *The Republican Senators!*

David Weigel's short story over at the Minnesota Independent provides some great inside Senate baseball reasoning why Coleman is being cast adrift by the McConnell-ites, but the headline is a thing of beauty: "Senate Republicans to Coleman: Drop Dead."

OK after yesterday's excitement and cold weather, it's great that the engine today actually turned over and started. Hope this will hold you and hold you warm (or cool you off for those suffering in the surf and along the Pacific beaches: watch out for windburn and pace yourselves in that scorching 75-degree stuff!) with all the latest from yust southeast of Lake Wobegon.

Shalom.

Courts & More Courts
January 15, 2009

Comments: 49 Recs: 51 Tips: 55

It just gets bigger and bigger, or "legaler and legaler"! Legal moves everywhere, court schedules, Republicans blowing out their molars mouthing the words, "election integrity" and "lawsuit", voters suing election officials, the MN Supreme Court sending both legal teams into their legal gymnasiums.

Election Contest Court – Episode VI
Maybe Big News

The 3-Judge Election Contest Court MAY begin hearing the case of Sheehan & Coleman vs. Franken Wednesday, January 21. NOT confirmed, only source is Camp Coleman so far (how much salt should THAT source have with it?)

> Also on Wednesday, in a filing, Coleman recommended conducting the trial in stages. He said the case should proceed to the next step only if he gains "a sufficient number of votes" in the prior stage. *(Star Tribune)*

Kossack BlueinMN posted this proposed Coleman schedule late in yesterday's comments:

JANUARY 21: If there's a Motion to Dismiss the contest, the courts will hear it on this date.

FEBRUARY 9th: Rejected Absentee Ballots hearing begins.

FEBRUARY 16th: Duplicate/Original ballots hearing begins.

FEBRUARY 16th: Missing 133 ballots in Mpls Ward 1/Precinct 3 begins.

FEBRUARY 23rd: Voter Intent Challenges hearing begins.

FEBRUARY 23rd: "Remaining Issues" hearing begins.

What the HELL kind of schedule is THAT? 18 days to argue Motion to Dismiss? In your DREAMS!

(Scream of over-revved engine outside as Jensen Interceptor does triple donut across a snow-slicked parking lot. Mescaline-crazed driver emerges, smelling of spilled Wild Turkey, running up to a petrified Fritz Knaak. Driver puts clawed left fingers on Knaak's neck just under right earlobe and screams in his face, "You sodden hulk of treacherous banal legalities! You think you can stall a Motion to Dismiss for 18 days? Lillehaug's motion and Pentelovitch's oral argument will be sharp enough to cut diamonds from across the room and will only take 18 minutes! If you get LUCKY, punk, Hayden will "take it under advisement" ...which means about 9:18 on the 21st your sorry case will need to be out of traction and in court! Trimble only has 6 more days, NOT till the 9th, of his St. Vitus dance to animate that corpse of a case...and then Elias will run through it like so much ground hamburger. Now where is that over-mortgaged Horse-Dentured lifeform?"

Driver releases a fear-liquified, collapsed heap of Knaak and takes off in madly fishtailing Interceptor before anyone can think to move...)

> So typical Fritz Knaak! I'm not sure who drafted Coleman's brief (probably some poor law clerk who was given minimum direction, no facts with which to work, and assumed that the attorney in charge would actually read it and edit it before it was filed), but Franken's attorneys have argued circles around Coleman's team. *(beastiemom)*

First Coleman wants to take up disputed absentee ballots. It is unclear if this includes the almost 400 improperly rejected absentee ballots (the famous 5th pile) that one or the other camp objected to before the Jan. 5 counting of the remaining. It likely DOES include Norm's favorite 654 cherry-picked ballots from piles 1, 2, 3, 4.

Second stage would be the duplicate/double-counted ballots that have yet to be shown to EXIST in this particular space-time continuum, let alone exist in sufficient numbers to make a difference and with a fair or even rational solution for counting them.

Third stage would be the "missing" 133 ballots from a Minneapolis precinct (which favored Franken NOT by +133, as the Reich-wing, the Wall Street Urinal editorial board, Slow Limbaugh, and any Joseph Goebbels Medal contender on Faux Noise would have you believe, BUT only by +46 Franken net.) ONE MORE TIME: there is strong evidence these ballots existed and the voters of the precinct DID sign in and vote. It is not "best evidence" (which would be the 133 ballots themselves--if we had those none of this noise would even be happening) but it is strong evidence.

Fourth stage and fifth stage "include deliberation over ballots with questionable voter intent and a probe into Coleman's argument that some voters had more than one ballot counted." The Coleman team estimates these stages could take the trial to the end of February.

"Ballots with questionable voter intent"!!?? THIS does not sound like a fishing expedition; this sounds like a fleet of Evinrudes drift-netting Lake Mille Lacs from shore to shore! This is the legal machinery Coleman would use to carry out Knaak's casual mention that "they have no intention of seeking to redo the entire recount." To me this stage is EXACTLY how they'd do it, for as long as Judges Hayden, Reilly, and Marben would let them–and if the judges put a stop to it before ballot #3,000,000 was re-examined for voter intent (WineRev--now VinegarRev Diary v. 1,622 dated Nov. 23, 2018) then they scream biased/unfair/in the tank/liberal/pinko/biased judges who are stealing the election from Norm. As I've said before in a diary title, in Brooklyn, "Da NOIVE!"

(Takes deep, cleansing breath; mentally goes to "happy place" and imagines shelling out horse dentures with rising cross from outside striker postion at edge of the box; feels good enough to resume diary.)

Three things on this "staging" idea.

1. It's not bad on its face and has something to commend it in terms of allowing for focus.

2. The Coleman provision about "sufficient number of votes" in each stage could well be Norm's undoing. If stage one results in the nearly 400 pile 5 ballots being counted, and Franken nets, say, +70 from them his lead is at +295. Then if *either* Norm's 654 cherries get run through the pitter and then chopped up in a legal Cuisinart, *or* Team Franken gets to dump all 10,000 rejected

absentee ballots (piles 1-4, except voters who showed up in person to vote, thereby canceling their absentee) onto the counting table and nets another +1,000 then Al is sitting at +1,300.

At this point stages 3 to "infinity and beyond" would be declared moot, Norm would be hoisted on Cullen Sheehan's petard *(sorry for the mental image)* and the words "sufficient number of votes" will be intoned upon his campaign carcass swinging slowly in an arctic breeze, and the case is over... on Norm's own terms.

3. Team Franken TODAY will propose their OWN and reportedly shorter timeline to the Court (presumably in stages of some kind as well.) Given prior history by both legal teams the Franken proposal will be brief, to the point, spelled correctly, judicious, efficient, and like most Apple Computer products, feature a REALLY cool fractal algorithm and a human friendly interface (*...uuummmmm, hmmm. Ok, where was I? And just what the heck IS a fractal algorithm and why does Apple have all the cool ones, while Bill Gates' always look like they've been squashed by a plastic pocket protector?*)

Republicans for Voter Integrity - HUH?

A group of MN Republican "activists" plan to file their own lawsuit (atty. Doug Seaton) over the supposed "double-counted" duplicate ballots, numbering maybe 150 votes. They also plan to put up their own website, although with Michael Brodkorb of "Minnesota Democrats Exposed" on board with their effort it sure looks like they've got their Internet presence already in place.

There's just a couple things: they admit they don't have any, you know, oh, what's that stuff called in court composed of facts, data, or measurements, photographs, lab test results... you know...ev-something... Everly brothers...Everclear for the still... Ev...Everett Dirksen...EVIDENCE! They ain't got any, just like Norm & Cullen. And second, under the law (just ahead) they have to propose a remedy...which would be what?

> **DK**
>
> The lack of specificity by Coleman: breathtaking!
>
> He proposes reconsideration of "the intent of the voter" with regard to an unspecified number of unspecified ballots.
>
> He and his people have seen every ballot that has been counted and their original motion should have indicated which items he intends to raise in question, as Franken argues. After all, Franken needs the time to prepare his counter-argument to every one of those ballots... *(Clem Yeobright)*

The 64-voter lawsuit

There are 64 voters in MN who cast absentee ballots which were rejected for no good reason (these 64 are part of the 392 noted above. The Franken campaign has helped them with paperwork and filing fees.

What's interesting in MN law is that such suits seem to get a fast track as they are filed in the Supreme Court, and remedies are to be acted on right away. Now in the case of these 64 voters their remedy in law seems self-evident: "I want my vote opened and counted as I cast it." I think any Brownie Troop meeting playing "Court" would jump on that remedy with both feet and declare things done with a bow on top, let alone a court of law.

Here's the (abbreviated) language of the law:

> 204B.44 ERRORS AND OMISSIONS; REMEDY.
>
> Any individual may file a petition in the manner provided in this section for the correction of any of the following errors, omissions, or wrongful acts which have occurred or are about to occur:
>
> ...multi-point description of grounds, and then...
>
> The petition shall describe the error, omission, or wrongful act **and the correction sought** by the petitioner. The petition shall be filed with any judge of the Supreme Court in the case of an election for state or federal office or any judge of the district court in that county in the case of an election for county, municipal, or school district office. The petitioner shall serve a copy of the petition on the officer, board or individual charged with the error, omission, or wrongful act, and on any other party as required by the court. Upon receipt of the petition **the court shall immediately set a time for a hearing** on the matter and order the officer, board or

individual charged with the error, omission or wrongful act to correct the error or wrongful act or perform the duty or show cause for not doing so. The court shall issue its findings and a final order for appropriate relief as soon as possible after the hearing. Failure to obey the order is contempt of court. *(MN State Statute, quoted in Pioneer Press, bolding for emphasis mine –WR)*

Supreme Court to Franken: Come In Out of the Cold

OK, Monday AL Franken asked Sec. of State Ritchie & Governor Pawlenty to award him a Certificate of Election. They both turned him down, citing MN law that requires all "election contests" (lawsuits like what Norm is trying now) to be resolved.

Tuesday in the MN Supreme Ct. Franken filed for an order from the Court to Ritchie & Pawlenty to award him such a Certificate.

Wednesday the Court answered Franken by **scheduling a hearing** on the request for Thursday, Feb. 5th (next episode of Must See TV on TheUpTake!). **Coleman's team was also invited** to say their piece. **Defendants are Pawlenty and Ritchie,** so presumably they will also be represented at this hearing–I'm guessing by MN Attorney General Lori Swanson. So there will be some REAL MN legal talent showing how good they are in front of Alan Page and the Court. (I would guess Magnuson and G. Barry Anderson will again recuse themselves from this hearing and its deliberations due to their service on the State Canvassing Board.)

> Then, in order, the court set this schedule: Franken has to file more legal documents on Jan. 20, Coleman, Ritchie and the governor get until Jan. 26 to file their responses, and the court set a hearing for Feb. 5. *(MinnPost)*

Now barring a 1 2 3 TKO in Election Contest Court the Coleman-Franken action will be going on **parallel** with this Supreme Court hearing. I think the High Court could have called a fair catch and said they would wait for the results of the Contest Court, OR they could have fast-tracked this hearing and scheduled arguments BEFORE the Contest Court got rolling (even order the Contest Court to wait). Instead, they showed everyone WHY they are the SUPREMES: "We hold our hearings whenever we want 'cause you're in OUR House now."

This will also be an interesting test for both camps' legal teams: how strong are they? How deep is their bench? After all, the Contest Court suit will be absorbing huge amounts of energy and attention from Trimble/Knaak/Magnuson the Lesser and from Lillehaug/Elias/Pentelovitch The Slavic Computer Processor Chip.

Can both teams keep their "A" game going in front of Hayden, Reilly and Marben and also BRING their "A" game to the Supreme Court?

Folks, there's serious money to be made in providing after-midnight coffee, Red Bull, Mountain Dew, pizza, cinnamon rolls and the "24/7 Legal Research R Us" franchise shop across from Mickey's Diner. The Great Waters Brew Pub takeout window could crank out Brie & Green Apple Chicken or Walleye sandwiches for everybody; I would hope for such an important case you could take out some Mr. Smooth Dark Mild or a Black Watch Oak Stout.

Let the last Serious Word on the Franken Supreme Court filing be this elegant summation:

> It was fairly evident that the request for a certificate from Pawlenty and Ritchie was not a PR blunder, but a necessary formality to ripen their request to compel the certificate. There was never any doubt that neither the governor nor SoS would step out on the ledge and contravert the plain letter of Minnesota law. They're bound by it... unless the MN S. Ct concludes that Franken's argument is valid and the language has no effect for Federal congressional races.
>
> I don't expect either to budge unless and until the MN S. Ct. rules on the question, or until the contest is decided, whichever comes first. *(underwhelm)*

Hard Times for MN's Senior Senator

You know, while all this is going on in MN, in DC there's a Senate happening. Minnesotans have issues they need help with at a Senatorial level and the Gopher State is short-handed. So far the Senior Senator and her staff are coping but the strain is growing.

> ...That's left Democratic Sen. Amy Klobuchar and her staff as the state's only Senate conduit for Minnesotans looking for help fixing problems with Social Security, veteran's benefits, passports, international adoptions or other bureacratic hangups.
>
> Klobuchar's State Director Zach Rodvold said the staff has seen a noticeable uptick in demand for help. So much so that staff members not normally directed to constituent case work, such as frontline receptionists, are taking on those projects.
> *(Pioneer Press)*

Thursday Morning Minnesota Media

The ice log dropped against the apartment door turns out to be the Star Tribune, which continues to run letters to the editor complaining about Sunday's story on Norm's 14 re-fis in 12 years. Kazuba and Doyle's story from B1, jump to B5 outlines the Coleman 5 stage plan, quotes Knaak as saying "the wheels are coming off the Franken victory train" and that Al "has not won this campaign.."... depositions of various election officials begin today.

The ONLY thing mentioned from the Franken Camp in all this is the Coleman proposed stages are "really interesting." That's a quote and that's all Team Franken said. I think their silence is loud and has an almost Obama-esque calm to it. Should be exciting when it breaks...

OK this has been WAY long enough but I hope it catches you up on the latest from yust southeast of Lake Wobegon.

Shalom.

Briefly Put (We Have a Date)
January 16, 2009

Comments: 116   Recs: 104   Tips: 85

AP Reports Election Contest Court will open Wednesday, Jan. 21. Franken's Motion to Dismiss will be up first.

Election Contest Court – Episode VII

TODAY, this morning both camps are going to **meet with the 3-judge panel,** get acquainted and, hopefully, in a long meeting, hammer out some basics like starting date, various procedures, etc. Lord have mercy on the judges (and even though it's not yet the court, maybe they should bring along gavels) and grant them strength, because both sides sure don't want to come out of their corners and make nice.

Norm Coleman's legal team filed a 204-page brief for an Election Contest Civil trial on January 6. By MN Law such a contest for a statewide race is heard by a 3-judge panel and begins 20 days after filing--so in this case, by no later than January 26.

Yesterday Team Coleman came out with a proposed trial schedule. The best part was they proposed starting on the 21st, saving everyone 5 days from the state maximum. Otherwise they seem to want to slow walk everything and not really start doing courtroom stuff until Feb. 9th.

Yesterday Team Franken proposed a rather different schedule. They want to start on January 26 (conveniently a Monday, and the legal maximum to start) and then chew through EVERYTHING in 15 "trial days" (weekends off), about 7 1/2 days for each side, and finish on Feb. 13 (that's FRIDAY THE 13TH – could be a VERY unlucky day for Norm Coleman!)

So they propose starting later (boo!) but finishing (off Norm) by the same week Norm really wants to start. (Yay!)

Franken lead attorney Mark Elias had a few things to say about the Coleman case as his side released this timetable. Now lawyers are supposed to do this, prop up your own side and bomb the other side, so a lot of this is standard boilerplate lawyer talk, but still: Duplicate/double votes? Missing votes? "They don't have any evidence.."...

More richly, "They have a theory but they don't have a case.."...

Coleman's case as a whole "lacks specificity."

> In a normal trial, they would present their witnesses," Elias said. Instead he asserts that they want a process in which they can slow down the process so they can find more witnesses and evidence that might help Norm. "If the court grants this delay, it will place an enormous burden on the witnesses. Some witnesses were involved in multiple stages or phases of the recount process. They would have to appear multiple times. Courts don't order this type of trial except in extreme circumstances. *(BigE at MN Progressive Project)*

You know, it's boilerplate, but when boilerplate is TRUE does that land on the other side like a street sewer= lid frisbee? CLANG! And Elias DID, you know, focus on the FACTS, and the CASE.

By contrast from under that sewer lid Knaak & Trimble threw up their usual chaff: "Franken did not win the election/is not a Senator/not entitled to an Election Certificate/has an artificial lead."

Knaak did wriggle free from the lid long enough to get off one nasty shot that to my nose has a whiff of desperation to it. Why does this sound like the old lawyer advice to the new kid in the firm: "If you're strong on facts and weak on the law, pound the facts. If you're strong on the law and weak on facts, pound the law. If you're weak on both law and facts, pound the table!"

> Claiming the Franken side merely wants the three-judge panel to rubber-stamp the Canvassing Board, Knaak said, "It's an insult to the intelligence of these judges and a big whack-a-mole over the head to the voters of Minnesota whose votes have yet to be counted." *(MinnPost)*

Soooooo...Judges Hayden, Reilly and Marben? Good luck (and some of us would LOVE to be listening at the keyhole!)

Franken's Gift to Texas

You know Sen. Barbara Boxer's quote: "Elections have consequences"? YES THEY DO, even when they are still hung up in Election Contest Court. Earlier this week Senate Republicans threw Norm Coleman to the wolves by agreeing with Harry Reid on committee assignments and ratios based on a 59-41 party division. (They assume Coleman will NOT be back.)

Now comes word from the Minn Independent that Franken's election has echoed all the way down Interstate 35 from Minneapolis-St.Paul to the Dallas-Fort Worth form of Texas Twin Cities. Texas Gov. Rick "GoodHair" Perry's (R-Nutso) term ends in 2010. Texas R's have seen the Lone Star Democrats' rising strength (Noreiga's solid run vs. Cornyn; Obama's notable improvement over Kerry; and I think some improvements in the Texas Legislature—subject to better info). So they have been making serious noises to ask Senator Kay Bailey Hutchinson to step aside from her Senate seat (term runs to 2012) and run for Governor. Texas Dems admit defeating KayBay would be a Texas tall order.

But now it sounds like the lady Senator is feeling counter pressure to stay in the Senate and out of the Texas Gov. race. Seems if KayBay steps down and Goodhair appoints an interim the calculation is the interim could well LOSE the Senate seat (and give Democrats that 60th filibuster-busting seat) in a special election. Because Franken's seat puts Democrats at 59 seats the Repubs don't think they can spare her. Wow.

Friday Morning Minnesota Media

The now bankrupt *Star Trib* (filed chapter 11) has a couple of stories up. One from Mike Kaszuba recounts (!) the legal maneuvering leading up to this morning's meeting with the three-judge panel. It's pretty balanced but he does cite this from Franken's filing regarding trial schedule:

> "Now, with the new Senate addressing the Nation's urgent business, Coleman still is not entirely sure what his case is about, so he proposes multiple trials that would begin on February 2, 9 and 16," said a nine-page legal document filed by Franken. *(Star Tribune)*

Also, as noted yesterday (*ahem*!, WineRev grins, takes small bow) Coleman proposes the trial in stages and at each stage could possibly cut it short if a "sufficient number of votes" ain't happening to swing Norm's way. I said that could be Norm's undoing if he hits the first hurdle and does a face plant instead of clearing it. Kaszuba reports somebody asked Tony Trimble if that is so:

> In court documents, (Coleman's) campaign said it might cut the trial short if any stage did not produce a "sufficient number of votes" needed to overcome Franken's lead.
>
> But Coleman attorney Tony Trimble downplayed the significance of that language. "No, no, it's not saying that," he said when asked whether the language indicated Coleman would continue only if he saw he was gaining enough votes.
>
> "It's saying that we want to conquer the biggest territory first [rejected absentee ballots] and, obviously, if we do well in that, we continue to move on. ... You can read a lot of things into it." (Star Tribune)

Tony, yes we can! And I think you're pounding the table some more. ("Methinks he doth protest too much.")

Also, the US Senate unanimously passed a resolution to allow Coleman's FORMER Senate office to be unlocked and reopened to Coleman's staff so they can archive files and arrange to send pending constituent issues and cases over to Sen. Amy Klobuchar's office, or in some cases, to members of the MN House delegation. Norm had asked for this for 60 days; Senate granted through Feb. 4.

And that's it. Really. It's so cold again I think even newsmakers are frozen up (although today's meeting with the 3 judges should thaw out LOTS of fingers and toes.) But for the moment that's the latest from yust southeast of Lake Wobegon.

Shalom.

Gone Courting
January 17, 2009

| Comments: | 31 | Recs: | 41 | Tips: | 44 |

You name a court in Minnesota yesterday and they probably issued some motion, order or ruling regarding the Franken-Coleman Senate contest. (Wadena County Traffic Court: "Guilty of aggravated snowmobile parking. $75 fine payable to either Coleman or Franken legal defense fund.")

For all you fans of *Law & Order* each segment opens with that cool, hollow, gavel-banging sound run through a Moog synthesizer "Tung-tong!" You can hear it all through today's diary.

Election Contest Court - Episode VIII

The last few days we've had dueling schedules for the ECC. Norm wanted to (kind of) start on the 21st, but not really until the 9th of Feb. Al wanted to start on the last starting date of the 26th of January but reach an end by FRIDAY the 13th. They both have ideas on how the trial should be run and both know the other side's ideas are wrong.

Well, guess what? The ECC heard both sides and then said, "We have our OWN ideas! And since we are the ECC, they are now YOUR ideas too!"

Up until now all we knew for sure was the deadline for starting the Election Contest suit in front of the 3-judge panel January 26. Friday morning both sides' legal teams met with each other and with the panel of Hayden, Reilly, and Marben for about an hour. The Election Contest Court *(ECC; has a Continental ring to it you know; Le Court di Eleczzione fur Kontestische Senatorii?)* issued a scheduling order and I have put them in chronological order because I'm so pro-time-line I'm actually... calendric (sounds like a KOS user/ screen name).

Contestant = Coleman. Contestee = Franken

"Tung-tong"

Monday, Jan. 19 (Legal holiday! But I would hope the ghost of Dr. King would understand working on his birthday.)

"Contestant's (Norm's) Answer to Contestee's (Al's) Counterclaims must be served (to Al) and filed (in court) by 4:30pm."

"Contestant's (Norm's) response to Contestees' (Al's) discovery requests must be served (to Al) and filed (in court) by 4:30pm."

That is, Franken gets to mount his own case (counterclaims) and Coleman has to respond by this deadline. *(To lawyers in the house, if you don't respond to a counterclaim does it then stand and win by default?)*

And if my many episodes of *Law & Order* are any help "discovery" means you get to look at the other side's documents, witness list, forensic data and stuff like that, am I right? Unfortunately this does cut down on the great Perry Mason move of "calling a surprise witness" and just kills the drama..rats. Anyway this is all due Monday, or barely 2 days from RIGHT NOW. So both of these items have Coleman's team of Trimble, Knaak & Magnuson the Lesser earning their fees this weekend. (More to the point their staffs are going to be drinking a lot of coffee & Dew in the next 48 hours.)

"Tung-tong"

Tuesday, Jan. 20 (Freedom Day starts at High Noon! Free from Bush! Free From Cheney, Free From Rice, Free From Proto-Fascists! "Free at last, free at last, thank God Almighty we are free at last!!")

"(Both sides) shall disclose the identity of all experts to be called at trial and the substance of the facts and opinions upon which they rely by 4:30pm."

So both sides have to tell the other and the court: "Horatio Caine, Dr. Quincy M.E., MacGyver, Dr. Lazareth and Graptar's Hammer, Gray's Anatomy of the Horse, and the 1957 Betty Crocker Cookbook." Again, it cuts down on surprise witnesses, but lets each side argue at trial from the same evidence: "Yes the defendant WAS found with Exhibit D, a bloody knife in his hand. Furthermore we stipulate his fingerprints Exhibit G, are on the knife handle..., but he's a union meatcutter and was on duty at the time...so?"

In this case I think any county election director would count as an expert witness; any other guesses? "Substance of facts and opinions" seems to me would certainly include the *Election Judge's Manual* put out by the Secretary of State's office for starters and sections of MN election law that underlies it. Other stuff?

"Tung-tong"

Wednesday, Jan. 21 (First Full Day of the Restoration of Constitutional Democracy; in honor of that Constitution:)

"The hearing on Contestee's (Franken's) motion to dismiss is scheduled for 2:30pm at the Minnesota Judicial Center."

NOW we're talking (or they are!). Norm filed his suit Jan. 6. Franken's team filed **motion to dismiss** Coleman's whole load o' lutefisk. Of course in our dreams not only does the Court agree to dismiss, but dismisses WITH PREJUDICE (Judge Marben: "You dragged me 71 hours by buffalo sled from Pennington County to listen to this?? Get outta here!") so Norm CAN'T refile. Throw it all out? I doubt it, but it could be great argumentation.

ALSO WEDNESDAY:

"Any briefs or motions filed in connection with any motions for summary judgment must be served and filed by 4:30pm."

Both sides have this deadline for written arguments pro and con regarding the **"summary judgment"** portion of Coleman's suit.

If I understand this correctly this is Coleman's home run hope, that the Court is SO impressed with the Coleman filing and feels the weight of their affidavits and the sheer justice and righteousness of Norm the Coleman that they decide "What further need have we of witnesses?" and rule in his favor on the spot.

...HAHAHAHAHAHHAHAHAHAHAHHAHAHAHAHHAHAHAHHAHA! Anyone who believes this has obviously found the purely mythical lifetime supply of Hunter Thompson's pharmaceutical life enhancements...

"Tung-tong"

Friday, January 23 (First Chance to TGIF Party in a Real Presidency! If you can't wait for after work, tune it to the Uptake to watch):

"The hearing on any motions for summary judgment is at 9:00am at the Minnesota Judicial Center."

OK *reading* the motions and briefs for/against summary judgment is fun but now they are going to argue it orally! And with straight faces! Really? How will Elias, Lillehaug & Pentelovitch keep from blowing their cuspids across the room? I mean can that much laughter really be suppressed for that long?

And after this is over:

"A pre-trial status conference shall be held... following the hearing on any motions for summary judgment."

It will be a busy week for both sides and the Court and this sounds like a nice way for all three sides to check in after the snowballs have flown.

"Tung-tong"

And then **Monday, January 26"**

"The trial in this matter shall begin on January 26, 2009 at the Minnesota Judicial Center."

Voiceover: "In the justice system two groups serve the public: those who think they get everything because they're babies, and the grown ups. In Minnesota election crimes are considered especially heinous. An elite squad of judges tries those cases. This is their story".

Coleman adds lawyer

Friedberg, Joseph. born 1937. U North Carolina 1959; JD, UNC, 1963, with honors. Order of Coif. Best Oralist, Jessup Competition, '63. Fellow, American College of Trial Lawyers. Admitted: MN bar, 1966; US Supreme Ct, 1974. Lots of credits/honors/ associations in criminal law.[7]

Norm doesn't have enough lawyers, poor guy. So he's hired on Joe Friedberg, who wasted no time sight-reading the "Anthem for Norm" song sheet for a 5-part, dragged-out trial:

> "Since there are multiple issues in this case, you pretty much have to know what issue you're going to try first," said Joe Friedberg, who is the newest face on the Republican's legal team. (Huffington Post)

Friedberg is not all that new to Norm... or Laurie Coleman. Turns out Friedberg is also Nasser Kazeminy's lawyer, and Kazeminy is the guy being investigated for providing Norm some great suits...and great free flights on a private jet...and great vacation trips... $75,000 to Laurie Coleman for "salary."...or something.

I wondered several diaries ago if either side might bring in a "ringer" for the trial portion. Looks like here's a partial answer. According to the *Star Trib* Freidberg will "take the lead" on the team of Knaak and Trimble—and I think this means in ECC, so we'll hear from him a LOT.

DK
> The selection of Joe Friedberg is interesting. Knaak and company ARE trial lawyers. Knaak has tried election contests before. Then why go with Friedberg-who is a very good CRIMINAL trial attorney. As he admits, he doesn't know election law. Does he have time to crash course it before January 16? Probably. But he won't have the knowledge that Elias and team have. Is this a signal that Coleman is doubting his legal team? I think probably... *(beastiemom)*

DK
> Coleman Grasping Straws? Is this a signal that Coleman is doubting his legal team? I think probably. I think most definitely. I read this as Coleman in full panic mode. His legal team has been sloppy, out thought and out lawyered. This is a desperation move. *(feebog)*

Will Team Franken counter? Or will they go with who they have right now? Both Elias & Pentelovitch seem to know their way around a courtroom. Will Lillehaug take a turn at bat? Or with their so far typical long-range planning does Team Franken already have their OWN trial pro already on retainer and will bring him or her out at the right moment? Stay tuned!

---

7   *Information from Lawyers.com*

Saturday Morning Minnesota Media

Kevin Duchschere gets an A1 column above the fold and a jump to A8, leading with the arrival of Joe Friedberg on Norm's legal team. Lots of stuff from Freidberg on how he thinks the trial could/should happen with very little balancing input from Franken's side. Not a pro-Norm piece by any means but an unusual angle on it, taking advantage of a fresh face on the scene.

Friedberg said "I don't know my election law and it looks like you've already got about 100 lawyers" and that Norm answered "Very few of them are trial lawyers." Hmmmm... sounds a little last-minute there, Norm...

There WAS one quote from Franken's main man David Lillehaug. (A rare sighting, so notable):

> Lillehaug, one of Franken's lawyers, said that the judges discussed the technicalities of the trial, such as motions and discovery, and how it should proceed.
>
> "Minnesota has an empty seat in the United States Senate, and the judges did comment that they thought this should be handled expeditiously," Lillehaug said. (MinnPost)

OK, I've actually got the day off so I'll be here with coffee and my bowl of oatmeal to ward off the "eh, so what" +3 outside. That's the latest for the moment from yust southeast of Lake Wobegon.

Shalom.

Inauguration Timeout & Ludwig
January 19, 2009

Comments: 23   Recs: 35   Tips: 28

WineRev's vivid imagination allows him to transport himself to Hyde Park, London: Speaker's Corner. (This country NEEDS an equivalent of Speaker's Corner!) He climbs on his soapbox to rant once more against the departing hyenas of Bush/Cheney. Then he will break into song for my country, your country, our country, so we can renew the promise of this land. (Despite his non-black, non-Baptist heritage, WineRev will gladly accept "amens", "hallelujahs", recommends if worthy, and the odd "preach it, brother" without being thrown off stride. *Clears throat, draws and points sword toward hyenas...*)

Out, Out Damned Spot!

The scheme of things today and tomorrow includes perhaps the most significant transition of American political power in the last century or more. At noon tomorrow a criminal mal-administration leaves power, not in blood (and as a peaceful man these skunk-jackals have driven me to the point of willing to entertain bloodletting) and not in chains (as they most richly merit) but they are **going**.

They are a dung-fly complot that has trampled the Constitution and looted the public Treasury for themselves and allies on Wall Street and international finance. They have subverted the law and suborned the federal judiciary and US attorneys to enforce their power, not do justice. They have treated the personal lives and private communications of Americans as criminals or slaves. They have attacked their domestic foes not with brownshirts in the streets but with anthrax in the mail, with persecution and jailing of governors, with interrogations and perverted medical science upon those they accuse. All this has been paid for by stupendous amounts of cash flowing as an acid bath of corruption among members of Congress, filling the pockets of Halliburton, crushing hope, dignity and perhaps life itself in the Marianas Islands of the Pacific.

By their illegal orders this pig sty cabal have murdered (*with malice aforethought murdered*) over 4,000 members of the American military in a war of self-aggrandizement, spat upon tens of thousands of wounded by refusing to properly treat their hurts, and treated veteran survivors of their malfeasance with contempt and scorn by denying them benefits, care or honor. They have taken funds, weapons and superior equipment from American soldiers, sailors, marines and airmen and given them to the mercenaries and soldiers of fortune of Blackwater, Inc. They have flung America's international reputation beaten and bleeding into the gutter of a delusional "war on terror."

This persiferous host has castrated the press into cuckolded sloths or raging Fox-agandists who defend the junta with cries of treason and disloyalty, just like their teacher Goebbels did for his regime. Their staging of Jessica Lynch's rescue and [the] suspicious death of Pat Tillman exceed in sheer gall and effrontery anything Lili Riefenstahl attempted.

This camarilla of machinations fulfilled to a high degree Sinclair Lewis' prophecy that when fascism comes to America it will come carrying the Cross wrapped in the American flag. Their religious leaders (morally reprobate hypocrites and financially flush liars who desecrate their God) have ignored all the scripture and tradition they claim to honor and re-enact all the disastrous acts of their wicked forebears. By their vacuous and contemptible blessing of secular power for unquestioned and unexamined ends they have added to the doleful human catalog of horrors done in the name of God that produced the Inquisition, the Hundred Years War, the 30 Years War, the Salem witch-trials and the Rhode Island Quaker hangings.

But they are going! and that is historic.

And there is not just their OUT-auguration.

(WineRev sheathes sword; doffs (DOFFS!) hat toward Lincoln Memorial)

My Country, 'Tis of Thee

Inauguration is at hand – the swearing in of a President. Presidents have been sworn in at various places (New York City for Washington, Dallas for Lyndon Johnson) and with various ceremonies (Jefferson and some friends rode their horses at a walk from the Capitol down to the White House while bystanders waved their hats, thus inventing the Inauguration Day parade.)

For the first time the American Presidency will be held by a man of African origins. While we can hope and work for the day when such an identification is no longer necessary that time is not yet. So we settle for a milestone...and what a milestone!

It is a GREAT day for all Americans but ESPECIALLY for Americans of African heritage. That heritage began in bondage in 1619, and continued in torment through the death of Crispus Attucks in 1770. That heritage includes the insult of being counted as 3/5 of a person by the Constitution of 1787, and reached a pit in 1857 when the Supreme Court declared Dred Scott and his people were not persons.

But in 1860 America began to live down her shame by electing a man from Illinois who held slavery should expand no further. Even this restraint was too much for slaveholders, and our Civil War began. In 1863 Abraham Lincoln declared as of January 1 all persons (Fie on you, Supreme Court!) held in bondage after this date would be "thenceforward and forever free," and he became the Great Emancipator.

Come Tuesday I will be at work but I will sneak looks at the ceremony, the swearing-in, a moment of fulfillment of the Emancipation Proclamation, the 13th, 14th and 15th Amendments. This day does not erase the bite marks of the German shepherds of Birmingham; it does not absolve the lynchings, nor does it excuse the cloud of endless indignities and cruelties...but it helps. This day is a huge shovel of dirt on the grave of Jim Crow.

I want the DVD of another man from Illinois becoming President. I want to take this in so DEEP that when I am ancient and my great-grandchildren look at my fading face, they will see tears as I tell them I saw history happen.

And come Tuesday, as on my last day on earth (68 years or so from now ;-)), I know the music ringing in my head will of course be Beethoven, the mighty 9th Symphony. WineRev is a pretty fair bass-baritone and it has been a lifelong dream to sing the solo part from the Ninth... not the whole thing, but right at the start of the choral section.

Partway into the 4th movement there is a storm of music: outraged trumpets, livid flutes, incensed cellos, bellicose tympanii, the whole orchestra having a furious musical seizure, like the Devil raging because a little person feeds a stray puppy. In his margin notes Beethoven wrote the baritone steps up and *"rebukes"* the orchestra. *("Rebukes!" as in "Shut up!/Go to hell!/Knock it off/You unbelievable bastard." And in Beethoven's native German..."Rebukes!" That must be deafening! Utterly cliff-collapsing, battleship Bismarck thunderous!)*

Yep, that's me. That's what I want to sing. *Rebuking* the rulers of the last 8 years: *(WineRev to crowd:)* "O Fri–ends," *(WineRev pivots toward outgoing gangsters and points)* "NOT these dreary tones!" *(Glares at Cheney. Spits toward Bush. Shakes fist at Condi, Rumsfeld, Addington, Feith, Gonzales, Rove...and I NEVER, in my life threatened a woman, so Condi, you're a personal first...)*

(Turns back to crowd)"Let us rather raise more dulcet tunes! ...Joy! *(Joyful!)*...Joy! *(Joyful!)*" ...and then the whole thing unrolls, a wonderful theme, a new administration, the Restoration, the Rekindling of hope, American History renewed. "O daughters of Elysium... All mankind shall be as brothers/ 'Neath thy tender wings and wide..."

I know, I know. We're not there yet. But we've got to keep moving that way, and Tuesday is a marker on the way. I'd like to make one circle around the Lincoln Memorial lay a single rose of apology next to a broken set of leg shackles, ask forgiveness from all the holies, and then keep on going. I hope America will too.

Shalom.

Ice Fishing for votes
January 20, 2009

Comments: 19   Recs: 29   Tips: 34

Inauguration Day. Both the End of an Error (as some Kossack as put it) and a milestone for human progress, American Division.

Although Scandinavian Lutherans tend to be rather reserved Christians (some wag has named them not "God's Chosen People" but "God's Frozen People") this is a day to stand on the pews, throw hymnals in the air and have the organist pull out one of those intricate scores that look like an inkwell was dumped in front of a fan and the spray captured on staff paper. (The final chord has a margin note: "organist throws body on entire keyboard except for middle C.")

Great God Almighty what a day!

Count Every Vote! So Says...Norm?

Monday the Coleman Legal Team decided their best friends in the Senate ECC case are...12,000 rejected absentee ballots. What? That's right. Having fought like a drunken moose for weeks over all 5 piles of rejected absentee ballots, having been given power by the MN Supreme Court to veto improperly rejected absentee ballots (the infamous "5th pile") and having had a hand (along with county officials and Franken's people too) in blocking about 392 5th pile ballots from being counted, NOW Coleman attorney Fritz Knaak has guts of iron to stand up in front of the press and say:

> Obviously, not every one of the 12,000 rejected absentee ballots was wrongfully rejected. ...If the absentee voter was alive on Election Day, and did not otherwise vote, then his or her absentee ballot should be counted — if the voter's intent can be determined from the ballot. *(from press conference, quoted in Power Line)*

(Strikes Dana Carvey puckered face pose:) "Well isn't that special!"

It's also a sign of weakness from the Coleman side and they're trying to put the best face on it by wrapping themselves in a "count every vote" absentee ballot outer envelope.

Two reasons:

1. Ever since the Canvassing Board made it clear they were going to count as many "5th pile" **improperly** rejected absentee ballots as agreed to by both sides (that was that run of 954 on 1/3 that raised Franken's lead from +49 to +225) the Coleman camp has been trying to shoehorn in their pack of 654 other **properly** rejected absentee ballots (that is, those rejected for one of the 4

statutory reasons, ie. "piles 1-4"). They have cherry-picked these from (in the words of attorney Tony Trimble) "precincts that by coincidence" happened to heavily favor Coleman on the non-absentee side. These 654 cherries also figure prominently in the ECC case opening Monday the 26th – they have to because the other fragments of Coleman's case are so weak they don't add up to enough votes to overtake Franken's 225 lead. So in bridge terms here they are leading out a queen of clubs against a dummy that shows ace-king of clubs...unless a ruffing miracle occurs the queen is toast.

2. This also interlocks with a second Coleman case weakness. Everyone with even a lizard brain has pointed out how hopeless Coleman's chances are in getting **any** semi-fair body (Canvassing Board, ECC, MN Supreme Court, even any federal circuit court slobbering over "equal protection") to agree to only count his 654 cherries without looking at ALL 12,000 rejected absentee ballots in all 5 piles, especially the 1st 4 piles. It's second guessing local election officials who ARE empowered by law to determine the status of absentee ballots. It also undercuts Coleman's OWN representatives who were present at every sorting of these same 12,000, starting on election day. And it sure as shootin' ain't equal treatment of a class of ballots.

So Monday they shuffled their hand, did a major pivot and yanked a used "Count Every Vote" sign out of some Franken supporter's backpack while the DFH was eating his yogurt and granola and said, "Let's look at all 12,000 and count every vote!"

...NO, they didn't say that EITHER, they just want you to THINK they did. "If a voter was alive"...OK Fritz I'll give you that one..."registered voter or registration card" (Pile 3)..."Did not otherwise vote" (Pile 4)..."if voter intent can be determined" (like if the oval is filed in and no stray marks? Shouldn't be hard, and Fritz? Nice quote of the legal standard: "voter intent.")

That's it? No pile 1 (name and address have to match between absentee application and absentee ballot)? No pile 2 (signatures have to match... including those 17 absentee ballots in Anoka County that have NO signature at all but Norm wants counted?

Nope it won't go. The Coleman ice-fishing hut is definitely tilted to one side and is slipping through a too-large fishing hole. First, if Team Coleman starts to get ANY traction on any of this the ECC is going to whip out those 64 absentee ballots of the 392 pile 5 that the Franken campaign is aiding and abetting. The Supreme Court handed them that scroll and the ECC court will unroll that pack of 64 like TP on a high school quarterback's house on a Thursday night and say to Team Coleman "Let's count these!" Franken could get +64 right on the spot, putting him at +289.

Then the remaining 392-64= 328 "5th pile" would be fair game and Franken could net a +30 without trying, so +319.

I can't see it. I think in an odd way this move actually increases (slightly) the chance that the ECC will move to dismiss Coleman's case. Franken has filed a **Motion to Dismiss** the whole bathtub full of lutefisk. Coleman has to show the pieces of his case (the 133 "missing" but accounted for Minneapolis ballots, the supposed 100-150 duplicate/double-counted ballots that are still riding around in the trunk of Fritz Knaak's car, since that's where all imaginary ballots hang out, and his 654 cherries) all add up to enough ballots to potentially overtake Franken's +225 margin.

But if the only way he can get in the 654 is to open the door to the other 12,000 absentees (which right off the top put 64 and 328 in play in a way that doesn't help Norm) all Team Franken has to do (a tall order to be sure) is to pound home the impossibility of Norm's position and so "Why waste everybody's time and Norm's money? Dismiss and let's move on." I still really don't think the ECC will dismiss, but I'd say the chances have maybe gone from 3% to 10% (9-1 against, but I like the trend.) As has been said often here, "We'll see."

And by the way the Franken side sounded like they smelled fresh lefse coming off the griddle:

> Andy Barr, Franken spokesperson: "We're not going to respond to any proposal they make until they figure out what, exactly, their proposal is...the shake-up of the Coleman legal team (adding Joe Friedberg) has resulted in even more confusion on their side.
>
> Yesterday (Sunday), one set of their attorneys proposed to our attorneys that they wanted all 11,000 rejected absentee ballots to be counted, regardless of whether

they'd been correctly rejected or not. And today, another set of their attorneys are telling the press that they want all 12,000 rejected absentee ballots to be reviewed by some other process." *(Star Tribune)*

Chessboard: Exchange of Pieces

When my Dad and Uncle Sigi would play they would make a couple moves early and then stare at the board for a while. Then they started swapping pieces. I always thought that was the best part of the game. Well the pieces aren't coming off the board but they sure are moving and talking!

The MinnPost play by play started at 3:26, Knaak & Trimble, knight & demoted rook for Coleman:

"We went back and looked at the other 11,000 [rejected absentee ballots] and convinced ourselves that there are many, many thousands, perhaps as many as 6,000 or 7,000 additional envelopes and ballots, that will be opened."

Trimble wants the judges to "re-examine every envelope again ... We have the right to bring these envelopes" to the three judges (of the ECC), he said. *(MinnPost)*

4:19, Andy Barr, pawn on the scathing diagonal for Franken:

"First the Coleman campaign said there were no wrongly rejected absentee ballots,"..."Then they said there might be a 'handful.'

"Then they went to court to stop any of them from being reviewed and counted. Then they rejected our proposal to count all the ballots identified by county elections officials as having been wrongly rejected.

"Then in their election contest, they questioned whether the court should ignore the 950 ballots that had been reviewed and counted by a process they'd agreed to – and substitute 650 ballots they pulled from thin air." *(MinnPost)*

5:41, Mark Drake, pawn on the straight ahead block for Coleman:

"It tells you a lot ... It tells you they're not really interested in every vote counting. They're interested in distracting and interested in the Franken area votes counting only." *(MinnPost)*

Media New & Old

All of them together! Just when you're ready to write off journalism as a waste of time, all of a sudden someone flips a switch and a major magnetic force field springs to life. "There's NEWS happenin' here."

They all line up: a perky Lois Lane chopping away at the microwave sized Royal; the hard-bitten police reporter clacking 2 fingers across the keyboard of a battered Underwood and a dead cigarette seccotined at the corner of his mouth; the camera hound getting a long-range shot of a helicopter loading on a Saigon roof; and (according to oppressors) the damned video cameras of citizens like the UpTake with an unblinking roll of tape or flash drive as Mike McIntee dares to ask the Coleman campaign to treat them with respect – ALL of them agree:

The Coleman-Franken trial is NEWS! *Consider* this list: the Minneapolis Star Tribune, the St. Paul Pioneer Press, WCCO, KARE, KSTP, KMSP TV stations, Minnesota Public Radio, the Minnesota Newspaper Association; the Minnesota Broadcasters Association; the Society of Professional Journalists; the Minnesota AP Association; and the Minnesota AP Broadcasters. All of them have signed a joint letter to the 3 judge panel of Hayden, Reilly and Marben asking **permission to have live cameras** in the courtroom for the Election Contest Court (ECC). They've asked for trial coverage; unclear if this also includes pre-trial motions (like the first arguments starting this Wednesday.)

Minnesota is more restrictive than most states allowing cameras in the courtroom although it's possible: we all got to watch Magnuson the Lesser and Pentelovitch argue a couple times in front of the Minnesota Supreme Court in the last couple months. (That WAS the Supreme Court and apparently there's a difference between the original trial – where all sorts of salacious or gruesome exhibits and testimony can happen, and the appeals level, where it's much more about the law and procedure rather than the evidence per se.) The rule is the court and both sides have to agree to allow such broadcasting. It looks like both the Coleman and Franken camps are on board (YAY! to both sides! Nice move, gentlemen! Well done.) so it's up to the court. This linked article hints that presiding Judge Hayden may well be on board.

Odds & Ends

US Senate Republicans chopped a hole in the ice of Lake Calhoun and dropped Coleman in there. That is, in negotiations on committee assignments and ratios they assumed a 59-41 split (i.e. NO Coleman.) Last week you also read here about the implications that has had on the Texas Governor's race.

Now the LameStream Media's Howard Fineman has a column up **ASSUMING Franken is IN** and urging Al to do in the US Senate exactly what he's been doing to get elected. This passes for news and wisdom in DC. I mean, being true to oneself, consistent, UN-hypocritical, principled, acting honorably and Constitutionally, providing good constituent service and honestly debating over the best means to advance the common good...WHO could be against any of THAT?

...Well, after the last 8 years of storm-troopers...?

Norm Coleman and his new lawyer Joe Friedberg have more in common than Nasser Kazeminy being their one degree of separation. Word is they've known each other better than 30 years and that the Coleman clan has been **using Friedberg's legal services** for some time:

> Friedberg, a longtime friend of Coleman's who said Coleman once came to his aid in a bar fight years ago, also represented Coleman's late father in a police matter. *(Star Tribune)*

Friedberg was in a bar fight? I gotta admit that's my kind of lawyer. And what exactly did Norm do? Kick the combatants apart? (Wouldn't want to risk those teeth... or maybe he did and that's why the current set of choppers?) And Coleman's Dad just a few years ago was rather in a situation *en flagrante*. Anyway it's a long standing relationship between Norm and Joe. Another snippet:

> That would make (attorney Joe) Friedberg Coleman's most important supporter. Except he's not a supporter. Friedberg's a Democrat, and he often disagrees with his friend's politics.
>
> "I would do anything for Norm, except vote for him," Friedberg said in a Pioneer Press interview before the election. "And I've told him that." *(Pioneer Press)*

Tuesday Morning Minnesota Media

Doyle & Kaszuba *(NOT attorneys-at-law; hmmmm... can you BE an attorney-at-something else?)* get only lower left corner of the *StarTrib* front page because some guy from Illinois is changing jobs today. D&K tell readers:

> The latest move also revealed the about-face both campaigns have made over the past month: When Coleman held an unofficial lead in the recount last month, his lawyers argued before the Minnesota Supreme Court that rejected absentee should not be part of the recount. Now, with Franken holding a lead gained in part by successfully arguing to include some rejected absentee ballots, the Franken campaign reacted coolly to reconsidering all 12,000 rejected absentee ballots. *(Star Tribune)*

Except... Franken's position hasn't changed. Only Norm's view has flopped across the ice like a just-caught 8 lb. crappie.

...A Hamline law professor and others think Coleman is moving this way in order to set up a FEDERAL court case once the ECC and/or the MN Supreme CT rule against him...still a maddening lack of specifics in Coleman's case (as in: "These 6 ballots from Otter Tail County should/should not be counted because..."), giving strength to the Franken defense that the ECC need not go on a fishing expedition...

> "What Coleman is trying to do is go through the whole universe of ballots to find more votes, there's no doubt about that," said Duke law Prof. Guy-Uriel Charles, an expert on election law. "I think they are going to press the Coleman camp to really figure out what are the ballots that are in dispute, and to focus on those. If you do have this sort of wide-ranging inquiry, we won't know what happens until April." *(Star Tribune)*

No wonder Al is in DC these days doing fund-raisers...

And why all this noisy maneuvering the last couple days? Well, other than helping your WineRev write a better diary,

> "Both sides are trying to intimidate the court," said Charles. "I think the court needs to quickly establish who's in control here, and say, 'This is what we're going to focus on, this is what the timeline is going to be. And if you don't like it, then you can appeal.'"
>
> One indication that the three judges took a dim view of Coleman's proposed court schedule was the panel's ruling Friday that trial would begin Jan. 26, not Feb. 9, as the Republican suggested. *(Star Tribune)*

Yeah, well I don't get the impression *both sides* are trying to intimidate the State Canvassing Board, local officials (except for 1 ugly 2-sided spat when 133 ballots went missing in a Lutheran church polling place in Mpls.), the ECC or the MN Supreme Ct. I get the feeling ONE side is, and a whole string of 0-5, 0-5, 0-5 decisions so far says that ONE side isn't doing very well with bluster and show.

Well gotta get to the shop in a few minutes and keep sneaking peaks at the DC news. Hope this will hold you with all the latest from yust southeast of Lake Wobegon.

Shalom.

"May it Please the Court…"
January 21, 2009

Comments: 116   Recs: 274   Tips: 231

All legal hands on deck! Today we go to Court. The **Election Contest Court (the ECC)** holds its first public hearing TODAY at 2:30pm.

Coleman Legal Team Gets Pushy

As in legally pushy. Tuesday the Coleman campaign said they want a **subpoena for a deposition** from Gary Poser. Poser works in Secretary of State's Mark Ritchie as the statewide director of elections, sort of the inside, nutsy-boltsy guy. If you were watching when the 954 "5th pile" ballots got counted (after a 7 hour wait) it was Gary Poser who got to flip over the ballots one by one and sift them into piles saying, "Franken, Franken, Franken, Franken, Barkley, Franken, Lizard, Franken, Coleman, Coleman, Franken…"

Anyway the Coleman Team wants a deposition from Poser claiming Coleman might be missing 10 to 15 votes because of discrepancies between local totals and the totals the Sec. of State posted on their website.

It is unclear how Poser will respond, or even if he will have to. First, MN Attorney General Lori Swanson came out [and] said she thought Poser should resist a subpoena. Second, Team Franken filed a motion to quash subpoena.

Team Coleman retreated just slightly and said if they didn't get a deposition (a sworn conversation beforehand) they would call Poser in the trial beginning Monday.

Meanwhile, Due Monday the 19th…

Attention all teachers and project managers! Do you set deadlines? "Turn in the answers to page 36 on Tuesday morning"? "I need an estimate on how many cubic yards of concrete for the phase 2 foundation by the 16th, Francine."?

And what happens if someone misses a deadline? "You get a "0" Bobby." "Dammit Francine! I'm sending you to our Provo office!"

Now Knaak, Trimble, Magnuson and Friedberg have been busy looking at 12,000 absentee ballots, figuring out how to repeal certain sections of MN election law, and getting a subpoena ready for Gary Poser. BUT they seem to have forgotten something:

Last Friday the 16th the ECC ordered a set of dates and motions leading up to the opening date of trial on the 26th. And *these* were top of the **Legal/Lawyer To-Do list** for MONDAY, January 19th. *You know,* **2 days ago?**

"Contestant's (Norm's) Answer to Contestee's (Al's) Counterclaims must be served (to AL) and filed (in court) by 4:30pm."

"Contestant's (Norm's) response to Contestees' (Al's) discovery requests must be served (to Al) and filed (in court) by 4:30pm."

That is, Franken gets to mount his own case (counterclaims) and Coleman has to respond by this deadline.

My question: Do Franken's **unanswered** counterclaims stand and/or win by default? And I add, how does a court look upon one of the parties that does not turn in their homework? Can they give extensions? Make up work? Impose sanctions? Rule summarily for the other side?

From all indications late Tuesday night the Coleman side **has NOT responded** to the Franken Counterclaims as ordered by the court. Is there a penalty or range of penalties?

I can't wait to hear what the ECC has to say!

Making Money Off the Inauguration

Al Franken was in DC for the Inauguration and doing some fund raising at a $/plate dinner. He also sent out a beggar letter to his mailing list to keep the money flowing for legal costs.

Norm Coleman's people are also raising money for their side of the courtroom and likewise sent out a beggar letter to their supporters. You've seen plenty of these so the language is pretty standard, just tweaked enough to recent events to keep it fresh.

That said, Coleman's letter is showing, well, a lot of Brooklyn NOIVE *(as Nahm would say in his native accent)* in the lines in original italics:

> Today marks an historic occasion for each and every American, from all backgrounds, all political philosophies and all walks of life. We all wish our new President well, and we will support him when we agree with him and be the voice of the loyal opposition when we do not.
>
> Unfortunately, the kind of change that President Barack Obama brings to Washington is worlds apart from the kind of change that Al Franken is seeking here in Minnesota.
>
> *Barack Obama won a majority of our nation's votes fair and square. Al Franken had to change the rules of the game to overturn our victory.*
>
> *Barack Obama was elected based on the principle of one person - one vote. Franken's lead exists because some votes were counted twice, while others weren't counted at all.*
>
> Franken's coordinated attempt to silence voices must not stand. But it might, unless I hear from you soon.
>
> Click here now to contribute $15, $25, $35, $50, $100 or more - up to $2,300 per person - to the Coleman for Senate Recount Fund. *(from the Coleman for Senate website)*

The Coleman Legal Team:
"With Friends like these, Norm..."

How good are they? They've certainly seemed tin-eared and lead-footed several times during this recount. Their reversals have been violent enough to burn out an alternator.

A blogger at the UpTake:

> If I had a penny for every position Coleman has flipped on during this recount, I'd be a millionaire. *(ct-dem)*

Legally trained Kossacks and others who have read through their various legal filings have called some of their work sloppy, with basic mistakes citing incorrect sections of MN law and bad spelling.

WE have NOT been impressed, or even confused:

> but see according to Coleman, the process is only fair and legal if they are in the lead. *(ct-dem at The UpTake)*

> Ok, so it seems to me that is a particularly dumb claim for the Coleman team to make *(northernMNer at The UpTake)*

And this elegant remark from the *Star Trib* comment string:

> I'm truly in favor of Mr. Coleman getting a fair hearing on his election contest. If he doesn't it will be his attorneys' fault for casting so wide a net for something - anything at all will do - to hang his legal challenge on. Each move they makes seems to imply more and more that they don't have any substantive or procedural evidence to justify overturning the current result in favor of Mr. Franken. *(Star Tribune online)*

But HEY, that's just us! Has the **Coleman Legal Team** impressed their supporters? *Power Line*, which publishes Hinderaker for cryin' out loud, has a typical, ...um..."Point of View" piece knocking both sides for their reversals on absentee ballots. Yet even THEY think Coleman is nuts trying to overturn MN law over the 12,000 absentee ballots (piles 1-5). Then they wind up with this great bit:

> Until yesterday, the Coleman campaign sought the inclusion only of other absentee ballots it claimed had been improperly excluded by local officials. Prior to the election contest, the Coleman campaign had no problem with the requirements imposed by Minnesota's absentee ballot statute. Now the requirements of Minnesota law are unfair! They are an impediment to equal protection.
>
> Knaak's statement is frankly ludicrous. It is nevertheless consistent with the Three Stooges quality of the work of the Coleman campaign following the canvas that has brought Senator Coleman to his current pass. *(Power Line)*

Tune in for today's arguments in the ECC, or maybe not

As we noted a couple days ago virtually every media outlet in MN signed on to a letter to the ECC asking for live cameras in the courtroom. It sounds like they would very much like to start TODAY and certainly on Monday for the trial formal. As noted earlier both Franken and Coleman have agreed to this (a prime condition for admitting cameras in MN) but it's still up to Hayden, Reilly and Marben.

As of Tuesday, according to Mike McIntee,

> We have still not had a decision from the 3 judge panel hearing the Franken/Coleman case on allowing a camera in the courtroom for tomorrow's motion to dismiss. *(The UpTake)*

Wednesday Morning

While some guy from Illinois was getting a new job yesterday (Hallelujah!) legalities kept flying. The Franken Camp formally filed their answer to the Coleman 5-part, slow walk, "let's not start really throwing stuff around until Feb. 9" schedule. The filing, signed by Franken's utterly main lawyer David Lillehaug, wrote in part:

> Coleman's side is seeking a "far flung re-re-inspection of ballots in the hopes of finding error where none has been identified."

That is NOT a typo. In an official court filing to try to get Al Franken to the US Senate Lillehaug used "re-re-inspection." It's a jewel of a semi-made up word that just might catch the eye and linger in the mind of a judge: accurate description, terse, yet with an air of foolishness in describing the other side that clings like an opened can of "Elk-in-Heat" Hunter's Aid.

DK

> Norm's new goal is to cast doubt on the whole process and say that a new election is needed. It works with the general population, but I don't think it is cutting it with the Senate or the courts in Minnesota. *(alswearingen)*

DK There is no authority for a recount. Windmills, meet Don Quixote. *(The Creator)*

Crack in the Case? Department

You know those duplicate/double counted ballots the Coleman camp keeps insisting a) exist, b) favor Franken? The Franken position has been consistent, most recently in Franken's last filing asking for a Certificate of Election:

> Franken lawyer David Lillehaug wrote, "Coleman has not only failed to prove that any double-counting occurred in any precinct; *they have not even attempted to do so.*" *(MinnPost; Italics are Lillehaug's.)*

But now the Coleman team's Tony Trimble has...read some of the filings and notes:

But Trimble points to one of Franken's very own legal filings from Jan. 12 to show even the Franken side thinks some votes were counted twice...

> On Page 28 of "Contestee's Answer and Counterclaims" Franken's side points to probable double-counting of 34 votes in 12 precincts that seem to have favored Coleman, Trimble notes.
>
> "They're not asserting that [double counting] occurred to their benefit, but they're claiming it occurred to our benefit," Trimble said. "That's a tacit admission that it does occur...
>
> "It doesn't take a genius monkey to figure that out," Trimble said. *(MinnPost)*

Well they've got something there so we'll see how Franken's side responds. Not crippling by any means but it sounds like an opening for the Coleman side.

Lazy headline in the Star Tribune: "Franken ratchets up legal fight". C'mon! BOTH sides are filing motions faster than a naked sauna user running back from the snowbank. Why hang it on ONE side?? Bleeh...

No word this morning regarding live video cameras in court, whether today, Friday, or trial starting day Monday. For the moment it's NO cameras, but if we get a change **The UpTake** has promised to be there turning their hand-cranks at **2:30pmCT** if allowed...

Hope this will hold you for now. I've got the late shift so I can stay a while while you read over the latest from yust southeast of Lake Wobegon.

Shalom.

Round 1, Lawyer clash
January 22, 2009

Comments: 140   Recs: 199   Tips: 172

We still have **Franken +225** and Harry Reid giving Al some Cliff's Notes of Senate committees, bills, motions & such so that WHEN he is seated he doesn't have to be seated for long but can get up and start running with his colleagues.

Election Contest Court – Episode IX

Just after 10am the ECC let it be known video cameras WOULD BE ALLOWED in for Wednesday afternoon's pre-trial arguments. Our new favorite the UpTake was there but local CBS affiliate WCCO had a better feed; so did KARE11 news and CNN (all at their respective dot coms.)

And why? Well the shoestring operation of the Uptake was at the end of its shoestring. As Jennifer pointed out, WCCO & KARE11 both have satellite trucks; THE UpTake is working off its wireless card picking up and sharing bandwidth inside the room. Here's a case where bigger, better tech wins – but the UpTake had a MUCH better liveBlog, so there!

> if al gore would have won we'd all have internet2 by now and bandwidth wouldn't
> be a issue anymore *(hopemonger at The UpTake)*

Hearing started on time at 2:30 and went about 1 hour & 10min.

Franken's Motion to Dismiss (take Coleman's entire soft taco case and let it melt in the nearest snowbank.) Arguing in favor of Operation Snowbank (both open and closing; Coleman's side got to do rebuttal in the middle of an A-B-A pattern) was Franken lawyer **David Burman** – a new name here, but apparently not new to election standoffs. Northwestern US Kossacks can fill us in on background but Burman was involved in the lengthy 2004 Washington State Governor's recount between Gregoire (D and now governor) and Rossi (R-Dead Salmon). That race ended up in court and was finally settled by a margin of 133 IIRC, so for Burman +225 must feel like a near landslide. Sounds like the right kind of guy to be arguing your side, and...extra bonus points...reinforces the Reich-wingers paranoia about a Vast Left Wing Conspiracy!

("Soros and Kos have this flying squad that goes around the country, staying in the basements of ACORN people, and stealing governors and senator elections. Why won't real conservatives fight back instead of making nice and caving all the time? McConnell and Cornyn are such wimps for not filing for impeachment of Obama! I mean it's been 48 hours! What more do they need than an improper oath of office?...")

(Burman: winner, 2003 Washington State Bar Association Award of Merit – their highest honor; 2005 Goldmark Award for legal work on behalf of the poor. Areas of practice: Constitutional law, civil rights, intellectual property. University of Wyoming, BA, 1974; Georgetown University Law, JD, 1977; clerked for US Supreme Byron White.)

General impression was Burman was plain-spoken and kept away from most Latin/legal jargon *(lawyer occupational hazard I'm sure; "Et tu, Brute?" was heard on the way to court I think)*. He did needle the Coleman side by reminding the ECC that at certain (weak) Coleman points the law "specifically requires that degree of specificity." *(I suppose the Coleman side would consider the point "picky" but the law is full of nits to be picked at, Norm, including some very specific ones.)* 3 judge panel pretty quiet through Burman's opening but a Motion to Dismiss is pretty drastic.

Team Coleman also sent in a new face: **attorney James Langdon**, part of a big Mpls Law firm Dorsey & Whitney. (Langdon: Northwestern U, BA, 1979; Columbia Law School, JD, 1984; Areas: Intellectual property, financial industry: banking, bonds, warranty law; arbitrator for NASDAQ and NY Stock Exchange). I'm not seeing how his qualifications/ background help his case...this lawyer for this case seems like (you'll excuse me) jury-rigged and makeshift.

Langdon had a tougher time of it on rebuttal. Both women on the panel (Hayden & Reilly) were vocal and questioning. Langdon seemed to spend a lot of time tearing down the Franken case (which is his job for Pete's sake) but doing it NOT by statute law or case law or precedents (which seems to me in a pre-trial is how you do it) but mostly by attacking Burman and Franken: "Alice in Wonderland"; "3 card monte on the streets of New York"; "Listening to Burman's lengthy and erudite speech..."(as in damning with faint praise); " human abacus"...

Bloggers were NOT impressed:

> I don't think he (Langdon) should be referring to Alice in Wonderland unless he's
> looking in the mirror. *(Ian at The UpTake)*

> I'm guessing he means anyone who reads the WSJ *(FrankenRulez at The UpTake)*

> 500 words of yakking from Coleman: 0 content, 0 legal force. *(guest at The UpTake)*

> Waiting for judges to tell Coleman "Were you expecting us to defend your case for
> you? Obviously your lawyer came armed only with political arguments, but this is
> not a political venue it's a court of law." *(ecostar)*

> That's probably what the opinion will say. Opinions in cases such as this are often
> very fun to read because the judge is able to, have shall I say this, express their
> displeasure in amusing ways... *(skywaker9)*

DK   I'm waiting to hear one of the judges interrupt Coleman's lawyer(s) and quietly ask, "Excuse me, do you have any actual facts to present?" *(Lashe)*

And somebody who maybe read my diary yesterday:

> Surely the onus is on the Coleman lawyer to provide some evidence that what they're seeking would change the result. This is ice fishing without a hole in the ice and without an ice hut. *(unknown at The UpTake)*

Judge Marben was fairly quiet all day but Denise Reilly and Elizabeth Hayden were pushing Langdon for specifics and some pointed questions.

> "How does your (Coleman) request now (to open up all 12,000 rejected ballots; or maybe Tony Trimble's 6-7,000 from yesterday) jibe with their earlier agreement that the smaller pool (1,600 or whatever) were the "ones" that were improperly rejected?" *(from either Judge Hayden or Reilly, quoted in live blogging at The Uptake)*

Things got, well, strained in the courtroom; on the UpTake's live blog things were, well, BLOG-like! No pie fights but mighty... open:

> I'm trying my best to listen to this objectively but Coleman's lawyer's arguments just make no sense. I think he's the one in Wonderland. *(unknown at The Uptake)*

Someone lowered the ultimate boom on Langdon's performance:

> Is Bush arguing this case? *(SM at The UpTake)*

[Then Burman got to do his rebuttal and everyone was impressed: tone of voice, argumentation, backing the right candidate, and, you know, the LAW:

> It seems Burman is bringing up specific MN law to back him up. Compare that to Coleman's lawyer, who couldn't state specific illegalities or errors that would benefit Coleman's numbers. *(WoebegonGal at The UpTake)*

AND...then it was over, recessed and "we will consider our decision." They *didn't grant* the Motion to Dismiss (I didn't expect them to) but they *didn't throw out* the Motion either. To use an old phrase I think they're putting it in a lockbox with 3 keys. They DID ask for a quick meeting with attorneys from both sides for "scheduling," which may mean something or nothing given Friday there is already a "pre-trial conference" on everybody's Blackberry and/or day planner.

Coming Attraction: Friday in Court with the ECC

Wednesday was Franken's Motion to Dismiss, a sort of "Let's see if we can spike this thing in one swoop and avoid the whole trial." Friday will see the same thing in reverse: **Friday, 9:00amCT** the ECC hears arguments in a pre-trial **Motion for Summary Judgment.**

This is the COLEMAN spiking effort to get the ECC to hear their side is so true and pure and the Coleman case is so strong, self-evident, self-starting, self-opening, self-arguing, self-closing and just all-around Sarah Palin You betcha WONDERFUL full of maverick-y Goodness!... that the Court might as well save everybody a lot of bother and just rule on the spot for Coleman.

They will be on the other side (I think) of the A-B-A pattern, so Coleman's lawyers will open and close, with Team Franken getting the rebuttal sandwich in the middle. Will we see Langdon and Burman again? Or some of the other legal teams for either side?

Oh and **what are the odds** the ECC will grant Motion for Summary Judgment? I thought Franken's Motion to Dismiss was no better than 10%, so the fact that the ECC didn't throw it out *en toto* is a partial victory in my book. But grant Coleman a Summary Judgment? HAHAHAHA...there are undiscovered subatomic particles that doubt the existence of micro-subatomic particles which still consider the micro-subatomics more likely than Coleman gets a Summary on his behalf...HAHAHA.

But there are **3 things** to watch for:

1. can Burman or whoever is speaking for Franken *really* keep from bursting out laughing during the Coleman open or close?

2. can the Judges also stay "sober as a judge" (in the non-laughing sense)?

3. Will any part of the Motion for Summary Judgment be retained...or putting it the other way, will the panel throw out the Motion for Summary completely?

Tune in **tomorrow.***(The UpTake will probably be broadcasting via Mike McIntee's "MacGyver" model wire-rim glasses linked to his Swiss Army pocketknife magnifying lens and iPhone FireWire Port, running a signal through an Apple Newton , beamed out to a waiting world of Kossacks through 11 twist ties wired to a window screen in a 4th floor janitor's closet.)*

OK I'd better get this up. For now that's all the latest from yust southeast of Lake Wobegon. Shalom.

Rulings & Lawyers 2
January 23, 2009

Comments: 89   Recs: 160   Tips: 144

Franken leads +225. Hearing today on Coleman Motion for Summary Judgment from the **Election Contest Court (ECC)**.

Election Contest Court – Episode X
We Have a Ruling

Wednesday the ECC heard arguments from both sides on Franken's **Motion to Dismiss**. Taking their tempo cue from the MN Supreme Ct. (who rarely let the snow pile up on their rulings in the Recount contest) the ECC court ruled late Thursday to **deny the Motion**.

In their 10 page decision the ECC asserted its jurisdiction to rule, showed they were Constitutional, and denied. Not a big surprise; to take a case of this magnitude and public interest and throw it out would just be TERRIBLE for ratings here on DailyKos! So they denied Franken's attempt to end this with a bang. Onward.

But I have to say on Friday Morning with the MN Media, THIS is the headline story, both Lamestream and New Media: "Franken Loses Ruling." Well yeah, but I think everyone has closed down their laptop too early...this was a long shot all along for Franken (although nothing like today's sidesplitter from the Coleman side) and so what? There's bigger news further down but no one's reacting to it. Maybe the WineRev has been left holding the cork here... but maybe...

We Have Filings and Motions.

On Wednesday, all eyes were on the first public appearance of the ECC and 2 new lawyers for each side. BUT lots of other lawyers have been furiously busy for both sides as well and they cranked out 21 (!) various motions for the ECC to deal with.

(Or maybe there was some confusion and they thought the day on the calendar meant they needed to turn in 21 things...)

Coleman Motions:

If you read through just the titles "contestant" means Coleman/ Coleman's side. They made motions to:

- answer Franken's counterclaims *("AHA! The Monday homework, turned in, good, but 2 days late. Normie, I'm going to have to take off points for that...")*
- law & precedents against the (Franken) Motion to Dismiss *(helping out the court here; what all good lawyers do)*
- motion for an order for counties/cities to turn in ALL their absentee ballots to the ECC *(here's that move Knaak & Trimble mentioned over the weekend to gather all 12,000 rejected absentee ballots from across the state)*
- motion for hearing summary judgments on **parts** of Norm's case *("We think these are our best shots, even if we don't get the whole snowball")*

- a set of motions and affidavits and notice of a hearing for the Coleman Motion for Summary Judgment (today's action; see more below) *including the "read the telephone book during a filibuster" motion (Motion to Exceed Page Limitations)*

Franken Motions:

Now while Al is in DC rubbing elbows with about 98 soon-to-be "distinguished colleagues" the Franken team ain't letting the slush build up and freeze in their wheel wells either.

The "contestee" (Franken) on Wednesday filed:

- Motion to Strike Unsupported claims, with the legal "whereas-es" and "becauses" *("Take these empty beer bottles off the table and here's why")*

- 5 motions, memorandums and affidavits (including a 76 pager!) and a hearing notice in support of **Franken's** motions of a partial summary judgment HIS way ("2 can play "summary judgment", Norm")

- motion arguing AGAINST bringing the 12,000 rejected absentees to the ECC (as in, "the local officials have already done this work, twice. Leave them alone"...in slightly longer sentences and backed up with citations & such.)

And some other stuff (which probably sounds cooler in Latin/legalese) was filed, noted and memorandumized too...

AND then came Thursday!

A bit quieter but only a bit. The **ECC court issued** a couple orders regarding the voters who are looking to have their absentee ballots counted (including I believe the group of 64 the MN Supreme Ct. sent over to them.)

The Court also took in a Coleman petition for a list of Inspectors (see below).

The ECC held a **mid-day hearing Thursday** on the Coleman motion to drag 11,000 (Down from 12,000, but the same batch) rejected absentee ballots to the ECC court. Langdon & Trimble for C: *"We bring everything to you and the Minnesota electorate depends on you for that purified result."* (Trimble really said that: "purified result." Sounds like he's asking for a restoration of virginity or something...)

Elias & Lillehaug (!) for F: Specific ballots, OK. 11,000? Major burden on local officials.

Langdon: No, it's not a burden.

Judge Reilly of the ECC to Langdon: "Have you worked in municipal government?" (Pretty sharply asked, acc. to those there.)

Ooohhhh, pretty...crisp there, Judge Reilly!

How to Do a Trial

The court also issued an *Order to Ensure Proceedings will be Conducted in an Orderly Manner Consistent with Minnesota Law and Court Rules*, which I suppose is kind of standard but also kind of not. This sort of proceeding, especially at a statewide level for a federal office, and one that has reached an "Election Contest Court" stage is a rather rare bird. So the ECC showed THEY can do homework and issued 75 pages of rules, so the lawyers will definitely have something to do on the weekend.

Not many lawyers have actually done a trial like this and not many judges have presided at one. There are 3 judges (like in appeals cases) but they are conducting a real trial: "Do you swear to tell...?". "On the night in question..." "I show you a lizard people ballot from Beltrami County..." "Objection!" "Sustained" and all that.

It is all together meet, right and salutary that the judges issue such an order and lay out the boundaries and rules so the attorneys know what they are doing and so the Court can call fouls and "Out of bounds." *("Half the courtroom shall be covered in 1/2" ice and any attorney over there shall wear or change into NHL regulation gear including protective cup at the lunch break halftime...The other half the courtroom will have 4 tiers of bleacher seats (including one aluminum one so McIntee can use it as massive antenna and consume all bandwidth in the room to broadcast to the UpTake) overlooking the regulation height NCAA net and hardwood floor. Judges Marben & Reilly will alternate dropping the puck and throwing in the volleyball. Presiding Judge Hayden will spend her entire time under the hood of the replay camera secretly watching the UpTake live-streaming...")*

So for those of you with OCD tendencies there's a WHOLE lot of reading to be done at the link. People around here love it when someone comments, "You know I just read on page 35 of the Franken Motion and I think..." It REALLY helps the rest of us so bless you for your efforts.

We Have a Hearing

Coming up TODAY at 11:00amCT. The Uptake (link: will give it a shot, and likely WCCO, KARE11 and CNN as well. **Subject: the Coleman Motion for Summary Judgment.** In a mirror image of the Wednesday hearing on the Franken Motion to Dismiss, this is the Coleman effort to end the whole thing in one stroke.

We will likely see a repeat of the procedure but with reversed roles: the Coleman attorney (Langdon again? Another new face? Or one of the knowns (Knaak, Trimble, Magnuson)? Or the semi-new, semi-known Joe Friedberg?) will make an opening argument with the 3 judge panel able to interrupt with questions at any point. (This will be more like an appeals situation than a trial; trial stuff opens Monday.) There is a time limit.

Then the Franken attorney (Burman again? He did a nice job Wednesday but there are a number of good alternatives at this table) will have a set amount of time to argue down what everyone just heard ("because of this, this and that..."). Again the judges get to interject ("Have you thought about this? What about that?").

Then the Coleman side gets one more turn at bat in a rather shorter closing. Wednesday's hearing took about 70 minutes. This one may well be about the same length.

Afterwards one of 3 things happen. The ECC judges:

1. stand and weep in awe of the Coleman case and ask for the privilege and honor to find in favor of Norm on all points, declare him the winner, adjourn, wring his hand and wish him "God's speed Senator!" and "Good luck, Bart!" *(patting the Gucci saddlebags)*

2. fling themselves onto the high bench and laugh convulsively while EMTs come forward to administer oxygen and veterinarian-sized horse shots of ANTI-nitrous oxide (laughing gas antidote). A brief recess is called while certified physical therapists enter to give soothing rib massages to all 3 jurists. After everyone reassembles the ECC denies motion for summary judgment. All 3 judges then strain to heft and swing Helm (Hjelm?) Hammerhand's Gavel with such force the high bench shatters and the sound causes a 13 mile rift in the Lake Superior ice at Duluth.

3. probably decline to rule immediately, take it under advisement, and move to the pre-trial scheduling meeting they previously put on the Friday calendar. Then sometime Saturday the ruling for denial is issued, WineRev has source material for Sunday's diary, and everyone waits for Monday's trial opening.

Coleman and the Inspectors

As part of its "Now Let's Count every Vote for ME" strategy, the Coleman team wants to have a look at all 12,000 absentee ballots that were rejected statewide. Or maybe it's 5,000...or 7,000, they're just not sure yet.

Anyway, this is where the famous 654 absentee Coleman cherry-picked ballots lie and even the lint brains running the Coleman legal effort have tumbled onto the fact that no court is going to admit only their 654 cherries into the recount. So now they have gone over to the other side of the horse and want the ECC (or somebody) to look at all 12,000. (Martin Luther once observed a drunk who has just fallen off a horse on the left side is the man who, having remounted, is the most likeliest in town to now fall off the right side of the horse.) So this is why their request that all counties and municipalities deposit their 12,000 absentee [ballots] with the ECC.

But if the ECC decides they don't want to do this the Colemaniks are willing to help the court in another way: the Coleman team has a **list of "inspectors"** *(given the Coleman tact one of them is probably named Javert or Clouseau)* they would like to fan out across 86 precincts (out of 4,131 in the state) to "examine" these unopened/uncounted absentee ballots (that were rejected for legal reasons by election officials following the law.) *Although they didn't say so, surely these 86 precincts were coincidentally chosen utterly at random starting in Michele Bachmann's basement.*

An UpTake blogger who is an atty. empties a bathtub of water on this move (and outdoors in January in MN this could be a serious attempt to injure!)

> Coleman wants the election contest "inspectors" to inspect voter rolls and rejected absentee ballots. But the statute says the court can appoint inspectors to "recanvass the votes cast for the parties to the contest or the question in issue in accordance with the rules for counting ballots in the Minnesota Election Law." You can't recanvass rejected absentee ballots, and voter rolls are not ballots. The inspectors are supposed to merely conduct a judicial recount. Coleman wants them to do a lot more than that – he wants them to conduct discovery for him. *(Chris II at The UpTake)*

I agree. This is more of the Coleman ice fishing expedition now aimed at one of 86 lakes near you. The ECC accepted the list but I think they'll either ignore it or throw it out when they deny Coleman's effort to look at all 12,000 rejected absentee ballots.

ECC on the Move!

Well THAT didn't take long! Team Coleman filed that motion to have the counties and municipalities send in their (total 12,000) absentee ballots to the ECC. That was Wednesday. Now comes word Thursday evening about 6:45: **Motion DENIED.**

Well OK. If the WineRev can survive HotAir[8] and Powerline, he can survive the ECC. *(WineRev reads entire 2 page PDF and summarizes.)*

> We the ECC heard this argued on Wednesday.

> Contestants' Notice of Motion and Motion for Order Directing Secretary of State to Deposit Original Documents with the Court **Denied.**

> Contestants' Notice of Motion and Motion for Order Directing Counties and Municipalities Possessing Original Rejected Absentee Ballots To Deposit Originals with the Court **Denied.**

> Signed, The ECC

That's it. No votes. No dissents. No comments. No review of why we the ECC are authorized to do this. Just NO. *(Well they'd never get past the Minimum Diary Reqs. here on DailyKos with THAT attitude!)*

Ahhhhh,... ya know, it's just me, (like nobody in the Minnesota media on Friday morning is saying this but I'm going out on a limb here. It's a big thick branch if you'd care to join me, or you can just gather by the trunk waiting for the cracking sound.)

BUT... I don't think this is a good sign for Coleman (only for John McCain.) I also think this means Coleman Inspector Agents are going to get bounced before they can even be fitted for trench coats and issued their magnifying glasses.

The ECC is NOT going there... and (praying to all the holies) this could mean a fast trial and decision. What will Trimble, Knaak and Co. talk about? They HAVE NO CASE with enough votes in it to overtake the Franken lead. Team Franken might reinstate their Motion to Dismiss or for Summary Judgment right after opening arguments on Monday. Maybe?

There will be some more writhing on the hook but in my book folks...this is serious. This is BIG. This ruling could be the equivalent of Sherman's telegram, "Atlanta is ours, and fairly won." (Not quite over but just mopping up to do.)

Things Norm

Just a quick wrap. On Thursday, Norm:

- got a day job with the Republican Jewish Coalition; Norm will be advising (but not lobbying) on matters of dress and deportment...
- put up a new video at his website that repeats all the usual shibboleths: "artificial lead" "double count" and "I can win"...
- said in an interview he thinks '08 having been a Democratic year he would likely have lost to ANY real MN Democrat, but because AL...

Busy day for Norm. Maybe he's jealous of the attention his lawyers are getting...

I hope this makes some sense folks but Thursday the news spread out like an espresso machine leaking onto the hockey rink and no one could find the shut off valve. Have at it with thoughts & comments

---

8 *hotair.com*

and enjoy the show at 11:00. OK that is some of the latest news, and not all of it is going to STAY latest today, from yust southeast of Lake Wobegon.

Shalom.

Voters, Lawyers & the Law
January 24, 2009

Comments: 39   *Recs:* 63   *Tips:* 57

Capsule: Franken leads +225. Coleman keeps losing pre-trial motions that would expand and distract the work of the **Election Contest Court (ECC). Formal civil trial** in front of this three judge panel begins Monday, 1:00 p.m.CT and will be aired live. Length: WineRev predicts less than 2 weeks; 3-0 Norm loses.

Appeals? Straight to MN Supreme Ct. WineRev predicts: Supremes take it immediately, hear it, rule 5-0 in less than 48 hours: NO, Norm.

Election Contest Court-- Episode XI
Voters First...

The ECC had a two-parter Friday. At 11:00 a.m. they had a hearing for about 20 minutes, with Coleman lawyer Langdon (who we saw Wednesday) sparring with Franken side's Kevin Hamilton.

There was also a bit of input from the "Nauen intervenors" and the "Kennedy intervenors." Unrelated to "revenooers" or "regulators" or even the "nullifiers" (and their snappy blue cockades) of American history, these **"intervenors"** are the lawyers' names on behalf of voters who have been notified their vote had been rejected/not counted and are now "taking it to court." By law the ECC is THE court for such voters and situations.

I believe the "Nauen" group are the 64 voters who the Franken team helped file their move last week with the Supreme Ct. (who made a nifty pass between the skates to slide their puck case over to the ECC.) The "Kennedy" group, I think, are 7 more voters making the same case (I love using clichés in their originating contexts, don't you?), but it's unclear if these folks are being helped by Franken, Coleman, Barkley or are skating on their own hook, funds and hockey sticks.

Subject to correction from wiser heads I believe these 64 and 7 are part of the 392 folks whose absentee ballots were wrongly rejected by their counties, then reinstated, but not yet counted because either the Coleman or Franken camp used their "veto" over admitting them to the count.

AND, just to make the lawyers wait in the lobby just a moment longer, these 392 (maybe 393?) improperly rejected absentee ballots that haven't been counted yet? Yeah, the ones left out in the cold (a terrible thing to do in MN in December and January) by the MN Supreme Court ruling of 12/18? According to some intelligent commentary from yesterday's diary, **ALL of these 392** MAY be heading to the ballot box! (If so it is no more than justice; NO VOTER should be denied because of "clerical error" or "broken machine" or other crap like that.)

Note this sequence (hat tip to those commenting, especially underwhelm, a MN atty(!) and the fine use of "confoozle". Nice job! :)

DK

> **Power to the Peeps and all, but** my concern is about Dentures perverting the system. I don't think many people think the MN SC's decision to give the campaigns veto power over the fifth-pile votes was sensible - the ruling on that matter was spineless, imo.
>
> That said, following on from that decision, it's concerning if the court reverse itself under pressure from voters who (I think it's pretty clear) are being prodded into action by the campaigns.

DK It plays right into Coleman's hands to start second guessing the fifth pile. Now, if they want to say, our bad, count all the fifth pile votes previously rejected by Coleman or Franken, then I could live with that (especially since they wouldn't break sufficiently for Coleman to make up his 225 vote deficit). *(HobbyWizard)*

DK **Not a reversal.** The decision to count improperly-rejected absentee ballots would not be a reversal. The S. Ct. specifically said that the erroneously-rejected ballots could not be counted unless (1) all parties agreed or (2) an election contest determined they should be. Some got in under condition 1, and the court specifically contemplated condition 2. *(underwhelm)*

DK **Okay, thank you for clarifying.** I still think it was a dumb way to do it because it undermines the authority of the canvassing boards.

My understanding is the campaigns did not have to offer a reason for excluding fifth-pile ballots. I hope I'm wrong about that, too, because otherwise it seems fairly obvious the courts, in theory, allowed the campaigns to exclude ballots for the vote contained within, rather than for cause. *(HobbyWizard)*

DK **It was a little bit the other way around.** The court basically said that no one but the ECC during a contest could order contested, rejected absentee ballots counted. So the only ones that could be counted were any that were completely uncontested. It's only because Coleman was then behind in the count by 20 or 50 votes that his side agreed to allow any of the rejected absentee ballots to be counted at all. And that just pushed him further behind. *(Ken in Tex)*

DK **Gotcha.** I've been confoozled about the finer points of this, I think, in spite of The Uptake, WineRev, et. al's best efforts. Thanks for the correction. *(HobbyWizard)*

DK **Cool.** So you see, that the ECC now counting those very same ballots is not a disagreement or an overruling of the supreme court's previous decision. In fact, the previous ruling sort of has already given the ECC a tacit OK to authorize counting any rejected absentee ballots that they deem to have been rejected improperly. *(Ken in Tex)*

SOOOoooooo...with a bit of luck, as the trial gets going next week, the ECC could decide on these 392 and call up Ritchie and Poser over at the Sec. of State's Office and have them hold another "Opening Party" with their stylish chant of "Franken, Franken, Coleman, Franken, Coleman..." *(in tango rhythm: slow, slow, quick, quick, slow, and in those proportions; "Jalousie" playing in the background, stirring the Argentinean soul of the WineRev...boy, that is strong salsa and Malbec...)*

OK, Let the Lawyers IN

At noon the ECC reconvened to hear the **Coleman Motion for Summary Judgment.** *("We are so great and our case is so good" just invoke the squirt hockey 10 goal mercy rule in our favor!)* As those filing the motion, the Coleman side got to open and also (after a slapshot for Franken's team) got to close. *(If you're watching the video replay on The Uptake, Team Coleman is in bright red uniforms, with lots of jersey names ending in "ov" and "off" and "enko". The inside tags say "Moscow Hockey Gear". Across the front: CCCP ("Certified Coleman Court Pretenders")*

James Langdon was center ice for the opening shift for Team Coleman. He was last seen in Wednesday's hearing thrashing around trying to convince the ECC NOT to throw out the entire case. (We're still here, so it was a partial victory.)

Langdon was arguing for including a LOT more LEGALLY rejected absentee ballots (piles 1-4, and oddly quiet on pile 5- gee I wonder why), anywhere from 4,000 to 11,000 (which would be ALL of them.) He *didn't exactly* say which ballots should thereby be counted for Coleman but *implied* mightily there would *likely* be *probably enough* to carry Norm over the top and (in a fast-talking finish) why not have the ECC *just accept* this list *and just rule* in their favor TODAY (before everything melts...like their case.)

The hockey/legal fans live blogging over at The UpTake did a wonderful job of summarizing how Mr. Langdon did.

> What is Coleman's argument? That they should redo the whole recount and let him pick the ballots that should be counted? *(unknown, at The UpTake)*

Sounds like Florida 2000 playbook to me.

> Does anyone else feel like Langdon just keeps talking and talking, going around in circles, rather than presenting evidence, just filling time? *(unknown, at The UpTake)*

Yes they did.

And even the ECC judges were... (ahem) straining to keep their judicial balance:

> Way to contradict yourself in the same sentence and yeah to the judge for calling him on it *(unknown, at The UpTake)*

This must have impressed:

> "You know it when you see it"?!?! Is this a recount or porn? *(unknown, at The UpTake)*

Coleman chief lawyer **Tony Trimble** skated onto the ice, met by the usual chorus of boos and catcalls that any team's "enforcer" gets when it's a road game. So naturally when "the enforcer" became the "enforcee" (to use the legal language; *WineRev buffs nails*) because of some body-checks to his logic and argument, the fans were cheering hard:

> Trimble's arguments are like an episode of "Lawyers Gone Wild." I can't believe some of this stuff! *(unknown, at The UpTake)*

> oh - We're sure there's evidence there, we just haven't found it! WMDs anyone? *(unknown, at The UpTake)*

> Basically, Trimble is still arguing that he has nothing yet. Is that enough to keep them from summary judgment? *(unknown, at The UpTake)*

And let me tell you, when the judges went down into the corners after the puck to mix it up along the boards with Trimble, the fans were rockin' at the ECC team's gritty play!

> "Why did you wait till yesterday?" *(Judge Reilly, quoted by rincewind at The UpTake)*

> That can't be good...... Is it bad when the judge is making fun of you?
> That lady judge (Denise Reilly) seems very skeptical of Trimble's games. *(Dennis at The UpTake)*

During the period break while the Zamboni was out laying down some fresh ice, we get some mid-game analysis:

> A lot of unanswered but specious allegations from Trimble. Voters voted both absentee and in person? Large number of absentee ballots, disparate rejection rates? Yes, Minnesota law expressly allows you to vote on election day despite casting an absentee ballot. That's why so many were rejected, and why it might happen more in one place than another. Not an indication of disparate treatment at all.
>
> Trimble's argument on Mpls and Maplewood is weak in one significant respect: no evidence. He complains that Franken's evidence is double hearsay, but he has even less--he has zero--and you need more than zero plus speculation to create a material issue of disputed fact. *(unknown, at The UpTake)*

In the Team Blue/Team Franken uniforms (jersey tags at the collar say, "Lake Placid Hockey Gear, 1980"; lettered across the front: USA: "Up Set Ahead") the stars yesterday had to be Marc Elias and, in a very smooth public appearance, (legal) team captain David Lillehaug. *(GREAT impressions of Neal Broten and Mike Eruzione!)*

Elias was methodical and historical, quoting PRIOR team Coleman positions on absentee ballots and pinning them to the boards by pointing out how *now* they were trying to skate down the other side of the ice. These Minnesota hockey/legal fans know good skating and hard-grinding when they see it:

> He is very organized. Good hire. *(Dennis at The UpTake)*

> bulldog... maybe because he has to prevent Coleman from muddying the waters every day... *(mikeinaz at The UpTake)*

Over a couple Molson Ice beers in the stands fans were talking about the Coleman strategy of claiming something "A" a few weeks ago, and now whining they are hampered or hindered because of "A". Unlike hockey, in court you have to stick with one line (fancy legal term: estoppel).

And they LIKED Elias' stick work and scrapping behind the net:

> Wow. Elias just blew up this motion (for Summary Judgment). Couldn't be argued more effectively. If "the universe isn't done", then there are material facts in dispute. A motion for summary judgment is so ludicrous that it might be sanctionable. Just because many litigants do file summary judgment motions doesn't make it appropriate every time. This is just an incredible waste of the court's time. *(Fisch Fry at The UpTake)*

> Tough to beat Elias's argument that equal protection does not require when one official makes a single error that the error be reproduced statewide. It would throw all elections into chaos. *(Chris II at The UpTake)*

Lillehaug was deadly from the slot, sniping at the goalie every shift:

> "Contestants (Coleman) claimed unqualified and ineligible voters voted for Franken. We asked 'Who are these voters?'" In what precincts did they cast unqualified votes.'
> They said, "We don't know."
> "They claimed some voters voted more than once. We asked who? and where? They said they didn't know." They have no evidence." *(quoted at The UpTake)*

Presiding Judge Hayden (I think it was her; voice sounded a bit different from Reilly's) broke in with something along the lines of "If you had gotten answers we might have to assign those voters public attorneys for their trial here on voter fraud charges." (Lillehaug smiled back and suggested Joe Friedberg from the Coleman table!)

Lillehaug was a scoring machine and he was hitting the corners of the net effortlessly. Looked like Mario Lemieux on a power play undressing the New York Rangers entire squad...he was that good!

The ECC has FANS!

You know sport referees or umpires have the thankless job; enforcing the rules is not a lot of fun. But so far the ECC is living up to the rave reviews Alan Page and the MN Supreme Court got on these boards and in many quarters.

Mental Image of the DAY here:

> These judges, I'm thinking, want to publicly display a full airing of everyone's issues, and then reach a sound judgment that way. So it's a good decision and everyone agrees, no grounds for someone to claim there was a voter on the grassy knoll that got disenfranchised *(Lilboyblue at The UpTake)*

ECC Decision

Mere minutes after the above session adjourned (final horn sounded; fans headed out clutching last of Labatt's for snowmobile ride home) another decision from the ECC. Coleman Motion for Inspectors (to go out to 86 randomly (hah!) picked precincts to look at some of those 11,000 rejected absentee ballots the ECC already said will NOT be coming to St. Paul): **DENIED.**

ECC said if Team Coleman wants to look at specific ballots, examine voter rolls, question election officials, they can do so via subpoenas once trial starts. (This also lets Franken challenge said subpoenas, cross-examine, etc.) But that little shack out on Lake Phelan named "Coleman Election Inspectors R Us"? The new one, being built, like all things Norm, from the roof down?

Yeah this ruling means the ECC just sailed their iceboat down the lake on a close reach with Judge Marben leaning out, the port runner hiked 3 feet in the air until Hayden slid them to a hockey stop in front of the Inspector's Shack, covering it in shavings. Then all 3 judges got out and Reilly started up the District Court Issue Poulan chainsaw and cut a circle around the shack until it broke free, capsized and sank like a Volvo-bound crime victim of the Stockholm Syndicate. *(Don't laugh. The Swedish Mafia has been making hits on inanimate objects like ice shacks and other structures for centuries. In 1628 a defense contractor tried to welsh on a deal with the Mob. Anders Svengaard took revenge by putting out a contract on a navy ship...and the pride of the Swedish fleet, the "Vasa" never made it out of Stockhold harbor!)*

OK hope this will hold you until the ECC rulings come down. I'll blog a bit with you and with all the latest news from yust southeast of Lake Wobegon.

Shalom.

Franken-Coleman Trial Eve
January 25, 2009

Comments: 36   Recs: 62   Tips: 67

Election Contest Court - Episode XI
still running from Friday

The ECC heard arguments Friday over Coleman's **Motion for Summary Judgment** *("Our case is so strong and the other side's is so pathetic let's not waste everyone's time. This is a gimme, so gimme.")* For those of you just tuning in, not to worry, the odds of the ECC granting this motion are less likely than Dick Cheney wheeling onto Fox Noise for an exclusive, live interview and breaking down: "It's all true: We tortured. We ordered troops into harm's way. Me and my buddies stole the Treasury blind. Here it is in writing and on computer CDs so you can take all of us to jail, starting today. Oh and everyone here at Faux News is being arrested in 10 minutes so we'll be going black".

I thought the court might rule Saturday or Sunday, but it looks like they might wait until Monday morning.

Reading Other People's Mail

In what I think is a real confession of weakness, Team Coleman has released an open letter to Team Franken.

> Norm Coleman sent his U.S. Senate opponent a "Dear Al" letter on Saturday, asking him to "join forces" and agree that 12,000 ballots that may have been wrongly excluded from the November election results be examined. "If you feel that tactically you cannot join this effort," the Republican told DFLer Al Franken, "we would at least ask that your campaign does nothing to block this suit from moving forward or makes any public statements which could be construed as standing in the way of this suit moving forward." *(Star Tribune)*

I think this shows the Coleman team is still woozy from the body check the ECC put on their case by denying their motion to bring the 11,000 ballots to the ECC. While they have filed a motion to join the "Nauen 64" case and add in their 11,000 ballots I think they know their chances of getting a class action suit loaded onto that 64 voter dogsled are less than a no-snow winter in International Falls. So the only thing they can do is go public, see if somehow they can get Franken to go along and say to the ECC, "Your honors, both parties agree bringing these 11,000 ballots to you would be in the interest of justice." If Franken declines, then the Reichwing Wurlitzer would crank up a storm of "Franken opposes justice for absentee voters".

Well this balloon is only going to float until about 1:01 p.m. Monday. Tony Trimble, lead attorney for Coleman, will get up in court and say, "For the sake of 11,000 voters we tried to get the other side to join us".....

At which point Elias, Lillehaug, Burman, Hamilton, and/or Pentelovitch jumps up and finishes the sentence, ".....in breaking the law about rejected absentee ballots, and in calling over 30,000 election workers across the state a bunch of moronic liars!"

After that the Coleman case will be all a Shakespearean idiocy: "Sound and fury signifying nothing."

DK Aren't Republicans supposed to hate frivolous lawsuits? *(wiscmass)*

OK I hope this will hold you into the evening. I'll crank away on tomorrow's news today (!) but for the moment that's all the latest from yust southeast of Lake Wobegon.

Shalom.

TRIAL Day 1
January 26, 2009

Comments: 218   *Recs: 560*   *Tips: 218*

Programs! Get Your Programs below the fold! Can't tell a judge from a lawyer without a Program.

Case No 62-CV-09-56

Coleman, Sheehan, et al. Vs. Franken, et al.

Minnesota Judicial Center, Room 300

Live Video feed: Allowed on a pool basis if unobtrusive

Cell Phones: MUST be off (vibrate does not count); violation: subject to confiscation by court security.

Laptops: OK, only if unobtrusive.

Jury: No. Three Judge Panel, appointed by MN Supreme Court.

Decisions: Majority vote; unanimous not required.

Appeals: Direct to MN Supreme Court, expedited track.

At Stake: United States Senator from Minnesota for 6 year term ending 2014. Court to determine if further votes should be added to State Canvassing Board certification of vote count (1/5/09). State Canvassing Board certified count: Al Franken leads by +225.

Issues:

- Shall 133 ballots from a Minneapolis precinct that were lost at time of recount but were recorded election day by voting machines and confirmed by voter registration logs be counted? 133 currently included in certified total. Coleman argues NO. Franken YES. Ballots favored Franken by net +46.

- Were 125-150 ballots from absentee voters that were duplicated under witness for purpose of running through voting machine counters counted twice? That is the duplicate run through the machines on election day but BOTH the original and duplicate counted during the hand recount? Ballots currently included in certified total. Coleman: Yes, they were and ballots should be disallowed down to one count. Franken: No evidence yet presented this actually happened. No precincts noted where this is alleged to have happened. "Theory in search of evidence." Without evidence, should be dismissed. Such alleged ballots alleged to favor Franken by net +100.

• Were 12,000 absentee ballots (out of nearly 300,000) across the state properly rejected for 4 statutory reasons? If not rejected for 1 of these 4 reasons should the "5th pile" absentee ballots be counted? Coleman: 954 "5th pile" ballots were already counted. 393 other "5th pile" ballots were excluded and should stay excluded. 654 ballots among the other 11,000 we think should be added but no others. Franken: 954 "5th pile" ballots were already counted. 393 other "5th pile" ballots certainly could be/ should be counted under law and under rubric of "count every vote." All other absentee ballots were rightfully/ lawfully/ legally rejected by the 35,000+ election workers across the state and they had 2 passes at it.

The Judges

Presiding:

Elizabeth Hayden, Judge, Stearns County (St. Cloud), appointed 1986 by Governor Perpich (D). BA College of St. Benedict ('68); JD Oklahoma City University ('78); Stearns Co. Asst. County Atty. '81-'86.

Elizabeth Hayden

Hayden, 62, is a member of a Minnesota Supreme Court advisory committee on general rules of practice... no kossack reports having practiced or tried a case before her, but a blogger from St. Cloud served on a jury where she presided and felt she was firm and fair toward the lawyers, kept them on task and moving, and was very kind toward the jury (like most trial judges I think).

> "She doesn't like sideshows, and she expects you to be prepared,"... when a St. Cloud lawyer was trying a case before Hayden, his client's cell phone rang in the courtroom. Hayden, he said, was not amused. "To this day I'm convinced that I lost the case because the cell phone went off." *(Star Tribune)*

Panel Judges:

Denise Reilly, Asst. Chief Judge Hennepin County (Greater Mpls.) Appointed '97 by Governor Carlson (R-Normal). BA College of Wooster, '75. JD, Wm. Mitchell College of Law, Cum Laude '83. Law Clerk & attorney, '83-89. Asst US Attorney, Narcotics & Firearms, '89-97.

Denise Reilly

Reilly, 55, was most vocal of the three judges during pre-trial motions and rather pointed in her tone with Coleman's Trimble. A kossack attorney reports Reilly is very precise about rules, procedure and precedents. An article at time of her appointment says

> she is kind to the new and nervous attorney (none in this case) and a bear on the unprepared (hmmmmm... now which side has had the most spelling errors in their motions? Late turning in their assignments?.)
>
> She currently handles civil and adult criminal cases, but in her 11 years on the bench she has spent the most time in juvenile court *(sounds like good training for THIS trial)*... She's good at cutting through the situation. She'll focus on the facts and she'll focus on the details."... teaches trial law classes at U on Minn law school. *(Star Tribune)*

Kurt Marben, Asst. Chief Judge, Pennington County (far NW; Thief River Falls, about 120 miles NNE of Fargo-Moorhead) Appointed '00 by Governor Ventura (I-very independent!). BS Bemidji State College, '74. JD, U. Minn. '77. Attorney, private practice, '77-'00.

Kurt Marben

Marben, 56, is a member of a Minnesota Supreme Court advisory committee on general rules of practice, from a Kossack who has practiced before him says he is very even-handed, careful and principled in explaining how he is applying the law in a given case...from a law clerk in 2001:

> "I think all the litigants and parties that came before him got a fair shake,"..."Every case before him, whether $100 or $1 million, you got the same treatment," ..."He's actually got the patience of Job. *(good quality for this case –WR (quoted in Star Tribune)*

Attorneys in the Court

Will you see all of them? Maybe.[9] Likely one guy (and they are all guys so far) will argue for each side while some of the rest of these sit at their respective tables, scribble notes, tap out stuff on laptops. We don't know who will argue which parts. I think they can switch more or less at will between witnesses or before and after recesses for various strategic reasons. Here's who you might see/ hear from in the coming days:

Attorneys for Norm Coleman (Contestant)

Joseph Friedberg (b. 1937) University of North Carolina, B.S., 1959; University of North Carolina Law School, J.D., with honors, 1963 Extensive criminal trial experience, late addition (1/16) to Coleman team, well known in Twin Cities law circles, no public statements so far, did not speak in pre-trial motions that I heard but was present at Coleman table.

Fritz Knaak (b. 1952) Rutgers College & State University of Florence, Italy/ St. John's University,(St. Cloud, MN) B.A., Summa Cum Laude, 1975; University of Minnesota Law School, J. D., 1978. Private Practice 1978-85. MN State Senator, 1983-93. Private Practice since. City attorney for Fridley, Maplewood & Newport, MN. Was attorney of record in Mower County state senate race recount. Client ended up losing by 5(!) votes. $7K in campaign contributions to Republican & Independent candidates since 1997. He has been the main public figure for the Coleman legal team at most of the pressers.

Tony Trimble (b.1953) Education: BA St. Olaf College, mid 70's. JD WM. Mitchell College of Law, maybe 1979. Admitted to bar in '80. Represented Mark Kennedy (R) in 2000 when Kennedy upset US Representative David Minge (D) and Minge decided to "step back" from a recount. $79K in contributions to Republican party/candidates since 1997. Chair, MN Republican Party, 1987-1989; took a lot of heat from fellow Republicans for focus on fund-raising rather than leading party in public way. A major critic: Fritz Knaak.

Roger Magnuson (b.mid 1950s) Stanford University B.A., Economics, with Honors, (no date but about 1968), Harvard Law School J.D., 1971, Board of Editors Harvard Law Review, Officer of the Harvard Corporation. Dorsey & Whitney (big name Minneapolis law firm); shareholder & fiduciary trust law, M&A, white collar crime, professional baseball, most notoriously, a player on the GWB Legal team in *Bush v. Gore* (2000). Author of several books (latest: Barracuda Bait). MN "Attorney of the Year 2003". $13K in campaign contributions since 2002. Argued 2 Coleman motions before Supreme Court in November & December, lost one decision 5-0, partial win 3-2 in case of who gets to decide on "5th pile" absentee ballots (the decision that gave an effective veto to each camp). Not heard from since.

James Langdon, (b. about 1957) Northwestern U, BA, 1979; Columbia Law School, JD, 1984; big Minneapolis Law firm Dorsey & Whitney. Areas: Intellectual property, financial industry: banking, bonds, warranty law; arbitrator for NASDAQ and NY Stock Exchange).Argued Wednesday pre-trial motion when ECC court heard Franken's motion to dismiss the whole case; (we're still here so in that sense Langdon "won"... but definitely praising with faint damns; no way was ECC going to dismiss). He liked to use a lot of cliches and tired phrases.

Attorneys for Contestee (Al Franken)

David Lillehaug (b.1954) Augustana College (Sioux Falls, SD), B.A., summa cum laude, 1976; Harvard University, J.D., cum laude, 1979. Paid staffer, Mondale campaign, 1984 (prepped Mondale for 1st Presidential debate, the one where Reagan looked BAD), joined Wellstone campaign in 1990, wrote speeches, coached Wellstone for debates, could also go heart to heart and do "tough love" so "Paul would stay Senatorial". White collar and construction law experience, former US Attorney, mid-90s, pro bono: won case for religious institutions who wanted exemption from new "concealed carry" gun law, ran for D nomination for MN Atty Gen. and lost, 1998. According to former law firm staffer and kossack, a tremendous debater and scary brilliant lawyer, so knows this case cold; hard to work for and hard to get along with but just the kind of sore-pawed bear you want ON YOUR SIDE. He was on the Wellstone campaign in '02 when Wellstone was killed; switched in last 2 weeks to help Mondale effort that lost to Coleman. Would he like some payback? Can you say Suh-WEET!?

Marc Elias (b.1969) Hamilton College, B.A., Government, 1990; Duke University, M.A., 1993 AND Duke University School of Law, J.D., 1993...campaign law, election finance, general counsel for Kerry-Edwards presidential campaign, general counsel for Chris Dodd presidential campaign 2008... attorney

9   *Three of the attorneys listed here (Roger Magnuson, William Pentelovich, and David Burman), while on the legal teams, apepar to have worked entirely behind-the-scenes and are not mentioned again in this book. They are included here for completeness.*

for DSSC... the public face of the Franken legal team... quick with a line (last week, "the universe is still expanding") and good with adjectives *(in one brief court address last week he described a Coleman legal move as inconceivable, miraculous, stunning, staggering, implausible, extraordinary and a "constitutional game of gotcha"--St. Paul Pioneer Press)* and with perhaps the most "election law" experience on either side...

William Pentelovitch (b. 1949?) University of Minnesota, B.A. Summa Cum Laude 1971; University of Chicago Law School, J.D., 1974. Extensive trial law experience, appeals, business law in areas of non-compete, antitrust, intellectual property, trade secrets, unfair competition, listed in Best Lawyers in America 1995-2008. Argued before MN Supreme Ct. in November & December as opponent of Magnuson. Apparently, he is quite focused & brilliant and a very nice person to be around; just don't get in his sights on the far side of a court room. He has not been seen since last Supreme appearance

David Burman (b. about 1952) University of Wyoming, BA, 1974; Georgetown University Law, JD, 1977; clerked for US Supreme Byron White. Areas of practice: Constitutional law, civil rights, intellectual property. Winner, 2003 Washington State Bar Association Award of Merit--- their highest honor; 2005 Goldmark Award for legal work on behalf of the poor; was a player for the Washington Democratic Party in their struggle in the governor's race recount in '04 that was decided by 133 votes in their favor; argued Franken motion to dismiss Wednesday. Bloggers liked his solid approach, almost home-y clarity and avoidance of legal mumbo-jumbo; it was unlikely the Motion to Dismiss would succeed but The Up-Takers were taken by the way Burman argued it.

Minnesota Law at Stake

You'll hear/read references to **Section 204 and Section 209** *(which after a while makes us non-lawyers want to join Corporal Klinger and file for a section 8)*. Basically 209 says the ECC's job is to determine who won (by as little as 1 vote) and then order a Certificate of Election. 204 "Errors & Omissions" is a detailed rule book of fouls and penalties in an election.

Team Franken will be working to keep the focus as narrowly as possible on 209. About as far as they want to go into 204 is in keeping with their "count every vote" approach with the "5th pile" absentees. This means they will be open to counting the 392/3 improperly rejected absentee ballots (and going on the prior 954 can expect to net maybe in the neighborhood of +50 for the Franken side.) Beyond this though, they will fight hard to stop at the beach-head in 204.

Team Coleman will be working to bring in as much of 204 for as long as possible: the properly rejected absentee ballots numbering 11,000 or so. (ECC in pretrial knocked down a straight attempt to bring these in. A "class action" back door approach using the "Nauen64" case is being tried but may get shot down this morning before the trial even opens.) Otherwise, this side will need to subpoena records and election officials (specifically, not en masse), and the Franken side has the right to oppose every last one of them and cross-examine any that arrive.

DK Overturning an election is a breathtaking event and requires breathtaking evidence. Coleman's case is as empty as his core values. *(Dr Colossus)*

UPDATE: Capsules on 2 more attorneys

There were late additions to both legal teams, heavy hitters both.

Coleman side: Ben Ginsberg

Ben Ginsberg — This national heavy-hitter has long advised the Coleman campaign on the post-election mess but did so behind the scenes until last week. Now the man who was a newspaper reporter for five years before becoming a lawyer has taken over the role as main legal spokesman to the media. He was national counsel during both of former President George W. Bush's campaigns and played a key role in the 2000 Florida recount. *(Pioneer Press)*

(What the HELL is it with the Florida 2000 legal beagles for Coleman?? First Magnuson and now Ginsberg??)

Franken side: Kevin Hamilton

The Washington state attorney has been one of the go-to lawyers for that state's Democrats for years. The Washington State Democratic Party has been an impor-

> tant client, and Hamilton was trial counsel in the 2004 fight over the governor's race. The Democratic candidate won. *(Pioneer Press)*

(So Hamilton helped beat back a Ginsberg-style "Florida ?" in Washington state? Hah! Game on!)

OK that should hold you until 1:00 p.m. CT, and then YOU take over this diary with reporting, comments and speculation (let's be RAMPANT people, RAMPANT!). For your morning coffee and lunchtime reading this is the latest from yust southeast of Lake Wobegon.

Shalom.

TRIAL Day 2
January 27, 2009

Comments: 120   Recs: 271   Tips: 177

The Elections Contest Court – Episode XII

"Tung-tong" (as we open *Law & Order* Minnesota style)

The Lawyers

Yesterday we had opening statements from both sides. Now opening statements are not testimony but rather like the preface to a really good book. A good preface gives a few explanations, sets a certain tone, and if done well, helps you smell the flat mud salt off the Thames and hear the skritching snick of tumbling autumn leaves being whipped across the cobblestoned lane toward you by a chill wind. A few stray raindrops spatter your sleeve as you pull your collar more snuggly and squint ahead at the gaslight, hoping it's the one by home. You quicken your pace against the rising wind and falling light and turn to the first page of the novel proper to read, "It was a dark and stormy night..."

In a trial there are two prefaces. Each side leads off with an opening statement to entice the court to read the evidence, understand the witnesses, and examine the exhibits THEIR way. Yesterday each side was given 45 minutes for their openings. Late addition Joseph Friedberg from Coleman led off. (The FORMER Senator Mr. Ordinary-Citizen-like-you-and-me Norm Coleman was in attendance.) Mr. Friedberg's preface/opening statement was ...delivered...deliberately...and ...slowly, in a medium deep, sonorous voice. Sonorous...as in drop the first "o" and say the word out loud and the man was a standing bottle of Ambien or "Let's Doze." The UpTake live bloggers:

> Friedberg has to talk slow, he has nothing but has to fill 45 minutes.
> 1:03 (3 minutes in) OMG Freidberg's voice is sooo soporifc. I feel myself nodding off already.
> How can he argue this with a straight face?!
> I just can't believe Friedberg did not show up today with a concise list of "we will demonstrate"s that pointed to a clear interruption of a fair democratic process.
> *(various live bloggers at The UpTake)*

Kevin Hamilton spoke for Team Franken. He invited the court to read the case rather differently and took the dastardly and daring approach of law!...facts! ... evidence!...logic!

> No, wait, this can't work, It's logical and orderly
> If this reading of the law is accurate, he's really delivered a body-blow to Coleman.
> Wow - you mean they actually have to show evidence that votes did change the outcome of the election? Strange that the Coleman folks didn't mention that.
> The judges look more attentive to Hamilton than to Friedberg

> Isn't it fascinating how much actual content and evidence the Franken team presents, as opposed to the Coleman team? Amazing how that works out.
>
> *(various, unknown live bloggers at The UpTake)*

Hamilton put the burden of proof where it belongs, on the Coleman team. He cited statutes, including some noted by Friedberg (as in "he said this, but as we all know by these precedents, it really means that"). He defended the process and those who worked in 4131 precincts across the state to make the election happen, happen right, happen fairly, and, when it was really close, happen to give it all a second look (3,000,000 times!).

> By reiterating the law, you are laying the foundation that there are laws and rules you must follow. It's a well skilled attorney that is bringing it up to keep the judges focused on the law and not baseless accusations.
>
> The best part of Hamilton's argument was the opening, citing statute and in effect demanding the Coleman team to produce EVIDENCE of a result changing error, rather than speculation that such an error might be revealed under the "right" circumstances. *(unknown live blogger at The UpTake)*

Well after that "always like to keep my audiences RIVETED", the judges took a 5 minute recess for 10 minutes. I don't indulge, but those openings, especially Friedberg's might cause me to take up smoking... something strong. (Judges' chambers voice: "Looks like I picked a bad week to give up drinking.")

Witnesses and Evidence

So on to actual "Raise your right hand. Do you solemnly swear" stuff. Two Coleman witnesses called to establish the Coleman side's "chain of custody" of photocopied ballots. They are trying to use these as a "sample set" of ballots to show the ECC how things went wrong with the Rejected Absentee Ballots in order to get the ECC to order all 11,000 sent in to the ECC for examination. The actual, physical ballots are still in the counties (all 3 million of them. You can't touch 'em (literally) without a court order, which Coleman sought in last week's DENIED motion. So they are trying again this way.)

Coleman requested photo copies of the ballots from the counties (and by rule of discovery, Franken side gets a copy too) for use in this trial, and abruptly the whole thing started to publicly capsize.

You see if you or I are working in a law office and FedEx delivers a photo-copied ballot from Otter Tail county this is EVIDENCE and you MUST play CSI: St. Paul. Open it, copy off as many copies as you need, log everything, and put the original in the vault (most law offices have one). Now everyone can eyeball their copy, ask about "FSM" on the margin, see if the envelope is signed, etc.

When the witnesses testified it became clear on cross-examination by Marc Elias that Team Coleman had not done this. Elias established the Trimble Troops had instead passed around *their original*, made notes, marked it with numbers, dates, etc. *Then* when they needed them in court, they had staff go back and try and erase/white-out those marks which they THOUGHT their own people had added to the photo copy from the county.

Elias was in excellent form POUNDING this mis-handling home which means things went rotten for Coleman's case. Given any judge's care for procedure, let alone the reputation Reilly has for prep & detail (Hayden too from yesterday's diary accounts; and don't tell me Marben will let something like this slide), this HAS to look really bad in the eyes of the court.

Indeed by the end of the day, the Norm side was reduced to saying the Franken side had clean copies, why don't they lend us theirs? Really!

More drama today! You can bet your bailout money on it. If the Coleman side can't get at least some of those absentee ballots into the case they are DOOMED, so they will be urgent in the coming days.

Dark Scenario Speculation

The Coleman side's main hope of getting enough "new" ballots posted on Norm's side of the ledger is to somehow mine the Rejected Absentee ballots. Their motion to get these in directly: DENIED.

Their motion to expand a 64 vote side case before the court into an 11,000 vote 'class action suit'? Unlikely, and Team Franken yesterday filed papers stating their objections to such an action.

The Coleman effort to get 5,000, 7,000 or 11,000 lawfully rejected absentee ballots into court via this proceeding using a sample set of "errors" to pry lose the rest of them? Stalled by their own incompetence.

Or is it incompetence? Most likely I think so. (In my life I have painfully learned just how fumble fingered and/or dense grown-ups can be.) But what if they run these messed up absentee ballots by the court? Bring in others in a haphazard, sloppy way? Get testimony from election judges that seem to show flat contradictions in the way ballots were ruled in and out?

Then they come pleading to the ECC "this is such a mess of conflicting approaches the only fair/just/honorable thing to do, (and we sincerely regret our own part and appearance in adding slightly to the situation) is for this esteemed Court to order the originals sent in so we can examine all of them in the light of your august wisdom?"

Frankly, I don't think they are nefarious enough to think up this on their own. Mostly I think it's slipshod preparation and law firm numb-skullery. But if the last 8 years have taught me anything it's to be slightly cynical enough to look for the outlandish conspiracy... it just might be afoot.

Tuesday Morning Minnesota Media

How messed up was the Coleman side with their copied ballots? So messed up the StarTribune headline writer (who has been no friend of fairness) has to write the banner on the top of B1 as "Recount trial, day 1: Copies of ballots don't cut it."

On those supposed, alleged duplicated ballots that may have possibly, allegedly been counted along with their originals in the recount that the Coleman side thinks might have happened a little/a lot/ at least enough times to give Norm a lead? One place the Coleman team named (they finally had to be specific) was Eagan a 2nd ring suburb on the south side by the airport.

> On Monday, Eagan officials said they had double-checked their election results and there was no such trouble in their city.
>
> "We're confident, based on the information available to us, that no votes were counted twice. They were counted only once," Eagan City Clerk Maria Petersen said in a release. (*Pioneer Press*)

Judge Marben presided yesterday from the center chair. Judge Hayden did so during some of the pre-trial motions. Judge Reilly today? Will they rotate all the way through? Sounds fair to me, very Minnesotan.

OK, hope this will hold you until 9:00 a.m. CT when the action begins. That's the latest for the moment from yust southeast of Lake Wobegon.

Shalom.

TRIAL Day 3
January 28, 2009

Comments: 128   *Recs:* 212   *Tips:* 98

It's still January – from the Roman two-faced god Janus who looked backwards & forwards. C'mon forward for a look backward at yesterday's trial...

Election Contest Court – Episode XIII
The Morning Wait

Court started at 9:00 a.m. CT and almost immediately disappeared from public view. Cameras panned uselessly, microphones warmed and cooled, bloggers blogged and lagged.

Monday's stumbling beginning by Coleman's team was a pathetic study in how to NOT win cases and influence courts. I don't think anyone wanted to go through *that again* so the judges and lawyers from both sides went into a no-kidding huddle for nearly 4 hours. There was no word what finally moved things forward but a court bailiff was seen bringing a 2 foot sealed case into the conference room.

(The audio in the Minnesota Judicial Building is still poor so this report MAY be a bit garbled. As the bailiff came out from the room a female voice (possibly Presiding Judge Hayden's?) was faintly heard to echo down the polished stone corridor: "Agreement or else." (Sonorous male voice--- Coleman atty. Friedberg?) "Or what, your honor?" "I'll open this case of lutefisk, and..." and the door closed. Court resumed almost immediately.

And what a resumption! Judge Denise Reilly in the center chair Tuesday after Judge Marben Monday, so they look like they ARE going to rotate the presiding task ("We'll take that under advisement"..."This Court does not believe...")so, it's likely Judge Hayden today. **The afternoon session** started with the ECC not SAYING what they had worked out with the two sides to re-start things.

Instead we moved straight to SHOWING what they'd worked out with **"Motion to Strike!"**. (NOT Session 3 of the DVD "Learning to Bowl", NOT the AFL-CIO battle plan to pass EFCA, NOT Robert E. Lee's final words to break camp). *The Coleman Team moved to strike their OWN witness testimony from Monday.* Huh?

Apparently this maneuver cleared the decks courtroom-wise, fulfilling all righteousness of court rules and procedures and got things restarted. Usually "move to strike" is an objection from the opposing side against a witness statement *("Mr. Smith is a scumbag!" "Move to strike the last sentence."),* or an affidavit, or I suppose, even an exhibit ("We offer these graphic audio tapes of former congressman Foley as exhibits 4 through 137." "Move to strike # 63 through 66 as NOT graphic").

As far as I know, a sort of unusual move. Any Kossack lawyer types ever done this? Seen this? I mean "move to strike" a whole day of your own case? Man that WAS a bad day! (Hope Norm got a refund on billable hours; really that's just awful and Coleman should NOT have to pay for it. I want Franken to win but that was pathetic, and if they actually charge Norm for "services rendered" for THAT day in court, well I will hold Norm Coleman's coat and find him a horse denture mouthpiece and tie on his gloves myself as cutman in the corner as he goes a few rounds with Knaak, Trimble & Co., "Da Noive" indeed!).

DK Norm's strategy reminds me of "Calvinball" from Calvin and Hobbes, where any player could make up or change rules at any time during the game. They act like it's all perfectly natural. *(TomK002)*

The restart DID let us get on to...

Witnesses: Coleman Case

The Coleman side called as witnesses 6 voters who had voted absentee whose ballots had been denied/rejected/refused. Much of the testimony circled around the "matching signature" criteria of MN law (this is #2 or "pile 2" of the 4 reasons.) For an absentee ballot to pass muster (pass all 4 mandated tests to be accepted) there has to be a match of signatures between application and ballot, subject to some narrow exceptions.

They all told their stories and, as FORMER Senator Norm put it at the presser afterwards, "put a human face on the absentee ballots." It did, but it remains to be seen if it helps the Norm case or becomes just a human interest interlude.

Eugene Markman of Waite Park, Minn., said he voted by absentee ballot so that he could spend 16 hours as chief election judge at a precinct in his former home town of St. Cloud. Coleman attorney Jim Langdon asked Markman to read aloud the reason (signature mismatch) another local official noted for rejecting his ballot.

"Whoever wrote this don't know how to write either," Markman said with disgust. *(MN Independent)*

One election judge couldn't read the handwriting of another election judge – ouch! And a well chosen witness for Team Norm.

The 6 had a diverse set of stories to tell (especially about the signature requirement), and what the Coleman side was driving at was **trying to show how loose** this criteria is. They are smart to focus here since asking election officials become handwriting analysts opens a real pack of pre-cooked linguini. THEN (a reach) if they can show inconsistent standards inconsistently applied it MAY (stretch that reach like a warmed up Gumby doll) open the door to them saying all 12,000 absentee ballots that were rejected for the 4 legal reasons ought to be examined (1 by 1) by the ECC. (They have to get some major fraction of these ballots or it's all over.)

WineRev on a Soapbox; *firm, soft tone of voice:*

They also used a hoary lawyer's play for the sympathy of the Court by leading off with Mr. Gerald Anderson, a 75 year old disabled voter. Nothing new about this shtick for the judges or lawyers; they've seen it/done it themselves before, many times. (Some lawyer-rabbi in front of King Solomon trying the Case of the Mystery Mothers probably brought in the baby in question and secretly pinched his bottom so the crying might sway the room.) But the blogger-folk over at The Uptake live blog were harsh, and in my book unfair. In their comments they were either mocking Anderson for his disabilities or furious at Friedberg & team for "exploiting those disabilities".

This is not worthy of good people. Mr. Anderson is part of WHY absentee ballots exist, just as they existed for the Franken voter in Bemidji --- remember the 84 year old woman whose signatures didn't match because she had had a stroke between application and voting? Her vote was being disallowed for this criteria and Kos bloggers were ticked off for the apparent injustice and heartlessness of the Beltrami County election officials. Yet no one was down on her for her medical situation. The story turned out to be garbled and the Franken camp dropped the issue fairly quickly, but the point is made.

Bad move, Uptakers, but kudos for moderators Jennifer and Jason for calling them to task for it. Disabled is disabled; allowances are made and the voter votes. Meet the criteria and **your vote counts:** *Coleman, Barkley, Lizard, Niemackl, or even Franken, and that is how it ought to be. Make your choice for your favorite or against your UNfavorite but VOTE!*

And if you've got a trembly hand like Sec. of State Ritchie's grandmother or a vision issue, let's invent a way of helping out these VOTERS that gets their vote and keeps it private. Anything else is cruel, anti-democratic and unworthy of a citizen who one day may themselves tremble or be blinded by age. Let us live up to the better angels of our nature folks.

(WineRev steps off "Democracy" soapbox, resumes diary.)

For their last witness of the day, Team Coleman had asked for a representative from the Secretary of State's office. The SoS's office sent over **Deputy Secretary of State Jim Gelbmann.**

(Fans of this series will remember early in December the State Canvassing Board was getting started on their work. Gelbmann's boss, Sec. of State Ritchie, had talked with the Board about sending out a letter to the county election boards asking them to examine and sort their absentee ballots. There was a certain "that sounds like a good idea if it's worded right" air from the Board. While the discussion was on, Gelbmann and staff put a letter together that was so crisp Ritchie was able to sign and send it the next morning. Gelbmann also led the staff when the Canvassing Board was ruling on challenged ballots and both sides were UN-challenging ballots. Gelbmann's team had to keep pulling the Un-challenges out and getting them back in the right stacks, and also keeping the challenged ballots that were ruled upon to THEIR proper stacks. The numbers moved so little (Franken one day +6 and Coleman +2 for instance) out of 6,600 endlessly shifting challenged ballots because of Gelbmann's work. Sharp, competent customer Mr. JG!)

A comment from the *StarTribune* blog put it well:

> I thought the big story today was Gelbmann, from the Secy. of State's office - Friedberg's (Coleman's) last witness. Gelbmann was called ... read more to show that there was no consistent standard in the way the rejected absentee ballots were reviewed under the Minn. SC order. Rather than show inconsistency, Gelbmann described a process that was controlled and carefully monitored, with the ultimate decision about validity of each absentee ballot resting with either a county election supervisor or a county panel, based on criteria that only allowed discretion when it involved signature analysis. Gelbmann's testimony, that continues tomorrow at 9AM, demonstrated an election system made up of dedicated public servants working tirelessly to canvass with deference to the law and each individual's right to vote. *(Star Tribune online)*

Coleman's side got a LOT less out of Gelbmann than I think they wanted. Also, if the commenter above is correct Gelbmann will open things today back on the stand at 9:00 a.m. defending his election officials across the state and the entire system. So more JIM POWER for fair, clean, transparent elections!

Cross-Exams & Objections: Franken case

Marc Elias handled a lot of the cross-examinations (a somewhat delicate task for these witnesses) and Kevin Hamilton did a good bit of the arguing over points of law. Together they raised the excellent point that these absentee ballots had been rejected by election officials under 1 of the 4 statutory reasons and that *those* folks ALSO had a story to tell. (Unclear if Coleman side plans to call such folks or Franken will for their own case.)

> Franken lawyers also objected to four of the six people who testified Tuesday, saying that they were not among the 654 people whose rejected ballots Coleman had initially wanted to review and were instead part of the campaign's attempt to reconsider a much larger number of rejected ballots. *(Star Tribune)*

They next invoked the idea that "equal protection" does NOT equal uniformity or perfection. Otherwise all 3 million votes would have to be cast in front of 1 election judge (and the Coleman team would probably argue that the 7:30 a.m. decisions were different than the 11:00 p.m. decisions...sigh). It was a nice *reductio ad absurdum (WineRev struts across diary, showing off at least one appropriate Latin phrase).*

They further argued MN has a 40+ year history of addressing these issues in practical terms and in case law and that experience and precedent all matter too. (And you know how legal types LOVE terms like "practical" "precedent" and "case law", so I think they held their ground here, even maybe gained some.)

They called foul on the Coleman team for their "shuffling the deck" of how many absentee ballots they want to have the ECC look at: 654 cherries, 4549 Trimble Taters, or all 12,000 shelled peas? They quoted the 204 page Coleman filing of the case *(ooohhh, don't you HATE when someone reads your own stuff against you? Petard hoisting and all?)* only called for the 654 and asked the court to hold Coleman to that (taken under advisement.) There are also rumors/stories afoot if the ECC agrees to look at Norm's 654 cherry-picked beauties from piles 1-4, asking the ECC to ignore the law-- because the law was improperly applied---- that Team Franken has a list of 770 absentee ballots they have grape-picked and are ready to drop on the sorting table for cuvee and reserve wine making.

That's the latest from yust southeast of Lake Wobegon.

Shalom.

Trial Day 4; Legal Update
January 29, 2009

Comments: 109   Recs: 171   Tips: 188

Election Contest Court - Episode XIV
The Gelbmann Affair

Wednesday saw a full day of trial, from 9:00 to 4:30. And on the witness stand for most of six hours was Jim Gelbmann, Minnesota's Deputy Secretary of State. The Coleman attorneys put him up there starting Tuesday, and David of Lillehaug for Team Franken got to cross-examine starting just before noon. Gelbmann may be back on the stand TODAY for even more.

Gelbmann was unrelenting in his defense of local election officials, their training, MN election law and the Sec. of State's office. He saw clearly Friedberg for Coleman was trying hard to show how haphazard, slipshod, and otherwise inconsistent absentee ballots were handled and Gelbmann was not having any of it. (And Team Coleman put him on the stand as a FRIENDLY witness.)

Friedberg at one point made a big deal of this:

> "Based on the order of the Supreme Court, based on the closeness of the race, based on the candidates' own wishes, desires and motives, people whose votes should be counted, in your expert opinion and in the opinion of the counties, have been disenfranchised, correct?"
>
> "That is absolutely correct," Gelbmann answered. *(MN Public Radio)*

As with so much of the Coleman case there is less here than meets the eye. Coleman's team spent and will spend hours trying to make this sort of statement the fulcrum of their attempt to drag in 654, 4,540, or 11,000 absentee ballots. ("See, even the Deputy SoS agrees with us!")

Stupid on a stick! What Gelbmann (and Ritchie and the Franken side and a whole lot of us) means by this is there are 1346 − 954 = 393 "5th pile" IMproperly rejected absentee ballots that should still be counted, the ones "vetoed" by one camp or another via the 12/18/08 MN Supreme Ct. order. The voters did EVERYTHING right but somebody at the local level messed up. The local officials identified their mistake and WANT TO CORRECT IT but so far have only been able to do so in 954 cases.

When these 1,346 were under discussion between Christmas & New Year's, Team Franken's consistent position was "Count 'em ALL!" It still is. Team Norm first said, "Only 131/133/136, ummmmm, maybe 787" and finally ended up at 954.

This is ALL that is hanging fire and these are the ONLY votes left to count. [A Kossack lawyer pointed out the 12/18 SC order specified that (what turned out to be) 1,346 ballots should be counted, a) as long as both camps and the counties agreed (which is where we are now and the source of the effective "veto"), OR, b) decided by an election contest court (ECC) in an evidentiary hearing (a trial.)] AHA! Great catch that OR. Guess where we are now?

For this reason I still say the ECC (probably next week in honor of my return from Florida) will order the 392 counted. WineRev predicts WHEN this happens Franken nets another +50 or better. At that point the RMS Coleman hears a gigantic scraping sound as a mountain of ice slides by starboard, the watertight doors that unfortunately only go as high as "E" deck are closed, and chunks of ice on top deck turn into impromptu hockey pucks.

The **ECC opened the day ruling on** a Coleman motion, and the Frankenites have reason to smile. This was a **Motion of Limine** ("at the threshold") to basically keep out certain evidence or other stuff and is usually done in jury trials to keep things in bounds. *(Suspect was seen in a blue suit at the scene of the crime. Defendant owns a blue suit of the same shade. That defendant also owns a brown suit is of no consequence.)*

Coleman's side had requested the ECC rule out... *their OWN previous public statements on absentee ballots!* Every time they get up to say something in court about including/excluding 933, 1,346, 393, 654, 4549, 11,000 proper/improper/statutory absentee ballots, you've noticed it's different and often contradictory. The Franken side has had the nerve to stand up in court and say "it's different and contradictory." The Coleman team asked the ECC to essentially gag the Franken side from using the Coleman's team own words against them...again, and again, and again.

Apparently a Motion of Limine is rarer in a panel trial (vs. one with a jury) like the ECC since a judge is presumably less influenced by irrelevant stuff. But the ECC remembered the precedent of Kirk to Savik in Wrath of Kahn: "Lieutenant you keep right on quoting regulations!" So, ECC: DENIED (again): "You said it. You unsaid it. You were against it before you were for it. You might be schizophrenic. *(Knaak was heard to whisper under his breath, "Well yes and no...")* You may have short-term memory loss and/or you might want to infect this Court with the same. But the Franken team has every right to bring all those back trackings, side alleys, reversals and cutbacks to the attention of the Court."

Reductio Ad Absurdum

This is a great Latin phrase: "to reduce to absurdity." While WineRev's Vulcan relatives are unemotional devotees of logic, even logic leads to certain intellectual cul-de-sacs: how many angels can dance on the head of pin? If two negative numbers multiplied together create a positive number, why DON'T two wrongs make a right? Why does lutefisk exist?

My dad the structural engineer taught me this. Now and again he would be called as an "expert witness" in a court case. I asked him about being an "expert" and he said, "Of course I'm no genius." I asked him the difference. He noted how experts are specialists, trading depth of knowledge for breadth. He said, "An expert is somebody who knows more and more about less and less. So a genius is somebody who knows everything about nothing." Reductio ad absurdum, with humor ever lurking at the absurdum like Inspector Clouseau about to burst in an attack on Kato.

A good deal of what makes the Coleman case so pitiful and the Franken effort so entertaining is Coleman's people are constantly having to avoid being reductio-ed into absurdums.

Coleman strategy:

> There must be ZERO! errors in this election! So because there were, Norm wins. That's the logic we're headed to. *(unknown at The UpTake)*

Reductio ad absurdum.

> "There must be one uniform standard to examine absentee ballots. Only one person can do this. Therefore all absentee ballots in the state (all 300,000 of them) must be examined by one person." *(Star Tribune)*

Reductio ad absurdum.

> "For equal protection all ballots must be treated the same. Since absentee ballots are handled differently because they arrive by mail rather than in person there should be not absentee ballots (Norm's case explodes)." *(Star Tribune)*

Reductio ad absurdum.

> "Since lawyers and judges are wiser and fewer in number than 1,000s of local election officials the entire recount should be done over again... by us in this courtroom." *(Star Tribune)*

Reductio ad absurdum.

Hypocrisy? "Nah! Just call me Norm."

Why do people hate politicians? Back in November the Franken team went to court in Ramsey County to force compliance with a MN law that states names & addresses of voters voting absentee shall be released to the public at the close of Election Day. Franken won, but the Coleman side wagged their finger, expressing GRAVE concerns the info might go into general circulation, that voter privacy would be compromised, and that campaigns contacting voters might frighten them. (Marc Elias got on the map at a presser by stating on the record he promised NOT to frighten Fritz Knaak by calling him up.)

Tuesday night/Wednesday morning the Coleman campaign (whose director is Cullen Sheehan, the co-filer with Norm in the ECC case), POSTED the spreadsheet of every absentee voter in the state whose ballot had been rejected. (Great respect for voter privacy there, Cullen!)

THEN late yesterday the Coleman website went down, off-line. Why? Answer is via Connecticut. Remember the Lamont-Lieberman epic struggle from 2006? Toward the end of that match Lieberman came out with a splashy accusation that the Lamont side had attacked the Lieberman website as part of the Soros/Kos strategy for taking over an expanding universe. After the PR damage to Lamont was done ("lies fly, but truth has to walk"), it turned out Lieberman dot com was indeed offline: a) because they hadn't paid their monthly fee, and b) because the server and infrastructure for the site turned out to be technically ultra lame. (I think the server was the brains to a digital gumball machine in the lobby of Mystic River pizza shop. Anytime someone was using the e-mail feature and a kid put a quarter in the machine it crashed.)

Yesterday Norm's team *(I smell the Sheehan Clearasil!)* claimed they were offline because of the VAST crush of Minnesotans logging on to find out their voter acceptance and to donate to Norm's righteous cause that they overwhelmed the computers.

NOT ONE WORD TRUE. They've handled much heavier loads, already paid their bill for the month, and from some technical stuff, *took themselves* off line. PURE PR! MNPublius was all over the story, complete with geek tech specs that once translated into English just hammer this one into the ground. In blogger-ese: "Epic Fail!"

And well, OK, this will have to do for today. A half day at the wine shop and then I'm off for Florida this afternoon. Packing the laptop so will try for the odd diary from Mama WineRev's spare bedroom. Will be back on Thursday the 5th (when the MN Supremes hold a hearing NOT related to my return.) That's the latest from yust southeast of Lake Wobegon.

Shalom.

Beach Blogging Minnesota
January 30, 2009

Comments: 75   Recs: 141   Tips: 146

Sheesh what is WRONG with these people?! No parkas. No long woolies. No gloves, mittens, scarves. I mean you can see faces, even SKIN. And ewwww, what skin! Soft, supple, smooth, . curved, *ahem*, instead of hard, stiff, cracked, splitting. If it weren't for the beach, Chapstick sales would be absolutely NOWHERE and you can't jump start an economy without that market.

And Florida's news is boring: 76 and cloudy, chance of showers. Obama governs THIS... Obama undoes another 1% of the 8 year catastrophe THAT...the President completes sentences in English without mangling his mother tongue.

All I can figure out by long distance is **Franken +225** and Coleman is still thrashing around in court like that swimmer out there tangled in a cluster of 14 meter strands from a jelly fish the size of a refrigerator, caught in a rip tide taking him out to that school of circling sharks.

Election Contest Court – Episode XV
Joe Power Returns

Team Coleman is/are slow learners. Witnesses Monday and Tuesday who whack their own case, followed by a day and half of Jim Gelbmann who offered a masterful defense of the entire MN election process. [All that cheering in downtown St. Paul – popcorn, nachos & salsa, the clink of beer bottles and the slap of high fives as The UpTake announcer Mike McIntee says in the background, "He could go... all... the ...way" – is NOT the official Super Bowl Rehearsal Party. All the noise is coming from the staff at the Secretary of State's Office as Mark Ritchie works on that form "How to Give a State Employee a 20% Retroactive Raise."]

NOW the Coleman legal masochists have called Joe Mansky, the Ramsey County (St. Paul) elections director, to the stand. No doubt they will try to get this 20+ year veteran of MN elections to say bad things about the process. Long-time readers from the single digit versions of this series recall JOE Mansky is the LAST MAN on earth you want to try to get to bad-mouth the system. (I think it's some sort of petty revenge for how Mansky verbally manhandled some of the Coleman operatives/observers as the Recount got underway. At one point Mansky laid down the marker, "If you don't like my decision you can take me to court over it." Looks like they're taking him up on that.)

WineRev predicts: you think Gelbmann helped the Norm Case? HAH! Well Mansky is like sending Dick Butkus into the defensive huddle AS THE BACK-UP second stringer (and he's hacked about being benched). NOT a lot of drop off between starting line-up and second string there!

ECC Morning News

During the recount 171 votes were discovered in a LOCKED cabinet in Maplewood, MN (N, NE, E suburb – endlessly running – suburb of St. Paul). Pristine condition and everyone on the scene (including Coleman lawyers who were summoned to the scene) agreed "nothing fishy" and they were added to the recount. Now as the trial has gone on Team Coleman has bruited (what a word!) these 171 as part of the dark doings of the Franken effort.

But now in the cold gray frozen light of the ECC court, Team Coleman has decided to NOT do one more flip flop (or maybe a 3rd one to bring it back to starting point). They are abandoning any efforts about these 171.

OK folks, it's not a full hit, just a little methadone from MORE THAN yust southeast of Lake Wobegon...back to that skin...those curves...

Shalom.

Suffering under a Florida Sun
January 31, 2009

Comments: 39   Recs: 47   Tips: 43

A brutal 50 degrees overnight here in Delray Beach, so the dog-walking neighbors are in double wind-breakers, turned up collars and hats.

More madness in the Coleman-Franken trial but they let out early being Friday. **Franken leads +225.** General feeling is Coleman is still trying to swim directly to the beach against an out-flowing riptide (instead of side-stroking parallel to the beach for awhile and then coming in on the diagonal.) Their legal flailing is getting kelp-covered.

Election Contest Court – Episode XVI

Remember that group of 64 absentee voters (the "Nauen" group) that also filed with the ECC to get their votes counted? (Team Franken provided legal & financial support.) Team Coleman has tried to use them as a vehicle for dragging all 11,000 (legally) rejected absentee ballots into court.

Well the group of 64 is down to 61 – a couple voters dropped out and at least one was informed their vote actually HAD been counted. There is concern Team Coleman isn't fighting these very hard so they can make some whiny claim (*you know, let Coleman campaign manager, co-contestant and all around fingernail-on-chalkboard screecher Cullen Sheehan speak in court*) that "Well, you let THOSE ballots in, you have to let OURS in too or it's not fair!"

Not to worry. Kibosh administered here with a dazzling use of the phrase "Statistical innuendo":

> There's a clear difference between the 6[1] and Coleman's equal protection claim. They are being offered on a case-by-case factual basis. Coleman doesn't want a case-by-case determination, he wants relief for classes of ballots, with no facts supporting the conclusion that any individual ballot except statistical innuendo. The difference is that the 61 deserve *de novo* review, while Coleman needs to prove that equal protection was violated first. (*BillW at The UpTake*)

The only sad note would be if/when the ECC rules against Coleman on this (again; and again 3-0) that they WON'T either use "statistical innuendo" or quote Uncle Scar from "The Lion King": "Life's not fair."

Shells Washed Up on the Beach

Jay Weiner at MinnPost wrote a fine round up of week one: "How to explore the universe without leaving your parents' basement."

The *elegantly dancing backwards in high heels* Grace Kelly at Minnesota Progressive Project reports in all the testimony by Joe Mansky over the Coleman jock-itch about "duplicate/double counted" absentee ballots there STILL has been NO EVIDENCE presented that this occurred! (*They NEED Joe Friday: "During the Recount on Tuesday, Nov. 19, in the Warroad, MN precinct 3 at about 5:45pm election judge Sigrid Torkelson did deliberately double count both an original and a duplicate ballot for candidate People, first name Lizard."*)

A great compliment to Marc Elias (turning 40 this weekend; way to go kid!) of Team Franken

The difference between a good attorney and a great one is that the great attorney will only deal with the issues needed to be dealt with, and will ignore the fray. Elias is a great attorney. (unknown at The UpTake

OK, hope that will hold you a bit longer.

Will stick around for a few comments and chaff from all of you who are not yust THIS FAR SOUTHEAST of Lake Wobegon.

Shalom.

February 2009

With a Rapier
February 1, 2009

Comments:	31	Recs:	51	Tips:	36

Another day of drizzle starting off at 47 degrees and a stiff north wind. No beach again but Monday is looking good.

Election Contest Court - Weekend Recap

One batch of voters in front of the ECC aren't wearing "Coleman" or "Franken" Jerseys, but "Nauen", the name of their lawyer. As required by law (*pay attention Friedberg/Trimble/Knaak and especially you 2 slime-covered land eels from Florida 2000/ Bush v. Gore legal team, Ginsberg & Magnuson*), the Nauen 61 have also filed a proposed remedy: Count their Vote! (What a concept – and sounds like WHICH Team's cheerleaders?)

I think the ECC may well rule on this part of the case this week. On Thursday the 29th, Team **Nauen moved for a Summary Judgment** on their effort to get these 61 votes opened and counted. As of Sunday afternoon the ECC had not acted. I've got a feeling the ECC will rule on this case this week: nothing solid, just a hunch, but maybe also to show things are moving ahead.

Blogger "Abbey" over at The UpTake liveblog has a personal stake in Team Nauen *(and Abbey? The Orange pom-poms and waving handkerchiefs over here in this deck of Kos stadium are cheering for YOU, including those 5 stripped-to-the-waist cute college-aged guys in...well not purple paint; that's just the effect MN cold has on skin... with A-B-B-E-Y spelled out on their chests!)*

> ...my parents voted AB (Absentee Ballot) - they went to city hall, filled out the application, got their AB forms, filled them out, turned them in. Found out later they were rejected. 1st reason they got was they weren't registered (they have been for 40 some years) then they were told they were rejected because they didn't have their applications. Now, they couldn't have gotten the AB if they didn't turn in the app (Gelbmann covered that yesterday) When mom called to find out why they weren't counted she was told by the clerk it wasn't her problem. So they joined the lawsuit. *(Abbey at The UpTake)*

"...*Wasn't her problem?*" Excuse me! Hey, you! In the election office? It sure as HELL isn't the voters' problem! What are you reading, "How to Lose votes and Influence Elections" by Rove, Baker, Harris & Blackwell? You don't know your job and that kind of snowball throwing and slush shoveling ("Not registered" "didn't have application") is straight off the stable floor (or [Katherine] Harris' rug) and has no place in this or any other election. Performance review coming anytime soon? Sheesh!

Alex Castellanos Article…Rant Warning

[WineRev was made aware of a putrid article on the MN Senate recount and ECC case by Re-dumb-lican "strategist" Alex Castellanos on cnn.com[10]. Time pressures last week did not permit a full treatment, but for Sunday afternoon Super Bowl pre-game festivity, here goes. Best enjoyed with Antonio Banderas accent in "Zorro," or for you REAL fans, Tyrone Power!]

---

10 *Castellanos' commentary is entitled "Minnesota recount's comedy of errors".*

Señor Castellanos, your first three paragraphs repeat some worn and some fresh MN stereotypes: eating lutefisk not for taste but as a cultural duty is well put. For this reason, I choose NOT to face you with a spoon but with a more manly weapon. *(WineRev slings off cape in a sweeping circle, landing it neatly on a convenient chair. Tosses Castellanos spare rapier in scabbard. Draws own sword. Cue flamenco flavored music.)*

You call Franken a credentialed clown?*(WineRev slices through candle burning in candelabra and heaves top 4" at Castellanos)* Given men like McConnell, Inhofe, and DeMint, or your Palin-pet who even Penthouse would turn down as too stupidly vacant, you certainly KNOW clowns. What you do NOT know is wit, humor, irony, satire or the ridiculous. You only know snide sarcasm and whining glee.

(WineRev with a left, left, right, left set of attacks shoulder high, all parried with suitable clangor.)

For no good reason you try to drag Blago and Illinois into your column, perhaps because you have so little to say and you have a certain word minimum?

(Castellanos moves in with right, right, left head cuts and a backhand belly sweep.) You quote a professor who was quoted in the Wall Street Journal editorial from 3 weeks ago.

(WineRev parries effortlessly, jumps back, and ripostes to the wrist so Castellanos' sword falls to the floor. He looks up in worry but WineRev pauses, reaches inside shirt, pulls out editorial. He draws dagger and throws. Dagger pins editorial to wood floor by Castellanos' hand. Dagger quivers in rising pitch: "brrrrrroooeeeet")

That editorial has been ripped apart by Kos blogger FischFry, then dismantled line by line by Nate Silver. A member of the State Canvassing Board, Judge Cleary, wrote an open letter to the WSJ board on how bad, how wrong and how moronic the editorial was. *(Castellanos rolls to feet with sword. His parry is slow and he shows blood on a knee, a thigh, the sword wrist and a long, thin scratch on the free arm forearm.)* Even Powerline's Johnson broke ranks with Hinderaker to lambaste this tripe. This editorial isn't good enough for paper training Rupert Murdoch's pet kangaroo and you dare to cite it??

(Castellanos lunges left just in time to escape a heavy WineRev thrust that crashes through the glass of the library bookcase.)

> The result in Minnesota is a crazy quilt of newly evolved standards that, in fact, have become no standards at all – and are constitutionally unacceptable.

Hah! *(WineRev just misses on sideswipe to head.)* There is only 1 standard, in 4 parts. It has been applied to over 300,000 absentee ballots and in 12,000 cases ballots were rejected. In the case of 1,346 errors, the state of MN and the Franken campaign have sought to correct those errors and have done so in 933 cases. The Coleman team has prevented the rest from being corrected and given "equal protection" under the election laws of the state of MN. This process will indeed pass Constitutional muster and NO federal court will even bother to hear the case on "equal protection" grounds.

> In some parts of the state, as a *Wall Street Journal* editorial observed, recount officials have accepted Franken votes tallied on election night, even when the physical ballots were nowhere to be found for the recount.

Again with the WSJ editorial! These would be the Minneapolis 133 for which we have strong evidence of their existence (both voter logs and machine tapes) as well as case law and precedent to support their counting *including the 50+ of those 133 that went for COLEMAN you drool of a burro! (WineRev & Castellanos in hilt to hilt clinch but WineRev leans back and uses free hand to punch available nose.)*

> In other jurisdictions, the election night tally was thrown out and Franken got to include votes he didn't have election night but his team subsequently discovered.

Son of a cactus! The election night tally in tons of precincts was changed (not thrown out) because of absentee ballots being added to the totals, arithmetical errors being corrected, recounted ballots being challenged by both sides.

(Castellanos ducks behind desk, then pops up with quick thrust along desktop. WineRev pivots, smacks own sword on top to freeze both, leans in and punches Castellanos in face again.)

Franken didn't discover votes and Team Coleman didn't either. Local officials doing their jobs caught these. The only thing the 2 camps did was rake 6,600 ballots out of the hopper for challenges. You are tequila-for-brains, Castellanos, if you think otherwise...but then, you ARE getting your pesos from Republicans who would send your relatives to jail, would shoot you on sight near the Arizona border, or would sentence you to mop floors for their friends at Wal-mart!

And your finish in praise of the steely-eyed character of MN civility *("HAH! Take THIS steel" WineRev shouts as he pins Castellanos face first to a wall. WineRev turns sword in hand, steps back and delivers ferocious swat with flat of sword to backside prominent.)* does NOT rescue you from your misleading, false, inaccurate, woefully slanted plate of re-fried Coleman talking points. Your column is a bilge-water barnacle of pureed jellyfish that deserves no notice, respect or attention.

(WineRev's sword rings slightly as it slides back into scabbard. Sound of Castellanos' stumbling feet and whimpering sores fade down stone corridor.)

Enough good friends! Yust something to hold you from REALLY FAR southeast of Lake Wobegon. Shalom.

The Spectre of Ginsberg
February 2, 2009

Comments: 41   Recs: 73   Tips: 45

Finally above 70 in the morning but in and out showers slated for the day. I'll take a leaf from Bill Cosby's routine on "Seattle" and stay out there and get a "rain tan."

Election Contest Court - Episode XVII

Week Two

Scheduled start today at 9:00 a.m...then 9:30 a.m... now heading to 10:00 a.m. BUT attorneys seen going into judges' chambers about 8:45 a.m., so there is action but nothing public yet.

And NOW, a report that Deputy Sec. of State Gelbmann and State Elections Chief Gary Poser and THEIR attorney are also in chambers with the ECC judges! This could be big... perhaps the 61 "Nauen" votes will be counted...perhaps the 393 remaining "5th pile" improperly rejected absentee ballots!

Visiting the Dark Side

No, not Dick Cheney's undisclosed location but a more public portal into the dark heart of proto-fascism passing itself off as the current Republican Party. Damn it is HEART-BREAKING to see a party of caution, patriotism and limited government being treated like a kidnap victim and forced into profligate spending, jingoistic chest-beating and "all the odious apparatus of Gestapo rule." (YES, I went there because the shoe/jackboot fits.)

A blogger over at The UpTake took a look at Ben Ginsberg's book An American Lie. Ginsberg is a lawyer/veteran of the Florida 2000 Bush legal team that Jim ("The Bastard") Baker put together. Ginsberg isn't in court for Team Coleman but he's at the pressers and shooting his Luger off on the PR front. HOW does someone like this avoid disbarment and charges of subversion when he writes:

> "Voting, for the State, is a nice tool to give the citizenry the illusion of control, while for the most part it is a meaningless exercise to convey legitimacy on government." *(An American Lie, quoted at The UpTake)*

Good Lord, in 1860 even Jefferson Davis accepted the *legitimacy* of Lincoln's election; even though he took several drastic steps after that, he never DENIED Lincoln had been elected by a plurality of voters.

Yet Sith Lord Ginsberg is Emperor Palpitane all over: "we allow the people the illusion of control... while we pull all the strings my young apprentice Magnuson the Lesser..."

MN Supreme Court

If ECC action is dull, the MN courts have scheduled a special: this Thursday, Feb. 5 at 9:00 a.m., the MN Supreme Court (once again led onto the field by the inestimable Justice Alan Page) will hear arguments from Franken and Coleman on a Franken suit to force Governor Pawlenty and Sec. of State Ritchie to sign a Certificate of Election.

The strongest leverage Team Franken has is the State Canvassing Board's Certified Count of Jan. 5 that put Franken at +225. They also make arguments about MN deserving full representation in the US Senate.

I understand the PR side of this and the need to press the Coleman side on all fronts but I'm not crazy about the case. To me, it comes across as grasping, even greedy. MN law is pretty clear that a Certif. of Election is issued either, A) 7 days after a Canvassing Board count is Certified, or B) after an Election Contest Court has ruled subsequent to such a count. Because of Coleman's suit we are in option B) and we haven't gotten there yet.

I suppose the best part might be to have this all in place and fresh in everyone's mind for when the ECC DOES rule. Then, even when Coleman DOES appeal his latest 3-0 loss to the Supremes, the decision of the ECC is on the books and Franken's position gets MUCH stronger. But still, it'll make for some drama and a few headlines but it sure comes across to me like an ice-clogged storm drain flooding the intersection; leaves me damp, cold and mushy in the boots...

OK that will have to hold you. I have a beach to apply to my body. I'll stay for a few comments but that's the vacation-abbreviated latest from yust WAY SOUTHEAST of Lake Wobegon.

Shalom.

Exploring the Universe
February 5, 2009

Comments: 41   Recs: 73   Tips: 61

Haunted by the fear that the Elections Contest Court (ECC) would finally heave the Coleman case through the ice of Lake Superior and the MN Supreme Ct. would not even give them a lifeline (or phone a friend), AND that he would miss the big "Franken Swearing In" Party, WineRev has oped back to MN for... more of the same old, same old.

Elections Contest Court - Episode XVIII

Crackin' a Move On.

While I was shivering in Florida (last night was supposed to be in the 30s in Delray Beach – maybe the coldest night of the entire year for Mama WineRev) the ECC issued 2 rulings.

The Court ruled the "universe" of rejected absentee ballots that the Coleman side can even open their mouth about is 4,797. Well "universe" is overdone. The ECC DID throw a cosmic rope around quite a bit of the solar system and declare everything from the orbit of Jupiter outward as out of bounds: "No Outer Planet Ballots!"

During Wednesday's testimony Coleman main mouthpiece Joe Friedberg made another move to once again go to the edge of the Oort cloud to bring in the 11,000. One of the judges pulled out his or her phaser set on heavy stun and said, "We already ruled on that. Move on." (As in, "Ain't happenin'!") Ppppp-pffzzzztttt indeed!

Many have pointed out the 4,797 are NOT being counted, only reviewed for possible counting. And many have noted the counting will NOT be pretty for the Coleman Team:

Finally keep in mind this motion to limit applies to the Coleman Camp. From what I can gather from some of the esquires on these boards (red Starfleet uniforms and insignia of balancing scales around a staff of winding precedents), if/when the Franken team needs to present their side of the case THEY can bring in other ballots from the rings of Saturn or the clouds of Neptune. (They've already hinted they have 771 absentees they will drop into the nearest di-lithium crystal chamber whenever they need to.)

The ECC also ruled that the 1,351 − 418 = 933 (their numbers) of improperly rejected absentee ballots ("Pile 5") that were counted back on Jan 3 by the Sec. of State's office are IN. As in "this rock from the asteroid belt of 933 is in earth orbit now and has been properly mined." They went so far as to dismiss any further claims/objections from the contestant Norm Coleman as "dismissed with prejudice." "With prejudice" is not a civil rights thing here but court talk for "WE have ruled and DO NOT bring this sucker back."...you can't re-file, or raise objections, or do a Cullen Sheehan patented whine because "with prejudice" is NO, NO and "no internet, iphone, video games, texting or anything with a TV screen for a week, Cullen, do you hear me?"

AND, the 418 (which have long been noted on these diaries as the 392/393 of the "5th pile" absentee ballots)? Well the ECC order regarding the 4,797 above also uses language about examining (and counting?) "absentee ballots that have been rejected through no fault of the voter." This means to me that the ECC has seen this 418-sized asteroid afloat between Mars and Jupiter and will sooner or later bring that rock into earth orbit for vote mining. The "Nauen 61" and even the "Kennedy 7" might well be caught in the tractor beam. (Team Franken is getting ready to say, "What YOU fail to realize, Sarris, is that I am *dragging mines!*")

Sooooooo... with those 2 moves, I think the ECC has begun asserting itself. The headlines have all been about the 4,797 and somehow this being a "big win for Coleman in his effort to retain his seat in the US Senate" but that's just hype for 2 reasons.

It's almost a word for word repetition from Ben Ginsberg at the daily Coleman presser. Just because Drake or Sheehan leads Ginsberg out on a straining neck chain to the podium so he can slobber out "Voters don't matter. Elections don't matter. Democracy only means illusions for little people and control by lawyers from Gorn like us, disguised as earthlings" doesn't make his slug-slime trailings anything like true or even significant.

Team Franken has been quite calm about this. Yes they tried to pin Coleman's side down to his little 654 cherries but the 4,797 doesn't seem to bother them. They don't look or sound down or sputtering to explain how this "mortal blow" is actually good news for John McCain. They are very much going on in a business-as-usual, running-the-starship sort of way, quite unruffled.

MN Supreme Court 9:00 a.m.CT

The MN Supreme Ct. will hear arguments TODAY. Since the Supreme Ct. gave the ECC THEIR courtroom for the ECC trial, the Supreme Court will hear the arguments in the old/historic Supreme Ct. chamber in the State Capitol; cool! Yay historic!...hope the video and sound are OK.

It is almost certain Justice Alan Page will preside and Chief Justice Magnuson and Associate Justice G. Berry Anderson will recuse themselves in honor of their service on the State Canvassing Board. (You may well hear from another "Justice Anderson" who is PAUL Anderson, same last name but a different justice.) Word is Marc Elias will speak for the Franken side and [James] Langdon for Team Coleman and the lightsabres are ready.

As in so much of the MN recount: "We'll see." It SHOULD be good watching though. Based on previous hearings the MN Supreme Court,justices seem to like testing attorneys in their Jedi training with pointed questions and tightly drawn hypotheticals. They also are quick to defend their own integrity: back in December Coleman's Roger Magnuson thought to draw on his experience 8 years ago on the Bush legal team in Bush v. Gore and began throwing around Florida 2000. Justice Paul Anderson cut him off with a sharp, "This is not Florida." When Magnuson persisted, Anderson nearly used the Force to lift Magnuson off the floor by the neck and was vocal about this hearing and this court being FAR from Florida and that the attorney was NOT helping his case AT ALL by persisting.

My guess is if it IS Elias and Langdon that Elias will need to be nimble but that the Court will enjoy questioning his sharp mind (even if they don't agree with him.). Langdon's reviews at The UpTake live blog have been dull: bloggers have seen him as plodding and simplistic, with bouts of condescension. If so he will need to sharply raise his game with the lively Justices who sit on the MN Supreme Court.

OK, great to be back to single digit weather. Hope the car starts and I can get to the wine shop on time. 9:00 a.m. CT for the Supreme Court hearing. And, the ECC MAY (unsure) recess proceedings while the Supreme Ct. hears arguments. Otherwise it's The UpTake on split screen. Meanwhile hope this will hold you until then with all the latest from yust southeast of Lake Wobegon.

Shalom.

Steadily Steady
February 6, 2009

Comments: 76   Recs: 169   Tips: 159

The universe stayed the same size yesterday (cosmologists take note!). Steady-state theorists fighting off "oscillating universists" and "endlessly expanding universists" now have FACTS emerging for their case. In the far corner of the (same-size) universe called "Minnesota" (a region of space that exists under an ice cloud and features slow-grinding legal masses chewing through space in time units called "Friedbergs") the universe stayed the same Thursday.

Election Contest Court – Episode XIX
County Auditors, Female

The ECC got rolling about 10:30 yesterday (even the judges wanted to catch the MN Supreme Court Special at 9:00 a.m.). Camp Coleman called 3 county auditors during the day, still trying to make their case about absentee ballots being badly handled in unequally protected ways. As usual they were getting as much flak as support from their own witnesses.

Ms. Corbid from Washington County (E of St. Paul to the WI line; Stillwater) had a chance to testify, and the Coleman camp sent 2 observers out on election night (Nov. 4-5), arriving at 2:00 a.m.; they stayed till 5:00 a.m. Sounds a bit odd now, but it also shows Team Norm had some really dedicated people working for him, which actually makes me proud. I may not like a given candidate, but I can salute that kind of middle-of-the-night dedication in anybody.

After the lunch recess Cathy Clemmer was called, auditor for Pine County (N of St. Paul, about 1/2 way to Duluth). Ms. Clemmer impressed the ECC, lawyers on both sides, and the entire The UpTake Live Blog universe with her sterling "Joe Friday/ Dragnet" impression that could not be shaken. She was "Just the Facts, ma'am" until it hurt (if you are a Coleman fan you KNOW how facts hurt). Even Franken Team's Kevin Hamilton could not reach her when he tried a Lizard People joke (told you she was tough).

She was defending herself by defending her staff and seemed mortified by the one glitch the county had election night when 100 votes were "lost" and then found a day or so later due to simple human error at 5:00 a.m. on Wednesday Nov. 5.

Your not-yet-intrepid WineRev had caught this in mid-November when the local Pine County press had called out and then clobbered the Reich-wing Noise Machine (and effectively too; I don't believe they've ever brought it up specifically again because they KNOW they've met their master in Pine County.)[11]

> The other (*StarTribune* letter to the editor) is from the publisher of the Sandstone, MN newspaper (Sandstone = about 1/2 way up the road between St. Paul and Duluth). He vents (by name) at O'Reilly, Hannity & Colmes, ranting about "100 votes" just showing up out of nowhere. The publisher hammers home 129 votes (for Franken) were counted in Partridge Township and delivered to Pine County. At 5:00 a.m., 11/05/08, the clerk receiving them wrote down "29." The county canvassing board caught and corrected the TYPO. End of story – and a very restrained, righteous rant. Way to go, Mr. Tim Franklin of the *Pine County Courier*.

That was Ms. Clemmons' county canvassing board making the catch and correction, Mr. Friedberg (like YOU never use the delete key on your laptop? Wait, let me translate that for you: you mean you never use the flat end of the stylus on your wet clay legal briefs?) Yeah, and when the *Pine County Courier* has you in its sights you'd better duck and cover because they have CLOUT!

Third and last called (and held over for Friday) was Anoka County Auditor Rachel Smith. Some of you stone-crazy fanatics will recall Ms. Smith from several weeks ago. Remember the MN Supreme Ct. on Dec. 18th issued a 3-2 decision re: the "5th pile", improperly rejected absentee ballots. The 1,346 of these would be counted IF the Franken, Coleman AND county officials involved agreed to count a given ballot. (A lot of pixels have been flung over the veto this gave each campaign. 933 DID get counted; the other ~400 are hanging fire.)

---

11   *See diary dated November 17, 2008.*

You may recall these 3-way negotiations didn't always go smoothly, and the most spectacular was from Anoka County. As I noted back on December 31:

> ...Anoka County (N of Twin Cities, exurban); Coleman lawyer: we aren't going to approve any of the 1346 statewide (including those from Anoka County) un-less/until we consider the 654 (Norm's cherry picked favorites from the remaining 11000 rejected ballots statewide) too. Franken lawyer: "Let me cut to the chase. We're not going to agree to any of the 654. The 654 is from left field." Anoka County election manager Rachel Smith: "I don't want to waste anyone's time here" and shut down the meeting. (Sent them home without supper? Way to go Rachel!) Total breakdown in talks. Anoka County has invited both sides back for Round II today...

The above took 8 minutes and Rachel Smith was the one swinging the gavel at the scene. THAT was the Rachel Smith on the stand Thursday.

Bloggers were impressed at how gently and carefully Friedberg handled her on the stand, as though she might, you know, grab him in a jiu-jitsu wristlock and throw him to the floor just for something to do. But the real news of the day came that 6 ballots had lately been uncovered in Anoka County. All 6 were Coleman votes and if allowed will take Franken's lead to +219. But there hangs the tale: have their dupli-cates already been counted? Maybe. (If so, "Petard, meet hoist... over there at the Coleman table.") Are they admis-sible since the Coleman universe by ECC order Monday is limited to the 4797 ballots already specified and these 6 are NOT ON THE LIST? More to come from Rachel Smith Friday.

How is the ECC Doing?

Not as fast as I would like, of course, but I'm not the one to ask. I was pleased to read this over (except for the April/June part) at one of the Live Blogs from a practicing attorney who can give some perspective (maybe we've got it better than we know):

> Because I have been involved in court trials, and observed the MN tobacco trial. The court system is not a fast and efficient arbiter. It is plodding and deliberative and that is a good thing. The tobacco case went on for 2 years before the trial that lasted several months. The Exxon case went on for decades.
>
> This will be all over, contest and appeals by June at the latest. I think the 3 judges will have a decision before April. 4 months from start to finish is lightning fast in the judicial system. Anyone here been involved in a civil dispute in district court? Divorce? Roof shingle case? You would be lucky if the court set a hearing date within 4 months. This is being fast tracked, but the internal process of taking tes-timony and creating a record takes time. Let give the process a chance, and lets give the judges credit for knowing how to conduct a trial. (No(ahs)VoteLeft Behind at The UpTake)

MN Supreme Court hearing

The MN Supreme Court heard the Franken case Thursday asking for a Certificate of Election. Only 4 justices present (Chief Magnuson and Associate G. Barry Anderson recusing themselves and Justice Helen Meyer not present – getting over ankle surgery – but WILL be in on deliberations and decision) but they were spirited in the old Supreme Court room at the State Capitol. Franken atty. Marc Elias (from DC) commented on the beauty of the room before he took questions afterwards at the presser.

Elias made his best case: Franken deserves a Certificate of Election because he is the certified count leader, MN is entitled to 2 Senators in DC. The Court reminded him that the ECC is not finished and MN law calls for that to be decided before a certificate can issue.

Elias offered the current situation as evidence itself: what prevents a contestant from dragging out an ECC for weeks and months while denying the leader his/her seat? Justice Lorie Skjerven Gildea (how much more Scandinavian can you get?): "MN law decides who's a winner. The US Senate decides who sits."

The Court asked Elias how they could issue a certificate. Elias had a clever answer: MN courts have REVOKED certificates of election in the past (at the state legislative and local level). If they have the power to revoke one don't they also inherently have then the power to create one?

Langdon for Coleman had the easier case to plead and did a workmanlike job of it by all accounts. The MN Solicitor General also appeared (from the Attorney General's office) to argue the state's POV (which matched up with Langdon/Coleman).

As expected, the Court took it "under advisement." They will round up Justice Meyer, deliberate, and if the past is any guide, issue a decision in the next few days (as they have on everything else in this recount that has come before them). If so I'd wager they will deny Franken's request.

Two things to watch for:

If they deny the request, is the vote unanimous (5-0)? Or is it a split decision (4-1/ 3-2)? If the latter, it gives encouragement to the Franken team (morale always goes up if, in a losing decision, at least 1 justice thought you had a case; very reassuring thing for a lawyer.)

Does the decision indeed come down in the next 3-4 days? Or does it linger? Do they chew on it, letting the ECC process grind on, maybe even reaching some decisions that give the Supreme Ct. grounds for saying, "In light of the on-going ECC trial and the direction that case is moving..."?

And now for something completely different...

In yesterday's MN Supreme Court hearing Franken attorney Marc Elias argued as well as he could (which is quite well, which still doesn't mean he'll win his point, but it was well argued) the MN Supremes should consider ordering a certificate of election for Franken on grounds that the US Constitution calls for each state to be equally represented in the upper legislative house and the Senate. To keep going the way things are going, Minnesota is deprived and under-served

This swings the spotlight briefly toward Minnesota's (soon-to-be-SENIOR) senator Amy Klobuchar. She and her staff are having to pick up extra work helping out Minnesotans with the usual sort of constituent services:

veteran's medical issues,

overseas adoption snafus,

a pointed letter on "Sen. Amy Klobuchar, Minnesota Senator" letterhead to the Federal Baitshop & Icehouse inspection agency ("the OTHER FBI", their business cards say; dress code is long-sleeve flannel shirts and cami overalls with dark goggles and a curled wire coming out of one ear down the front to the battery heated socks), politely telling them to lay off Lars Fjelsen-Hakkonnen's "Rent-a-Shack" ice-fishing business on Gull Lake. (The FBI(ia) is worried Lars may be renting to Winnipeg terrorist sympathizers who are leaving leaflets around saying "Single Payer Health Care for Everyone, eh? You should try it oot and aboot YOUR hoos too!")

But people, we REALLY need to get Al Franken to DC before the load crushes Amy. Now comes word she is picking up Al's comic load as well. I mean, how much more can we expect from 1 Minnesota senator? Sure she was good, excellent even (among others she told a Barney Frank joke, with Barney Frank in the room, and Barney Frank laughed himself off his chair! You go girl!), but we can't burn her out.

ECC, if you are reading this...MN Supremes, I beseech you... send Al Franken to the Senate now before Amy Klobuchar undergoes comic burnout. America needs the laughs, now more than ever.

OK hope that will hold you until we all meet around the hot stove at The UpTake blog starting at 9:00 a.m. for day 10 of the ECC. Time for coffee and the early shift at the wine shop; that's the latest from yust southeast of Lake Wobegon.

Shalom.

Light Space Opera
February 7, 2009

Comments: 124   Recs: 168   Tips: 187

Election Contest Court – Episode XX

The trial...excuse me *(yawning)*...the trial *(nods off)*...the trial was BORING as hell, even with the Anoka County Auditor on the stand all day *(Rachel Smith, known by her fans as the hearthrob: "Coffee Cup Girl" – and the inevitable "CCG" by those desiring fan club membership).*

The six found ballots in Anoka County look like they are THREE ballots, not six. Still unclear if they will be counted. And as several posters noted thinking these are a +3 for Coleman is stretching things a LOT. Anoka County (3rd most populous in the state) has nothing but cross-currents:

part of the Michele Bachmann 6th district,

AND contains city of Blaine, who's mayor is Elwin Tinklenberg who ran against Bachmann, so there are normal people there,

AND was the home of Jesse Ventura and gave the man a strong vote in '98 to put him in the governor's mansion,

AND saw a record absentee ballot count this year due to the Obama and Franken campaign's efforts to encourage this.

So to say these 3 ballots are in the tank for Coleman if the ECC will admit them at all for: a) not in the Coleman universe, b) chain of custody issues, but also c) count every legal vote, is a stretch under any scenario.

So how long before this approaches resolution? Duchschere of the StarTribune quotes Judge Denise Reilly:

> Reilly let slip a couple of clues in court Friday, when she reiterated that the panel plans to "make sure that every legally cast and wrongfully rejected ballot is opened and counted."
>
> As for legal and procedural questions that have been churned up, Reilly said that the judges "have talked about a motions day when we will consider these issues." *(Star Tribune)*

Now how they are going to count "valid, legal ballots" is also up for grabs but Duchschere has an idea for the ECC:

> Minnesota's last big recount, the 1962 governor's race, might provide some ideas. In that case, three judges were appointed to oversee the recount and appointed bipartisan teams around the state to slash the number of disputed ballots from 97,000 to 3,851. In the trial that followed, those ballots were sorted into categories – all those with strange voting marks were put together, or those apparently marked for two candidates. Instead of considering every ballot by itself, the judges agreed to turn thumbs up or down on entire categories of ballots. That trial was over in three weeks. *(Star Tribune)*

Grace Kelly tuned in late at The UpTake (which by the way is also being watched by Al Franken himself!) and capped it all:

> Wow, it looks like I missed nothing in the trial, and everything on the blog: movie plans, Minnesota spice, discussions of passive voice and position, and even Gilbert and Sullivan! *(The UpTake)*

All of which goes to show once again that nature abhors a vacuum (like the Coleman case) and that human beings can fill it with Kunin/Kumin/cumin vs. cilantro spats and handy light opera (here follows WineRev's attempt at doggerel via *HMS Pinafore*):

> Joe Friedberg enters, with Trimble, Knaak, Magnuson, Langdon & Ginsberg following closely behind.

Joe Friedberg	I am the captain of the Coleman case
Trimble, Knaak, Magnuson, Langdon & Ginsberg	And a right good captain too
Joe Friedberg	I can blabber by the hour and always looking dour and never make a point at all
Trimble, Knaak, Magnuson, Langdon & Ginsberg	He blabbers by the hour, and always looking sour he never makes a point at all
Joe Friedberg	Every witness I call undercuts my case and makes Norm look like a fool, I play to the base and keep a straight face and I'll never let AL get his Seat!
ECC Judges	What, never?
Coleman lawyers	No, never!
Coleman lawyers	What, never?
ECC Judges	We'll decide whenever!
Entire cast at The UpTake Live Blog and Daily Kos	So give 3 cheers and 3 cheers more, for the hearty judges of the ECC, Let them bring this mess to an end, so Al can sit as Minnesota's friend!

Hope this will hold you for the week end. If there's no news, I'll wait till Monday to put up a diary. Enjoy Saturday like we do yust southeast of Lake Wobegon.

Shalom.

Trial Day 11, with rant
February 9, 2009

Comments: 33   Recs: 74   Tips: 75

Friday in ECC Court

Bless them, The UpTake legal fans were at it again Friday, following Coleman attorney Joe Friedberg and his cast of self-destructing witnesses. How do The UpTake people stay awake through hours of Joe Friedberg? I think at least some of them have fallen back on a Civil War method. When Union army units were scheduled for a dawn attack, officers prohibited the men from lighting fires to boil coffee (and also give away their positions). So the men simply chewed the coffee beans and sipped from their canteens until the order came to move out.

When the Coleman witness (Rachel Smith of Anoka County elections) wasn't poking holes in the Coleman case, Friedberg seemed to be maneuvering toward a staggering idea. The UpTake watchers (some with little black granules between their teeth) offered thoughts:

Witness: Rachel Smith, Anoka County Elections Director. Contestant: Norm Coleman. Requirements: for an absentee ballot to be accepted and counted as cast.

> The witness said that to ignore the requirements as suggested by the contestant would be against the law
>
> I love how Friedberg objects every time the witnesses are asked if they feel the count was handled correctly and then he gets overruled
>
> Friedberg wants to allow late absentee ballots, are we suddenly going to have a ton of late absentee ballots admitted into evidence, anybody who didn't vote on election day could vote now???
>
> *(various, unknown live bloggers at The UpTake)*

The Coleman side basically wants all reasons for rejecting an absentee ballots struck down. Yep. Anybody can vote anytime (no deadlines) from anywhere (Michele Bachmann's basement?) regardless of signatures (so Mickey Mouse = Tom Cruise?) and no checking to see if they have voted in person first (or also?).

I kid you not. That is the desperation level of the Coleman case. This is so breath-taking and anti-American (you know, like so many things over the last 8 years) that at the close of business Friday the ECC asked both sides for written arguments over admitting absentee ballots that have been (twice) rejected. The Franken side will have to make "follow the law as passed in the 60s and added to by case law since then" sound sexy and legal all at once. For Lillehaug, Elias, Pentelovitch, Hamilton, and their staffs that could actually be rather fun.

On the other hand, Team Coleman is trying to make the case to set aside all that, you know, LAW stuff. After all, laws are for little people, right? Not for big, aristocratic, important, Republican people, right?

Well let me just say this about that: *(Instead of a soapbox WineRev climbs on 6 massive volumes on Western Civilization by Will and Ariel Durant and uncorks a magnum of* **Chateau du Rant, '09**. *TASTING NOTES: For a new vintage very pronounced: flaming aromatics with hints of brimstone; full-bodied scorn opening at the lips and pungent outrage mid-palate; closes with a tangy bile d'upchuck and a long-lingering rankle of HST '72.)*

To: *Norm and "friends" Trimble, Knaak, Magnuson, Friedberg, and especially YOU, Ginsberg (who the ECC has the good sense so far not to let in to stink up their courtroom)*

What the freakin' hell do you want now? You are honestly going to file a Motion asking the ECC to void MN election law for absentee ballots? Not ALL ballots of course, just the 4,797 in your particular universe?

Are you out of your American jurisprudential minds?

Your tedious and lately wildly misnamed "Republican" party has spent 8 years stuffing the "Bushista Defense Panel" (formerly known as the US Justice system) with "graduates" of "Regent University Law" & "Liberty University Law", *(law degrees worth a $49.95 "freewill, tax-deductible LOVE offering" and 6 box tops from Rice Krispies.).* Your Clear-Channel/Murdoch/Faux Noise graduates of Propaganda U *(summa cum Goebbels)* have screamed "voter fraud", "cemetery voting", "stolen elections", and "ACORN activists" for a deafening six years.

Yet all the radio ravers, all the small-screen screamers, and all the slobbering gum-chewers who barely have the brainpower to unsnap their briefcases (Exhibit 1: Monica Goodling); those putrid jackboot-ers haven't yet come up with a SINGLE CASE of voter fraud or "double voting." But NOW you want a court of the United States, State of Minnesota, to COMMIT voter fraud for you?? You want absentee ballots that were rightfully rejected under LAW now to COUNT?

Ballots whose signatures (as required by LAW) do not match because the voter was in Arizona tending his sick mother so his girlfriend signed it for him? You want THAT in? What's next? An absentee ballot from, "Bachmann, Michele" on the application but signed by "Jesus H. Christ"? By your theory, why not?

Ballots that arrived LATE? Secretary of State Ritchie is willing to enforce the LAW against late ballots (with tears in his eyes and a choking in his throat when they have arrived postmarked Baghdad) but you want him to BREAK THE LAW? I tell you Colemaniacs, that Ritchie is a real man, with so much integrity and honesty that he could transfuse each of you a pint of his character so you would give up chasing ambulances and he'd still have enough left to run a clean, transparent election w/recount as needed.

Ballots from UNREGISTERED voters? You want registration dropped as a requirement, but only in 4,797 cases? You frozen pond-scum lickers!! I, WineRev (you can address me by my nickname, "Equal Protection"), **demand** you include my second vote in your Motion. I already voted in person Nov. 4 as a registered voter. Now as a matter of "equal protection" I want to UNREGISTER and cast an absentee ballot (or maybe *several*; or has it JUST occurred to you this is one reason registration exists?) And I want to do it now, late, and I'll get my almost 16 year old son "WineRev-ER" to sign it for me as "WineRev-ER" so the signatures won't match! But for "equal protection" I want it counted, again. After all, my voting should certainly count twice as much as that treacherous Cullen Sheehan! (For that little snot-picker's vote, I can make a case for 5 or 6 of mine.)

Yours is the latest in reprehensible legal bilgewater. By your Motion, you sneer at the People's legislature of Minnesota who put this together. You dismiss with a hiss and a chop of the hand your fellow barristers who have built 40 years of case law on the sturdy foundation of the People's legislation. You treat with arrogant disdain THOUSANDS of precinct workers from around the state, many of whom were VOTING before Norm was born, some of whom lost husbands, sons and relatives in wars fought to preserve the rule and votes of the People.

If the FCC judges *don't* handle your Motion with iron tongs while wearing gas masks, you should count yourselves fortunate. But then you have run your entire case like this, first with Trimble and his "coincidental" ballots from overwhelmingly Coleman precincts, then "Sominex" Joe Friedberg and his cast of self-inflicting witnesses, and finally the Florida 2000 Coupmaster, "Ginzu Knives" Ben Ginsberg with his blatant words and outrageous acts against democratic rule.

Just watching you these last 2 weeks as a team of lawyers has been an exercise in tedious gagging, like being downwind on the street while a circus elephant with diarrhea splatters by.

In the words of the master Hunter Thompson your case has been "an ugly, low-level trip that hovered somewhere between dullness and obscenity - like a bad pornographic film that you want to walk out on, but sit through anyway and then leave the theater feeling depressed and vaguely embarrassed with yourself for ever having taken part in it, even as a spectator."

(*WineRev hurls empty bottle of Chateau du Rant out apartment window with perfect aim into recycling dumpster three stories down. The heavy glass shattering against the inside steel wall is enough to wake the dead. Driver of Volvo 245 with Doberman in back and Woody Creek, CO plates parked by dumpster rolls down window, unleashes string of hair-raising epithets and returns fire with empty bottle of Wild Turkey... hell of a neighborhood.*)

Tremor in Universe
February 10, 2009

Comments: 146   Recs: 254   Tips: 236

Most Coleman testimony Monday was from Kevin Boyle, elections officer from Dakota County (ex-urban, S of St. Paul). They actually covered a few dozen absentee ballots (a new ECC record). Most of the attention was on signatures matching or not matching. This is easily the most subjective part of the law and Team Coleman is doing Norm good to focus on it. If they can show enough variations between ballots, precincts, and counties, they may think they have a chance. Of course, many of these should have been covered earlier in pre-trial filings and motions and all sides were reminded of that Monday.

Election Contest Court - Episode XXI
Queen to Queen 3

In chess, the pawns make the opening moves, the knights do their odd one-step square/one-step diagonal stutter, the bishops set up for long diagonals. Eventually the rooks get to show their long sweep on the ranks and files. But when a queen moves (she can go both on the diagonal OR rank AND File) good players pause, even if she only takes one step.

Monday morning Knight Langdon opened for Team Coleman, shortly followed by the new Queen piece, Friedberg, listlessly flogging another witness about another ballot. Usually for Team Franken Knight Hamilton runs his lance in Court with objections, and occasionally Rook Elias flings his trebuchet in an objection or motion to the Court.

But Monday morning, just as the Friedberg Drone was setting in again for another day of ennui slathered with tedium, David (Franken's legal Queen) Lillehaug rose and stunned Team Coleman, the ECC and even The UpTake bloggers.

Says Lillehaug:

> "The problem is (Coleman) hasn't sat down and figured out which (rejected absentee ballots) they are really going to pursue and which ones they are not...
>
> "The fundamental purpose of the discovery rules, adopted almost 50 years ago, was to end the practice of trial by ambush. Parties are required to disclose their evidence prior to trial so that other parties can fairly prepare to meet the evidence," Lillehaug wrote in a memo to the judges...
>
> ...the Coleman legal team has flouted the basic rules of evidence and given the Franken team only "sweepingly uninformative and nonresponsive answers" to the Democrat's demands to know more about the ballots and the reasons Coleman believes they should be counted. *(Pioneer Press)*

With a dazzling and elegant sweep of a royal-blue lightsaber he stood and called, **"Objection! Move to strike** all this Colemanistic Crapola!" (OK it was a bit more formal than that) and then lopped off the nearest leg of the Coleman legal table in a shower of blue and white sparks and a crash of wood, binders and laptops. Friedberg, red lightsabre flickering with 3 D-cells clicking in handle, rasped back, "It's all Franken's fault we don't have any evidence since they won't give us their clean ballot copies." (One lone spark floats in air above Friedberg then winks out.)

As in chess, everyone paused when the queen made a move. Friedberg blamed Team Franken, Langdon, county officials and the ghost of Mata Hari for the current procedure. Team Coleman called Lillehaug's move of, you know, pointing out how overdue their PRE-TRIAL homework is, "grandstanding" and both sides almost did a "is *not* grandstanding", "is too", "is not", "is too!" sequence.

The ECC was so amazed something happened in their courtroom they took a 20 minute recess to consider Lillehaug's objection. When they came back Judge Marben spoke for the Court: "Objection overruled...for the moment."

For the moment, eh? I think that means the Judges had just time enough to take Lillehaug's objection down to Lake Nokomis on a snowmobile and put it under the ice in suspended animation. Not kill it, but suspend it. For the moment! Hmmmmmm. Maybe nothing... but maybe the beginning of something... I'm not sure what. These judges have been so careful and guarded in their statements that this is NOT casual... for the moment...

Bishop to King-Knight 4 - on the Slice

And lest you think that a "for the moment" was the only effect of the Lillehaug Queen move, the ECC later called counsel into chambers over lunch. They talked over "ways to expedite" the trial and move beyond this 1-by-1 introduction of absentee ballots, but no one in the afternoon session or at the pressers later gave any clues if this went anywhere. So, we'll see.

But over lunch, while no one could approach chambers, an unearthly light was seen glinting several times from under the door sill. A low hum was heard and all the press, between bites of their fried walleye with tartar sauce sandwiches (from the McDonald-berg's Sled-Thru Window?), wondered what it could be.

The UpTake's intrepid Mike McIntee whipped off his "MacGyver" model wire-rim glasses, bent them into several twists, aligned the two lenses at 67-1/2 degrees, and licked one ear loop before snapping it into his iPhone. Jennifer back at The UpTake headquarters pointed the aluminum garbage can lid to the southwest until Mike picked up the Chinese GPS satellite link. Back came the iApp from Starfleet Academy, accessed through a future-oriented wormhole. Running the Tri-chorder iApp McIntee ran the data through the Atari sub-routine, then mused under his breath to Kunin, "Now why would the ECC need a tunneling anti-boson gamma beam generator?"

The heat was enough to raise Twin Cities air temperature in early February to near 40, so thank goodness it didn't go on long. When ECC reconvened, they announced (since confirmed by astronomers at Arecibo Radio Telescope, PR) that the (Coleman) **universe has just shrunk by 174 ballots.** Whatever goggles they wore let them see into the asteroid belt beyond Mars to declare 174 ballots LATE (as in NOT ON TIME, Norm) and stipulated by both sides as OUT. So 4,797 – 174 = 4,623 ballots are left in the Coleman Properly Rejected 2 Times By People Who Have Done This Before And Are Sick And Tired Of Having Their Integrity Questioned...Universe.

(Is that two weeks of trial ROPE being tugged just a bit around one side's neck? Hmmmmmmm...)

PxP, P-QN4, P(5)xP(ep), N-Bishop 6 "Check": Motions Day

You know, since the Great Minnesota Recount has moved into Court there has been a certain loss of drama. Oh I know, Ben Ginsberg does his best every day when he fouls the air with his latest anti-democratic fumery but the witnesses, ballots, and questions have been less than riveting. *(Yesterday even Friedberg was reduced to "I un-withdraw this ballot" and confessed at one point, "I'm confused. What am I asking?" Sounds like Early Stage Stockdale to me: "Who am I? What am I doing here?")* I think the Court senses this as well and they are worried about their ratings. Being clever judges they have come up with a plan hinted at late last week by Judge Reilly.

Monday, Feb. 16 is a legal holiday and all these county auditors and county election folk are entitled to the day off with pay. Calling them as witnesses seems onerous and costly. Indeed the day even suggests itself as a day off for the ECC.

Instead the ECC is going to have **Monday the 16th be "Motions Day"** in Coleman vs. Franken. Just the lawyers, and the court, and the press, and the public. The panel wants to hear and dispose of all sorts of pending, hinted at, threatened, withdrawn, un-withdrawn, re-instated, submitted, and potential motions without making a witness sit there in the dock while everyone debates.

This could be GREAT for ratings! Think of the Coleman Team... now think of the Franken Team. Who do YOU want making motions and arguing coherently, rationally, with case law, precedents, and even evidence at the ready? I mean look, Franken's (White Knight) Hamilton could "Move opposing counsel (Black Knight) Roger Magnuson be removed as an attorney from this trial and stripped of US citizenship on grounds he aided and abetted the Bush v. Gore legal team coup of Florida 2000 in violation of the Constitution." *(Finally Bush v. Gore would get a useful workout!)*

Team Coleman could bring out all of Al Franken's books, video-taped programs and scripts in a leap and ask Al to recant them. Humble Pawn Franken could stand there ("he could do no other!") and say, "Unless I am convinced of error by Scripture or right reason I will not recant." As Queen Friedberg sputters incoherently Al goes on, "If a devil will not yield to scripture, nor yield to prayer, then mock him. His pride that made him a devil will not allow him to be made fun of." Then he launches into, "There once was a lawyer named Friedberg..."

If there is to be courtroom drama, Monday the 16th could well be a red letter day to watch while contemplating the Paraguayan gratitude for the presidential acts of Rutherford B. Hayes.

God Talks to Norm?

As a religious body, the Jewish faith has always featured a strong intellectual component. The highest title among the religious is "rabbi" – teacher, which implies students, and study. There is a place for the Spirit blowing in a life, but Jews are not generally noted for a conversion experience that is a litmus test in some Christian circles.

Even when it happens in the Old Testament usually somebody is doing some explaining, teaching or even rebuking: God calls Samuel but old Eli has to explain who is calling. David thinks being called king by God lets him get away with murder and adultery, but Nathan the prophet can tell him off so vividly ("Thou art the man!" – and this was NOT a compliment) that the King is reduced to sackcloth and ashes, literally in those days. (2nd Samuel, Ch. 11 and 12).

Sooooo... now when word comes Norm believes "God wants me to serve" and in the context, "in the US Senate," well that's news. As Paul Seltzer of the Minnesota Independent points out this sounds like Norm has been hanging out with Michele Bachmann or even Sarah the Pale.

Norm, I think God values all sorts of service. In my tradition, "a charwoman scrubbing floors is doing work to the glory of God as great as that of a bishop consecrating a priest." But the Senate, Norm? You sure? Do you have a prophet in the house who will NOT tell you what your itching ears want to hear? Have you not studied the following?

An Iowa farm lad, a good and devout fellow, was feeling restless about life, wondering as he approached manhood what he should do with his life beyond farming. One hot summer night he couldn't sleep and went outside to work off some energy. He also took some time for prayer which helped calm him. In the still of a dark starry night he then looked up and saw clearly 2 letters floating there: "P" and "C." He told his family and friends about this encounter and finally decided this was a message from God: "P C" meant "Preach Christ."

Off he went to Lutheran seminary in Minnesota full of zeal and devotion. He did miserably in his studies, struggling with Greek and Hebrew, sweating doctrines and failing on all fronts. Finally, Dean Sorensonberg had him in for a talk and the lad recounted his vision of "P" "C."

"And you believe this was God telling you to preach Christ?"

"Yes."

"Hmmm. Given your background, and how you've done here, perhaps He did speak to you."

"You think so?"

"Yes. But "P" "C" for you might well mean "Plant Corn.""

So Norm... serve, yes. But maybe, plant corn?

OK that is quite a load for a Tuesday morning when "not much" happened Monday. I'll have a 2nd cup of coffee, watch yesterday's rain and drizzle freeze solid this morning, and think about sliding to the wine shop for the late shift when there are enough fender-benders on the roads. Until 9:00 a.m. CT when you all gather at The UpTake hot stove in the back of the ECC courtroom, and that's the latest from yust southeast of Lake Wobegon.

Shalom.

Day 12: The Court Acts
February 11, 2009

Comments: 148   Recs: 260   Tips: 195

And NOW for something completely different: meaning, action, movement.

By order of the **Election Contest Court (ECC)** certain ballots shall be counted; **Franken's lead** of +225 is now an "all over but the shoutin'" **+249**.

Election Contest Court – Episode XXII

Change in Karma

How boring has Coleman attorney's Joe Friedberg's case been? On Friday Friedberg asked a question of a witness so slowly he lost his own place in it. Courtroom observers say he has looked physically quite tired; the man is over 70 and has been showing it. Standing for hours on end at peak mental function IS tiring and it doesn't help when your case doesn't have anything to say.

So Tuesday saw Friedberg give way to Tony Trimble for the examination of Dakota County Auditor Kevin Boyle. But the change in lawyers seems to have altered the chemistry in the courtroom and the judges of the ECC made some moves. At the MN court website ten (10!) items are suddenly listed: affidavits, orders, motions, all dated Feb. 10.

Ballots IN!

There has been a parallel case unfolding alongside the Coleman/Franken collision in ECC: the 61 "Nauen" petitioners. By MN law such voters are entitled to petition an Election Contest court for relief (typical remedy: count my vote!) and these have done so.

Tuesday the ECC **ordered** 23 of these to be added to the totals the candidates received in the Certified Count (although they left open the actual DATE for this to happen). The Secretary of State's Office will apparently do the honors. Also implied was "These 23, but not yet, because there'll be *more coming* and you might as well do them all at once."

The 23 voters in question had filed detailed affidavits telling their "ballot story" and the Court approved. Scott Wente of the *Duluth New Tribune* had one of those stories:

> Eila Nelson of Two Harbors said her ballot was rejected because she improperly filled it out. The 83-year-old has blurred vision because of glaucoma and said she couldn't see that she accidentally marked Coleman when she intended to vote for Franken. Nelson's friend pointed out the mistake before it was submitted, and Nelson scratched it out and marked Franken. *(Duluth New Tribune)*

(Two Harbors is a lovely little resort sort of town on Lake Superior. Not so much fun to visit right now but delightful in the summer: June 24th to July 11th... you know, summer on Superior.)

Another Ballot IN!

While dealing with the "Nauen 61" and approving 23, the ECC also provisionally approved one more ballot. The voter here also affirmed in her affidavit all she had done to pass muster for her vote to count but with one hitch.

A voter must be registered to vote absentee. If they are not registered, or have reason to believe their registration is not current (just moved 2 weeks ago, for example), the absentee ballot packet includes a voter registration card. The deal is your ballot goes in one envelope (the "secrecy" envelope) and then that envelope and the registration card, etc. go in the outer mailing envelope.

This voter did all that but sealed her registration card in the inner "secrecy" envelope. When election officials opened the outer envelope: no registration card, and by checking voter rolls, she was not registered, so, quite properly, "Pile 3" rejected: by reason voter not registered.

Voter says she IS registered by virtue of her registration card that is in the (as yet) unopened "secrecy" envelope. The ECC ordered this ballot be provisionally included with the other 23 and be opened with the others. If her card is indeed there, and in order, then her vote is IN.

GREAT CALL by the ECC! (We pro-democracy types get very excited when the rule of the People gets affirmed.) But it's not just me saying that: **BOTH Team Coleman and Team Franken applauded** this act by the Court. Here's why:

For Team Franken they can continue their mantra "Count Every Legal Vote" with a clean heart. More practically, when precinct election officials sorted their absentee ballots into 4 piles, one for each legal reason for rejecting such a ballot, there were reports of this same situation (registration card inside secrecy envelope) in other locations. Some bloggers on these boards dubbed such cases the "Pile 3A" ballots and there were reports of about 41 of these floating around. As absentees have generally been favoring Franken (if the sampling is random and not cherry-picked), Team Franken can expect more votes.

Then too, as these ballots were admitted because they had been *set aside by mistake* on the part of election officials that sets off "good, good, GOOD, good vibrations" regarding those famous 393 "5th pile" ballots. I think the odds rise in favor of the 393 being admitted as well.

"But don't get cocky, kid." Team Coleman applauded too and for sound reasons. *First,* just getting these 23+1 ballots officially "IN" breaks the legal ice for this Court to actually add to vote totals. That power has always been there but it's just cozy to see it actually exerted.

Second, the Coleman case has been to get in previously rejected absentee ballots (from all the piles 1-4, not just these "3A"s.) They have been chary of the "pile 5" ballots (IMproperly rejected absentees), no doubt in part because they broke against them in the big Jan. 3 count of 933 (and Franken's lead went from +49 to the until-yesterday current +225). But the rest of their case lives and dies on getting other rejected absentee ballots added in. (Of course they have VERY definite ideas of just which particular ballots should be added in, and no others.)

Third, such "pile 3A" ballots may well be from more Colemanesque precincts and counties and so help their cause. Indeed, these are the sort of ballots Joe Friedberg early on mentioned might be worth physically weighing. He caught some flack for that but it wasn't a half-bad suggestion. The registration card would increase the weight of the "secrecy" envelope so you could make a fair case for saying such ballots, even unopened, were from voters who were wrongly denied their vote counting.

So bottom line: a good day for Franken fans but the Coleman side is right to smile too. With some of these ballots the numbers will move Coleman's way on some days to come (just not today, since the pool these 23 +1 came from was strongly Franken.)

On the other hand, the Colemaniks should be sobered by today's rulings. The 23 + 1 were admitted because their affidavits were detailed, precise and in conformity with the law. (Three attributes often majorly lacking in the Coleman testimonies so far.) "Substantial compliance" as the Colemaniks have been flinging around WON'T cut it. Do all 4,623 Coleman Universe ballots have affidavits with this detail? I doubt it.

So we may be on the road to Franken in the Senate and all of us celebrating, in Shamballa, but best leave the three dogs in the night a bit longer. :-D

More Rejected Ballots

The ECC got on a roll. With a view toward "expediting" the trial *(YAY!)* the Court yesterday issued an order to both camps ordering them to show why ballots in 1 of 19 (!) circumstances should or should not be counted.

> Should a ballot be barred if it went to the wrong precinct? Should a ballot be excluded if cast by a non-registered voter? And what about an unsigned ballot where the instructions for signing were obstructed by a pre-printed address sticker?
>
> Those are among 19 questions that District Judges Elizabeth Hayden, Kurt Marben and Denise Reilly want lawyers for Coleman and Franken to answer this week in a major development in a dispute over thousands of ballots that one side or the other wants counted. *(Star Tribune)*

This sounds like the Court is getting both sides to sort the Coleman universe (and obviously argue over individual ballots) 19 ways and then RULE on the 19 groups. *(Might I suggest the classic Roman "thumbs up/ thumbs down" group photo over each of the 19 piles? Makes a lovely documentary moment.)*

But what's really cool is the speed demanded. The Court issued this order YESTERDAY, close of court, 4:00 p.m. Due date? TODAY, close of court, 4:00 p.m. In the words of George Carlin and events pre-death: "24 hours. Get your **act** together!"

Now while "past performance is no guarantee of future results," I for one will NOT be surprised if about, oh, the 10:30 a.m. ECC mid-morning recess and cookie break, Lillehaug, Elias, and friends say, "May it please the Court (and it WILL!) Team Franken hereby submits their 19 slices of the Coleman universe." *(Beat the deadline again!)*

"Your Honors will note they are color-coded, tabbed and cross-indexed for easy reference. We hope your honors do not find the fine Corinthian leather bindings and *(Sotheby's and National Archives attested)* John Marshall autographs on the flyleafs ostentatious. Also, we enclose these ballots in virtual form on DVDs and in a searchable, cross-platform database. They are available by voice command in 3-D holographic form via your Honors' iPhones using the supplied "iBallot" software McIntee & Kunin hacked together last night on The UpTake's Apple IIe server (512K!) running MacOS System 4."

(During the cookie break the Judges discover if they run "iBallot" in a linked, 3-way iPhone network, the Judges' Chambers becomes a holodeck and they can virtually visit each of the 4131 precincts around the state and personally interview any local election official or absentee voter in real time.)

About 6 hours later (4:00 p.m. or so), the ECC turns their eyes to Team Coleman. Cullen Sheehan wheels in a warehouse dolly stacked with 19 peck and bushel baskets. [James] Langdon keeps going in and out the back doors, each time entering with more armloads of ballot photostats, slightly damp, warm to the touch and smelling pungently from the ditto machine. Trimble and Knaak step forward and desperately sift ballots into the pecks and bushels quietly muttering, "Red, green, horsey, the number 7, apple, star-shape, the letter C..." Joe Friedberg strikes a pose and says with Perry Mason-esque gravity: "Your honors, the Coleman Universe has arrived. The case speaks for itself. We await Norm Coleman's travel voucher." Court adjourns.

This order has real potential for moving things along. It may also figure in Monday's "Motion Day" arguments. By then the Judges will have had a chance to make up their own minds and be able to push back against both camps with their own position.

OK, I hope that will warm your coffee until 9:00 a.m. when so many of you gather at The UpTake for Trial Day 13. Gotta get to the early shift at the wineshop so that'll be the latest from yust southeast of Lake Wobegon.

Shalom.

Trial Turning Point #1
February 12, 2009

Comments: 130   Recs: 228   Tips: 204

Election Contest Court - Episode XXIII
An Order and Arguments

Late in the day Tuesday, the ECC issued an order to both sides in the case: by 4:00 p.m. Wednesday (24 hours!) each side was to supply written responses to the Court.

The Court laid down a marker in its Order:

"We the ECC put before the 2 sides 19 possible situations where an absentee ballot might have been rejected. Discuss in essay form each of the 19 and give reasons why such a ballot in 1 of 19 situation should be accepted and counted, or be rejected. Show your work."

The Response: Coleman

So each side had to submit written arguments which they did.

And what does each side say? In layman's brief (not boxer - and not lawyer style brief, which can be lengthy and intricate):

Coleman's side has been throwing around various groupings/classes of these ballots, by some reports numbering as high as 45. Their purpose has been to throw so much dust in the air using their own methods of confusion they can argue, "Look, these ballots have been SO arbitrarily handled, sorted, included, excluded (and made into paper airplanes) that to be fair, for the sake of 'equal protection' (i.e., same standards for same ballots) the ECC should re-do all 10,929 absentee ballots."

So the Coleman side LIKES categories and LIKES the list of 19 (not as much as their 45, but more than the boring Franken list of 1: "Count every legal vote"). In their written response they agree **17 of the court's situations** *should have ballots included and 2 should not.*

The Response: Franken

Franken's side has all along been calling for IMPROPERLY rejected absentee ballots to be counted, BUT, says the Franken team, there are VERY few other remaining absentee ballots that should be counted. Nearly ALL of the 4,623 were rejected for rightful reasons (i.e., came in late, voter already voted in-person, etc.) Because of this Team Franken is saying: "The local officials knew what they were doing in almost every case. Even when there's some question, here are some precedents and case law from the last 40+ years that applies and settles things." In their written response they hold **2 of the court's situations** *should have ballots included and 17 should not.*

What the Court could well do

Well you can't get much further apart than that! So TODAY the fun really begins as the ECC has scheduled **ORAL** arguments starting at 1:00 p.m.

Now mind you the 19 pieces of the Coleman Universe don't have any ballots in them. The Court has gone to their baking closet and brought out a big mesh frame with criss-crossed wires that make 19 pieces. They are proposing pressing this down on the Coleman Cookie Dough case that Friedberg, Trimble & Knaak have been rolling out the last 2-1/2 weeks. (The Court hasn't asked for lists of ballots to be put in the 19 pieces...yet. You can bet both sides could produce such a list from their view on short notice. You can be sure both sides will argue a LOT which ballots should go where.)

But they are doing something important: this gives the court the chance to break the universe of 4,623 into 19 pieces covering all the bases and affording both "equal protection" ("all the ballots were sorted in this manner") while (as Kossack beastiemom, Esq., points out) closing another avenue of appeal ("the ECC found a way to place these ballots in group 6 under this statute and applied the statute correctly") .

Instead of looking at each "Friedberged" (you know, droned, bored and withdrawn) ballot 1-by-tedious-1, the Court can look at groups. Then after arguments they can call for both sides to submit lists of ballots in each of the 19 pieces. And THEN they can rule "All ballots that are part of section 13 are OUT!" *(To put it another way, they fire up the anti-boson gamma generator first detected by Mike McIntee and slice off that part of the Universe.)*

Where the Court might Go

In ruling OUT 174 ballots that were late, and ruling IN 23 ballots from the "Nauen" group of 61, the ECC has shown strong signs of sticking with the statutes, so a number of their "19" will be slam dunks (e.g., voter NOT registered and NO registration card = OUT, end of story). They have also been careful in honoring the principle of "voter intent," not so much WHO a voter chooses but that they vote at all. So they have shown favor in the case of the +23 yesterday from the Nauen group to count ballots of voters who did everything right but foul-ups occurred on the election board side of things.

This last is potentially good news for the 393 "5th pile" ballots that are still outstanding. Given how the ECC has been ruling the ballots on that road may be humming the last verse of Edwin Starr's "25 miles" ("5 more miles to go now, over the hill, just around the bend...").

Underwhelm, Esq., on these boards first caught a detail in that 12/18 ruling: all the 1,346 will be counted when each side AND the county agree to count it (hence the veto) OR "when an election contest court so orders them counted." In other words, "work it out among yourselves being 'Minnesota Nice' and if you can't/won't, I'm pulling this judicial system off the road and coming back there to settle it!" And here we are in an Election Contest Court...

The Court's stance in favor of voters also is good news in one of their 19 situations where the ballot arrived ON TIME to the county courthouse Board of Elections. But because of some circumstance it was NOT delivered in time to the particular precinct where the voter is registered. When the precinct folks got it, it was late, so they didn't open or count it but that is no fault of the VOTER. So, the Franken Team will probably argue in favor of accepting such a ballot.

You can see how this could cut things down to manageable size. *In our dreams* of course the ECC antiboson gamma universe slicer lops off so many pieces that the ones left hold less than 249 ballots. Then Lillehaug stands up for Team Franken and "Move to Re-Submit our Motion for Summary Judgment. Even if they get 'em all it won't be enough." The Franken Team won't even have to mount their defense because (a delicious legal term this time) "the case is moot."

Well this isn't as tight as I'd like but I had the late shift yesterday and choir practice last night. (The tenors and basses are singing Sunday so we had to stay late to boot.) So that's the latest from yust southeast of Lake Wobegon.

Shalom.

Judges' Writing Day
February 13, 2009

Comments: 83   Recs: 180   Tips: 205

Election Contest Court - Episode XXIV
A Great Debate

ECC opened with Dakota County auditor Kevin Doyle winding up his testimony. They switched to Plymouth city elections director Sandra Engdahl. (Hennepin Co. includes Plymouth, a western, 2nd ring suburb.) She will continue Friday morning.

Here's another witness that will probably do more to help Franken's case than Coleman's. Here's why the Internet is so cool that notes like this happen in real time! Check this opening line:

> I was a recount observer in Plymouth for both days it took there. Sandy was a terrific manager of the recount process. She was extremely well organized, efficient, and she ran a really tightly disciplined ship! A lot of people there, it would have been a zoo if she had not been such a strong disciplinarian holding down all idle talking while people were sorting and counting. And she read the riot act to both Coleman folks and Franken folks when they got too loud or broke any of her rules - scrupulously fair. Anybody who saw it as I did would say it was absolutely fair. I fell in love with her. Unrequited love, sadly. *(unknown at The UpTake)*

In other words, if Sec. of State Mark Ritchie ever needs to hire someone for MN elections, here's somebody you want!

Lawyers Written, Lawyers Oral

The real action was in the afternoon. The Court heard arguments for over 2 hours from both sides over the 19 "circumstances" that might lead to an absentee ballot being rejected. Each side had filed briefs at the end of business Wednesday and bloggers took a look. General consensus:

> As I read the competing briefs, it seems to me that Franken's response directly addresses each question posed by the court while Coleman's response hedges. Coleman's brief might seem on its face to support the counting of 17 categories, but that support seems to really be for special cases in many cases. *(unknown, at The UpTake)*

Friedberg and Langdon opened for Coleman. Freidberg made an impression:

> They never should have allowed Friedberg to present in this hearing. *(aonanodad at The UpTake)*

> I can't believe the judges will buy that *(WaltAz at The UpTake)*

> So ends the creationist version of election contests... *(Joe in GB at The UpTake)*

Lillehaug & Elias answered for Franken. Elias' specialty is "election law" and I have to think that is rather esoteric, so Al has an edge here. The bloggers agreed.

> oh great argument - we aren't here to challenge the rules, we are here to establish whether votes followed the rules! *(Mrs B at The UpTake)*

> I'm liking Elias's argument. He argued with passion and with authority. He just gave the court a clear template for taking "strict compliance" view. Concise, logical and well-argued. Well done, Mr. Elias! *(VA Atty at The UpTake)*

Fate Takes a Hand

About 10:00 a.m., Presiding Judge Elizabeth Hayden announced things were going in a new direction. Both sides would make their oral arguments Thursday afternoon as planned.

THEN: Friday morning: witness testimony (continuing with Sandra Engdahl, Plymouth.)

NO Court Friday afternoon because the ECC will be writing one or more court orders.

By Monday morning, Judge Elizabeth Hayden indicated, the judges will have their order ready for the Franken and Coleman attorneys. The panel has given the attorneys until 1 p.m. Monday to change their cases in reaction to that decision.

So a writing day for the Court. A sweating weekend for the paralegals. A blogging day for The UpTakers and Kossacks. Sounds like a great President's day treat. And Motion Monday could really rock.

I gotta go. To all of you from yust southeast of Lake Wobegon.
Shalom.

Valentine's Day: Chicago Style
February 14, 2009

Comments: 167   Recs: 123   Tips: 124

The Election Contest Court (ECC) ruled on 19 categories of rejected absentee ballots. They asked both sides for briefs Tuesday, deadline Wednesday, heard orals Thursday afternoon (with a Coleman atty. admitting to the Judges, "You're not buying this are you?"), and took a half day Friday afternoon to write.

In honor of St. Valentine's Day, Chicago-style in the 1920's, I would invite youse to **"Talk like a Gangster Day."**

Election Contest Court – Episode XXV
Da Court's got Somethin' to Say dat youse guys should Hear.

Foist they all spent the morning hearing more from Sandra Engdahl, da Plymouth city election gal. (Plymouth is in Hennepin county, which is mostly Franken turf, but it's a suboib, where the Red State mob is tryin' to muscle in.) They had about 800 absentee ballots and nixed about 171 of them. Coleman's mouthpieces keep tryin' to show what kinda hanky-panky might have gone down but Engdahl wasn't showin' any cards.

When Hamilton from Franken gave her the old morning cross-exam she wasn't havin' anything from him either. Some a da bloggers thought she spent too much time lookin' over at the Coleman table for help when Hamilton was leanin' on her and she clearly didn't like being up there, but everybody got through it.

Then, the Judges sent everybody to lunch and said, "We'll call youse when we wants youse!" About 4 in the afternoon they let it drop.

Ya know those **19 categories** of absentee ballots? The ECC has said we ain't gonna walk through every damn one of these 4,623 absentees dat Coleman wants. *("It'd be like takin' a trip through da whole universe if you know what I mean.")* Nope. We're gonna cut 'em 19 ways, and then we're gonna throw out bunches."

The Coleman stiffs wanted 17 of the 19 to make it through. The Franken hired guns wanted them to knock off 17 and just leave 2.

The ECC brought the gavel down and said: 10 are dead.

But then everybody read the thing and can see they put a few together and that 13 are out. Then Franken's main talker Elias came out and said they way they saw it **13 are out** because the ECC said they were out...and 4 more are out if you read the Order the right way, you know, by implication and logic.

The Coleman mob sent out Knaak, for the first time in a while instead of Ginsboig, to say the 4,623 is only down to 3,500 and they are sure Norm "The Teeth" is going back to the Senate soon.

The bloggers who like to run the numbers (when they're not runnin' numbers for us) are figurin' Norm lost at least 800, and maybe as high as 1100 off his stack.

Big issue hangin' fire is still how the Court is goin' to look at the **signature matches of Pile 2,** and there's a lot of those. But the Court also took a pretty hard line one what's in and what's out. They look to be pretty strict on following the law, so if the law says: No match, no vote, dat's what they're going to do. And THAT is not what the Norm gang wants. One writer put it that the ECC were singin' Franken's song and a lot of their order sounded like a straight lift from Elias' song and dance.

And I'll tell ya, da Court liked da way things happened in the election and anybody who says uddawise... well the Court ain't afraid to muss ya up:

> The Court is confident that although it may discover certain additional ballots that were legally cast under relevant law, there is no systemic problem of disenfranchisement in the state's election system, including in its absentee-balloting procedures. *(MN Election Contest Court ruling, quoted at MN Progressive Project)*

AND, da Court looked at all that hot air da Berg Boys (ya know, Joe the Fried-BERG and Ben the Ginz-BERG) have been spewing out the sewer grate about "equal protection" and said... nuttin'. Dey ain't goin' dere, like it ain't here, it ain't happenin' and we ain't gonna flap our gums talking about any of it. Dey don't think "equal protection" is at issue at all.

AND the Court laid another hit on the Coleman mouthpieces, like Kunin from Da UpTake writes up here:

> ."...the court raised the burden of evidence shouldered by the Coleman campaign in adding additional ballots. Coleman attorneys must now prove that a ballot was legally cast, not just improperly rejected. This means showing evidence that the voter did not submit an additional absentee ballot or arrive in person on Election Day to vote." *(The UpTake)*

Monday, Feb. 16th

So now it's on to **Motion Monday**. Da schools, post office and banks are closed (lettin' some of us get on with diggin' under the 2nd National vault over on Toity-Toid street) but the Court is gonna hear motions from both sides. You can bet a case of bootlegged Canadian rye Team Franken is going to try to put the squeeze on da last categories and see if they can't pull Coleman's numbers down to where he can't win. Coleman's side is gonna have to play nuttin' but defense even though it's their suit, their case and their turn to put on their side of the argument. Not a good spot for dem.

I still think Franken's boys are actually going to have to present their case (and woid is they got 771 ballots to put on the pile from their side if they need to) but they won't have to go too far until it becomes mathematically impossible for Norm and his teeth to win it. Then the ECC will decide...

When dat happens; A) Coleman takes his one shot with the MN Supremes (less than 15 days by law I believe) and I think the Supremes will give Norm his final 5-0 pasting, B) Franken moves to get his Certificate of Election and puts the heat on the Senate to seat him provisionally – which they might just do at that point. Even chowderheads like McConnell will see how pathetic Norm's case is (and for McConnell to see pathetic is DAMN pathetic.)

DK The more we watch, the more we see that Coleman has no idea how to win Nice story there, it'd be a shame if somethin' happened to it. *(freelunch)*

DK I wuz jist gonna give youse muh poysonal feelin's on dis subject an than ah decided it wud be more fun ta jus' tell youse Happy Valentines Day. *(funluvn1)*

Dat's da latest from yust southeast of Lake Wobegon (and ya know, Chicago is southeast of Lake Wobegon too).

Shalom.

PS. The ECC ruled Friday on the 19 categories using legal language. But I think the hit really went down something like this:

(Roll music: sad, minor key, Big-Band on a mellow break, bete-noir kind of film)

> "Ok then," rasped a low, female voice. A hand featuring polished red nails reached through the pool of light to hang up the phone. The down light on the desk also briefly showed a grey cuff and a pearl cufflink, both poking from a black pinstripe jacket. "We'll have to take care of it ourselves," she said to the gloom beyond the desk.

> She could just make out a brief smile playing across the lips of "Scapel" Marben. She watched his silhouette against the grey light coming in from the high window: wide-brimmed fedora, broad & pointed charcoal gray lapels, black shirt and ivory tie in a careful four-in-hand knot. In the dusky light he crossed over to a closet and pulled out 3 violin cases. He put one on the desk and handed another to "Stickler" Reilly.

> Reilly nodded briefly, her chin bobbing over a cream-colored silk blouse. Her arm, encased in a burgundy jacket with a touch of brocade at the shoulder, hefted the case with a familiar ease.

> The "Presider" looked up from her desk. She hoped the semi-darkness hid the flinch in her eyes as "Scalpel" said, "Like the old days. We're gonna operate."

> Marben wore a thin smile. "Stickler" swallowed hard and her mouth went dry as it usually did at Marben's icy humor. The "Presider" turned back to the phone, picked it up and growled, "Louise? Yeah, get me Maplewood P-6171..."

> A dying splash came off the tires of the square-backed 1929 Oakland rolling on the rain-washed bricks. Pools of light from the streetlights on Ireland Boulevard reached only faintly into the alley. As the 5 inch whitewalls brushed against the curb Hayden let the American Straight Six idle for a moment before she killed the

ignition. She took a last, long drag on her Lucky Strike then she flicked the butt out the window into the flowing gutter.

"What didja tempt 'em with?" Reilly asked from the front seat.

Hayden grunted back, "20 cases of Jack Daniels, 15 of French Clicquot and 4 Oban scotches."

"Think that's enough?" Marben hissed from the back.

"Enough to get 'em interested," the "Presider" answered. "I clinched it when I said I had 40 cases of Absentee Ballot."

Reilly whistled low past the toothpick in the corner of her mouth. Marben's soft, deadly "heh, heh" from the back seat broke off as he snapped his fingers. He pointed toward the yellow cone of light over the outside steps going down to the basement of St. Paul's Judiciary Building.

"There they are," he rasped. "Right on time." Several shadowy figures moved out of the midnight gloom. They slipped along the edge of the light circle and then went down the concrete steps. The gang in the car could just see the top of the basement steel door open and close several times.

Stickler kept count, then threw away her toothpick. Presider took one more long look around. They both heard Scalpel pull back the bolt on his gat. All three got out and tucked their Thompsons inside the fronts of their black robes. They didn't zip them, just held them closed for the few seconds they walked along the alley. They went with a quick, deadly silence down the steps below street level. The steel door opened and closed once more and a muffled chatter ripped the night quiet for a few seconds.

"CNN Headline: Modern Valentine's Day Massacre in St. Paul? Developing."

Just beyond the yellow police tape marked "CSI St. Paul, Do Not Cross," Lt. Horatio Cainenen pointed and asked, "What is that?"

Technician "The Kid" Wolfenberg took several photos of a small piece of steel that was carefully, even deliberately, perched on one of the bodies. Then he used a pair of tweezers to pick up the polished crescent and put a few drops from a small bottle on the surface. He peered at it through the lens of a small, blinking metal box.

"High quality steel, hardened with vanadium. Surgical grade I'd say. You could make a scalpel out of this."

Cainenen stared off in the distance and whispered under his breath, "Scalpel?" His footsteps took an urgent pace as he walked quickly over to Sr. Tech Kalli Duquesnedahl.

Kalli was just pulling something out of a heavy wooden post with a pair of rubber coated needle-nosed pliers.

"That is an unusual slug I'd say," Cainenen remarked as he came up. Kalli nodded as she squinted at it through her Swiss Army knife pocket magnifying lens. ."45 caliber with a long, right hand twist." She placed a pair of calipers on the faint ballistic marks. "It's about a 16 inch twist so it's not a pistol. This rim says it came from an automatic weapon."

Cainenen's eyebrows lifted as Kalli dropped the slug in a white box for weighing: "230 grains?" Kalli muttered, puzzled. She punched up her iPhone, tapped the application labeled "iBullet" and waited a few seconds.

"Horatio, this doesn't make any sense. This kind of bullet hasn't been made in 70 years but I'll stake my reputation that it's freshly fired. What's going on?"

Horatio looked over her shoulder at the iPhone screen and a little detail caught his eye. Then he looked around the scene: cases of Veuve Clicquot and Jack Daniels piled high, a large tarp covering a heap over by the wall. On a sudden impulse he went over and yanked down the tarp. 6 cases high. 6 wide. 4 more in a short stack over here. The letters A B everywhere.

Cainenen holds both sunglasses in his hands and fixed his eye on both Kalli and "the Kid."

"What we've got is murder. Those old style bullets are nicknamed "Orders." They were made by a British firm Tryal & Court. Like we used to say back in New York, (slips on sunglasses, gestures toward body bags on floor) what we have are 13 ballot categories killed off by "Court Order.""

(Cue Roger Daltrey scream. Roll music: "Won't Get Fooled Again.")

Less Than We Hoped
February 16, 2009

Comments: 189   Recs: 343   Tips: 210

Well THAT was fast. The Elections Contest Court spent all morning in chambers with attorneys for both sides. Then at 1:00 they all appeared - with a witness. Three absentee ballots were flashed (not actually entered into evidence). Atty. Hamilton for Franken kept his vicious cross-examination down to "Were you contacted by the Coleman campaign before your testimony today?"

At 1:18, "Tung-tong" (From *Law & Order*) Court recessed until 9:00 a.m. Tuesday. Motions? None in open court today. Orders? None issued so far (although to be fair they may be being written as we speak. The ECC HAS issued Orders rather late in the day on several occasions.)

So as has been often the case with the case of the Recount: "We'll see."

UPDATE 1

In some cases the absentee ballot application is missing at the local level. (You apply for an absentee ballot and leave/mail in the application to the local elections board.) The two sides will argue over this and the Court will earn its pay:

If the application is missing (through no fault of the voter) should the vote count (Team Coleman)? There is something here; the ECC has been sympathetic to voter intent when there has been error by the officials. And it is only fair.

Or is the applicant's signature needed for comparison to prevent fraudulent voting, (*i.e. prevent someone from going to Kinko's with a blank absentee and running off 50 copies for each member of the Fergus Falls "God Loves Only Republicans" Club*). Team Franken? There is something here too. Fraud prevention is even on the GOP list (today) and this court will take this quite seriously.

Darker scenario: Suppose a county auditor named Kathleen Harris/Blackwell knows God wants Al Franken to be senator. So she "arranges" for absentee applications that are from a precinct that usually votes 80% Republican to "become lost/disappear" in a way that seems plausible/innocent. The auditor is disenfranchising voters (through no fault of the voter) but the fraud is at the local official level.

If the ECC allows the ballots w/o matching up the applications (1) then a (2) scenario is possible. If the ECC turns down the ballots because of missing applications (3) then voters are disenfranchised because of fraud and through no fault of their own (1).

So esquires and everybody else out there: how does a Court rule on 1,2,3? How does a legislature write laws to ferret out a crooked local official?

I actually think this is a rather close call...will we see our first ECC 2-1 decision? Will the losing side on this issue cite this on appeal to the MN Supreme Court? As in all things Recount: "We'll see."

Prospects: The sun is setting on the Coleman case. This may become much more visible after today.

The Legals

What are the motions we might hear today? One motion already in the hopper is this Franken "Motion in Limine" to exclude testimony of "King Banaian." The "Motion in Limine" (limine = Latin for threshold/entryway) is an attempt to fight him over there so we don't have to fight him in here (on the witness stand). King Banaian is the man's name (and what is it with Republican first names? "King," "Cullen,""Tucker"? I first read "King Banaian" as a variant spelling of an oversize example of that tropical/Indian sub-continental tree with the extra trunks under each main limb).

Team Coleman apparently want to call Banaian (an economist at St. Cloud State University) as an expert witness to testify how the variations between counties and their absentees is so wacky that the ECC has no choice but to look at the entire "universe" of 11,893 ballots.

Team Franken will argue; a) the variations are not statistically significant, b) that Banaian is only an economist not a statistician, c) the ECC has already ruled the "universe" down to under 3500, d) why have this guy come in at all?

Judges Hayden, Marben, & Reilly

The three judges have truly earned their pay by their patience and silence. (Me, I would have been lashing Freidberg with wet spaghetti from day 2 when I wasn't laughing.) They have really lived up to the old adage "sober as a judge." (Not referring to their drinking habits, but a facial expression that is poker-faced, somber.)

But they are human and those little flashes can give us some read on the judges' inner life.

For instance: Thursday, Coleman attorney Langdon was faltering in his argument and blurted out to Judge Reilly, "I see you are not buying this, are you?" She cracked up and made a joke about it. But our legal eagles on these boards have been unanimous: a judge laughing at a lawyer is NEVER a good thing for that lawyer's case. EVER. Sooo... this could mean something. We may know when they rule.

The Laughs (to keep from Screaming)

Finally, until things start at 1:00, or if things get tedious in ECC today, here are a few lawyer beauties that maybe Noah or Mike at The UpTake can drop on the Coleman table when they are not looking to improve their case.

Q: Have you lived in this town all your life?

A: Not yet.

Q: Now doctor, isn't it true that when a person dies in his sleep, he doesn't know about it until the next morning?

A: Did you actually pass the bar exam?

Q: ALL your responses MUST be oral, OK? What school did you go to?

A: Oral.

And finally, for ALL of Team Coleman's ballots proffered and then withdrawn, for their striking of their entire first 2 days of their own case in ECC:

A Texas attorney, realizing he was on the verge of unleashing a stupid question, interrupted himself and said: "Your honor, I'd like to strike my next question."

OK. Hope this will hold you all until 1:00 p.m. CT. That's the latest round-up from yust southeast of Lake Wobegon.

Shalom. (Oral.)

Flattened Balloon
February 17, 2009

Comments: 107   Recs: 229   Tips: 201

Election Contest Court - Episode XXVI
Can Coleman Present Completed Legal Homework?

Well after an 18-minute court session yesterday (MAJOR letdown) we'll see how proceedings go to-day and forward. Team Coleman (actually both sides, but Coleman is putting on his case right now so it affects him first) will now have to meet the standard laid down by the Court on Friday: it is not good enough to show a given absentee ballot was rejected by local officials.

Now for a ballot to be accepted by the Court either side has to show a rejected ballot:

a. was rejected because of error by election officials and NOT because of an error on the part of the voter (sounds tougher than it is; the local officials did not make many of these mistakes and nearly all of them are pretty obvious) AND

b. otherwise meets the legal tests for a properly cast absentee ballot (all 4 legal tests, and assumes it arrived on time).

This b) is, if not new, at least explicit now. The Court will no longer buy the Coleman song-and-dance that asks a county auditor on the stand, "I show you this rejected ballot. Do you NOW believe it should have been rejected?"

Instead the Coleman lawyers (actually their paralegals and staffers have to do some real digging and work) have to say something along the lines of "I show you this ballot from Ingabord Larson. She filled out the application and her signature matches between the app and the absentee ballot. The address on the application and on the outer, mailing envelope match. She is registered to vote (either according to county rolls or via the enclosed voter registration card). She did not vote in person according to the voter sign-in log from the Yucatan Township (really!), Houston County, precinct 6. The vote arrived in the Caledonia, MN courthouse on Nov. 2 in time for the election. Why was it rejected?" So we'll see . . . .

Morale Issues: Each Team

Yesterday was disappointing and the grind is wearing. But consider 2 items from Horse Denture Brigade:

a. The Coleman attorneys yesterday gave the ECC a letter asking them to reconsider last Friday's Order (excerpted from MN Democrats Exposed (MDE); nothing like going underground once in while!).

In a letter asking the three judges to reconsider their ruling today, attorneys for Norm Coleman noted that the panel's holding overrules decisions already made to count similar ballots cast in the Minnesota Senate election.

> "The current situation would result in a widespread equal protection problem by disqualifying a large numbers of ballots that are the exactly the same as hundreds, if not thousands, that have already been counted," said Coleman recount attorney Ben Ginsberg. "Without a proper review and remedy of this situation, we would end up with many votes being counted that do not meet the new standards now set by the court. It is critical that we get an immediate review of the standards so this issue can be addressed. Without a remedy, we will be faced with a widespread equal protection problem that would not only violate the law, but create Constitutional legal issues that would only delay this process further." *(MN Democrats Exposed)*

Once again they are projecting on a perceived foe (this time the ECC), Rethug standard operating procedure the last decade or so. Team Coleman wants all of the 12,000 ballots reviewed (including, for instance, 933 ballots they already stipulated should be counted, and another 174 they stipulated were late). Estoppel anybody? Invited error apply here? They want a whole "new" set of standards, and if they don't get them, they are going to run to the federal courts on a 14th Amendment "equal protection" squeal.

But from a morale standpoint, this brave blogger over at MDE notes:

> Leroy Jenkins Says: Friday: Norm Coleman is confident, got the bulk of the ballots he wanted. Monday: Norm Coleman is wetting his pants. Admits that he lost a lot of votes that he needed to make a legitimate run at winning. *(MN Democrats Exposed)*

b. CNN reports Al Franken is having conversations with Harry Reid and letting himself be called "senator-elect" at a meeting of Minnesota mayors. He's looking at committee duties and being posted on pending bills. Meanwhile Norm Coleman has some invisible job with a Jewish Republican lobbying group that apparently pays him well and requires him to sit in Minnesota courtrooms for long stretches of time.

Hey Team Coleman! If what the Berg boys say is true (Joe the Fried-BERG and Ben the Gins-BERG) and "we look forward to Senator Coleman's return to Washington," why isn't NORM meeting with Mitch McConnell, talking over committee assignments, doing his homework on upcoming legislation? After all, if he's going to be "resuming" his duties why isn't he getting ready? Or is this a sign?

c. And Al Franken's Team? Well at the press conference afterwards:

> DK
>
> The presser was longer than the hearing today.
>
> The best part was where Elias related that Hamilton and Lillehaug were debating whether the ever shrinking Coleman Universe of rejected ballots was a Black Hole or a Red Dwarf. He seemed to enjoy describing the Red dwarf as small and the least powerful. He seemed very loosey goosey in the presser while Ginsberg demeanor lacked his usual snark . . . although he did call Franken's discussions with MN communities on stimulus a "cute political stunt." He would know about those. *(glassbeadgame)*

Why so long?

Everyone's burning question. A late commenter in yesterday's diary may have hit on it (and if true I am immensely sorry!)

> DK
>
> The challenge exists because (pick 1):
>
> Coleman was leading, and he still thinks if he can cherry-pick the right ballots he can still win. Remember such men really do live in a bubble, and he may really think this.
>
> Coleman is sucking wind financially, and if he gives up now he loses everything. He has to keep this going to get enough money to save his house, etc.
>
> The GOP doesn't want another Democrat in the Senate, and this is convenient.
>
> The judges on the EEC love reading WineRev's column, and realize that if they render a decision NOW then the column will go away...forever. They aren't going to let that happen! *(lostboyjim)*

If lostboyjim is right, then I am a living example of "no good deed goes unpunished." Sack cloth and ashes for me - fortunately Lent starts next Wednesday, so I'll be inconspicuous among the Lutheran wine buyers...right?

(PS. Pre-emptive joke of pennance: A few years ago we hosted fellow Lutherans from Germany. Coming from state church Germany with magnificent but empty cathedrals to free church America with stuffed churches and a crazy-quilt of denominations is a heavy shock.

We told them if they remembered three things they could cover about 80% of American church life:

"In America, Catholics do not recognize the Lutheran sacraments.

The Lutherans do not recognize the authority of the Pope.

The Baptists do not recognize each other in the liquor store.")

Tuesday Morning Minnesota Media

Pat Doyle in the *Star Tribune* has the solo article and was given top billing. The headline writer might have been a President's Day rookie replacement: "Coleman asks court to reconsider ruling on rejected ballots since it was; a) news-y, and b) not slobbering over Norm.

Some nice reporting by Doyle, filling in some pieces:

> On Friday, the three-judge panel excluded 12 categories of rejected absentee ballots from reconsideration. But the Coleman legal team said Monday that those banished categories would have fit about 100 ballots that were accepted last month during the recount.
>
> While the campaign could challenge the 100 accepted ballots, it would prefer that the panel allow similar ballots to be introduced in court and counted. *(Star Tribune)*

This says to me, at 100 ballots in this part, the Coleman side is squirming over small potatoes and is trying to re-inflate the universe. Lots of hot air to be sure, but I don't think the Court is buying it.

Coleman's lawyers also said the judges applied a looser standard earlier last week!

> These would be the 23+1 votes from the "Nauen" group and this is really bogus. The Nauen group is 61 voters. 24 of them had affidavits so detailed that were airtight that the Court ruled the ballots IN. It is the Coleman side that has waved around ballots unsigned, voters who had girlfriends sign in for voters, etc. No, no. Any "loose" standards are NOT from the Franken or Nauen side... *(Star Tribune)*

General agreement in article (including Hamline Univ. law professor, David Schultz) that this is mostly posturing to set up an "equal protection"/14th Amendment basis for appeal.

Marc Elias delivered an X-ray analysis:

> Elias said the Coleman campaign's bid for the panel to reconsider the ruling demonstrates that the decision went against them. *(Star Tribune)*

More significantly, number cruncher TomTech on these boards (with rough concurrence offered from Vote for America and other stat heads) said in a comment he believed only about 650 of the Coleman ever-shrinking, red dwarf universe of ballots would ever get counted by the ECC. The Franken number folks have been right on for months calling their shots, so notice (especially the last line):

DK

> He (Elias) called 3,500 ballots "the high water mark" for Coleman from now on during the trial. Elias said about 2,000 of the ballots involve mismatched signatures or questions about registration and predicted that the vast majority of those wouldn"t survive a court test. He said it was possible that 500 to 1,000 would end up being counted. *(TomTech)*

If so...WOW! This would mean Franken's case might need to be minimal, or best case scenario, UN-NEEDED! This last would come about if we get down to say, 762 ballots finally are opened and counted (Coleman's last gasp) and they DON'T break his way by at least +250 (to overcome Franken's current +249). Then it would be "Motion to Dismiss" and "hello, Senator Franken." (With an obligatory victory lap in the MN Supreme Court.)

Rachel Stassen-Berger at the *St. Paul Pioneer Press* writes the Coleman strategy now is . . .. you know, Republican "Backwards Day" Speak. She quotes Ginsberg:

> The court could correct those alleged problems by removing the hundreds, perhaps thousands, of now-invalid ballots from the count.
>
> Coleman attorney Ginsberg said that's not the Republican's goal. "We are not asking to have the votes uncounted," he said. Nor, he said, is it their goal to pave the way for a federal court challenge once the state case concludes. *(Pioneer Press)*

Not asking to have votes UN-counted? YES THEY ARE!

Pave the way for a federal court challenge? YES THEY ARE!

So it is on to 9:00 a.m.CT. For The UpTake and friends they are having a meet-up Wednesday night for staff and friends and the shy ones are planning to come early and stake out corners to text each other all night long from 6 feet away.

Hope this will hold you with the latest from yust southeast of Lake Wobegon.

Shalom.

Plugging Along
February 18, 2009

Comments: 125   Recs: 188   Tips: 165

Election Contest Court - Episode XXVII

I don't know. The ECC keeps making noises about streamlining the case so it slips through the air with less resistance and more speed; you know, going from a station wagon to a Ferrari. (Maybe even a Ferrari-Carano Siena for a red blend? Or the Chardonnay on sale @ $21? Even the Reserve Chardonnay (delectable if you like chardonnay at all) is on sale @ $34, down from $49.)

The ECC keeps saying "streamline" but then every day Trimble, Knaak, Langdon and Friedberg keep showing up in court at the Coleman table. With those guys around the best the ECC can do for streamlining is riveting chrome "Dagmars" on one end and 14-inch tail fins on the back end of an oversize chest freezer skidding down the black diamond run called "Resurrection" at Crested Butte, CO. Such a beast doesn't ski well at all, banging from tree to ballot and screeching to a halt on a rock outcrop. It sinks up to its lid handle in a snow bank at every witness

Tuesday everyone started late. (10:00 a.m. rather than 9:00; a bit unusual, the ECC has kept pretty good starting and stop times.) Friedberg had Robert Hiivala (GREAT Finnish name that one!), the Wright County auditor, on the stand. (Wright County, NW of Minneapolis; Bachmann district and strongly R; went for Coleman about 51-29 - rest to Barkley & Niemackl.) The Coleman attorney at least was saying, "This GROUP of ballots was rejected for mismatching signatures." (Yay for "GROUP of ballots." - streamlining!)

BUT the Court order on Friday said rejected absentee ballots that either side introduces need to meet EVERY criteria for acceptance (i.e., pass all 4 legal tests.) So David Lillehaug of the Franken Team objected to Friedberg's group of ballots since they didn't meet the other criteria. (As in "there's other failures here so why even bring these up?" - more streamlining) Lillehaug then got up and laid out how some of these ballots had additional problems, such as a residential address in another precinct (or even another county), which the court has already ruled would disqualify them.

Objection was sustained as the opposing counsel showed the Coleman Team what Friday's order means in court. Friedberg even apologized to the Court for not knowing the ballots had other problems. In hockey terms this is, "Lillehaug staples Friedberg to the boards in front of the Coleman bench. Puck pops loose. Lillehaug over the blue line and now a vicious snapshot just under the crossbar! Oh, buy Sam a drink and get his dog one too! What a goal!" (With a hat tip to the great Mike Lange, radio voice of the Pittsburgh Penguins.) NOT good for your case when attorney for the other side takes you apart like that and the Court agrees. (Sounds like double streamlining with ECC and Team Franken on a 2 on 1 rush at the blue line.)

Well Friedberg finished with Mr. Hiivala around 11:25. OK, pretty speedy for one of the Berg Boys. Then Presiding Judge Hayden called one of those judge plays you all know, (Friedberg, play right wing on Trimble"s line this shift. Change it up! C"mon! Get your breezers over the boards! . . . OOPS! Wrong play) "Mr. Friedberg, call your next witness."

And silence fell on the room like a tent with a snapped ridgepole. "Mr. Friedberg? . . . You don't have another witness until 1:00 p.m.? . . . Court is in recess until 1:00 pm." Judge Hayden was NOT a happy person as she called this recess. Again, the ECC judges have been pretty good at keeping start and stop times and the lunch break. There was PLENTY of time for a witness late morning, and Team Coleman was NOT ready. Yes they have been NOT ready a lot in this case, but this is the first time it really impinged on court management and time keeping and Judge Hayden was annoyed and everybody knew it.

Lawyers in the room, correct me if I'm wrong, but when one judge in your case (Thursday) laughs at one of your attorneys and says through a faint smile, "I'll ask the questions here," and another judge cracks the gavel at you like she'd like to have your thumb on the gavel's sound block, is your case going well? Is the Court making up its mind?

Coleman Strategy?

Is there one, other than ennui rampant on a field of tedium? The Big E over at MN Progressive Project thinks there is: the current Coleman shadow-boxing is NOT trying to win the case in the ECC. It is trying to set up grounds for an appeal, not so much to the MN Supreme Court (where their batting average has been less than stellar) than in FEDERAL court, on the "equal protection" line.

Jay Weiner similarly reports:

> Ginsberg (Tuesday) criticized the judges" Friday decision. At that time, the three judges wrote there was "no systemic problem with the election." Today, Ginsberg said: "I don"t know how you can say there"s not a systemic problem when you have Scott County saying one thing and Carver County saying they do something completely different."
>
> . . . Is Ginsberg laying the groundwork for an appeal?
>
> No, he said, although Elias opined otherwise. (WineRev agrees with Elias. This is Republican Reverse Projection all over the place: "We have no intention whatsoever of . . ." until tomorrow when they do just that.) Ginsberg said he wants these three judges to address the problem.
>
> But he called the election "fatally flawed if we go along on this path" of different counties counting differently. *(MinnPost)*

Oh Rot and Rubbish, Mr. Ginsberg! This election was fairly, openly and meticulously run. The recount was likewise carefully done; mistakes were discovered and corrected (except in about 200 cases where YOUR side PREVENTED them from being corrected!) The law was followed. AND as of Friday the Elections Contest Court of the State of Minnesota in the Matter of the United States Senate Seat of November 4, 2008, said unanimously, in their considered legal opinion, there was "no systemic problem with the election."

Now you get up in front of microphones and start bleating, "this election was fatally flawed." What nonsense! Did you scrape that idea off the back floor of a South Philly taxi? Flawed? Why? Because your guy ain't winning? Because you couldn't game this one? Because there are too many legal barriers erected against "people" like you for you to break through?

"Fatally Flawed"?! Fatal to continued development of proto-fascism, yes. Fatal to your idea that elections are shams, a modern "opiate of the people" to let them think they actually mean something, yes. Fatal to power unbridled, yes. Fatal to manipulation, trial by media, yes. Fatal to bringing in Jim "The Fixer" Baker to bail out another Bush-style lint-brain, yes. (One day the hammer is gonna fall on that gangster mouthpiece too.) Fatal to flying in a gang of penny-loafered, polo-shirted, two-legged noisemakers hired from "Jackboots R Us" like you and your mob did in Miami 8 years ago, yes.

You're in trouble, Ginsberg, and your case is sagging like Friedberg's white belly over swim trunks on a Florida beach. All you've got left is to try and get this carcass out of the Minnesota Courts where its being sliced apart like Bruce Lee and 6 knives meeting a side of beef and into the Federal District. (Quick strum of Spanish chords on a guitar . . .) But this time, gringo, the federales ain't gonna save Norm's bacon either. (For one thing, it wouldn't be kosher.)

A New Measurement of the Universe

You've read a lot about the "universe" of rejected absentee ballots. After 933 improperly rejected absentees (as in correcting some mistakes by local officials) were counted on Jan. 3, the universe had just under 11,000 ballots. It shrank to 4,797 as of Jan. 23 (last day of pre-trial filings, confirmed by the ECC on Feb. 2.) Another 174 late ballots were excluded Feb. 9, bringing the size down to 4,623. Friday's Court order lopped off some more, to about 3,300, according to Ginsberg for Team Coleman yesterday.

It is out of these remaining 3,300, or so, that the Coleman side MUST convince the court to admit and count at least 250 in order to overcome Franken's +249 lead. Since Coleman does NOT know how those 3,300 ballots are cast (they are still sealed; no one has opened them since the voters sealed them up), although he has chosen them from pro-Coleman precincts, he needs more than 250 for cushion. A lot more. Maybe 15% of those ballots will be for Barkley or other 3rd party candidates and thence of no use to Norm. Absentee ballots opened so far have favored Franken net due to Democratic party efforts and the Obama campaign to push for early voting. (Since MN does not have early voting, absentee voting served as a substitute.)

But for Coleman's hopes, the votes have to come from these 3,300. (And shrinking. We may see more exclusions.)

Now all of the above has applied to the Coleman case. Coleman is suing Franken in this civil action so he has to put on his case: call witnesses, expert testimony, forensics, the whole bit.

But in a court of law, in a case like this, the "contestee" (Franken) gets to mount his own case as soon as the Coleman side announces, "Plaintiff rests." So Franken gets to call witnessesand BRING IN HIS OWN ABSENTEE BALLOTS from among the rejected ones.

How many? Ah, the Franken side in theory gets to start from the opening 11,000. Their "universe" is NOT cut down to 4,797/4,623/3,300 - that is truly the COLEMAN universe. Or to put it more crudely, if Norm gets to pick cherries (like his original 654) AL gets to pick grapes too.

Now Franken's team originally knew the Coleman side was flaunting these 654 super Normie ballots. In response, during the pre-trial maneuvering Franken's side notified the Court (and perforce Coleman's side via "discovery") that they were prepared to drop 771 grape-picked ballots into the wine vat.

As court opened Tuesday, Judge Hayden announced for the ECC that the Franken side will be allowed to amend their initial filing of 771. The specific ballots Franken's side wants to ADD to his Universe are due to be filed by this Friday. Sooo... the Franken "universe" looks to be expanding some (in line with most astronomical theories; man, talk about reality based!).

Given how tight the legal work of Franken's side has been so far you can believe these ballots will be; A) grape picked from every Franken vineyard from Pipestone to Grand Marais, B) will be in order, will strongly support the Franken effort, and will have a higher than average chance of being admitted, C) will probably be EACH engrossed on parchment.

If pressed together correctly in the final stage of this case and allowing a fairly quick fermentation by winemaker Lillehaug et Cie., these ballots should produce a luscious Frankenia Beaujolais "09. (Saucy, smile-making aroma; Minnesota lingonberry and northwoods fruit notes with full-bodied celebration; deep, satisfying and long-lingering finish. Drink now through 2014. 1 case made (and how!), but endlessly reproducible every time a progressive vote goes our way in the Senate.)

That's the latest from yust southeast of Lake Wobegon.

Shalom.

Grinding
February 19, 2009

Comments: 198   *Recs: 225*   *Tips: 222*

Elections Contest Court - Episode XXVIII
The Dark Lord Arrives.

Last Friday the ECC ruled 12 or 13 of 19 categories of absentee ballots inadmissible, thereby shrinking Coleman's universe of potential ballots from 4,623 down to about 3,300. On Friday the Coleman legal team called that ruling "a victory." Monday they wrote the Court a letter asking them to reconsider their victory from Friday. (Don't you just hate victories that won't stay victorious?)

Well yesterday the Court replied in writing to the letter from the Coleman side: DENIED. This is almost the entire order!

(Has an almost eerie resemblance to: From: the commander of the military forces at Bastogne TO: the commander of the German military forces surrounding Bastogne, regarding your request for surrender of Bastogne: "Nuts.")

While the Court heard more testimony and saw more ballots flashed and then withdrawn, Ben Ginsberg held pressers in the lobby re: the Court's action. He was very wound up about them, invoking as much gloom and doom as possible that the "Friday the 13th" court ruling is denying equal protection to MN voters who voted absentee. Indeed, after invoking cheesy shlock movies, now comes word that Ben

Ginsberg, legal eagle in Bush v. Gore in Florida 2000 and the mouthpiece of record for the Swift Boat team of 2004 is pro hac vice!

This means more than being ANTI hac vice. Ginsberg has now been officially entered as a member of the Coleman legal team for this case ("pro hac vice" is prounced pro hawk VEE-chay, I believe) "for this instance/case." An out of state lawyer is allowed to try "just this case" without being actually admitted to the state bar. Elias and Hamilton are PHV for the Franken Team.

We'll see if Big Bad Ben makes an official appearance in court today. But this probably means the Coleman pressers will be duller. I mean Ginsberg could at least throw around terms like "fatally flawed" and "Friday the 13th horrors" with gusto, even if they were aimed at the Court rather than at Team Franken. As a citizen he still has right of free speech. But now he is officially part of the case, an "officer of the court." Standing outside the courtroom and bashing the other side in the case is standard stuff and we've seen plenty of it.

But it seems to this non-lawyer that going after the Court that is hearing your case is a definite no-no. The most you can say is something like, "Well the Court unfortunately decided against our motion. We are disappointed but will continue the case seeking justice for my client." Saying, "The stupid poopy heads in the judges" chairs were really mean and wrong by shooting down our motion" goes down hard with a court, whether inside or outside the courtroom.

King Banaian out.

The Court also bounced the Coleman witness Banaian, the St. Cloud State Univ. economics professor. "Bounced" as in agreed with the Franken side not to have him called. No need apparently for statistics on voting anomalies between counties from an economics guy who did well in stat class. Not that his analysis would be "fatally flawed" or anything. . . .

Equal Protection defended

The Coleman case now seems more and more aimed at an appeal to federal court on grounds of equal protection. The Court in its Friday ruling already slapped this down saying (among other things) that they found no systemic problems with the election.

Team Franken filed a 6-page memorandum yesterday supporting the Court by arguing equal protection has been met and that (as the closing line has it) contestant/Coleman's argument fails "both as a matter of law and of procedure." It's surprisingly easy reading for us of the non-esquire persuasion (you just sort of slide your eyes over the (Marbury v. Madison 1803; Dred Scott v. Missouri) parentheses stuff, like you just did.) You can tell whoever wrote it (Elias probably); A) knows his law cold, B) enjoys law, and C) can write with flair, brevity and microscopic focus from across the room.

OK, hope this will hold you. Gotta get a shower (and why is water so LOUD?), scrape my face and pretend I like the early shift at work. Will try to check in at lunch. That's all the latest (good GOD the late . . . the damned early) from yust southeast of Lake Wobegon.

Shalom.

The Ice Groans
February 20, 2009

Comments: 184   Recs: 284   Tips: 292

Election Contest Court - Episode XXIX
Flying Counties

No really. The ECC's admonitions to both sides (you KNOW how both sides are BOTH putting on their cases simultaneously? NOT!) to streamline and move from tail-drag to walk to trot to canter seems to be having an effect. Thursday Team Coleman kept rolling through county auditors and city election directors: Olmsted (SE MN, Rochester), Steele (straight S of Mpls. about an hour; Owatonna); Stearns (NW of Twin cities; St. Cloud) Cass (N Central part of state; Walker) Hennepin county (Mpls.) cities of Minnetonka (due W of Mpls.; the original Lake resort - which up until 1955 you could reach by light rail/trolley from as far away as the WI line; all destroyed by GM); Eden Prairie (SW of Mpls.; home of the state's richest zip code) and Bloomington (S side sprawling along outer-belt, reaching east to airport & Mall of America).

Now of course this IS the Coleman legal team we are talking about, so all this may mean simply flooring the gas in your pickup right next to the ice fishing hut. The engine roars and the tires spin at 83 mph - but the actual progress is measured ice crystals per meter thrown off the rear wheels as the tailgate falls open, slews right and tips over the *neighboring* ice hut and the 3 Harley's parked in front.

The roaring engine sounds are provided by Big Bad Ben Ginsberg (now an official member of the Coleman legal team since his "vice" (VEE-chay) got "pro hacked" yesterday. Even though Ginsberg is now subject to a closer scrutiny by the Court he is still throwing "illegal votes" and "the Court's Friday the 13th decision is leading into legal quicksand" since we want this matter "concluded as expeditiously as possible" at the presser afterwards.

Veterans among you KNOW this is utterly for the neo-con, proto-fascist base. It's also a roadmap of Team Coleman's next steps when read through the Republican Reverse Projection machine. May I?

"illegal votes" = non-Coleman votes *(that felon in Roseau without voting rights who voted Coleman? WC Fields: "Go away kid, ya botha me!")*

"Court's decision leading into legal quicksand" = our entire strategy is to lead this case into legal quicksand. We are swamp rats and that's where we do our best work.

"Concluded as expeditiously as possible" - the stalling will go on until our money runs out

The bloggers can dump sugar in Ginsberg's gas tank without even trying:

> Really, Mr. Ginsberg: How many "illegals"? How many how many how many?? And tell us: How do you know how many? Please, let us know how you came up with this number. Oh, and...and please: What difference will it have on the outcome? *(Yippee Skippee at The UpTake)*

> **Court strict on law**. What Ginsberg said in his news conference is that because some precincts did not check carefully to see if witness was a registered voter, then all votes rejected because the witness was not registered should be counted. He must really be nuts. This court has been vigilantly following the letter of the law. So the idea that the court is going to allow ballots that are clearly illegal to be counted is stupid. *(ABowers13)*

This lawyer was not impressed either:

> "What evidence do you have the Coleman was unequally affected" This is just the problem with Coleman's higgledy-piggledy election contest, and what Franken complained about when it said the notice of contest was not specific enough.
>
> Just whose rights is he asserting here? His own? Every absentee ballot voter? Every voter? Every rejected absentee ballot voter? It's constantly shifting, which makes it impossible to determine if he has a valid legal claim, much less whether he's proven his claim, or what the remedy ought to be. His theory has never been determined with any specificity. It's a moving target. *(Chris II at The UpTake)*

Nor was this one:

> The Coleman position is simply untenable. An important case is Berg v. Veit, 136 Minn. 443 (Minn., 1917). In this case 20 votes were illegally cast in a county-level election. The court said "...the burden was upon contestant to show that purging the election of these illegal votes would change the result declared by the canvassing board." *(annie esq at The UpTake)*

1917 eh? Lawyers & judges LOVE precedents so it may be a bit moldy, but, ah, Norm? Like the song says, "Moldy oldie/just another brick in the wall" of the case against you.

The ECC BUSTS a move:

King Banaian rejection take 2

Lawyer types have attached a fair weight to the Court's Order rejecting Professor Banaian from testifying. (He is the St. Cloud State economics professor who did well in some of his sadistics classes, so Team Coleman wanted to call him as an "expert witness". Wouldn't want to call an actual, you know, *statistician* after all. I mean somebody really knows stats and is not a member of the Minnesota Neo-Cons Forever By Jesus Club might somehow hurt the case.)

The Franken team filed a Motion In Limine (Latin "at the threshold") to exclude Banaian's testimony completely, as opposed to either crushing him on cross-examination or using him to dump a truckload of bricks onto the Coleman case. (*"We could do it, you know, but... why bother?"*)

Well the Court ruled to exclude and I thought, OK, another nice backhander on net from the slot for the Blue Team. But the lawyers around here are pretty taken with the Court's move:

> Last night's Banaian ruling was the beginning of the end of Coleman's case on the absentee ballots. The court reminded everyone, but especially Coleman (and me) that they are not a court of general jurisdiction.
>
> This thing should wrap up very quickly now. The court has all but said they are not going to decide whether previous conduct in the election violated equal protection, so they aren't going to give Coleman a remedy for it. They're just there to count, and give a final number. (*underwhelm*)

> I've been wondering what practical effect the court's limited statutory jurisdiction would have (to determine who had the most votes). The court's order seems to suggest it means that it may not consider or remedy any purported equal protection violations that took place during the election. I think that about does it for Coleman's absentee ballot issue. (*Chris II at The UpTake*)

You see the Court could have simply said to the Motion in Limine "Granted" and stopped there. (They were quite terse, for instance, in responding to the Coleman letter asking them to reconsider Friday the 13th's "victorious" ruling; they said simply, "Denied." Full stop with signatures.) But this time they went on and put in a bit of reference material ("this is what's at stake and what each side is asking for"). Cool.

Then they wrote part 2 briefly (and it really is brief) "here's the law on evidence and why we think this sort of testimony can be excluded." They closed with the line, "evidence which is not relevant is not admissible." Hmmm... I like how this is unfolding... Cool again.

But then they said, "We are going to use our arithmetic skills to see which number is bigger on which candidate." Period. Whoa!

"Irregularities between counties are irrelevant" YOWSER!

"The Court will be reviewing all ballots presented according to the uniform standard contained in MN law..." Wooden stake in the heart!

I have to agree with the lawyers, this is BIG. The court seems to be going out of their way to say:

1. All, and I mean ALL, of the last three weeks of Coleman mumbo-jumbo, buck-and-wing, "hoc est pecorum meum" (fondly known as "hocus pocus") having to do with discrepancies between counties are IR-REL-E-VANT! And those "discrepancies" and "irregularities" are the absolute heart and soul of the Coleman case and the fulcrum they are trying desperately to build for an "equal protection" appeal to federal court. (The ECC just walked over to the Coleman Fulcrum Cement mixer and added about 22 extra bags of sand. You pour that as concrete and it will NEVER set up or harden.)

2. And then the court will be proceeding according to the "uniform standard contained in MN Law." Yes there is a standard, written, with case law attached since 1963 when the law was enacted. (*Hey ECC! If you want to get hard-nosed, take a look at the annie, esq. post above if you'd like a 1917 bit of case law!*)

If the Berg Boys (Joe Freid- and Ben Gins-) want to argue "equal protection" one way to do it is to say (as in Florida 2000) "there is no uniform standard." Indeed a lot of the microphone mist the Coleman team has been blowing around at their pressers has been *calling for* "a uniform standard" for recounting ballots/judging absentee ballots.

(The Franken Team all along has been answering there IS a uniform standard in place and it is MN law. The *StarTribune* in particular and the lamestreamers in general have considered this dull and not worth reporting.)

Now the Court has come down and said (3-0, mind you) yes, there is a uniform standard and come hell or high water WE the ECC are following and will follow it. ("You don't got no problems wid dat, do youse?" - sorry. Left over comment from "Talk Like a Gangster Day.")

Many of us would LOVE to see, say, Judge Hayden snap her gavel down on Ginsberg and say, "Mr. Ginsberg, in the Court's opinion you haven't thought through those fatally flawed comments about legal quicksand. I am finding you in contempt and sentencing you to 72 hours in solitary to find the flaws in your thinking. Bailiff? Remove him now."

But courts are about laws, and at their best, about justice. This court is saying, "We are following the law. We are observing equal protection. We are being uniform. If your case is saying the opposite, you are day old lutefisk left on a steam radiator." That means Norm's legal strategy is sunk AND (important) any reversal on appeal (or an appeal even being granted for hearing) is VERY unlikely.

Friday morning Rachel Stassen-Berger for the *St. Paul Pioneer Press*

    a. has a good headline writer ("Judges shoot down Coleman.."; MY kind of fair and balanced because it happens to describe facts)

    b. notes Ginsberg from Wednesday is being a gas bag:

> Ginsberg didn't outline how or why the court would reconsider its refusal to reconsider its decision, but he insisted the three judges must. *(Pioneer Press)*

    c. showed Team Franken at work counter-mining the Coleman effort by actually, you know, helping the Court by citing, you know, law and reason.

> "Under (Coleman's lawyers) theory, any mistake by a local election judge ... any misapplication of the statutory standard to a particular ballot would constitute a constitutional violation and draw the entire election into question. Not only would this result in an untenable rule that would make democratic government impossible, it finds no support in the case law," Franken's lawyers told the judges in a memo. *(Pioneer Press)*

I tell you RSB keeps this up and the people of St. Paul are going to end up as an informed citizenry.

Over at The UpTake, McIntee gets a half-hour show these days at 5:00 p.m. on KTNF the local, rather low-power, but feisty outlet for Air America. Thursday he had on some ir-REV-erent WINE-o as a call-in interview. Despite the guy's obvious condition and unlikely work history (wine sales and a pastor? C'mon!) he had some decent things to say. (Probably not worth archiving though.) But more like him and another pool of informed citizenry might be forming. :-)

That's the latest. Keep warm out there; here it's still single digits but daylight is up over 100 minutes since the 8 hr. 48 min. bottom on 12/21, which is how we know spring is coming yust southeast of Lake Wobegon.

Shalom.

Battle! Gloves Off
February 21, 2009

Comments: 144   Recs: 225   Tips: 198

Wolf poop? Meet spinning air distribution device.

Yikes! Team Coleman surprised (mostly by acting like lawyers rather than continuing to act like lint-heads) and filed a motion for a restraining order to undo a stipulated agreement and so begin UNCOUNT-ING ballots. Team Franken was opposed (and HOW!).

Clashing paper, followed by lawyers arguing the motion in court.

Election Contest Court - Episode XXX

Drop the Gloves; Center Ice.

OK. Another ho-hum Friday in the offing, made even ho-er-hummier knowing Coleman's minions would be once again flogging a 4 million year old petrified *eohippus* of a case again in court.

> Someone suggested the other night that court be held ON Lake Minnetonka. As the ice gets thinner, the participants will talk faster, guaranteeing completion by ice-out. *(BillW at The UpTake)*

As happens, there was a delay until nearly 10 a.m. as another "in chambers" head-to-head between lawyers and judges was thrashed through. But this time we got the thrashing and the fallout.

Back to "Pile 5"?!

To review: MN requires absentee ballots meet 4 tests in order to be considered valid. Twice during the Recount local officials were directed to sort rejected absentee ballots into piles, 1 for each of the 4 reasons a ballot failed. Well there was some slop in the system: statewide 1,346 absentee ballots were rejected locally but NOT for a legal reason. Local officials wanted to correct their earlier mistakes and open and count these.

Franken agreed - all of them. Coleman said, "Some of them, maybe." A legal wrangle ensued and when the snowballs finished flying in the courts both campaigns and the local officials agreed to open and count 933 of these ballots.

They were opened and counted on Jan. 3. It took a stinking 6 hours because the Sec. of State's office first took time to mark each ballot and the secrecy envelope it came "just in case" (some shorthand like: "Cottonwood Co, Jim Beam Precinct, ward 2") AND - important - *why (of 4 reasons) this ballot had initially been rejected*. Then we had that glorious 45 minute read-off of "Franken, Franken, Barkley, Coleman, Franken, Coleman, Franken, Franken, NIEMACKL!" and Al's lead went from +49 to +225.

With me so far?

Now everybody AGREED to all of the above, in writing, and even used lawyer talk:

Agree to - "*stipulate*".

NO crossed fingers, No take backs, NO do-overs, which in lawyer talk is "*stipulate with prejudice.*"

Because it's *really* strong you make REALLY sure of before you "stipulate with prejudice": "Yes this is a 1951 Evinrude outboard motor, serial #... found in the victim's boathouse." If you are trying an inter-solar case you stipulate with prejudice "the sun rises in the east... ON EARTH" particularly when suing in a Uranian Court (since there it doesn't.)

Both sides agreed to stipulate with prejudice this count of 933. And on Feb. 3 both sides also agreed via Court Order the SoS's office could go ahead and redact (erase, cut out, black magic marker) those ballot shorthands (including reason for rejection, if any) in order, by law, to preserve voter privacy once the ballots are returned to their localities. The SoS office notified EVERYBODY some time ago (the ECC and both camps) they would be doing this on Friday the 20th.

Friday morning Team Coleman trooped into judges' chambers about 9:00 a.m. with a Motion for a **Temporary Restraining Order** (TRO) to prevent this. But their timing was so unusual that several 100 of the 933 had already been so redacted.

It was such a surprise (and the real skullduggery seems here) that it was The UpTake's Mike McIntee who first broke the news to Deputy Sec. of State Gelbmann - and mostly by accident! McIntee called him up and said, "Have you really stopped redacting because of a TRO?" Gelbmann said, "WHAT Restraining Order? Are you kidding?!" (puts down phone, yells down the dungeon steps, "Put...the candle..BACK! Put the magic markers down NOW!")

> ...about half of the 933 ballots and votes have already had their identifying numbers redacted.
>
> (Gelbmann) said his staff began removing the numbers on the ballots around 8:50 a.m.. When they received the TRO papers at about 9:30 a.m., they halted the redaction effort.

> Gelbmann said the court order to begin removing identifying numbers came Feb. 3. The attorney general's office thought a three-week window to redact the identifying marks was sufficient. So, today was the day *(MN Post)*

LOTS of speculation the timing was *intended to interrupt* the redacting so Team Coleman can claim "unequal protection", "differing standards", "broken rubber", "no way to tell how this all went so we should just reduce Franken's total by -100".

> Several of us theorize that Coleman waited until too late to move for the temporary injunction because they did not believe the motion would actually be granted, and this way they can whine about injustice because the redaction has already begun. *(annie esq at The UpTake)*

MAN! Is this the depth of arrogance or WHAT?

If this is the first evidence (!) of what having Ben Ginsberg INSIDE the courtroom means, well then Florida 2000 has just had jumper cables clamped to the bolt on its neck.

The basis for the TRO by Team Coleman? "Well since the Court on Friday the 13th threw out a bunch of absentee ballot categories and since maybe some of the 933 were in those categories that got thrown out those votes should now be equal protection-wise thrown out too." AND "stipulation with prejudice" doesn't count since the ECC is making new law here.

> Lord have mercy! You just don't go back on a Stipulation with Prejudice. We're talking an absolute stipulation as to the facts. Only if huge new facts which changed things suddenly came to light would you even try a Motion to reconsider. A last second TRO application? Damn, sanctions are in order. This is as low down as it gets in trial hustles. Amazingly well explained by Wine Rev. *(Rolfyboy6)*

The request itself stinks like moose poop on ice, steam still rising and ice melting in shallow circle. The mind boggles (and yatzees!) at the effrontery and condescending trumpery and leaves one speechless.

THE Response (Lap and Shoulder Harness Required)

One may be left speechless. But not another.

The bloggers climbed all over Team Coleman within minutes:

> *"Any absentee ballot envelopes so identified that the local election officials and the candidates agree were rejected in error shall be opened, the ballot shall be counted, and its vote for United States Senator added to the total votes cast for that office in that precinct"* The Supreme Court's Dec. 18th order rendered the 933 legal. The end.
>
> What matters is that Coleman dismissed any claim about the 933 WITH PREJUDICE. Where I come from that means he doesn't get to go back and get a do-over on those 933. *(Chris II at The UpTake)*

But HANDS DOWN the response of the MONTH/YEAR came from where it should have come from: Team Franken.

Where are your donations going? Want to see your donation dollars at work?

You want a lawyer? You should check their written work when they have time to really crunch through facts and law and precedents. Go hear a few in court. Watch The UpTake for reverse knowledge ("What to Avoid in a Lawyer").

But do you want a crackerjack/ "won't get fooled again"/ think on your feet/ command of the facts and law/ keen mind and moral outrage in one gleaming laser beam focused through a fist sized diamond really GREAT lawyer? Call **David Lillehaug** of Team Franken.

> Ahh, nothing like a brief from Mr. Lillehaug to get the blood boiling. I see he hasn't changed a bit in the years since I worked with him...David stalking the halls, pacing, waiting for the brief to be finalized, and him to be satisfied, which never happened until the messenger was waiting for the package to be airlifted to the court.
>
> He is a stickler for the law and will not deviate even when to the benefit of his own client. And he does not mince words.
>
> Yeah for Mr. Lillehaug. *(GrandmaJ)*

Holy Mother of St. Olaf! By the thundering reindeer herds of Lapland! Lillehaug was not just en fuego. He's like the remote picture from the bottom of the blast pit when the space shuttle is just launching. En fuego? His kind of heat could turn a mile high glacier into Lake Calhoun in 10 minutes.

On extremely short notice (like, walk into Court and be told: "take a look at this/what should we do?" short notice) he turned out a scorching 6-page rebuttal.

Sentence 2: "the motion flies in the face of a stipulation…"

Sentence 4: "Contestant's effort to renege (!) on stipulation… (and) eviscerate the binding order warrants imposition of sanctions."

(**Sanctions:** For making such a motion Lillehaug wants the ECC to lay the lumber on the Coleman legal team: a fine paid to the Court; "3 days in the cooler, Hogan!" for contempt; reprimand—"Goes on your permanent record—" - by the State Bar Association; all the way up to and including lifting law license. Sanctions are HEAVY.)

And that's just prelude. Then he gets onto those pesky FACT things of "**Factual** Background". He runs down all the details of how we got to today, including all exhibit numbers and paragraphs of the stipulations.

Then he gets to the arguments from LAW in "**Legal** Background." Lillehaug holds nothing back:

"Contestants seek to breach the Stipulation, defy the Court Order…and make the Court party to the breach." (YEE-OUCH!)

"Irreparable harm to voter privacy will occur if motion for TRO is granted…indeed the 933 should never have been marked up in the first place" (YOWSER!)

I am not a lawyer, but I will poll the house here of those who ARE esquires if they've seen motion language like this before: "This is the Contestants' second, and even more egregious, flip-flop on the 933 ballots." (recommended for "EGREGIOUS FLIP FLOP"!)

The outraged, compressed fury goes on and on: "reversed course again"… "no basis whatsoever" "in this case or any other" … stipulation is not "null & void - it is fully enforceable and *should be enforced against* Contestants"… (emphasis in the original)

Lillehaug caps the climax by going on a doff-my-hat RANT that would pull Hunter S. Thompson out of a mescaline drug buy:

> "Contestants' latest strategy is to attack the legitimacy of Minnesota's electoral system and the decisions of this Court. Until now, that strategy has been pursued outside the courtroom through the voice of a spokesperson. Now, the strategy has entered the courtroom, through this motion…This is a direct attack on the integrity of the Court and the entire judicial process." *(quoted at MinnPost)*

By the robe of John Marshall and the ghost of Daniel Webster! The man can write, preach, proclaim and argue a case…WHEW!

[And a final coda: "Contestee (Franken's side) advised counsel for the Contestant that this motion is baseless and warrants the imposition of sanctions." I think this is lawyer talk for, "Your honors, let's take along opposing counsel and step outside in the alley. I'll hold your robes."]

Had Enough?

The ECC hadn't. They took the Request for TRO. They took the Motion to Deny the TRO. And then they said, "Enough with paper! We will hear **Oral Arguments** on the motion…Today, 4:00!"

And so it was. Both sides had 10 minutes to open. Langdon went first for Team Coleman…his side "read in the paper that the SoS was going to redact today" (THAT'S a hell of an argument!)… we think we want the court to see it our way… used 4 minutes; NO questions from ECC judges.

Lillehaug retells his motion but with gestures (hard to add to his words!)… "This motion is the next step in attacking the MN election system"… "motion is brought in bad faith."

Langdon (5 min to close) miffed his side is misunderstood in their efforts to aid all MN voters to actually cast their votes for Norm Coleman, real American (certified by Michele Bachmann) or something. But he WAS resentful Lillehaug could question the "utmost good faith" of Team Coleman in stipulating with prejudice to the counting of the 933. It's just that the Friday the 13th order of the Court had opened the door to overturning that stipulation...If reading faces counts for anything, the consensus was the ECC judges were less than enthralled by Mr. Langdon's presentation or facts. Adjourned right after orals. Decision on TRO anytime.

Looks like about 4 inches of snow last night with some nice powder. Hope this will hold you until the ECC comes down with a ruling on the TRO. That's some of the latest from yust southeast of Lake Wobegon.

Shalom.

Universe de Franken
February 22, 2009

Comments: 42   *Recs:* 63   *Tips:* 62

After getting an extension, the Franken camp Saturday afternoon filed their motion for the **size of their universe** of absentee ballots: **1,585.** If/when the Franken side puts on its counter-case in front of the Election Contest Court (ECC) these are the ballots they will be working from and seeking to have counted.

They look to trump Coleman's originally cherry-picked 654 with 804 of their own. They want to knock out a group of 64 votes that favored Coleman and knock IN a different group of 64 votes that favors AL. And...they don't think felons should vote.

Forget the "Al Franken Decade" (that is SO '80s). Today we join together to explore the Franken Universe (NOT to be abbreviated to the FU unless referring to the Berg Boys; let's go with ""**Universe de Franken (UF)"**. If you get tired of the trip you can exclaim in Minnesotan to MRS. FRANKEN: ""*Universe de Franken? Frannie, Dat's Alot!*"...which of course abbreviates to UFFDA :-D!)

First, while we were waiting for this to be filed by Friday at 5:00 p.m. the judges of the Election Contest Court (ECC) took into account the dramatic needs of the WineRev series and realized David Lillehaug's tour d' force would figure prominently in their Saturday morning reading. (They DO read DailyKos don't they? After all these are intelligent, informed and wise judges. They (*ahem*) read the WineRev series to keep laughing. You have to look forward to something while waiting for Coleman mouthpiece Friedberg to impeach his own witness, the Kanabac County Auditor from Mora.)

So since the Franken team had to produce their answer to the request for a Temporary Restraining Order, the judges gave them an **extension until 2:00 p.m. Saturday** to file.

(Hat Tip to Nola Sue for first snagging the AP report on KARE-TV Channel 11.) Instead of the 771 we have been hearing rumors about for awhile, the Franken filing (not posted online anywhere yet; when it is somebody will no doubt link it in the comments) came in at **1,585.** So to go with your 1,346, 933, +225 and +249 we now all have a new number to play with: 1,585.

You'll notice this makes the UF an *expanding* universe, aligning with most astronomical observations and various cosmological speculations. In other words, it is reality based.

Known Features of the UF

The former 771 expanded to **804 rejected absentee ballots** that Franken would like considered for counting that are NOT on Coleman's list. (TomTech or Vote for America are likely hard at work on Venn diagrams.) They are from the 6,100+ ballots that lie between Coleman's former frontier of 4,797 and the total edge of the rejected absentee ballot universe of 10,962.

 Venn Diagram? I haven't heard that since I don't know when. You get tips just for that! This case is spawning a new entity known as a "Coleman diagram," maybe something like if you could combine a Venn diagram with a Mobius strip? *(Fiddle-girl)*

DK   Venn diagram + Mobius strip? Sounds a little one-sided to me! (Unless you cut lengthwise of course!) *(WineRev)*

DK   That's twisted...but only just a little. *(floundericiousMI)*

Are these 804 as grape-picked as the original 654 Colemans were cherry-picked? *You bet your sweet ass they are! This is how tango is done! This is how poker is played!* (""Call 654. Raise you to 804."")

> Those ballots seem to lean heavily on areas favorable to the Democrat.
>
> (Marc) Elias, essentially, admitted as much Saturday.
>
> "The other side put before the court a cherry-picked list that was disproportionately Republican voters from red counties, and we have helped restore a balance to the electorate," Elias said. *(Pioneer Press)*

The Horse Dentures Brigade was shocked (SHOCKED!) to be accused of cherry-picking ANY votes whatsoever. Their hearts are pure, covered with lint filtering down from their braincases.

> Coleman spokesman Mark Drake dismissed that notion
>
> "Their motto is simple: If it's a vote for Franken, count it. If it's a vote for somebody else, disenfranchise the voter. The time has come for all the valid votes of Minnesotans to count, not just the ones that favor one candidate over another," Drake said. *(Pioneer Press)*

Right, Mark. You really said that, huh? Anybody injured by flying enamel as the reporters' teeth exploded trying to hold back laughing?

The 64 times 2: Doing the math leaves 1,585 − 804 = 781 that ARE part of the decrepit, shrinking Coleman universe as well. But as usual with all things Recount connected, it's not as simple as both sides *actually agreeing,* at least this far. Now follow carefully as we look at a couple features of these 781.

This is messy because "64" keeps popping up. There were 64 absentee ballots in Becker County (**"Becker 64"**) that were apparently **kept in an open cardboard box** from Nov. 4 (election day) to Nov. 7. *(Becker County: NW, 60% for Coleman; Detroit Lakes - stole those lakes from Michigan).* These Becker 64 have been counted and ARE part of the state certified count. (They went Norm +22 net.)

Team Franken believes they were not secured, that anybody could have walked by and messed with these. (Hell, somebody could have put them in the trunk of their car and taken them for a ride so they could invent a Republican Reverse Projection talking point!) Therefore, Team Franken is asking these Becker64 be UNcounted (the tango indeed!) on chain-of-custody issues. Are they valid, legal, countable votes?

Both sides will argue of course, but this shows Team Franken (if you had any doubt) can play offense too.

As the Recount began (when this series was still in single digits!) the Franken team made some court moves, claiming there were ballots missing here and there in certain precincts across the state.[12] They now claim in their filing *(in these 781 I believe but maybe not; it's not clear if these are absentee ballots or IN-Person votes)* that 64 (!) votes in 17 precincts around the state WERE counted on Election night but were NOT counted/included/went missing in the Recount. (The **"64 of 17"**; The Borg really have arrived on Earth.)

As the Coleman team has pointed out this is the exact opposite of the Minneapolis precinct where 133 voters cast their ballots (and were recorded so doing by the machine tape tallies) but whose paper ballots could not be found for the Recount. Currently these 133 are IN the Recount total (and broke for Franken +46 net). The Coleman Team is trying to get these 133 thrown OUT.

I have no clue where the ECC might go with this. My own guess is still the 133 are in and will stay IN. The "64 of 17" are a long shot for the Franken side on their own grounds for including the 133.

But it IS another example of forcing the Coleman team on the defensive. They are behind by 249 and their universe of possibilities is shedding votes faster than a teenage snake in a growth spurt. They MUST hold everything they have; 64 (of 17) off their pile would be disastrous.

---

12   County list for those wondering: Hennepin (Mpls.), Ramsey (St. Paul), Washington (Stillwater), Stearns (St. Cloud), Olmsted (Rochester), Hubbard (N Central; Park Rapids), Dakota (S suburban; Hastings), Clay (W-N border; Moorhead, the MN answer to Fargo), and (Chisago; N of St. Paul; Center City.

Single ballots in the UF

No kidding. The Franken filing is going after every single legal/illegal/miscounted/uncounted/recounted vote. They moved to have 1 vote (not an absentee) removed from Coleman's total from Roseau County *(Canadian line NW; breeding ground for some of America's greatest hockey players; see Broten brothers).* One voter was a **convicted felon**, on parole if I recall, nearing the end of his sentence. Like in many states since he was still under sentence he has lost his voting rights, but he went to the town of Roseau (he lives there), registered Election Day (perfectly legal under MN law, and rather common) and voted. In a newspaper interview he noted he voted for Coleman but since his ballot (which should NOT have been run through the counter but was) is in the stack somewhere it can't be pulled.

Team Franken wants the ECC to put a minus 1 on Coleman's pile because of this. My guess: they might well do so, crisply covered under election law. This is clear cut example of *voter fraud/ballot box stuffing/the collapse of legalities/dogs and cats living together/the crumbling of the galaxy!!!! ...*according to those of the Reichwing whose brainstems are connected directly to their voice box (bypassing even the amphibian growth of neural tissue, let alone reptilian, mammalian, primate or Australopithecus - - "the common clay of the New West... you know...morons.")

And another **single ballot... with a name** attached: Cullen Sheehan. Yes THAT Cullen Sheehan: Coleman Senate campaign director AND Co-Contestant in this case pending before the ECC. That snot-nosed whine-bag moved here 2 years ago from Iowa (grumble, grumble; not your fault, Iowa, but next time a dumping notice would be nice).

Since he was so busy with the campaign he voted absentee here in MN. He says he was informed it was invalid (for some reason; one of 4 maybe?) and so he cast another, valid ballot. (Unclear if in person, or another try at an absentee.) At least he says this 2nd ballot was valid.

> "Franken is without information as to whether contestant Cullen Sheehan...Coleman's campaign manager who came from Iowa for that purpose, is a Minnesota resident qualified as an eligible voter under Minnesota election law or as to whether he cast an absentee ballot in the election." *(Franken Filing, quoted in Pioneer Press)*

I tell you that Franken team of lawyers can zing with the best of them - they are putting on a clinic in legal zinging!

Unknown Features of the UF

Does this filing have anything to say about the "Nauen"61 *(formerly 64- whew! Dodged a bullet there.)*? This is that separate filing before the ECC that Team Franken has supported with some legal help &money. 24 of the 61 look to be IN (ECC so ruled; they just haven't been actually opened and counted yet.) The remaining 37 were hanging fire as the ECC asked for more information.

Has the Franken filing of 1,585 bootstrapped these 37 along? Are they included in the 1,585? Or are they still in a parallel dimension? Wait and see.

Does the UF of 1,585 include the 392/393/418 (depending on how you count) remaining "Pile 5" absentee ballots? Over 1300 absentee ballots statewide were IMPROPERLY rejected by local officials. When they sought to correct their errors the MN Supreme Court gave each campaign a say-so in which ones would be corrected. 933 were IN (although see yesterday's diary for the explosion as now the Coleman side is trying to "welsh on da deal"), but the remainder are not. *(In universal terms these 392-418 are beyond the 10962 in the Oort cloud of 1,346 that goes on to the end of the rejected ballot universe which is only theoretical of course.)*

Franken was and is willing to have ALL the remaining counted. So does the UF consist of 804 Franken grapes +392 to 418 "Pile 5"= 1,196 to 1,222? If so, then the actual overlap with the Coleman universe of rusty tin cans is down to 363 to 389. (Ooops; a fair chunk, say half, of the 392-418 are Coleman rejected absentees, so perhaps this number would be more like 563-589.)

OK hope this is something to absorb with the Sunday funnies. No word from the ECC on the TRO motion, so likely Monday. That's the latest from yust southeast of Lake Wobegon.

Shalom... with an uffda.

The Empty
February 23, 2009

Comments: 61 *Recs:* 93 *Tips:* 91

Talk about thin. EVERYBODY has taken the last days off: *The StarTribune, The St. Paul Pioneer Press,* The *Hooterville World Guardian,* and, bless them, the judges of the Elections Contest Court (ECC).

Don't worry folks, this is just a breather. All eyes and ears will be on the ECC this morning.

In a last minute move Friday (and the timing itself smelled like Team Coleman's locker room an hour after a bean, bacon and bean session from *Blazing Saddles*), the Colemaniks moved for a Temporary Restraining Order (TRO) that would undo a stipulation with prejudice and open the door to UN-counting ballots already included in the state certified total. The ECC took written work and held about 30 minutes of orals on the issue Friday.

Nothing came down over the weekend so will the hammer fall this morning? This was SO over the top for lawyers that David Lillehaug for Team Franken asked the Court to **sanction** the Coleman lawyers. As vigorously as lawyers argue with each other in court you often see them mingling in the lobby with a genial air, even being friends as they clash inside.

But to ask for sanctions is QUITE the step. This is something nasty happening in the rink and the fans are littering the ice with crumpled beer cups and wadded programs. Boo birds are roaring and the glass is thumping as fans pound their fists on it. This is the coach standing on the bench with one foot on the side boards calling the ref to skate over so he can say, "Are you going to let Ginz LeBerg cross-check like that? That's a major! Throw him the sin bin!!" accompanied by a few choice gestures learned in the Major Junior League in Halifax.

I don't know we'll GET sanctions but we WILL get a ruling, if not today, then soon, on the request for a TRO.

Until that comes down its all quiet in MN and that's all there is from yust southeast of Lake Wobegon. Shalom.

Franken edges; Norm sags
February 24, 2009

Comments: 169 *Recs:* 302 *Tips:* 293

A so-so day in Election Contest Court (ECC), but there are signs the Coleman case is finally approaching its finish line like an fresh-landed walleye writhing across the ice.

Franken KEDGES another 18 votes

Kedges? Kedging?

In the War of 1812 the *USS Constitution* was caught at sea by a British fleet. As the British closed for capture or destruction all the vessels were becalmed, no air stirring at all. They bobbed & drifted on what currents stirred the waters. The American captain made a desperate decision: he lowered longboats and then gently let down anchors into them. Sailors then rowed ahead to the length of the anchor chain and heaved the anchors overboard. The *Constitution* moved ahead a few ship-lengths until its anchors hung vertically. The longboats returned as the crew raised anchors and lowered them into the longboats again.

The British also began kedging and it became a test of American vs. British backs. The Constitution pulled away far enough it caught a slight breeze, retrieved her longboats, and sailed away to fight another day.

Monday, the Nauen 61 filed new papers with the ECC. In a Monday motion 18 more strong-backed sailor/voters from the longboat "Nauen" complied. No answer yet from the ECC but it sure looks like those hearty tars are rowing out ahead. When the ECC rules they'll toss the anchor overboard and the USS ("United States Senator") Franken's lead will KEDGE out another +18. I'll leave it at +249 for now but the oars are dipping and pulling folks.

(Math & physics whizzes can enjoy creating a formula for calculating how far forward a ship will move given the length of the anchor chain and until the sinking anchor is in a vertical position.)

Election Contest Court - Episode XXXI

The Drone goes on

How is it going in ECC? Well the trial itself is more of the same-old same-old. But number cruncher TomTech believes the Coleman side only has about 425 ballots to offer and take back and a limited number of their own witnesses left to impeach (What a way to try a case!) and believes they will wind up sometime this week! (By all that is holy, let it be so...)

This was somewhat confirmed by the Gins-iest of the Berg boys at a presser. Asked when they might be done with their case he said as soon as Friday. "How done?" came the question (the reporters have been burned before.)

"Done, done," Ben the Gins responded. (Does he mean the Minneapolis 133 done? (The alleged duplicate ballot/double-counted maybe 100-never-seen-a-shred-of-proof, done?)

If it were just Ben Ginsberg I'd dismiss it as unimportant, an early arriving robin that will die in the next cold snap of 14 below. But TomTech saying so?...Hmmmm... we'll see.

The bloggers over at The UpTake are somehow staying awake:

> as long as we are in a chess analogy, I'd say the position on the board is as follows: The match has been won, and the losing side is now suing for a urine test to be administered. The winning side counters that there are no provisions for doping in chess but here's some ...ahem...go ahead, analyze this *(Latte Liberal at The UpTake)*

Franken team lawyer David Lillehaug on cross-exam continues to mock Team Coleman:

> Just a layman's view, but Lillehaug seems to be doing a minute dissection of what the Coleman camp in turn agreed to, then disagreed, then un-agreed then mis-agreed and finally non-agreed. *(Patricia at The UpTake)*

And finally, NO WORD from the ECC late Monday night as the Coleman Motion for a Temporary Restraining Order to prevent the Sec. of State's office from redacting the 933 "pile 5" ballots that were counted back on Jan. 3. (Gory details, including a legal tour de force by Lillehaug in opposition in the Saturday diary (v. 82).

I still think the ECC will deny the request. There is a school of thought on these boards that Team Coleman is being deliberately provocative, almost hoping the ECC will come down on them like the wrath of Odin. Even sanctions have been asked for (minor to major penalties imposed by a court on a lawyer(s) whose conduct goes out of bounds.) The idea is if the ECC rules against and slams the Berg Brothers, Trimble, Knaak, and Langdon with fines, a visit to the Ramsey County holding facility, or worse, then the Coleman team can appeal to a higher court alleging ECC bias against them and citing the "excessive/disproportionate/unbalanced etc." sanctions themselves as proof of the court's animosity.

That plan may be the ONLY thing keeping the court from landing on them like a chopped-through Norway pine. The ECC does not want to see these guys again and do NOT want their capers back before another Minnesota judge or court

Coleman Universe Shrinks again!

YEP! From 10,962 back on January 3, the Coleman universe of possible rejected absentee ballots (his only hope) was limited to 4,797 as of Jan. 23 by filings with the ECC. In early Feb. the court shrank it to 4,623 by striking off 174 ballots that were late. On Feb. 13 the Court ruled 12/13 categories of ballots OUT, which took the number down to 3,500, then 3,300 as admitted by the Coleman side.

NOW the Coleman side is saying:

> Coleman's attorneys now say they believe there are about 2,000 valid, yet uncounted, votes on those ballots, which had been originally rejected by local election

> officials. That's down from their original estimate but still a significant number.
>
> Franken's attorneys say there are an additional 800 or so valid absentee ballots that should be counted but that the Coleman legal team hadn't highlighted.
>
> The judges haven't yet indicated how many of that universe of about 3,000 ballots they will order opened and counted. *(Star Tribune)*

I gotta tell ya, I LIKE the trend line even if it's not from Research2000!

Marc Elias took note of the cosmological shrinking and is NOT worried the sky is falling:

> But Franken attorney Marc Elias said that the ballots submitted by Coleman showed that the Republican's pool of possible ballots continued to shrink.
>
> "The smaller that his universe becomes, the harder it is for him to make up that margin ... That might explain why as we've gone along, the Coleman campaign seems to have shifted more and more towards claiming fundamental errors in the process as opposed to trying to focus on those counts," he said. *(Star Tribune)*

Might explain why you've gone along!? Yeah, it DOES fit!

On a different note, we've all admired the legal work of the Franken team and blown rotten lingonberries at the sloppy stuff coming from the Coleman side. But it's not all perfect and there may be an oopsie in the Franken universe (although the source for this IS the Coleman side and a significant probability exists that; a) they are wrong, or b) Elias & Lillehaug are REALLY good at resurrections).

> According to the Coleman campaign, the Franken legal team has some problem getting absentee ballots straight. Late Monday, the Republican posted three ballot envelopes Franken included on his list of votes that should be counted. Each of the envelopes came from voters who the Coleman campaign says were, in fact, dead on Election Day. Minnesota law requires all voters to be alive on the day of the election to have their votes counted. *(Star Tribune)*

(If this gets ANY traction at all stand by for the Reichwingers to start screeching "Dead people voting for Franken! Just like Chicago.")

OK that's the latest. I hope it will hold you until The UpTake starts broadcasting at 9:00 a.m. for day 22 of the ECC. You can skip to the comments because this is all the latest from yust southeast of Lake Wobegon.

Shalom...and RAHU (RAW-hoo) in honor of Estonian Independence Day! Elagu Vaba Eesti! ("Long Live FREE Estonia!")

Orders from the Court
February 25, 2009

Comments: 112   Recs: 289   Tips: 233

Election Contest Court - Episode XXXII

The Coleman team is nearing the finish of their case (in more ways than one!) They called Gary Poser to the stand, the state elections director under Sec. of State Mark Ritchie. (Poser was the gentleman who got to read off all those "Frankens", not so many "Colemans" some "Barkleys" and 1 or 2 "Niemackls" back on Jan. 3 when the 933 "pile 5" ballots were opened and counted.) Friedberg brought out over 100 rejected absentee ballots that they believe should not have been rejected. Poser was stubborn in clinging to the law and holding they had been properly, legally rejected.

He had great help from David Lillehaug from the Franken table, both via objections and on cross-examination. Better than 80 of the 100 were pretty clearly knocked out of the game.

The bloggers thought so too:

> I think Lillehaug is just trying to drive home the point that appropriate standards were applied quite uniformly. The equal protection argument (weak as it is already) is being demolished. *(expat Minnesotan in NY at The Uptake)*

If you could hum "Sweet Georgia Brown" while reading this:[13]

> Lillehaug - this is just cruel. Knocking Coleman voter after Coleman voter off the list. I bet Norm just wants the pain to stop. Franken's legal team against Coleman's looks like when I saw the Globetrotters against the Washington Generals in my high school gym. I think Marc Elias is the Meadowlark Lemon of the team, while Lillehaug is Curly Neal. *(headlight at The UpTake)*

In 1984 Ronald Reagan looked bad in the first presidential debate against Walter Mondale (who was prepped for only that debate by a super sharp, hard-talking, early 30s aide by the name of David Lillehaug!) He recovered in the 2nd due in part to a genuinely funny crack while looking over at the silver-haired Mondale (and still being several years his senior), "I am not going to take advantage of my opponent's youth and inexperience."

In a DELIGHTFUL reverse pivot off of that in this trial:

> I've only been practicing law for 37 years, so I may not understand what Ginsburg and Coleman's other lawyers are doing because of my lack of experience. But it sure looks like a total waste of time to me. *(Stepper at The UpTake)*

Lazy/Cheap student gets ballot smacked.

You know, there are still certain things in life that require HARD COPY: certain legal documents, car loans, WineRev's great novel, AND Minnesota absentee ballots. You can do a lot online but the state of MN requires you to print out and sign your absentee.

Printer out of paper? Jump drive to a friend's printer! E-mail to iPhone to Mr. Coffee to dot-matrix ditto machine! You're in COLLEGE man, you're smart, you can think of something! Of course you can, unless you are this guy (as reported by Jay Weiner at MinnPost):

> On Feb. 13, a North Dakota State University student, who voted absentee for Coleman, testified. He initialed his absentee ballot application online with a computer mouse, rather than print it out and copy it so he could sign it in full.
>
> The Coleman side wanted his ballot accepted. The Franken campaign said that computer initialing wasn't valid.
>
> Then, under questioning, Peter DeMuth, who is from Plymouth, said he didn't copy the application and sign it because it cost money to do so.
>
> Well - and here's the Perry Mason moment - Lillehaug Tuesday, while questioning (state election director Gary) Poser, produced an affidavit showing that, in fact, NDSU students get 500 free copies per semester. And, thereafter, it's 3 cents per additional page.
>
> When Lillehaug produced that, Coleman lawyer Joe Friedberg threw up his hands and didn't object.
>
> The three judges, who have not smiled a whole bunch the past five weeks, all broke out in broad, teeth-baring grins. *(MinnPost)*

Final Pieces? Minneapolis 133

On Tuesday and no doubt continuing today and longer, Team Coleman moved to the Minneapolis "133" part of their case. *(We are taking a well deserved break from absentee ballots to look at PRESENTEE voters.)* This is that precinct where 133 voters came in and voted IN PERSON (among over 2,000+). In the Recount the envelope containing 133 ballots went missing (and remains so to this day.) We know they signed in to vote. We know the voting machines recorded their votes. So we have strong evidence they were there. But since the ballots are gone, Team Coleman is pushing to have all 133 votes ousted. (Some were Coleman & Barkley, et. al. but they totaled NET +46 for Franken.)

---

13   *For those of you too young to know, Lemon was the prankster and Neal was one in a long line of unbelievably gifted, "how did he do THAT?" amazing ball dribblers the Globetrotters have had.*

The ECC agreed to hear this (earlier turning down part of a Franken Motion for summary judgment to settle this that way) but already cited precedents in *law* from 1913 and 1915. (WOW! The judges do homework the way Team Franken does homework! Now in school didn't the good homework kids usually hang out together, date each other, and stay away from the bad homework kids? Hmmmmmm.) Those precedents in law seem to favor keeping these votes IN (and they currently are IN) but they want to *hear facts* argued. *(Which means the Coleman side just fell through the courtroom ice fishing hole...again. They seem allergic to facts and clumsy, like trying to feel the texture of velvet while wearing hockey gloves.)*

I'm confident Franken will prevail on this and the 133 stay in, BUT it's going to be an ordeal of pushy questions and embarrassment for Cindy Reichert, the Minneapolis city elections director. She'll be on the witness stand, called by the Coleman team, trying to explain what happened. The Franken team will support her with objections and whenever they get to cross-examination. But even on cross from a friendlier Lillehaug, Hamilton, or Elias, she'll still be on the wrong end of Desi Arnaz's accusatory, "Lucy? You got some 'splainin' to do!"

ECC Rules: Temporary Restraining Order (TRO): Denied

The ECC ruled as expected on last Friday's Motion from the Coleman camp for a Temporary Restraining Order. This order would have kept the Sec. of State's office from redacting (editing) information on 933 ballots in the office that connect them with the envelopes they came in and the reason why the ballot was initially rejected. This is BIG because if granted it might allow the Coleman side to argue certain ballots the court has already excluded are EXACTLY like certain ballots in the 933 that are INCLUDED in the count. So it would open the door to UN-counting ballots already included in the state certified total.

The ECC ruled: DENIED, 3-0. ("Lou Groza with that classic straight-ahead kicking style (not like those sidewinding soccer-style booters like the kid, Pete Gogolak) is good from 44 yards for another 3!")

The Court worked through every angle in their denial. They said Coleman MAY have a couple MAYBES but nothing solid. They note the request fails "on likely to prevail on merits" but then are very careful and quick to add this failure is ONLY about this request for a TRO and says NOTHING about the merits of their case as a whole. *(Harumph! C'mon ECC! If Kossacks and The UpTakers can't rampage about the "failing on merits" what are we gonna talk about today? Where's your sense of "feeding the Internet beast"?)*

Oh, and after the whole Lillehaug tour de force on this Friday (where he asked in writing for sanctions against the Coleman lawyers), sanctions did not appear in the Denial. It would have been pretty drastic, might have set up grounds for an appeal on the basis of judicial bias, but HOLY SMOKE would it have been GREAT to see Ben the Ginz led away by the bailiff for three days in the brig!

Oh well... but damn it, I'm glad they tried it. SOMEBODY's got to throw a flag on these Yukon Jack Yaks!

Wednesday Morning Minnesota Media

You KNOW Norm Coleman had a bad day in court, either with witnesses or court orders when; a) Doyle and Duchschere at the Star Tribune write a rather somber but balanced story on the proceedings, b) the StarTribune (in the tank/ bought off/owned/ stupid/biased/ lackey of a: choose your favorite progressive epithet) headline writer can only get off a topper of "Setbacks for Coleman Grow at Trial," and c) D&D close their article running down the Nauen ballots, the 12 the court has put on the Ready to Count pile, and noting Franken's lead is up to +261!

Yumpin' yimminie uffda, Norm! If YOU of all people are losing the Star Tribune, you might want to look into, say, lobbying for Jewish Republicans as a job. I've heard the job requirements are big on sitting in courtrooms, is that right? WHEW!

OK, I hope this will hold you until 9:00 a.m. CT when all of your browsers will of course be pointing toward The UpTake (part of the stimulus package has been announced in MN that could have been a LITTLE better focused):

> *Duluth Tribune & St. Paul Pioneer Press* receive $238k to train workers on how to better use the Net. That's more than 2008 The UpTake budget. *(The UpTake)*

That's the latest from yust southeast of Lake Wobegon.

Shalom.

Fire & Ice
February 26, 2009

Comments: 174   Recs: 305   Tips: 278

Slam and Bang yesterday in Election Contest Court! A Coleman witness testifying for a couple hours, cross-exam and then, (BODY-CHECK into the boards) Team Franken, "Move to strike the entire testimony of this witness." GRANTED! WOW!

The New Swamp Fox: Charles Nauen!

After the British captured Charleston, SC in 1780 they set up a string of forts and strongpoints to hold what they'd won and continue re-conquering America from south to north. Late in the year Gen. Washington was able to appoint his own man to lead the resistance: Nathaniel Greene. Greene confused British General Cornwallis by splitting his already outnumbered force. The western wing under Daniel Morgan delivered a smashing American victory at Cowpens. Cornwallis took off in pursuit of Greene and Morgan across North Carolina all the way to the Virginia line. (A forgotten but epic march by both armies.)

Meanwhile natural-born guerilla fighters Andrew Pickens, Thomas Sumter (they eventually named a certain fort in this man's honor, which figured in another war) and Francis Marion (the "Swamp Fox") began unraveling the British defense system. Marion and "Lighthorse" Harry Lee (later father of another military man, Robert Edward) took Fort Motte by setting it afire with flaming arrows.

They captured Fort Watson by taking up Col. Hezekiah Mahan on a genuine backwoods idea. While Marion & Lee kept up a siege (neither side had cannons) Mahan and a crew of marvelous axmen spent five days logging in the nearby woods cutting and notching timbers. On a moonless night they tapped together their creation.

At dawn the British awoke to find a 50 foot tower looming over the fort. A squad of riflemen (not those smoothbore muskets but those "Pennsylvania" long rifles that could kill with precision at over 100 yards) was firing DOWN on the fort (can you say fish in a barrel?). As the rest of the Americans battered down the opposite gate without opposition surrender was the only option.

While Team Coleman/Cornwallis (The Berg Boys, Trimble & Knaak playing his Lordship and Gen. O'Hara) are grappling with the main force of Team Franken/ Greene (Lillehaug, Elias, Hamilton & Pentelovitch are Greene, Morgan, Otho Williams and Wm. Washington, a distant cousin, to call the roll of the neglected) **attorney and Swamp Fox Charles Nauen** brought in a case of 64 (later 61) absentee voters and their ballots to the Franken side. The ECC has already ordered 24 of these onto the "Ready to Open" pile growing at the Sec. of State's office, and another 18 are looking possible.

But while those 42 ballots are still burning at Fort Motte, *Swamp Fox Nauen has struck again!* He is now attorney for *another* 30 group of voters *(all on the Franken Universe list)* and their absentee ballots who want their votes counted. Petition was made to the MN Supreme Court. If the Supremes follow their prior pattern (and no reason they wouldn't) they will refer these **"Nauen30"** to the ECC for disposition. So while Cornwallis, Ginsberg & Trimble are falling back on Guilford Courthouse, deep in their rear another 30 long rifles are up on a Mahan Tower firing down on Fort Watson and the ever-shrinking stockade of the Coleman case.

Like Marion, Nauen's efforts can't win the case. But also like Marion, Nauen's wasp borings can make it a LOT harder for the British/Colemaniks to win. (No offense to our cross-pond readers; hope we can let that war rest in peace.)

Election Contest Court - Episode XXXIII
Evidence? And Strike that Witness!
In Chambers

The thinking was casual among the bloggers as Court opened:

> I think this court has made it (plain) that there will be no "uncounting" of ballots. That was Coleman's "Hail Mary" pass, and it fell flat. The panel stressed the binding character of a stipulation *(regarding the "933" and the Friday the 13th motion for*

> *a Restraining Order - WR),* as well as the importance of preserving the secrecy of ballots. Moreover, in their ruling, as in past rulings, they freely adopted the language of Elias' and the other Franken attorneys' arguments. I can't help but feel that they find Franken's side more logical, crisp, and convincing. *(Gordon at The UpTake)*

Court opened with a bang by... recessing...what? Yep. Not long after things started there was a side-bar and then lawyers and judges headed into chambers. People scurried around with excitement. Word came soon after from McIntee at The UpTake that what all parties were looking at was possible **"new evidence"** using information from Gary Poser's testimony from yesterday (Poser is state elections director in the Sec. of State's office): 19 voters may have voted twice.

You can vote absentee in MN, but if your plans change you can show up and vote in person. Your in-person vote CANCELS your absentee vote. Election officials are supposed to pull your absentee and reject it ("pile 4" for those of you keeping score in basements.)

Coleman contended that in 19 cases they believe they have evidence local officials did NOT do this and so the in-person vote AND the absentee vote of these voters was each counted, either on election night or in the Recount.

> Of course it would be illegal. The question is did the counties miss some that fall under that category. *(Noah Kunin at The UpTake)*

Well if true that IS pretty serious and it was enough to get everybody into chambers.

(Of course there was a more likely possibility I think the judges needed to recess to have a round of Linie aquavit straight up with their morning pop-tarts. I mean the idea that the Coleman lawyers would actually *recognize evidence,* let alone present it in court, has such an infinitesimally small chance of occurring in any known or imaginable universe that you really need a stiff drink to even consider the cosmological possibility! It's enough to make you question your entire weltanschauung, re-order your categorical imperatives, and wonder if the square root of 2 is rational after all. It's pretty big.)

About 11:00 everyone came back to court and... things went on like none of that ever happened. No announcement, no court order. Big false alarm? We may never know until the tell-all book comes out.

At the Curling Rink

After the lunch break little did witness Pamela Howell (on the stand for Coleman) know that Judiciary Building Room 300 had been converted into a curling rink.

(Republican) Howell has been an election judge since 1977 in Minneapolis. Friedberg swept the ice ahead of her testimony as Coleman's side of sweepers worked on the "duplicate ballot/ double counted" part of their case. (They contend in about 100-150 cases, mostly in Minneapolis and other Franken-heavy areas BOTH the original absentee ballot AND the duplicate of it that was made on a blank ballot so it could be run through the counting machine were counted in the Recount and that only 1 should have been, the original.)

Howell's testimony was smooth and nuanced toward the button, if a bit partisan. She was almost gleeful when it looked like a duplicate counting error (for Franken) was happening (so she could wreck things, she wanted to be a take-out stone.) It was pretty clear she could be in the "God only loves Republicans, who are the only real Americans" camp. But when Lillehaug got up for cross-examination, she was short with him, almost curt.

Now this is usually no big deal. Any trial lawyer will prep their witnesses: what to say, even how to say it, where to look, when/if to smile, etc. You go over their testimony and assure them that ONLY stuff brought up by the calling side can be asked about by the other side. ("We are only going to talk about the green Toyota in the garage. We will NOT ask you about the little red wagon in there and don't mention it either. If we don't and you don't, they can't ask about why the little red wagon's left rear wheel is missing and such a wheel was found next to the victim...")

But Howell's contrast was so sharp people wondered if this was the same person.

> I swear I'm trying to be objective but I've never heard such a pile of incompetent, untruthful garbage in my life - except Gonzales. Amazing how selective memories can be. Reminds me big time why I'm a democrat and proud of it. *(Andrea at The UpTake)*

Then about 2:18 or so Lillehaug asked her about her prep for today's testimony. (Cross-examining lawyers ALWAYS do this. If a witness gets nervous and says, "Ben Ginsberg never talked with me" and it turns out he has done prep, then the cross-examiner can clobber the witness with, "Well you were untruthful earlier about your own sides' lawyer preparing you, so how do we know you are being truthful now?" A prime example of "honesty is the best policy.")

Howell stated she had been contacted in January by the Coleman team and had been making notes to herself on her computer about what she could recollect. (Not a bad move at all.) Did she provide this file to Team Coleman (Tony Trimble it turns out) as part of her preparation for testifying? Yes. *(And skip Dave delivers an 18kg ailsite stone down the ice!)*

Lillehaug to court: **we never got our copy of this.** (Both sides share with the other side info and documents before trial: "Discovery." You have to lay it all out.)

BIG brouhaha over this. "Suppressing" information in discovery is "sanctionable" (YAY! DL brought back that idea against the Coleman lawyers.) This is a HUGE taboo, right up there with trying to UN-stipulate a stipulation WITH PREJUDICE. (I mean NO one would try that…).

Joe Friedberg hustled forward with a sheet and said, "Here's a copy." (For both the court - who apparently didn't have one either (!) - and Team Franken.) Lillehaug asked for a recess "so I can study this information I've just been made aware of."

Everybody took about 10. When they got back, Lillehaug opened with "Since this witness's testimony is based on these notes and notes were not shared as part of discovery, **I move to strike this witness's testimony."** WHEW!

Friedberg argued against (big surprise) and Court said they would rule "shortly." (How shortly? Surely the judges aren't brooming this stone for action today?)

> Friedberg can ask when they received it but it doesn't matter. The judge (Hayden) is not amused, responds that the issue isn't only prejudice, also a violation of rules. *(guest at The UpTake)*

Winning the hearts & minds of The UpTake bloggers…NOT:

> I have to say, until today I have been advocating that Friedberg is actually competent and all his amateurish behavior is part of the evil plot to delay seating Franken. But after today - that was really egregious and I'm seriously reconsidering my position. *(nikip5555 at The UpTake)*

But then **a second stone thrown down in the ice**!

Lillehaug resumes cross-exam and in a couple minutes it comes out that *during the recess* Friedberg had taken said notes OVER TO THE WITNESS so she could "refresh her recollection." She hadn't brought them with her on her own (which I think would be OK.) But opposing counsel take advantage of a recess to help a witness like this???

Lillehaug, "I RENEW my motion to strike on grounds of…" (well he didn't QUITE use the words *"tampering* with a witness" but damn near.),"and for other penalties as well" (which he let hang there; penalties against the Coleman case? Against their legal beagles?)

Succinctly put here:

> Attorneys prep witnesses all the time. That is their job if they are at all competent. Not turning over documents that are requested, and then using the same to refresh a witness at break during cross, those are other matters. As far as her testimony is concerned it wasn't very persuasive. A poor witness, but not everyone is used to testifying in court, let alone in a proceeding such as this. *(LandslideAl at The UpTake)*

Boiling down about 2 hours into a paragraph:

> Under examination by Friedberg Howell was composed and answered quickly. Upon cross she became nervous and unresponsive. Sounded like Gonzales with the old "I don't recall routine."
>
> Lillehaug asked if she had notes or she had been coached by the Coleman Camp.

> She stated NO to both. As he went on she admitted to notifying the Coleman Camp, building a file of thoughts called "Testimony" and talking several times to the Coleman camp as late as January. She had sent her thoughts to the Coleman Camp. The Coleman Camp forgot to give a copy to the Franken Camp. They also didn't mention that there were several phone conversations between Howell and Coleman Camp. I guess that was a BIG OOPS. *(evad dnats daeh at The UpTake)*

Tony Trimble damn near threw his broom and tried his best to explain and squirm out of this mess, calling the notes a "work product" so not subject to discovery.

The mighty UpTake bloggers were NOT impressed!

> Still has not explained how it is work product if the witness used it to refresh recollection. Slight oversight! *(John TX at The UpTake)*

> say as many words as possible in hopes that no one will notice that three of them were "we screwed up" *(nikip5555 at The UpTake)*

> "Let me make this perfectly clear, I did NOT have email relations with that woman..." *(Politjunky at The UpTake)*

NEITHER WAS THE COURT IMPRESSED!

Judge Hayden: *For violation of the rules the testimony of this witness is stricken from the record. Ms. Howell you are excused.*

Get that? NO "take this under advisement." NO "objection overruled...for now" NOPE. A ruling, within the hour of the motion being made, "strike this testimony; excuse the witness" (we will hear no more from her; and to Trimble/Friedberg: As it is written in Psalm 50, verse 9: "I will accept no bull from your house").

Well now! Team Skip Lillehaug has knocked a witness out of the Coleman house with a beautiful incurl takeout draw! Coleman wants to build this final part of their case about the "duplicate/double count" ballots and I think they were using Howell as momentum or maybe a guard stone to set up the following witnesses and now they have to start over. The fact the Court ruled (still deliberately, with 3 judges in the house they wanted to check signals with each other instead of Judge Hayden simply snapping out something on the spot) says once and for all they WILL enforce the law and the rules of evidence, which sure sounds like bad news for Coleman to me. Soo... we'll see what comes next!

Best drama of the trial. Who knew curling could be so riveting?

OK, hope this will hold you. Another "end" to be played today on The UpTake starting at 9:00 a.m. Bring your stones & brooms to the curling house and see if the mate or skip can knock another Coleman witness out of the house with a little in-swing spin. Mind the hog line. That's the latest from yust southeast of Lake Wobegon.

Shalom.

Too Long Madness
February 27, 2009

Comments: 113   Recs: 208   Tips: 209

Election Contest Court - Episode XXXIV
Moves on Moves

The ECC kept everybody on their toes yesterday with their rulings. Pamela Howell's testimony **that was stricken Wednesday by court order** has been re-instated.

Her testimony was thrown out

- Because she had made notes about it ahead of time (OK) and shared the notes with Team Coleman (OK) who had NOT shared these with Team Franken in pre-trial "Discovery" (MAJOR NOT OK). [*Rules of evidence say both sides show the other side and the court the evidence, affidavits, witness lists, documents, reports, exhibits, etc. they are bringing into trial. This is automatic, always done, no exceptions. NOT sharing is like showing up to play goalie without your cup (not coffee; think VERY personal), you never do this and if you do, you'll never forget to wear it again.*]

- Because on the break after this revelation (to give the court and Franken's attorneys time to study copies of the notes) Coleman atty. Friedberg went over to the witness with the notes and talked them over with her (MAJOR NOT OK; bordering on witness tampering).

Now it's back in and the general internet opinion is this closes another door for Coleman on any appeal.

> **DK**
>
> Not to worry - the court did this because they know Coleman will most likely lose and they do not want this to be an issue on appeal, nor do they want to leave an opening for the wingnuts to howl about an unfair trial and the court ignoring evidence.
>
> Even though it is back in, the court is not going to allow this dubious testimony to change the outcome - they will either rule that the testimony was not credible and/or the issue is moot because 46 votes is not enough to change the final outcome. *(Allen03)*

> **DK**
>
> Well I'll be damned. 'Inadvertent' *(Clem Yeobright)*

> **DK**
>
> **The court does not want to wander into the weeds.** I chafed at "inadvertent," too, but I think they said that to keep the trial on track. If they had said it was intentional, Coleman could have argued they did not get the benefit of the doubt, or Franken could have continued to argue for sanctions. All of that would have been a sideshow that simply delays the trial. They would prefer to stick to the merits and get this thing over with. *(Allen03)*

And since Ms. Howell was being cross-examined, I would think Lillehaug could get her back on the stand and say, "And now Ms. Howell, I'd like to resume my questions. With your co-operation these shouldn't last more than 6 hours or so..."

> **DK**
>
> **Actually, this is horrible news for Coleman.** Ms. Howell's testimony was stricken in the middle of cross examination. Lillehaug is nowhere near finished with her. Her testimony was so weak and non-specific that I could poke major league holes in it. If she does get recalled, Coleman's case will suffer even more. *(mswojo)*

The Court ruled on a Franken Motion

In Limine (Latin "at the threshold"). We've had a few of these from both sides. These are motions to exclude a witness or something else on grounds of relevance before it even gets to court. ("Fighting them over there...").

The Colemaniks are apparently sending/wanting to send out e-mails to all 87 county election officials asking them their OPINION about certain absentee ballots and how they handled them. The Frankenites objected; a) not best evidence (get them in here so can be cross-examined), b) not qualified to give legal opinions, and c) hearsay evidence (rarely allowed; If Helga testifies, "I said to Inga..." OK. If you want Inga's answer you put Inga on the stand, NOT a quote from Helga.)

Motion granted to Franken ("Field goal! 3-0")

Nice summary here from ABowers13:

> **DK**
>
> Apparently Coleman has sent a list of questions to county election officials about ballots cast in their counties.Questions like: 1. Was there an absentee ballot application for this ballot?If not, in your opinion was there one which has been lost?
>
> Franken says that Coleman cannot be asking legal opinions of county election officials. And that Coleman cannot enter evidence received by mail which would not allow for cross examination.

DK

Franken is probably right about the law. He always is. But this brings up an issue for me:

WHY is Coleman only NOW trying to gather actual evidence for his case? Has he really not gotten any proof for any of the absentee ballots he has been trying to get entered into counting? *(ABowers13)*

Go Ye Forth and Find votes!

Late in the day the Court ORDERED (and both camps expressed delight, as do ALL of us in favor of "Count every vote") county & local election officials to **examine "pile 3"** absentee ballots for possible valid votes!

This is important. Pile 3 are absentee ballots that were rejected because the voter is not registered to vote. OK, so far, so cool. BUT the absentee ballot packet includes a voter registration card for people who have just moved, etc. or just want to ensure their registration. This gets mailed in with the absentee ballot.

The registration card is SUPPOSED to be in the outer, mailing envelope, not the inner, secrecy envelope – which is supposed to have only the filled in ballot and nothing else. No registration, or no card = no vote. BUT there seem to be several cases where the voter put the registration card in the INNER envelope. (You can tell because it's a bit stiffer and if you have a fine scale it will weigh more.) In political junkie parlance these have been nicknamed "Pile 3A" ballots. How many ballots? **Maybe 1,500 ballots! WHOA!**

And a first bit of analysis from our Kossacks:

DK

Lets peek inside secret envelope! Yes! Yes! The court ruled late today, according to MinnPost, that election officials are to look inside secret envelope of absentee ballots cast by unregistered voters. TomTech thinks there may be 1,300 of these with as many as 50% holding a registration card. This means we might get an additional 600-700 absentee ballots sent to count. I have been predicting this ruling for weeks and again just today!

The order is not up yet so do not know details. I assume the SOS will set out procedures - Peek only, no fair looking at who vote is for, remove with tweezers, seal immediately...

More importantly will the election officials also check for other three reasons for rejection? Will ballots go to court, to lawyers or both?

Most important - who does it help? Our man Franken!

1. Coleman suburbs already checked - they have too much time of their hands... Busy city of Minneapolis did not.
2. Democrats ran huge voter registration drives and also encouraged absentee ballots.
3. First-time voters - young people - were not registered and went 2 to 1 for Obama.
4. Absentee voters went for Franken.

I say, Franken could net as many as 150 votes from this. TomTech says not so much. Love it when my predictions come true. *(ABowers13)*

I think ABowers13 could be right (and TomTech too). Franken's current +249 lead could grow past +350 and stretch toward +400.

The kedging goes on with the Nauen longboat but now this ruling could mean a very slight wind is catching the sails of the USS Franken. We'll see, but on balance this is GOOD NEWS for (*Sit down Mr. McCain!*) Al Franken!

The court earned its pay

Just for reading through a title like this: *Letter to Judges Requesting Permission to Request Permission to File a Motion to Reconsider Ruling Striking Testimony of Pam Howell.* Got that? Or do you want to reconsider? Do you have permission to reconsider?

I think this is "legal humor" (a slim pamphlet filed in the library right next to "papal humor.")

Motion WITHDRAWING Ben Ginsberg's "pro hac vice" from the Coleman team.

Ben has been the raving spinmeister at the daily pressers. Last week he filed his "pro hac vice" to be in the courtroom as an official part of the Coleman courtroom team (he's been on the team on background a long time, but this let him go into court.) [Pro hac vice; Latin: PRO hack VEE-chay if I've got it right. "For this case," the way you bring in an out of state lawyer without them having to be admitted to the state bar. Elias and Hamilton (from DC and Wash. State) are Pro hac vice for Franken].

Of course when your "vice" is "pro hac"-ked that means you are an officer of the court and your words and actions *inside and outside the courtroom* are subject to a stricter, court-enforced guideline than if you are just being Ben the Ginz. This has been apparently too much for Ben, too much cramp in his style. Or to play on the words, maybe his pro hac vice was met by too much anti hac virtue from the Franken side and from the court. Maybe his involvement with Florida 2000 put too much Miami Vice in his vice for a Minnesota setting.:-)

Or... (oh no! I feel the rush coming on, the endless ennui, lack of sleep, the adrenaline/caffeine/pinot noir combo, the smell of lutefisk next to speed, Yukon Jack and mango juice with six aspirin all at once, and there at the foot of the bed, the drug-twisted ghost of Hunter S... no, no rant, just a nightmare of pro hac vice, anti hac vice, vichay...vee-chay... veni, vidi, vici... why not vici? Why not Vichy, the resistance vive la France... Hunter, let me at least mark the puns with "!," ok most of them) a partly burned script recently uncovered...

.....then by train, or auto, or foot across the rim of Africa, to Casablanca in French Morocco. Here, the fortunate ones through money, or influence, or luck, might obtain exit visas and scurry to Lisbon; and from Lisbon, to the New World. But the others wait in Casablanca... and wait... and wait... and wait.

"Rick, Rick. You must help me Rick!" came a nasaled male scream, followed by two pistol shots. From behind a door another male voice said in the sudden quiet, "I hope when they come for me Rick I can count on somebody."

Rick Blaine growled back, "I stick my neck out for nobody."

In the far reaches of Rick's storeroom next to the alley sat WineRev, his white sport coat rumpled and his tie askew. He took a drag on an unfiltered Lucky Strike filtered unlucky Strike and blew the smoke out with a heavy sigh. The table in front of him was littered with bottles of gin, vodka, scotch and wine. He gazed despondently and said to the back-up piano player Scott, "I'll never get out of Minnesota Casablanca. I'll die in Casablanca writing for that Orange fiend. That Russian is such a Kossack!

"Oh c'mon boss. It'll change. You'll see," Scott answered, tickling the ivories on the battered upright piano.

(WineRev suddenly flings shot glass across the room. Shouts)

"Whats the use? The pro hac vichys have everybody under their thumb and the anti hac vichys let 'em. Hacs, thats what they are, hacs. All of 'em."

"Ya gotta keep hopin', boss'."

"I haven't hoped for a long time, and then Ingrid Bergman walks in tonight with Victor Lazlo." WineRev throws back his 5th gin & tonic (Tanqueray 10) and a tear comes to his eye. He shakes his head and growls at Scott, "What's that you're playin?"

"Oh, nuthin."

"Yeah you are."

"No I'm not."

(WineRev pounds table, face twists into a grimace.)

"Of all the gin joints, in all the towns, in all the world, she walks into mine. Why, Scott, why?"

"Don't know boss"

"Well, play it then."

"Play what?"

"You know what, If she can stand it, so can I. Play it Scott!"

The sounds of "As Time Goes By" are interrupted from the alley by loud voices. Sound of glass breaking. WineRev and Scott go to a nearby window and look out through the blinds. Angry gangs are shouting, armed with sticks, week-old baguettes and broken bottles. Dogs bark and growl. Distant pistol shots are heard. A sudden rush of live farm animals from the market stampede through the square.

The battered figure of a man staggers around the corner and WineRev recognizes Fritz Knaak. Knaak is waving someone to come join him. Knaak and his partner huddle beneath the window, not realizing they are being overheard.

"Fritz! Fritz! Thank god they didn't get you too" came a slurred voice past a swelling lip.

"Tony get a hold of yourself. Stop it. Don't trimble, Tony. Get a grip man. What happened to the others?"

(Gasping) "It looks awful. I was down at our seafood place..."

"Leni's?"

"Yeah. Leni's. Well a couple weeks ago 'Leni's Reef' installed (!) a shortwave and we heard some stuff. Herman's gone."

"What happened?"

"Sounds like he was at the farmers market when the animals stampeded. Last anybody heard a bull was goring Herman (!)."

"Thats awful."

"Yeah it is," Tony answered. "The new girl was listening with me and the news left Sarah pale in the face."

"What else?" (Sound of beer bottle smashing against wall nearby.)

"Somebody reported on the trial. That damn Minneapolis election director Cindy Reichert wouldn't give poor Joe any help at all. Just sat there smiling and giving straight answers or quoting the law"

WineRev could see Knaak shake his head in disgust, then pull out a witness list and calendar.

"How long has she been on the stand anyway, Tony? What day is she? First day Reichert or second Reichert?" Tony shakes head back.

"Worse. Third Reichert(!) day on the stand and Joe couldn't shake her."

Suddenly Tony began to sob and he whimpered, "But that's not the worst. They got Ben."

Knaak sat straight up and WineRev could see the color drain out of him. "Who got him? How?"

"Who else? The anti-vichy hacs! The anti-viches broke into the hall shouting "Down with Pétain. Death to Blum!" All sorts of anti-Vichy crap while tearing down easels. Then they saw Ben and all the pro viche hacs in Casablanca couldn't help him and he got himself out of the courtroom."

"Unbelievable," Knaak said staring off.

Tony began crying again. "Oh that was so bad, so bad. I mean they got Ben. Knaak, worst(!) of all they got Ben."

(Crowd noises increase and both Knaak and Trimble stand.)

Knaak: "They're coming."

Trimble: "Yes, thats them, I'm sure of it, the anti hac Vichys! Damn them." They listen a moment, the 2 in the alley with fear, the 2 inside the window with a growing hope.

"Can you make out what they're chanting?" Knaak asks.

"It must be that hac French of theirs," Tony said, pulling out his Berlitz guide. "It sounds like..."Libre France! Libre France!"

"We can't transmit that. Whats the German translation?"

"Wait, let me see," Trimble mutters, flipping pages and mumbling.

"Ok here it is. In our report to Berlin we'll tell them the anti vichy hacs were chanting, "Frei Franken. Frei Franken. FREI FRANKEN!"

"Maybe if the Franken goes free from this trial of a town," WineRev muttered to Scott, "I will too...

(script breaks off at burned edge. Scribbled notation visible: "Burn at all costs. DO NOT USE, Signed, Michael Curtiz."

OK, got the early shift so off to the wineshop in a few. Hope this will hold you until The UpTake time at 9:00 a.m. CT. The latest from Casablanca and other points yust southeast of Lake Wobegon.

Shalom.

This came in the comments after the diary was posted, courtesy of JDog42...the missing pages, perhaps?

WineRev: Last night we said a great many things. You said I was to do the thinking for both of us. Well, I've done a lot of it since then, and it all adds up to one thing: you're getting on that plane with Franken where you belong.

Readers: But, WineRev, no, I... I...

WineRev: Now, you've got to listen to me! You have any idea what you'd have to look forward to if you stayed here? Nine chances out of ten, we'd both wind up in Court. Isn't that true, Kos?

Captain Kos: I'm afraid Mr. Coleman would insist.

Readers: You're saying this only to make me go.

WineRev: I'm saying it because it's true. Inside of us, we both know you belong with Franken. You're part of his work, the thing that keeps him going. If that plane leaves the ground and you're not with him, you'll regret it. Maybe not today. Maybe not tomorrow, but soon and for the rest of your life.

Readers: But what about us?

WineRev: We'll always have St. Paul. We didn't have, we, we lost it until you came to Minneapolis. We got it back last night.

Readers: When I said I would never leave you.

WineRev: And you never will. But I've got a job to do, too. Where I'm going, you can't follow. What I've got to do, you can't be any part of. Readers, I'm no good at being noble, but it doesn't take much to see that the problems of three little people don't amount to a hill of beans in this crazy world. Someday you'll understand that. Now, now... Here's looking at you kid.

Norm Staggers
February 28, 2009

Comments: 317	Recs: 313	Tips: 324

Personal Breather and Reflection

February 28th? You must be mad! Yes I am, in both senses. If someone would have told me I'd still be writing this series after WineRev-ER got his driver's license (Thursday: loose on the roads! Look out America!) I never would have signed on. Grrr... a grind and time hog (but since I have no other life...)

And this is driving me mad ("leave the driving to us."..."Hey Dad, can I drive to Target?"...Fahrfugnugen "joy of driving."..."'49 Roadmaster, Straight-Eight. Fireball Eight. Only 8,095 production models. Dad lets me drive on the driveway, but not on Monday.") Oh yeah, that kind of mad too...

But then maybe that's why I wasn't told and it's better just to sit down and do the next piece, which isn't so bad. And then the one after that. It's just one at a time that builds up to something... sort of like living life. We are not told how long or how many days we have, and those who have been told are either tortured or transformed by the knowledge. Ignorance isn't exactly bliss but some things are better known when they are unknown to start with and pieced together on the way.

And along the way are all sorts of incidents, accidents and people you encounter: a skinny kid in Orange with a small user number and a big website; people who will step up and tell you about Neti pots, prop you up in a chapter 13, cheer you on with Beethoven in a grieving moment, critique and improve your letter writing, supplement your diary with number crunching or legal citations, laugh/groan at your jokes, and sometimes completely miss the really GOOD puns.

So it's been a long, twisting trip and it's not done yet. It's also been an education, a comfort, and a healing and growing for me in ways I don't even understand yet but that you have contributed to.

(WineRev rises, bows, doffs (DOFFS!) hat to DailyKos community)

Thank you one and all.

Election Contest Court – Episode XXXV
Strike! UN-Strike! Re-Strike! and …Say What?!

We got about 6 inches of new snow Thursday night and all that shoveling, blowing and plowing affects people, even lawyers.

(It also affects Ole & his wife Lena. A big snowstorm came down and the mayor announced for plowing purposes parking would be restricted to the odd-numbered side of every street in New Narvik. Ole put on his coat and hat & moved the car.

About a week later came another storm and the mayor declared another snow emergency, this time restricting parking to the even-numbered side of streets. Ole went out and shuffled the car again.

A third storm came through (being March and state tournament time, this is required) and Ole and Lena were having a TV dinner as the mayor announced once more parking would only be

on the odd-numbered side of the street. Ole rose and started putting on his hat, coat and gloves when Lena said, "Oh c'mon Ole, you've done enough. This time yust leave the car in the garage.") :-D

Pamela Howell was back on the witness stand Friday morning. She testified a good while Wednesday on direct examination and then after lunch with David Lillehaug on cross-examination. Things turned into a major lightsabre duel when it came out:

- Ms. Howell had made notes to herself on her computer about her testimony (perfectly fine and a good idea for anybody),

- she had shared these notes (a computer file and/or hard copy) and had a phone call or 2 with Tony Trimble of the Coleman legal team (still OK; she's their witness and they want to prep her testimony) but

- the Coleman team had NOT shared her notes with the Franken team or with the ECC (MAJOR NO-NO; Rules of evidence on pre-trial discovery REQUIRE each side to share this information with each other; not the attorney's working notes, flowcharts and other in-house stuff you use to get ready, but the document itself MUST be shared.)

This produced a major hole in the ice, like heaving a refrigerator off the IDS tower onto the frozen Mississippi, so everybody took a 10 minute break to look everything over. When court (and cross-exam) resumed it came out almost immediately Joe Friedberg of the Coleman legal team had shown Ms. Howell the notes again while everyone was at recess on the swings and teeter-totters. (If they would have been her own notes which she brought with her herself I believe this would be acceptable.) But that it came from counsel made it a MAJOR NO-NO.

The ECC (who have shown repeatedly they are REALLY tight on stuff like…the LAW, courtroom procedures, Rules of Evidence, etc.) **granted Franken's Motion to Strike** the witness's testimony.

By all accounts and comments from lawyers on these boards andThe UpTake, a Motion to Strike like this is pretty rare because the offense has to be pretty severe, so everybody agreed this was a BIG DEAL. Even the court was a bit nervous at how big a deal it was, since this is just the sort of thing that gives one side or another grounds for appeal (even reversal) in a higher court. ("See? The court was prejudiced against me and my client because Motion to Strike was beyond the bounds.") Judges HATE to get their rulings reversed.

Sooo… they were in a somewhat receptive frame of mind on Thursday when Tony Trimble (in particular) came crawling to them (because a big chunk of their case rests on this story about double counted ballots) to beg forgiveness. He claimed he didn't share the Howell notes not from bad faith but from simple oversight. Apparently his apology and willing to eat a plate of lutefisk in penance (It IS Lent after all, the season of repentance, of contemplation of one's sins and unworthiness before God) moved the court to **vacate their order** granting Motion to Strike.

SOoooooo, now Friday morning rolls in. Ms. Howell is again on the stand because Lillehaug had not finished (indeed hardly begun his cross-examination when he had been so rudely interrupted by a violation of the Rules of Evidence), he still gets to question her until he is satisfied with her answers and/or runs out of questions.

Not far into it, the witness, Ms. Howell, (gad; sounds like, "the virgin, Connie Swale"), said under oath she had had SEVERAL conversations AND e-mails with Tony Trimble about her testimony, notes and recollections. Lillehaug climbed all over this with the court pointing out this was NO MERE OOPSIE from the Coleman legal team.

> Meehs - This is pretty bad conduct. Trimble represented that the failure to provide the document was inadvertent, the emails suggest otherwise. Whether Trimble or his paralegal or junior assoc messed up, Trimble's representation in court to the judges was at worst a lie, and at best given without Trimble knowing whether the representation was true or not. This will lead to a sanction against Trimble. *(Landslide Al at The UpTake)*

Coleman attorney Tony Trimble ends up looking like the guy who drives the tractor at the driving range to sweep up the golf balls. Usually these Lawn-Boys have a steel mesh cage so the driver doesn't get hurt while everyone keeps improving the slice off their 6 irons. But now the place was packed on Sunday afternoon for Kiwanis "50 Cents a Big Bucket O' Balls to go with a Tall Beer" fundraiser, every pad is firing, and there was no mesh cage out past the 125 sign for the ball boy Tony.

Rats off a sinking ship? Rattlesnakes starting to eat each other?

Again, Coleman lawyers? INADVERTENTLY? Multiple e-mails and phone calls (which Lillehaug was given Friday morning). Lillehaug alternated between focused furious and genuine sadness toward the Coleman Team but was relentless in nailing them for this "strategic decision not to disclose" the info in discovery.

It was so bad (How bad?) Joe Friedberg got up and basically said, "Your honors, all this stuff happened in the case BEFORE I WAS BROUGHT IN, so it's not my fault." Yep! Nothing like Team togetherness! Yowser.

What might the court do? After all they were taken in by Trimble's sackcloth and ashes mea culpa so that they UN-struck the Motion to Strike. The bloggers offered these suggestions:

- Reinstate Motion to Strike" - not bad.
- Entertain "Motion to Strike" not ONLY the testimony (as before) but also strike the "CLAIM' in the testimony: that there was duplicate ballots/double counting; you know, saw off that entire leg of Coleman's case. (That would bring the case down to a pig-on-stilts-on-ice with only 3 stilts), would leave an opening on appeal ("not all the evidence was heard...")
- Sanction Tony Trimble, maybe after the trial end... fitting too.
- Let in the claim and other testimony from other witnesses so the ECC can then rule against ALL of them while showing their even-handedness? They might find that attractive. We'll see.

The ECC took Howell off the stand and said they would rule on her testimony, her claim, Tony the Trimble, the Coleman team's abuse of discovery, on Monday. What a weekend of sweating...for everybody except Al Franken and friends!

Coleman's universe nears Supernova stage

Out in the far reaches of the galaxy there are times when a star is shrinking in on itself. With the right combination of spin, mass, and rate of collapse there are times when the whole thing undergoes a cataclysmic collapse which crams the atoms in so close together and under such heat and pressure the entire process reverses and explodes: a supernova, where all the matter bursts out in all directions lighting the sky (as in sometimes visible on earth to the naked eye in daylight visible!). But then the atoms of like the Crab Nebula (a former supernova) dissipate into a cold dust cloud.

The Coleman universe has shrunk from 12,000 rejected absentee ballots to 11,000 to 4,800 to 3,500 to maybe 2,000. Friday in court, attorney Langdon proposed a supernova finish to the Minnesota Senate race.

(Watch this 3 1/2 forward in pike off the 10 meter tower!) Given the court's Friday the 13th ruling (they keep coming back to that so they REALLY didn't like it) of ruling in and ruling out certain categories of absentee ballots;

...and given such a set of categories amounts to a de facto set of statewide standards for absentee ballots

...and given those standards were only invented by the Court 2/13

...(ready?) the ONLY way for the court to be fair and avoid a claim of "unequal protection" (that some scumbag candidate's lawyers might file for) would be for the court to re-examine **all 286,000** absentee ballots by those standards!

First to recover his voice was Judge Kurt Marben: "How can we undo something once these votes have been cast and counted?"

Langdon was ready with a Ginsberg/Rube Goldberg answer: reduce the absentee ballot count precinct-by-precinct in mathematical proportion to how the precinct voted overall. If I get this the side with more absentee ballots would take a greater reduction. Hmmm... now which side is leading by +249? Which side has done better among absentee ballots?

Second to recover her voice, Judge Reilly threw the first ballista at Langdon by noting MN law doesn't really allow for such a thing. *(Totalitarians of all stripes HATE the law for just such reasons.)*

Langdon was ready with #2): If #1 is too hard the judges could change or lift their Feb. 13th order (they REALLY don't like what that did to their case!)

Third to recover his voice was Franken attorney Marc Elias, albeit haltingly:

> "I am frankly almost without words, which is rare, very rare, I'm almost without words to know quite what to do in response to this motion," Elias said.
>
> "I couldn't even begin to tell you which ballots out of the 280,000 ballots that were cast by absentee they believe were illegally cast," he told the judges. "I don't think they know. I think they what they want is we'll sort of take all 280,000, put them on a big forklift, we'll take them, we'll plop them here in the courtroom and then the court will do something."
>
> ...
>
> As for asking the court to "fix" the Feb. 13th ruling on its own, Elias said that's because the Coleman side doesn't have a remedy:
>
> "Instead they wish to simply cast doubt on this process as it comes to the conclusion of their case," Elias said, glaring at the Coleman table as he sat down at his. *(MinnPost)*

The ECC will rule on this, maybe by Monday. It may take them that long to find a forklift big enough to pick up the carcass of the Coleman case, load it on a triple set of Saturn V rockets, and blast the whole schmeer directly into the Sun for incineration.

Duluth City Clerk behaving oddly

Joe Cox is City Clerk for Duluth and hence the local elections director. On Monday, Team Franken (who was given word Team Coleman might rest their case as early as Wednesday the 25th), subpoenaed Cox to testify for their case and be ready to drive down on Thursday. Witnesses get a $20 daily rate and mileage both ways from New Narvik or wherever.

Cox moved to quash the subpoena (what?) on grounds it didn't pay enough! No really. He wants a minimum of $1,100 UP FRONT, based on $60/hour of his time, on a 24-hour clock while he is away from Duluth. (He wants to get paid $60/hour while sleeping in his motel room if necessary.) And he's not crazy about a motel room either. He wanted guarantees(!) he could drive down, testify and drive back all on the same day or else he won't come at all.

This is all before the ECC and another thing for them to rule on this weekend.

What is with Mr. Cox? I doubt he's some crazed and drooling knuckle-dragging Rethug because Duluth is quite a "blue" city and I imagine the various officials are likely Democrats. So does he not want his face onThe UpTake? Doesn't he like St. Paul motels (result of an unfortunate childhood incident with a "Magic Fingers" massage unit and a tiny bar of soap?)

Does he think St. Paul-ites will make fun of his out-of-town clothes? [*Duluth Power Dressing for Men: black fisherman's cap over dark blue blazer, orange shirt and eye-stinging sunburst yellow tie all riding magnificently above lime-green slacks. Accessorize with multi-holed white belt and gleaming white patent-leather shoes when snow not present. Otherwise match tie with lemon yellow steel-toes from Red Wing (MN!) boots – about $85 in finer sporting goods stores*].

OK. I hope that will hold you for the weekend, although if something breaks, I'll put up a post. That's the latest of the late from yust southeast of Lake Wobegon.

Shalom.

March 2009

Norm's Case Rests
March 2, 2009

Comments: 211   Recs: 294   Tips: 299

The Transition Point

Thank GOD! (Druids among us can simply rap knuckles on the nearest piece of oak to invoke their protectors; ha! and now you know "knock on wood" for good luck) We are at the Legal Inflection Point! Perhaps even today we will hear the third sweetest words any MN political junkie can hope for from Joe Friedberg/Fritz Knaak/Tony Trimble/Joe Langdon: "Plaintiff Rests." [If you are wondering, #2: (Norm Coleman speaking:) "I will fight no more/ concede/ need to spend more time with my family/ seek new opportunities..."; #1: From the floor of the US Senate: "I, Al Franken, do solemnly swear..."]

If not today then Tuesday/Wednesday but the words are at hand. There will be a flurry of motions from both sides but 2 that will merit attention.

First the Coleman side will move (Summary Judgment, I think) they have made their case with such factual clarity, spiritual force, legal brilliance, moral integrity and perspicacious rodomontade (buffs fingernails!) that the ECC should make a finding for the Coleman side on the spot, rule from the bench they need not even HEAR the Franken side of the case, send Norm to the Senate, and send Al packing to St. Louis Park (where we love him.) Really; I think they will move this, pro forma if nothing else.

Prediction: Court will be recessed immediately for 30 minutes. Muffled, endless, shrieking laughter will be heard down the hall from the judges' chambers. 1 male and 2 female licensed physical therapists will be seen entering chambers. Their white jacketed supervisor will give Noah Kunin an UpTake update explaining the 3 are specialists in rib massage, rubbing away hurts after a particularly convulsive session of prolonged laughter.

Second the Franken side will likewise move (*either Summary Judgment or Motion to Dismiss; esquire types among us can give us the refinements and distinctions*) to end the case NOW on grounds Coleman has NOT met the burden of proof (which rests on the contest-ANT) to show Coleman can overcome Franken's +249 lead and so has "the highest number of valid, lawfully cast votes," which is what the ECC exists for.

Prediction: ECC will not grant this because the stakes are too high. ECC will not dismiss this out of hand (which they should do to #1 above). ECC will "take it under advisement" just like they do with the Coleman Motion.

AND in the next few days the ECC may well "Grant in Part and Deny in Part" Motion for Summary judgment for both sides. They have done this on other motions and it seems to be a careful way of proceeding. They seem to like to let the legal glacier move forward here 10 meters over night, move there 3 meters one day, and then crush a particular boulder at 2 in the morning with explosive force that rips the tents of the ice watching team with granite shrapnel. (*I still think the Coleman side is facing this mile-high glacier in a box canyon and this will not end well.*)

Too Good to Pass Up

You know how Norm Coleman "won on election night" that the Reichwingers keep chewing their cuds about? Well here's something from the NW suburb of Maple Grove (ex-urban, fast-growing McMansion territory) that was on the *Star Tribune* blog:

> Here are some election night fun facts. I was an election judge in Maple Grove. We didn't even get our absentee ballots delivered to our precinct until 11:30pm. By that time Coleman had declared himself winner. By the time we had prepared the AB's for scanning it was 1am. We didn't finish tallying our precinct results until 3am. If you look at the election results in the Strib the next morning you would have seen results showing 0 precincts reporting in Maple Grove. In case you don't know, there are a lot of people in Maple Grove. That is why you can see a huge swing in vote tallies overnight. So when Coleman declared himself winner, to cite an old adage, he was counting his chickens before they hatched. *(Star Tribune Online)*

At the Wineshop (no kidding)

A quiet morning (it's February) and this 40-ish guy comes in, suit and cellphone conversation, "Yeah, I forgot, but I'm here at the wine shop." Hangs up says to me, "I'm running late and I forgot to pick up some wine at Trader Joe's. You don't carry any '3 buck chuck'?" "Sorry I don't."

"Ok, let me, ah, have 2 bottles of Beringer White Zinfandel (bleeh! 10% alc. and maybe 15% sugar water added; really) and 2 of these and 2 of those." Whole thing came to under $40. "Great. That'll be just what I need." Picks up bag, gives me odd, earnest/bragging look that made me think this *might be* a gag gift. Says seriously (so I believed him), "Need these for Governor Pawlenty's meeting with us here in (name of suburb) later this morning."

I put mouth in motion before brain in gear: "Pawlenty? That explains the White Zinfandel." He stopped and laughed till he sagged against the door frame. Didn't say anything else and left. Dodged a bullet I hope...

DK What kind of champagne would you suggest when this is all over? Cold Duck? *(Fiddlegirl)*

DK Maison d'éléphant mort - 2009 *(edgeways)*

That's the latest from yust southeast of Lake Wobegon, not far from New Narvik.

Shalom.

An End; A Beginning
March 3, 2009

Comments: 159   Recs: 375   Tips: 306

Election Contest Court - Episode XXXVI

The End of the Beginning

The Coleman team dragged the last of their case like milfoil infestation clogging the propeller across the ECC floating dock Monday, a few more questions for state elections director Gary Poser, and one more round with Minneapolis election judge Pamela Howell.

The Poser testimony had one telling moment. Apparently a few absentee ballots were rejected because a state data base showed the voter had voted in person (Reason/Pile 4 legal reason to reject and absentee ballot, in-person takes precedence over absentee by law.) Apparently due to a data entry error some of these voters had NOT voted in person, and therefore their absentee ballots should have been accepted.

OK it's a human system and errors happen. Normally it wouldn't matter but at a margin of 249, little errors matter. It LOOKS like a small problem (9 votes so discovered). The Coleman team did NOT offer evidence it is a BIG problem, but it's something for Norm, and it IS part of the case record, and so the ECC is going to have to do something about it. Kudos to the Coleman team for digging this out. It won't help them much but the MN election system can be improved and here's one way how.

On the other hand, outside the courtroom the no-longer-accredited, got his "pro hac vice" ("for this case" permission to appear in court while not a member of the MN bar) "Anti hac virtued" Ben Ginsberg told everybody in earshot not only was this a HUGE problem, but that the state of Minnesota's entire data system is "corrupt and it is impossible to have faith in (the information) in the system." *(Which is different than the entire Republican party being corrupt and it is impossible to have any faith in its leaders and most of its members... but you see where Ben got it from.)* It is for the freedom to make whacked off remarks like this that Ben the Ginz withdrew as a lawyer trying the case. Yeesh!

Another Yeesh to Ginsberg came from Jim Gelbmann, deputy Secretary of State. Jay Weiner caught it:

> At first, the secretary of state's office declined comment. But the word "corrupt" proved to be a fightin' word.
>
> Deputy Secretary of State Jim Gelbmann reacted to Ginsberg's allegations, calling the notion of corrupted data "false ... Minnesota's elections system has been recognized as one of the best in the nation for decades. Many states look to Minnesota as they attempt to improve their own systems." *(Minn Post)*

You GO, JIM! Don't take that off Ben the Ginz. You slap him with a fresh caught northern...still alive and hungry!

The Howell testimony was regarding the possible "duplicate ballot/double counting" issue which Coleman contends was worth 100-150 votes for Franken, mostly in the city of Minneapolis.

She actually made it to the end of her testimony today. Franken attorney David Lillehaug did NOT start 5 steps back, a black leather brace on his right wrist and a 16 pound ball with a 3 foot by 10 foot loft and make a Motion to Strike her testimony today. (He spared her that! :-) No "gutter"-al remarks now.) He DID work hard at undermining her credibility as Noah Kunin reported:

> The Franken cross-examination was long and contentious. The main thrust of the Franken argument was that (Howell) had no first hand knowledge the labeling (of duplicate and original ballots) did not occur. David Lillehaug, representing Franken, also raised questions on the timing of her report of the incident. In other precincts an incident report was immediately filed when ballots were not labeled "duplicate" - Howell did not recall filing an incident report and no such report can be found. *(The UpTake)*

At MOST Ms. Howell contended the duplicate/double count MIGHT have happened in her precinct on **14 instances** and not all these on Franken ballots. The Coleman side has held the issue was widespread (100-150 ballots; still a mystery where this number came from) but offered no other witnesses or evidence that it was, which left the whole claim limper than cheese off the edge of hot pizza.

It also appears **Ms. Howell had reason to be leery** of testifying and had cause to be borderline hostile (in the legal sense) when being cross-examined. Noah's paragraph above closed with THIS little pointed icicle:

> During the recount, the Franken campaign issued a complaint against Howell's handling of ballots. *(The UpTake)*

Really? Being a little sloppy or snappy even then, Ms Howell? (Not as overt as the woman in Dakota County who was caught putting 26 Franken ballots in piles meant to be 25.) But whatever Ms. Howell was or wasn't doing during the recount was apparently enough to trigger a formal complaint. So was she on the stand in, payback? Reluctant to face more of the same? Hmmm. Speculation welcome.

Sanctions Delivered on a Lawyer

When we last left the ECC Friday afternoon they took under advisement a Franken motion: a) to strike Howell's testimony, b) to strike the CLAIM in her testimony (that is the issue of double counting duplicate ballots), and c) to *sanction* Coleman's attorneys for violating court rules on discovery and coaching/tampering with a witness.

When Ms. Howell first thought she saw double counting of duplicates she had started a computer file of her thoughts (and labeled it "testimony.") She contacted Team Coleman about it, Tony Trimble's office. She showed them her notes and they had several e-mails and phone calls with her about it (including phrases like "we don't want to lock you into your testimony"). NONE of this was passed on to Team Franken or the Court in pre-trial "discovery" - major no-no. It got her testimony stricken, then re-instated after Trimble apologized to the court for not sharing her notes, then re-exploded when the e-mails came out.

Court started late Monday as lawyers and judges met in chambers to hear the decision. When court opened, Ms. Howell was allowed to testify and the court "sanctioned" the Coleman lawyers (Trimble in particular, I believe.) Late in the afternoon came word: **sanctions for $7,500.** This is payable to the court I believe and, can a MN lawyer fill in, is it due at the end of the trial, or in 3 days, or...when?

The fine comes from the lawyer (who, yes, I know, is going to collect it in fees from Norm Coleman) but Norm has EVERY right to expect to see on his bill, just before the grand total in the lower right hand corner, an item like "Attorney Sanction, pd to Court" and a BIG MINUS $7,500.00.

Go get 'em NORM! Yes it's just a drip off the ice dam backing up under your shingles, Norm, but Tony a headslap! That is REALLY BAD lawyering when the COURT lays down a 75 C-note marker on YOUR mouthpiece.

GRrrrr... this is the kind of crapola that gives lawyers a bad name. If lawyers are necessary (and it seems they are) well let them be honorable, diligent, vigorous and meticulous. Getting sanctioned by the Court? $7,500? Hey, this is the NFL giving a two-game suspension without pay to your cornerback for that nasty hit out of bounds. Ya like the guy, you're going to miss him against the Steelers and the Browns, but even a red-hot home fan in purple braids reeking of spilled Summit Pale Ale will say the league made the right move.

So, here too, Norm. We will all turn our backs for 10 seconds while you wind up for a sharply-struck corner kick, well delivered to the gluteus splaticus. There will be no witnesses. (Then we'll go back to cheering for Al, Norm. But this is a freebie.)

Hey! Lawyers are Human too!

And oddly continuing a streak of saying nice things about the other side, Court was on a break near noon when singing broke out. Both tables in Coleman vs. Franken joined in. Really. As hard core as its been sometimes IN court these people are still people and, thank the holies, they check their lightsabers at the door going OUT of the Court.

> About noon, led by Franken lawyer Marc Elias, attorneys from both sides and – dare we say some of the media corps – sang "Happy Birthday" to Coleman lead litigator Joe Friedberg, he the veteran Minneapolis criminal defense lawyer.
>
> He turned 72. *(Star Tribune)*

So Mr. Friedberg, on the occasion of a perfectly timed birthday at a natural break in the trial, for all you have tried to do for your client and thereby contributed to justice being served in a court of law rather than on a rack, or via vengeance, or by fire or water, or by duel to the death (all kind of ways humans have invented before law for all), WineRev offers you a Happy Birthday salute! (Today of course it's back to cheering for Hamilton, Al, Marc and Lillehaug...*wait, didn't they do "'Don't Pull Your Love Out on Me Baby" in another life? Hmmmm, how DID they pay for law school?)*

> **DK** I'd say the Coleman lawyers were more like a bad polka band playing a cover of "Feelings." *(Fiddlegirl)*

The Contestant Provisionally Rests

That's what they said just before 1:00 p.m. and school let out early. "Provisionally."... man, can't we ever get SOMETHING solid from these people? OK, I get it. You do this "provisionally" so those last minute or final papers you had due can get turned in for a grade for THIS nine-weeks.

And that's what happened. If you go to the MN Court webpage for the trial, you'll see 5 items the Coleman side downloaded into the ECC in-box.

And they have been busy little lawyers! Three of the items are related to a **Rule (9) both sides agreed** to for the Recount. Specifically, in the Recount there were many situations where a duplicate ballot had been made of an original so it could be run through the counting machine. SO, on election night, original ballot saved, and its duplicate run through machine for the count in the precinct. OK?

But for the Recount it is a HAND Recount, no machines. All 3,000,000 ballots shall be tallied by hand. OK, for this one, no duplicate for the machine is needed since the machines are not being used. Human eyeballs will do the reading. Both sides stipulated (agreed; I DO NOT know if this was *"stipulated with prejudice,"* which we have all learned is lawyer talk for "no crossed fingers, no givebacks and no do-overs.")

Rule 9 said both sides agreed for the hand recount we should **use the original ballots.** Fair enough and, as the Coleman lawyers point out (with all the excitement of announcing "the Sun rises in the East") the originals are "best evidence." Cool, and so it was in the Recount.

NOW in their 3 inter-locking items Team Coleman **wants to throw out Rule 9,** claiming the agreement itself was in violation of MN election law. And they have memoranda and legal citations and 14 pages worth of stuff and really actually sound like lawyers.

This isn't half-bad. Stipulation or no, if it's in violation of law then the stipulation is void, even I can see that. As near as I can make out (jump in anytime Oh Perry Mason wannabes, Matlock mavens, LA Law longers; you can say it better than I) they are claiming this use of original ballots was not done, or was done haphazardly, or inconsistently. They are using this to get after the Minneapolis 133 (again!) because of course those original (in-person instead of absentees for once) ballots are missing. It also supports their "equal protection" claim they seem to be readying for state or federal appeal. It is of a piece with their on-going "no uniform standards" mantra *(which reductio ad absurdum would mean only PERFECT elections would be acceptable and therefore elections should never happen.)*

This also fits with another item filed with the Court, a **letter from Coleman attorney James Langdon.** Langdon argued last week that one remedy the court could use to clean up the absentee ballot "mess" (messy only because of the efforts of TEAM Coleman) would be to reduce the count of absentee ballots (all 286,000 of them!) by mathematical formula. Failing that the court should overturn its 2/13 ruling (that threw out certain categories of absentee ballots that the Coleman side had obviously been counting on heavily.)

Much of this was repeated in Langdon's letter, citing neighboring states (and cases back to 1912! Good work, James!) who had used a mathematical approach. He does keep calling these issues "illegal" ballots. And he now offers in writing what the Reichwingers have been clamoring for in their talking points: if there are so many "illegal" votes in dispute, well, with a heavy heart, the court can **"set aside an election"** ... and call a new one.

OK, there it is in black letter Letter, folks. THE forlorn hope of the Coleman campaign, an official request for a statewide "do-over."

Sooo... while the Franken side of the case launches today the court has these items on their back burners and can rule on them at anytime.

Odds & Ends

Signs of...something I guess. Last week PR guy Luke Friedrich quit the Coleman campaign to take a PR job with newly elected congressman Eric Paulson (R) MN-03. Then over the weekend, the office closed for the "Coleman for Senate" campaign. Word officially is that their lease ran out. Now comes word that Mark Drake, another PR guy, has left the staff. No job upcoming but he's going to explore opportunities.

OK, all these people and offices cost money. The offices seem superfluous at this point. And with a PR ball of fire like Ben the Ginz well, what further need have we of anyone else? But still, is it a sign? We'll see...

The ECC also ruled Monday afternoon on **Jeff Cox, the Duluth city clerk** issue. Mr. Cox's is city elections director and Team Franken has called him as a witness for their case. The city admin. and city attorney got involved. It sounded bizarre when I posted it in Saturday's diary (complete with a Duluth Power Dressing guide) but the reality is much sadder.

In a case like this "court costs" you hear about include the court paying a witness mileage & compensation as permitted by law. (Same sort of thing as happens for jury duty.) MN Law (like a lot of states I'd wager) is pretty lean on this: $20/day + about 30 cents/ mile round trip. A court can pay more but it's under unusual circumstances, and this case doesn't count.

Duluth's city attorney filed to get more, like $1,100 to offset expenses and loss of labor. It was calculated on a 24 hours running clock (so Mr. Cox would get paid for sleeping at the Motel 6 if he had to stay overnight.) That's what came off as so bizarre.

But Duluth asked for this because the **city is so broke!** As Kossack and Duluthian rincewind puts it, "the city is so far down, Normie's bellybutton looks like up." To try and get another 1000 bucks or so covered in the city budget they went and asked for more.

The ECC, sticklers for the law that they are, **turned them down,** but then their hands are tied by the law. Raising these compensations isn't real high on anyone's list and you can see what an easy target they would make for budget cutters in hard times particularly.

And what will today look like on The UpTake and in Room 300 of the Judiciary Building? Well Jay Weiner of the MinnPost quotes Mark Elias of the Franken team, who says that in five weeks Team Coleman managed to get about 20 voters on the stand to testify about wanting their vote to count (and sometimes blowing it too). 5 weeks, 20 voters.

Elias says Team Franken plans to call 20 voters too ...**TODAY** *and more* if there aren't too many objections from the Coleman side. Wednesday one of those called will be The UpTake's own Noah Kunin (East Baltic power!). All wait to see if Noah will learn how to tie on a tie for the occasion...

OK hope that will hold you until 9:00 a.m. CT at The UpTake when the 6th grade orchestra of the Cool Coleman Cids has finally been ushered off the stage, earplugs are unplugged, gum scraped off, and there is a hush. Tuxedos, floor-length gowns, and patent leather here and there. A baton rises, swings in tempo, and the entire hall knows the Academy of St. Martin's in the Fields is here and THIS is how Vivaldi should be, THIS is how Sibelius should flow, and THIS is how a case should be played, sung, presented and tried. To harmonious case-ifying from yust southeast of Lake Wobegon.

Shalom...2, 3, 4...

Shalom.

Real Trial, Real Law
March 4, 2009

Comments: 169   Recs: 229   Tips: 236

Try the new prescription contacts: **Election Contest Court (ECC) looked like... a court!** That's because Team Franken is putting all those reruns from Perry Mason to Boston Legal that they watched for 5 solid weeks to good use. 24 witnesses... *in one day,* but a popcorn chance missed.

Election Contest Court - Episode XXXVII
Rehabilitating Lawyerdom

For five excruciating weeks legal groupies have watched and wondered how badly can a court case be handled? Have law schools REALLY deteriorated that much? Is "Boston Legal" actually fantasy TV if this is legal reality? Cripes, kids playing pond hockey will settle a "puck on the goal line under Emily the goalie" dispute easier than this, and get back to having fun on the rink behind the St. Louis Park Fire Station #2.

Well, folks, on January 20, 2009 at noon ET, the restoration of American democracy began. Yesterday at just after 9:00 a.m. CT the rehabilitation of lawyers in America began in earnest. **Team Franken opened its case.**

They called 17 voter/witnesses in the morning, in under 3 hours, almost matching the Coleman 20 witnesses called in 5 weeks. Clicked along at about 8 minutes apiece. Witnesses were sharp, respectful, coherent, informed, occasionally nervous. Lunch break and 6 more voters. Gary Poser from the Sec. of State's office was back testifying and the Franken Team played a 40-minute DVD for the court (*no popcorn observed or heard*) used in MN Election Judge Training.

THIS is case management! Trial Law! And already they have met the WineRev mark of true profes-sionalism and talent: *they made it look easy.* [It really isn't. I'm sure as in most great displays the effort is terrific, but if you're bad, the effort shows (see last 5 weeks in ECC). If you're good, well, then it's Peggy Fleming throwing an "effortless" double-axel and gliding away like a swan on water.]

I only read about it on The UpTake and I am almost as limp with relief and verging on tears as I was on Inauguration Day. FINALLY! Competence. Order. Logic. Clarity. Yea even under it all, HOPE!

It sounded familiar, voters who voted absentee and whose ballot was rejected testifying why they believe/want their ballot counted. Hell, it was SO familiar on cross-examination *(now from the Coleman side; after yesterday's "Coleman rests," the teams switch ends to even out any sun or wind advantage).* Joe Friedberg! agreed with a (Franken) witness in wanting her ballot opened and counted.

> Does anybody else find it funny that Freidberg is agreeing to count a ballot while at the same time his team member Langdon is asking the court to set aside the election. *(RC at The UpTake)*

But then current Rethuglicans claim, "a foolish consistency is the hobgoblin of small minds." (Actually for the current Reichwing, "a foolish foolery is the hallmark of large asses.")

But why these witnesses from Team Franken? At least 2 reasons.

To put more votes on the board for when the ECC rules on which rejected absentee ballots be finally opened and counted. The lead is +246, but getting some insurance is a good play. The court has said they will (and has) rule on individual ballots so here are 2 dozen today, telling "their story." (One was from a resident in assisted living whose ballot was rejected because his address had changed: he had moved from one floor to another in the same place. Team Franken can play some heart strings too!)

You know how "some attorneys" endlessly said, "Unfair. Unequal protection. No uniform standards. My client has been grievously injured by the unfairness of inconsistencies between Traverse County elec-tion officials and Koochiching County officials."? [You know, the Ginsberg Flambé Gasconade du Jour in the outer hallway ("where they will wail and gnash their teeth")?]

> **DK** However, since all of these folks are likely Franken voters, it shows that the mis-takes are evenly distributed and did not materially effect the outcome. *(jmacatty)*

Yeah, there may have been unfairness and inconsistency but it was EQUALLY so (Team Franken's stance); both sides got nicked BUT there is no pattern here for or against one side or the other. Therefore "equal protection" is preserved under "equal injury." I'm not sure if that is a legal doctrine (I'll find out in the comments) but I think jmacatty has called it just right. It also gives the ECC a road to travel as they move to rule on the case.

More about Sanctions on Lawyers

Monday the ECC sanctioned the Coleman legal team $7,500 for their trampling of the rules of evi-dence/discovery from Wednesday to Friday last over the testimony of Pamela Howell. Given the millions be-ing spent (and collected) on this case $7,500 does seem like, well, like "cigar money" as the MinnPost put it.

> **DK** If you really want to get the lawyers here going, post the links to the Trimble-Howell emails, if they exist. I heard Lillehaug read through them when he made the second motion to strike last Friday. The media has not grasped how bad they really are and why the Court is so pissed at Trimble. I think that is one of the big-gest under reported elements of the trial. *(speet)*

Sanctions are available to a court to punish lawyerly misconduct and can range from a stern public lecture (perhaps the most common) to fines (like what we have here, although pretty nominal usually) through dismissing a lawyer's case *(which the ECC specifically noted in their order as a possible final resort if the Cole-man team keeps pulling this crap; YOWSER!)* all the way to causing a lawyer to lose their license.

But I put it in yesterday's diary to the legal types reading here, "What about sanctions? Pretty rare? How does this compare? How often does it make the "Lawyerly Times" news that a lawyer was sanctioned by a court? What is the practical effect?"

A couple of Kossack replies in the comments I thought you might like so you get the insider view:

DK

This is highly unusual. I have not personally seen a fine like this in over 20 years of practice. I first note that the court has opted for a sanction that does not bar evidence. This is to preclude a Coleman appeal issue that could affect the ECC's final determination on the election outcome.....

Trimble's bigger potential problem is that this may portend an ethics complaint/investigation with a likely result to be a stern public admonishment (yes the equivalent of a wet noodle lashing) or suspension (that one would hurt). *(speet)*

A Couple of Matters:

On monetary sanctions. Seventy-five hundred dollars doesn't sound like a lot of money when you consider how much is being thrown around in the overall Contest. It's probably about ten hours of Ben Ginsberg's time at his regular billing rate.

But it isn't really the money. Hard to believe it, but it's the shame. Here in California (and I suspect Minnesota is similar) if a judge sanctions an attorney for more than a thousand dollars, the attorney has to report that sanction to the State Bar. It is considered bar discipline and it is entered into the attorney's permanent record.

DK

Each time I use the California State Bar database to look up an attorney I do business with, the entry contains not just name, address, telephone number and e-mail address, if also tells you whether the attorney has ever been sanctioned. And every time you file a brief in a Court of Appeal, the court checks the same database.

In a business where a lot of money is at stake and the clients and general counsels of clients are always looking to cover their asses, having this blot on your record just makes it all the more likely that a potential client will look elsewhere for representation, not wanting to take the chance that this shameful sanction (which it is) will unnecessarily handicap your case by causing a judge to distrust your lawyer.

And this is the kind of thing that the kind of dweebs who become lawyers will sit up in bed in the middle of the night, sweat running off their foreheads, thinking, "why did I do that?"

...So in the bent universe lawyers inhabit, seventy-five hundred dollars in sanctions is a big deal. *(kaleidoscope)*

So YES, even a $7,500 sanction is a FREAKIN' BIG DEAL among lawyers, so if the lawyers are going "OUCH! That hurts from here" watching the 62-inch TV in the bar when the ECC plastered Team Coleman to the boards, well then the rest of us should cheer too.

WOW!

AND, for **MORE SANCTIONED** goodness, here's just a little more butter on your kolache:

The judges also said they would be willing to consider making Coleman pay for three days of Franken's attorneys fees at the end of the trial even if Coleman wins his case. *(Pioneer Press)*

To this non-lawyer this says the Court is hacked-off enough to not only fine the Coleman team (fine paid to the court) but that Al Franken's time and the time of his attorneys was ALSO wasted (and so compensation for "lost wages" to be paid to Team Franken!)

(If so, and if I were on the Franken legal team, I'd get a couple of CPA types to work right now so they can prove to the court that just by coincidence those 3 days in question just happen to be the MOST expensive legal fee days for the Franken effort. You know, sliding scale with a first-hill-up-the-roller-coaster-hump in the middle of it. WHO KNEW Marc, David, Kevin, William, and the rest were ACTUALLY worth, oh, $55k those days...each day... apiece? Gives new meaning to the phrase "flextime"!)

And finally *("Alex, let's finish the category, "Legal Cases and Monetary Fines" for $1,000")*, to follow on we've known for some time that in an ECC case **if the contestant (Coleman) loses they must pay** the *cost of the case.* (A major disincentive for every losing candidate running for 3rd assistant dogcatcher in Lost Fjord, MN to file an ECC action willy-nilly.) Court costs are pretty clear to me. But it's always been just slightly hazy in my mind if the contestant loses do they also pay the contes-TEEs costs (like legal fees). In a nice catch in the footnote to the order imposing sanctions:

The footnote[14] in the sanctions Order explained everything to my delight. No attorneys' fees yet (for the 3 days of stunts the ECC sanctioned Team Coleman for) because if Franken prevails, Coleman will have to pay his attorneys fees FOR THIS ENTIRE MESS!!!

To clarify, the footnote indicates Team Franken will be able to bill Coleman for these 3 days of Franken attorney's fees, a rare and stinging rebuke.

Written Clashes

As Canadian, Minnesota, Michigan, and Massachusetts readers especially know, any good hockey coach looks for players by position: offense (center or wing) or defense (left or right side). But they don't want players who are "one-dimensional," that is, a dangerous shooter on the attack but no help in their own end, or alternatively, a bruiser who will clear out the prime scoring area ("the slot") in front of his own goalie, but is no help in taking the play to the other end of the rink. Really good "two-way" players are called on for extra duty, like when a team is short-handed due to a penalty. Then you have to "think defense" but have that talent and anticipation to make an unexpected quick steal and make a short-handed rush and maybe catch THEIR goalie napping.

Today in court was the first day for Team Franken to really go on offense and present their case. 25 witnesses and a 40-minute DVD for the court's education was a great first (day) shift.

But Elias and Lillehaug swung back to do some checking in their own end as well. The **Coleman Team sent the Court a letter** at the hand of attorney James Langdon, 3 pages on how/why the court

- • could reduce the count absentee ballots that are "illegal" by mathematical proportions; he cited case examples from neighboring states.

- • could *"set aside the election"* from Nov. 4 because of the "irregularities" which the Coleman team showed were rampant, corrupting, and riddled the integrity of the vote (not, Not, and NOT!!!) (This part is the formal effort to get a "do-over" of the entire election.)

Well, Langdon was working the puck and got the shot off. Elias stick-checked it into the corner. He and Lillehaug wrote a 2-page letter in reply, stating what Langdon asked has little support in law. Specifically the "pro-rata" mathematical idea *is not allowed by MN law.*

Langdon's scrapped in the corner for the puck and took that "election do-over" move he's been working on in practice. But Capt. Dave "Give 'em Ls" Lillehaug is tough to beat. How about this elegant deflection, reaching with a poke check and then a jazzy "behind the back" pass right onto the stick of Elias to start the break?

You know that Motion Team Franken argued in front of the MN Supreme Court a month ago today? The one where they asked for a Certificate of Election *apart from* the Sec. of State and the Governor? It hasn't been heard from since (or ruled on) but it's still out there. Part of the argument was based on US Constitutional grounds, that only the US Senate has the right to determine the makeup of its members (mascara? blush?) so let's let the 99/98 decide this, not the Court, Sec. of State, or Gov.

Sportswriter Jay Weiner over at the MinnPost looks at Langdon's letter and the proposal for an electoral "do-over" and called the action this way:

> As for the setting aside of the election, Elias and Lillehaug write that the three-judge panel's jurisdiction "is limited to deciding which party received the highest number of legally cast votes, and therefore is entitled to receive the certificate of election ... Any other remedy lies within the jurisdiction of the United States Senate." *(MinnPost)*

Great block by the "L" man, followed by a body check to shake the puck loose! An unexpected bank off the MN Supreme Court side wall and Elias gains center ice...

Diving Under the Ice

Just to make sure global warming isn't causing the lake scum clinging to zebra mussels to grow brain cells, I put on the insulated wet suit and took a swim under the ice of Lake DerBunker.

Yep, they're still stupid. According to Ed Morrissey at "HotAir" the StarTrib got it wrong when they reported Team Coleman is seeking an election "do-over." [According to comments, another example of liberal media bias in the "Red Star" (and Sickle)]. Morrissey writes he talked with Ben the Ginz himself to

---

14 *Footnote is on the Order on Contestee's Motion to Strike, dated March 2, 2009.*

get the straight story (STOP laughing!) and Ben told him the *StarTrib* was wrong. (Engage Rethug Reverse Projection Mode, Denial Sequencer.)

> Ginsberg told me, "We're not asking for a new election, or anything like that." *(Star Tribune)*

YES THEY ARE and I offer as evidence Langdon's letter to the Court, and Norm's own pensive demeanor and statements as reported in the StarTrib. "We are not" in modern Rethug discourse MEANS "WE ARE." "Anything like that" MEANS "Exactly what we are denying."

Got the early shift the rest of the week, so I've got to get to the wineshop. Until the UpTake broadcast starts at 9:00 a.m. CT, that's the latest from yust southeast of Lake Wobegon.

Shalom.

Razzberries and Beans
March 5, 2009

Comments: 149   Recs: 257   Tips: 212

Well, today is the day! That's right, and you get to celebrate with razzberries; not the eating kind (my absolute favorite fruit), but the kind like Archie Bunker used to do: farty, sloppy ones sprayed loudly.

To whom, you may ask? Why **Norm Coleman** of course!

Today is **4 months TO THE DAY**, the morning after the election, when the unbeknownst (!) to himself-ness (Nearly Former) Senator Coleman stood before TV lights and reporters and noted that while close, he was leading the count for the US Senate seat. He said with as much dignity as his horse dentures would allow that his opponent Al Franken should spare the people of Minnesota the expense and aggravation of a (state-mandated) recount, "let the healing begin" and "step back" like I would if the situation were reversed.

RRRRAAAAAZZZZZZZZZZZZZZZZZZZZZBBBBEEEERRRRRRRYYYYY!

Norm, in your honor last night I cooked a can of Bush's baked beans in order to personally reenact Blazing Saddles in the bad guys' camp. And today's diary sections will feature 1–4 razzberries and scoops of beans for ratings!

Election Contest Court - Episode XXXVIII

The Beat Goes On

The Franken case beat went on, with another 14 absentee voters called to the stand, including The UpTake's Noah Kunin. But court was overall, almost...routine. Not quite boring, but already a certain ho-hum quality is there because there is a certain common ground right now.

The Franken witnesses (not necessarily Franken voters, but a decent probability) are rejected absentee voters who want their votes counted.

Team Coleman (**1 razzberry** for thinking like this) is pretty quiet about this because

several of these voters testifying appeared on Coleman's list of possible witnesses,

this trickle of voters keeps Coleman's universe from shrinking any further, and

they think *(according to Mr. Echo Chamber in the outer hall, Ben Ginsberg—always worth* **a scoop of beans** *by himself)* rejected voters make it easier to uphold a claim of "unequal protection," "fatally flawed system," "poor, rejected voters who did nothing wrong." They probably think (delusionally) this somehow improves their chances of a "do-over" election ("See, even Franken voters/witnesses are disenfranchised...").

But most of the reasons things were quiet was a combination of Franken Team competency coupled with...

The Quiet Return of Joe Friedberg (1 razzberry)

Joe Friedberg has taken a LOT of snowballs and shaved ice down his breezers for his handling of the case the first 5 weeks. He has stumbled, struggled, been woefully unprepared and awkward. People have rightly wondered how this man got to his 72nd birthday as a trial attorney.

Well, that's a lot of it right there. Friedberg does criminal defense, and in this case he has been plaintiff/contestant lead.

The difference is this: in a criminal case (and most of the TV dramas are criminal law) the burden of proof is on the prosecution. It is the DA who has to gather enough evidence to indict the Bush Crime Family, present the Cheney energy task force "Rape America" notes with witnesses, find the bloody knife with Pat Tillman's blood on it in Addington's desk with Rumsfeld's, Rove's, Libby's, and Feith's fingerprints on it. And the prosecution has to meet the standard of proof "beyond a reasonable doubt"; in math terms (although no one can measure it like this), if not 100% certain, then 99%, or 98%, or... something beyond a "reasonable doubt."

Joe Friedberg has spent his entire career on the other end of this. That means he does NOT need to bring nearly as much evidence. He does NOT need to prove the case or even disprove it, but needs to only raise doubts and questions enough to get up to that threshold of "reasonable doubt"—but from the other end. Not the 97%+, but only 5% or 7% uncertainty. His natural stance is counterpunching, not leading with the jab.

And THAT is a big part of why the last 5 weeks went so badly. He had to LEAD. He had the BURDEN of PROOF. Instead of having to only "disprove" the other side's case a few percent he was in charge of presenting enough stuff to convince the ECC of a "preponderance of the evidence" (the standard in a civil proceeding.) So he had to get to somewhere to the high side of 50%. By training, inclination, and decades of experience he was just not ready or able to do this.

Kossack (and attorney) beastiemom has been in the courtroom with Joe Friedberg and offered a telling couple of comments yesterday:

> **Friedberg is an excellent attorney with a great** reputation. I have said before I think it is odd that Coleman chose a defense attorney to be the lead counsel in this case because the burdens and approaches in the two instances are completely different. As a criminal defense lawyer, he doesn't have to prove anything. The burden of proof is entirely on the prosecutor. His only job is to poke holes in the prosecution's case, not carry the burden and prove his case, as he has had to do for Coleman. As speet wrote, you will see his brilliance emerge in this next part of the case.
>
> I am not surprised that the court went out of its way to note that Friedberg had nothing to do with the non-disclosure. Although Friedberg and I practice on opposite sides of the fence, I know for a fact this is nothing that he would ever do. Clearly he was blindsided by Trimble, and the incompetence of the others on Coleman's legal team.
>
> ...
>
> Remember, Friedberg is a criminal defense lawyer, and spends a lot of time at the federal courthouse. He has clients that have done despicable things, but that doesn't mean that Friedberg is despicable. He is a very important part of our legal process. His job is to protect the interests of his clients within the ethical rules. I haven't seen anything in this case that says HE hasn't (no comments about Knaack & Trimble and gang). *(beastiemom)*

Fritz Knaak and Tony the Trimble (3 1/2 razzberries, 2 large helpings of beans and a $7,500 sanction)

ON THE OTHER HAND it's coming out more and more that these 2 guys have REALLY put the sand under Norm Coleman's double-runner skate blades.

The Big E over at the MN Progressive Project:

> The fault mainly lies with Coleman's original legal team, the inept duo of Fritz Knaak and Tony Trimble. They were the ones who were unprepared for the re-

count. Unlike Al Franken's campaign, they didn't have watchers at every recount location. Consequently, they were incapable of performing analysis of recount trends. They just put the blinders on and insisted they were winning. Until they weren't. Then somebody panicked... *(MN Progressive Project)*

Beastiemom also provided some sourcing for the Coleman recount effort being in deep water from the start (i.e. starting with Knaak and Trimble):

DK

Scuttlebutt at the courthouse yesterday (from someone deep inside the Coleman legal team) is that they realize that they are being completely manhandled... they lost this case during the recount when they did not see the forest for the trees.

The smartest thing that Franken did was bring in lawyers immediately that had done this type of statewide recount before and understood how each decision in the recount would later affect the recount. They strategically outmaneuvered Coleman's team from day one.

The most interesting comment made is that Coleman's side concedes that Franken's side knows what is in each ballot. They know that Elias's numbers are dead on... you can take that to the bank. *(beastiemom)*

The Paper Wars

Now while things in the courtroom may settle into a routine with both sides playing to their strengths, the real drama looks to shift to the clerk's office next to the ECC court room. Papers, motions, filings, e-mails, boxes, faxes, FedEx, and UPS (hell, things could arrive in saddlebags or be delivered in the teeth of the 2 lead dogs of a sled from an election official practicing for the John Beargrease Race in the North Woods).

This battle has a written component that is just as important as the typical courtroom stuff out front of the cameras.

Two major items and a promise of a 3rd:

(2 razzberries and a medium helping of beans) Remember Monday when mercifully the Coleman side rested its case? Actually they *"provisionally rested"* their case. They asked (and got) permission to bring some final affidavits to the court's attention as evidence (I think). ECC said, "OK. Deadline: Wednesday noon."

Well, it turns out a lot of this was those e-mails the Coleman campaign sent out to the 87 counties trying to get election officials to express their OPINIONS on absentee-ballot issues. The ECC already shot these down after objections from the Franken side. But, at about 11:58 am they delivered...the same stuff AGAIN... and basically UNSORTED.

Blogger (and attorney) annie over at The UpTake had a crisp roundup (Note especially the second paragraph):

Northern, to answer your question from 1.5 hrs ago, the judges were discussing the attempt by the Coleman lawyers to offer into evidence some boxloads of email printouts they had obtained from the counties. These email responses had already been ruled by the court as largely inadmissible because they would be hearsay and would contain conclusions without adequate foundation. The court gave Coleman until noon today to get their act together and submit what they wanted entered into evidence (this was the provision in the provisionally resting Coleman did the other day).

The Coleman atty wanted to offer them anyway with the understanding that they would have "inadmissable parts" and essentially leave it up to the Franken team to object to the inadmissable parts and the court to sort it out.

The judges and the attys chatted a bit about this latest episode of sloppy lawyering from the Coleman camp. That's what was going on just before the break. The attys were supposed to chat during the break about the feasibility of them sorting it out between themselves as to what Coleman would actually offer and in how many exhibits (they had proposed offering the whole shebang as one exhibit). If I were a judge I would be totally fed up by now with this sort of behavior from the Coleman people. Sloppy, sloppy, expecting the other atty and the court to do their work for them. *(annie esq at The UpTake)*

The ECC **ruled to deny** these box loads of old electric bills from 1977 found in Uncle Ingmar's attic qualified as evidence...AND they declared the Coleman case "rested" (removing the "provisional." As in, "Time's up! The icicle as fallen.")

Over in the Secretary of State's office lists were arriving up to the afternoon deadline from all across the state. Friday the ECC ordered local election officials to open AND THEN RESEAL without looking at the ballot the **"pile 3" absentee ballots.** These are absentee ballots rejected for the 3rd of 4 reasons, the voter is not registered to vote.

However, the absentee-ballot package INCLUDES a voter registration card so a voter can update things along with their ballot. The card is SUPPOSED to go in the outer, mailing envelope, but apparently a number of voters may have put it in the inner, secrecy envelope with the ballot.

The ECC ordered local officials to carefully open these ballots, extract a registration card (if any) and reseal the ballots. Then officials were to make 3 lists:

a) ballot with no card (voter not eligible to vote; reason #3, not registered).

b) registration card found but incomplete or defective somehow.

c) card found and complete.

All 3 lists were due in to the Sec. of State's office close of business yesterday.

Total ballots involved: maybe 1,500 or so (!)

a) list—these votes will not count.

b) list—need to take these one by one; how incomplete? No zip code? Probably OK. Middle initial present or absent? Probably OK. Out-of-state mailing address—maybe not; but a college student choosing to vote at home?

c) list—so far so good, but officials to determine if ballot passes muster on other 3 reasons. (e.g., registration may be good, but if voter voted in person on Nov. 4, then absentee does not count.)

Best guess how many may pass muster? I've seen 600–900, but your mileage and the ECC's will vary.

Eric Black at MinnPost caught this promise of more paperwork to come TODAY:

> Franken lawyer Marc Elias said that he would file, Thursday morning, a motion to dismiss portions of the Coleman's case. He wouldn't preview the argument, but this much is obvious. Coleman's side officially rested their case today. Elias will argue that Team Coleman failed to prove the basic allegations that Team C. made in its original petition for an election contest. *(MinnPost)*

The Noisy Return of Ron Carey (2 1/2 raspberries and large helping of beans)

Except for serving as the soil-stack pipe for the RNC funneling $ to Norm Coleman's side (the other week they handed on $250,000) the MN GOP has mostly confined itself during the Recount to sending out talking-point memos to its "letter to the editor" writers across the state.

Oh there was one stupid moment back in December when chairman Ron Carey was last heard from. The State Canvassing Board was reviewing challenged ballots from both sides (doesn't THAT seem like a different lifetime ago??) and it was being broadcast on the MN Judiciary building closed-circuit system. Any organization that wanted to tap into the feed was welcome, and plenty of outfits did (WCCO, KARE 11 locally, CNN, and even the Murdoch Mob on the national side). But it was Christmas week and the tech folk who run the equipment had the days off for holidays.

Mike McIntee and the UpTake techs volunteered to turn on the lights and cameras, aim, and focus them in place of the state workers for free, and Sec. of State Mark Ritchie took them up on that.

Well, Carey blew the muffler off his snowmobile and issued a statement that such a move by Ritchie showed he was in the tank with a leftist, Acorn-related, socialistic, pinko group like The UpTake... because The UpTake was going to run the live feed! (No reporting, no commentary, just point & focus.)

Well, apparently **Carey has gotten jealous** of the Ben Ginsberg show outside the courtroom. I mean Ben the Ginz is hogging all the limelight (lemonlight? orangelight? How do citrus fruits rate?) and talking points are getting boring.

So yesterday Norm spent the morning in ECC at his team's table. A few blocks away in St. Paul, Al Franken was at a breakfast receiving an award... a do-gooder sort of thing but a nice "thank you" to the *Franken for Senate* campaign and how they ran things for a certain often-overlooked set of voters.

Carey and the MN GOP are just despicable (said with Daffy Duck juiciness):

> With Al Franken set to receive an award from the Commission of Deaf, Blind and Hard of Hearing Minnesotans for having the "Most Accessible Campaign," Ron Carey, Chairman of the Republican Party of Minnesota, announced another award that Mr. Franken won today.
>
> "During each phase of the recount and election contest, only one candidate can claim to have tried to disenfranchise as many Minnesota voters as Al Franken. After initially supporting the counting of every wrongly rejected absentee ballot, Franken sought to only count those ballots from heavily DFL areas, leaving thousands of Minnesota voters disenfranchised. He also has the dubious distinction of trying to disenfranchise every Minnesota voter by attempting to force the Governor and Secretary of State to issue an election certificate in violation of state law. It is for these reasons that we present Al Franken with the Republican Party of Minnesota's 'Most Disenfranchising Campaign' award." *(MN Democrats Exposed)*

[A hat tip is NOT right... a scrape off the shoe (sots) to MN Democrats Exposed for providing this bit from the business end of a Roto-Rooter power snake.]

Thursday Morning Minnesota Media

Whoooo, last night got late with the diary, with timeout for Lenten services and choir practice, so I hope this is fairly coherent.

Duchschere and Lopez (where are the Scandinavians?) in the StarTrib are still writing back on page B5. Since that's about where these stories were the last couple weeks of "Trial by Norm" I suppose that's fair. D&L point out that while the witnesses sound a bit like the Coleman case what the Franken Team is doing is pointing out how rare and isolated these foul-ups were out of 3 million votes cast.

Best of all they close with a quote from the Senator-Elect himself! And on a topic Team Norm keeps trying to make into an issue:

> Meanwhile, at an event at the State Capitol, Franken was asked about a possible do-over of the race. He said that "instead of really addressing and meeting the enormous economic challenges that face us, it seems that Senator Coleman has chosen instead to attack the Minnesota court system, attack election officials and try to erase voters' votes."
>
> Franken added: "I know he's disappointed, but we've come through a fair election and a fair and very meticulous recount and we're going through now a very fair court challenge and I think it's time we address the people's business." *(Star Tribune)*

Another day of the early shift (but late-afternoon walks are nice now that the sun is out and UP) so this will need to hold you until The UpTake roars into action at 9:00 a.m. CT. That's the latest from yust southeast of Lake Wobegon.

Shalom.

A Nine Vote Universe?!
March 6, 2009

Comments: 159   Recs: 302   Tips: 266

Election Contest Court – Episode XXXIX
Origami

Life in front of the court cameras continues clicking along like the reel on a fishing line on a slow troll (the good kind), just click, click, click. It's starting to give people hope that Al Franken's comment over the weekend that the trial might finish in 2–3 weeks might be true... and even better, it might be on the shorter end of that.

Soooo... looking at the calendar, 2 weeks from the opening of the Franken case would be Mar. 17...St. Patrick's Day. OK, I'm game. Nothing like the luck of the Irish to bring good fortune to a "New York" Jew running for Senate from Minnesota.

"May the fumes from the Guinness keg waft over your pastrami on rye and wash down your krumm-kakke."... I'll send that over to Temple so the rabbi can warm up for the Wednesday Night Lenten Services in Latin at the Lutheran church. (The choir will sing a Bach chorale in plainsong mode while dancing to "Hava Nagila, Have 2 Nagilas..." Oy vey!)

Rats! The entire lead screwed up royally. No hope of recovery... just move on...

Duluth's Day in Court

More voters/witnesses whose absentee ballots were rejected. But as the afternoon session came on so also came Jeff Cox to the stand. Cox is City elections director for Duluth, and the person at the center of Duluth's effort to get paid more for his time testifying. (Duluth lost that battle; $105 for the day is going to be IT. Worse, testimony did NOT finish; Cox resumes today, so another day of lost time, offset only by the statutory $20/day).

While Cox's testimony may seem routine the issue at stake in Duluth is not. Apparently several dozen (I remember 77 but that could be off) absentee ballots were rejected by Duluth election officials because the DATES did not match between the voter signing the secrecy envelope and the witness's signature.

BUT then officials went and read the manual (and underlying law) and found such a match of dates did not appear and was not required. BUT when they sought to correct the error and admit these ballots Team Coleman objected and they've been in limbo ever since.

Now, Duluth is heavily Democratic and there is good reason to believe these ballots if counted would break strongly for Franken, so here is a chance to get IN a group of votes wholesale rather than retail—and Team Coleman will fight this for the same reasons. So don't be fooled by the debates and arguments over this witness—it's a bigger stake than usual that both sides are playing for.

Motions on Paper

The paper-folding is getting fierce. Team Coleman filed a "motion to intervene" (which I haven't read; I'm tired of crayon) and Mr. Nauen ("the Swamp Fox") filed papers for his latest group of 30 voters.

But the BIG news at the filing window was from the Franken side. As promised Wednesday and predicted earlier, the Franken camp delivered a **Motion for Dismissal.**

I am not a lawyer and anyone who IS has seen my ignorance in these posts and has been kind to correct me. Before this series I think the only published legal document I ever sat down and read through was the execrable *Bush v. Gore*.

But folks, if you have never read one, follow the link in the footnote, take a long pull on the coffee cup and take it slowly. It restores my faith in the LAW and how it should be practiced.

Of course, having a few... leanings... in this case I can also appreciate the **utter demolition** this piece does to the Coleman case. I know, I know, it's only one side of the argument, but if the ECC rules for Franken in the end as having the most votes, it wouldn't surprise me a bit if they lifted phrases, even lines, from what is written here... it's that well said.

What Franken Asks to Heave Across the Ice

As predicted Monday here Team Franken filed to have the ECC **dismiss the whole Coleman claim** towed away like a lutefisk-stuffed '87 Yugo (Joe Friday, Dragnet: "representing the cutting edge of Serbo-Croatian automotive technology"). Failing that they ask for **summary judgments against parts** of the Coleman case.

Now since "even a drunken moose finds a tree once in a while" theory, even Ben Ginsberg agrees with me that *some of this is routine* when a case switches from one side to the other presenting. SOP for lawyers to cover all the bases (and you never know!). But more serious is the request for partial dismissals.

Running down several of the particulars, Team Franken asks the ECC to dismiss specifically:

- the Minneapolis 133—the precinct where the ballots were lost but the voters signed in and voted on the machines;
- the claim of "duplicate/double-counted ballots."

They ask these mostly on grounds Coleman DIDN'T PROVE THEM, which Ben the Ginz will no doubt complain is a vicious example of the liberal bias of reality.

Somebody (likely a BUNCH of somebodies) on the Franken Team has spent days dismantling the original Coleman "Notice of Contest," that is, THE original filing to launch the entire ECC. This is where you lay out just exactly what you intend to "conTEST," point by point.

And point by point the Franken Motion goes under the hood like an auto mechanic on 4 hits of speed and 3 espresso ultra grandes who has just won a brand-new set of platinum pneumatic power tools made by Porsche:

- "Unidentified errors, mistakes and other irregularities" including "matters and things"—Team Franken is ready to respond but...to WHAT?
- Improperly rejected absentee ballots (A Lenten penance).

Team Franken points out an absentee ballot must climb several circles of "Il Purgatorio" before it can pass into the globes of "Countedness."

They (gloriously) note the ever-shrinking-ness of the Coleman universe of ballots as these fell short of blessedness, stricken by their ballot sinfulness. (Remember how good the Franken Team's numbers have been? Well, the crew has been saving up for this part!)

- **4,787** (1/23: Notice of Contest)
- **4,623** (2/3: 174 late ballots not allowed)
- **3,687** (2/13—Friday the 13th Order, eliminating a dozen categories of absentees).

Then Coleman **withdrew 136** during the course of the 5 weeks (of legal dentistry without benefit of painkillers) and **another 601** initially claimed for signature mismatches, so down to **2,950**.

THEN, "Contestant failed to introduce ballot envelopes for 1,473 (of the 2,950)"—and THAT alone (no introduction into evidence) TAKES THEM OFF THE BOARD.

- **Down to 1,477** (Easily the lowest number yet)...BUT 5 of these were part of the 933 opened and counted on 1/3 and so are IN... but no longer at issue.
- **1,472**: of these in *1,151 instances* (YIKES!), Contestant did not introduce both the ballots AND the absentee ballot application, which makes it impossible to compare addresses (which must match: legal reason #1 for rejection) or to check of the signatures match (part of legal reason #2 for rejection.)
- **Leaves 321**... and almost all of these fail for registration lack (legal reason #3) or the voter voted in person (legal reason #4)...

LEAVING 9! Yep, NINE!

By the beard of St. Olaf and the iron ore of Kiruna, is that ALL? MAN! Let Norm have his 9, move AL to +237 and I will GLADLY hang up my keyboard TODAY!

The Motion shoots down (by name) the votes of 16 of the 21 voters who testified for Norm, and notes the other 5 were withdrawn by Team Coleman.

As they wound down I was tickled at how they went after EVERY Ginsbergian claim, even shooting down both the "let the ECC recount all 286,000 absentee ballots" nonsense and the "let's set aside this election and order a new one," an opium eater's delusion of preposterous dimensions.

"Contestants offer no Minnesota authority in support of their position" but the Franken team offered a couple precedents from the opposite side, one from 1986... and one (I KNEW they were good but this is really cracking the law books) **FROM 1865!** That is not a typo... they cited a case in their favor (Taylor v. Taylor) from 7 years after MN became a state. (Good grief, I half expect them to produce a handwritten comment on *Taylor v. Taylor* from Abraham Lincoln!)

DK Citing precedent from 1865? Dang, they ARE good! Color me impressed. Good to know my donations are being put to good use! *(Vacationland)*

DK Just watch. For final arguments NOT ONLY will Lillehaug cite precedent from the Peter Zenger trial of 1735 (noting rulings from COLONIAL law!), but Elias will summarize by citing the Magna Carta....spoken in Latin and sung in Middle English... to the tune of the "Law Code of Hammurabi"... *(WineRev)*

OK, I hope this will hold you. This diary had to be one of the hardest to write in the whole string. I've been hit by a HUGE wave of "GET IT OVER WITH" and it's hard to swim against surf like that.

Off to the early shift at the wineshop. That's the latest from yust southeast of Lake Wobegon.

Shalom.

Courts: ECC and Supreme
March 7, 2009

Comments: 238   Recs: 192   Tips: 194

After a morning of testimony Friday afternoon in the Election Contest Court (ECC) was lawyers arguing over the Franken Motion to Dismiss the Coleman case, on grounds they hadn't MADE the case. (Under advisement, but partial granting of claims likely.)

The MN Supreme Court RULED (5 0): Al Franken will NOT get a Certificate of Election by going around the Governor, Sec. of State and the state election process...but to coin a phrase, "This is GOOD NEWS for Franken" since the Court said plainly (!) such a certificate will issue APART from federal court moves by either party (cough Norm cough).

Election Contest Court - Episode XL

Before court was even gaveled to order the bloggers had ALREADY caught Team Coleman blowing more bilge water out of their bugles.

Charles Nauen continues to be the "Swamp Fox" to Team Coleman's Greene & Morgan, picking off little clusters of absentee ballots and bringing these voters to the attention of the ECC. First it was the "Nauen 64"—3 of those were disallowed and 3 more withdrawn, but 21 of those ballots are in and 37 are hanging fire. Then Nauen came in with 30 more.

I see a filing at the MSC site by Coleman yesterday that appears to be attempting to prevent legally cast votes from being counted—these are for the voters represented by Nauen—Say it isn't so, I thought Ginsberg said they wanted every vote counted! *(Jim at The UpTake)*

Hard to know if this is actual hypocrisy or more of the Coleman-side incompetence.

Friday's morning session featured testimony from Joe Mansky, director of elections for Ramsey County (St. Paul). Joe struck everyone as calm, competent, and well-versed on election law. (In other words, the perfect witness for Franken and a nightmare for the Coleman side.)

The real action in ECC got rolling after lunch. Thursday Franken filed a Motion to Dismiss (Involuntary Dismissal) Coleman's case on grounds he hadn't met the burden of proof, also known as "coming up with enough ballots to overtake a Franken lead." Coleman answered in writing in the morning

Both sides used various lawyers to argue the points. Joe Friedberg led off for Coleman.

> You are now seeing Mr. Friedberg in a different role, as an advocate in oral argument. He's arguing in support of the Coleman motion to set aside Rule 9 from the SOS recount rules. He should be delivering a somewhat scripted speech to the panel and punching the points that should have already been made in the written brief. *(annie esq at The UpTake)*

And how was Joe doing?

> His entire argument will fail simply because he is trying to overturn a stipulation and the court will not do that.
>
> Jason Barnett: Coleman lawyer is not afraid to say "the State Canvassing board violated the law"—is that what was just said?
>
> In summary Friedberg argued Rule 9 should be thrown out and we should trust the election workers and we proved that by showing where election workers messed up. *(Candide at The UpTake)*

And then came a Minnesota Moment. If you try this case in a boring place like my home state of Ohio and you think the other side has nothing you might say they are "All talk, no action." If you try the case in Texas you can be more colorful: "All hat, no cattle."

David Lillehaug created an instant "old saying" (the way "Edelweiss" was never an old Austrian folksong until Sound of Music became a money-making smash—then the Austrians admitted that, yes, "Edelweiss" had "always" been an old Austrian folksong) that will be heard around 10,000 lakes as soon as the ice goes out this spring:

All of Coleman's talk is "BIG BOAT, NO WALLEYE."

There you go, big boat, no walleye. Walleye is the state fish and excellent eating. And big boat? Well, maybe David was watching a rerun of Jaws. When the shark was first identified a reward was posted for the first person to catch it. A MOB of saltwater nincompoops show up and practically kill each other just getting launched from the dock—the Keystone Kops on water.

Where is the proof of double counting? Evidence? There is NO BEEF to the Coleman case. They had their chance in open court and after 5 weeks they got "nuthin."

After a quick recess the court took up arguments over the Franken Motion to Dismiss. Marc Elias took his turn:

> not giving enough evidence and not clear enough evidence; looks like a show then a contest in court. *(MNsense at The UpTake)*

> Go Marc!! "A full or even partial determination of what votes remain will streamline the rest of the case." *(memiller at The UpTake)*

He ran down the points of most of his brief including the big countdown of the Coleman universe down to 9 ballots. The Court asked him about the ballots Team Franken is introducing in their case. Elias said they don't matter BECAUSE it was up to the Coleman side to come up with enough ballots to overtake Franken's lead and they didn't do that... so if the Court accepts the Franken motion and its countdown to 9, then they can rule and everyone go home...

James Langdon for Coleman was met with a question from the bench within 3 minutes of starting, with the Judge quoting Marc Elias.

CAN'T be a good sign when the judge starts quoting your opponent...OR when more than one judge is after you:

> Three skeptical judges is not a good sign Mr. Langdon. *(Harry in NC at The UpTake)*

> All three judges questioning Langdon in detail. This can't be good for him. *(shlif at The UpTake)*

> Dang, triple-teamed by the ECC. *(middlewest at The UpTake)*

Somehow the ECC judges seemed less than impressed by Langdon's assertion "there are 1,725 absentee ballots that we presented that ought to be counted." When did we see those 1,725 (a new low number for Team Coleman) entered into evidence? Langdon: Right now as I'm arguing it before you... Uh-huh...

What Will the ECC Do?

Take it all "under advisement" of course.

> For my two cents, I don't think the panel will grant any part of the motion to dismiss, they are keenly aware Coleman is angling for an appeal, and they will not go forward knowing that dismissing his contest might become a basis for an appeal. Better to let the weight of all Franken's arguments swamp the Coleman boat at the end of the contest. (*NorthernMNer at The UpTake*)

I think the ECC might rule on parts of the Motion. The easiest is the fact that Franken puts forward 14 points on which they move for partial or complete dismissal. The Coleman side in their brief agrees they are NOT pursuing #1, 4, 7–14 of the Franken motion. If Franken in essence agrees, the Court can bless these pretty easily.

What would be left to struggle over?

#2 Improperly Rejected Absentee Ballots: The whole "shrink the Coleman universe down to 9" deal, and knocking down 15 of the 21 Coleman voters who testified.

#3 Duplicate ballots (double counted?? NOT yet any evidence)

#5 the Minneapolis missing "133"

#6 Some of the 933 ballots opened and counted Jan. 3, which the Coleman team want UN-counted.

Do you recognize this list? After ALL the fume and sputtering, the droning and the spastic lurching, after 5 weeks of excruciatingly BAD lawyering, they are arguing the SAME 3 items they started with, and a piece of the Friday the 13th ruling which Coleman claims means some of the 933 ballots counted on Jan. 3 are "illegal." ALL the rest of it? Smoke and mirrors. As Bugs Bunny would say, "What a bunch of maroons!"

MN Supreme Court Decision

The other BIG news came in while these debates were being argued. The MN Supreme Court rendered a decision on Franken's request for a Certificate of Election apart from the Secretary of State and the Governor. One month to the day after hearing oral arguments the Court handed down a unanimous, 5-0, decision: NO.

This was hardly unexpected. This petition was a Franken long shot all the way, but that won't stop the Reichwingers from turning handsprings at this "defeat" for Al. Ben the Ginsberg shot across the rink with a fresh batch of ditto-ed purple press releases still smelling from the ammonia (what cutting edge technology!)

> "The Minnesota Supreme Court's decision is a victory for Minnesota Law and Minnesotans. This wise ruling will ensure that Harry Reid, Al Franken and Chuck Schumer cannot short-circuit Minnesota Law in their partisan power play... (WineRev: Blah, blah in the middle about the case talking points)...
>
> "Despite Al Franken's efforts to disenfranchise thousands of Minnesota voters, Norm Coleman is committed to ensuring a legal and fair election. This ruling stops the Franken/Reid/Schumer power play in its tracks, and puts the decision back in Minnesota where it belongs." (*quoted by Eric Kleefield at Talking Points Memo*)

Marc Elias, an attorney for Franken that is actually TRYING THE CASE (you gasbag Ginsberg!) said about what most attorneys say at such times, "We appreciated them hearing the case as quickly as they did and considering it as thoughtfully as they did. Obviously we had hoped for a different result, but we accept the ruling of the Supreme Court and move forward."

Intelligent comments came here on dKos:

> **DK** Certificate after final judgment enters in ECC? The decision of the MN SC, see in particular page 11, seems indicate that a certificate would issue as soon as final judgment is entered in the Election Contest Court, i.e., it will not have to await

DK

> any appeals. At minimum, the certificate would issue following appeal to the MN SC and would not have to await a US SC appeal. See first full paragraph on page 16, the last paragraph before section "II." *(Allen03)*

WOW! MAYBE this whole thing could end with a bang as the Hayden, Marben, and Reilly reach their decision on the case BEFORE any appeal to the MN Supreme Court!

Eric Black at the MinnPost quotes a Hamline University law professor that it is significant the Court said the Election Certificate issues upon resolution of an Election Contest in STATE COURTS. That seems to point toward: ECC rules, Franken asks for Certificate, Coleman asks MN Supreme Court for a stay, Court rules and story ENDS, regardless of appeals to federal courts.

So the END moved visibly closer, but all of you will still see your fondest wish fulfilled: Not only will Al Franken go to the Senate, but WineRev will make it to diary 100 in this series :-D!

OK, I've got the late shift today so I'll hang around a bit. Chat away over Saturday morning breakfast because that's the latest from yust southeast of Lake Wobegon.

Shalom.

Screed
March 8, 2009

Comments: 180   Recs: 134   Tips: 140

I need to tell you of and dispute the UN-fun, stooopid sellout of the *Minneapolis Star Tribune* to the Reichwing Wurlitzer Talking Points Machine.

This morning reporter Pat Doyle makes the front page, A-1, above the fold, and a big jump write-up on A10, under the headline "Is Another Election the Answer?" The first seven little paragraphs (albeit some of them a longish sentence or two), EVERY ONE OF THEM THAT ARE ON A-1, do not mention the name or party of the state-certified count leader, Al Franken. (But the former Senator gets 3 citations and the line under the headline.) If you're standing in front of the steel box at Perkins' Pancake House deciding whether to spring for the Sunday edition, the headline stories are "Lost Jobs" and an election do-over.

Yes Doyle did some research. He quotes Dr. David Shultz of Hamline University (on page A-1) as describing the odds on this as "less than me winning the lottery." He also quotes Dr. Ed Foley from Ohio State as saying it looks like Coleman has "put on enough evidence to show that there's potentially a sizable number of ballots that should not have been counted given that order" (the Friday the 13th ECC order throwing out a dozen categories of rejected absentee ballots). Hey Foley? Take it from a fellow Buckeye ('75) NO, he has NOT put on enough evidence. Hell, Norm's legal team can barely spell the word.

Hey Doyle old man! St. Patrick's Day is almost here. In honor of your ancestors from the "old sod" who have a brawling reputation in some quarters, THIS WineRev from the East Baltic, this son of Estonia, takes off the gauntlet and SLAPS YOU IN THE FACE! I invoke the ghost of Kristjan Palusalu for aid and call you into the lists for either Greco-Roman or freestyle grappling. (Palusalu won gold in both in '36. Mat men among us can say how easy or difficult it is to win this particular Olympic double.)

Yours is a slimebag of execrable journalism! Thirty-three paragraphs in your story and Franken's name appears in just 7 of them. It takes you until paragraph 9 to mention him, and then only in passing as the friend of Norm Ornstein—from the American Enterprise Institute in DC. The AEI? Whose policies implemented for 8 years have destroyed those 100s of thousands of jobs the rest of your front page is lamenting? The AEI? Home of the "Albert Speer" school of Fascist Economics? The AEI, charged by the Reichwing to redesign the American economy into a pathetic copy of Greater Mexico?

Doyle, yours is an abomination to the written art. You Coleman-kissing scum-sucker! (Beg pardon; I repeat myself.) You finally quote Ornstein (in #12!) as saying a do-over is illogical, that there is no assurance it will have any fewer "problems" than the one from Nov. 4. SO WHY THE HELL BOTHER!? And the LAW doesn't allow for one (paragraph 14, sort of: might "prompt the Legislature to call a new one." REAL crisp writing there, Doyle!) Why not write about finishing THIS election, Doyle, instead of writing like a (to quote the master HST) "limp-wristed Nazi moron."

Doyle, your despicable, demented doggerel says the MN Supreme Court might (a LOT of these qualifying words in your patsy piece by the way: might, possible, concern, suggest) "provide Coleman (there's the MASTER's name again, one of 14 mentions, a nice 2:1 ratio; is that the minimum reading requirement on the Slant-o-Meter?) with a forum for getting beyond the nitty-gritty of examining specific ballots..." (Correct; but your readers would never discover that. The Supreme Court doesn't DO trials, or evidence, or findings of fact, or objections, or sustained, or overruled. They are the court of APPEAL. Did the ECC apply the law, equitably and correctly? If so,... APPEAL DENIED.)

But get "beyond the nitty-gritty of examining specific ballots" and actual evidence of systemic breakdown or inequity? EXACTAMUNDO! Let's get beyond all those ballots that don't say "Norm for senate." Let's get beyond evidence. Let's leave FACTS behind. Let's ignore the MN LAW that is being followed by a MN court charged with determining the MN candidate with the highest number of votes in a MN election. Let's get beyond all that "democracy" stuff. Let's go out into the hallway where Ben Ginz Spinz, a twilight zone of the intersection of mind and imagination; where facts, law, logic, and reality are all bendable, warped to the need to promote a soulless cruelty of self-aggrandizing power.

Although Doyle you actually get around to mentioning (in paragraph 20) that Coleman has "the burden in the trial of proving the State Canvassing Board was wrong when it certified Franken the leader in January" you make sure you quote Shulz as calling Franken the winner of a TIE. RIGHT! Like an NBA game that ends 109-108 is a TIE? Close? Hell yes! A tie? Did your mama or Shultz's mama drop one of you on your head when you were a baby?

Doyle! Your loathsome, mouth-breathing old sod-brainer of an article! In the trial it's the "burden of PROOF"— facts, evidence. Norm and his Klown Kar attorneys have to bring in this ballot, that ballot, those nitty-gritty ballots over there and say/argue/demonstrate/show "these should be IN, those should be OUT" and do it enough times to overcome a 246 lead.

For this next part, Doyle, let me get down on all fours and LOOK YOU SQUARE IN THE EYE: And Franken's side GETS TO DO THE SAME. It's called "fair" and "equal" and "justice" and "the rule of law" and yes, "equal protection under the law"—for BOTH Coleman and Franken. It is written in Leviticus "You shall have ONE law for you AND for the stranger who sojourns among you, for you were once sojourners in Egypt."

Doyle, BOTH these sons of Israel, and a WHOLE hell of a lot of the rest of us, ALL qualify—one law, for all. The judges will hear it and they will decide. Appeal? Sure. More judges. But based on law. Facts. Logic. Evidence. Precedent. NOT the bleating of lint-brained agitprop-meisters. Not the fevered rantings of drug-addled, piss-ant microphone morons, whose brainstems are directly wired to their vocal cords. (That leaves in question whether their skulls actually contain amphibian, reptilian, mammalian or primate neural clusters.)

So have Norm bring his case and strut his stuff. And he did. For 5 freaking weeks, Doyle. You wrote about it, slept through it, tried your best to make it interesting.

And right now, Doyle, we are in the other side of that same case. Fairness, equality, justice and rule of law: Franken is putting on HIS case. He brings evidence, ballots, witnesses, affidavits, exhibits, just like Norm got the chance to do.

And the courts will decide, and it will be fair, just, reasoned, meticulous. Their masterpiece of case law will be cited again and again in years to come...while your article from today, Doyle, will be dust in the wind... and in a just world it will sift in the high barred window of Karl Rove or Dick Cheney's cell where they still rave in a Thorazine haze...

Doyle, your noxious nattering across the front page and spuming speculation among possible delusions that somehow get Coleman another election, let alone into the Senate, is yellow journalism at its nauseous, wretched worst.

Turn in your laptop, Doyle. Go empty grease traps at McDonald's... if you qualify.

(Here endeth the rant. WineRev slings the singlet over his shoulder and walks off the mat.)

From yust southeast of Lake Wobegon to wherever you are blogging from today,
Shalom.

Ballots In, Ballots Out
March 10, 2009

Comments: 152   Recs: 284   Tips: 247

Election Contest Court – Episode XLI

Joe Mansky, Ramsey County (St. Paul) elections director, spent much of the day on the stand, interspersed with occasional voter/witnesses.

As of late Monday, NO ruling on the Franken Motion to Dismiss. That ruling hangs like a winter storm warning over the trial right now, but it's just wait and see, watching the trial.

And IN the trial a much-overlooked group needs your karmic thoughts and support (besides the WineRev Acapulco & Tahiti Fund). The real grunt work in the trial is happening as you are reading this. Really. There are a raft of unsung paralegals and junior lawyers ON BOTH SIDES who are endlessly pulling all-nighters researching legal precedents, readying exhibits, checking witnesses, preparing Motions and briefs and memoranda. While all the attorneys you see in court (and the judges too!) are working very hard they get a bit of down time. But the judge's clerks, aides, and both teams offices are at it 24/7 and every weekend.

A very nice reminder and shout-out from yesterday:

> I once worked as a paralegal on a trial where our side had poor facts and crappy evidence. It was hell. The attorneys had to make up new evidence and change their case every day to cover up their losing case, which meant the paralegals had to work literally 36-hour days cranking out new versions of the evidence for every day of the trial. I feel so sorry for the Coleman paralegals; I can only imagine what they've suffered through. *(middlewest at The UpTake)*

So all friends of justice! For the labors being done in the courts and offices and law libraries, we doff (DOFF!) our hats to you who toil unknown, unseen, but no longer unsung! L'Chaim to the staffers!

Pile 3A Ballots Go Kinky

The ECC about 10 days back ordered local officials to open rejected absentee ballots from Pile 3—those rejected because a voter is not registered to vote. Statewide there were 1585 of these. There were reports some of these contained a registration card in the inner, secrecy envelope.

The Court ordered officials to open these, feel around inside and, if present, extract the card, and do it without breaching voter privacy. (Whew! I mean, "ordered," "feel around," "extract," "do it" ... sounds like a leather-and-dungeon scene from a bad dominatrix video in the clearance bin at the pawn shop.) Results were due in to the Secretary of State's office last Wednesday.

Monday came word: 1,585 opened.

1,436 (90.6%)—nothing, so these ballots will NOT count because of legal reason 3, voter not registered to vote.

72 with a card BUT the card incomplete, damaged, or defective in some way. Will any of these ballots count? Very doubtful, but maybe a few.

89 with a completed card. These ballots are LIKELY to be added to the "Ready to Count" IF (and the ECC has been quite pointed about this) a ballot passes the OTHER requirements for an absentee ballot. (For instance, if one of these 89 voters had a change of plans and was in fact able to vote IN PERSON, then the properly completed absentee ballot here will NOT BE counted for legal reason 4, voter voted in person.)

> More than 1,500 previously rejected absentee votes in the 2008 U.S. Senate race have been opened, and the result is something akin to Geraldo Rivera cracking open Al Capone's vault. *(Jason Hoppin at Pioneer Press)*

So any way you cut it (like cut it down) the universe of absentee ballots available to both sides shrank noticeably. I expect either or both TomTech and Vote for America to crunch the numbers overnight to see how many of these came off each campaign's list.

By the way, and not at ALL to run down in the least the work TomTech & VFA have been doing on the numbers, how about Team Franken? When the ECC issued the order regarding these Pile 3A ballots Marc Elias went in front of the press and bloggers who were buzzing about the 1,585 votes. The Franken numbers squad, whoever they are, have been Nate Silver Gold Standard good all the way through the Recount. So when Elias came out and said, "Well, maybe 100 will qualify," that was taken fairly seriously but everyone put it at the bottom of their estimate range.

And now we get... 89! YOWSER! Nice shootin', Tex! 1,585 to start, estimate of 100, final 89. Diff. of 11, so stat types? Would "margin of error" then be 11/1,585 = 0.69% ? Not sure if that's the formula but any way you cut it the numbers team for Franken is GOOD!

(By the way, on the Coleman side, Ben Ginsberg continues his rant and rave act out in the hall. Notice how former Senator Horse Dentures is never seen there with him... especially when Norm is having a health food bar off camera? I guess they don't want the prowler of the hall and the chewer of grain together in the same picture... because then we'd have to call them... Hall and Oates! Ducks, runs for life... singing "She's Gone")

DK

How about some analogies? Coleman universe of ballots is sinking faster than:
1. Polar icecaps.
2. A 401K in February
3. A mafia hit with cement shoes
4. My wool sweater washed in hot water put in dryer. *(ABowers13)*

MN Supreme Court Ruling: Franken Loss

"We fight, get beat, rise, and fight again."—General Nathaniel Greene

Again harking back to our American Revolution in the South, as Greene and Morgan (played by Elias & Lillehaug) continue campaigning against Cornwallis (the Horse Dentures Brigade) from the Dan River to King's Mountain to the environs of Charleston, Swamp Fox Charles Nauen continues his guerrilla warfare in bringing in smaller stands of voters. Early on he brought in the "Nauen 64." Three of them later withdrew from the petition, 3 more ballots were found by the ECC to not qualify to be counted. Twenty-one ARE on the "Ready to Count" stack (probably over at the Sec. of State's office) and 37 are still hanging fire.

A couple weeks ago Nauen bought ANOTHER group of 30 ("Nauen 30") to the attention of the MN Supreme Court, asking they also be referred to the ECC for disposition.

However there is clear law (Sec. 204) that states any voter seeking relief needs to file the case within 7 days of the certification of count (in this instance Jan. 5).

Coleman filed his case in 1 day (Jan. 6). Nauen brought his 64 to the Supreme Court (since the ECC had not yet been named) within days. Now Nauen was asking for his 30 to be admitted too and the 7-day requirement be waived.

Monday it became clear the MN Supreme Court would NOT make this exception so Nauen withdrew his petition. The Court affirmed the withdrawal "with prejudice" so it can't be filed again.

So, as in battle so in law, and Team Franken lost one here. Nauen has been doing yeoman work in the twilight ambuscades and with dawn hit-and-run raids, but this time Lord Rawdon came up to support John Cruger at Fort Ninety-Six and Marion, Greene and Lee had to retreat......

......and yet, in a surprise development noted in the Star Tribune (the surprise is the Star Tribune discovered it and printed it) of these 30 voters? 10 of them so far have been called as witnesses by the Elias & Lillehaug to testify about their vote. The ECC has been quite clear they will rule on EACH such voter and ballot, so 10 of these 30 may still have a musket shot. Huzzah! Huzzah!

So Mr. Nauen? Great work and fine effort. Keep up the fight (those 37 captives might still be sprung onto the winning pile!). You'll see the backside of Cornwallis yet!

Funny Pages: It's been a while but yesterday rocked! First:

Everyone is doing their best to keep patient as the trial continues. There are recesses and lunch breaks and the minds live blogging over at The UpTake pass the time by...being creative. Poets are strutting their stuff to the point there is an effort to collect and publish all of them. For all I know at the next UpTake drinking event some of it will not only be read but performed in interpretive dance: the lovely Jason Barrett in lavender tutu performing "Trimble on a Microphone." I can't wait.

The humor/snark level is getting pretty high (as are some of the UpTakers perhaps as they wait for the next swing of the gavel.) From the lunch break, consider this...including the screen name:

> I was so happy to hear Michele Bachmann on the radio the other morning. Every time I hear her on the radio it sends tingles down my spine! She explained how liberals were using the discredited theory of evolution (punctuation and equations?) to promote socialism. She finally had the guts to say what right-thinking folks have been saying for decades: FDR and LBJ were filthy bohemian socialists. If only she had gone that one last step, and blasted that scourge of states rights, Abraham Lincoln, for being the RINO he was. *(Jindal-Bachmann 2012 at The UpTake)*

Second:

And the outbreak of online snarking even leaked into the courtroom itself. For some reason everyone ran late getting back and it was crowding 2:00 when the afternoon session started. The judges came out and banged home the gavel... and only the Franken team were in their places. Yep! Court was in session and the Coleman team was not yet in the room.

Franken attorney Kevin Hamilton SEIZED comedic potential by the throat, rose to his feet and said,

> "May it please the court? It seems we are missing opposing counsel. We'd be happy to second Mr. Elias to their side." *(quoted at MinnPost)*

Nice round of laughs in the room.

But every good stand-up knows you build on the previous laugh and Kevin Hamilton, the Seattle Sonic Boomer, DID.

> "It would be a rare instance of a net gain for both sides!" *(quoted at MinnPost)*

Brought the house down! Way to go Kevin! WineRev doffs (DOFFS!) hat in salute of good humor. (God knows we can use all we can get right now.)

Third:

Finally, inspired by his opening of the afternoon session, Kevin Hamilton continued his light needling as part of court procedure. Yep! Somebody from Team Coleman said something a bit vague and Hamilton pounced like a cat on a catnip-dusted ball of yarn:

> Hamilton sure is perky today: "I don't know if that was a statement or an objection. If it was a statement I object. If it was an objection it is meritless." *(nay nay at The UpTake)*

OK, I hope that will hold you until The UpTake goes on the air with today's trial show. A winter storm is coming with a foot of snow predicted NW of the Twin Cities, so Lake Wobegon and New Narvik will be blanketed. (No doubt Ole is warming up the car to move it to the other side of the street.) Here it is supposed to be an absolute rotten mess, maybe starting as rain or freezing rain and THEN changing over to 3–6 inches of wet cement. I just HATE (as in Ben-Ginsberg-is-a-farting-horse hate) that mix—just let it snow and we'll handle it fine. Rain & ice? Yuck!

Oh well. As of today it's three weeks left until APRIL... and that I can believe in...

That's the latest from yust southeast of Lake Wobegon.

Shalom.

Franken Rests
March 11, 2009

Comments: 142   Recs: 326   Tips: 259

Election Contest Court - Episode XLII

Minneapolis city elections director Cindy Reichert returned to the stand yesterday for more testimony. Also several more Franken voters testified. No decision on the Franken Motion to Dismiss from last Thursday.

An interesting point found by a blogger who IS a lawyer:

DK Been surveying 50 state SC rulings. From state precedent throughout the country, it would be highly unusual for a Court to "uncount" votes short of fraud or negligence. *(aonanodad)*

DK Franken has entered 250 of his ballots into the record in open court, 150 of which came during the last week. There has been multiple examples like this morning where large chunks of ballots were put on the record without witness ballot by ballot testimony. Coleman did the same predominantly with his final submission which will be allowed or not (probably in part) based on the last Friday motion hearing. *(TomTech)*

You've noticed the contrast between the Coleman and Franken presentations? Well, it's not ALL perfect on the Franken side. Yesterday Lillehaug made a mistake with an exhibit and:

I liked when Hamilton (Lillehaug?) said, after an error was discovered in one of his exhibits: "I've been waiting to do this. Withdrawn!" It was a great way to tweak Friedberg for all the dozens (hundreds?) of times he's had to say "withdrawn." *(Shlif at The Up Lake)*

But the big story was at the pressers afterwards. Franken attorney Marc Elias said plain as day their side will provisionally "rest their case" today. (Assumes no last minute snags or some lengthy legal argument from the Coleman side.)

Really? REST? What an amazing 4-letter word! Rest! Let lie. Repose. Requiescence. Tranquility. I am SO in favor of the motion I will signify by lying down... on a beach somewhere.

So Team Norm took 5 weeks and 1 day to put on their case. Team Al went Biblical, created their own universe and on the 7th day rested. (OK, so they worked ON the seventh day and rested at the end of it. But with court starting today at 1:30 for a 1/2 day session they are moving toward the "Six days shall ye labor and on the seventh day shall ye rest.")

Jay Weiner at MinnPost sums up thusly:

By the end of (Tuesday), Franken's lawyers brought in 62 voters, most of whom seem to have submitted legal ballots. They brought in 11 county auditors or election officials, most of whom seemed to suggest Franken's witnesses—and other voters' ballots in their counties—should be counted. Another 40 or so election officials statewide have been certifying the validity of ballots from afar. *(MinnPost)*

They rest because they believe they have added ballots to their side, because they lead, because, to quote another Testament, "what further need have we of witnesses?"

Stormy Thoughts

One thing that might delay the case today is some of the witnesses Franken has called are traveling from western parts of the state where the storm has been the worst. (One reason court begins at 1:30 p.m.)

(Minnesotans are a hearty bunch and good "storm" drivers but they know bad when they see it and they're smart enough to pull over. I was coming back from Des Moines a few years ago in just this kind of sleet/freezing rain/snow crud doing a careful 25 mph. About 20 miles this side of Iowa on I-35 I saw 4 semis jack-knife before my eyes and another roll over in about 15 minutes. I got a motel right then and beat the rush: 35 rooms vacant when I checked in, 0 45 minutes later.)

It's quite possible some witnesses may be stranded on the way to St. Paul and be unable to testify. So we'll see and hope for safe travel for everyone.

While you're hoping for them please send up prayers, blessings, karma, whatever you've got to Whomever you've got for the judges and lawyers in this case as well. If something awful should happen to Friedberg on his way in or if, say, Judge Marben would be injured on his way in from the hotel what then? Legal types help us out—what would happen?

If one of the lawyers were incapacitated somehow (I mean physically; Ben Ginsberg's mental/psychic delusions still leave him able to walk and talk), I suppose the rest of the team could/would pick up the slack. But what about one of the judges?

In a jury trial there are usually a couple alternate jurors who have been hearing the case and can step in as a replacement. But what about here? Is there a replacement judge? Would the remaining 2 be able to finish and render a verdict that would hold up? Or (Gaak!) would the whole bloody thing have to be retried in front of a fresh panel? Anybody have an educated guess? Is there statutory provision for this?

Possible Sequence/Timeline

Just so everyone can set their calendars here's a guess on what comes next and how many days.

Today: Court convenes 1:30. Franken brings in more evidence for its side and puts a few more witnesses on the stand. Provisionally rest case.

Nauen 64: ECC hears from Charles Nauen representing 37 voters and their absentee ballots remaining from their original group of 64. (3 withdrew, 3 more were ruled invalid. 21 were ordered by ECC to be put in "Ready to Count" stack: presumably in Sec. of State's office.) Both Franken and Coleman camps can support or oppose voters Nauen is bringing in. Begins Thursday—1 or 2 days?

Rebuttals: Contestant (Coleman) opens and closes a case. So Coleman has presented and rested. After today Franken will have presented and rested. Coleman gets to offer rebuttal of Franken's case/witnesses/evidence. Rebuttal is limited to direct testimony & evidence that offsets Franken's witnesses, testimony, and evidence. Franken gets to do the same with same limits.

Neither side may introduce NEW evidence (like Ben Ginsberg as a witness offering a copy of Barack Obama's "Kenyan birth certificate" supposedly produced on AL FRANKEN's ditto machine. Neither can Coleman call Michele Bachmann as a Coleman character witness ...BBWAHAHAHAHA!!! Bachmann recognizing character? When she has none of her own? Hee-hee! Wicked thought department: I would be willing to be homeless for a year just to hear David Lillehuag and/or Marc Elias on cross-examination. That would be the best 10 days of the trial, bar none, and worth this entire series! Whew!)

Rebuttal time: Weiner thinks maybe 1 day, some other legal types around here maybe 2 days.

Closing arguments. Both sides will get a chance for the lawyers to sum up their case and poke holes in the ice under the other side's skates. What do you think, legal types? This is a high-profile, major case, so 1 day for each side to close? Too much? Too little?

Orders from the ECC: There are motions pending that the court needs to resolve. In so doing, and in light of the case now resting before them, the ECC must DECIDE and order certain ballots to be opened and counted. (In the wildest fantasies of the Colemaniks, also order certain ballots UN-counted.) There is no set time period in which the ECC must do this but my guess is that it won't be long, maybe a day or 2.

Whichever ballots finally make it into the golden circle, the ECC will most likely order the Sec. of State's office to do the honors. At this point ballot copies (either clean from Team Franken, or crayoned, coffee-stained, and tic-tac-toed from Team Coleman) will not do. The court will want best evidence: the ballots themselves, which will need to be transported from 87 counties across the state to Mark Ritchie's office. (Maybe a few of them will even arrive in the trunk of a car, you rat bastard Reichwingers!) That will take maybe 2 days.

That will give both sides time to read (and maybe argue) the rules the ECC will set about the ballots: will both sides be able to challenge (just like in the old days in December)? Since there is no longer a State Canvassing Board to rule on challenges, who will? (Recall the Board?—so "equal protection" of same standards by same persons is preserved? Just Ritchie in his capacity as Secretary of State? The ECC itself?)

Whenever this happens it will be absolute MUST-SEE TV on The UpTake. Strap on the extra servers at the UpTake computer central! You're gonna need 'em to broadcast the last chance for both Niemackl and Lizard people to overtake Norm for 2nd place!

But having counted the ballots in question, then it's back to court. The ECC will need to resolve any challenged ballots and rule on motions: Kick out the Minneapolis "133"? Franken goes down net –46. Hold there was no double counting of duplicate ballots proven? Coleman's side takes another shovelful of dirt on the grave.

And then finally DECIDE the statutory question and purpose of an Election Contest Court: "Who got the most valid, legal votes?"

There is no legal time limit for this. A court can take as long as it wants (but my own feeling is they will not dally. A few days certainly; they'll want to get it just right, sleep on it, and tweak it once more).

Sooo 1 + 2 + 2 + 2 + 2 = 9 court days to get us back into court after that final, great, openin'-up mornin' (hat tip, ABowers13) so... maybe around the 24th or so? Could we then have another week until a final decision?

And how will the court announce? Just written? Post it on the website? Or orally? (I hope the last. They should have the chance to finally speak and have everyone listen.)

Morning thoughts: Now that we're in the end game of this suit (barring, of course, preternatural turns of events), I'm hoping for well-written, extensive, and pithy Findings of Fact and Conclusions of Law from this court.

While it isn't properly the court's job to reply to "hall court" ravings of Be Ginsberg's pressers, I really hope this court can produce some eloquent and memorable ways to express just how vacuous Coleman's case has been from the beginning. A few quotables to shove down Cornyn's throat would be much appreciated, O judges of the ECC.

(I can't say that I've seen much in the way of outstanding legal writing from this court to date, but I can only hope they'll rise to the occasion.)

Reactions to Coming Rest

News of the coming rest of Franken's case touched off reactions from here to Washington.

Al Franken was in DC yesterday sitting in on a lunch meeting of the Senate Democratic Caucus, invited by Harry Reid. MinnPost writer Cynthia Dizikes (Dizikeo? Ya know, Lena, dey have some pretty unusual names out dar in Vashington. Some of dem don't even end in "son," "sen," or "nen" like they're supposed to. Maybe da Minnesota Post could only find a Czech to work for dem dar?)...reports:

> "The light at the end of the tunnel is that the case will wrap up and the court will make a decision," said Franken, adding, "I believe that we are going to win the election contest and that after that [Coleman] can do what he wants. And if he does choose to appeal, it will be to the Minnesota state Supreme Court, and if they rule in our favor, then I imagine that I will be certified, and it won't be very controversial that I will be seated. But, no, we are not attempting to be seated before that." *(quoted at MinnPost)*

Dizikes also noted the Senators were interested in a personal update and satisfied how things are going. Said the SENIOR Senator from MN, Amy Klobuchar:

> I believe that the Minnesota process is very clear," said Klobuchar, adding, "So there was no talk about the Senate intervening." *(quoted at MinnPost)*

Election Contestant Cullen Sheehan (Norm's partner in the case and campaign manager) had to step up in place of the 2 PR flacks the Coleman side has lost in the last 2 weeks (Friedrich and Drake). Fortunately he can read (!) talking points from Limbaugh as well as those 2 could:

> "Al Franken doesn't know the difference between a light in the tunnel and the freight train that is coming right at him," said Coleman's campaign manager, Cullen Sheehan. "The freight train is coming, and it's Senator Norm Coleman being reelected to the United States Senate. And, if the contest court results are fair and legal, that freight train ..." *(quoted at MinnPost)*

WHAT? Cullen!? You calling out the court? You sayin' they ain't being LEGAL? Hey fella, you are on ALL the court papers there, you know? I mean implying the court would be "unfair" and "illegal" IF they don't find for me and my case, well, Cullen, it's just the way I was raised but I don't think that kind of talk is going to help my case.

What kind of attack is THAT on the judiciary? Cullen, where do you get off questioning the court like that, a court that has bent over backward for your case, letting your lawyers strike their own first 2 days of the case, NOT smacking your overpriced gang around any more than they did for not having witnesses ready to testify. Really STOOOPID, Cullen...

But while Cullen Sheehan (a name I want to quit typing sooner rather than later and never want to type again) is just being the typical south end of a northbound Republican horse Ben Ginsberg took things to another level. Its just I'm not sure I've ever visited that level personally (or at least I don't remember it... but enough about my college life), that level where he would say:

"I take joy of heart, lightness of heart, even in the Franken campaign deciding to rest their case tomorrow," said Coleman's legal spokesman Ben Ginsberg, but he reserved comment on the overall merits of Franken's case until, he said, Wednesday's conclusion.

I only read of Ginsberg's comment. I did not see video of him making it so I don't know if he looked like Jack Nicholson with a certain look rasping "Here's JOHNNY!" but it sure SOUNDS like that. Same glint in the eyes, same smile, "I take joy of heart..."

Whew, that's just creepy. I've joked about the Coleman side being on or off psychotropic drugs like thorazine or stelazine but this sure sounded like evidence that sometimes humor is damn close to the truth... Yeesh!

Stuff like that from Ginsberg makes me appreciate who Franken has handling his side, and this Up-Take blogger put it well:

> Actually, that's one interesting distinction between the Franken lawyers and the Coleman lawyers, both in the courtroom and in the hallway. Franken folks are invariable polite, observe all court protocols completely, apologize even for minor errors, etc. Friedberg and Ginsberg are rude, presumptive, and (especially Friedberg) seemed to think they have every right to say what they want to and act like they want to. *(Shlif at The UpTake)*

Wednesday Morning Minnesota Media

Both Twin Cities newspapers knocked the ECC trial to the B sections for the holiest of reasons. Front page A1 top streamer is: The High School State Hockey Tournament opens today! Little Falls; Hill-Murray; Totino Grace; Roseau; Warroad. They will ALL be here. The '84 Edina state champs will hold a reunion to bless their sons and nephews in this year's tourney. (And you outlanders say we Minnesotans have no life. HAH!)

Doyle & Duchschere for the StarTrib are still writing from the B section (B5). They avoid the Ginsberg quote above since it's a family newspaper and would scare the children. Instead they settle for a tamer Ginsberg quote on the rebuttal, "I think there were a lot of subjects that were raised in the Franken case that we have the opportunity to follow up on." No word if that follow-up will happen INSIDE the courtroom or be confined to Ginsberg in a striped leotard turning somersaults in hall to the floor-exercise music of "Springtime for Hitler."

Well, I've got the early shift and I'll need to leave early to slide on over to the wineshop. It's a little long today but you need something to keep you until 1:30 for court on The UpTake. Stay warm. Skate hard. That's the latest from yust southeast of Lake Wobegon.

Shalom.

PS. Good grief, can't Norm do ANYTHING right? Now it appears his Senate campaign has leaked credit card information of contributors out into cyberspace, just in case anyone needs to hack into some Colemanik's account. Yeesh!

Franken Rests Again
March 12, 2009

Comments: 242   *Recs:* 334   *Tips:* 323

Election Contest Court – Episode XLIII
The Unresting Resting

Court was scheduled to begin at 1:30 for a 1/2 session Wednesday. Franken's team would call a last few witnesses, get its last bits of evidence lined up and submitted, and then "provisionally" Rest their case.

Didn't work out. For one thing, one of their final witnesses was Auditor for Clay County (Moorhead, as in Fargo-Moorhead, way up on the MN-NoDak line. Minnesotans in that area sometimes describe it as "Fargo is across the river from US.") The 8–12 inches of new, blowing snow on top of new ice made travel down I-94 impossible. They hope to reschedule for today; if not, there was even talk of conducting examination by phone.

Last Minute Subpoenas

The ECC did lay out a brief timeline: This morning the Nauen side case will get a hearing (see #4 below). Franken will get final witnesses after lunch and then rest provisionally. Coleman will open rebuttal on Friday.

Coleman lead attorney Joe Friedberg complained Friday for rebuttal was too soon (basically the old: "no one could have anticipated we'd have to be ready so soon.") The Court said have at least 2 witnesses ready to go. (They didn't say "or else" but there was a faint echo of "Talk Like a Gangster Day" in the exchange.)

Now rebuttal is just that: Coleman gets to call limited witnesses to answer back Franken testimony and evidence.

But the Coleman team continues to perform "Leona Helmsley does St. Paul" and act like laws and rules are for "little people." It came out the Coleman legal team on Tuesday night beginning around 11:00 p.m. (WHOA! and one ECC judge asked, "What time did you say?") sent out a series of e-mail, fax, maybe Blackberry (and hell, as far as I know, carrier pigeon and dogsled) SUBPOENAs to various county election officials around the state asking/demanding them again provide answers to Coleman questions. (We saw this show last week, trying to get into evidence answers and opinions without allowing cross-examination or even court appearances.)

Franken moved to quash them all on grounds this is UN-resting the main Coleman case ("case in chief") and has nothing to do with rebuttal testimony. ECC took it under advisement and then issued a late day order turning down a bunch, allowing a little (about a rebuttal-sized portion.) I know, I know: fairness by the court; give every opportunity; cut off routes of appeal; all of those apply to the ECC action and I do appreciate them. But it's wearing...

Last-er Minute Spreadsheets; Ahhhh, Norm?

Yesterday was also the due date for Team Norm to submit their final (in their case ALWAYS semi-final; semi on so many levels) list of ballots they believe the court should open and count, that is, the last reading on the Coleman Universe. Total count: 1,360, down from 1,725, from 2,000, from 3,300, from 4,623, from 4,797, from 10,962.

And of all people, Pat Doyle (gasp!) of the *StarTrib* is up with some analysis of the 1,360. Taking Pat with a big gnaw off the corner of the salt block, he slices the 1,360 two ways:

Nearly half of the ballots on the list had no documentation of absentee ballot applications, and about a third no evidence of ballot return envelopes.

Half of 1,360 = 680; 1/3 = 453. The ECC has been very particular about things like undocumented applications and return envelopes. So the math here is 1,360 − (689 + 453 = 1,142) = 218!

Ahhhh Norm? That's less than the lead...

The *StarTrib* also did a county-by-county work-up of where the 1,360 are coming from, how many might have gone/will go for Barkley etc. and summarized:

If the ballots identified by Coleman were allocated to the candidates based on the percentage of the vote they got in each county, he would pick up 596 votes, Franken would pick up 539 and other candidates would get 225.

Since Doyle decided NOT to do the math for his readers, allow me: 596 – 539 = 57 Net to Coleman.

Ahhhh Norm? That's less than the lead…

Not content to leave spreadsheet analysis in the uncertain hands of Pat Doyle, Mark Elias of the Franken legal team at the presser also offered an analysis of the 1,360. He noted that ALL of them had been covered in last Thursday's Franken Motion to Dismiss (Day 8, still no ruling from the ECC), covered in the "Great Coleman Countdown." Having recapped that, Elias felt the number of ballots on the Coleman spreadsheet that will be counted will be…ZERO. Zip. Nada. Nil. Mitte midagi!

Ahhhhh Norm? That's less than the lead…

Charles Nauen's Trial Day

Today is the day "Swamp Fox" Charles Nauen gets a longer turn in front of the ECC to argue the "Nauen 61" voters cases to get their absentee votes counted. The Franken team has provided $ and legal support to these voters and to Nauen. Nauen is the guerrilla leader out in the forests and back alleys of MN picking off little clusters of Franken votes. 21 of his group of 61 have been ordered put on the "Ready to Count" pile over at the Secretary of State's Office.

Well, yesterday the court made a move and issued an ORDER on behalf of the latter-day Francis Marion: 14 more ballots of Nauen's 61 will be added to the "Ready to Count Pile." Voters of the 21 and of the 14 have all indicated they voted for Franken, so it ain't official yet, but you can at least pencil in +35 to the state-certified lead of +225 or +260.

By my count, 61 – 21 – 14 = 26; Nauen will be making his case for these 26. Both Coleman and Franken attorneys will be in the room and can support or raise objections so this morning could be rather multi-sided.

[Cripes! With 3 judges and 3 groups of attorneys they should lay out a huge Chinese Checkers board and hand out 60 marbles in 6 different colors. "Yellow (Judge Reilly) forward left, right, left, and a side left, stopping between a red and a green. Objection sustained."]

Given Nauen's tireless efforts, anybody willing to bet against him getting in a few more of these 26? Mr. Nauen, "well done, good and faithful servant."

The Great Coleman Computer Hack/Flap

Back in January the Coleman camp tried a "Lieberman" maneuver: put up a fund-raising appeal on their website and then report the site had crashed due to overwhelming response by Minnesotans and Real Americans everywhere rushing to make a donation to Norm.

MN Publius was on top of that before sunset (and in January in MN that is getting on it RIGHT AWAY) pulling back the computer geek curtain and showing nothing like that happened. Instead the Coleman IT people had basically had their computers query themselves in a loop and then they turned them off, claiming overload. (It was a bit more sophisticated than that, but a sham all the way.)

Well, a quick blurb (again at MNPublius, under the great headline: "Coleman Campaign Lying") yesterday morning built up all day long that the "Coleman for Senate" website had been hacked (spin story); no wait, had left some of their donor spreadsheets (300 page download) available for reading: like donor name, address, amount, employment place last 4 digits of a credit card, and the CREDIT CARD SECURITY CODE (that 3-digit number on the back of a CC you enter sometimes to prove you are looking at the physical card.) This last is a MAJOR, FINE-ABLE No-no in the credit world and in all 50 states.

> Coleman donor data breached in January, but donors alerted by Wikileaks not campaign.
>
> After Wikileaks put out a report that Coleman's donors' credit card data had been stolen in January, and after Wikileaks posted information to people warning them of that data breach in March, Coleman's people are now saying that they want an investigation into how the information got posted onto the internet (i.e. the Wikileaks posting), rather than admitting the campaign had a data breach in January and failed to report it to potential victims as required by law. *(Shlif at The UpTake)*

I know NOTHING about computers except I like my Mac, but a blogger with IT expertise posted that a stunt like this apparently is in the "slap my face, I can't believe they did that" category. (Ole runs up to Sven waving a magazine article: "Sven, look at dis. It says here lots of Norwegians have low, sloping foreheads. Vy do you tink dat is?" Sven gives himself tremendous, full-on palm slap above his own eyebrows and answers, "Danged if I know, Ole!")

> I'd also just like to point out, as someone who has web/database admin experience, the fact that a backup of the database was simply tarred and gzipped in a folder that was accessible is the stupidest thing I've ever heard. Even if the directory listing wasn't available, that's just a very, very bad idea. It's not like it's hard to backup to somewhere outside of the web root. Backups do not belong in varwww! *(Palpitations at The UpTake)*

Well, now I speak English, Estonian, and Southern, some Spanish, a bit of Greek and Hebrew, and a touch of German and Latin. But have not the FAINTEST idea what "Palpitations" means by this. It sounds awful (you know, like having to be Ben Ginsberg's dentist without a mask) so I'll take his/her word for it. Anyone who can translate at least from Geek to Greek I would appreciate (just get it into aorist subjunctive – Koine if you can – and I can dope it out from there).

> One of the Wikileaks e-mails cited a blog post by Adria Richards, a Minneapolis-based technology consultant who said she read in January about the supposed breach of Coleman's site and went there herself out of curiosity.
>
> Richards said in an interview that she quickly found private information, including a link to a database, that was accessible to anyone with a decent understanding of Web servers. She took several screen captures of the pages and posted them to her blog.
>
> "I'm not a hacker. My goal is not to dig into other people's insecurities, but just to identify them," said Richards, who added that she didn't download or even open the database.
>
> Richards said she had nothing against Coleman. "I would have done this if it was a Republican or a Democrat," she said. *(MN Independent)*

> According to a friend whose opinion I trust, the fact that the Coleman donor database contains credit card security codes is a violation of their agreement with Visa/Mastercard. Those numbers are not supposed to be retained by anyone. *(Andrew in VA at The UpTake)*

> I think it's important to note, as often as possible, that it's not just a list of credit card information. It's a list of credit card information that was illegally stored in violation of the Minnesota Government Data Practices Act. All of the comments talking about breaches of security, and blame being placed on others seems to ignore that fact. Simply put: if Coleman was in compliance with the law, that sensitive information would not have been there for anyone to find. *(Palpitations at The UpTake)*

Court is back at 9:00 a.m. CDT. Hope this is enough for the morning for all of you from yust southeast of Lake Wobegon.

Shalom.

Milestones & a Revival
March 13, 2009

Comments: 241   Recs: 328   Tips: 331

Cue up Neil Diamond's "Brother Love's Travelin' Salvation Show"...

"Hot August night and the leaves hangin' down..." WHAT? August? Hot? NO. March... Minnesota. (rewrite, rewrite...)

"Maaaaarch frozen night and the stars glintin' down and the snow on the ground gleamin' fresh..."

And it is evening, a plain frame structure with light golden shining through the windows, and you move quietly in the door and slip into a back pew. At a nearby microphone in the side aisle stands a be-spectacled young man, a Tri-Lambda frat ring on his finger, speaking in tongues, which sounds like:

> Misconfigured the web server so it only served the page when requested by do-main name, not IP.
>
> Misconfigured the web server to allow anonymous directory browsing.
>
> Misconfigured the web server root in such a way that the database was under-neath it *(MN Independent)*

A woman with an Omega Mu pin in her lapel rises beside him, her eyes closed and rocking in ecstasy:

> Dr. Adria Richards said she discovered the database by entering normcoleman. com, into OpenDNS' cache-check tool, which gave her an IP address where the Web site lived.
>
> Simply copying that address into a Firefox browser revealed the Web site directo-ries for colemanforsenate.com.
>
> Richards didn't download the database herself, but she posted a screen capture of what she'd found online after she made the discovery. An I.T. consultant for 10 years, she published her findings on her blog to educate others about the risks of improperly managed websites, she said.
>
> "All you needed was a Web browser," she said. "It's like I walked over to Norm Coleman's house and saw his door was open, took a photo of the open door and posted it on the Internet." *(MN Independent)*

As attendants lead these two gently to their pew a man, lean and bony with a "JedL" nametag, stands and says with authority, "St. Paul writes, 'Let no one speak in tongues unless there is someone to interpret tongues.'" 197 Amens broke across the room.

And another stood up and said unto us all, "It has been given unto ME to interpret the utterances of "Coleman Credit Card Debacle."

And the crowd pressed upon this one pleading, "Say it to us and we will update thee, yea unto 6 times we will update thee." And the blogger "Eman" then said, "The interpretation is in the plain tongue of Bri-tannia called English if thou wilt linketh unto me to the article."

And by 9:00 p.m. Central Daylight time last night over 250 had so linked and been moved unto com-ment upon the dastardly deeds of the database of Normshame.

And behold a lawyer stood up to test the database of Normshame and said unto the people, "It is writ-ten in the law that should thou asketh for the card of credit, thou SHALT keep the numbers of said card hidden in the bosom of thy servers. If they be NOT hidden and left where thief may steal or moth consume, then the law is written thusly:

> The 12 aspects of the PCI-DSS (with violations highlighted) are:
>
> Build and Maintain a Secure Network
>
> Requirement 1: Install and maintain a firewall configuration to protect cardholder data (VIOLATED)
>
> Requirement 2: Do not use vendor-supplied defaults for system passwords and other security parameters (password? What password? VIOLATED)

> Protect Cardholder Data
>
> Requirement 3: Protect stored cardholder data (VIOLATED)
>
> 3.2.2 Do not store the card-verification code or value (three-digit or four-digit number printed on the front or back of a payment card) used to verify card-not-present transactions. *(MN Independent)*

And many did click upon the link and behold for themselves the words of the Minnesota Independent and the comments upon them, and read in the comments not just the 3 but the 12 Aspects for themselves. And then a curly haired man arose and said with great force, "Follow after me and I will show you links and background, yea even videos of the lies of Normshame and the truth of the words of Adria." And many shouted, "It is Noah. The Kunin speaks! Let us UpTake links unto him for all his great words and moving videos." And they did.

Then many who came to this diary passed beyond the dark place of the database of Normshame and came unto a place of majesty. As they drew near they saw first a black turning cloud, a whirling dervish of great spinning, with clouds of thick smoke scattering broken easels in all directions. Some doleful persons with pads and recorders and cameras pressed (!) upon him hoping to hear not only olds, or spinz, but news. Alas and alack for the doleful "reportarii" who must wait upon the dervish ben-Ginz.

> Coleman attorneys have suggested the judges need to loosen their standards, which they have said they are unwilling to do, or uncount some votes.
>
> Attorney and Coleman trial spokesman Ben Ginsberg acknowledged, "The court has not shown a great deal of sympathy on these arguments." But he said the court still has to deal with the problem. *(Pioneer Press)*

But entering into the majestic place where all is LAW, behold, on high sat three in black robes, 2 women and a man. And each held a wooden Hammer in hand and listened closely. And before the 3 were 2 tables at which sat 3 men each.

And the sojourners drew near and uptook(!) for themselves seats as near as they could to hear from the 3 in black, for they said little, but when they said at all, the 3 and the 3 at the tables did stand and bow and nod.

Now the table of 3 at the right hand of the 3 in black were "Frank in" their speech and did call unto witnesses and questioned them closely and in good order.

And behold a small group of Nauens entered, and spoke and witnessed. The 3 of Hammers heard the Nauens with great respect and showed them good courtesy and even called them "voters."

> Catherine Brigham, who lives in a White Bear Lake senior living apartment, needed a little assistance walking to the witness stand. But she needed no help expressing her desire to have her vote counted.
>
> "I felt really cheated. This was a really important election in my life ... and now I wasn't a part of it," said Brigham. "They told me two days after the election that my vote wasn't counted, and I'm not a very quiet person, so I started calling everyone up to the Secretary of State."
>
> She registered at her White Bear Lake address — and got a registration postcard in the mail to prove it — but her vote was rejected because local officials decided she wasn't a registered voter. *(Pioneer Press)*

And while the Nauens spoke the Frankens looked on pleased but the Coal men had dark looks and hard words for the Nauens. And the Nauens gave back hard words and would not be frightened by the Coal men. And when the Nauens were finished yea even in just the morning and no longer, the 3 of Hammers said unto them, "Your pleas we taketh under the advisement and we will DECLARE in days to come whether thou shalt join the other Nauens in the Pile of "Ready to Count.""

And at 8 minutes past 2 in the after of noon Lille of Haug of the Frank men did stand and say they RESTED from their labors.

"I'm honored to say that contestee Al Franken rests his case," David Lillehaug, the attorney for Democrat Franken, said this afternoon in court.

And it was so, and those watching from afar uptook themselves in much rejoicing.

The 3 at the left hand of the 3 in black were black in their own way, black as Coal men they were. And these did offer cross words against the witnesses of the Frank men but did not prevail. And when the 3 with hammers said unto the Coal men, "A witness for the Franks is delayed in coming. Begin now thy butting and do it again so that it be Re-butted." And although they wailed that the time was too soon and too little they did indeed butt and butt again unto re-butting.

They called to witness a Gelbmann from the SoS (so is an "office" called in their tongue) and a Reichert (from a city of small, yea even mini, apples) and a Manskey (from a county of Ram's Ee, where Paul the St. doth reside). And their words to their own witnesses were small and few and not ordered and signified only dust:

> This is Coleman's rebuttal case? Not much substance *(Abbey at The UpTake)*

> What is Friedberg offering? *(WaltAZ at The UpTake)*

> Your honor: Even before I begin giving you this evidence, I will admit that it is flawed: wow. *(VA Aaron at The UpTake)*

And while there was eating and drinking at the high sun of day some said hard words against the Coal men and uttered the egregious name of Sheehan and thought the Franken men had been too gentle with the men of Coal:

> Franken should have pursued claim that Coleman Campaign Manager, Cullen Sheehan, was not qualified to vote in MN. Sheehan came to MN for a temp job but has maintained his Iowa(?) home. His intent to return to Iowa would make that his official residence. Having Sheehan declared unqualified to vote would force his removal as a party in this case and prevent deep pocketed Republicans from skirting campaign finance laws by paying the court costs and legal fees through gifts to Sheehan. *(TomTech at The UpTake)*

And one thought the Normshame should be sent to a far country, but others thought his words but a snark:

> Don't know if its true or not but a deal is in the works for Norm to quit this challenge. No quid pro quo but Obama will then appoint him to be the US ambassador to Japan. Apparently Norm is wildly popular there as he evokes the memory of those Japanese WWII soldiers in the Philippines and other Pacific islands from the 1970s who refused to leave the mountains and surrender even though they knew the war was over. *(JFS at The UpTake)*

And even after the last of the Frank witnesses arrived and did speak, and after the Lille of Haug did REST still the Coal men did Re-butt until at the end of the day.

And then the 3 with the Hammers DECLARED, first unto the Coal men, "Only one morning more shall ye butt and re-butt and no longer." And the morning is the one upon us now on Friday.

And then they declared unto BOTH the Coal men and the Frank men, "We shall hear from each of thee 1 hour on the Friday. Argue while ye may that hour for then the time will have passed and the arguments shall be called "CLOSING ARGUMENTS." And then both ye shall rest and we the 3 of the Hammers, called by some the ECC and by others the Election Contest Court, shall take unto ourselves thy case and all thy words and papers. We shall DECLARE which papers with seals shall be UNsealed and counted, some for the Coal men and some for the Frank men. And then WE shall declare who has the more of the Papers of Ball-ot."

Lord, We Need a Revival![15]

And now, "move on up the road/to the outside of town/with the sound of that good gospel beat/Sits a ragged tent, where there ain't no trees"[16]

And if you enter your feet will stir the sawdust and a sweet pine-y aroma arises. As you take your seat on a bench people are clapping in time to the music, the choir is swaying and the organist strutting her stuff across the stops and keys.

---

15   *When a diarist at DailyKos breaches the "100 diaries on one topic" mark, he or she is allowed to post a donation link (preaching optional).*

16   *Neil Diamond, "Brother Love's Travellin' Salvation Show"*

"the room is suddenly still/and when you'd almost bet you could hear yourself sweat...he walks in"

"eyes black as coal and when he lifts his face every ear in the place is on... him"

My friends, the time of trial is at an end. *(Amen! Hallelujah!)* No more shall we learn of pro hac vices *(No more)*. Not again do I want to hear of motion in limine *(Lat. "at the threshold")* for I don't want such a motion to come anywhere NEAR my threshold. *(That's right.)* I have had it up to my threshold with motions and objections and sustainings and advisements. *(Me too!)*

As this retelling began it began as a revival of hope, a revival of the hope of democracy, a hope of the people ruling themselves. And somebody had to write it down, and somebody had to write it up, and somebody had to write it 90 times and nine, and I am here to tell you for the 100th time I have written it again! *(Right on! You go Rev, write on!)*

There have been times when I have been moved by the Recount *(yes sir)*, times when I have been frustrated by the recount *(yes sir)*, times when I have been left weeping by the recount *(say it brother)*. But brothers and sisters it has been you who have sustained me, you who have encouraged me, you who have egged me on, you who have corrected me, you who have added your wisdom to my poor mite.

DK Congratulations on becoming a centenarian with most your faculties still intact (we've all lost some listening to the Cole men) *(blueinmn)*

That's the latest from yust southeast of Lake Wobegon.

Shalom. *Doffs (DOFFS!) hat to Kossack community.*

We Wait for the Court
March 14, 2009

Comments: 237   Recs: 233   Tips: 206

The Election Contest Court (ECC) heard closing arguments from both sides Friday, an hour apiece, posed for pictures, and then... took the case into chambers. It's in their hands now.

We could get answers and move toward an end anytime, yea even this week.

Election Contest Court – Episode XLIV

The Closings

After some legal "housekeeping" early in the day there came the Main Event: the Closing Arguments of Coleman vs. Franken.

A closing argument is NOT evidence and NOT testimony. It is basically a sales pitch, an attempt to persuade the court to use YOUR lens, YOUR field guide to look at the evidence and testimony. If justice is rightly shown as a woman blindfolded holding scales (whether or not she wears the "Full Ashcroft" or is in classical "au naturel" Greek) then you have to appeal to the ear. Rhetoric, even oration, are tools of the trade.

Both sides chose their champions: For Franken: Kevin Hamilton; For Coleman: Joe Friedberg. Each side was allotted one hour and both sides took full measure.

Just a thought. Team Franken is very effective. Lillehaug is great on examining and cross-examining witnesses. But Hamilton really can deliver an argument, and I think he is the right choice for closing. *(feebog at The UpTake)*

Hamilton closed first. He moved through his introduction—"No election is perfect, so errors were present"—as smoothly yet defining-ly as the cowbell, then drums, add bass and then lead guitar in the first measures of "Honkytonk Woman."

Hamilton took aim at the courtroom-and-hallway Coleman strategy focused on alleged errors (to the point of wanting the "fatally flawed" "error-riddled" election set aside and a new one run.) He laid it before the Court: the Berg boys' "advocacy" of that strategy "had outrun the evidence" for it:

- the errors have to have changed the outcome of the election
- the burden of proof to demonstrate this is upon the Contestant Coleman
- the Contestant does not have evidence to prove it.

The contestant "has [so] woefully failed to carry the burden of proof" that the Court should grant Franken's Motion to Dismiss (from last Thursday.) It was done with real style, the legal equivalent of Mick Jagger's opening snarl after the instrumental intro, "I MET a GIN-soaked BAR room QUEEN in MEM-phis..."

Hamilton dumped THAT freighter-full of iron ore from Duluth onto the Coleman table and then proceeded to crank through EVERY last challenge the Coleman side raised. He used the index of a Coleman (!) spreadsheet to show how weak their argument was over rejected absentee ballots. "The failure of proof is breathtaking."

He used photos of witnesses like Pam Howell, the Coleman witness and election judge whose testimony (entered, stricken, restored, re-stricken, pieces restored) was the only limp link to the claim of "double counted" votes.

He swatted away the Coleman mosquitoes around the 133 Minneapolis ballots that had disappeared. They should still be counted because the voters who cast them exist, signed in, and the voting machines noted their ballots.

> My god, it's like a closing argument on Law and Order. It's that good. But he needs to bang his fist more :). *(lostboyjim at The UpTake)*

He NAILED Team Coleman (like an tenor hitting the high note on the National Anthem) with the Coleman attempt to back out of Rule 9[17], which they had stipulated (agreed to) when they were leading in the recount, but now wanted to get out of since they are trailing.

"Contestants' attempt to back out of their agreement ... is as cynical as it is groundless."

It was a masterpiece of methodical, never boring, detailed, factual, logical "leave no stone unturned and leave no turn un-stoned," relentless, "Karl Rove would gulp in fear if he were the defendant (a fond wish of mine)" Closing Argumentation.

> "As the record before this court vividly demonstrates, Al Franken received the highest number of votes in this election. Al Franken is Minnesota's senator-elect. He is entitled to the certificate of election." *(quoted at MinnPost)*

And then it was Joe Friedberg's turn to close for Team Coleman. Joe Freidberg is no Kevin Hamilton, he is Joe. And he stayed within himself. He railed against the ECC's Friday the 13th decision as "changing the rules in the middle of the game" (They REALLY didn't like that ruling. Ben Ginsberg's spinning in the hall after that date started to drill through the marble like a core sampler drill with a fresh diamond bit.)

Joe was charming and self-deprecating. You could see he would play well to a jury. You can see if he has only to raise doubts so one juror has doubts beyond a reasonable level a Friedberg client may be found innocent by reason of a hung jury.

He didn't do PowerPoint. He didn't do spreadsheets. He worked from a yellow legal pad and his own handwriting in a time honored way.

He asked the court to come down off its standards of "strict compliance" on absentee ballots to the Coleman position of "substantial compliance" with the law. He argued that if the court kept to the strict standard they have shown so far (particularly in those Friday the 13th rulings) then errors were made and ballots were unequally treated.

On the other hand, if the court moved to "substantial compliance," then the Coleman camp knew of about 1,360 ballots that substantially meet the requirements (and implied they should be equally treated with the other ballots already counted.)

If the court insisted on a strict standard then let the Minneapolis 133 be strictly excluded because we do not have the physical ballots. If they be allowed in then fairness/justice/equal protection calls for other ballots to also be admitted.

---

17 *Rule 9 had to do with how to Recount absentee ballots and their machine-readable duplicates. What stinks like an un-tuned chainsaw burning swamp gas is the Coleman side's effort to "UN-stipulate"; lawyers and courts DON'T DO THAT.*

His charm and self-effacement led him (perhaps inadvertently) to undercut much of his case. He was praising the judges for their learnedness and noted they knew much more about election law than he did. In fact he himself had learned a great deal about election law in the last 7 weeks because when they started "I knew nothing about it."

As with all things Recount-related: "We'll see."

Afterwards there was an impromptu photo session, judges standing by their chairs, lawyers and (bless them all) the clerks and court reporters. Everyone realized it was historic and deserved a photo for the ECC ruling on the closest Senate race in Minnesota history. Friedberg said in his decades of practicing law he'd never posed with the court and counsel like that.

Oh, and then, as everyone was getting ready to pack up, Jay Weiner from MinnPost reports:

> After that fuzzy picture-taking, there was still one final legal proceeding. It had to do with evidence that had been in dispute.
>
> The courtroom was empty save for the lawyers, clerks, the judges and some hangers-on.
>
> Franken lawyer David Lillehaug offered boxes and boxes of evidence.
>
> Friedberg, to make the event official, objected.
>
> (Presiding Judge Elizabeth) Hayden looked over her red-framed reading glasses. "Overruled," she said, with a slight smile.
>
> "We rest," said Hamilton.
>
> Bang went the gavel of court clerk Christopher Channing, who added: "All rise, the court is in recess."
>
> Now, we wait. *(MinnPost)*

Next Steps

What can we expect and when? ABowers13 likes making lists and his prognosticating has been pretty good. His/Her take on the immediate future (like... wrap-this-before-April future??!!)

> Actual schedule—from my crystal ball—
>
> 1. Friday— Summary arguments from Coleman & Franken.
> 2. Monday —Court orders the two sides to come up with 3 lists:
> 1. Ballots BOTH sides agree should be counted.
> 2. Ballots Coleman wants counted and Franken challenges.
> 3. Ballots Franken wants counted and Coleman challenges.
> 3. Wednesday List#1—ballots stipulated by both sides get sent to SOS for counting. Lists #2 & #3 are reviewed, one by one, by the our 3 judge court and sorted into two piles—One pile accepted and off to SOS. Other rejected and put back into black hole with other 11,000 rejected ballots.
> 4. ???Day—SOS has ballots from all over Minnesota sent to his office. He rounds up the usual suspects and schedules that great opening-up day. They will be counting less than the 900 previously and will NOT mark ballots so whole thing should be over by noon.
> 5. ???Day—Court rules Dinkytown ballots IN (the lost net 47 Franken); rules Duplicates count unchanged—no uncounting; apartment numbers don't matter UNLESS apartment complex divided into precincts; election was clean, thorough, fine—no equal protection violation. And all other issues moot.
> 6. Wednesday 25?—Court rules Franken got the most votes and adjourns.
>
> Again, it's one blogger's opinion but worth considering. *(ABowers13)*

A Fife and Drum

Yesterday in the comment string I was moved by these two comments by the same Kossack (edited together for your reading pleasure):

One thing no one has really talked about is how the judges will handle the counting of the remaining [absentee ballots]. There will be around 600 or so to count, as we've been saying from the beginning.

But, I am hoping they will stage it such that they have written up their decision without naming a winner and allow that final counting to be the deciding moment as to who gets the certificate. You know, the judges take themselves out of the picture and we go back to that January 3rd atmosphere of "what is actually contained in those ballots?"

That way, in the media at least, there will be this sense that impartial justice has been done and Coleman has a chance to overtake Franken, only to have his whole world turned upside down as Franken stretches his lead beyond 300 votes.

DK That's my hope anyway. It really should not be about the court; it should be about the people in the final analysis. We are the ones who voted.

...

I hope that there is considerable drama and "suspense" built into the counting. I want the public to sense that the decision was not made by the judges, only that they ruled certain other ballots were legal and should be counted.

In the public's mind it is much better if they sense Franken won because of "counting" not because of the "judges." That's what gives him stronger legitimacy.

...

I know one thing. The MNSC is not going to take very long once this ECC process runs its course. They do not suffer fools gladly, and with two Supremes on the Canvassing Board and now three very careful judges wading through all this paperwork, they understand that Coleman was given a fair hearing in a close election, and that, he lost. *(Mi Corazon)*

Mi Corazon is RIGHT ON! I started this series because I was caught up in the coming drama of the Recount and thought Kossacks would like to keep up on it. Being political junkies around here it seemed a natural fit.

And yet something changed in January as the whole thing moved toward the ECC and I think it's because it moved from the political to the legal realm. It was harder to write about the deal, and maybe harder to read about too. Oh there was plenty of action, many twists and turns. I learned more than I ever wanted to about "Motion in Limine," "pro hac vices," and precedents and Rules of Evidence.

But all that, important as it has been (and is yet to be) has been in essence a massive detour. Mi Corazon's remarks are the first sighting of those delightful signs "End Detour" and "Resume Speed."

Back in the day of WineRev's youth, my sister and I enjoyed laughing over the comedy show Green Acres. Eddie Albert played a lawyer disgusted with modern urban life who moves himself and his glamorous wife (Eva Gabor, complete with heavy Hungarian accent) to a farm. The laughter came from the clashing outlooks between the locals and the new exotics.

About every 3 or 4 episodes Oliver Wendell Douglas (Albert) would wax rhapsodic about farmers: "the backbone of the country," and "here the embattled farmer stood and fired the shot heard 'round the world." As he did a fife and drum would start up in "Yankee Doodle" manner which everyone except Albert could hear playing.

Well, strike up the drum and fife, the WineRev is going to preach a moment.

The Recount has been the long end game of the MN Senate election. But that election and the whole election that went on around the country was of course an exercise in democracy, of "demos"—the people and "krasis"—to rule, of "the People ruling themselves."

The last 8 years have been a terrific assault not just on the legal system, not just on American idealism, not just on the Constitution. They have been an Empire Strikes Back assault on aspiration, on ordinary people living ordinary lives, on the entire concept of democratic rule.

By the narrowest of margins (5-4) a people-loathing, power-grasping regime came to power in the home of a great democracy, our home, our democracy. Wars were started. Dissenters were trampled (the Republican campaigns and National Conventions of '04 and '08) and even murdered under suspicious conditions (Pat Tillman). People were jailed arbitrarily (Padilla) and languish still. Senators' offices were biologically attacked. Governors were railroaded out of office and into prison. The Treasury was looted for private gain and our currency debased. Mercenary armies were raised while true soldiers suffered from scaled-back medical care and died from inferior equipment. A propaganda behemoth of Goebbelian depravity still spouts and spumes acid on the idea that power belongs to anyone other than the few.

But "the people" would not submit. Amid the humiliating airport searches and across their wiretapped communications they voted down, voted out, argued back against the bastards. Unevenly, haltingly, but steadily. For the last few years all those stories from American history, our history, have been unusually lively to me. For good reason I have felt a kinship to Francis Marion the Swamp Fox, and Greene, and Washington.

The MN Senate election ended up breathtakingly close. Who won is actually NOT as important as the fact of the Recount itself. A law, drawn up by the people of Minnesota, was in place, with procedures and plans and rules and clarity of what was to be done—so that the voice and vote of the PEOPLE would be expressed. Those 3 million votes would be counted... and recounted, carefully, patiently... by poll workers and election officials from Pipestone to Baudette... by the people... for the people.

The whole machinery cranking up and going forward was a smashing defeat for the smashers. "Brooks Brothers" rioters would NOT carry the day. (The only people I really called out in these diaries, daring those jackboot wannabes to come here for a round to offset Florida 2000. The gasbag cowards never showed.) The Jim Baker (Bush family fixer) Money-and-Lawyer machine would NOT clank their panzers to another blitzkrieg win. Ben Ginsberg's loathsome contempt and arrogance would NOT intimidate or stampede the Secretary of State or those in the courthouses. (Interesting that Ginsberg was hired on back in November but scurried in the background all through December during the actual Recounting and only emerged into light when the court maneuvering started. When these last ballots get counted I don't think Ben will be visible at all. Ballots being counted and democracy in action are like garlic and a silver cross to a vampire like Ginsberg.)

The arguments of the last 7 weeks and the orders and decisions yet to come are merely (MERELY!) an extension of that democratic impulse. Mi Corazon is right. The ECC and even the MN Supreme Court should step back and let the votes, these finally settled upon, LAST votes of 2008, be counted in front of the PEOPLE. Its their election, their vote, their state, our democracy. Huzzah!

OK, now we wait... for orders and decisions. I'll post when there's something to post so this series may not be quite daily. In the meantime I'll work on thank-you notes and the "collection" project as noted last weekend in v. 95.0. But that's the latest from yust southeast of Lake Wobegon.

Shalom.

Need a Good Lawyer?
March 15, 2009

Comments: 259   Recs: 207   Tips: 218

The Mighty Mississippi starts its life in Itasca State Park and is currently frozen solid. From Mark Twain (yea, from Hernando DeSoto) we think of the "Father of Waters" as a southern, broad, twisting even lazy river. But here in the north country it's like most other rivers, the Minnesota and the St. Croix—typical, average, and frozen in winter.

Now spring arrives and the ice cracks and breaks up in fair sized pieces on the Mississippi. So likewise the river of the Minnesota Recount, frozen for seven weeks in the Election Contest Court, is cracking. Judges Hayden, Marben, and Reilly are drilling holes here and there, setting charges, using sledge hammers, to break the up the ice so the last votes of the 2008 election can be counted and the final senator of the class of '08 can be seated.

Before the flow starts, consider with me some of the ice slabs piled up and jammed along the shore, the chunks heaped by the abutments of the Stone Arch Bridge in Minneapolis. You know...the lawyers. They will drift out of sight downstream pretty soon, so before they do, I thought I'd put my feet up in the ice house and consider them.

The Law is as diverse as human activity: corporate, labor, contract, real estate, divorce, juvenile, medical. A lawyer has to pick an area of concentration because being a "general practitioner" just isn't possible. And even these areas are so vast that practicing in one of them is almost routine and provides a steady or even lucrative living (like doing divorces in Hollywood).

You can also do well being a specialist, practicing law in a niche where you get good at the subtleties: David Lillehaug does a lot of construction law—e.g. the legal issues connected with putting up a skyscraper. I have a cousin who is married to a lawyer who does "social security" law (a dependable niche in Florida I'll bet.)

Election law is esoteric and yet very diverse: all 50 states conduct their own elections by their own standards. I suspect it can vary also at the county level. Cities can have their own rules for choosing water commissioners that will be vastly different than the water control board in a rural area. If ever you need a specialist, a close election is the time to get somebody on retainer and have them start boning up the particulars.

Assessment: Team Coleman

Fritz Knaak

A MN native and has practiced law here for decades. He has been politically active in state GOP affairs, been a state senator for several years. He has tried at least one case under MN election law, complete with a recount and an election contest court (ECC).

We all got to meet Knaak early on as the public face of the Coleman press gatherings. He was straightforward, plainly advocating for Norm as you'd expect, and handled himself and the press quite well, with a certain wit and charm from time to time.

Yet when the entire Recount ended up in the ECC Knaak was mute, practically invisible. He was at the Coleman table almost as part of the furniture. His remarks this week on the credit card fiasco for Team Coleman were both the first time we've heard from Knaak at a presser in ages, and a reminder of how long it's been.

GRADE: C–; started solidly and had potential but declined noticeably.

Tony Trimble

Hard to see from the outside why Trimble was on the Coleman Team. He runs a law practice out of Hopkins (Trimble & Assoc.) that appears to handle a general gamut of law. It's hard to tell because Trimble & Assoc. does not have a web presence, which seems old-fashioned but in a bad way. It may suggest a certain allergy to things computerized and may account for the Team's difficulties with spreadsheets, use of Powerpoint for exhibits, etc.

Tony was the "inside guy" to Fritz Knaak's "outside" guy in the opening weeks of the Recount. He doesn't wear well publicly so it was a smart move to send out Knaak for the PR side of things. He has some familiarity with MN election law and emerged when the Recounting ended and the issue moved to the challenged ballots. He was the point man in arguing issues with the State Canvassing Board and was often seen opposing Secretary of State Mark Ritchie.

Trimble may have been the original lead attorney for the ECC but somewhere a decision was reached to bring in a "name" for the lead, sending Tony to a sidekick role. He did carry some of the witness load during the trial and raised and argued at least a few objections.

And then of course Trimble was at the center of the Pamela Howell disaster, where not only was the witness' testimony twice (!) stricken from the record but also caused by Trimble mishandling of pretrial Discovery. The court's $7500 sanction had Trimble at the center of the bullseye.

GRADE: F, for poor preparation, and for the sanction.

Joseph Friedberg

Joe Friedberg was the "name" attorney brought in as lead. He is well known and well liked in Twin Cities legal circles, folksy, humorous and rather clever in many ways. But he was brought in late to the case, only 10 days before opening and just days before pretrial filings were due.

In the trial Joe was overwhelmed. His line is criminal law, and defense at that, where the task is to just move the needle enough from "She did it" to "Are you sure beyond a reasonable doubt? If there is a doubt you must acquit." To move from this to having to handle reams of paper (which the team was not good at in providing him), carrying the burden of proof, and having to pile up that proof to a height and weight that it constitutes a "preponderance of the evidence" was a tall order—too much of one for Friedberg. He admitted as much in his closing argument noting that he started from a zero base 7 weeks ago on election law.

GRADE: C–; Joe was outworked and overwhelmed and in some ways it was sad to watch. It was like kidnapping the pilot of an ultralight and strapping them into an F-14 on the steam catapult of the USS Enterprise and the first words he hears in the helmet are "Clear for launch. 3-2-1..." It'll fly but it may not end well.

Ben Ginsberg

Ginsberg came on board in November but stayed very low key all through the Recount. He seemed to want to play the mastermind without leaving fingerprints. He emerged from the cave in mid-January, not to take the lead on the case but to become its public face. (I wonder if bringing on Freidberg was Ginsberg's idea? He may have sized up Knaak and Trimble and decided the Team needed a late-season acquisition for the playoffs.)

In that public role he was... visible. He spun like a figure skater, almost an incarnation of Faux News: any development in the case is "Good news for Norm!"

Strike your own first 2 days of testimony?

"Great head-fake by Norm, eh?"

An absentee voter testifies his girlfriend signed his ballot for him?

"A system riddled with errors that has injured my client Norm the senator."

A genuine case of vote fraud in Warroad, where a convicted felon on parole without voting rights votes for Coleman?

"It is a fatally flawed system that keeps men who have paid their debt to society from voting for Norm Coleman. The state should be ashamed." It didn't work.

GRADE: Past F to W, with his friend. (For a "Z" he'd actually have to stand in front of a mirror and NOT see his reflection.)

Assessment: Team Franken

Kevin Hamilton

Washington state attorney who came on the Team in early December I believe and was not heard from at all until basically the ECC opened. But with election law being as obscure a field as it is there may well have been a LOT of behind the scenes work going on. Vitally important, Hamilton has extensive, intense, and fairly recent experience in a drawn-out recount battle on a statewide level. Not many do and the Team was very smart to get him early and set him to work. Between Hamilton and Lillehaug I imagine it is the 2 of them who really assembled some first-class clerk/paralegal and junior attorney talent behind the scenes to do research, line up witnesses, assemble affidavits, etc.

And when you have a top-drawer staff it lets the in court team pull off "stunts" like this (and make it look easy!):

Sometime during Friday's proceedings, a question came up as to whether or not one of Coleman's pieces of evidence had been actually been accepted by the court. After a couple of minutes, Lillehaug! came up with the answer.

DK   It had been accepted. Lillehaug not only gave him the date, but the exact time. *(mswojo)*

DK   I laughed out loud, he was so precise. *(rincewind)*

Hamilton carried a fair bit of the witness examination and cross-examination load. He knew what to ask and how to ask, so the Franken case clicked off witnesses about every 9 minutes. He even let a bit of wit shine through [when "offered" to trade Marc Elias to the other team :-)] and was picked to do the closing argument. That close was methodical, detailed, relentless, and compelling.

GRADE: A; would put a REAL notch on his holster if he ends up on the winning side of a second statewide recount case.

Marc Elias

Elias came in early, days after the election ended and was the public face of the Franken campaign from beginning to end (easier to stay on message that way when it's just one person). He dueled in the PR wars with Knaak, Drake, Friedrich, Sheehan, Trimble. Ginsberg...it didn't matter, there was Marc, making the case, answering back with facts, law, and wit. No doubt he was the principal advisor on all things Constitutional and has been guiding his side of the case as tightly as possible to leave no toehold for an appeal to the federal courts (equal protection and all that). He has been Obama-ly focused on MN law, MN procedures, MN courts, studying them with all the intensity of a customer at the Mustang Ranch making a choice. (Just a metaphor; Mrs. E would kill him and no prosecutor would even indict for such a case of justifiable.)

He was in court but let Hamilton and Lillehaug carry most of the witness load. He did weigh in with objections from time to time that were masterpieces of the lawyer's art. He often wrote and argued the motions from team Franken, working over the Coleman team like Steven Seagal taking apart a martial-arts bad guy.

GRADE: A; just the right man both public and private from beginning to end.

David Lillehaug

Lillehuag was there from the start but you never knew it. Passionate, abrasive and behind the scenes all the way. The mainspring of the whole Franken effort and probably the guy who thought of going to Ramsey County court eight days after the voting machines cooled to force the county to release the names of absentee voters.

Lillehaug (no doubt helped by Elias and Hamilton) assembled the legal staff, chose the best and brightest, and ordered intravenous lines installed from Caribou Coffee (MN answer to Starbucks). Undoubtedly these people are good, motivated, and energetic. Lillehaug would have left them exhausted; the man is the incarnation of relentless.

Lillehaug also carried a lot of the cross-examination of the Coleman witnesses and argued objections rather calmly... a dead-flat, ice-down-your-spine kind of calm. When the explosion came over the Howell testimony and lack of discovery he didn't scream or jump, just turned to the judges and said, "I move to strike the testimony of this witness.." and bit off the reasons. He just coolly kept tossing sticks of dynamite onto the fire and wetting it down with gasoline. After the recess, when it came out in a few minutes that Team Coleman had in effect tampered with the witness during the break, Lillehaug let his voice rise just slightly, "I re-NEW my motion to strike on the further grounds of..." That $7,500 sanction on the other side in a case of this magnitude is one for David's trophy case.

GRADE: A; what else is there to say? Wow.

Until there's something from the court, that's the least of the latest from yust southeast of Lake Wobegon.

Shalom.

MN-Sen Non Events
March 16, 2009

Comments: 159   Recs: 219   Tips: 232

The Minnesota Senate Recount is in the hands of the three judge panel of Hayden, Reilly, and Marben. They have motions to decide, orders to write. They also have testimony of 134 witnesses to review, supported and contradicted by 2,182 exhibits (mostly photocopies of ballot envelopes).

Both legal teams for Coleman and Franken have homework assignments due. By noon today Team Coleman has to turn in certain certifications from county officials or some of their evidence will be tossed.

As with all things Colemanik look for this to arrive at the clerk's window (if at all) about 11:57 a.m. Team Franken also has some stuff to turn in (affidavits I think) but it's likely done already and will be beamed in a transporter beam as soon as the clerk's window opens around 9:00 a.m.

Both sides have one major piece due by noon Tuesday BUT this may have been moved up to today. You see when the court will rule the decision will feature 2 major chunks: Findings of Fact and Conclusions of Law.

Those are the 2 elements of any legal case: based on this evidence (the facts ..."The temperature was 4 below zero..." and certain inferences ."...therefore the ice under the fishing shack was not melting from natural causes") we think this and this and this happened.

Therefore the law that applies here is (citations ."..MN code xx.03" and precedents ."...however, in Barons v. King John (Runnymeade, (1215); obviously Team Franken at work) the court held instead..."). Putting the 2 together, we the court decide the following ...

Both sides get to turn in a set of proposed Findings of Fact. Both sides get to help the court by saying on paper, "Look at these facts, these exhibits, this evidence because they are the important stuff." That of course IMPLIES the other stuff (like the stuff the other side brought in) is less important. I don't know (and the legal eagles around here will tell us) but each side may even have been allowed to write up: "Here's the good stuff and why (OUR stuff) AND here's why the court should ignore, dismiss, or downplay the other stuff (from the other side.)" In other words, one last chance to throw a tachyon grenade over the wall at the other side.

The Court will produce its own Findings and is likely already come up with a draft. But they'll look at both sets and decide whether they want to modify their own; you know, go with a 0.2 update, or a complete v. 2.0. or go with what they've got.

As in all things Recount-related, we'll see.

The senator-elect is in the news too. The Franken campaign (and to be fair, the Coleman campaign too, but Al started it) got a ruling from the Federal Elections Commission allowing him (and by extension Coleman) to fund-raise beyond the $2,300 individual limit in order to pay for the Recount expenses, lawyers fees, court costs—you know, his side of the whole show we've been enjoying (?) for the last 131 days since the election.

(Norm gets to do the same, but his website does not currently have a credit card option available. That could slow things down for him, ya think?)

So that's all that's happening as far as I can tell. We all wait upon the court. Yesterday's diary featured a great set of legal thoughts and casual betting as to how the court might rule, appeals to the MN Supreme Ct. (if they'll even agree to take the case), equal-protection issues (damn hard to find), etc.

Hope this will hold you until news breaks from the Court. That's the latest from yust southeast of Lake Wobegon.

Shalom.

Irish Scraps
March 17, 2009

Comments: 148   Recs: 226   Tips: 231

Gorgeous weather! At 60 degrees and I had the day off to enjoy it. Ahhh! It was the same kind of spring weather when Ole and Lena got married in New Narvik, Minnesota. For real excitement they decided to honeymoon in the Twin Cities. They were on the freeway nearing Minneapolis when Ole put his hand on Lena's knee. Giggling, Lena said, "Ole, you can go a little farther now if ya vant to.".. so Ole drove to Duluth.

Election Contest Court – Episode XLV

No orders or decisions from the Court as of first thing this morning. But here and there were a few scraps that emerged from under the melting snowpiles.

Scrap 1

The UpTake (no webcast/broadcast but they put up a live blog as political methadone for the junkies in trial withdrawal) picked up that Deputy Secretary of State Jim Gelbmann has informed the Court the SoS office would need four days to collect ballots from around the state that the court would order opened and counted. (The opening and counting will be done in St. Paul but the ballots themselves are in city and county vaults.)

No doubt at least a few of these would be brought to St. Paul in the trunk of somebody's car to finally make somebody's wish come true. I don't suppose they should stop by ACORN for a cup of coffee, huh? (For all 12 new readers very early in the Recount process a story circulated—possibly started by Coleman attorney Knaak—that certain ballots had been mishandled and been left insecure in someone's car trunk. Even Republican Governor Pawlenty shot this one down but in the Reichwing mind, weeds have strong roots.)

Scrap 2

As noted yesterday both camps TODAY will turn in something called "proposed findings of facts." Each side gets to point the court toward the evidence entered and emphasize certain bits and urge the court to skim over other evidence (like the other side's).

The MinnPost reports that a mini-version of this has been going on during the trial. Apparently each Friday both sides handed in some paperwork reviewing evidence (and maybe legal points as well; they too will figure in the final decision) from that week. That way the court has some running, intermediate sheets they can be drafting as they go along and not have to do it all in one massive effort here at the end.

Cool. Smart management breaking this into some smaller pieces.

But... as you might guess there has been a, um, CONTRAST between the 2 camps: During the course of the trial, weekly findings of fact have been filed with the court. They are not made public, and neither side has shared its documents with the media.

But we know this: The Franken side's findings have been far more voluminous than the Coleman's side. We hear that one week, the Franken side had nearly 100 pages of findings of facts; the Coleman team, four.

HA HA HA! I can't stop laughing...:-D

Scrap 3

The MN Progressive Project has a little something on the ECC from Washington DC (!) We were not the only ones watching the closing arguments. It seems the Democrats in the Senate also saw Hamilton vs. Friedberg and drew the same conclusions you did. So did the Majority Leader:

Friday, Senate Majority Leader Harry Reid (D-Nev.) issued a statement saying the decision of the three-judge panel should be respected ...

"The decision of the 3-judge panel"! Oh REALLY!? Harry, do you mean if the ECC lays it down the way a whole lot of us think they will, you and the Senate Democrats will NOT wait for an appeal to the MN Supremes? You will NOT insist on a certificate of election? Harry! Let me slap you on the back and see if that side of you offers any resistance...

News like this calls for a drink, maybe at the Laplander Lounge in New Narvik. Ole and Sven were there for St. Patrick's day getting really plastered and talking bar talk. Ole looks meditatively at the ice cubes floating in his Skyy & tonic and says, "You know, lions have sex 10 or 15 times every night." Sven slams his fist on bar in disgust. "Is that right? Damn, I yust joined the Elks."

PRE-miniscing Things Norm

Little things just keep showing up about Norm Coleman. Maybe it's anticipatory nostalgia—so soon he will disappear and no one will pay anymore attention, so they're "pre-miniscing" now instead of reminiscing later.

Two more items connected with the Coleman credit card database release.

1. When this first hit the news Coleman's attorneys (particularly Fritz Knaak) came out snarling about the secret service is investigating and these criminal hackers should go to jail and all that.

    Well, one of the heavy players in things hi-tech has weighed in. The Electronic Frontier Foundation legal arm has said as far as they can tell neither Adria Richards who first discovered the hole or the Wikileaks website did anything wrong and are not liable legally for anything. Am

I right that the EFF is a pretty sharp outfit on things like this? If so now the focus can go back to where the question should be: what were they THINKING on the Coleman tech team??!! Because this retention of credit card security numbers is still a MAJOR deal and if anybody's going to be arrested...

2. There is a little item that might deserve a gentle look. You know how the Reichwing has used the Christian fundamentalist churches as a source for "boots on the ground" and grass-roots fundraising?

Well, Joe Bodell at MN Progressive has eyeballed the famous Coleman database list of names, the 50,000+ withOUT the credit card info (that affected about 4,000). He finds what looks like a block of 20,000 names added en masse in September of 2007. The column header is notated "gopjew" and there are many names that have a Jewish-sounding flavor to them. (A Minnesota list that featured all sorts of names ending in "son" and "sen" could be described as having a lot of "Lutheran sounding" names.")

I say this carefully because I will NOT tolerate any anti-semitic CRAP being flung around. There's still WAY too much of that in the world and I won't give it any room at all.

But with that BIG caveat, this may be a sign of a parallel effort among the Republicans to use the Jewish community for funds and boots like they have with the fundys. The fact the list of 20K names came in all at once may be a glimpse of how these lists circulate. Finding out where it came from before Norm got it might be another piece of understanding and dismantling the gang...

Tuesday Morning Minnesota Media

Kevin Duchschere goes solo for the *Star Tribune* in an article that basically it's all up to the judges. The paper has been rather more pessimistic on the speed of the ECC decision and believes it may not come until April. That's OK, someone has to keep us from getting too giddy too soon. He quotes from Hamline University professor David Schultz (a frequent contributor to the I) for a fair reason to look for a longer waiting time:

> Schultz said that may not come until April.
>
> "The judges will have to be writing this opinion fully cognizant that there will be an appeal. They won't write it overnight," he said. "I'd even say, for these judges, it will be the most important decision they'll ever write. The pressure will be on them." *(Star Tribune)*

Not bad thinking and I agree. I want the ECC to get this right and get it tight. I just think they'll move faster than the "delay, delay" strategy than the Rethugs want.

May the luck of the Irish be with us so we get some developments soon. Hoping on a 4-leaf clover this will hold you with the latest from yust southeast of Lake Wobegon.

O'shalom.

More Ballots? More Money?
March 18, 2009

Comments: 180   Recs: 217   Tips: 212

As on Monday, yesterday saw no news from the Election Contest Court (ECC). The scraps and tidbits from around the web I tossed you yesterday you managed to make into 137 comments. This place IS full of political addicts! Until about 8:00 last night I really didn't think there would be a diary today—BUT it's OK! You're reading it now, so it's OK.

(Slow deep breath in...hold it...now slow exhale through the mouth. Whew! Gotta be careful around here and quick with medical advice or someone could go into tantric withdrawal...which has NOTHING to do with...stop that!)

Fall of St. Paul, Rising Mini-Apple

A weird phenom is happening in the Twin Cities. The *Pioneer Press* in St. Paul, which has shown signs of balance, journalism and dissemination of information (mostly thanks to Rachel Stassen-Berger's reporting) has fallen through the ice the last few days. Over the weekend they ran a stinky editorial of Coleman talking points. Yesterday their main story reprinted verbatim Manu Raju's Politico column, passing it off as news.

You Kossacks were already dismantling Raju's garbanzo beans yesterday in the comment string, noting his 11 references to Republicans on the Hill and only 4 to Democrats.

And Raju writes: "Top Republicans are encouraging Coleman to be as litigious as possible."

So there's your Re-thug stalling tactic confirmed. AND the Kos nation pulled up the roots of the funding behind Politico—another in the dreary string of wingnut money guys who are funding "Junior's" little project. (We have 8 years of proof that would fill the Grand Canyon that shows this doesn't work!)

But while the *Pioneer Press* paid $25 for services rendered and 10 more for the room, the *Star Tribune* (REALLY! I kid you not) the *Star Tribune* had an outburst of journalism. (They would have won the daily award just by showing up but they went further than that; ran up the score a bit. GREAT!)

In Friday's closing arguments attorney Kevin Hamilton of the Franken team cited 252 rejected absentee ballots they believe meet the ECC's criteria for strict compliance with the laws for voting absentee. Well, according to Doyle, Team Franken filed the details of the 252 with the ECC in written form on Saturday (busy beavers they are!) But not just the 252... but another 131! (Tuesday—presumably alongside their proposed "Findings of Fact" that were due from both sides—the Franken team submitted the Revised Standard Version of those 252 + 131 ballots.)

In identifying the 252 ballots last week, Franken lawyer Kevin Hamilton described them as having proven all of the requirements for counting. The additional ballots included Saturday (the 131) may lack some of those elements but were identified by Franken and admitted into evidence during the trial.

We're putting them all before the court for consideration," said Franken spokesperson Jess McIntosh. "We're directly asking them to count 252."

Those more marginal ballots could help Franken if the panel accepts a version of the Coleman argument that it use "common sense" in deciding which ballots to count, rather than a stricter interpretation of state statute. Such a ruling would allow the judges to count many of the ballots the Republican has identified that otherwise might remain rejected, and Franken's marginal ballots could be used to offset them.

Apparently about half of these 252 + 131 = 383 are from Franken counties and cities where Al's margin was better than 10 percentage points. In other words they are grape-picked (preparatory to making wine).

On the flip side Doyle reports about 1/3 of the Coleman 1,360 that THEY want the ECC to count are from areas where Norm's margin was better than 10 percentage points. In other words they are cherry-picked (preparatory to making Wisconsin Door County yucky sweet cherry wine... while singing that song title (better than the wine) from Tommy James and the Shondells—perhaps one of Norm's musical idols from those magical days of the late 60s.)

Now mind you these 1,360 Coleman-chosen rejected absentee ballots are the ones Team Franken ran through their spreadsheets like a Lightsabered flour sifter and ginned those 1,360 down to 6(!) valid ballots. Then too, 1/3 of 1,360 = only 453 ballots are from where Norm could reasonably hope to score some gains.

This points to the continuing weakness from the Coleman side in doing numbers. I'm no Nate Silver, TomTech, or VoteforAmerica but look:

Franken: 252 solid

47 solid-er (voters have stated they voted for AL)

131 Ralph's Pretty-Good Grocery Store ballots

Total: 430 ballots

To really understate it, suppose they go 75-25 for AL, or 322 to 108, net +214. Add Al's existing lead of +225 = +439.

On the other side: Coleman

453 congealed (not exactly solid)

907 iffy

Total 1,360 ballots

If Norm gets the 453 NOT by 10% points but by 20% points, that is, they break for him 60-40 that = 272 to 181 net +81 to Norm.

On the iffys, if Norm gets THOSE breaking his way 55-45, that is, by 10 percentage points then the iffys would be 499 to 408 net +91 to Norm.

And honey, 81 + 91 = 172 is still less than Franken's CURRENT lead.

Good move by the Franken Team but I really think it's basically insurance against a really stretched ruling by this Court. But good on them for thinking of it...just in case...

...Oh, and before leaving the *Star Tribune*, their comment had one patriot standing in defense of democracy and the law and fair elections whom the WineRev would be proud to go into the trenches with and slide my musket alongside his:

> *"I'm so sick of both Franken, Coleman, their Lawyers, Election officials..."*
>
> **Reply:** The election was a virtual tie and the balance of power in the U.S. senate hinges on the outcome. Should both sides give up? I love you guys pretending to be above it all. Let this process run it's course it's the only process we have on our books right now. I would expect both campaigns to fight fiercely for their guy. Even though I hate Al. *(allen2u at Star Tribune online)*

Well done, allen2u, well done sir! Huzzah, and a tip of the three-corner to you! I'll buy the first round at the tavern to explain to you why you are all wrong about Al. You buy me the second round and tell me why I'm all wrong about Al. And I'll flip you for the 3rd round for the honor of the Constitution at work to let us have the first 2 rounds!

You know, we really are going to have to practice for withdrawal someday soon. If it stays quiet, and the next diary does not appear on Thursday, you'll know why. Hope that'll hold you (especially the filings) because that's the latest from yust southeast of Lake Wobegon.

Shalom.

Starting a 12-Step Program
March 20, 2009

Comments: 209   Recs: 191   Tips: 229

> *The group shuffles in, takes chairs quietly. Everyone looks at each other sideways, then breaks eye contact, stares at floor. Finally one brave soul takes a deep breath and steps to the front. Everyone else sighs secretly in relief as the standee says,*
>
> *"Hi. My name is (your name).*
>
> *The group responds with mostly genuine enthusiasm,*
>
> *"Hi (your name)!"*
>
> *"Um... OK, here goes. I've been reading WineRev."*
>
> *Entire group applauds.*
>
> *"I've been clean one day."*
>
> *Another round of applause...*

Holy cow! I came back last night to look over the Wednesday diary and found 40 MORE Comments—the bulk of them posted Thursday.

But then e-mails!? People dropping little messages saying I could at least post SOMETHING (one suggestion was to do a WineRev treatment "The sun rose in the east"... over the MN Senate recount. Well, yes it did but...)

Another made a truly tender and utterly sincere inquiry after my physical health (4th floor ICU for 7 hours, but I finally convinced them it was only a flesh wound!... NOT! I kid, kid.)

Oh and no I was not abandoning you (as someone put it).

It's just there really was NOTHING happening. Zero. Zip. Mitte midagi! The cobwebs grew up on all the media sites because there was no news from the ECC and until there is the news will be scarce. And there's no need to emulate the blond pole-dancers on Faux Noise and breathlessly pout out the latest twisted brain-plaque scrapings from McConnell or John-90%-is-not-a-high-enough-tax Boehner (What a maroon!)

What News There Be

And there actually is, just a little. On Thursday Coleman filed an answer to a request for summary judgment filed by the Nauen group.

Coleman (ironically) objected to 2 voters because they failed to meet the court's requirements for strict compliance with absentee voting law.

Katie Kaszynski is a MN absentee voter and college student in Illinois. They question if a) she is registered, b) her signature looks a LOT like her mother's c) the date Mom signed as a witness is several days after the ballot itself was signed so Mom could not have been present "witnessing" the signing.

Tempest Moore [really; that's her name. Hmmmm... The granddaughter (sequel of a sequel) of "Stormy" by the Classics IV?] goes to college in Chicago. Team Coleman claims a) her witness did not register to vote until election day and the absentee ballot is dated late October, b) the ballot date and witness date are both Oct. 28 but the Ramsey County "date received" stamp is Oct. 27, and c) Tempest apparently misspelled her own name on the certificate card.

Coleman's side is not being petulant here [and certainly not petillant here; that would be the very slight, tongue-tickling effervescence found a delightful, light and softly fruity white vinho verde from Portugal (about $7)—I expect both words descend from a Latin root having something to do with the tongue; after all a petulant child may well stick out their tongue.] Actually Coleman's team here is on pretty solid ground.

In fact, even though this is a defensive effort for Coleman (keeping Franken from adding votes, rather than going on offense and Coleman either adding his own votes or pulling some off of Franken's pile) it's a good one, one they should have been doing all along, every single day of their case.

And I'll give 'em a point or two for table turning. They've been backed into a corner by Franken and the Court insisting on a strict compliance standard. Now they get to knock down 2 ballots on just that ground UNLESS (as they point out in making the motion) the court wants to move toward a "substantial compliance" (Coleman's only hope) standard. Indeed they even cite the Feb. 13 order as being the pivotal reason the court needs to strike down these 2 ballots.

Well played, Team Coleman. Too little. Too late. Shoulda, coulda... but solid lawyering here.

Now fair warning again. If there IS NO NEWS I won't post, but if something breaks you'll get it on the diaries and I'll have at it the next morning. Take it easy with all the latest from yust southeast of Lake Wobegon.

Shalom.

Just Waitin'
March 21, 2009

Comments: 206   Recs: 134   Tips: 149

Talk Radio with ...Joe Friedberg?

On Wednesday KFAN radio here in town took a time out from all things basketball and all things sport and had an interview with Joe Friedberg, Norm Coleman's lead attorney. (On the other hand maybe it was still sports, changing over to boxing?)

The heart of the conversation was this:

> ROSENBAUM: Joe, are you done?
>
> FRIEDBERG: Yes (laughing), I'm done.
>
> ROSENBAUM: Let me ask you in a different way. Is Norm done?
>
> FRIEDBERG: Well, I think that we've been trying this case with the appeal record in mind, and that's where we're going, and it's going to be a very quick appeal, and then I'll know whether or not it worked.
>
> ROSENBAUM: Well, when you say quick appeal, are you confident that you are going to lose the case in front of the three-judge panel? By losing the case, I mean Norm ends up with less votes.
>
> FRIEDBERG: I think that's probably correct that Franken will still be ahead and probably by a little bit more. But our whole argument was a Constitutional argument, and it's an argument suitable for the Minnesota Supreme Court, not for the trial court. So we'll see whether we were right or not. *(quoted at MinnPost)*

That is Coleman lead attorney Friedberg admitting a) Franken is ahead and will likely be ahead-er b) they were playing for an appeal all along.

Now how can you tell a political campaign/legal case has said something smelly? They issue a CLARIFICATION! ("What the President really MEANT to say was..." the mantra of the last 8 years)

> On Friday, Friedberg issued a statement of "clarification" stressing that he believes Coleman's legal strategy has merit.
>
> "I feel confident that if the court proceeds with wisdom and with decisions based on the facts, and on the law, that we will succeed in our case," Friedberg said in the statement. *(WCCO)*

People who know Joe Friedberg say that "aw shucks" folksiness is genuine and that he is a really likable fellow. So could this interview and clarification be an assertion of that? Could it also be Joe distancing himself from the smell of the Coleman Legal Team dairy barn where all the livestock have the farts? Recall Joe was quick to his feet to distance himself from the rest in the Pam Howell lack of discovery fiasco. The Court agreed and was careful to swing the sanction club PAST Friedberg onto the rest (but close enough Joe could feel the breeze).

I wonder if this could also be an indicator that when this goes to appeal Friedberg will NOT be arguing it. After all the appeal is a rather different hearing. Five MN Supreme Court justices in a half circle taking no guff off nobody and sharper than hell themselves.

(Back in December they heard a Motion argued by Roger Magnuson for Team Norm. Magnuson hasn't been heard from since but he was on the Bush 2000 legal gang along with Ben Ginsberg. About 2 lines in Magnuson invoked Florida. Assoc. Justice Paul Anderson right there said, "This is NOT Florida" with a look that boiled the varnish on Magnuson's podium. Sort of like finding out early on, "May it please the court?" "It may or may not...").

You have to be very sharp and quite nimble and I'm not sure Joe Friedberg fits the bill.

Rampant Speculation: What We Do Best at Daily Kos

Yesterday in the comment string was a nice set of questions to ponder. While we wait for news from the ECC, what do you think?

> **Beyond The ECC** Not much discussion about what happens after the ECC judges come out of their self-imposed isolation and issue their rulings, so I thought I would get it started here with a few questions tossed out into the ether for anyone who wants to gaze into their crystal ball and predict the Senatorial future:
>
> 1. Will Coleman appeal (or if you want me to be non-partisan here, will Franken appeal)?
>
> 2. Will the ECC instruct Governor Pawlenty to issue a certificate to the winner, or will they simply declare who had the most votes?
>
> 3. What courts, State and/or Federal, could appeals wind their way through (up through SCOTUS?), and what sort of time frames are we talking about?
>
> 4. Will Governor Pawlenty issue the necessary certificate to the "winner" based on the ECC findings, or will he hold out until all appeals are exhausted?
>
> 5. If Pawlenty refuses to issue the certificate based on the ECC ruling and declares he will wait until all appeals are exhausted, how many days (or hours) will it take before Minnesotans march on the Capitol with pitch folks and torches demanding they be given a second Senator?
>
> Inquiring minds (of political junkies) want to know! *(Doctor Who)*

For myself:

I think the loser appeals (and if this is AL, I will be in serious doubt about the sanity of the legal system). Appeal is straight to the MN Supreme Court and must be filed in 10 days or the ECC decision is FINAL. If filed then the trial records have 15 days max to get to the Supremes (so they can read up on it).

Apparently loser has to post a bond equal to at least costs incurred so far. Can Team Norm afford this?

ECC will pronounce who has the most votes. When the MN Supreme Court denied Franken's request for an Election Certificate they used some language that left the door open to the Certificate being issued at THIS point, BEFORE an appeal to the Supremes.

Majority leader Harry Reid last Friday used the phrase "respect the decision of the 3 judge panel"— again ignoring the appeal route (or at least not mentioning it.) Does this hint the Senate (Democrats) might consider an ECC decision good enough for them?

I think the federal courts will wait until the end of any state appeals. THEN EITHER the loser files in federal district court, OR, if the MN Supreme Court took the appeal and ruled—I believe such a state supreme court ruling CAN go directly to the US Supremes. But the pressure on Sec. of State Ritchie and Gov. Pawlenty to issue a certificate to the winner of the court cases in MN would be immense. If they would, or if the Senate seats AL on the strength of the rulings apart from a certificate, no federal court, even the Supremes, will touch it, on the basis of Article 1 of the US Constitution.

Pawlenty has been carefully ambiguous in his wording that I've seen (like any politician.) He didn't sign a certificate when Franken was certified the count leader because Coleman filed an Election Contest. Right move by the Gov and an easy call. (May have accounted for Norm filing as soon as he could to forestall anything else.)

He has said he will wait for the appeals to run their course BUT he has been notably silent on whether he means STATE appeals or FEDERAL appeals. State appeals he can sit tight and proper. But after the MN Supremes would rule he really has to make a call. He might hold out for a little until Franken files for a writ of mandamus from the court FORCING him to sign. That way he could go to the Reichving pleading, "Those damn liberal activist judges MADE me sign..." Personally I don't think he'll wait that long. He'll sign after the MN Supremes rule.

Nothing in the news media to report. I hope this will hold you.

That's the latest from yust Southeast of Lake Wobegon.

Shalom.

MN-Senate NOT Events
March 23, 2009

Comments: 52   Recs: 126   Tips: 121

Franken leads +225 (+21 and +14 of the "Nauen 61" the Election Contest Court has ordered into the "Ready to Count" pile at the Secretary of State's office; all these voters have indicated they voted for Franken) = +260.

The waiting continues, not because Coleman is stalling but because the court is deciding—a different flavor of waiting.

DK   Every week of delay in seating Al Franken is time lost that can never be recovered. It is becoming clear that the objective is delay. *(livoshl)*

Like an expectant mother 6 days past her due date, all Minnesota waits upon the Election Contest Court. No news but our good thoughts, wishes for karma, and prayers if you've got 'em rest upon them.

Cynthia Dizikes of MinnPost in DC reports Al Franken will be in her town on Wednesday to do what politicians love to do, but also what any real mensch deserves: receive an award.

Al is going to be honored by the USO for doing his level best to fill the shoes of Bob Hope; he's been entertaining the troops.

Good on you, Senator-elect!

That's the latest from yust southeast of Lake Wobegon.

Shalom.

Snips/Waiting
March 24, 2009

Comments: 76   Recs: 114   Tips: 75

Media Reporting on Media I

The UpTake blog posted a tantalizing little link to, of all places, CBS News! They have an unnamed source from the Franken campaign and this (possibly informed?) speculation:

> A source close to Franken tells CBS News' Mary Hager that "the court will virtually certainly rule in his favor, and he will likely add significantly to the margin, maybe up to 500 votes or so," at which point Coleman will likely appeal to the Minnesota Supreme Court.
>
> The source says that Minnesota state law allows the Supreme Court to drop all other business to quickly hear and deliberate on Coleman's appeal.
>
> "Give a week to prepare briefs, a day of oral argument, and a few days for a ruling. Then they will probably call for a certification. At that point, perhaps mid-April, he comes to DC," the source says... *(CBS News, quoted at The UpTake)*

"A source close to the Franken campaign..." Hmmm. This has been a tightly run, on-message effort so it's a bit unlikely this is accidental or someone talking out of channels. Is it perhaps slightly MORE likely this is deliberate? A controlled play?

"...margin up to 500 votes or so..." certainly plausible.

"law allows Supreme Court to drop all other business..." That's new. Any legal eagle like to pry loose the likely relevant statute? Or is this within the discretion of the Court of call a recess in the legal review of pollution standards applying to commercial lutefisk processing plants to take this up?

"The week of briefs, orals, and few days to ruling...certificate" seems to fit other thoughts around here.

Sooooo...speculate away!

Media Reporting on Media II

Jay Weiner at MinnPost reports Esme Murphy of WCCO raised the issue in her blog whether either side should appeal the ECC ruling. As a non-scientific, non-statistical sample of nothing, 109 people commented in her blog and the vast majority of them said "Hang it up NORM." So there's at least SOME sentiment to get this over with by having the former senator BE former. And also a report of a FaceBook page saying goodbye Norm with 2,000 (!) subscribers (or however that works). Maybe the anti-Norm folk are more blog- and FaceBook-savvy, but there's some sort of reading of Minnesota sentiment.

Media Reporting on Media III: Pathetic

Remember in Young Frankenstein when the doctor ordered himself locked in the cell with the monster because he was going to show him love or die trying? Gene Wilder fights down his terror when he finally points at Peter Boyle and says, "Hi, handsome!" Smart, sophisticated, man about town, puttin' on the ritz.

And why are Kossacks smart, sophisticated, and puttin' on the ritz around the Lamestream media? Because Pat Doyle of the Star Tribune has a story TODAY about Al Franken getting a USO award—which was in diary 109! AND he is reporting the FEC ruling allowing both camps to do more fund-raising for their legal costs—which was in my diary several days ago!!

You come here to read these franken-nutso diaries and leave several steps ahead of the game. HAH! Way to go Orange readers! Buff those nails, put on your dancin' shoes, and show 'em how it's done everyone!

And WHY is the media covering the media? Because they have nothing else to cover.

So that's the latest from yust southeast of Lake Wobegon. Hoping for news.

Shalom.

Waiting
March 25, 2009

Comments: 48 *Recs:* 73 *Tips:* 59

Comment from an Interested Party

Norm Coleman was in DC yesterday for lunch among the rancid cream of America's elite (hat tip to HST for that phrase), otherwise known as congressional Republicans. The Capitol is right across the street from the US Supreme Court. When asked over lunch if he thought how far his ECC case could go, Coleman gestured and said, "I'm not anticipating, at this point, being across the street."

Uh oh! Using the Republican Reverse Projector Ray we can see Norm is saying he IS hoping/planning this whole election court case DOES end up at the US Supreme Court.

Now for once this may be wishful thinking. You need GROUNDS to get across the street to the US Supremes, as well as 4 of them to agree to hear the case. Now there is the stink of the "STAR" lineup of the Reichwing: Scalia and Thomas for sure, Alito damn likely. Roberts? I think there is at least some question whether he would join the first 3, especially the tighter and narrower the decision of both the ECC and any appellate ruling by the MN Supreme Ct.

Make of it what you will.

News of the Dumb

My sign-off line "from yust southeast of Lake Wobegon" might move out of the blogosphere toward a DUMB reality. MN State Sen. Tarryl Clark (D from St. Cloud; showing in Michele Bachmann's district there are enough Democrats to elect an "anti-American" state senator) has decided economic catastrophe, crumbling health care, deteriorating infrastructure and state support for schools is too short an agenda for the MN Legislature. She has introduced a bill to combine 2-1/2 counties into one for "efficiency" but mostly so it can have a working name of "Lake Wobegon County."

This is silly, and not in a joking way, it's just dumb.

(For tax dollars spent on fun, years ago Reader's Digest noted the state bird of Iowa is the goldfinch. The state flower of Kansas is the sunflower. One lazy summer afternoon the Kansas Legislature passed a resolution declaring the goldfinch to be a "public nuisance" and mailed it to Des Moines. In an equally relaxed mood a few weeks later the Iowa legislature declared the sunflower to be a "noxious weed" and mailed that to Topeka... Now that makes me smile. Tarryl Clark makes me wince.)

So we wait. That's the littlest and least-est from yust southeast of Lake Wobegon.

Shalom.

A Lawyer You'll Love
March 26, 2009

Why Is It Taking So Long?

We are 9 days since the attorneys filed "proposed Findings of Fact" with the ECC and 13 days since closing arguments.

One thing that occurs to me is the fact this was a "bench" trial rather than a jury trial. Now I may be all wet here and you lawyer types can stand over there with Gatorade coolers and dump on me in a minute, but here's my thinking.

Any trial includes 2 elements: facts and law. We expect/know the ECC will produce BOTH "Findings of Fact" and "Conclusions of Law" as parts 1 & 2 of their decision (which will be part 3).

In a jury trial the jury does the fact part. They retire to the jury room, talk over testimony, weigh witness credibility *(Henry Fonda: "The old man COULDN'T have gotten to the door as quick as he said he did." 12 Angry Men; fabulous, tight drama & all star cast!)* examine exhibits, and critique the lawyers.

Meanwhile, AT THE SAME TIME, the judge is boning up on the pleadings, checking citations the lawyers threw into the case, researching precedents, case law, and certain statutes that may figure in an indirect way.

That allows not only for drama but a bit of speed when the word buzzes through the marble corridors from the bailiff Louis Nizer (!): "The jury returns." Everyone assembles for the "Findings of Fact." Jury Foreman Mark Slackmeyer, called away from his radio host chores on Doonesbury 100.7 for jury duty, stands up and reads carefully from a sheet, "In the case of the People of the United States vs. Karl Rove, Donald Rumsfeld, John Yoo, Dick Cheney, David Addington, Doug Feith, Alberto Gonzales, Condi Rice, and the Former First Puppet, on the charge of TREASON, we the jury find the defendants individually and collectively guilty as charged...that's guilty! Guilty! GUILTY!!"[18]

Then it's up to Judge Roy Bean to apply the Conclusions of Law, which will be ready to roll: "I sentence you each to swing at dawn tomorrow!" *(And there is much rejoicing...).*

BUT in a bench trial like the ECC, the judge(s) need to do BOTH functions in series rather than in parallel... I think. Courtroom types, does that make sense, at least in part? Yes they want good orders and a tight, non-reversible ruling, but would this be part of it too? Just asking... or do I now get to walk around drenched?

---

18   *For those too young to remember, this comment refers to a famous Watergate-related Doonesbury comic strip by Garry Trudeau, dated May 29, 1973., which is available at Wikipedia as of this writing.*

Retrospective Recount and Fun Gossip

We are all waiting, of course, and writers are trying to fill the space. Some lunatics with a laptop like Winerev serialize their novel. Jay Weiner of the MinnPost acted like a REAL REPORTER (*Lamestream media take notes; lookin' at you, Star Tribune!*) and tracked down a man named Terry O'Toole, an 87-year-old St. Paul Irishman and as rock-ribbed a Democrat as you'll ever meet. O'Toole came to room 300 in the Judiciary Building for the last couple weeks of the ECC trial for professional and historical reasons.

The professional part is O'Toole is a retired trial lawyer and still enjoys the "game." He is also personal friends with that kid who was lead attorney for Coleman, 72-year-old Joe Friedberg. (Now Friedberg is a Democrat too and said on the public record he did not/would not vote for Norm Coleman.) But O'Toole is a Democrat's Democrat:

> When (Franken attorney Kevin) Hamilton completed his closing argument 12 days ago, O'Toole lifted himself out of his seat. Cane in hand, he marched over to the swinging door that separated the lawyers' well from the public seating area.
>
> "You did an excellent job, and I should know," he told Hamilton. "I practiced law for 50 years. I've seen a lot of closing arguments, and that was one of the best." *(MinnPost)*

WOW! But there's more!

O'Toole is a Democrat who was still active in the early '90s when an East Coast transplant wanted to run for mayor of St. Paul. O'Toole and Ramsey County (St. Paul) Democratic chair Mike McLaughlin helped launch Norm Coleman to his first win in public office.

In 1996 Norm decided to make...the SWITCH to the Dark Side. He called in both O'Toole and McLaughlin to break the news to them:

> "He was a wild, anti-Vietnam protester from the East and he's going to become a Republican?" O'Toole said, reliving the moment of Coleman's transformation. "I couldn't believe it."
>
> And O'Toole and McLaughlin made it a point to be in attendance days later when Coleman formally and publicly announced his party switch.
>
> "What are you two doing here?" Coleman asked them, as O'Toole recalls.
>
> "McLaughlin and I both said—almost simultaneously—'We're both Irish. We have an old habit. When a friend dies, we go to his wake.' " *(MinnPost)*

Hah!

AND there's more: O'Toole was *part of the 1963 governor's recount won by 91 votes* statewide. That mess led directly to the enacting of the present recount law we are watching play out.

Hope that will hold you as here yust southeast of Lake Wobegon we wait for the ice to break up and the ECC to order, rule, and decide.

Shalom.

MN-Senate Speculation, with Drinking
March 27, 2009

Comments: 55   *Recs:* 76   *Tips:* 73

Republican Party, Democratic Party, UpTake Party

Things are REALLY slow when the biggest news on the MN Senate Recount is the UpTake Meet & Greet party. Another gathering of maybe 40 political junkies (BillW, Grace Kelly, Jack, EdBradley7, MidContinentalRift, woebegon gal, liebshuist & Christopher, MsGeek, TomTech, and 51stWardPrecinctCaptain in from Chicago, to name some) along with Mike, Noah, Jason & (ahh!) Jennifer from The UpTake. A large time had by all.

General table-hopping consensus: a court order from the ECC to count X number of ballots—which would take 4 days (per the Sec of State's office to round them up from around the state). At the same time the ECC readies its final decision with a couple spots left blank: "Based on the count the candidate with the most legally cast ballots is _____; by a margin of _____."

Less likely but still possible: The ECC decides that the number of outstanding ballots yet to be counted that meet all the criteria for being count is LESS THAN 225 (Franken's current edge). Therefore the case is MOOT and over, per the certified count from January 5.

Unanimous question in the room: "When are they going to rule?" This sounded much easier to take over burgers, beer, and wine, so on your behalf we asked it over (munch) and over (gulp) and over (sip). So we here at ground zero feel the progressive nation's pain and we did our best for HOURS to address it, drown it, and guzzle it... on your behalf... you're welcome.

New Media 1

Paul Schmelzer at Minnesota Independent answers something asked around here in early January, when the new Congress took over.

Franken can't expect to chip away at the debt through Senate back pay, WCCO's Pat Kessler reports. Yesterday, the Secretary of the Senate's office told him that back pay is no longer possible and Minnesota's next senator will get paid — at a rate of about $464 a day — starting on the day he's sworn in. Kessler estimates that whoever wins will miss out on around $37,000. And counting.

Some other tidbits on the sniping increasing in DC over Franken being seated, and that Mitch McConnell is being the infected boil on the butt of the Senate:

> "Republicans have made it clear they will hold this Senate seat hostage in order to pursue their political agenda—at the hefty expense of Minnesota having full representation in Congress," says DSCC spokesman Eric Schultz...McConnell predicted Minnesota won't have a second seated senator for months, stating that Republicans will use a Bush v. Gore-style defense in state and possibly federal court to appeal on Coleman's behalf. *(MN Independent)*

Months, huh? Mitch, as in all things Recount connected: "We'll see" (you sanctimonious, Alabama carpetbagger of Kentucky horse droppings...)

New Media 2

Eric Black at MinnPost has an interesting think piece revolving around "the presiding officer of the (US) Senate" which may be VP Joe Biden, but more likely Majority Leader Harry Reid. Black reads a bit farther into MN Statute 209, by which the ECC is formed and will rule on the question "who got the most legal votes."

> "Evidence on any other points specified in the notice of contest,... must be taken and preserved by the judge trying the contest... After the time for appeal has expired, or in case of an appeal, after the final judicial determination of the contest, upon application of either party to the contest, the court administrator of the district court shall promptly certify and forward the files and records of the proceedings, with all the evidence taken, to the presiding officer of the Senate..." *(MinnPost)*

I think what Black is driving at is this: after the ECC rules, and Norm takes his 3-0 field goal loss to the MN Supreme Ct. and loses there (5-0), ALL the evidence/exhibits of the case go straight to the Senate. They will be on the spot to decide their membership (per Article 1 of the Constitution).

Since by LAW all this is now in the hands of the Senate doesn't that make it even tougher for the losing side to file anything in federal court? It gives such a court ample grounds to deny even hearing the case "since it's in the hands of the Senate"/ we defer to the separation of Powers/branches etc.?

OK, lawyers in the house, your chance to educate the rest of us...

I'll be leaving for the early shift at the shop shortly. That's the latest and the least-est from yust southeast of Lake Wobegon.

Shalom.

Waiting
March 29, 2009

Comments: 45   *Recs:* 61   *Tips:* 71

Sixteen days since final arguments were heard and not a peep from the Election Contest Court (ECC). All we have is our speculations and wonderings.

Intelligent Journalistic Ponderings (you know, the complete opposite of the Lamestream Media and the Faux Noise pole-dancing company)

Jay Weiner writes for the MinnPost and has been covering the trial in depth for weeks. He has a think piece up at the link below and sketches out some scenarios:

a. The ECC is being picky in looking at anywhere from 300 to 1,300 absentee ballots. (They were quite strict in their rulings so far). Having picked the nits down to the last bit of navel lint they *issue an order to count* X number of ballots...these (and they note every one of them, county by county, name by name.)

The Secretary of State's office would do the counting and they have stated they need four days to collect the ballots from around the state and get to it.

This much has been expected for some time so there is some mystery why this HASN'T been ordered already.

b. Because of the (apparent) delay could a larger ruling/decision be in the works? The ECC could order a), above *AND also add some decisions* on:

- the Minneapolis 133 ballots that went missing (favoring Franken by net +46) but for whom we have voter sign-in logs and machine tapes

- the alleged duplicate/double counted/never actually shown to have happened/Pam Howell testimony ballots that might favor Franken +100 net

- some equal-protection issues

Since this would be more work they need longer (although it's getting rather longish for this scenario, I think).

c. The ECC could order A) and *see how they come out.* If Franken's lead grows to say, 500, and THEN rule on the Mpls 133/duplicate 100 *when it wouldn't make any difference.*

Does seem a bit out of character for the court.

d. The ECC might have the Nauen 35 and the 12 others from early on counted. Then they *nerve themselves to accept* Franken's Motion to Dismiss from 3/6 and say "Coleman did not prove his case. Failed burden of proof, presented insufficient evidence, etc." No need to count any more ballots because Coleman didn't give us any reason to...

The political fallout would be noisy but judges/courts often ignore political noise.

e. *Is the ECC divided?* A 2-1 majority is all that is needed to decide the case but they have been unanimous so far and a 3-0 decision strengthens their decision against reversal on appeal. But what if they can't agree? What if one of them really wants to, say, throw out the Minneapolis 133 and the other 2 want them kept in?

Here the reason for the delay might be simple/complex debate and negotiation. I still think they want to be unanimous on all points if it is at all possible (not the least of which is that if, say, the MN Supreme Court would reverse their ruling on some points the case would be sent BACK to the ECC for further trial—and I think Hayden, Reilly and Marben do NOT want that. They're as tired of this as we are...)

Franken Sighting

The Senator-elect has kept a low profile for virtually all of the Recount, just an odd appearance here and there, no real press conferences. But last night he did attend a Young Democrats (DFL as the party is known in MN) deal and said:

> "We will be seated," Al Franken told a gathering of young Democrats in Minnesota today. "And by 'we,' I mean me." *(Minnesota Independent)*

That's all we got right now from yust southeast of Lake Wobegon.

Shalom.

April 2009

Ruling from the Court, on Skis?
April 1, 2009

Comments: 145   Recs: 235   Tips: 220

The Election Contest Court handed down a ruling midafternoon calling on the Secretary of State to collect, open, and count about 400 ballots. Deadline for gathering, 4/6; Count on 4/7.

More, much more, now that there's something to write about...

Just reading DailyKos last night and thought to myself:

NY-20 Events v. 1.0

Its been 232 years since the smoke cleared from the battlefields near Saratoga, but another battle in Upper NY looks to be entrenching. Democrat Scott Murphy and Republican Jim Tedisco are feeling their way towards Freeman's Farm and Daniel Morgan is gobbling like a turkey to rally his sharpshooters. In the same way Murphy has called in his own sharpshooter, a DC attorney named Marc Elias...

AAAaaaaaauuughhhhh!

Somebody stop me!...

DK   And let somebody else winerev New York 20. *(vets74)*

DK   "Winerev" is now a verb! winerev \'wɪn-rev(v). to report, analyze, and mock any election recount effort through internet blogging. winerevved, winerevving, winerever *(Word Alchemy)*

DK   That's when you know you've really arrived. *(Heart of the Rockies)*

DK   And an active verb at that! *(Leftovers)*

DK   Transitive, as opposed to the Ginz's intransigent. *(NM Ward Chair)*

ECC Order: Lets Count Some Ballots!

The news broke at 3:11 on the UpTake Twitter, and Kossack Rieux was up with a diary by 3:40. The Great Orange One himself put up a front-page story *(man! Who does he know!? He acts like it's HIS website or something!)* within the hour.

The Election Contest Court issued a 32-page ruling on rejected absentee ballots. Counties and cities have until **noon on Monday, April 6** to get the specified absentee ballots to the Secretary of State's office.

(The SoS's office had already informed everyone they would need 4 days from an order to do this, so this interval is just a bit longer than expected.)

THEN (in the words of ABowers13) on that great, countin' up morning, Tuesday, April 7, 9:30 a.m. the Sec. of State's people will open and count the LAST BALLOTS OF THE MN SENATE RACE AND RECOUNT. (Must-See TV at its finest!)

How many? The Court ordered 400 sent in BUT they carefully reserved the right to review each of these and decide exactly which ones will make the cut. Both sides will again be able to challenge ballots (but for the opening of the 933 on Jan. 3, only 1 was challenged, and that was withdrawn).

Factors favoring Franken:

Apparently these 400 INCLUDE several of the "Nauen 61" and 12 ordered counted early on in the trial by summary judgment. Marc Elias at the presser afterwards said this would be about 50 or 51 of the ballots. YET virtually all the "Nauen" voters have stated publicly they voted for Franken AND the 12 of the summary judgment were brought by the Franken team.

OK, AND a first take on the counties where these 400 are coming from shows 119 from Hennepin county (Minneapolis), 43 from Ramsey County (St. Paul) and 40 from St. Louis County (Duluth). Franken carried in all 3 (especially Duluth city) BUT there are strongly red suburbs in both Hennepin & Ramsey, so there's probably an edge there but not overwhelming. And now a later reports says only about 20 of these ballots are from the city of Minneapolis proper (Franken turf) with the remainder from the various 'burbs (a mixed lot). Likely the spreadsheet mavens TomTech and/or Vote for America will have some specifics shortly (no word on Venn diagrams).

From an UpTake blogger:

> The court order reaffirms the court's position that evidence needed to be presented for ballots to be opened. Since the Franken team presented evidence, with a few exceptions by the Coleman team, the vast majority are probably Franken votes. *(bungalowmike at The UpTake)*

And now, a little fun with math. Franken leads by +225. Let's add the 50 from the Nauen group and the summary judgment = +275.

This leaves 350 (assuming the ECC orders all of them in; no guarantee there). So, for Coleman to overtake Franken's +275, he would need 276 NET out of 350 (yeah, right!). Take it one step further: 350 − 276 = 74. If Coleman and Franken EACH split these 74 down the middle (and assuming NO votes for Barkely, Lizard, Niemackl, etc.), that's 37 each.

So in the counting, assuming the 50 are in, if Franken gets to 38 (or what you'll hear 38 + 50 = 88) his lead is insurmountable. 87 ties it... and there are 87 counties in MN...one vote/ county...every vote counts indeed!

Why Did It Take Until Now?

One clue is on page 5 of the order:

> At the close of trial Contestant and Contestee gave the Court their respective lists of identified rejected absentee ballots the parties believed should be opened and counted. (Coleman 1,360; Franken 430)
>
> Upon the Court's initial review it became apparent that the parties spreadsheet identification of the relevant exhibits were inadequate and unreliable. This required the Court to complete an exhaustive review of all the records and documents submitted by either party throughout the course of the entire trial.
>
> 19,181 pages of filings, pleadings, motions & memoranda
>
> 1,717 individual exhibits admitted into evidence
>
> 142 witness examinations
>
> The trial evidence in 3 ring binders came to over 21 feet of paper *(Order for Delivery of Ballots to Office of the Minnesota Secretary of State for Review by the Court)*

There were a lot of pixels spilled around here about the contrast between the Coleman spreadsheets and the Franken ones (favoring Al) but apparently the Court was not so impressed by either side. OTOH plowing through 21 feet of evidence in about 17 days is pretty steady work I'd say, although the lawyers on these boards could say more about that.

Bad News for Norm?

Reading through the Order complete with crystal ball, tea leaves, goat entrails, Ouija board pointer, and Magic 8 Ball, there may be some straws in the wind blowing toward Team Norm... actually, they are hay bales caught in a twister hurling toward Norm's Team. If these are hints of what the final decision will look like... on pages 6–7 the Court notes,

> Each party knew or should have known the scope of the Court's review by February 13, before Contestants rested their case. *(Order for Delivery of Ballots...)*

Or in other words, "Norm, your team should have known 3 weeks in you were in the ice-fishing hut without beer AND you should have changed your approach right then..."

Further on page 7 the Court notes the countdown in Coleman's numbers from 4,800 to the 1,300 which was left at the end and then says,

> This number, however, was contingent upon the Court making certain presumptions regarding whether an absentee ballots was legally cast... Contestants' presumptions are not reasonable in light of the small number of absentee ballots at issue... and the fact that these absentee ballots have been already carefully reviewed as many as 3 times by state and local election officials. *(Order for Delivery of Ballots...)*

Not quite, "You are wasting our time" but close... AND a GREAT affirmation of the election crews across the state! Yay Court![19]

And if "the devil is in the details" how about this great shot from page 10: "Contestants themselves recognized the importance of ensuring that only registered voters are afforded the right to cast a ballot."

Since an awful lot of Norm's effort was on "substantial compliance" with the law (instead of strict compliance) in order to get in as many rejected absentee ballots as possible, well, this stuff on page 10 and footnote 32 is a prime case of "Petard, meet hoist!"

What Was NOT Said

ECC did NOT rule/order or say a word about: the Minneapolis 133 ballots lost (which Norm would like to get thrown out, reducing Franken's lead by 46) or the alleged duplicate/double-counting issue (which Coleman claims would move things toward him by 100 or so—but offered no solid evidence this actually happened). Of course now that they've finished wading through the ballots and other evidence to come up with this Order they can take on the rest of the case in fairly short order, I would think (but that's just me). Needless to say the Court could rule on these at any time, or wait for the ballots to be counted Tuesday, or put them all in the final decision. We'll see.

Reactions

Marc Elias for Team Franken phoned in a presser from DC. He nicely kept using the term "former senator Coleman" with some frequency. He got really pointed in saying the Coleman team had their chance to conform their case to the Feb. 13 rulings *and chose not to do so.* They just complained about it. When asked if this was a win for Franken he graciously called the ruling a win for the people of Minnesota, and that this entire process has affirmed MN's election system as among the best in the country.

Ben Ginsberg's presser was about what you'd expect: "the Court is wrong," the decision/order is on that "needs to be fixed on appeal."

Jay Weiner quotes Ginsberg:

> "the court has reached an unprincipled decision ... the court was subsumed with its own logic ... We believe the court is wrong in their entire standards of review ... We just think they're wrong to sweep the problems of this election under the rug." *(quoted at MinnPost)*

Yet even Ben the Ginz had to admit this makes things a "much longer shot" for Coleman. When asked about an appeal to the federal courts (after the MN Supreme Ct., or starting a federal case at the district level) Ginsberg was interestingly in a strict, "No comment" mode...Hmmm.

---

19   Footnote (32): See Feb. 4, 2009 @ 68 (acknowledging that "[Contestants] are not trying to get unregistered voter's votes counted"); Feb. 12 @ 148 (representing that: "[Contestants'] view is that a voter being registered is an absolute requirement.") Contestants' counsel recognized this fundamental requirement prior to the issuance of the Court's Feb. 13, 2009 Order."

Wednesday Morning Minnesota Media

As has been the case since the case went into court Jay Weiner has the best write up by far, including these sweet words:

> (Ginsberg) demeaned (the Order) because all the calculations for Coleman now can only be public relations and legal ones. If there were ever a doubt on the numerical calculations, it ended today. They all add up for Franken. *(MinnPost)*

Pioneer Press looked good because Rachel Stassen-Berger came in with a comprehensive story that focused on the Minnesota angle of the recount, complete with voter quotes and quotes from the court, and laying out how we got here:

> "The election contest is a civil action, and the burden is on the party seeking relief to introduce evidence to the Court sufficient to meet its burden of proof. ... The court gave both parties every opportunity to meet this burden."
>
> The judges had said they would need proof the voters were registered, that they voted only by absentee, had submitted absentee ballot applications, appeared to have registered witnesses and properly completed and signed their ballot envelopes.
>
> Coleman's attorneys did not submit such meticulous evidence. During his week-long case, Franken did.
>
> Ballots from both men's lists are included in the judges' Tuesday order. Nearly 150 names were on a ballot list Franken submitted; 125 were from Coleman's list, and 50 were on both. The rest did not appear on either candidate's list. *(Pioneer Press)*

The *Star Tribune* put Pat Doyle's story under an ominous headline, "Coleman All but Concedes...but Will Appeal."

At the end of the piece he quotes a Cornyn crony that is just a despicable replay of all Rethuglican LIES! [And big John, in MY CHURCH we have commandments about lying. Maybe you can get away with that SINNING at the First Self Righteous Egoists of Tumbleweed, Texas, but among CHRISTIANS, JEWS, MUSLIMS (to name a few) what you are doing here is burn-in-hell crap!]

> "The NRSC has and will continue to support Norm Coleman's efforts to ensure that thousands of Minnesotans are not disenfranchised, that ballots exist before they are counted, and that every legitimate vote that was cast is counted once in Minnesota." *(Star Tribune)*

That's from Cornyn man Brian Welsh. Say, Brian, you come up here to MN and I'll give you a left jab of disenfranchised, a knee to the groin of ballots that exist, and a bicycle kick of counted once...that'll just be in the airport and after that I'll get MAD, you lizard-vomiting cactus prick... *(Fumes!)*

Well, that's the straight view of the news. You are welcome now to skip down to the comments and add to all the news from yust southeast of Lake Wobegon.

Shalom.

PS. In the moanings with the stomach flu and unable to sleep at 2 in the morning, this fever mirage grabbed me by the temples and said, "Write me."

> *It may be March but it's the snowiest month of the year in MN. Head to the North Country:*
>
> *A slate gray sky. Snowflakes flutter through bare-branched birches, sift through pine needles. Tree trunks in every direction loom dark gray, fading to black at a distance. The sound of boots chucking through snow is all that breaks the stillness.*
>
> *From somewhere comes a faint hissing, rhythmic, pulsing. Tree branches rubbing? But the sound is not random. It is a regular hiss and hiss which slowly grow louder. Now added faintly, a gentle "chick" "chick."*
>
> *The sounds come from everywhere, from nowhere. In every direction only black trunks against white. Sss-chick sss-chick.*
>
> *And then...a faint clatter, maybe wood on wood ... followed by absolute silence. Look around. Still nothing. Trees against snow. Black against white.*

Step aside from the line because the boot lace has come loose. Kneel for a moment to retie it. In that instant, where the head was just an instant before the kneel began, the air ripples with a sonic boom and the man to the left topples over dead, the bullet spilling his blood bright red on the snow...

Bronze Medal for guessing this is the Finno-Russian war of 1939–40..Stalin's troops seized Petsamo in the north. Then 20,000 Soviet soldiers went into the "waist" of Finland to cut the country in half. The Finnish ski troops, dressed all in white, operating in endless forests, shot down over 15,000 of them in 6 weeks..

Silver Medal for guessing biathlon is the sport that came out of that war. You ski cross country for several kilometers, then pull up to an outdoor shooting range and unsling the .22 rifle you have on your back. You shoot 5 targets with 5 bullets at a range of 50m one time standing, the next time prone. Miss a target and for each miss you go over to a 150m "penalty track" and do a turn for each miss. Fastest time wins.

Gold Medal for guessing that of course what you are reading about is... the Election Contest Court of the MN Senate race between Coleman and Franken! Let's tune in Mike McIntee and the UpTake gang for the coverage from the North Woods... Mike, are you there?

Mike: "Yes we are here, WineRev, and a very exciting competition it is! It's been a long rivalry between the Big Bad Reds of Team Coleman and the Dress Blues of Team Franken. But today the upstart ECC team of Marben, Reilly, and Hayden have set the pace. Noah Kunin, what happened at the first firing range?"

Noah: "Well, Mike, all three squads in the first round shot clean on all targets. So off into the woods they went for the next skiing leg of this contest for what seems like better than 2 weeks. Now Jennifer has a report from the penalty track. Jennifer?"

Jennifer: "Thanks, Noah. We see Ben Ginsberg loosening up for the Big Bad Reds. A veteran senior like Joe Friedberg for Team Coleman lets them us a substitute to take any penalty laps over here. Since Team Norm shot clean, Ben is staying loose. Back to you Mike."

Mike: "Thanks, Jennifer! Yes today's competition is an obscure version of biathlon called "Contest Court." The Big Bad Reds threw down the challenge January 26th and they, the Dress Blues and the ECC team have been at it ever since. Noah, any surprises so far?"

Noah: "Well, let me get the binoculars on the trail...Yes, Mike. I can see some Red... and some Blue too, a couple kilometers away ... but no sign of Team ECC. n the other hand their jerseys don't stand out very much under the cloudy sky. We'll see when they get up here to the range."

Mike: "Say, Jennifer, that's a different vantage point for you. Where are you?"

Jennifer: "Mike I'm up here in the old forest fire watchtower with Toivo Kekkonnen, a 91-year-old veteran of the Winter War. Toivo's up here not only for the view but also just in case...shhhh,...(intense whisper) Mike, Toivo is slowly moving into the front chair... strapping himself into the seat with the hooks and the leather like Quint on the 'Orca' smelling shark... he sees something with that mirror over the front edge....and he's reaching for the flare..."

Three shots crack out and Toivo's flare gun booms into the air as the stunned spectators gape over their shoulders.

Mike: "Noah? Jennifer? Was that THE flare gun?"

Jennifer: "Yes it was, Mike. Toivo Kekkonnen has just signaled Team ECC has fired prone from the knoll from 250 meters! Maybe a Petsamo Bonus!?"

Mike: "Amazing! Noah?"

Noah: (panting) "I'm running back toward the firing range, Mike and there! I think you can see the judges out on the scaffolding looking at the high targets, and...yes! YES! 3 green flags are up! Team ECC has shot clean from 250 meters! Holy Smokes!"

Mike: "And it's true! Over here at the judges' table the flag is up, and the judges have awarded Team ECC a Petsamo Bonus. I'm looking it up but it looks like...yes there hasn't been a successful Petsamo since the 1978 World Biathlon in Kiruna, Sweden

" William Pentelovitch of the Dress Blues just started skiing penalty legs for each member of his team. That's the Petsamo Bonus, make the other teams pause until all 10 penalty laps are completed. And Ben Ginsberg is protesting for all he's worth but the judges are having none of it. They keep waving him toward his barrel staves with the workboots nailed on and telling him he'd better get skiing."

Jason: "Mike it's Jason Barnett here at the pursuit mass start. We know Team ECC is coming because the fans are roaring them on through the woods. The cry everywhere is 'Sisu! Sisu!'"

Mike: "Can you give us a translation, Jason?"

Jason: "It's a tough one, Mike, but it means a combination of moxie, nerve, street smarts, and guts. And to try for a Petsamo takes plenty of sisu! Miss on a Petsamo Bonus try and each team member has to eat a plate of lutefisk, so it's a very high-risk move.

"And Mike. Now we see why Team ECC were able to gain their lead. Mike, they're in their road uniforms."

Mike: "What do you mean, Jason?"

Jason: "Mike, you've only seen Team ECC on their home course at Judiciary Room 300. But they are treating this competition in New Narvik as an away game, so they are in their traveling uniforms with the colors reversed."

Mike: "You mean...?"

Jason: "That's right, Mike. Dress white judicial robes from the Helsinki Winter War and Confirmation Gown Company! (www.sisuRus.fi) although they didn't fool old Toivo. Team ECC are really digging in, Mike, breaking out of single file and lining up 3 across for the finish line. They are digging deep, slogging through evidence and testimony but charging hard. The crowd is roaring and the pursuit skiers are anxious to take up the relay. I see Joe Mansky and Cindy Reichert and, ah, oh there's another Finn, Paul Tynjala representing St. Louis County, ready to go.

"And ... across the line comes Team ECC! They fling off their pouches and Ritchie, Gelbmann, and Poser from the Secretary of State's Office sprint forward with them and are handing out the orders. All 87 counties are here for this one and several cities as well. The 3 are working their way down the line... still lots of cheers for a tired but happy Team ECC now resting on their poles. Now Poser's done, now Gelbmann and Ritchie and BANG! Yes the Silver Axe has been thrown into the picture of Stalin and they are off into the woods across the state. We'll see them in six days. The Boston Marathon has its 'Heartbreak Hill.' We'll see these folks doing the herringbone up 'Final Count Mountain' on the 7th. Back to you, Mike..."

Toasted Norm & Appeals
April 2, 2009

Comments: 186   Recs: 292   Tips: 251

Out in the back lot of the Minnesota Judiciary Building a large crowd gathered behind police lines yesterday. Cameras were everywhere and little folk were hoisted on Dad's shoulders for a closer look at the vehicle-sized mass.

One little girl pointed a 4-year-old finger and said, "Mommy, what is it?"

Mommy looked very closely at her and said, "Remember when you asked me once, 'What's a universe?' and I said, 'Everything there is.'"

"I remember."

"Well, there once was a silly man who said, 'I believe the universe is made up of pieces of paper called "ballots."'"

And the little girl's eyes lit up and she began to giggle because Mommy was using that "funny story" voice of hers.

"And the silly man said, 'My universe has 11,895 ballots in it.'" And the little girl laughed and said, "That's not a big enough number!"

"And the silly man said, 'Wait, I mean it's 10,962 ballots.'"

The little girl was laughing hard now.

"'No wait,' the silly man said, 'it's 4,797 ballots...no wait, 3,698 ballots, no...wait...2,900...'"

The little girl was starting to sit down because she was going weak in the knees laughing so hard.

"Maybe it's 2,500...no, wait, it's 1,700, no it's, 1,369."

The little girl was in tears when Mommy held up a finger and said, "Then one wise magicians and one wise magi, who giggled as much as you do but only when they are alone with each other, decided to bring the silly man's universe to the ground."

The little girl's eyes went wide and she said, "You can't bring a universe onto the ground! It won't fit."

"Of course it won't, but the two and the one were not only wise and magical but they also like to laugh. And so they waved their arms and made writing appear on paper and pointed out the back window of their tower and said, 'Let the silly man's universe land on the ground.'"

Mother pointed to the blackened, smoking heap of black rock, glistening here and there with melt marks from air friction upon entry and said, "And there it is: A silly-man universe of 400 ballots. It not only fits on the ground but it's so small it won't even get the silly man a seat in the Senate..."

Signs of the End?

While the last of the MN-Senate ballots are being collected from across the state for counting, the *Star Tribune* has decided to begin preparing the faithful for the inevitable. Kevin Diaz's story itself is about Norm's increasing odds... that he plans to appeal, and quickly...that at some point MN patience will run out and see him as stalling...which would damage his prospects for further MN political office (ya think?).

We also KNOW the new Rethuglican MEME for covering up the stall in the US Senate/WWIII etc. straight from the horse's Bluegrass rear:

> Coleman's GOP allies in Congress, meanwhile, are urging patience. "Although we all want finality to this historically close election, patience must outweigh partisanship as Minnesotans continue the process to attain the accurate results from Election Day," said Senate Republican Leader Mitch McConnell of Kentucky. *(Star Tribune)*

So: code word: "patience" = "stall Franken"

Several poli sci profs cited... people may feel like a "pox on both their houses" mood... "could look like a denial of democracy"...why Coleman voters' neighbors might be getting fed up...all in all not a bad bit of ground prepping for the inevitable, Kevin.

And you KNOW SENATOR Franken is looking good when the shriek level on the Reichving is coming from... Bill O'Reilly! Megan Gamble at MNPublius put on the Hazmat suit and used the iron tongs of Barad-Dur to bring back news that if Franken is seated, O'Reilly wants the Reichving to...wait for it... *boycott Minnesota!* I'll worry later after I stop laughing to scorn.

Back to the Future, Recount II, NY-20 Events v. 2.0

I DO NOT want to go here BUT dammit the GOP is frosting my cookies!

First, Guy Harrison of the National Republican Congressional Committee (NRCC) sent out an e-mail fundraiser in the NY-20 squeaker between Scott Murphy (D) and Jim Tedisco (R). Yeah I know you whip up the troops by throwing a boogeyman in front of them but... *democracy in action in Minnesota is NOT a bogeyman!*:

> Don't let the Democrats steal this election. Less than 80 ballots separate Republican Jim Tedisco and his Democrat opponent. We cannot afford to allow the Democrats to steal this election.

> We need your support to ensure we can overcome the Democrats' legal maneuvers.
>
> Democrats have almost succeeded in stealing the election in Minnesota and seating Al Franken. We cannot allow them to manipulate electoral results to seat another tax-troubled liberal. *(quoted at Pioneer Press)*

"Stealing the election in Minnesota"!? Hey, Guyyyyy! Does that mean you think (hah!) "Republican loses = stealing election," slimebag? You got any, you know, EVIDENCE of that? "Manipulating election results"? Here's a COURT sitting, with ONE item on its docket: THIS election. Get your case, your witnesses, your ACORN hoods, your ballots in the trunk in here NOW, man. 3 judges stand ready to "hang 'em high"... if you've got the goods... or evidence.. or ANYTHING.

Otherwise tell me one thing Gar-eee. Why SHOULDN'T the ECC swear out a bench warrant for contempt of court against you right now? You're calling the whole process crooked. That's contempt of court in my book. Indeed, I'll be happy (oh BOY would I be happy) to serve that warrant personally upon request of the ECC and drag your sorry butt before them. You think $7,500 on Trimble was light? For you my man, it'll be heavy, and not just on the wallet. Maybe Judge Marben would offer the hospitality of the Pennington County Jail in Thief River Falls, a place you probably would go insane in because it's normal. Father Inqvist from Our Lady of Perpetual Sorrows in Lake Wobegon would come by to hear your confession, 6 hours at a time...

THEN: The NY GOP got a NY Supreme Court injunction to impound all the voting machines and voting materials in NY-20 until all the absentees are in and to ready for a recount. OK, a little drastic but not bad overall. But then comes the crap via Newsmax:

> In Minnesota, allegations that different standards were used by different precincts in the state to determine which absentee ballots would be counted have played a central role in the election dispute that now appears likely to be appealed to the state Supreme Court, and possibly beyond. *(Newsmax)*

Hey Newsmax! Like to add that ALL, EVERY LAST FREAKIN' ONE of those allegations were raised by the GOP? And not the state GOP but by the COLEMAN GOP? You know, one of the 2 parties "in the election dispute that now appears likely to be appealed"...by NORM the Republican?? What a selective bunch of sewer-line backup!

> Michael McCormack, chairman of the Dutchess County Republican Committee in upstate, tells Newsmax it is "fairly accurate" to say that New York Republicans sought the impound order to head off a repeat of embarrassing complications that afflicted Minnesota's electoral process... "It's a matter of putting rules in place that are fair, even, and even-handed. Obviously in Minnesota that was not the case." *(Newsmax)*

Now from this distance, and not knowing Newsmax at all, I'll cut McCormack one length of slack. Mike, if you haven't been paying attention up here, there has been NOTHING embarrassing coming OUT OF Minnesota. Ben Ginsberg was an embarrassment that came INTO Minnesota. AND we are NOT afflicted...except by Ginsberg, Guy Harrison, Brian the Crony of John the Cornyn and Mitch the 'Bama Hitch in Kentucky... and even these are only from afar. Mike, our rules ARE in place, and have been fair, even, and even-handed for 45 years. Can you say the same in NY?

OK, Empire State Kossacks and bloggers! It's up to you. Murphy is digging in for the absentee ballots and the recount. That's waiting for Gentleman Johnny Burgoyne/Jimmy Tedisco at Saratoga. But those are the formal troops. So what say you bloggers? Tell us the Recount rules. Who will open the absentees? Are there challengers? Is there a recount law in place?

Rally the Oneidas again! Warm up the keyboards! Demand transparency! Answer back the Harrisons and McCormarcks. Blog them down demanding fairness, a clean count. What is the traditional media like? *Albany Times-Union* worth the read? Can they be prodded? Who is on-line "New Media"? Anybody like The UpTake cranking out stories on hand-held cameras over the Internet in NY-20?

Strike up that fife and drum. And, if it gets really nasty, we'll send you the ultimate weapon: sealed containers of lutefisk. But only as a last resort. Go get 'em Word Alchemy! And Gaspare! And Ex Real Republican! If the Brooklynites join you (Eds in Brooklyn), well the Empire State has glory for many.

Hope this will hold you with the all the latest from yust southeast of Lake Wobegon.

Shalom.

On the Ice in DC: Norm vs. Al
April 3, 2009

Comments: *113*   *Recs:* *206*   *Tips:* *191*

Today's ravings have the excuse of mentioning Michele Bachmann as reason for their... "meandering" quality as you'll see...

The End Is Near

No, no, not the MN Senate Recount, although that may be included. But rather **THE** END. You know, 4 horsemen of the Apocalypse, "earthquakes, floods, famine! Chaos! Dogs and cats LIVING together...!" kind of END.

Because...Michele Bachmann, execrable Congresswoman from (sigh; sorry)MN; wingnut-ETTE, self-righteous, airheaded, mock-moral, plastic patriot...

because Michele Bachmann, like fellow linemate Sarah Palin, both of whom probably first tasted fame and adulation as one of the leggy backdrop girls with eye makeup applied with a trowel swaying suggestively behind Robert Palmer in his smash MTV video "Addicted to Love"...

THAT Michele Bachmann, who never found a Reichving position or Brownshirt male politician she didn't love and go kissy face on,

THAT Michele Bachmann... has publicly AGREED on a political issue... with President Barack Obama.

"President Obama's rhetorical spanking of the American auto industry yesterday hit the right chord," Bachmann wrote in her blog.

Whew! Well, after that kind of reverse spinning of the current solar system, I'm just getting my balance back here, so what follows may be a bit woozy. And looking around it seems the after-effects are still echoing.

Opening Shift

While county and city election officials across the state are skiing hard toward Monday's killer climb up "Final Count" Mountain, we can only cheer them on. Those of us who are patriots can. The political types ... not so much. They have politicking to do, but there is a distinct smell of sweat rising from inside the hockey gloves of the games being played in DC.

Take (please take) a PRIME example of a politician, Norm Coleman. He hasn't had an interview with his "hometown" newspaper (the St. Paul Pioneer Press) or even taken questions from them in weeks. But Norm was in DC yesterday and managed to be on 3 radio outlets there... after appearing at the National Republican Senatorial Committee for a session, accompanied by everyone's favorite greaser, Ben Ginsberg. Norm's still skating without a mouthguard (in a couple of ways), dropped his stick and is fighting for his balance while fast approaching either the side glass or a court decision:

> Coleman, who is trying to overcome a 225-vote deficit, believes that Minnesota's expansive election law is on his side and that he will eventually prevail...
>
> "He believes that he won the race and won't concede until there is a fair and accurate accounting of all properly registered voters or a new election is held, whichever is cleaner," said one GOP source. "If he wanted to protect his political future he would drop it, but this is about justice to him, not a political seat."
>
> Coleman will hold today's briefing partly because he wants to counter the public perception that Tuesday's ruling by a state judicial panel puts his legal case on shaky ground and is unlikely to net positive results. The Coleman camp is circulating talking points to that effect. *(Roll Call)*

As Norm sailed by windmilling and clutching for help, the Senior Senator from Illinois reached out to give him... *a firmer push toward the boards:*

> "No one should have to go through what [Franken] is going through and what the state of Minnesota is going through. But it looks like it's nearing the end of the Minnesota chapter when their courts will have the last word," Senate Majority Whip Dick Durbin (D-Ill.) said Wednesday. "I hope that at that point that fair-minded people will prevail, that the governor and secretary of state will step forward and give the state of Minnesota the two Senators that they need." *(Roll Call)*

Thank you, Senator Durbin.

Some of the homestate Democrats, sporting the popular "DFL" logo (Minnesotan for "Democratic") also skated over to shove Norm along:

> "We had a very good meeting," Coleman continued. "We went over where the case is at and the position of the courts and we talked about the next steps."
>
> The Minnesota DFL Party responded later to the closed-door session.
>
> "Rather than being transparent regarding his intentions, former Senator Coleman is hiding behind closed doors in a secret strategy session with national Republicans," DFL Party Chairman Brian Melendez said in a statement. *(MinnPost)*

Thanks to MinnPost's Cynthia Dizikes of the DC Bureau for leaning down close enough to the ice there to hear the exchange.

First Line Change

Now Southerners have some excellent traits but I must say hockey is probably not one of them, especially in the growing up days of Republican Senator Jefferson Beauregard Braxton Stonewall Lee Hill Longstreet Stuart Sessions. Does he sound a little wobbly on the ice yesterday in his first 8 words? You know, like his laces aren't quite tight enough above his double runners? *(Hockey fans know I am slapping the man bald with impunity here!)*

"I think if there is a realistic prospect for a complete count that's fair that would give Sen. Coleman the victory, we should not give up until the last avenue of appeal is over," said Sen. Jeff Sessions (R-Ala.). "Everybody on our side believes that."

Hmmm... that sounds like a loophole to me.

Next Line Change: Hometown Heroes

And while Minnesotans are a people who honor the Law and respect this process our patience is taxed(!) by those who do neither. (Those idiots who have forgotten so much will also have forgotten the adage "Beware the fury of a patient Northern state.")

Indeed, our rather overworked Senior Senator is showing a bit of "Beware" herself.

> (MSNBC) Host David Shuster said to (MN-Sen. Amy) Klobuchar: "Your colleague, Republican Senator John Cornyn, said that if Democrats try to seat Al Franken before this goes all the way to the (US) Supreme Court, he threatened World War III. What's your reaction?"
>
> "Well, one of the other things he said, David, he said that we could go on in Minnesota with one senator for years. And I would love to know how Texas would like that. I think that Minnesota would prefer to make its own decisions." *(MinnPost)*

I know, I know. We would all prefer Amy flame throwing to a level of "Mesquite Crisp" on Cornyn, but around here this counts for getting edgy.

Cornyn has skated into the corner of the rink throwing elbows pretending to scrap for the puck. But Klobuchar knows the corners are a place AWAY from the referees for throwing back: does the skate blade kicking at the puck come up just a little higher than needed to slice through somebody's boot lace? (Try skating on one blade, you hoser.) Butt end of your stick slide inside your own elbow and snap up into somebody's solar plexus...leaving them, a little breathless? And just how did that Lone Star Stick get the first 6 inches cracked off so abruptly that you have to drop it on the spot or else?

And the overworked Senior Senator is not alone on the Congressional ice either. Teammate (D) James Oberstar is working the boards too and giving "Klobs" some help against those Washington Senators (trying to make them look like the Washington Generals):

> "The Republican Party nationally and in Minnesota is playing not just with fire, but with dynamite," said Rep. James L. Oberstar, a Democrat and the dean of Minnesota's congressional delegation.
>
> Oberstar—like a lot of Democrats—says November's election should finally be over as soon as the Minnesota Supreme Court rules.
>
> If Pawlenty and the Republicans push it further, he says, "this thing is going to blow up in their face." *(Politico)*

In my time in MN this sort of statement is NOT Oberstar (although I haven't paid a lot of attention; he's in another district) so for the Transportation Committee heavy to start throwing around "dynamite" and issuing warnings... folks, for Minnesota, "Klobs" and "Obie" both going on record like this on the same day is skating past the other team's bench for a whistlestop line change... and dragging your stick along the top rail. (The football fan equivalent is from Remember the Titans, when in the semi-final Julius flattens the quarterback and Guy runs to the opposing sideline to point a snarling finger in the face of the racist coach.)

Even the Senate coach had something to yell at the other bench when the ref was fixing a bad spot on the ice during a stop in play:

> Majority Leader Harry Reid (D-Nev.), whose spokesperson Jim Manley said:
>
> "It's not fair to the people of Minnesota to be represented by only one Senator. And, it's about time a Senator from Texas stop telling the people of Minnesota what's best for them. Enough is enough." *(quoted at MSNBC)*

Grinder/Checking Line

AND Paul Begala of the Democratic Senatorial Campaign Committee has also skated over, flexing, with a bit more reputation than Klobuchar for throwing hard body checks:

"How many more recounts does Norm Coleman want? How many more delays? How much longer will the Republican Party hold Minnesota's Senate seat hostage?" Begala asks in an e-mail and invitation to sign a petition called "Give it up Norm."

And AGAIN in DC, Aaron Blake at Briefing Room Blog of The Hill is loudly asking "How is Coleman LEGALLY paying for his Recount effort?" The first quarter just ended and reports are due OUT (published and public) later in the month. Well, Norm?

And still MORE from DC, Chris Cillizza of the Wash. Post asks the doom question of should Norm concede? Leaving aside any considerations of "premature," "legal appeal" Cillizza goes for the throat (by DC standards) and asks the Beltway angle: what is Norm's political future and on THAT basis thinks Norm should do what's best for NORM. That has seldom been a problem for the former mayor, former Democrat, former New Yorker, former loser to a pro wrestler for governor.

Minor League Exhibition Line Change

Finally, in MN (you know, where this period of hockey started on this diary) Manu Raju of Politico thinks the hockey player *really* facing some rough ice ahead is a guy who actually does skate and play a nice club version of the game, Governor Tim Pawlenty. I still think T-Paw will sign off on a certificate of election but he's going to try to skate off with as much limelight as long as he can without having to actually do something until he absolutely has to.

Old Timer's Line Change

Why did your WineRev read through all these (and more) to bring you these clips and links? Well, aside from my sense of duty to all of you (really), sheer curiosity, love of politics and the affection I genuinely feel for you who continue to tip, rec, and comment, it's also the hope of coming across something that will distill this all down. Mark Bannick over at the UpTake blog is looking for it too. If somebody (Bill Moyers? Keith Olbermann?) wants it, here's the nut of it (edited for spellings, grammar):

> The hope is one, just one anchor will say something to the effect: "The recount in MN was automatic, transparent, and fair. There is no "stealing" involved. It was the right of either losing party to challenge the results via an "election contest" as

provided in MN law. Former Senator Norm Coleman chose to force an election contest to try to overturn the recount. The cause of the delay and the person trying to overturn, or, as you said, "steal" the election, is former Senator Norm Coleman, not Al Franken. To steal the election, the person doing the stealing must be behind in the count. That definition fits no one other than former Senator Norm Coleman. *(Mark Bannick at The UpTake)*

Eastern League Wire Report: Out-of-Town Game NY-20: The Bloggers build!

It's like giving birth, watching the last couple days in the comments as the Empire State Upstaters around Albany mobilize for their own election drama. Blogger NYlawstudent put up a comment on NY election law vs. MN, was answered, asked to put up her own diary and got comments and recommends done to a turn.

Donna over at The UpTake came up with a PDF on ALL the absentees in NY-20 hanging fire, which is begging for the emergence of a spreadsheet wizard like TomTech to take it down and bring it up (Venn Diagrams optional).

OK, OK so NY-20's Word Alchemy begged off "winerevving" the whole thing. But Albany Project, javelina and other bloggers are on the way, revving up. Just add the wine (or other chemical assistance) fill us in on the players, timelines, and guesses and lay it out for us to read!

[BTW, Marc Elias' wife blogs regularly on The UpTake so she can keep up with Marc's life while he's in MN. (They live near DC.) On her birthday yesterday many bloggers sent good wishes...and wanted to know if Marc was going to Upstate NY for Murphy's side as an election lawyer with any fresh experience?

Mrs. E laughed, but DIDN'T say no, but she also said she's usually the last to know where he goes next.]

Now see? There's a GREAT rumor to start in Tedisco's backyard! And a bug to e-mail to Murphy's ear. "Fresh off a bracing 5-month election win in MN, Marc Elias today announced in Albany..."

Not much of this happened in state, but it was plenty to read about here just southeast of Lake Wobegon.

Shalom.

72 Hours
April 4, 2009

Comments: 75   Recs: 164   Tips: 174

Cornyn Capers and Follies

Not a lot today; everyone seems to have released their trebuchets on Wednesday and Thursday with all the stuff out of DC. But some of that is still echoing and in contrast with the Cornyn "WWIII" bronco-riding a lot of it is coming from the left side of the street.

Manu Raju at Politico apparently so liked getting printed in the *St. Paul Pioneer Press* s/he came up with a hypothetical and shopped it around various Congressional offices: "How would Norm Coleman's return to the Senate be received?"

While this sounds like the premise of a great 5-minute skit on Jon Stewart or *Saturday Night Live*, Raju was actually able to get people to give serious answers.

> Separate and apart from the ongoing legal dispute over November's election, the Minnesota Republican faces several unresolved investigations:
> - a reported FBI probe into his dealings with Nasser Kazeminy, a friend and benefactor;

> - a potential Senate Ethics Committee inquiry into his Capitol Hill living arrangements;
> - a federal elections investigation into his use of campaign donations for legal expenses; and
> - a possible state probe into his campaign's handling of donors' financial information on its website. *(Pioneer Press)*

Good grief! MN would STILL only have one Senator because the other one would never get out of court or away from the various panels.

Bless her heart the Senator from Michigan took aim at the Horse Dentures gleaming across frozen Lake Superior (used as a night navigational beacon in Marquette):

> Sen. Debbie Stabenow, D-Mich., echoed those sentiments, adding, "I think it appears he's got a number of challenges in front of him. I would think it would be wise for him to make a decision to accept the outcome of the voters in Minnesota." *(Pioneer Press)*

And back at the Saphead Saloon in Plumb Dumb, TX (next town over from Crawford?) Sen. Big John Cornhead of Texas was seen dancing in the saloon. You know, when you just wanted to humiliate somebody you didn't shoot them but you pointed your six-shooter at their feet and said, "Dance, pardner!" After all the Colts, Winchesters and Remingtons going off this week from Klobuchar, Oberstar, Durbin, Begala, lots of the DC press, Harry Reid's office and now Stabenow of Michigan... well, the following is QUITE a contrast from "This will be World War III and go on for years":

> On Thursday, Cornyn chalked up the Democratic attacks to "saber rattling."
>
> "I think maybe it's possible that the litigation concludes (and) there is a clear answer that's been decided in court by an impartial tribunal," the Texas Republican said, "and everybody can just put their guns on their table and walk away." *(Pioneer Press)*

"I think maybe it's possible...?"

Now them's fightin' words, Big John!

Those are words to lead off a WEEK's worth of Slow Limbaugh's show!

Those are words to send out on RNC fund-raising letters to make the red-meat faithful howl with delight and rain down contributions!

Whew! Those words will give pause, dry-mouth, hard-swallowing pause, to ANYONE who would question the essential rightness of Norm Coleman's place in the Senate.

Big John, let them tremble before your milk-soaked zweiback and your bowl of pablum.

I shudder at what comes next.

Takedowns Internet style

Actually all the fireworks this week in DC quarters was several weeks behind...the INTERNET community![20]

Remember the HUGE flap over Norm Coleman's website crew leaving a donor database lying around cyberspace with the sign on it, "Rip me off, Please"? This is the one where Norm and his people are in hot water because the credit card security codes were retained... and available.

Right. Well, apparently there were something like 4,000–5,000 donors affected by that security breach that Wikileaks sent up the flare about. But these were a subset of a database that had over 50,000 names, addresses, e-mails of people. (Obviously most of these did NOT have any credit card information.)

These were names Coleman was accumulating in a typical, political way as a target for mailers, contacts, etc. Nothing new about this. EVERYBODY in politics builds lists.

But according to MN Independent what's fun about Norm's list is that people could leave comments— again, nothing new in these high-tech days. The Independent combed through the 50K names and found an entertaining slice of them were FRANKEN supporters, who let that be known.

---

20   *See diaries dated March 11 and March 12, 2009*

A batch of contact names came in response to a full-page newspaper ad during the campaign:

About 800 of the records, including some duplicate entries, have the word "Franken" listed for "signup_type." These appear to be contacts generated after Coleman placed a full-page ad in the Star Tribune in September 2007. Titled "'Ridiculous,'" the ad takes Franken to task for using that word to describe a U.S. Senate vote that condemned MoveOn.org's own full-page ad, titled "General Petraeus Or General Betray Us?"

> Coleman's ad asked readers to "Send Al Franken a message to condemn these ridiculous personal attacks on our military ... Log on to www.colemanforsenate.com/ridiculous to find out how." *(Star Tribune)*

See the date? How far ahead of the DC crowd is the internet crowd? (Takes off shoes for Big counting; Sept. 07 to Apr. 09 = 19 months! The internet isn't reading next week's newspaper in advance this is...I don't know, but MAN, are we good!)

September of 2007? Fighting the good fight **14 months** before election day. MN progressives were already sniping and throwing off-season snowballs (the kind every MN kid makes in winter and keeps in the freezer until the 4th of July picnic; the MN Snowball Fight tradition just before the fireworks show behind Ingmar's Bait and Snowmobile Showroom. Ah... the memories...).

Hope that will hold you for a bit. That's the latest from yust southeast of Lake Wobegon.

Shalom.

24 Hours
April 6, 2009

Comments: 176   Recs: 290   Tips: 304

TODAY, all counties and cities are required to have specified absentee ballots delivered to Secretary of State Mark Ritchie's office. (Due by noon.)

The Election Contest Court (ECC) judges Elizabeth Hayden, Denise Reilly, and Kurt Marben want to have a personal look at these 400 ballots and see if they meet all the criteria for being counted. We already know 12 do, from an early summary judgment granted by the court to Franken, as do another about 36–38 from a parallel case brought by attorney Charles Nauen, so about 50 will be perfunctory.

The remaining 350? That's where the action will be... action *probably* out of sight of the public, but The UpTake will go on the Internet with live blogging today at 11:00 just in case (and ready to go with cameras too.)

Then **TOMORROW, Tuesday, 9:30 a.m.** all of the 400 that pass judicial inspection will be OPENED AND COUNTED. These will be the LAST ballots counted for the MN Senate seat decided on Nov. 4th. And just to roll up the newspaper and take a few practice swats (you should do likewise so you are loose and ready for tomorrow), these are the FIRST TIME and ONLY TIME these ballots are being opened and counted. The swatting is for any nearby Reichwingers.

Republican Screech Level Goes National

The Hill reporting site went all RNC on the weekend and lined up a bunch of quotes from all quarters and you'll see delusional reasoning is a national Republican disease. The commonality of quotes does seem to stem from Norm's visit last week to the National Republican Senatorial Committee.

> "I'll back Norm as far as he believes he should go," said Sen. Sam Brownback (R-Kan.). "He's there on the ground, he's the one with the best information." *(The Hill)*

Uh-huh. Best information I have is Brownback has spent too long strapped to a windmill blade in a high wind.

> Sen. Bob Corker (R-Tenn.): "I know it's not damaging the party because I don't hear that. But I do think Norm is a very sensitive, thoughtful person." *(The Hill)*

Take the fingers out of your ears, Corker. You'll hear better. And thoughtful/sensitive has nothing to do with who has the most VOTES!

> "They know what to do based on their intimate knowledge of the case," said Minority Whip Jon Kyl (R-Ariz.). "I wouldn't presume to give them advice." *(The Hill)*

"They know what to do..." didn't watch any of the trial, did you, Jon?

> "...I have no qualms about saying that if he can, he ought to push it all the way," said Sen. Orrin Hatch (R-Utah). "We're so sick and tired of having one set of rules for Democrats they don't abide by, and then another set of rules for Republicans." *(The Hill)*

You're right by dammit, Orrin! If the Democrats could just get it in their thick skulls that the rule is Republicans should always win, life would be easier...Go sit on a cactus while contemplating how many lines of scripture Joseph Smith stole from the Bible to "write" the Book of Mormon.

Monday Morning Minnesota Media

Having insulted most of the human species on earth by giving Michele Bachmann (!) a huge, Sunday front section write-up, the *Star Tribune* puts the Recount on the front page with a story from Doyle and Duchschere. It's a tale well told of tangled assumptions and a tinge of sadness. Doyle & Duchschere prove they **can** write rather than simply reprint Coleman campaign press releases.

> Tim Stocke, whose multiple sclerosis makes him a prime example of the need for absentee voting, got a reprieve last week, when his rejected ballot became one of 400 from across Minnesota that judges in the U.S. Senate recount trial decided to consider for opening and counting this week.
>
> Not so for the votes of Karen Stocke, Tim's wife, or Karen's aunt, Jessie Zirkle, who all share a lake home outside McGregor in north-central Minnesota. A combination of good intentions, faulty assumptions and misinformation conspired to ensure that the two women's ballots remained rejected.
>
> Tim Stocke, 53, operated heavy equipment for the University of Minnesota before multiple sclerosis made him an invalid. Karen Stocke, 54, works occasionally in the schools and has landed a job with the Census Bureau, but much of her time is spent caring for her husband and looking after Zirkle, a retired Wisconsin teacher in her 80s who is legally blind and moved in with them last summer. *(Star Tribune)*

I haven't said this often but even a blind squirrel finds an acorn now and again: this is a good read in the *StarTrib*, right down to the last line.

Got the early shift down at the shop so I hope this will hold you. Waiting for Tuesday morning's great moment of democracy.

That's the latest from yust southeast of Lake Wobegon.

Shalom.

Count Ballots
April 7, 2009

Comments: 358   Recs: 336   Tips: 289

Today, 9:30 a.m. CDT in room 300 of the Minnesota Judiciary Building, where 7 weeks of trial were held, the Secretary of State's office will open and count the last ballots of the 2008 election for US Senator from MN.

Democracy Unleashed

After 154 days, or exactly 22 weeks since November 4, the last ballots of the 2008 MN Senate election will be counted TODAY. 400 ballots have arrived from across the state, including 5 that arrived yesterday just before the noon deadline in a car from Freeborn County (due south of Twin Cities, on the Iowa line; no word if said ballots were *in the car trunk for the drive!* Some Reichwingers early on the recount accused the Franken folk of just this and have kept it up even after the governor denied it.)

DK If your election lasts more than four months, see your physician immediately. *(Ed Drone)*

Deputy Secretary of State Jim Gelbmann announced 13 of the 400 ballots had already been counted, either on Nov. 4, or during the hand recount. No word on how/why these 13 have been included in the 400.

Judges Hayden, Marben, & Reilly of the Election Contest Court (ECC) have examined these ballots and their accompanying paperwork (ballots applications, information from the county if an absentee voter was registered, etc.) as they have come in. We should hear THIS MORNING just how many of the 400 have been ruled IN and will be counted. (And they may even rule on a last few this morning. We'll see.)

State elections director Gary Poser, last heard and seen January 3 reading off 933 absentee ballots "Franken, Franken, Barkley, Coleman, Franken, Coleman, Franken, Barkley, Niemackl..." will once again do the honors.

Once opened, outside envelopes—which contain voters' names—will be separated from the security envelopes that contain the original ballots, said Secretary of State Mark Ritchie. Poser will then sort the ballots into three piles—Franken, Coleman and other. By noon, judges should have an actual count and add the numbers to the candidates' tallies. *(Star Tribune)*

DK Lizard People? Again? Those guys must have a lobby or something. *(phenry)*

DK Well, the scaly overlords are the obvious choice to get us out of the economic situation. Being used as food really negates the need for job doesn't it. *(delver rootnose)*

DK When this is all over, I want a Lizard People t-shirt. *(crystal eyes)*

The Numbers

Jim Lovell, played by Tom Hanks, floats in the LEM alongside a feverishly working Fred Haise. Lovell calls back through the tunnel to the Apollo 13 Command Module to Jack Swigert (Kevin Bacon), "Jack, I'm gonna need your gimbal numbers BEFORE you shut down the command module!"

He switches on his radio, "Houston, I need a check of the arithmetic on these conversions. My roll/cal angle is... pitch is...yaw is..." and on the ground mechanical pencils speedily scribble down Lovell's numbers. As the music strains, engineers squint anxiously at...their SLIDE RULES, working the multiply, exponential, and/or logarithm sticks, and take a close look through the magnifying lens of the hairline cursor in the slider. A series of "thumbs up"s and "OK" hand signals go up to reinforce the head nods and the capsule communicator says, "OK, Jim. We'll go with those numbers."

WineRev floats in a third-floor apartment in St. Louis Park, MN *(using WHAT for anti-grav you ask? HAH! This MAC OS X update REALLY rocks!)* feverishly scratching a quill pen across parchment and signals the Kossacks, "Houston, I need a check of the arithmetic on these conversions because our Colemanizer has been hit by a spinning Ginsberg."

"Copy the spinning, Rev. You've got serious time pressure here so let's go with the numbers."

"Roger that. My Franken lead is +2-2-5. My last Frank-Cole-Bark reading from the ECC OrderCount was exactly 400, but with a minus 13 that I can't assign yet. My Coleman Overtaker is +2-2-6. So Houston, what I'm getting is 400 total, 226 from the Coleman Overtaker leaving 174 to go. Do you copy?

"Roger that, Rev. Copy you at 174."

"So Houston, for the Coleman Overtaker to really blow out the entire SM (Service Module or Senate Member) no more than half of 174 can feed into the Franken Booster, or 87? Do you copy, Houston?"

"Hang on Rev, we're checking it now…" *(Faint, tiny sound of slide rules moving; muffled sounds of fast huddle of engineers, TomTech, Vote for America)*

"Ah, Rev, this is Houston. The engineers say yes, if the Franken count reaches 87 you, Swigert, Haise, and Lovell and the Markos Mob can rest easy about the Coleman Overtaker. No chance for that to happen… Standby Rev…WineRev? Additional point from Purdue Slide Rule & Mathematics Department. 87 is the threshold with a 400 total. If your total ECC reading is below 400, you can lower, repeat lower, your threshold by 0.5 for each number below 400. Copy that?"

(Sound of orders: "Fredo, go with those last numbers. Jack? OK to shut down the Command Module.") "Roger, Houston. So you're saying if our ECC OrderCount at 0930 hours Houston time is, say, 390, then our threshold Franken Senate Booster number goes to 82?"

"That's affirm, WineRev. You and your crew can rest easy when the Franken count goes to 87, but it could be less than that. It will not, repeat not, be more."

"That is good news, Houston, good news. 87 is a clinch."

"Roger that, Kos."

"Say, Houston, Jack wants to know about the condensation issues in powering up the command module. We swing through the ECC Decision Belt past final, but then… Supremes, Houston?"

"Rev, tell Jack ah… we'll see. The Colemanizer may quit after the ECC, or after the Supremes. The Ritchie-Pawlenty Certificatus Electionus crater could issue. We'll just have to take that as it comes."

"Roger that, Houston. Jack says it still sounds like driving a toaster through a car wash and believing it won't short out…"

After Today

The Election Contest Court (ECC) needs to rule on a couple groups of ballots already counted that Coleman wants out (the Mpls 133 and the supposed double-counted 100) which, if allowed, would take 146 off of Franken's lead (net loss). They may well rule on these by themselves OR

The ECC issues its final ruling on all the disputed points AND declares one candidate has received the highest number of votes. Loser has 10 calendar days from the date of this decision to file an appeal to the MN Supreme Court or the ECC decision is FINAL. Appeal to the Supreme Court is preceded by a bond being posted by the losing /appealing party.

A bit unclear as to the SIZE of this bond. Some here have said it is merely nominal, like $500 to cover the cost of officially generating papers and serving them on the other party and notifying the court with an official filing. Others hold bond is in the amount of costs incurred SO FAR (in the ECC; side issue if this would also include winning side's attorneys fees—unlikely but I've not seen anything definitive so far) PLUS something more to cover the MN Supreme Court costs.

MN Supreme Court is the first court of appeal so anything further goes to them directly. If it happens appellant has 15 days to forward ECC transcripts and evidence to Supremes. MN Supremes would schedule oral arguments, probably rather quickly, then take it all "under advisement."

Lawyer TerribleTom raised an interesting angle a few days ago. At this point it seems it's possible the MN Supreme Ct. could *rule on the case* and issue its opinion with all the details and legal stuff LATER (like months from now). This would let the case be considered FINAL.

Whenever the case becomes FINAL by MN law for a US Senate election the Governor's office prepares a certificate of election, the Governor signs and it is countersigned by the Secretary of State. If either won't sign the winner of the senate race could file for a Writ of Mandamus *(as in "mandate, mandatory" "You must…"; from the Latin mandatum, which by the way, also lies behind the Christians' day this Holy Week of "Maundy Thursday," where Jesus has a final meal with his disciples and gives them several mandatums: Take. Eat. Drink. Do this in remembrance of me.*

Love one another as I have loved you. All imperatives or mandates...). The MN Supreme Ct. could so issue such, that a state official perform said duty on pain of felony and imprisonment. Pretty drastic, but on the books.

Winner takes Certificate of Election to US Senate. Senate seats winner as McConnell and Cornyn both fold like a couple of worn-out lawn chairs in a high wind.

Pawlenty Speaks

Governor Tim Pawlenty had an MSNBC interview yesterday with Norah O'Donnell and said he would not move to issue a certificate of election now (which is quite a legal and reasonable position).

Much less reasonably, he said it could take "months" until the appellate process is finished, and hinted strongly that would mean the federal courts.

The nut of it here:

> O'Donnell: If this three-judge panel tomorrow, after counting these ballots, says that Al Franken has the lead, will you sign the election certificate that makes him Senator Al Franken?
>
> Pawlenty: The Minnesota Supreme Court said in a recent decision that a certificate shouldn't issue or—isn't likely that it should issue until the state court process has run its course. That would include the appellate process. It's pretty clear that one side or the other's going to take that next step, Norah, and it wouldn't be appropriate for me or anyone else to step in front of it. It's frustrating that this has taken so long but we need to get a proper and just and accurate and legal result and it's going to take, it looks like, a few more months to get that. *(from transcript, quoted at MinnPost)*

Sounds like Pawlenty has gotten a pointed e-mail or 2 from the RNC or Mitch McConnell. This is the strongest he has yet said he will wait for the process to play itself out in federal court (although he didn't put it that point blank. Tim IS a politician you know.)

The Ballots

But enough about governors and senators of blather!

Let the lawyers rise but also... let the Court enter and stand aside.

There are 400 votes here...from the people. 400 from the lame, the halt, the blind, the afflicted. 400 votes from 400 voters who are old, hurried, harried, victims of strokes or disease or accident.

But 400 votes of the people... by the people...to help decide which of their fellow citizens SHALL BE REDUCED IN RANK for a period of six years and be made their servant. If rule is not by blood, if rule is not by might, if rule is not by wealth, but if rule is by the PEOPLE, then those elected SERVE... the people.

Call me naive or a hopeless, mystic romantic. Yes the people make mistakes: how else to explain 59,000,000 in 2004 reelecting the *shrubus patheticus?* Or Inhofe? Or Liebermann? Yes they can be seduced through a sexy grin like Bachmann or Palin or by a bourbon in the lemonade called "Old Earmark" for the home district/state like Stevens or Murtha. They can even be whipped into a jingoistic frenzy against some perceived foe like by a Cheney most Foul.

But not always and not for long. Someone will always stand in front of tank in Tiananmen Square in '89, or hold hands 300,000 strong along 600 miles of the Baltic in '89 to say, "WE decide." Someone in '02 will put up an Orange website and say "I'm here to talk politics and elect progressives." Just enough somebodys in '06 will get together enough to say, "We CAN elect a servant like Jim Webb; George Allen—go home." All kind of somebodys in '08 can stand together and say, "We CAN elect a black man president and begin to live down our shame and live up to our calling, and we can do it in Virginia... and North Carolina... and Florida..." Yes. We. Can.

Mr. Lincoln? It has been 7 score and 6 years since you spoke of a nation "conceived in liberty and dedicated to the proposition that all men are created equal." We are still "testing whether that nation or any nation so conceived and so dedicated can long endure." And Mr. Lincoln? On this day, starting at 9:30 in the morning, in your frontier town of St. Paul, MN, just down river from Ft. Snelling, there will be a counting of votes... of the People. Votes from equal people created as men ...and as women too, Mr. Lincoln, as Cady Stanton & Susan Anthony made a ruckus about in your day. Votes from people created equal with color bold enough to endure an African sun, the children's children's children of those you emancipated. Votes from those who came from everywhere to dig in the mines, log the forests, plow the land. Votes from those who fled here because there was no place else in the world to flee.

And Mr. Lincoln? You can watch them do it on a fancy little machine that uses some of the ideas of the telegraph machines of your day. (Cue Aaron Copeland's "Fanfare for the Common Man.")

*WineRev stands and doffs hat in presence of the votes...*of the PEOPLE, all of them, even those I disagree with, and even those who live yust southeast of Lake Wobegon.

Shalom.

Franken has Most Votes: Final
April 8, 2009

Comments: 292   *Recs:* 397   *Tips:* 428

Franken leads +312.

Number of valid ballots (absentee or otherwise) remaining to be examined by a court of law and counted by the Secretary of State's office of Minnesota: **0.**

The Count, Finally and Final

EVERYBODY was ready for Tuesday! Judge Reilly brought her mother to court to watch. Judge Hayden's husband (who is also a judge) came too. Sec. of State Mark Ritchie came but sat in the visitor's benches while Jim Gelbmann and Gary Poser did the honors like they did back on Jan. 3 and the opening of the 933 absentees then.

And yes, Team Coleman was there (although without Norm himself) and attorney Tony Trimble showed that while the ice is going out on lakes across MN, his brain and courtroom tactics continue in frozen brainlock. FIVE freakin' minutes after the session started Tony was on his feet asking the Court for a 15-minute recess. Why?

> Trimble, "Your honor, we didn't know you would be counting today." sheesh. *(KevinS at The UpTake)*

Judge Hayden decided to show off with her husband in the room: "Denied. Sit down, Mr. Trimble."

If Coleman PR flack and election thief-in-chief Ben Ginsberg would have been in court, an UpTaker guessed the motion might have been:

> Ginsberg: "Your honor, I move for a recess. Our case in hallway court is more important than this one." *(Chris II at The UpTake)*

Obviously the day started well!

It took about 45 minutes to open the 387 ballots in question and for the court to rule if any of them had "issues" and a few did so that the final FINAL number of ballots that would be FINALLY counted was...351. (Franken began the day with a +225 lead.) Live bloggers passed the time with gems like this:

> Many absentee ballots will have written in George W Bush for senator. The almost physical separation pangs have driven countless Americans to tears. *(Jindal-Bachmann 2012 at The UpTake)*

Yes, I too have been moved to tears at being separated from the image, the thought, the idea and the insult to the human species that IS George Bush, but those tears... have a different chemical composition than what JB2012 is snarking about. (It has been shown there is a measurable chemical distinction between sorrow, and pain, and "tears of joy." And brothers & sisters, I paid my dues in the first two for 8 LOOOOOOooong years!)

At 10:35 a triple gaveling called all to order. Gary Poser, flanked by Trimble for Coleman and Marc Elias for Franken (Marc flew in for the day from DC) so either side could challenge a ballot (neither did), began sorting into Franken, Coleman, and Other piles. Nearly 2,000 were on the liveblog or video at The UpTake alone. At 11:07 the words to Poser: "You may begin."

The Franken-Coleman-Other numbers were 10-3-1 after 3 minutes.

> You can see that this process is biased because more ballots are going in the Franken pile than in the Coleman pile. (*EV Debs at The UpTake*)

By 11:24 Franken had 63. With a +225 starting lead and 351 to be counted, that was the clincher. The rest came to a final of 198-111-42 or 56.4%-31.6%-12.0%.

> If anyone here from Western Pennsylvania remembers Bob Prince, the radio announcer of the Pittsburgh Pirates in the 1970s, you will recognize this, as the Pirates win in the bottom of the 9th on a steal of home: "We had 'em AAALLLLLLLLLLLLLL the way!"
>
> billw: It took Norm Coleman nine weeks to prove they Franken's lead should have been 87 more than the State Canvassing Board said it was. (*Jeff in CA at The UpTake*)

Aftermath I

We all knew there would be pressers afterwards and there were. For a brief moment they sounded like they would be terrific as moderator Jennifer Wingham at The UpTake promised:

> After this, we'll bring press conferences galore, and Noah (Kunin) and Mike (McIntee) will recap, take questions and do tap dances. (*The UpTake*)

I, like several others, slightly, oh so slightly, misread the 9th to last letter as a lowercase "L" not a "T." I couldn't WAIT for those two guys to start in on Ben Ginsberg and Marc Elias with THE most suggestive set of reporter's questions EVAH... and maybe even give the Faux Noise Pole Dancing Co. of augmented gum-chewers a run for their money but alas... it was all a misreading.

Marc Elias for Franken made ongoing use of "FORMER senator Coleman" and had the unmitigated temerity to... name FACTS:

> The problem that Senator Coleman has is he lost fair and square. He lost because more people voted for Al Franken than voted for Norm Coleman. No amount of lawyering or sophisticated legal arguments is going to change that.
>
> I think this is going to be a decision that former Senator Coleman is going to have to make about what he wants, how he wants to be remembered for this process ending, what he wants for the state of Minnesota. I suspect that, more than Washington, D.C., political considerations will come into play.
>
> Coleman brought a nonmeritorious claim...Franken has been elected the next MN Senator. (*MinnPost*)

On the other hand, Ginsberg for Coleman was more entertaining than usual. Oh, not because of this:

> "The decision [to press the case forward] is Senator Coleman's," Ginsberg said. "He has received much support and advice and good cheer from the members of the Republican Party, but it's Senator Coleman's decision." (*MinnPost*)

Not because of this:

> "What happened today in the sphere of this election is really inconsequential. There's a much larger universe of ballots that should be opened." (*MinnPost*)

Last votes of the election being counted: "inconsequential," huh? Right.

No, actually Ben was entertaining because Rachel Stassen-Berger (RSB) of the St. Paul Pioneer Press had hot sauce on her luncheon enchilada and came on like the granddaughter of Helen Thomas! Ginsberg got off some crap lines like those above and called on RSB for her question. She asked, "Do you have anything other than rhetoric to back that up?" YOWSER!

Ben went into total duck-and-cover mode... NOT a happy man facing the PRESS with its blood up for the hunt. He snarled back at RSB something about "reporters who do their jobs in digging out these stories."

Rachel hit him again! "You want ME to do YOUR research? Show me the numbers."

I've said it in a different setting, but Rachel, now THAT is how tango is done! THAT is how poker is played! And THAT is how a reporter grills at a press conference! Charbroil the subject like a walleye for a shore lunch by Split Rock Lighthouse. You go grrrl!

Aftermath II

Deep from under the overturned table at the Sap Head Saloon in Plumb Dumb, TX comes the voice of Sen. Cornyn on Tuesday's events:

> Events today do not address the main issue that remains unresolved: Over 4,000 Minnesotans were disenfranchised by this three-judge panel. That's why it's so critical for this process to move forward before the Minnesota Supreme Court and why Senate Republicans fully support Senator Coleman's efforts. *(John Cornyn (R-TX), quoted at MN Independent)*

NO, you Two-Bit Texas Tumbleweed! 4,000 Minnesotans didn't properly fill in their absentee ballots, or were NOT registered to vote (if that's how it's played in TX, Big John, I'll get on I-35 ratt now and drive down and start votin' agin' ya!).

Much more important than Cornyn...ooops! Excuse me... Interstellar dust 90,000 parsecs beyond the Delta Quadrant that the Borg haven't even thought of visiting yet, THAT interstellar dust is more important than John Cornyn. Let me try again.

Far more politically significant is an editorial in the Albert Lea Tribune after yesterday's count. Albert Lea is county seat of Freeborn County, straight south of the Twin Cities on the Iowa line. The Tribune endorsed Coleman in his senate run but came out yesterday calling for an end. They end like this:

> For a time many Minnesotans followed the case closely, but now, after five months, they mainly see stalling. As for the rest of the country, at first, Americans thought Minnesota looked like a diligent place for vote recounts. Now, it's starting to seem like an election laughingstock.
>
> And Coleman, who rails against career politicians, is looking like a career politician who is losing his career. A good politician knows when he is looking bad and making his state look bad.
>
> Throw in the towel. *(Alberta Lea Tribune)*

Oh, and you know how the judges had family in court today? Well, some other Minnesotans, those who voted, watched, and endured these months of maneuvering, some of them wanted some action too. A couple guys from Carlton County (yust SW of Duluth) drove 3 hours to St. Paul to be first in line for public seats yesterday... arriving by 8:15 a.m. (The math says that's gettin' up good and early!)

They were first through the metal detectors, got seats not far from Ritchie, watched the whole thing and the spin stuff after:

> As the post-courtroom news briefings ensued, Peterson and Gerard, the gentlemen from Cloquet, watched from the marble steps of the Minnesota Judicial Center. On a landing below them, Elias, Ginsberg and Ritchie met the press.
>
> It was fascinating. It was historic. They both said the three-hour drive was worth it.
>
> "It was fun seeing the system in action," said Peterson. "We here in Minnesota take this election stuff very seriously." *(MinnPost)*

Yes you do! The WineRev doffs (DOFFS!) his hat to you and says next time I'm headin' to Superior I'll pull off at Cloquet and meet you at your bar. First round of drinks and food is on me. First toast is to Madison, Jefferson, Franklin & Lincoln.

Whew! Well, the people have spoken, and by 312 votes Mr. Al(an) Stuart Franken is their choice as the next senator from the Great Frozen North State of Minnesota! (I know, I know: lawyers, courts, appeals, etc. But for the moment: The People have spoken; the rest is commentary!)

That's worth a second cup of coffee here yust southeast of Lake Wobegon—maybe even with a bit of Bailey's or Drumgray to liven it up!

Shalom.

While Waiting for the ECC
April 9, 2009

Comments: 124   Recs: 173   Tips: 152

Afterglow is definitely the word after Tuesday's open & count session has moved Al Franken's lead in the MN Senate race to +312. We can do just a bit of basking while waiting for the ECC to either a) rule on the Mpls 133 and/or the 100 alleged "duplicate/double counted ballots" or b) roll those issues and other points into a final decision. No word as of first thing this morning, but I personally am hopeful we will get a decision yet this week.

Reactions and reflections are showing up in various places for your casual perusal.

Doug Grow, once of the StarTrib and now writing for MinnPost, has a pair of pieces. The first is a short article on how the Franken campaign was ready with a plan for a recount from Nov. 4.

> Volunteers—including lawyers and everyday Franken supporters—were quickly trained so they could attend every district where ballots were to be recounted...
>
> Volunteers, hundreds of them, also were involved in carrying data from each recount station in the state back to Franken headquarters, which was operating 24-7, according to Jess McIntosh, Franken's press secretary. *(MinnPost)*

Marc Elias was already on board on Election Day as an attorney. And unlike most campaigns, the Franken headquarters got BUSIER after Nov. 4 than before.

But the real story is a wonderful profile piece from Grow on Franken's campaign manager, 36-year-old Stephanie Schriock. (First noted by Allen03, hat tip.) If you're on Franken's e-mail list she's the one who's been signing and sending fund-raising e-mails.

Schriock is a rising star for sure, so much so that Bob Shrum and other Muskie leftovers can leave now... and take the DLC with them. Schriock is MN born (Mankato), grew up in Butte, MT, came back to MN for college (Mankato State). Fresh out of school she became finance director for a (D) campaign to unseat MN-01 (R) Gutknecht in '96. (Close loss.) In '98 (age 25) she was campaign director for (D) Bill Luther's win over John Kline in MN-02 (Kline won the rematch in '00).

Then in '03 she signed on as treasurer for an obscure VT governor's try to become president, Howard Dean, and rode herd on the idea of using the Internet for fund-raising for politics.

In '06 she managed another long-shot campaign back in her "other" home state: John Tester's 3,000-vote cliffhanger win for Senate in MT. (She and the staff & the DSCC prepared a recount plan and strategy since it looked so close. She assembled a team for what turned out to be an unnecessary effort when Burns conceded...but that's when she met...Marc Elias!)

I tell ya that is one HELL of political resume for age 36!

While we wait, so does the other side. Now while generally the term "think piece" and the current Republican mindset go together about as well as Alaskan seawater and the Exxon Valdez, Scott Johnson's piece at the National Review is more than passable. Sure, it's written from a pro-Coleman view, but doggone it, this is what the "other side" used to look like and sound like and for the sake of the health of American Democracy SOMEBODY better start sounding like this again.

Johnson incorporates some of his language about the MN State Canvassing Board that he wrote at the time of a certain Wall Street Journal excuse for an editorial. I saluted him then for it and I'll give him props for sticking up for Magnuson and Anderson now against the mouth-breathers of the "moran wing" of American politics. (At the time I wrote him an open note and gave him a doff of the hat even though I said flat out he & I probably saw very little in common politically.)

And speaking of Chief Justice Magnuson and Associate Justice Anderson (Barry, not Paul, also an associate Justice), word comes from a Supreme Court spokesman confirming that if either side appeals the ECC decision, both will recuse themselves from any involvement.

And what do I mean... "if either side appeals the ECC"? The WineRev glue-sniffing has finally reached Lloyd Bridges' levels in the control tower of Airplane? Either side?

Well, yes. Yesterday I put up a scenario to get some speculation/feedback from the legal eagles who have been hanging around here, and from what I can make out in nearly 300 comments, no one took me up on it. So I'll reprint it here and ask again: If there is an ECC decision that **does not** include a Certificate of Election...

The ECC will rule finally who got the most valid ballots. I'll grab a shower and head off for the early shift at the wineshop and bring the Mogen David leftover wine/grape syrup from the Passover table to church tonight. (Very odd the link between the two should be Mogen David... I mean a charming merlot from Carmel winery on the slopes of Mt. Carmel, sure, but Mogen David? I just report what happens.) Hope that will hold you until the ECC rules (fingers crossed... or if you are Estonian, holding your thumbs). From yust southeast of Lake Wobegon.

Shalom. A blessed Pesach to the Star of David folk!

Dueling
April 10, 2009

Comments:	62	Recs:	91	Tips:	81

Closing arguments by both sides were heard by the Election Contest Court 3 weeks ago TODAY. This past Tuesday saw the opening and counting of the last 351 ballots of the Coleman-Franken Senate race. We have speculated and surmised on these threads what might come next, could come next, should come next.

Well, personally, I'm ready for a "come next." I'm all for the court making a good decision and writing it as tightly and non-reversible as possible BUT

C'MON!

Even my patience is fraying at the edges and I'm wearing down toward my frazzle level. Sheesh! [Fortunately according to Allen03 today is NOT considered a court holiday despite the religious impact of Good Friday/Passover. Then too, recall the ECC met on President's Day (honoring Franklin Pierce and Benjamin Harrison!) back on Feb. 16—a "legal holiday"] so at least they're chugging away.

But if this keeps up I'm going to start taking drastic measures.

First I might start posting chapters of my novel again.

If that doesn't move them, I'll start winerevving the NY-20 race just because the ECC stuff has gotten... boring. Ignoring them might goad them.

If that doesn't do it I'll go down to the Minnesota Judiciary Building with a boom box, dressed like John Revolting, take Ben Ginsberg in a wristlock and force him to be my partner as we reenact the dance scenes from Saturday Night Fever... (you can see I AM willing to cross the nuclear threshold...)

Dueling Pressers

The MN Democratic Party (spelled MN DFL) scheduled a "Give It Up Norm" presser for 2:30 yesterday. Just to show they still read the Rove Book on Politics, the MN GOP hastily announced they would hold a 1:00 presser.

(Both sides were cruelly handicapped by Michele Bachmann's district "forums" on cap and trade. Michele and her flunkies lectured everyone who came about galloping socialism in the guise of environmentalism that would cost the average MN-06 family $3,000/year payable in cash this week... or something. That circus sucked most of the air out of the political room.)

The useless Ron Carey, MN GOP chair, came out and said he wanted a fair election, that 4,400 ballots should be counted, that the Reichwing wants letters to the Editor (LTEs) across MN, but that he/they are not trying to sway the judges. Right.

Carey said the public information campaign is important because, even though citizens can't vote on how to conduct the recount or on how it's adjudicated, "public pressure can influence you in the back of your mind." He later said he wasn't trying to influence the judges handling the case.

Look, Ron. Let me put it this way to you and the rest of the rabid ankle-biters in a propaganda way you'll understand. *(Snark follows)*

MN GOP calls for VOTER FRAUD.

The chair of the MNGOP today invited John Cornyn, Mitch McConnell, Tom DeLay, Karl Rove, Dick Cheney, and George W. Bush among others to cast ballots in the MN Senate race between Norm Coleman and Al Franken.

"We believe every vote should be counted, regardless of MN law," Carey said to startled reporters at the MN Judiciary Building. "Inviting these illustrious leaders to vote in our election will enhance the prestige of MN.

"In the 4,400 we called to be counted today, we invite the ECC to allow voters who already voted in person to also vote by absentee ballot because busy rich people deserve 2 votes don't you know? And we also feel registering to vote is such a crock and waste of time, so 20th century, so we welcome anyone to vote in our free, fair and clean elections.

"In fact I have here an absentee ballot application which I have already filled out in crayon with the last name, first name of 'Mouse, Mickey'. The MNGOP is honored to present this application to the former president of the United States George W. Bush. When he signs it we want his ballot counted because we all know MN laws are irrelevant."

When asked by Rachel Stassen-Berger of the St. Paul Pioneer Press why such an act by His Shrubness would NOT be voter fraud, Carey replied, "We believe none of MN election laws are relevant to voting for Norm Coleman. If there are no laws being broken it is not possible to commit voter fraud." *(End snark)*

> An hour later, state DFL Chair Brian Melendez took his turn, in the same Capitol hearing room, and introduced a new website that includes a minute-plus video outlining why it's important that Norm Coleman accept the pending court ruling from a three-judge panel hearing the recount appeal...
>
> Melendez did say that if Coleman plans to appeal only to the Minnesota Supreme Court and not go the federal route, DFLers probably would not be pursuing this website/public information campaign.
>
> "Former Sen. Coleman had every right, under law, to contest the recount results. And he got his day in court. He got seven weeks," Melendez said.
>
> "Minnesota needs to have Sen.-elect Al Franken seated so as many voices as possible are speaking up for our state and its people," he said. *(MinnPost)*

So we wait.

I'll be assembling the gold chain necklaces and humming "Stayin' Alive" this morning here yust southeast of Lake Wobegon. Hope yours is a blessed Good Friday whether or not you are of the Christian persuasion.

Shalom... by a cross.

Thumbs? Meet Twiddle.
April 13, 2009

Comments: 97   Recs: 175   Tips: 185

The ECC Orders

Yes, they actually issued an order but obviously NOT the one(s) we are all waiting for. The Court addressed the "Nauen 61." The order, issued Friday, dismissed the rest, formally and officially. So that's that... except of course that decision can ALSO be appealed to the MN Supreme Court. SOoooo... we'll see.

(The court clerk who brought in the order to an anxious press crowd also announced "no further orders were expected for the weekend," so the media all got to spend the weekend doing Easter/Passover/ Pastafarian stuff.)

Gaming the Norm Game

While you're over at the MN Progressive Project, check out Grace Kelly's piece. Grace thinks the ECC will rule this week but even if they don't, the equation is turning against Coleman and the Republicans. Their big plus at the national level has been of course keeping one more Democratic vote out of the Senate. At the moment of course with Congress in recess for Easter/Passover the advantage is moot.

But according to Grace the minuses keep gaining weight:

1. The Rethug "image," already putrid, will NOT be helped by Norm's ongoing legal problems with Kazeminy down in Texas. That case has skunk oil flying off it like a propeller blade and Norm is standing on the tarmac.

2. Pawlenty's presidential prospects (both his own and those "handlers" who think a nice-looking Midwest governor might be an appealing face for 2012) are in a bind on whether and when to sign off on an Election Certificate.

3. In the courts (esp. federal) the Rethugs would have to publicly support transparent, auditable elections and have to come out AGAINST having 5 times more voting machines/voter in gated communities than in inner-city "ethnic communities..". on grounds of "equal protection"! Not only would that be genetically impossible but they would never win/steal another election... even in JesusLovesMe, Alaska.

So Grace thinks the calculus is swinging toward the puppet masters telling Norm it's time to concede. Hope so, Grace... and we'll see.

Well, as you can see, there's not much. but I WILL have a second cup of coffee with you from here, yust southeast of Lake Wobegon.

Shalom.

THE Ruling: Franken ROCKS!
Tuesday, April 14, 2009

Comments: 285	Recs: 521	Tips: 474

Franken WINS by +312.

Who says so? The Election Contest Court (ECC) of Minnesota says so, that's who! In a 68-page decision the ECC has declared Franken the candidate who received the "most, validly cast votes" and deserves the Certificate of Election.

DK YEAHHHHHHHHHH!!!! Hurrah! Yipee! Eureka! Voila! SKOAL! I take back all the mean things I said about this wonderful, beautiful, magnificent three judge court. It is a good thing you have done this day. *(ABowers13)*

There I was, having gotten off the phone with a long chat with an editor of mine about the WineRev diaries book collection, ready to do a filler diary on that while we wait forever for the ECC to decide. Went out for a haircut and dinner... and the heavens have opened, the bush was burning but not consumed, the waters of the Red Sea parted and the stone is rolled away from the Tomb...

That's right! The Election Contest Court delivered of themselves a 68-page decision. According to Jennifer at The UpTake they promised the press no decisions after 6:00 p.m. SOOooo...The UpTake shut down their LiveBlog at 5:56 p.m. with a sweet round of good-nights. ANDddd... the clerk of courts made sure the twitter for the media went off at 05:59:59! Obviously planned ALL THE WAY!

And as so many have hoped, they have laid it down for Al Franken while burying Norm Coleman's hopes like so much leftover sand-and-salt mix for Highway 169.

Where to start?

The Court took 18 pages to lay out Findings of Fact, 3 more for Conclusions of Law, and 1 for the Order for Judgment. They also attached the next 40 pages of memoranda dealing with various points and closed with 10 pages of names of absentee voters.

They dismissed the Coleman case and claims "WITH PREJUDICE," which we have all learned means Norm's set of claims and evidence can NOT see the light of another courtroom (barring a reversal by the MN Supremes). They dismissed the Franken counterclaims without prejudice but also moot. I think that means Franken can use all the parts of his case (warp engines, lightsabers, photon torpedos, holodeck transporter beams—all running through David Lillehaug's iPhone) anytime he wants to and it's all admissible... but since Norm's mess has been officially, legally shot-to-hell it's a moot point for Franken since the Court thinks he won't need it.

Findings of Fact

This is the evidence presented, contested, and argued over. VERY important since appeal courts give VERY high deference to findings of fact/evidence/testimony and rarely question a trial court's record of this. Appeal courts wrestle mostly with the law part and how the evidence and law intersect, but the evidence as considered by the trial court is usually taken as GIVEN THESE FACTS.

Here the Court breaks into Ancient Persian/Farsi and takes 18 pages to say (to Norm Coleman's side), "Mene mene tekel upharsin" (Book of Daniel; God's finger writes on the wall at the King's party: "Measured, measured, weighed... and found wanting!")

Opening phrases from the Findings of Fact, Conclusions of Law, and Order for Judgment, in favor of a GREAT election and DAMN accurate Recount:

> #69: The record [in court] is devoid of any evidence that election officials did not perform their duties on Election Day in good faith and to the best of their abilities. *(Findings of Fact... Final Ramsey County District Court Order)*

> #70. The Court has received no evidence or testimony to support a finding of wholesale disenfranchisement of Minnesota's absentee voters in the November 4, 2008 general election. *(Findings of Fact... Final Ramsey County District Court Order)*

Then they swung to the (in)famous absentee ballots:

> #86. In their Notice of Contest, Contestants [Coleman] alleged that county election officials wrongfully accepted absentee ballots that were opened and counted on Election Day. ... Contestants failed to identify any such ballots in response to Contestee's [Franken] interrogatories [written questions and answers]. *(Findings of Fact... Final Ramsey County District Court Order)*

Failed to identify ANY such...? Right. The Court is just doing scales for vocal warm-ups. ANY such?

> #88. No evidence *[Picky, picky, Ginsberg would say]* was presented by either party that facially invalid ballots *[sounds like Extra Strength Clearasil is needed]* were wrongfully included in the vote totals certified by the Board. *(Findings of Fact... Final Ramsey County District Court Order, editorial comments mine - WR)*

In other words, they swat down the **duplicate/double count** allegations and note only the shaky testimony of Pamela Howell in support of the idea.

Minneapolis 133/132?

> #120: Given the evidence presented, the Court finds that 132 ballots from Minneapolis Precinct 3-1 were cast and properly counted on Election Day and were lost at some point after they were counted on Election Day but before the administrative recount. *(Findings of Fact... Final Ramsey County District Court Order)*

Then, breaking into full-throated trio that rings like archangels humming for progressives, co'
~~ives, liberals, democracy lovers, and those who live by the law everywhere, but which sounds

arch-fiends like scraping iron fingernails across acres of slate blackboards for totalitarians, Reichvingers, trotskyites, leftover Kim Jung-Il–ians, certain skinheads and advocates of force, violence, and might-makes-right (lookin' at you, Dick the Cheney!):

> #125. There was no evidence of fraud in the conduct of this election and no show-ing of bad faith on the part of any election official at any point during the election or recount. *(Findings of Fact... Final Ramsey County District Court Order)*

Then vote totals: 1,212,629 vs. 1,212,317, "Franken received the highest number of votes legally cast...is entitled to receive the certificate of election."

How soon? We'll see, of course...

Conclusion of Law

Now for all of us non-lawyer types, here is where the Court launches into deep water and sails over the law books and precedents in case law. The citations can get so thick they can be more than the words in a sentence.

BUT... ya gotta love some of the stuff they threw around... or threw AT at least one of the parties.

In the memoranda starting on page 28, the Court comes on like a baseball-pitching machine that has been turned up to "fastball" and plugged into the 220-volt outlet instead of 110 so the batting cage is a reenactment of the ancient Olympic sport of Shotput/Hammerthrow Catching.

Both sides agreed to adopt Rule 9 for counting original ballots instead of duplicates for the hand recount. Starting with the recount on Nov. 19, Coleman "insisted on the strict application of Rule 9." He didn't object until Dec. 16, and then began to claim double counting. SMACKED down on laches, as many Kossack legal types argued here. [Meaning if you go along with a rule, or don't object, right at the start of the process (when you think you're winning) you DON'T get to change your mind later (when you're losing).]

Then, while we're at it: "Contestants did not prove by a preponderance of the evidence that double counting occurred." DID NOT PROVE! Take THAT!

Like, the star witness, Pamela Howell "did not have personal knowledge on whether judges marked duplicate ballots or how many ballots were potentially affected by this error. No incident log was intro-duced during the trial, and no other election officials from this precinct testified."

Equal Protection!

Yes, the ECC went there. This is where Coleman's team wants to go, to the MN Supreme Court and their bruited (!) idea to pursue this in federal court.

Well, from what I can tell as a non-lawyer, since the Coleman side wanted to make such a big deal out of this, the ECC grabbed this one by the throat. (IF they missed and only got the earlobe or collarbone let me know, OK, lawyer types?) They DID say "this Court lacks jurisdiction to make findings or conclusions on these points and the matter is preserved for the United States Senate." (HAH! We are going to throw this one curving right past the Supremes and hand it to the First Branch of Government.)

> It says that "to the extent" the claim alleges material and intentional violations of state law they have no jurisdiction, but that they do have jurisdiction to consider it to the extent it pertains to who has the most lawful votes. So they do consider and decide the eq prot claim. *(Chris II at The UpTake)*

First they acknowledged the equal protection clause and 14th Amendment of the US Constitution. Then, the right to vote is regarded as fundamental because it is preservative of all rights. (Citing a case from 1886—now we're rolling.) And under MN law it should be "liberally interpreted" (MAJOR screech-ing sound from the Faux Noise Pole Dance & Pundit Company) "so as to secure to the people their right to freely express their choice." (1950 cite.) Nonetheless the states get to set their own rules and regs, and absentee voting can have more restrictions on it.

But, having said they don't have jurisdiction, the ECC proceeds to run equal protection through the ~~aces~~ like a kid running a stick along a picket fence. (The chattering sound you hear is Ben Ginsberg try-~~g~~ to say something.)

The ECC admits errors will happen but simple errors do NOT rise to the level of a constitutional violation of equal protection. They cite "no matter how hard we try, regrettably we may never be able to guarantee a perfect election." [This is Bush (yeah that one) vs. Hillsborough County FL in 2000!] And to cite the old with the new: "There is hardly an election held in any county at which in some town irregularities do not occur..." which is Taylor v. Taylor, MN 1865 (! and which Chief Justice Magnuson brought to the very first meeting of the State Canvassing Board back in November; I LOVE citations from almost TERRITORIAL law; MN became a state in 1858).

THEN they go for the big one. There ARE MN statewide, uniform standards that were followed, implemented by uniform training, yet adapted to local conditions. The local variations? The ECC cites, "The question before the Court is not whether local entities, in the exercise of their expertise, may develop different systems for implementing elections...the Equal Protection Clause does not forbid the use of a variety of voting mechanisms within a jurisdiction, even though different mechanisms will have different levels of effectiveness in recording voters' intentions."

And where is that citation from??? Bush v. Gore!!

Yep. The ECC cites Bush v. Gore like a cactus boxing glove on the Coleman legal position.

SINCE there are statewide standards, and

SINCE there is statewide training in those standards, and

SINCE the local expertise will implement the election process differently but within the law, and within the standards and within the training,

Bush v. Gore holds the election outcome is fair and an expression of equal protection.

DAYAMM! It strikes me they are almost daring the Coleman side to take this to the US Supremes. It seems to me the ECC is saying, "Look, Bush v. Gore said because Florida didn't have (STILL DOESN'T HAVE?) statewide law, uniform standards, haphazard training and implementation, we the US Supremes need to intervene/interfere."

SINCE we here in MN HAVE all that stuff in place and it was all used in the US Senate race, Bush v. Gore ITSELF would imply a) the USSC has no cause to intervene/interfere and b) equal protection was observed because NONE of the Bush v. Gore crap was present.

If I've got it right THAT is a fastball just under the chin of the Norm Legal team. "Here's your Bush v. Gore, which you cited in your arguments, coming AT YA! Swing, batter, or bail out, but decide NOW!"

Finally, having smacked down or swatted aside all the rest of Coleman's case, the ECC finishes once more with a quote from the 1865 Taylor case: "The public good demands that the will of the people as expressed at the ballot box should not be lightly disturbed."

"The overwhelming weight of the evidence indicates that the November 4, 2008 election was conducted fairly, impartially, and accurately."

And for a coda, the Court says words worthy of a plaque in every voting precinct in the state [WineRev rises and doffs (DOFFS!) hat]:

> The citizens of Minnesota should be proud of their election system. Minnesota has one of the highest voter-participation rates in the country. The Office of the Minnesota Secretary of State and election officials throughout Minnesota's counties and cities are well-trained, fair, and conscientious and performed their duties admirably. Minnesota could not conduct elections without the hard work and diligence of its dedicated professionals and citizen volunteers, and the Court is proud of their service. (*Findings of Fact... Final Ramsey County District Court Order*)

Whew! Well, THAT's a bit of a rundown for you. I hope that will give you something to chew on with your coffee this morning. I've got the early shift today and the spring sale coming up Thursday but I'll try & check in over lunch. Go ahead and add your thoughts, tips, and recs to make this one of the bigger reports from yust southeast of Lake Wobegon.

Shalom.

Reactions from All Over
April 15, 2009

Comments: 265   Recs: 270   Tips: 271

Franken wins by 312 votes.

So said the Election Contest Court late Monday.

In true rabbinic style, those words at the top are THE text. What follows below is merely commentary...

TODAY is DAY 2 since the ECC handed down its decision in Coleman v. Franken. Coleman has 8 days left to file an appeal with the MN Supreme Court or the decision becomes final. The clock ticks. The leaves fall from the calendar. The cookie crumbles. The pickle drips...

Fallout Landing like Turkeys from a Helicopter

Well, the echoes of Monday evening's decision from the Election Contest Court declaring Al Franken the senator-elect from Minnesota continue to reverberate like the shouting of a hung-over Norwegian calling in the North Woods for more aquavit. LOTS of "names" weighing in.

RNC Chairman Michael Steele had something to say:

> "I am glad that Senator Coleman is appealing the recent court order in Minnesota. More than 4,400 voters remain disenfranchised because judges ignored equal protection concerns and the facts from Election Day. The Republican Party will continue to strongly support Senator Coleman's appeals until we are confident that no voter is left behind." *(quoted at Politico)*

DNC chair Tim Kaine answered:

> "Enough is enough. It is time for Norm Coleman to concede and for Al Franken to be sworn in as the next U.S. Senator from Minnesota. The voters of Minnesota months ago elected Al Franken to the Senate—and during every step in the legal process that judgment has been confirmed." *(quoted at Politico)*

But more than that, the DNC is set to begin running a radio ad in Minneapolis & St. Paul calling on Coleman to give it up.

> (The ad) accuses the incumbent senator and national Republicans of wanting "to thwart the will of the voters" and delay the outcome.
>
> "Enough is enough," says the announcer, noting that Franken won the original election, the recount and a legal challenge. "America is in an economic crisis—and Minnesota faces unique challenges of its own. Minnesota deserves two Senators and voters deserve to have their verdict stand without delay." *(Politico)*

The Coleman campaign sent out a new spokesman to reply to the ad using the same wet-dishrag rhetoric we've learned to expect:

> Asked to respond to the new ad, Coleman spokesman Tom Erickson said: "We'd invite them to spend that money to join us to ensure that the 4,400 hard-working disenfranchised Minnesotans, who care about the future of this country, are afforded their due process and equal protection rights. Perhaps the DNC and the President would support an electoral stimulus package that ensures that each and every Minnesotan who cast a legal ballot in the last election has their vote counted." *(Politico)*

Joe the Scarhead(!) on his morning TV show:

> "When are the Republicans going to give up the ghost on this? Seriously. Norm, I like you. Ya lost, OK?... Can we seat?... Making Amy Klobuchar carry all the load... It is not fair to the constituents in Minnesota..." *(Joe Scarborough at MSNBC)*

Joe?! Nice to see the old adage still has force: Even a blind pig finds an acorn once in a while.

Chuck Todd from MSNBC is impressed by Franken:

> Franken's discipline: By the way, and it's a point we've made before, but it's been pretty impressive how Franken has been so disciplined during this recount period... Clearly, the GOP thought they were dealing with the stereotype that was Al Franken—not the guy who proved to be a candidate who, well, got more votes than Norm Coleman. In fact, this has been a problem for the GOP in general the last few years when it comes to dealing with Democrats: They believe their own stereotypes about their opponents, rather than actually dealing with their opponents at face value. *(MSNBC)*

Nothing like believing your own propaganda... after all, once you've been greeted as liberators, life after is just dull...

Michael Brodkorb of Minnesota Democrats Exposed (title says it all) reports he "did an interview with WCCO-TV (the big local station) on the Recount (aired at 6 p.m.)...Senator Coleman should keep on fighting, keep on (the) march to victory." Ah, it's spring and the lemmings are in heat...

Nate Silver, the Holy Odin of Numbers and Crunching Thereof, believes Norm's chances of pulling this one out are "in Calista Flockhart territory."... the woman who casts no shadow on a sunny day.

Lawyers Swinging Lightsabers Episode ??

Its been quite a while, since before the ECC convened, since the lawyers on both sides got to swing their lightsabers at each other in public. Oh, Ben the Ginz has been doing hula-hoop shimmies with his, but it's just not the same when there are no Jedi around.

Ginsberg is still delusional or dizzy from all that spinning:

> "If you read this opinion, the court was very defensive of the Minnesota system. The purpose of the contest is to be protective of the rights of voters ...In spending so much time kind of patting themselves on the back about the Minnesota system the court, I think, kind of missed what the real picture is." *(MinnPost)*

Ginsberg got off a press release/public statement for the Team Norm at 7:00 in the morning, Tuesday:

> "As the record in this trial shows, the volume and significance of the equal protection violations is great enough to turn the results of this election," Ginsberg said. "You cannot know who won this election without coming to grips with the equal protection issue." *(MinnPost)*

Excuse me, Mr. Sith Lord? The ECC gripped the equal protection issue like Darth Vader doing a choke hold using the Force at five meters. The Court gave equal protection pages 33 to 58 in their decision, addressing every angle. They gave it a stun gun blast, used Bush v. Gore to slap it seven ways to Sunday, cited precedents and case law from here to Alpha Centauri, laughed "robotic sameness" off the roof of the IDS tower, allowed for humans to be human and local conditions to be adapted to MN law, and showed equal protection as grounds for ANYTHING in this case is a delusional fantasy that would be an insult to the paper upon which it is filed. Harumph!

Ginsberg also argued that the ruling by the three-judge panel wrongly ignored double counting of ballots, as well as 132 Minneapolis ballots that were lost but still included in the final vote tally. "Regrettably, this court decided to take expediency over accuracy and never wanted to kick open the hood and look at the engine," he said.

Actually Ben, they WERE accurate, excruciatingly so, and as transparent as 20 inches of ice under your pickup on Lake Minnetonka in January. Ben, you're just addled because Norm, Joe, Fritz, Tony, and you on the Spaceballs 1Starcruiser have found the Court pulled the emergency brake ("Warning: Never use") on your case as it was doing Ludicrous speed. You think it still is going at "plaid" but actually you and your Dark Helmet have hit the dashboard and you haven't called for the 5-minute smoke break yet.

Meanwhile one of our heroes, Marc Elias, weighed in with a presser from his home in DC. He swung the blue lightsaber that hummed musically:

> "We are extremely pleased with the court's final opinion," Elias told reporters. "Al Franken won this election fair and square. Al Franken won this election because more Minnesotans voted for him than for Norm Coleman or for any other candidate." *(quoted at MinnPost)*

More Minnesotans voted for (Franken) than for Norm... well, that is obviously Elias doing one of the roll-on-the-floor moves with the lightsaber blade apt to come flailing out at an unexpected angle. It's necessary to make a low, rolling move like this sometimes, not to go for the legs, but because it's the only way to look some of the "morans" straight in the eye!

> "It's extremely unlikely that the U.S. Supreme Court would have reason to take this case," Elias said, noting that the nation's top court has only heard two election cases in recent memory. "If former Sen. Coleman chooses to appeal to the Minnesota Supreme Court, I think that will be the end of the road for him." *(quoted at MinnPost)*

And it's STILL, for all of you usage mavens, "FORMER Senator Coleman"! Right on, Good Jedi Elias!

Eric Black of MinnPost sees the pressure building steadily on Governor Pawlenty and tries to read the cross-currents building on him, along with some possible deals that could be made by T-Paw and Norm and/or with Cornyn or the national GOP.

And Politico reports Franken's victory has been noticed at a VERY high level:

> ...for the first time, the White House weighed in on the matter, if gingerly.
>
> Press Secretary Robert Gibbs repeated the judges' opinion that the election had been conducted " 'fairly, impartially and accurately' and that Al Franken received in that election the most votes."
>
> "We look forward, hopefully soon, to having an additional U.S. senator representing the people of the state of Minnesota," Gibbs said from the White House podium. *(Politico)*

You know, looking back over this list of quotes there is an interesting amount of pressure building here...

Hope this will hold you while you finish up your taxes (and remember, Form 4868, Extension to File, is your friend if things get too harried). That's the latest from yust southeast of Lake Wobegon.

Shalom.

Longer, with wine
April 16, 2009

Comments: 119   Recs: 180   Tips: 168

TODAY is **DAY 3** since the ECC handed down its decision in Coleman v. Franken. Coleman has **7 days left** to file an appeal with the MN Supreme Court or the decision becomes final.

And what if Norm doesn't? Could happen, you know. This entire thing ends...with a whimper, a quiet "for the sake of the people of Minnesota I choose to step back" sort of speech. Unlikely? Yeah. Impossible? Not sure I'd go that far...I mean Norm IS a bend-in-the-wind sort of politician and he has been...um, EXPEDIENT and flexible in his political path. But he has been visible (Franken has been much wiser in this regard) and been visibly unhappy. Of course kowtowing to the likes of McConnell, Cornyn, Steele, & assorted members of the Goebbels' School graduates on the air would be miserable. Having to be around a sheet of human sandpaper like Tony Trimble or downwind from the human feedlot that IS Ben Ginsberg would be adding lutefisk to the lash wounds.

But can he be pushed "too far"? Does Norm have it in him, either from being whored one time too many, or from some tattered sense of human dignity or personal self-worth, to tell these meretricious marble-brains to go to hell and call off the whole sorry mess short of the Supreme Court? I don't think so... t I might put it at a 20% chance this morning. Just saying...

Minnesota Opinion I

One factor that may be making its weight felt is public opinion in MN. David Brauer writes over at MNPost. Back in the fall he was tracking newspaper editorial endorsements around the state. In late October Norm had an 11-0 endorsement lead until Winona's daily paper weighed in for Franken.

Well, Brauer has been calling around the state the last couple weeks as the ECC trial ended and as the decision came down Monday asking those same editorial boards where they stand on should Norm call a halt... or go on through the court system?

Call it off:

- *Worthington Daily Globe*
- *Albert Lea Tribune*—we heard from them the other day
- *Winona Daily News*
- *Faribault Daily News*
- *Owatonna People's Press*—sounds like a name the Right would hate

Battle on:

- *Minneapolis StarTribune*
- *Mankato Free Press*
- *Crookston Daily Times* (with plenty of snark)
- *New Ulm Journal*

Overall, like the election itself, slight edge to Franken.

Minnesota Opinion II

Public Policy Polling (is this PPP in the Nate Silver nomenclature?) took a MN survey of 805 people, Tuesday and Wednesday morning (AFTER the ECC decision came down Monday evening). 63% of Minnesotans would like Norm to concede: virtually all voters who voted for Franken and Dean Barkley (42% & 15% respectively) and 1/3 of those who voted for Coleman! Margin of error 3.5%.

So, for what it's worth, here's another piece of info for Norm to add to his calculus (or at least his algebra).

Other Voices

The BigE over at MN Progressive Project disagrees with me in thinking Norm might quit. He leads off:

> Those of us who have been following the Minnesota Senate race (MN-SEN), its recount and subsequent election contest suit know former senator Norm Coleman's chances of overturning Al Franken's victories in the recount and election contest are extremely slim. Of course, we also know that winning is no longer the point. (MN *Progressive Project*)

No real disagreement here, just thinking out loud about another scenario. BigE does a swift but pointed rundown on just how much a lapdog Coleman has been in his term as Senator and so rates his likelihood of "doing the right thing" as nil.

The BigE is also willing to slap around a decayed Pioneer Press columnist named Joe Soucheray. Joe just came out with an opinion piece that is heavy on delusion (Coleman's chances of getting to the Senate are close to 50-50... uh huh!) and the usual Ginsberg pack of lies and talking points. BigE gives him what for (and what five and even what six; whatever it takes).

Paul Begala of CNN but writing for Huffington Post opens his piece with a line sure to tip you off his column will not end well for a former senator: "If character were oil, Norm Coleman would be a quart low."

Thursday Morning Minnesota Media

Diaz & von Sternberg put together a story for the StarTribune noting both sides combined have raised about $12 million SINCE election day to pay for things Recount-related (I am STILL waiting for my cut!). They also go over the PPP results.

And shooting down my idea at the top of this diary is Rachel Stassen-Berger's story in the Pioneer Press. Norm sounds like he's going to appeal and they are "working on the briefs right now." Coleman sat down with the P-P editorial board for a talk and RSB writes it up here: (P-P wins the Twin cities newspaper competition by default since the Pioneer Press got an exclusive.)

OK, a fast shower, some coffee, and then off to face the public... (Lord give me strength!) Hope this will hold you with some of the latest from yust southeast of Lake Wobegon.

Shalom.

Coleman writhing on the hook
April 17, 2009

Comments: 233   Recs: 312   Tips: 328

TODAY is **DAY 4** since the Election Contest Court (ECC) handed down its decision in Coleman v. Franken. Coleman has **10 days left** to file an appeal with the MN Supreme Court or the decision becomes final.

The Soap Opera

SOOoooo, like sands through the hourglass so are the days of Norm's lives... um, could we get a little input here from the legal profession? Coleman has 10 days to file—not the whole barrel of briefs and lutefisk, but apparently a Notice of Filing/Appeal—something like that term, right? OK, 2 mechanical questions:

Does this mean filing with the Supreme Court (like the clerk of court's office?) ONLY, or also filing with the opposing party by serving them notice as well? Is there a stack of these forms at the clerk's window, so, say, Coleman lawyer Fritz Knaak (a name from the past!) goes by and says, "Hey Sven? Let me have a number 203B with a side order of 319 WITH the glossy white & gold seal, not the purple one because we're out of Lent now?" And Sven Svenson says, "Ya sure, you betcha dar Fritz. Yust put down your $500 bond and yew can haff 'em." How does that work, exactly?

Is our timing correct? The Election Contest Court twittered the press/public famously at 5:59:59 p.m. on Monday, April 13. The decision was dated the 13th but with no time-of-day stamp. Did the clock start ticking at straight up 6:00:00 p.m. on the 13th in 24-hour increments, so that the last possible second to file timely without the ECC decision turning into Norm's personal pillar of salt (Genesis 19:26) is 5:59:59 p.m. on April 23? OR did the clock start ticking on Tuesday the 14th when the courts opened for business at, say, 9:00 a.m.? If the last day is indeed the 23rd and the clerk rolls down the steel window cover and snaps the padlock shut at 4:00 or 4:30 p.m. does that mean the hammer has fallen?

Inquiring minds who are planning the MN REVERSE replay of the infamous "Brooks Brothers" Miami riot want to know. Just exactly WHEN should the troops be in place to swing into the "Sting" line at the clerk's window immediately ahead of Doyle Lonnegan/the Coleman crew to shut them out of the action at Paul Newman's place down the alley? Or if it's Ben Ginsberg leading the bad guys, we want to know when Theoden's riders need to appear and blacken the ridge with mounted warriors? (Ginsberg will say to Trimble, Friedberg & others, "Form ranks, you maggots! Pikes in front! Archers in the second row!" And we will fear no darkness; spears will be shaken and shields will be shattered but we will call down "death" on the enemies of democracy, ride for ruin and the world's ending shouting "Forth Eorlingas!!")

Spring is here and DeNial is rising - old Egyptian proverb?

Oh, and that shout of "Forth Eorlingas" will be in a reality-based kind of way. Yesterday PPP released a poll of Minnesotans that showed people wanting Norm to call it quits by 63%-37%, which is dang lopsided. (BTW also reported Obama's approval in the 60s.)

In that 37% that are in the 5-3 minority are the "real American/true believers/utterly self-righteous"— Bachmannites, Kline-dinks, minions of MNGOP chief Ron Carey and the common clay of the new West...

you know... "morans!" Scientific polling from a firm with a good track record that conflicts with their own opinions MUST have something wrong with them.

According to Ryan Flynn at MN Democrats Exposed, PPP's poll is "bogus and misleading," PPP president Dean Debnam is a Democrat, has contributed to the NC "Democrat" party, and his wife has run for local office as a Democrat. (All of which proves...?) In Oct. of '08 he had the gall to point out the NC governor's race is "neck and neck" and will continue to seesaw up to election day. This stunning news is a result of PPP controversial polling methods that involve cost-cutting measures for the company...

Yeah, well even at MN Democrats Exposed the commenters take Flynn apart.

Denial flows, but money flows like the Nile

Yeesh, linking to those guys sure leaves my hands gummy on the keyboard. Well, some leftover lye & water from the first soak of the lutefisk should take it right off... yep.

Cynthia Dizikes of MNPost (both a MUCH nicer person and site to link to) scanned over the Fed. Election Commission financial filings for Coleman & Franken that were published this week. Not only have Cornyn & McConnell chipped in for Norm but Coleman has support in the Senate from Georgia to Idaho.

Franken has his own geography working for him from Nevada to Massachusetts and stops in between. AND, just to put the Reichwing's teeth on edge, Hollywood has also been dropping dollars in Franken's microphone bucket from Jane Curtin to John Grisham.

A little chippy on the soccer pitch

Chris Steller at Minnesota Independent gets off a rather edgy piece for the land of Minnesota Nice. After Coleman met with the St. Paul Pioneer Press editorial board, Steller quotes him as saying "We may never know" who won the Senate race—which is infuriating!

NORM—who is that "WE" you are referring to? Damn near all of us in reality land KNOW who won. The ECC knows who won and took 68 closely reasoned pages to tell you in excruciating detail who won. A minimum of 63% of Minnesotans know who won. Editorial boards around the state know who won. "What you mean 'we,' Kimosabe?"

In the same piece Steller quotes gawker.com, apparently a New York City edgy website (which is thereby several parsecs of magnitude edgier than what we hear in MN). They take a Manhattan swipe (and that is SOME roundhouse right, youse guys!) at Governor Pawlenty, calling him an "amiable prick." I know, I know. In midtown Manhattan that could be taken as a term of affection or as a description of a surly Nathan's hotdog pushcart vendor, but out here that's a pretty heavy shot.

Friday Morning Minnesota Media

Kevin Diaz of the *StarTrib* is up with an expanded version of MNPost's listing of donors to both campaigns in the last quarter. (Let it be noted that Coleman reports cash on hand on 3/31 of $469K, having spent well over $3 million during those 90 days.) More names of corporations and individuals including—GASP!—confirmation that Al Franken got $10K from George Soros. (Every Reichvinger's suspicion confirmed! Dang disclosure laws!)

Having met with the *Pioneer Press* editors Wednesday (where Norm Coleman stated "we can never know who won"), Norm continued his personal charm offensive by meeting with the StarTrib board. (Obviously he's trying to offset the impact of the *Albert Lea Tribune*, *Worthington Daily Globe*, and *Hooterville World Guardian* coming out against him carrying on the fight.)

He thinks "the law is on our side"—which is actually the dawning of reality since this implicitly acknowledges THE FACTS are nowhere to be found near his side of this galaxy!

Also:

> "I don't spend 30 seconds worrying about my political future," he said. "I don't define myself by the office that I hold. ... If it weren't to continue, that would be fine, too. I'm not looking for another office." (*Norm Coleman, quoted in Star Tribune*)

Norm, I've got your 30 seconds beat cold.

Also:

> He said that he expects an appeal to be filed early next week, well within the 10 days that state law gives him. Joe Friedberg, the noted defense lawyer who led his legal team during the trial, will argue the case before the state Supreme Court, Coleman said. *(Star Tribune)*

Despite this I will continue the countdown clock at the head of these diaries. And Friedberg to argue the case before the Supreme Court, eh? OK, I started this diary asking for input from the legal eagles here. Let's close the same way.

How good a move is this, people (assuming it's true)? Joe Friedberg in front of 5 razor-sharp judges who can fire questions at will? 19,000 pages of transcripts to keep straight?

What's your take? Mine is, this is enough to get Norm's synagogue to go Catholic and take on the name of St. Jude, the patron saint of hopeless causes, but that's just me.

Staying within Talmud: to ask Joe Friedberg! to plead this case in front of the MN Supreme Court with your political life hanging in the balance...oy vey! It is written for the feast of Purim (Book of Esther) one rabbi invited another rabbi in town to the party. It was a rip-roaring affair and somewhere in the night the visiting rabbi was killed. The next morning the host rabbi found the body and was stricken with grief (and a massive hangover). He prayed that his friend be resurrected from the dead... and he was, and went on with his life.

The next year when Purim came around again the same rabbi invited his friend AGAIN to come for a party. The other rabbi politely declined this time with the words, "A miracle doesn't happen every time."

The wine sale is on big time down at the shop but I've got the late shift this morning so I can stay & chat a bit with you. Hope this will hold you with the latest from yust southeast of Lake Wobegon.

Shalom.

Pull a Coleman
April 18, 2009

Comments: 112   Recs: 158   Tips: 168

TODAY is DAY 5 since the Election Contest Court (ECC) handed down its decision in Coleman v. Franken. Coleman has **5 days left to file** an appeal with the MN Supreme Court or the decision becomes final.

Cultural Phenomena

I really wasn't going to post a diary today since not a lot is going on here in the Paint Drying Universe. But then I came across this GEM from the Minnesota Independent linking to CNN.

First we had Al Franken's delightful phrase of the "lying liars who lie about lying while lying around" (not the exact quote but close). Then there are all the possibilities using "Franken" as a stem: I've mentioned/coined "Frankenites" but also a title suggestion using "Franken Sense" (for the Christmas chapters of the book), "Frankenly my dear, I don't give a damn," sending out mail via the congressional privilege is Franken franking his constituents. LOTS of other possibilities.

But now comes word from the other side of the street. Ashton Kutcher, an actor I've never heard of (see how limited I am) has apparently been in a friendly competition with CNN to see which one, Kutcher or all of CNN, will be first to gain 1,000,000 "twitter" links/connections (something; again—totally clueless on this end).

Well, apparently it was quite close mid-week and Kutcher said on Larry King he now knew how Al Franken must feel. But THEN Kutcher crosses the double comma line first. Larry King has him on his show and says on behalf of CNN, "I'm not a sore loser. I'm not gonna pull a Norm Coleman."

"Pull a Norm Coleman!" WOW! Now THERE is something that needs to go Internet viral by yesterday.

"Mr. Tedisco, how long do you intend to Norm Coleman the race in NY-20?"

"The EFCA passed the Senate today in Washington. Senate Minority Idiot Mitch McConnell Norm Coleman-ed the press corps by releasing the following statement..."

"Did Paul Warfield have both feet in bounds on that last catch for the Browns that won the game? Eagles fans are Norm Colemaning the airwaves this morning and bombarding the Commissioner's office with letters and phone calls..."

"As Karl Rove was led away from the courtroom today in shackles to begin serving his sentence in Blistered Rock Federal Prison in the Arizona desert he Norm Coleman-ed nearby reporters by calling out, 'I've got the math for my appeal. You'll see...' "

Public Pressure

The DNC's radio ad is running in the Twin Cities, calling on Norm to concede. MN Democrats Exposed seems to be hacked off about it and some of the comments here and there at the StarTrib and Pioneer Press are pretty whiny too, so GOOD! It's working! You throw a rock at a pack of charging iguanas and the one that gleeps the loudest is the one you hit.

According to Joe Bodell at MN Progressive Project the gleeping could increase by 1 magnitude. He says flyers will be going up around MN with the simple message "AL WON." MN Progressive Project is calling for folks to send in photos of where they spot them. (Myself I'd love to get a photo of one plastered to the front door of Michele Bachmann's home church: First Self-Righteous of Delusionals, but that's my religious side coming out.)

For Shame

Flyers? Fine! Radio ads: Give it up Norm? Excellent! "Pull a Norm Coleman"? Delightful.

Go by Norm's house and throw eggs at it? Dumb. Stupid. Insulting. (Karl Rovian trick? Egg own house by own supporter in order to blame it on opposition? Sort of like planting a non-functional "bug" in your own office, Karl? Yet to be proven.)

Taking it at face value: BAD form!

> Dear Mr. Coleman,
>
> I'm sorry to hear some fool came by and egged your house. This is demeaning, insulting and moronic. As a public servant you should be immune from such knavery. On behalf of politically interested people of Minnesota who believe in free speech, the rule of law, and the exchange and debate of ideas, please accept this apology that this incident happened to you and your family.
>
> Politically yours,
>
> WineRev.

Linguistics

DK   Yesterday someone thanked me for "winereving" the NY-20 election vote count. My head spun. Highest praise possible. *(Ken in Tex)*

DK   I am STILL adjusting to the idea I'm a VERB. Odder than hell. *(WineRev)*

DK   You're American. We verb nouns here. *(Xapulin)*

OK, back to the wine shop and wine sale in a little while for the late shift. Hope this will hold you for the weekend. That's the latest from yust southeast of Lake Wobegon.

Shalom.

Sunday Crossword
April 19, 2009

| Comments: | 19 | Recs: | 55 | Tips: | 68 |

Lazy, cloudy Sunday here, a bit damp (we could use the rain to green things up). Thought I'd look at the crossword, the jumble and the sudoku today.

Let's see.

The Former Senator: Mr. 11 Across (A) Modern eohippus// 14 Down (D). Set of artificial teeth.

TODAY is DAY 6 since the Election Contest Court (ECC) handed down its decision in Coleman v. Franken. Coleman has **4 days left to** 2D. "Rank and __" an appeal with the MN Supreme Court or the decision becomes final.

1.(A) Old time furnace fuel delivery man. Var. C-o-l-e-m-a-n met with the 3A. "Burning gas ball in space."..s-t-a-r 4D. second letter from 3A: "Roman official."..hmmmm (T)...r-i-b-u-n-e for an 16A. Opp. of outer-view.

Mr. 11A + 14D: We believe very strongly that there are thousands of Minnesotans who voted through absentee ballots and didn't know that their ballots had been rejected until these proceedings began...

There was no malicious intent; good judges made decisions that resulted in the disenfranchisement of voters—that's a constitutional problem.

But one of the chief grounds for a constitutional argument for equal 31D. Opp of anti-tection is malicious intent: election officials who say these voters shouldn't vote because they are 14A. Not male 17A. Not white 26D. "_____ and paid for." If there is no malicious intent that 11D. "Iran-____: Reagan era scandal"-dicts the idea there was UN-equal protection, yes?

There ARE statewide standards that are implemented locally. That is NOT an equal-protection issue. As Franken attorney Marc Elias said to the *Pioneer Press*:

> Virginia requires voters to show photo ID, but Minnesota does not. Yet no one would argue that this variation in administering a national election invalidates the result in a national presidential race. "You're always going to have variations between jurisdictions," he said. "There's nothing in the constitution that says that's wrong." (*Pioneer Press*)

When all the absentee ballots were in, 10,962 of them were 26A. Not accepted, r- d for one of 4 legal reasons. Norm, when you filed your court case you only wanted 4,797 counted. Isn't that UNequal protection for the other 6,165, because yours would be counted and the others would not? Or are you arguing all 10,962 should be counted? The ECC called that 41D. a-b-s-u-r-d. If all 10,962 get counted, then we have no state standard, just like 57A. Capital is Tallahassee. If none can be rejected, the law passed by the MN legislature to govern elections is 48A. "__ and void" See 41D. Then the need for a legislature is 29A. "All or __" which is also 35D. See 41D.

I know, this is what 43A. Author of "Das Kapital"___ Marx Rove means when he says "permanent Republican majority." Fortunately Mr. 1743A. 3rd US President and Mr. 1751D. 4th US President set up a democracy, NOT a 26D. Ancient tyrant ship/"d-i-c-t-a-t-o-r" ship.

> The (Election Contest) court was wrong to say it didn't have jurisdiction to deal with equal protection. As a result, we weren't able to introduce the full range of evidence. (*Norm Coleman, quoted in the Star Tribune*)

Mr. Furnace Fuel Delivery Man? The ECC spent 46A. Number of cents in a quarter pages on equal protection, utterly 19D. Display contempt, street slang: __mantling every piece of equal protection they could reach. And for cryin' out loud: "we weren't able to introduce the full range of evidence"? You had 5 full freakin' weeks! What a bunch of 37A. Male bovine droppings.

> ON POLLS THAT SAY HE SHOULD STEP ASIDE
> I'm not going to stick my finger to the wind and say here's a poll, here's what we should do. (*Norm Coleman, quoted in the Star Tribune*)

22D. "X, _, Z" 33A. "Here's _____ back from your dollar"

52A. "Every _____ and then."??

> ON HIS POLITICAL FUTURE
> I say this humbly: I don't spend 30 seconds worrying about my political future.
> *(Norm Coleman, quoted in the Star Tribune)*

When you have to point out a character trait it usually means you ain't got it. Sort of like shopping at "Honest John's Used Cars." But I have to agree with the second part; indeed, I'll beat it. I don't spend 19A. "4, 3, 2, _" second worrying about that 36D. "Past, present, _____" either.

The Governor of MN

Patricia Lopez of the *Star Tribune* got a front-page, under-the-fold story on Governor Pawlenty, looking at how the waters are rising around him as the Senate race grinds into the 22A. Diana Ross and the _____ Court. Lopez quotes T-Paw as waiting until the court stuff plays out before he has to face the music. We may not like it, but it's completely true and a fairly safe spot for him.

Where he heads off for trouble is when he starts saying stuff like, "the federal courts might stay the (state) court proceedings. We want a chance to see."—to Rachel Maddow.

He also says once the Supreme Court hands down its ruling, "I will evaluate genuinely and seriously at that point. It's quite unfair to say what you would do in advance of all that."

> But elections law expert Raleigh Levine, a professor at William Mitchell College of Law, said Pawlenty may not have any such purview. "The [Minnesota] statute does not give him any grounds for saying 'Wait for the federal court,' " Levine said. "I think he'd be on pretty shaky ground saying he needed to do a review once the state Supreme Court decides the case. He has mandatory responsibility to issue the certificate when all the requirements have been met. There isn't any discretion there." *(Star Tribune)*

Sounds like T-Paw is trying to create discretion...is that creating an indiscretion?

Oh, an another quarter heard from... from the man who likely has "666D" tattooed somewhere on his scalp:

> Would a federal court appeal prevent an election certificate from being issued?
> That's "an open question," said Ben Ginsberg, Coleman's lead attorney and a player in the Bush vs. Gore recount. *(Star Tribune)*

Fortunately, appearing in the Gregory Peck role to answer Damien,

> Marc Elias, Franken's lead recount attorney, said he finds it "curious" that Pawlenty would imply that the decision is his to make.
> Pawlenty "does not get to apply his own, independent legal analysis to this issue," Elias said. "The governor's role is ministerial—to prepare the paperwork. He's not the decider here." *(Star Tribune)*

Thank all the holies that are out there! I am HEARTILY sick of self-proclaimed deciderers littering the American political scene like a rat-infested, overturned dumpster. Governor, if it gets to your desk, sign the certificate and just ...shut... up. If you need help NOT talking, just go see Michele Bachmann. She hasn't kissed anyone like a $10 "sex worker" since the '07 State of the Union and she's probably in the mood.

OK, that's a weekend edition. Hope this will hold you with the latest news from yust southeast of 87A. Garrison Keillor locale.

7D. "Peace" in Hebrew.

Appeal Week
April 20, 2009

Comments: 88   Recs: 201   Tips: 195

TODAY is DAY 7 since the Election Contest Court (ECC) handed down its decision in Coleman v. Franken. Coleman has 3 days left to file an appeal with the MN Supreme Court or the decision becomes final.

OK, so I got up a Sunday diary around 11:00 yesterday morning but some of you missed it. (I know this because it's been a LONG time since a series diary generated only 18 comments.) But that was a GOOD thing! Shows you all have a life, you enjoyed the weather, started gardening, raked dead leaves, went out drinking, put the cell phone on "OFF" (or took the phone off the hook; I AM dating myself) and locked the master bedroom door for some winerevving (*SUCH a fun verb!*) ... well, whatever.

Everyone is waiting for the galosh to drop, as in Coleman files his appeal with the MN Supreme Court. On the one hand Norm said he would "not take the whole 10 days before we file"—but he's working on in it. OTOH when he had 7 days to file for an Election Contest Court appeal he took 1 and that gave me at least some grounds for thinking there might be streaks of dignity in the guy. Looks like those streaks are mere oil stains on the garage floor of the Judiciary Building parking ramp.

The Mighty Wurlitzer of the VRWC is still blaring awful notes like a raw steak tossed on the keyboard. MN SENIOR Senator Amy Klobuchar has enough (double enough) to do these days without having to swat at flies circling the meat like Nev. Senator John Ensign.

> Appearing on CNN, Klobuchar sparred with Sen. John Ensign, R-Nevada, who repeated GOP talking points that "votes [of all Minnesotans] should be treated the same. And I at least think that his appeal to the Minnesota Supreme Court should be heard." *(Star Tribune)*

DID YOU SEE THAT? Holy Smokes! It's like finding news in Pravda! Or truth in Izvestia! Amazing since those sources are the last place on earth those usually appear. (Just like a M*A*S*H episode where Hawkeye & BJ get hold of an entire side of beef enough for the whole camp. BJ: "Let's serve it in the mess tent. It's the last place anybody would expect to find real food.")

What, you say? Bob von Sternberg's article from the Star Tribune cited above. BVS says... "repeated the GOP talking points...". HAH! Informing readers for once that Ensign is being a shill, a tool, a parrot, a (well-tanned) lapdog, or simply Dana Perino with lousy, hairy legs.

BTW as overworked as she is, Senator Klobuchar found time to praise the holies for her staff and keep up her (excellent) crystal-ball gazing. She may be having to work twice as hard with half the help to get only a quarter of the praise she merits, but fortunately as a woman this is not difficult. It also means she's likely working about ten times harder than Ensign does on his tan and golf handicap. (Insert jokes here.)

> "Since December, our staff, I'm so proud of them, they've had double the case work," she said. "Everything from veterans benefits cases to people who have lost their Social Security checks to people who are trying to adopt babies in Guatemala that are stalled out."
>
> She noted that she had originally predicted that the Senate race would be resolved by the time ice-out was officially declared for Lake Minnetonka—which occurred last week on the same day as the ruling of the judges.
>
> "Now I predict this will be done when Minnesotans are allowed to swim in our lakes, which is Memorial weekend," she said Sunday. *(Star Tribune)*

And in honor of Memorial Day settling the whole thing, Norm Coleman's entire legal team should be thrown into a Minnesota Lake that day... Lake Superior, so they can "enjoy" swimming in the 56-degree water. (It's so deep that's about as warm as it gets even in August.)

Nothing else going on in the media, new or lame. Nothing to report so I guess the staffers might have been off winerevving with their favorite (drink/eatery/person/etc.). Hope this will hold you with the latest from yust southeast of Lake Wobegon.

Shalom.

Coleman Files Appeal
April 21, 2009

Comments: 271   *Recs:* 257   *Tips:* 236

At 3:30 p.m. Monday Team Norm held a press conference announcing their appeal of the ECC decision to the MN Supreme Court.

Team Franken answered at 4:45 p.m.

The Coleman Appeal (sounds like a rejected Aqua Velva TV ad)

The Countdown calendar is GONE because Norm Coleman (henceforward to be known as the "Appellant" in place of "ContestANT") filed his appeal with the MN Supreme Court (MNSC) Monday afternoon. And not just the Notice of Appeal, but an Appellant's Statement of Case.

The Statement is 7 pages, sort of a precis (!) or first sketch of what their case will look like. It is supposed to be rather limited but it sure seems to this non-lawyer to be dang limited. They fill in all the required notifications and briefly review the trial. Then on pages 4 & 5 they get to the heart of what they are asking:

The Election Contest Court erred:

1. by excluding evidence local officials applied the statewide standards of law differently varying by locality, resulting in "illegal" votes being included in the certified total.

2. by counting so many "illegal votes" that certifying Franken the winner was incorrect. This violates (they claim) equal protection and due process.

3. by requiring a strict compliance standard for counting absentee ballots (in its Feb. 13 ruling; they REALLY don't like that ruling!). Since other ballots were counted under another, looser, standard this denies equal protection to all ballots.

4. by not ordering inspections of precincts to investigate "double counting."

5. by allowing the 132 "missing ballots" Minneapolis precinct ballots to be counted.

Everybody can play "Supreme Court Justice" on these! I'll start, OK? Starting from the bottom, #5—not a chance. These are in and will stay in until John Cornyn grows more than 80 grams of functioning cerebral tissue (you know, not in this space-time continuum?).

#4—not a chance. It is NOT up to the Court to order investigations that produce evidence for one of the parties in a case. You want something (like evidence) done, ya gotta do it yourself, Norm.

#3—not a chance. You want a court of law to ignore/evade/wink at the law? That might work in Alabama, son (Justice for Siegelman!), but it ain't going to work here, not for 20 cases of Surly beer or 2 ounces of lutefisk. No way.

#2 & #1—the only hope on equal protection/due process grounds and the only part of the appeal worth hearing. Is there a statewide set of standards? Yes. Can human beings enforce these standards? Yes. Did they? Yes. Were civil rights violated for an identifiable GROUP of people? (Afro-Americans? Nope. Women? Nope. Native Americans? Nope. Residents of New Narvik, MN who are left-handed, Norwegian, Baptist, teetotaling gopher kissers? Nope. Students in Dinkytown whose 132 ballots were lost by election officials but who actually showed up and signed in to vote, and the machine tapes show they did indeed vote?—happened and addressed in #5.)

BTW, Colemanik lawyer types? If you win on #5, you disenfranchise 132 MN voters. They are denied equal protection and due process by YOUR acts. Your appeal against them is by (WineRev's) definition a denial of Constitutional rights under the 14th Amendment. You double-dealing, Janus-faced, two-bit, forked-tongue, soulless Ginsberg kissers! Knock it off!

I have no idea (although like you, I am about to get a world of education) how the MNSC works, but it sure seems to me they could look at #3, #4, & #5 "under advisement" for, oh, about a day, and then issue something denying them on the spot. (Don't know what it would be called, or even if they could lop ~rt of the appeal this way. But it sure would be efficient.)

MN attorney for Coleman James Langdon (the best of the Coleman bunch; a lawyer who deserves a better client IMHO) was quoted as saying he thought the MNSC would hear the case in 2 weeks to 2 months (and pointed out 6 months would normally be typical) but that he doubted it would be even 2 months.

> "I'm sure they're very sensitive to the passage of time in this matter and will do it as soon as they think it is reasonable under the circumstances," Langdon said. *(WCCO/AP)*

Ben Ginsberg blathered by remote from Europe (he's vacationing there; sorry, Europe!) and raved about the usual things on disenfranchisement of the 4,400, equal protection, and satisfaction that finally this would get heard by a court that could really act.

Yeah, right. Comment of the day from the UpTake Live Blog from North Carolina:

> Ginsberg is representing ME. I feel like a Minnesotan, and my ballot for Minn Senator was not counted. Of course I didn't cast one, nor was I entitled to, but damn it all, I wanted to vote in Minn. *(Harry in NC at The UpTake)*

And a favorite from the Star Tribune blogs, spotted by a fellow Kossack:

> My favorite comment in *Star Trib* today:
>
> The election day judges were wrong. The recount judges were wrong. The three judge panel was wrong. They were all wrong, wrong, wrong because I'm not winning...The right thing to do is to count illegal ballots that have been found to be illegal three different times by three different groups of officials and judges, until I'm ahead; then we can stop counting. *(Jimbob21a at the Star Tribune online, quoted by Zinger in VA)*

The Franken Response

Marc Elias held a presser by phone from his home in VA about an hour & half after the filing. He was brief and pointed.

The Franken team (Franken at this level is known as "Respondent," replacing "ContesTEE" in the ECC) will file a motion TODAY asking to expedite the case. (They are tired of waiting too; after all, they have a Ginsberg to crush! Ah-HA!)

To keep things moving, team Franken will ask for the Coleman briefs (not just the Statement of the Case) **by Monday April 27** (I think that's forcing the tempo; not quite the Ohio State Marching Band entering to the drum corps hammering at 180 beats/minute, but judicially moving at "double quick step").

They join Team Coleman in asking for oral arguments, also in an expeditious way. (Coleman formally requested orals in their Statement. It's only a request; the Court does NOT need to grant and can go on just the written briefs. I myself think they want to hear it in the flesh.)

Elias was feisty and dismissive in turn:

> Four of five Coleman claims actually call for disenfranchising voters, Elias said: "When it comes to disenfranchisement, no one holds a candle to the legal team assembled by Sen. Coleman."
>
> Al Franken's attorney dismissed Norm Coleman's appeal to the Minnesota Supreme Court today as "same old, same old" and the "death throes" of the Coleman legal effort.
>
> "It's not easy," Marc Elias said of being on the short end of a disputed election. "But at some point you have to accept the reality."
>
> "What we have now is the death throes of the Coleman legal effort," Elias said. *(MN Independent)*

"Death throes," eh? Well, Marc, next you'll be calling Norm's legal team a bunch of "dead enders" (which they are of course)... but enough about Senate republicans! Let's move on to...

Supreme Court Questions

Subject to correction in the comments from our legal pros hanging around here, I think the sequence is:

Notice of Appeal; **Coleman** (done, 4/20)

Statement of Case; **Coleman** (done, 4/20)

Motion to Expedite; **Franken** (coming, 4/21)

Appellant's Brief; **Coleman** (Franken requesting, 4/27)

Respondent's Brief; **Franken**. Elias states they could have this by May 2. *[In their massively thorough way, I think when they do, Elias, Lillehaug, & Hamilton's brief will cite a Peruvian Inca legislative from 718 AD; and Egyptian case law: Cheops vs. Giza (−2533 BCE), recently found next to the map room in Tanis. (Also found: medallion with markings on BOTH sides ("Take BACK 12 kadem in honor of the Hebrew God whose ark this is"), broken staff, shredded swastika flag.]*

The first 3 are set. Starting with 4 & 5 the Supreme Court will set a **Briefing Schedule/Calendar**. Both sides will do 4 & 5, and there may be a round (or even 2) of responses by each side (e.g.: "Appellant's Response to Respondent's Brief" or some such title; then "Respondent's Response to Appellant's Response") (Elias for Franken mentioned 4 & 5, and even said if Coleman has a response to 5—by May 2—that they produce it by May 4.)

Sometime among the flying briefs (or maybe after?) the Court can order **oral arguments**. THAT will be MUST-SEE TV (and if The UpTake can make budget they will have it, along with the best-running live blog in the business). The High Court has been generous in allowing televising (of earlier arguments over various motions). If there are oral arguments, 3 things:

1. Norm Coleman already mentioned last week Joe Friedberg would appear for him to do the honors. No word so far from the Franken side. Who do you like? Kevin Hamilton (who did a masterful job on closing arguments in ECC)? Marc Elias (best election law mind in the country)? David Lillehaug (perhaps the sharpest, think-on-your-feet mind we saw in the whole trial)?

2. When the Supreme Court has heard earlier arguments in this election they ordered 1 hour of arguments total. Each side's attorney faced a 30-minute grilling from the 5 judges over certain rather narrow motions. Do the appeal lawyers have a sense if the Court might order longer oral arguments, just because it IS the Appeal, and because they KNOW this case will be studied and cited for a long time? Could they order, say, 1 hour/side? Or "Appellant, 2 hours in the morning; Respondent, 2 hours in the afternoon"?

3. Is that the order they would bat: appellant, then respondent? (Is there rebuttal at all?) And if this IS the order, is there a slight advantage for the respondent's side? They would get to hear Friedberg and could shape some of their argument on the spot as reply, yes/no? Or are the questions from the Court likely to be rather different to each side so there is not a lot of overlap?

Have the late shift at the shop today, so I'll have a 2nd cup with all of you. That's the latest from yust southeast of Lake Wobegon.

Shalom.

Buckle Up!
April 22, 2009

Comments: 170   Recs: 307   Tips: 287

Buckle up, here we go... vroom!

Pop the Clutch, Let's MOVE!

Tuesday was the Franken Team's turn to file a motion with the MN Supreme Court, as promised by attorney Marc Elias. (David Lillehaug's signature graced the bottom.) You kind of get the feeling they were ready with maybe 85% of it already written and were just waiting for the Coleman formal appeal to tweak the remaining 15%.

It's only 5 pages with a cover letter and a closing affidavit of the attorneys on the Coleman side who got it and pretty easy reading here, top item:

Two things caught my nose like a ring on a bull. The motion's first sentence is:

> "Cullen Sheehan and Norm Coleman ('Appellants') have appealed the unanimous decision of the three-judge election contest court...which...affirmed the unanimous Minnesota State Canvassing Board certification that Al Franken ('Respondent') received the highest number of votes... (that is, he won)." (*Respondent's Motion for Expedited Schedule*)

OK, they don't say won, but you get the idea. But did you see "unanimous" twice? Already laying down a marker and raising the heat on the MN Supreme Court? (Sort of like opening the front door of my brother-in-law's house on an August afternoon in Dothan, Alabama; heat hits you right away like a blanket straight from the dryer.) In a not-so-subtle way, kind of making the High Court wonder a bit if going against all those "unanimous-es" is a good idea.

And the second thing is the proposed schedule to the Court, not just asking them for a speedy schedule, but also why and HOW speedy.

Now, as we all know, courts move at their own tempo (seldom even andante; largo or lento is more like it). That's not bad; they need to think things over and be careful.

But the Franken Motion points out they've had opportunity to track this case and that there's no particular reason for delay on the court's part. The Motion notes the speed (6 days, 5 days) in which the MN SC ruled on earlier motions, and commending the Court for showing that kind of moderato tempo.

As far as the lawyers are concerned, they note both sides have been prepping for this appeal for weeks and that the lawyers on both sides are from big law firms, so plenty of staff power is available.

So then Lillehaug & Co. gets to the heart of it and comes on like a Wernher von Braun protegee from the Redstone Arsenal of Huntsville, AL.

ECC Trial Record: the famous "15 days" to get this transcript, documents, and exhibits from the ECC to the MNSC. Motion asks this be done by close of business... TODAY! Whoooooooooweeeee! What a sforzando!

Coleman's ("Appellant's") brief 5 days after the Trial Record arrives, or Monday, April 27; Franken's ("Respondent's") opposing brief 5 days after that, or Saturday, May 2; and (if there is one) a "Reply Brief" from Coleman 2 days after that, or Monday, May 4.

"Respectfully suggests" Court call for Oral arguments (which both sides would like, although it's up to the Court) "very shortly after the reply brief is submitted" (i.e. May 4).

Wow! Now the Court has not answered yet but in judicial terms this is definitely allegro, bordering on presto!

We'll see. Next move is up to the Court.

...n to the Wine Shop *and* win sale! Hope this will hold you with the latest from yust southeast of ...obegon.

...om.

Flying Motions
April 23, 2009

Comments: 101   Recs: 162   Tips: 171

The Wednesday Motion

The vitamin people had something else in mind with their One-a-Day slogan, but that's what we're getting right now in the MN Senate Recount final lap.

Monday Team Norm filed official notice with the MN Supreme Court they would appeal the decision of the Election Contest Court, which found for Franken receiving the most votes (to quote the statute—which is very different from quoting a statue—they don't talk much) by a margin of +312. They also filed a sort of overview of their appeal, a 7-page Statement of the Appellant's case. (Of course if Ben Ginsberg had attorney standing to file this, it would have to be renamed "Statement of the Repellant's" case.)

Tuesday Team Al filed not a direct response, but a 5-page Motion for an Expedited Schedule. (More in a moment.)

Wednesday Team Norm proved they could be concise too, and filed a 1(!)-page Response to the Motion to Expedite.

Now mind you these last 2 are simply requests of the Court, and proposals. The MN Supreme Court will set a Briefing Calendar/Schedule (not sure the exact term) that will be binding [with I believe a few really narrow exceptions for change—but I may be wrong. Obviously if your lead/only attorney is felled by appendicitis and has to be three days in the hospital, I think any court will grant an extension/revise the schedule. I would also imagine (subject to wiser heads) that if BOTH sides work hard at an ambitious schedule and agree between themselves, "we can do this but we just need another 24 hours," I believe a court might grant that.] *(If not, both sides could say to the Court, "Just 24 hours, that's all we're asking... You'd do it for Randolph Scott!" **Gasp** Music: "Randolph Scott")*

Where this gets interesting are the times proposed. Consider this the 10-meter platform for 3-1/2 forward twisting RAMPANT speculation as to what it means.

Record of Trial. (Transcript of the ECC case, evidence, exhibits) to be officially submitted to the MN SC (by appellant: Coleman).

Tuesday Franken proposed WEDNESDAY for this to happen. (It did NOT happen.) But this forklift beeping over to the SC clerk's window is the first real step.

Team Coleman's Wednesday response did not even mention Record of Trial or suggest a date. (Maybe 1 page was a little TOO short.)

Appellant's Brief. THE case for appeal as seen by Coleman, complete with citations, whereas-s, therefore-s, and those Latino additions to Anglo-American jurisprudence, the inasmuch-as-s. Franken proposed Trial Record +5 (or, starting from Wednesday, Monday, April 27; perforce now Tuesday, 4/28 IF Trial-Rec day is TODAY).

Coleman offered Thursday, April 30 for their Brief.

Not a big deal, something I imagine happens a lot. Each side has an idea/suggestion, there's a little variation, and the Court in question makes a call: A, B, split the diff, something else.

So the difference here is Franken proposing T-Rec +5, and Coleman offering T-Rec +7/8, depending how you count. Not a lot there and strikes me as a normal variation between 2 parties, although as usual Norm's side wants to be slower.

Respondent's Brief. THE case against the appeal as seen by Franken, complete with similar verbiage and citations and ANSWERS to the Appellant's Brief. ["Appellant repellantly argues A, but the Court should deny because of B." B is supported by precedents and various prior laws. The way things have gone in this case, the Franken team will have precedents from MN law, Sioux tribal election law from 1827 (delivered on the original tanned hide from the MN Historical Society), a citation from Hernando DeSoto in the original Spanish that affected all elections in states on the Mississippi River, and (in a stretch move) case law precedent from the Hanseatic League meeting from Tallinn in 1383.]

Franken offered 5 days after #2 above; just being as even-handed as possible: "You guys get 5 days for your brief; we'll take 5 for ours."

Coleman proposes 11 days! For Franken's reply!

WHAT ARE THEY THINKING? "Take your time. Our brief is gonna be so supercalifragilisticexpialidocious it'll take you guys 4 days just to read through it! The issues at stake will be SO monumental you'll fry your servers! Our brief will be SO intimidating/complex/brilliant/(or so senseless it'll take you a week to stop laughing), you guys'll need 11 days."

If there is a case to be made for the Coleman/Rethuglican STALL, this is ahem...prima facie evidence. 11 days my butt!

The Court should take up Franken on his 5-day offer and smack those other 6 days on Tony Trimble as a contempt-of-court sentence just for, well, contempt. Bleeh!

The Reply Brief. Appellant gets to answer Respondent's brief ("This is why our original argument stands and why this response is inadequate/misleading/wrong/weak/irrelevant"). Apparently this is usually a rather shorter bit of work and takes less time to prepare.

Franken proposed Coleman have 2 days to "Reply."

Coleman offers 4 days.

Now this could be one of three things:

The obvious: Coleman is stalling, and here's another piece of it.

Team Norm is a bit worried at how good the Respondent's Brief could be (it really COULD include the Hanseatic League citations!) and that it will be some hard work to answer it.

Team Norm is tacitly admitting they are outclassed, outgunned, and generally just not as good a legal team as Team Al, with a lousy case and a crummy client.

Me, I vote D, all of the above. The Court could very easily split the diff on this one.

Oral Arguments. Coleman's "Statement of Case" requested orals and Franken's Motion to Expedite was also in favor. Neither side put a day on it (REALLY up to the Court; after all they are the ones who have to listen to these guys) but Franken proposed basically ASAP after the Reply Brief.

Coleman now proposes after the above Briefs, "The Court may then schedule oral argument at a time convenient to it."

Both sides are being as respectful as possible to the Court, but it sure strikes me there is a limp, open-ended, "when you get around to it" air to the Coleman offer. Now I may be all wet on this and my bias may be showing—for the first time in this series, I think. This sentence from the Coleman side may be a bit of "boilerplate" lawyer language that was easy to plug in and means only what it says. (Lawyers who have appealed at this level can fill me in on the protocol and language.)

But it still doesn't come across to me as "let's wrap this up as soon as possible." Am I off base here?

SOooooo... for today's parlor game let the guessing begin. Does the Court Briefing Schedule/Calendar split the difference between the 2 camps to show how even-handed they are? Do they go Oriental menu and order 1 from Column Norm (like the time to reply) and 1 from Column Al (like 5 days to respond)?

If they adopt the Coleman proposal, are they a bunch of utterly sold-out/in-the-tank/bought-off losers? If they adopt the Franken list, ALL the same words will fill the air from the Reichwing Wurlitzer (along with some "Move-On"s and "ACORNS").

Since both camps each got to say something Monday, Tuesday, Wednesday, I hope the Court takes its turn today and says, "THIS is how it's going to be." (It'll give me something to write about tomorrow.)

DK

Triskaidekaphobia? The true reason for the proposed Coleman schedule is probably something different. His case has always been based and conducted more on superstition and fear than on facts and logic. This can be seen most clearly in Benny the G's monomania about Friday the thirteenth.

In truth, the thirteenth day of a month has rarely been a good one for Coleman:

* April 13 The Ruling
* March 13 The closing arguments
* February 13 The Friday

DK

The only other item was the Senator-elect at an Earth Day rally giving a speech. (One of the sponsoring groups was Aveda—a health and beauty products company here in Minneapolis. They also operate a cosmetology school near where the speech was given. Al opened by thanking all for coming, noting the Aveda folks and then saying, "I've spoken to a lot of crowds but this one has the best hair and skin tone of any of them!"

In a few questions afterward he was optimistic the MN SC stage will be the last stop and that he's anxious to get to work. He said he thought Governor Pawlenty would sign the certificate of election.

OK, hope that will hold you. Minnesotans, be careful out there. Monday was 41, Tuesday 53, and yesterday 63. Today is forecast for 83, followed by 2 days in the 70s. Beware of grass growing and trees leafing out and budding before your eyes. (It'll be like living in a Disney nature film with time-lapse photography.)

That's the blooming latest from yust southeast of Lake Wobegon.

Shalom.

Follow the Money
April 24, 2009

Comments: 101   Recs: 230   Tips: 206

Redford hears the click of the Zippo lighter, then spots the faint glow of the cigarette by the pillar in the parking garage. Hooded by shadows, Hal Holbrook rasps out, "Follow the money."

All the President's Men. In the days when the press was still feared by politicians and reporters gave them reason to fear.

A Bill Comes Due

An affidavit was circulated yesterday, filed with the Court and served on Team Norm (Langdon, Knaak, Trimble & Friedberg). Not your usual, dry, arcane legal stuff but something to make you reach for the liter-sized "Ein Mass" at the Hofbrau Haus (or maybe the Black Forest Inn about 10 blocks down the street from the wonderful Jerusalem Cafe). An affidavit dunning Team Coleman for $16,132!

This stems from the Pamela Howell testimony of the ECC trial. Howell was a precinct judge and the Coleman side's star witness to prove their allegation of "double-counted/duplicate" ballots (which Coleman claims would be worth about +100 votes net for Franken, and hence should be removed from his total).

David Lillehaug, Franken's main attorney here in MN, swore out the affidavit. He said he prepped for the testimony with other attorneys in the office, AND noted that Team Coleman had not sent over anything to the Franken side about her testimony, any affidavits, etc. (Pre-trial both sides do "discovery," that is, show the other side what evidence/witness/exhibits they plan to introduce at trial. You don't HAVE to use everything, but ahead of time you DO have to SHARE everything. If you don't: BIG, BAD NEWS. All attorneys know; DON'T go there.)

Team Coleman went there. As Lillehaug began cross-examining Howell on 2/25 it became clear there was stuff Team Norm had NOT shared with the Franken side. Lillehaug moved to strike the Howell testimony because of this breach of discovery. GRANTED! (Unusual!)

Coleman's side (esp. attorney Trimble) crawled to the court and asked forgiveness. Thurs. 2/26 the Court agreed and reinstated the witness and her testimony.

Friday, 2/27, Howell is back on the stand for cross-examination and it becomes clear Team Norm has withheld e-mails etc. in discovery. Lillehaug: "I reNEW my motion to strike the testimony (and her CLAIM—the double-counting business) from the trial." GRANTED! (Double unusual!) AND the Court sanctions Team Norm (except for Joe Friedberg) $7,500, which is payable to the Court (ECC). (Sanctions: According to lawyer types around here, you NEVER want to have these on your record. To have a $7500 one splattered on there in a high-profile case is grounds for practicing for a new job: "DO you want fries with that?")

AND for wasting the Franken attorney's time for this fiasco and major violation of rules of discovery (although Howell's testimony was finally re-re-admitted and then cross-examined into insignificance), the ECC in their Final Decision on April 13 ordered Franken's court costs AND ATTORNEY'S FEES for those 3 days to be paid by the Coleman side whenever the Franken Team provided an affidavit of how much these would be.

THAT size-16K shoe dropped like a lead-soled wingtip from 30 stories up yesterday.

Who says legal documents can't be fun reading in a dry-humor sort of way? On page 4, "the time of Howell's testimony, arguments by counsel and the Court striking the testimony was approximately 1.4 hours."

Yeah, it took a little while for the Court to load the ballista and let it fly at Norm Coleman's team. Gad, Lillehaug sounds like Calvin Coolidge on a casual day! (The notoriously tight-lipped President came out of church one Sunday and was met by 2 reporters who hoped to catch him in a little better mood.

> 1st reporter: "Been to church, Mr. President?"
>
> "Yep."
>
> 2nd reporter: "Enjoy the service, Mr. President?"
>
> "Yep."
>
> 1st: "Enjoy the sermon, Mr. President?"
>
> "Yep."
>
> 2nd: "What was the sermon about, Mr. President?"
>
> "Sin."
>
> 1st: "Oh really? And what did the minister have to say about sin, Mr. President?"
>
> "He's against it.")

And THEN we find out why Team Franken is SO good: You get what you pay for!

Lillehaug: Prep time for Howell testimony 10.5 hours @ $418/hr = $4,389.

Trial time for Howell (actual time in front of The UpTake cameras; makeup NOT included) 3.7 hrs. @ $418/hr = $1,546.

By the way, David Lillehaug, being, you know, the local talent, from backwater MN... well, he just can't command the legal fees the BIG BOYS can and has to settle for $418 per. Kevin Hamilton, being from a saltwater state like Washington, commands a more robust $464 per, and Marc Elias from the Big City of DC pulls down $538 per. AND since each of these 3 (and others) were in the courtroom, their meters were ALSO running for 3.7 hours' worth of Howell-ing fiasco time (that's $1,716 and $1,990 respectively, Tony Trimble, for screwing up rules of discovery).

Following Other Interesting Money

And just where is the Coleman camp going to come up with that kind of scratch to pay for their legal maneuvers? Well, that's what the MN DFL (Democratic Party with old allies Farmer & Labor) wants to know too, and in a kind of nosy way. Yesterday they filed a complaint with the Federal Elections Commission alleging Coleman is using campaign funds from his Senate run to pay for his legal fees in this Contest and Appeal. (A major no-no EXCEPT under certain circumstances.) BUT Coleman, having promised in December to ask the FEC for a ruling on just those circumstances and seeing if they apply to his situation, has never done so. So the MN DFL has gone to work on the FEC to press for a ruling (and NOT a favorable one to Norm). We'll see.

And Still MORE Interesting Coleman Money

Now HERE is the change... we need. Here is the kind of outside-the-box thinking that not only made this country great, but will change this country's future AND will be hell on the current Republican Party. Now we're talking!

Joe Rosenberg over at MN Publius is reporting on a wonderful idea from WCCO-TV's Esme Murphy. (Legal types at the front; here's the ball; slant over left guard while the tackle blocks down on the linebacker; break clear and run LONG; on 2!)

> My theory is that since Minnesotans are paying taxes to support two US Senators we should get a refund for the days that we have only had one...Right now we have not had a senator for 107 days. At $8,000 a day, that's about $856,000 we, as taxpayers, have funded for a Senate office that doesn't exist. *(MN Plubius)*

AND since Norm is the proximate cause for this lack, HE should pay most of this as a reimbursement to the state of MN.

GREAT IDEA!... although methinks the lawyer types will have seven reasons to Sunday why it won't/can't work. But let's be positive for once! Grounds FOR this? Class action? I myself am willing to play the victim on this as a MN resident if it will help (neck brace; arm in a braced-out metal prop/sling; shuffle painfully with a cane; moan about my bad back) that can ONLY be remedied by having my pain and suffering relieved. No longer do I want to be "Colemanized"; if I had two Senators I would be able ("I do believe it") to rise up from my chair, leave those crutches behind, take off the neck brace, and feel the everlasting healing power flow through me like Chevy Chase playing Claude the faith healer.

Friday Morning Media

Just about to skip this today when we get word of an editorial calling on Norm Coleman to give it up. Always like to report comment like that... but now, from the far eastern suburbs of Stillwater:

> Editorial in Newark NJ Star Ledger this AM: "Hey Norm, it's over" ... He's being egged on by Republicans in Washington determined to deny Democrats a 59th seat in the Senate. But they're doing their party no good, as many state-level Republicans understand, at a time when the GOP needs desperately to shed the image of strident partisanship ... *(Thomas J Marlowe at The UpTake)*

New Jersey? Newark? THEIR newspaper thinks Norm's gotta go?? .

Whoa! I mean when you've lost the Star Ledger it shows the Puritan descendant vote going against you! (IIRC the place was founded in the 1670s as a place of refuge for the righteous fleeing corrupting Dutch influence—hence the name "New Ark," as in Noah and the flood. I'm sure the natives think of themselves in those terms every day.) It really is all over. Hang it up, Norm!

OK, hope that will hold you until the Supreme Court says what THE schedule will be. Back to the wine shop for the sale this morning so that's the latest from yust southeast of Lake Wobegon.

Shalom.

June First
April 25, 2009

Comments: 43   *Recs:* 61   *Tips:* 65

The MN Supreme Court came out Friday with their schedule for briefs and oral arguments.

MN Supreme Court Schedule

As many of you have pointed out (starting with Allen03 in yesterday's comment string), the high court has ordered briefs and oral arguments in Coleman v. Franken. We speculated about both sides' requests & proposals to the Court.

Coleman's ("Appellant's") Brief is due on or before (hah!) Thursday, **April 30**. Franken's Team had proposed 4/27 and Coleman's side about 4/29 (depending on how you were counting) but those were a few days ago, so 4/30 is pretty dang quick.

Franken's ("Respondent's") Brief is due on or before Monday, **May 11**. Franken's side themselves had proposed 5 days after the Appellant's brief and Coleman proposed 11 days, which is what came down. Major disappointment! Look, I know Team Franken can and most likely WILL beat this deadline, but even if they turn in their brief on May 1, 24 Randolph Scott hours after Coleman's (and they shouldn't for PR reasons), it doesn't speed things up any because of the next 2 items.

Appellant's Reply to Respondent's Brief is due by **May 15**. As I read it, this is a fixed calendar date (like Christmas Day, Dec. 25) and NOT a date tied to the preceding filing (for which the Court would have said "4 days later"; so it's not a movable date like Easter—the first Sunday after the first full moon after the Spring Equinox (no paganism there!) IIRC swinging across 37 possible days).

So even if Coleman files 4/30 and Franken responds on, say, May 3, by this Coleman still has until 5/15 to Reply.

And then the Court ordered **Oral Arguments for June 1,** which is a really fixed date. I think rincewind was first to dig through the SC calendar the other day to see what else was already scheduled for them in May and it looked pretty full. TerribleTom noted that while the MN statute calls on the Court to act "expeditiously" it does NOT, in fact, REQUIRE them to drop every other case and put an ECC appeal on the top of the docket.

Unhappily Terrible Tom also points out this schedule IS an expedited one, that the Court really is moving at quite a clip.

Both camps claimed to be pleased with the Schedule.

Coleman spokesman Tom Erickson:

> "We're pleased that the court has granted an appropriate amount of time to prepare for this historic and consequential case to enfranchise thousands of Minnesota citizens who still wait for their voices to be heard, and their votes to be counted." *(quoted at MN Progressive Project)*

Except for the fillip of "historical and consequential" it's the same old, same old talking points. SHUT UP already!

> Franken lawyer Marc Elias: "We are grateful that the court has issued an expedited scheduling order, and we look forward to the process continuing to move forward so that Sen.-elect Franken can be seated as quickly as possible." *(Minnesota Public Radio)*

Bravely said, Marc. Stiff upper lip, good form and all that.... but a bummer.

> *(From the old Laugh-In opening party scene:*
>
> *Texan to umbrella-toting, bowler-hatted Englishman:*
>
> *"Why do you British always keep a stiff upper lip?"*
>
> *"Well, you see, there's a definite hesitancy about British dentures.")*

MN Supreme Court Issues Expedited Schedule

I agree the Court is moving at an excellent clip. Good for them. I am bummed.

So, in my bummed-ness WineRev proposes the following:

I will post on the Recount when there is a significant quantity (like a brief) of news or quality of news (Tim Pawlenty and Norm Coleman are caught on video in a 3-way with Michele Bachmann at the No Tell Motel in White Bear Lake, complete with leather, hoods, 2 pounds of chocolate mousse and.... a slice of lutefisk on jumper cables clamped to a car battery. Should be enough to sweep them all out of office and wreck the MN GOP for about 70 years.)

I can go visit my mom in Florida for Mother's Day weekend in some peace, KNOWING nothing is going to be settled before I get back. I will NOT be haunted by the fear this whole thing ends and the swearing-in party at the Convention Center (complete with Surly & Summit beer, aquavit, chocolate mousse, and lutefisk served across a leather tablecloth....) happens without ME.

Newspaper Senate Race Now Tied; Recount Looms

David Brauer over at MinnPost has been tracking MN hometown newspapers and their editorial board positions on the Senate Recount. While many of these endorsed Coleman for his reelection bid last fall, they are now split 9-9 (2 + 8 outstanding) in calling for Coleman to concede, vs. fight on. So there has been a swing in the MN position against Coleman (as much or as little as such newspaper views mean) but it's still in the hands of the Court.

When Republicans Had Honor

Chris Steller at MN Independent has up a blast from the past that is nostalgic, noble, and such a contrast with the current fascist-infected blowhards that claim to be Republican that it makes you weep. Steller dug through some microfiches or drawers or maybe clay tablets and unearthed incumbent Governor Elmer Andersen's concession statement from 1963. He and Democrat Rolvaag ended the 1962 governor's election 91 votes apart after a recount. (The thrashings that caused were so deep the legislature created the current system to avoid that sort of pain.)

Who, I ask you, among the current crop of Republicans in office now, would issue a statement that contained a paragraph like this?

> On the other hand, when a competent and fair tribunal, which the district judge panel most certainly has been, renders a judgment that skilled representatives of mine feel cannot be successfully challenged in a higher court, then no one could expect me to appeal in order to gain time or keep possession of this office until the last possible moment. *(MN Independent)*

How FAR they have FALLEN!!

Masterfully written, generous, praising of others..... in a political way a distillation of "Minnesota Nice." It's what public service used to be before cheapjacks like Coleman carpetbagged their way here, Bachmann was hatched in some Stepford Wife lab, and all those polyestered and penny-loafered, pimple-faced, petulant, pony-hating, puppy-slapping, pootie-torturing, piss-drinkers destroyed a party that used to have honor and a political system that actually (albeit imperfectly) served the PEOPLE! (*Fumes!*)

Well, I hope that will hold you for a while. The sale looms on (until the 2nd) and I want some breakfast and a 2nd cup of java. I'll see ya when I see ya and post when it seems good. Here's the latest from yust southeast of Lake Wobegon.

Shalom.

Grumblings
April 27, 2009

Comments: 122   Recs: 198   Tips: 210

So here I have Monday off from work to listen to the drizzle leak down in 50-degree weather. (I know. Probably considered beach weather in Seattle, but still....) I've noted to the Kos Community from Saturday that these diaries will be more occasional/sporadic since there will be NOTHING worth mentioning for a while. (MN Supreme Court will hear oral arguments June 1.)

But then the *Star Tribune* (dying) newspaper goes and screws up my day off!

The last few days they did a good thing: They commissioned a MN Poll, a good in-state polling effort (sample of 1,042) that has a nice track record on politics in MN. They are releasing the results over a couple days; Sunday they used it for stuff on the Franken-Coleman struggle. (Today they have front-page coverage on how President Obama and his policies are seen in MN; good reading.)

Sunday the page-one headline above the fold read "Most Want Coleman to Call It Quits." The story says 64% of those polled want Norm to GO AWAY! (This confirms a separate poll by the Alliance for Better MN from about 10 days ago that says 60% feel this way.) Further, the Sunday story manages to get in above the fold(!) that only 28% of Minnesotans consider Coleman's appeal to the MNSC "appropriate." (Those are Bushistic numbers for sure.)

Well, now the Monday headline writer has reported for work in the on-line section of the StarTrib. This lobotomized cretin with the Faux Noise/Nancy Grace model vibrator glued inside his shorts decides the real story is "Favorable Ratings for Franken and Coleman Drop." Compared to November, Franken's favorables have dipped from 47 to 43%—4 points: which is the margin of error, you quarter-witted toe-sucker!

Coleman's favs went from 46 to 38—outside the margin of error and sadistically significant.

Unfavs for Franken is at 47; for Coleman 55. So Franken is net negative 4, and the margin of error is 4. No doubt some stat slinger will tell me those 2 numbers have damn little to do with each other except they are in the same article, but any way you slice it this ain't half bad for a Senator-elect who hasn't been able to legislate or serve his constituents one inch—because of Coleman.

OTOH the FORMER Senator who can't find an equine orthodontist is net negative 17. Minus 17! NORM! Go stick your tongue on the steel pole of the swing set at MINUS 17.....after you double-dog dare that headline writer to go first. Then the rest of us can get on with fixing the country now that the First Puppet with 28% of the sawdust for brains of the average puppet has left the White House. (*Fumes*)

A Fair Idea Shot to Hell

Columnist Eric Black over at MinnPost last week had an interesting proposal: a deal between Franken, Coleman, and the US Senate. The Senate agrees to provisionally seat Franken while Coleman pursues his legal options all the way to Ninth Circle of Il Inferno. If the final appeal of the final court rules in Norm's favor that he won the election (and that Ninth Circle might be the only one in the metaphysical universe that might), the Senate would then UN-seat Franken and seat Coleman. This would show that Coleman TRULY was interested ONLY in pursuing justice while allowing MN to have 2 US Senators. (There would be NO question then that he was stalling for partisan purposes.)

It was sort of bar talk from Eric but readers urged him to "give it a shot" with Team Norm. So he did.

> I am now officially informed that Coleman—who is giving a lot of interviews these days and who, to his credit, has often tolerated my impertinent questions—will not discuss the merits and demerits of my modest proposal. *(MinnPost)*

Stymied here, Black decided to see if the Coleman side might have something more general to say on the matter. Well, yes, generally generically talking-point-stupid as in a written statement from Cullen Sheehan, the Coleman campaign manager AND co-appellant in the court case:

> "We are pursuing the legal avenue that has been prescribed under Minnesota law. We are disappointed that Al Franken or anyone else would be so shrill to suggest that the due process and equal protection rights of 4,400 Minnesotans should be swept under the rug. The time that we are taking to get it right is well within the prescribed limits allowed under the law, and any suggestion to the contrary is wrong and misleading." *(MinnPost)*

Uh, Cullen? Shrill? Eric asked about the Senate seat and MN representation in the Senate. He did NOT ask about equal protection, due process, rug sweeping, complain about time limits, or suggest ignoring the law (Rethug Default Position 1). Shrill indeed!

OK. For what it's worth, here's some of what passes for news these days on the Recount. No real action until Coleman's Brief gets filed later this week, so that will be the next diary FOR SURE. Any other postings will be hit-or-miss; you have been warned.

The latest to you from yust southeast of Lake Wobegon.

Shalom.

Pennsylvania Ricochet
April 29, 2009

Comments: 156   Recs: 224   Tips: 259

"Pardon me, boy? Is this the Pennsylvania station?"

I really, really wasn't going to post anything Recount-related until Coleman's brief was filed. That would be actual hard news. OR, it could be fabulous hard news if several 100 Minnesotans and their attorneys found they HAD to file various motions with the MN Supreme Court and got in line WAY ahead of Fritz Knaak and the other Coleman mouthpieces so that the window shut at 4:30 p.m. (or whenever) and they opened an Emerald City porthole and said, "Come back tomorrow!"

But then PA senator Arlen Specter (my senator for 7-1/2 years when I lived in Clarion, PA) decides to give the Reichwing Occupiers of the Republican Party a swift knee to the groin by switching parties. Needless to say, Joe Lieberman is incensed since now he'll get even LESS attention for switching from D to CfL. *(And why the Grey Cup League allowed him in at the 55-yard line in Montreal is beyond me.)*

SOoooooo now counting Sanders, Lieberman, and now Specter on certain organizing issues, the Democrats have 59 votes. If they can pry one more loose from the far south shore of Lake Gitchee-goomi (St. Paul is just a fringe suburb of Duluth really), they hit the magical "take your Southern-fried filibuster out to the grease dumpster" 60 level and sharply cripple G-NO-P's ability to prevent real political, economic, and legal reform.

Odds are they will up the pressure to force Coleman to slow-walk everything in the MN Court and then run like hell to jump into the LaBrea Tar Pit of the "speedy" federal court system.

I haven't thought that much about it and I'm on a tight, early schedule today, but you are welcome to talk about it.

OK, back to restocking the shelves for the last days of the wine sale. When Norm files his brief let's chat, OK? That's what there is from yust southeast of Lake Wobegon.

Shalom.

Coleman's Brief Due
April 30, 2009

Comments: 160   Recs: 215   Tips: 214

Coleman's Appeal Brief

TODAY is the day set by the MN Supreme Court for Norm Coleman's appeal brief to be filed. Back on 4/23 we had his Statement of the Case, a 7-page sketch of what his appeal will be about. But today the whole bowl of oatmeal is due, complete with law, precedents, case citations, footnotes, "therefore"s and "insofar"s. No doubt this will be THE news of the day; feel free to post info and comments here when it comes down.

Now WILL it come down? Norm COULD ask for an extension of time and lawyers around here have pointed out courts do grant these. I doubt it given the high profile of the case and Coleman's statements from a couple weeks back that his attorneys were already constructing it, BUT this IS Team Norm we are talking about; a legal team that can earn themselves a $7500 sanction from a court in the highest-profile case tried in MN in 40 years. Would he really risk the uproar WE would raise about "stalling," "legal filibuster," etc.? It might be legally permissible to ask but not politically possible.

And if he asks, does the Court grant? Grant less than he asks "48 hours, not 10 days"? And what will that say about the court?

If this date moves, do the other dates (like Franken's response due 5/11) move with it? Does the date for Oral arguments stay June 1? Non-lawyers among us want to know.

Specter of Fallout

Norm's tin ear is in excellent working condition noting what Arlen Specter's party switch means to him is...... money.

> Republican Norm Coleman said Wednesday that Sen. Arlen Specter's decision to become a Democrat wouldn't mean big changes in his fight for Minnesota's vacant Senate seat—except in his quest for cash.
>
> "It probably makes fundraising a little bit easier," Coleman told the Pioneer Press. *(Pioneer Press)*

Al Franken's had a reaction too. Not a statement or press comment. Maybe it's better described as a PRE-action.

Yeah, yeah. Officially he had this to say:

> Democrat Al Franken spokesman Andy Barr released the following in response to Senator Arlen Specter's switch:
>
> "Sen.-elect Franken looks forward to working with Senators of both parties to make progress on President Obama's agenda and move our country forward." *(MN Progressive Project)*

But Chris Steller at MN Independent dug out his copy of *Rush Limbaugh Is a Big Fat Idiot* (still true since 1996) and looked up Specter. Franken thought Arlen had a shot at the 1996 Republican Presidential nomination under the right circumstances. Those circumstances?

> I've been giving this a lot of thought. As I see it, there are two possible scenarios that could lead to an Arlen Convention. The first is a plane crash. A 747 carrying Dole, Gramm, Buchanan, and Alexander crashes ... on top of Newt Gingrich and Colin Powell.
>
> The second is a bus crash. It plays out kind of the same way. *(Al Franken's* Rush Limbaugh is a Big Fat Idiot, *quoted in MN Independent)*

Thanks Chris.

Bits and Bites

Al has provisionally hired a chief of staff. Hired is too strong. Franken is NOT a senator and has no money to pay for staff. But he has named Drew Littman as chief of staff who will start collecting a paycheck whenever Al does

Michele Bachmann is so unsettled by Al(an) Stuart Franken becoming Senator she's been watching "Stuart Smalley" reruns and believing (*sigh*; She is the MN answer to Reichwingers who say, "There's morons in MN too and they deserve a representative in Congress") that "SMALLEY" had something to do with the Hoover administration that could be blamed on FDR... or something. Whatever the hell this is, it is vintage Bachmann.

Late night last night. Long days in the wine sale. Not a lot to report to you and I have an early appointment but I hope this will hold you until the briefing breaks. That's the latest & least from yust southeast of Lake Wobegon.

Shalom.

May 2009

Coleman's Appeal
May 1, 2009

Comments: 191   Recs: 355   Tips: 441

Franken wins by +312 votes.

Number of days Norm Coleman seemed to lead: 43.

Number of days Al Franken has certifiably led: 134.

Number of days since election day (Nov. 4): 177.

Team Coleman filed their Grief of Appeal.....

The Appeal

Norm Coleman's legal team beat the April 30 deadline for filing their Brief by less than 2 hours yesterday. It's 62 pages along with references to various parts of the ECC Trial record, exhibits, evidence, etc.—you know, what a legal brief is supposed to look like. (No sign of crayon.) It falls into arguments on 5 points, all of which you have heard before (and before, and before, and...).

1. They object to the 132/133 (depending on how you count; the ECC said 132 but for a long time everyone got used to saying 133, so I'm using both) Minneapolis ballots being counted. These were cast by 132 1/2 voters who signed in and put their ballots through the voting machines and the machines counted them (maybe all but 1/2?). Then the paper ballots were lost before the Recount. They favored Franken by net +46.

    The State Canvassing Board ruled these IN (because the voters voted them; there is good evidence they did; the problem comes from the officials losing the ballots for the sake of the Recount). The Election Contest Court (ECC) ruled them IN.

    Prediction: Team Coleman's hand for 5-card stud is from "The Sting": Doyle Lonegan (the great Robert Shaw) drawing a 3 of clubs. This card has already been clubbed twice and the Supremes will put the 3rd punch in it: No way.

2. They hold (AGAIN!) that duplicate ballots made from mailed-in absentee ballots were "double counted" along with the original absentee ballots in certain Minneapolis precincts, favoring Franken by a net of about +100. (The Pamela Howell testimony was the key piece of evidence; yep, that strong!) They did not offer any other witnesses to this, any physical evidence, and Howell's testimony amounted (barely) to hearsay.

    Since courts LIKE things like evidence, facts, etc. and there WEREN'T any entered by Coleman's side, and despite Coleman's request that the Court discover these for themselves, the ECC said there is no evidence this occurred, so the vote totals stay unchanged.

    Prediction: Team Coleman draws a 4 of hearts. None of the 4 attorneys in court brought any evidence this happened, however much they want to truly believe it DID happen. The Supremes will frisbee this across the room into the far wastebasket.

3. ....

I am sorry, folks. Too many late nights for some personal things and too little sleep, along with the endless restocking at the wine sale, have left me a shell.

I wanted to rant on about the "equal protection" crapola Coleman is raising: that on the one hand there was no fraud or intentional effort to discriminate, on a second hand there ARE statewide standards (unlike Bush v. Gore), and on the third hand (!) serious errors were made by non-fraudulent, non-discriminating local officials applying statewide standards that resulted in 4800 Coleman-identified voters (who will probably break in favor of Franken by +700) not having their votes counted.....

...but I just can't this morning. I'm shot.

Anything worth reading for analysis is going to have to come from YOU today in the comments. Let it be strong & vigorous & concentrated.... all things I am NOT today. Whew...

> **DK**
> A prayer for Al (and WineRev) :
> Though I walk through the volley of briefs, I shall fear no weasels,
> my staff and legal team comfort me,
> my fundraising cup shall overflow.
> Surely Norm will find another hobby
> and I shall dwell in the Peoples House for 5 and 1/2 years. *(the fan man)*

OK, that's the latest and most I can do today. (It is going to be a LONG day at the shop, I can feel it right now.) Bless you for your reading-ness and take a look at the links; they'll give you the latest from yust southeast of Lake Wobegon.

Shalom.

Coleman's Mirror
May 2, 2009

Comments: 94   Recs: 169   Tips: 171

Franken **wins by** +312 **votes.**

Number of days Norm Coleman seemed to lead: 43.

Number of days Al Franken has certifiably led: 135.

Number of days since election day (Nov. 4): 178.

Hoooooo—wweeeeee.

Sleep is SUCH a good thing I'm recommending it to all my friends. I needed that.

Thank you SO much for all your support (hat tip to Bartles & Jaymes) in yesterday's diary. My tip jar overflowed with good Karma and strength. The sensation of being supported was almost mystical "The Kossacks want you to be...... conscious!"

You people are great and I am grateful.

Norm Coleman's House of Mirrors

Kossack TerribleTom did a terribly good dismantlement of the Coleman brief in yesterday's comments, with a great moment here:

> **DK**
> Throughout the entire argument, Coleman conveniently conflates two processes: The first is the election-day system of poll watchers, election judges and county auditors and so forth. The second is a court of law, bound by rules of evidence and procedure.

DK

> In effect, Coleman argues that the two processes should be identical. If a court requires evidence of a particular element, then the election day process should have required the same evidence and, thus, always produce an identical result. Otherwise, there are two standards, and we can't have that.
>
> It's nonsense, of course, and it makes my head hurt. *(TerribleTom)*

And the proposed remedies (since on appeal you have to propose one or more) have all the properties of patent medicines before the Food & Drug Administration was established about 1908. *(One of the early 20th century best sellers was "Radiathor": a great little tonic based on the latest scientific discoveries. It contained grains of pure radium in the alcohol and not only cured everything from lumbago to baldness to toenail fungus, it also provided a soft night-light glow in your medicine cabinet. Really.)*

> Norm argues that because some counties used different standards than others, a statistical method of altering the count should be used which is based upon how well each candidate did in the county in question. This is pretty bizarre and would be an unprecedented solution.
>
> Another way is to allow properly rejected absentee ballots to be counted to make up for the absentee ballots that Norm now claims shouldn't have been counted in the first place. In other words, illegal votes should now be counted. This is also unprecedented and very unusual.
>
> Considering how weak Norm's arguments are, I can't really see the MN Supreme Court ever getting to a point where they will be analyzing Norm's remedies. *(MN Progressive Project)*

You go to the MN State Fair or the carnival comes to town and often one of the trailers is the "House of Mirrors." Step right up. Pay your money. Try to make your way through the maze while meeting yourself coming and going, in double profile, and while seeming to be 2 foot 3 or wider than tall. Of course if you just keep glancing down you'll see where the gray/grey (spelling war!) paint has worn off much more to show you where goes the path through the maze.

The Coleman Appeal [the legal one, not the personal angle; also no truth to the rumor that Norm (unlike Ben Ginsberg) is reptilian by genetics and periodically sheds his skin, which poetically is described by Chaucer as "Coleman a-peal-in"] makes a big deal out of "equal protection." The phrase is from the 14th Amendment to the US Constitution, ratified in 1868, just after the guns had cooled from the Civil War. The newly-freed were usually being treated as the still-oughta-be slaves. The Republican Party (!) put through the legal, yea bedrock Constitutional, basis for laws to be enforced equally for all persons "regardless of previous condition of servitude" and apart from considerations like race, sex, etc. (like state laws in Lincoln's state of Illinois that limited the number of persons of color who could settle in the state to an annual quota). In other words, it's an amendment that the elite, the aristocratic wanna-bes, the biased and the hierarchical are always going to despise because it demands EQUAL treatment under the law.

Well, Coleman argues at length (as his side has done at width, at sprawl, in the hall, bouncing a ball; could you, would you, Ben, at the Mall?) since local election officials made decisions on the spot on absentee ballots, based on statewide legal standards, and that those decisions came out differently between, say, Baudette County and Wadena County, there was something wrong. He looks in this mirror, sees that quadruple reflection over there and says, "Hey! Must be bias. Must be discrimination."

Then he holds up 1,300 ballots from his back pocket, and if you look toward this mirror they look like 4,000, and in that mirror they look like 4800 AND if you look at them in this TINTED mirror 3 reflections over there, they don't look like they came out of his pocket. And he bleats, "Disenfranchised. Gotta count them. Equal protection for the rejected."

OTOH his brief turns a couple corners and stands where 2 mirrors face each other square on. If you lean your head in and look either way, the image of your head is repeated into infinity.

The 2 mirrors here are the 133/2 votes from Minneapolis where the paper ballots have been lost for the recount (but we have fine evidence the voters voted IN PERSON).

These votes Coleman wants UN-counted. Why? Well, there's no real good way to say, even using Latin in a legal brief, "I'm losing so I want some of the other guy's votes thrown out." Ego non victoriatum, ergo desirio votati Frankenisti heave-ho-rium doesn't cut it somehow. (Subject to the Latin grammar police, but I think I'm as close as Brian putting up his "Romans go home!" graffiti in his first "terrorist" strike.)

BUT look! Norm! (Slaps Tony Trimble/Ben Ginsberg upside the head, partly to get their attention, partly because they deserve it in general.) If every vote should be counted regardless of legalities, you CAN'T have the 133/2 thrown out! Those voters would have screaming loud grounds to beat you to a bloody pulp with "equal protection." "May it please the court, these voters exercised their RIGHT to vote in person, not by privilege of absentee. They were registered. They voted. To take away their vote denies them the franchise, discriminates against them as a group/class of identifiable voters." If there's any justice the Court should not only agree, they should stick a rolled-up copy of the 14th Amendment up Ginsberg's nose.

For a much more elegant demolishment of Coleman's "equal protection" claim, Kossack and actual MN attorney "underwhelm" put up a diary back on January 29 (3 days after the ECC trial opened). S/he (and I think he's a he, but not positive) takes the Mirror Maze Coleman is trying to lead the court into and lays down those airplane-floor lights that "will activate to lead you to the nearest exit," the little glow-in-the-floor string that blinks "walk this way." I think the Court will do just that, Aerosmith-style, "Walk this way, talk this way! Walk this way, talk this way, and gimme a kiss!"—a kiss-off, that is, to Norm's whole argument.

Hope this will hold you for the next day or two with all the latest from yust southeast of Lake Wobegon.

Shalom.

Breakfast with Franken
May 4, 2009

Comments: 73   Recs: 249   Tips: 238

Franken Days

ENOUGH about Norm Coleman, horse dentures, Ginsberg the spinning top and the limpest election appeal since Mom put the linguini in the 10 -liter pot and turned up the heat – an hour ago.

Pat Lopez of the *Star Tribune* had a nice interview piece with Al Franken, the, you know, *Senator-elect!* from MN. The weekend- page assembly crew seems to be much more evenhanded in their news treatment and headlines (unless Pat Doyle is vomiting up some screed about Coleman's path to the US Supreme Court) so Lopez got page 1, lower- left corner with a color picture of a thoughtful Al Franken.

They met at a famous St. Paul breakfast shop called The Egg and I.

Al is "tantalizingly close" and yet so far. Instead of legislating he's having to wait...and wait...and wait, just like us, only worse, since he's in the middle of it.

> "A lot of people ask me and Franni [his wife], 'Are you OK?'" Franken said, his face crumpling into a caricature of someone inquiring after one's health. "As life's challenges go, this is pretty low on the totem pole. Our kids are OK, we're not in danger of losing our home to foreclosure. We're fine." (*Star Tribune*)

He has named a chief of staff and a director for MN constituent services, but he can't pay them. When he travels it's on his own dime. But he keeps looking ahead, how he's going to handle celebrity (been talking with Hilary about that), and how he's going to relate to the rest of the MN congressional delegation.

> One challenge will be maintaining at least cordial relations with a congressional delegation that spans the political rainbow from Rep. Keith Ellison, recently arrested while protesting Darfur, to Rep. Michele Bachmann, whose controversial pronouncements have earned her a near-permanent berth on the talk-show circuit. (*Star Tribune*)

And then to sort of act out "a day in the life of Senator Franken" Pat Lopez sat in the booth while a pair of lobbyists met with him over toast and coffee to pitch him why cap and trade on emissions is a bad idea... followed by a pair of lobbyists who pitched him why cap and trade on emissions is an excellent idea.

Odds & Ends

Your ever-lovin' WineRev decided to go Communist over the weekend and attend the Powderhorn neighborhood May Day parade in the delightful company of my mental institute's nurse-and-Kossack who signed me out for the day. Weather was fantastic as father Sun was rowed across the pond in the manner of the closing credits from "Hawaii 5-0". Jousting boats of snow and winter rowed out to duel the Sun but the Sun pushed on through to kiss mother Earth in a Tree of Life ceremony. We weren't close enough to the Kremlin Wall to see who was in "bad health" and who was the coming man, and I did miss the Red Army Chorus and the SS-22 missiles, but the band "Machinery Hill" was excellent.

There were tents set up from all sorts of MN organizations... including the MN Republicans. (Good for them for turning out.) Their tent with tables was a good 25 feet apart from every other tent in the row (most were like 6 feet apart) and in 5 full minutes NO ONE went near their tent. Kossack SageHagRN and I watched the 4 white males stand there inside their "U" shaped tables talking earnestly with each other, backs to the outside world. Great symbolism.

OK hope your Cinco de Mayo tomorrow is a good one. That's the latest from yust southeast of Lake Wobegon.

Shalom.

Predictions?
May 5, 2009

Comments: 108   Recs: 146   Tips: 181

Come the prophets

How long will this take? We all want to know and we have a few dates. May 11: Due date, Franken (Respondent's) Brief Due. May 15: Due date, Coleman (Appellants's) Reply to Respondent Due. June 1: Oral arguments.

Nothing to be done about those but let the pages fall from the calendar. But after that?

Well, the Wicked Witch of the West (your choice of nominees) has sent out her brother the Wicked Warlock of Waco to gaze into the dusky crystal ball and prophesy doom. Texas Senator John Cornyn (R-Prick) came out from his shell at the start of April to predict "World War III" if the Senate tries to seat Al Franken without a certificate of election. With Arlen Specter switching parties Franken becomes the critical 60th vote that, should all the Senate Democrats stick together on certain votes, they can squelch a Republican filibuster.

> "I expect they (Coleman's legal team) will pursue the appeals until they are exhausted, whenever that may be. ... I would assume if they were unsuccessful in the Minnesota Supreme Court, there may very well be an appeal to the United States Supreme Court." *(John Cornyn (R-TX), quoted in Politico)*

Further,

> National Republicans are eager to see Coleman continue fighting as long as he can - even to the federal level, a process that could take many months. But they are wary of being viewed as directing the fight out of Washington, saying that the decision remains up to Coleman, who can expect the full party's financial and political backing should he appeal to the U.S. Supreme Court - or wage a new lawsuit in federal district court...

> NRSC Chairman John Cornyn, who views the race as his first of the cycle, added that he's "not advising them, I'm just watching. That will have to be determined by Sen. Coleman and his legal team." *(Politico)*

And...

> Cornyn, the chairman of the National Republican Senatorial Committee, acknowledges that a federal challenge to November's elections could take "years" to resolve. But he's adamant that Coleman deserves that chance — even if it means Minnesota is short a senator for the duration. *(Think Progress)*

Infuriating as ever, John. Thanks. It's so nice to see you like reruns too, you playing Archie Bunker when you and Edith go to visit Edith's cousin Maude (the recently departed Bea Arthur.) Archie let fly with some stupid, bigoted remark and Maude gave him that STFU look and said, "Still fighting mental health, Archibald?"

Rebuttal from on High

Meanwhile, the MN Independent may have uncovered a Cronyn counterweight from out of this world. We all recall the Coleman "universe" of absentee ballots, a vast, pulsating region of space marked by clouds of dust being thrown toward judges, great, spinning masses of super heated gases (Ben Ginsberg), and numbers of absentee ballots that shifted with such rapidity and scale (from 10,962 to 6 and all points in between) not even the on-board computer on the *USS Enterprise*, sporting giga-quads of memory and computing power behind an Apple logo, could keep up.

Well, the black-box recorder of the not-so-scientific-but-venerable vessel called the *USS Astrologer* has been recently recovered. Vulcans, Mr. Data and various reality-based folk dispute the significance of the data but others want to believe in a Mulder/ Scully kind of way.

Or maybe Chris Steller at the MN Independent is getting as desperate as anyone to find anything to write about between now and May 11/ May 15/ June 1. Blogging astrologer Terry Lamb is (sort of) predicting June 14 as Al Franken's good day.

I'm not partial myself to astrology (since I never indulge in anything but the most prosaic of descriptions of events; my diaries make a Coleman attorney like Joe Friedberg come off like a genial auctioneer, but you already knew that) but I can't deny there are folks who put stock in it. Those same folks probably aren't partial to my fusion of Jewish-Pastafarian-Lutheran (JPL, Reformed; the OTHER JPL, not those rocket guys with the fancy Hubble Telescopes and cool slide rules) but they are willing to leave me to the red sauce/white sauce theological struggle as long as I support Al Franken. Live & let live.

OK, that's what little we've got. I leave tomorrow night for Florida for a few days with Mama WineRev, but I'll take along the laptop for when the inevitable news of the Franken Respondent's Brief breaks. Hope this will hold you for now with all the latest from yust southeast of Lake Wobegon.

A raucus Cinco de Mayo to the Latinos and Latinas from our friendly neighbor to the South (Greater Iowa.)

Shalom.

The Specter of Arlen
May 6, 2009

Comments: 77 *Recs:* 188 *Tips:* 191

Today I feel like Father John Francis Patrick Mulcahey from *M*A*S*H* in the episode where Radar is hurt after Hawkeye sends him off to Seoul for some "action." Radar gets wounded on the way and is evac-ed to MASH 4077 and a guilt-ridden Hawkeye has to step out of surgery to vomit partway through the serious (but not life-threatening) surgery to repair the damage. Later in post-op he ends up yelling at Radar for his hero-worship and "Iowa naivete." The whole camp is upset and Fr. Mulcahey comes to see Hawkeye.

> "Hawkeye, I know you work under terrific pressure here and please take this in the spirit it is intended but *have you lost your mind?* Where's your decency man? That boy is lying there wounded and you talk to him like that? I tell you I'm not just upset, I am acrimonious!"

It's the same way with news from Senator Specter, the newest quasi-Democrat in the US Senate. In an upcoming *New York Times* interview he gets a softball question about being the last Jewish Republican in the Senate. He answers it bugs him and could have waited for the next question. Instead:

> Q. With your departure from the Republican Party, there are no more Jewish Republicans in the Senate. Do you care about that?
>
> A. I sure do. There's still time for the Minnesota courts to do justice and declare Norm Coleman the winner.
>
> Q. Which seems about as likely at this point as Jerry Seinfeld's joining the Senate.
>
> A. Well, it was about as likely as my becoming a Democrat. *(New York Times)*

Arlen! *Have you lost your mind?* Really!

First, why is being Jewish and Republican even a question? Yeah, it's as unlikely as a Big Mac at a vegan dinner but so what? No big deal. And Norm "Les Faux Dentales du Cheval" Coleman would be holding that last rag of honor, Jewish Republican Senator? Its a damned small caucus as it is, but fortunately neither Talmud nor the Constitution require a *minyan* to pass EFCA, universal health care, or to (keel)haul a fair percentage of the last Administration through any number of courts of justice.

Next, Arlen: "Do justice"? *Have you lost your mind?* On what grounds do you raise this? Were you joking and the gum-chewing reporter thought you were serious? At what point has there been INjustice? Is it not written "if the diff between 2 candidates is less than 0.5% a recount of votes is required."? Was this not done, Arlen? Was it not done openly, transparently, with challenges and arguments and quick runs to the MN Supreme Court?

"Let there be a State Canvassing Board of 5 to decide the challenges." And it was so. Arlen? *Have you lost your mind?* Haven't you heard of The UpTake? They covered it live, challenge by challenge. There are tapes, videotapes. Arlen, you should watch them. Don't pull a McCain Internet here and let it be said, "Senator Specter is aware of the UpTake."

And Arlen? It is written, "You don't like how the Canvassing Board rules? So sue me. I'll set up a court just for you." The ECC set up shop and heard 5 weeks of Norm-andies AND, to be fair and just, 2 weeks from Mr. Franken. It was no injustice that Norm has Tony Trimble at his side being unjust with evidence and being slapped with a sanction from the Court...that WAS justice. The fact that Tony came off as somehow fulfilling the proverb "A lawyer who represents himself has a fool for a client" is unfortunate, but no injustice. (OTOH it is also written [here] that "The client who has a Ginsberg for an advisor is a fool" but that is still not injustice.)

NOW, Arlen, the Supreme Court will hear the appeal. 2 members of the Sanhedrin who were in on the case earlier have stepped back (!) from the bench to avoid even the appearance of bias. Briefs are being written and filed. Laws are being researched. Precedents are presented and scrutinized. And all this is unjust ... How? *Have you lost your mind?* Slow, yes? Unjust to Al Franken? Perhaps you should consider THAT angle Arlen? Unjust to the people of MN and being represented in the Senate? What of them, Arlen?

And then Joe Bodell reports

> Said Specter: "In the swirl of moving from one caucus to another, I have to get used to my new teammates. I'm ordinarily pretty correct in what I say. I've made a career of being precise. I conclusively misspoke."
>
> Asked who he's backing now in elections, Specter said, "I'm looking for more Democratic members. Nothing personal." *(MN Progressive Project)*

Not smooth Arlen, but that's what happens on this side of the street. You get the Great Orange One himself to put up a diary on the front page; you get a recommended diary with over 600 comments in about 4 hours; you'd BETTER issue a "What I really MEANT to say..." kind of statement.

After all, it is written, "Better to be *thought* a fool than to open one's mouth and remove all doubt."

Acrimonious indeed!

Gotta finish packing for Mama WineRev's in Florida, get to the early shift and catch a plane south. YOU have mere days to get something in the mail or ordered for your MOM, so get on it. And THAT is the latest from yust southeast of Lake Wobegon for this morning.

Shalom.

Responding Respondents Who Respond in Brief
May 12, 2009

Comments: 126   Recs: 247   Tips: 229

Franken wins by +312 votes.

Team Franken FILED their Respondent's Brief on Monday.

Coleman can (optional) file a Reply to Respondent's Brief By THIS FRIDAY, May 15.

Oral arguments, MN Supreme Court: June 1, 20 days from this morning.

The Respondent Responds (take that, you hacks!)

Monday afternoon Al Franken's legal team did the usual lawyer's appeal thing-y and ran the clock down to the last hours before filing their Respondent's Brief. (For those of you keeping score: it sort of helps to take it to the last minute. IF Coleman is going to file an official Reply to Respondent's Brief, the due date is this Friday the 15th. Filing right up against this May 11th deadline means the Coleman side has the minimum number of hours to work on their Reply.) If you've got the time, you might as well use it, right? Besides for Lillehaug, Elias & Co. it takes longer. Their pride prevents them from submitting a Brief done in crayon. OTOH it takes a while to fit a Brief with 1.21 gigawatts of power...especially since DeLoreans are so hard to find these days.

Just in formatting (from this nonlawyer's view) it is elegantly written. They give a Table of Contents and then list all the cases they are citing, the statutes they are citing, all by page number, and then get down to a brief review of the Recount from Nov. 5 to yesterday.

A Respondent has to do a few things in their Brief. Since the Appellant gets to go first AND they can even Reply (as a sort of final rebuttal; it's rather fair, since the "burden of proof" is on the Appellant---it's the tougher job so they get some extra opportunity) the Respondent has to play both defense and offense. Defense means doing your best to dismantle the Appellants' case. Offense means counterpunching, showing the Court why they should not only dismiss the Appellant but also buy into the Respondents' line.

> I thought the tone was perfect. They (Franken's Team) effectively refuted the Coleman claims but did so through citing evidence from the trial and precedent in other legal cases. It wasn't vague in any area so I don't think they overplayed the notion the Coleman case fell short. *(katelync at The UpTake)*

And Kossack TerribleTom offered:

> One test I like to apply to an appellate brief is this: If I were a judge, to what extent could I base a sound opinion on the holdings set forth in this brief? With that in mind, Franken's brief approaches a pre-written opinion. Coleman's brief does not. Not even close. *(Terrible Tom)*

The defense/dismantling (sounds like removing a shelf above the fireplace) starts early in the Brief:

> With the voluminous record before it (142 witnesses, 1,900 exhibits, 20,000 pages of transcript) the trial Court (Election Contest Court: ECC) issued a unanimous decision on April 13 dismissing each of Appellant's claims on multiple, independent grounds. *(Respondent's Brief)*

As in, *"you gonna mess with the work of those 3 judges who put up with / weeks of this lutefisk and decided it really does stink on ice"*? I think that's called "burden-ing the proof."

And the next sentence is

> The (ECC) rejected Appellants' central attack – involving the treatment of absentee ballots – for a multitude of reasons, including improper pleading, insufficient proof and failure on the law. *(Respondent's Brief)*

I don't know law at all but these three sure sound like a Joe-Curly-Moe triple cheek-slap to me... and all this is 2 1/2 pages in among the narrative (with 43 to go!).

The next page David, Kevin & Marc really rev out the old Evinrude there in drydock, with the competition clutch and a flathead mill, walkin' Thunderbirds, and lettin' the lake pipes roar:

> (appellants') claim that this Court should substitute its judgment for the Legislature's by rejecting clear statutory provisions in favor of an invented regime that finds no support in the facts, has no basis in the law, and suffers from a host of procedural problems. *(Respondent's Brief)*

This is heading off for contemptuous...not of the Court, but of their "worthy opponents". In carefully crafted legal language they are indeed "telling us how they REALLY feel." I mean: "no support in facts... no basis in law...invented regime". WOW. That is serious calling out, sort of like going on DailyKos and calling someone a "pootie-hating Cheney-kisser who hates Young Frankenstein"... you know, serious fightin' words.

Fourteen pages into their PDF Team Franken really gets rolling and passes from defense to counterattack (like Longstreet holding out until midday on the 2nd day of Second Manassas, and then smashing Fitz-John Porter with a tremendous drop punch that wrecked the "Army of Virginia" as an organized body and sent John Pope chasing Indians for the rest of the Civil War).

They really get down on the Coleman legal team:

> Appellants' statement of the case pays little heed to the record on review. For this reason, Respondent provides the following restatement of the case. *(Respondent's Brief)*

In other words, *"we are going to cite the court record up to this point and do your work FOR you."* Whammo: leaving the tennis racquet with busted strings collared around their collective heads...

They are relentless and yes, even contumelious (!) of the Coleman side:

> Moreover, MN has, for over 100 years, required that contestants bear the burden not only of proving "that there were irregularities," but also proving "that they affected the result" *(citing the 1865(!) Taylor v. Taylor case in MN law - WR)*... since the Coleman side did NOT so prove it's a lot of bogus billingsgate and gasconade. "This rule is settled, clear, and undisputed. *(Respondent's Brief)*

DK

> Ah, WineRev. I wish this had been in the brief verbatim: "since the Coleman side did NOT so prove it's a lot of bogus billingsgate and gasconade" Succinct, accurate, on point and devastating. Perhaps you missed your calling, WineRev. *(TerribleTom)*

And again (page 25):

> At the outset, Minnesota's statutes are presumed to be constitutional...A court will not strike down a statute...unless the challenging party demonstrates its unconstitutionality beyond a reasonable doubt. Appellants have not even come close to making this showing. *(Respondent's Brief)*

The "even" is REALLY harsh, a forward roll upthrust of the light saber...

Then they REALLY throw it back in the faces of Team Coleman (*"Mud on your face, big disgrace!"*) in refuting Coleman dragging in *Bush v. Gore.* They point out that *Bush v. Gore* as an argument regarding Equal Protection not only does not support Coleman, but

> In other words, Appellants' expansive reading of *Bush* not only finds no support in the(ir) case; it directly contradicts it. *(Respondent's Brief, emphasis mine - WR)*

A MAJOR "read between the lines of my Boy Scout salute" moment for sure.

And finally, in a moment of flawless, Vulcan -level logic, Team Franken clobbers the Coleman team for...wait for it...NOT bringing in all nearly 300,000 absentee ballots to be ruled on by the court, but only a "mere 4,800 rejected absentee ballots." If the Court were to make ANY decision about those 4,800 it would deny "equal protection" to the remaining 295,200 because the same "standard" was not applied to them. Yowser!

Nuggets all over the place: p. 47:

> Appellants' claims are incoherent, and there is nothing in either the record or in Appellants' offers of proof that could rehabilitate the factual deficiencies. *(Respondent's Brief)*

As to the missing 133 Minneapolis ballots: page 49:

> Where the original ballots are missing the official results are the best evidence"... This principle is clearly established in both Minnesota and across the country-- and has been for well over a century *(and then they cite Newton v. Newell from MN... from 1880; FACE, man! - WR)* *(Respondent's Brief)*

In other words burying this whole "missing ballots" (and likewise the supposed "duplicate/double-counted" ballots) under the ice rink about 4 Hoffa Units down under the concrete.

And as they go on into mashing the equal -protection argument they go *THERE*... yep, right to the dispenser in the men's room in the Judiciary building.

> Even by comparison to the minority of states that still require an excuse (for voting absentee) Minnesota's Legislature has imposed stricter prophylactic standards." *(Respondent's Brief)*

("I do not think that word means what you think it means." Well, maybe... but still...)

Finally, the Brief closes by asking the MN Supreme Ct. to back up the ECC finding that Franken won and is entitled to the Certificate of Election, and that the court "direct" the governor and the secretary of state to issue and sign the certificate in their "ministerial" capacity. That is focused lawyer talk for what so many of you have been saying here: "Sign the damn thing NOW and be done with it." (The "ministerial" language is calling on them to perform the function of their office WITHOUT further deliberation, aimed directly at the Pawlenty hemming and hawing. "You don't GET to deliberate, Tim.")

To go to the far end of Paul Bunyan's crowbar for maximum leverage the Brief adds a couple things. First the Brief calls on the Court to expedite the certificate of election by waiving a 10-day notice to recon-sider/rehear the case (apparently a little provision that SOME appellant might reach for) INCLUDING offering to waive any reimbursement to Franken from Coleman for costs of the appeal. Whoa! Lawyers turning down money? Yeah, it happens, but I think it's rare enough that it might get somebody's (eg.the Court's) attention. AND the Brief cites the Court's OWN ruling (a ruling *against* Franken in *Franken v. Pawlenty* (an ancient precedent from February, 2009) that the certificate not issue until the STATE courts are done with the matter. When the MN supremes rule, they ask for the certificate REGARDLESS of any federal court action or maneuvers-- in other words, Norm can appeal till a Cornyn Doomsday, but the certificate of election should issue now. We'll see.

Personal Notes

Winerev is back from 4-1/2 humidity choked days with Mama Winerev in south Florida. I tell you there is NOTHING like mulching plant beds and laying sod under the double 88s (you know, degrees and percent humidity?) But the beach was wonderful.

OK back to ye olde grindstone at the wine shop this morning. That's the semi-latest on the MN Senate Recount to hold you from yust southeast of Lake Wobegon.

Shalom.

Oddly Endlies
May 13, 2009

Comments: 66   Recs: 190   Tips: 208

Odds & Ends

It's all odds and ends today as we await Friday at the MN Supreme Court's clerk window. Back on April 30 the Coleman Team filed their Appellant's Brief. Monday the 11th was Team Franken's turn to file their Respondent's Brief. The Court set this Friday the 15th as a deadline for the Coleman side to file their Reply to Respondent's Brief. Since the side making the appeal carries the "burden of proof" (known in Missouri as the "Oh yeah? Show me!") they get to both open and close around the Respondent's paperwork.

If this sounds familiar it is. When we've watched oral legal arguments on The UpTake during the Recount on various motions whoever brought the Motion opens and gets to reserve part of their time to a closing (which they usually do.)

Around the blogosphere learned legal minds are weighing in on both Briefs and as you might guess the consensus is building that the Coleman case looks like a pig on stilts... on ice: not pretty.

Pat Doyle at the *Star Tribune* continues to prepare his dwindling circle of readers for the inevitable defeat of former Senator Horse Dentures by reporting actual facts:

> Franken also said Coleman's lawyers never adequately raised a constitutional due process argument in seven weeks of testimony during the trial.
>
> Coleman claimed a due process violation during closing arguments, saying the three-judge panel that heard the trial imposed different standards for counting ballots than were used during the election and recount.
>
> Franken said Coleman should have raised the issue in a more serious manner earlier in the trial if he wanted it to be considered. *(Star Tribune)*

He closes with:

> Election and constitutional law experts Fred Morrison of the University of Minnesota, Guy-Uriel Charles of Duke University Law School and (Rick) Hasen (of Loyola Law School) said Monday that it's unlikely Coleman will prevail before the state Supreme Court because he hasn't proven violation of constitutional rights or state elections law.
>
> "I thought Coleman had an uphill battle, and it's only reinforced by my reading of the Franken brief," Hasen said. *(Star Tribune)*

Meanwhile a law professor at Ohio State's School of Law has spent time combing through the Coleman Brief from the other week. I haven't always liked Dr. Foley's take on things but this is a thoughtful piece, sort of like reading over a judge's shoulder while she works out a next-to-last draft of a ruling:

> If local officials acted properly within their scope of discretion under state law, then there is no wrongful conduct to remedy even if some of them rejected ballots that others would have accepted, and vice versa. Only if this exercise of discretion were a violation of federal law would a remedial issue arise. *(Election Law @ Moritz)*

Odder End

The whole question of issuing a Certificate of Election is headed for the governor's office and Tim Pawlenty is being the last kid on the one side of the gym in a game of dodgeball. While he keeps trying to have it both ways ("I'll sign when the appeals are done... but I didn't say WHICH appeals") the heat in state is growing on him.

At the corner of I-94 and Snelling Ave in St. Paul some folks have bought up the rights to a billboard and are using it for a hot-pink challenge to T-Paw that thousands of commuters a day can ponder while zipping by at 17 MPH riding each other's bumpers.

The sign puts Pawlenty in the crosshairs by challenging him to choose between MN and his personal ambitions.

Oddest Yet

Of course in MN you can't REALLY do "odds and ends" until you do Jesse Ventura. Monday night Jesse had a guest appearance on "Larry King Live" and was vintage Jesse. You want to know why a former Navy Seal (yes, he's that tough and that smart; the Seals don't take weaklings and they do NOT take stupid for members), former mayor and, yeah, former ring rat showed WHY he attracted a certain percentage of the vote in '98? The man comes off as speaking his mind and speaking other people's minds as well. In the embedded video he flat out calls Dick Cheney a "coward" for having ducked Vietnam (FINALLY! somebody willing to nail that fascist son of a bitch... not that I have an opinion about the former Vice-President...*fumes!*). He says waterboarding is torture and anyone who did it OR ORDERED IT should be jailed or worse. He calls out Cheney on the waterboard/torture issue by offering to **use the technique on Cheney!** ("In one hour I'll have him confessing to the Sharon Tate murders." I would sleep under a bridge for a year... in Minnesota, through the winter... to see that particular hour carried out on the carcass of Dick Cheney.)

BUT, to bring this back to all things MN, Ventura also calls his former opponent in '98, Norm the Dentalated, a **hypocrite** and says that is nothing new. Coleman is only doing what he has always done, said Jesse, looking out for Norm.

That kind of straight talk will get you votes in a lot of places, even if you govern like you've been hit with a metal folding chair on the head a few too many times.

Well, the Coleman Reply is due Friday. The next couple days? We'll see if there's enough to put something together to hold you from yust southeast of Lake Wobegon.

Shalom.

Coleman's Reply
May 16, 2009

Comments: 64   Recs: 174   Tips: 180

The Coleman Reply

As the one making the Appeal Coleman bears the burden of proof and has to open the case (April 30). Once Franken responds (May 11) Coleman can (optional) file a Reply. Yesterday afternoon he did.

When you sift through the 33 pages in PDF some things are noticeable right off. They repeatedly state "the trial court (Election Contest Court: ECC) erred…" which sounds like name-calling or denial of reality but I think is actually lawyer's boilerplate. Coleman is appealing the lower Court decision so his side HAS TO say, "the lower court got it wrong, here's where and here's how." If the lower court got it right and Norm agreed with it there would be no appeal. (If the roles were reversed, Franken's team would be saying the exact same thing: "the ECC erred when they said A, because of B"). So while it's a bit jarring to read the phrase repeatedly the Justices will slide their eyes right past those words; for them it's language as routine as Alberto Gonzales saying "I don't recall" to anything.

There is no mention of "let's do the whole election over since it was too close to call." That idea has floated around throwing off pixels and ink blots for a while but in their last written word before oral arguments on June 1 the Coleman side does NOT go there. I suppose that's a gain of some kind but sort of hollow, rather like a Honolulu homeowner announcing "I've decided NOT to shovel any snow off my front walk today"… to which the proper reply is, "Still feeling that surfboard on the head from yesterday, eh buddy?"

One more time they add the Supreme Court should look for duplicate/double-counted ballots AND throw out the Minneapolis 133/132 (depending on who's counting) ballots that voters signed in and cast (according to voting-machine tapes) but that were lost. Both requests are right at the end, barely a paragraph each, and have a tacked-on feel to them, like they were added because, say, Coleman attorney Tony Trimble was standing there saying, "If you don't put these in I'll hold my breath 'till I turn blue and then you'll be sorry." So they added them just to get him to shut up.

But as a late friend of mine liked to describe the Lutheran inner life, these 2 issues are mostly here out of guilt, fear, shame, dread, and remorse. In the matter of the "duplicate/double-counted" they alternate between whining and effrontery. *"We brought out one witness to this widespread problem, who maybe overheard some other election officials in her precinct who worked for her maybe say something that sounded like some duplicate ballots were possibly being counted alongside the original ballots. We object that she was cross-examined by the Franken side, object her testimony stricken from the trial record by the Court because we messed up discovery, object the trial court struck her testimony again because we got sanctioned $7500 for tampering with her testimony. We decided NOT to call any other witnesses to this problem and offer no other actual evidence this actually happened BUT the Supreme Court should take, oh, maybe 100/125 votes off Franken's pile because of it."* What a bunch of grease trap cleanings! The whole position is about as meaningful as Deputy Sheriff Barney Fife trying to enforce a city noise ordinance at the Sturgis, South Dakota biker's week.

> **DK** You nailed the Lutheran inner life! But since I grew up with the "Wisconsin" brand, I was spared the lutefisk. *(Fiddlegirl)*

> **DK** Went to a Lutheran funeral a couple years ago after maybe 20 years of entering the church generally only for Christmas Eve midnight services.
>
> Ohmigosh did I have the nastiest flashbacks during the church basement 'lunch' ceremony! Ham sliced too large to fit on the little 'buns', miracle whip but no mustard, individually-wrapped cheese slices, you know the type of meal. Beverage choices were water, lemonade-type-drink (since it was summer), and coffee.
>
> My wife, California-raised, looked upon this scene in horror. All she could think to say was 'where are the fresh produce?' Me, I just felt like I was eight years old again. And did not like it one bit. *(TheOtherJimM)*

The Coleman side has been also loudly trumpeting their appeal as the opportunity to enfranchise 4,400 *(stand by for tomorrow's number! Changes daily!)* voters who have been wrongfully denied their ballots being counted. But the Minneapolis 133/132 have rightfully had their ballots counted under law: so said Cindy Reichert, Minneapolis director of elections, supported by an opinion by the Attorney General; so said the State Canvassing Board by 5-0; so said the Election Contest Court by 3-0.

Not ONE person in a position of authority and expertise on MN election law has supported UN-counting these ballots as Coleman wants, not one! And THAT goes to the heart of why this point is added in a mumbled, back of the hand way to their Reply...it completely undercuts the rest of the Reply's argument regarding equal protection.

See, Norm is at pains (mostly OUR pains; we're on the receiving end of statements by Ginsberg & Friedberg) to highlight that while there IS a set of standards in place in MN law regarding absentee ballots (UNlike Florida 2000 and therefore making *Bush v. Gore* irrelevant to *Coleman v. Franken*) and while election officials across the state ARE trained in applying those standards (UNlike Florida 2000 and therefore...), they did not apply those standards with machine-like regularity to all 286,000 absentee ballots AND that the variations are enough to swing/cast doubt on the election. It's the only shot they have and they actually make a half-decent argument in the body of their Reply. They offer as a remedy that the Supreme Court "remand" (send back) the case to the ECC with their 4,400 absentee ballots *(soon to be another exciting number!)* with a set of instructions/standards on how to count a few/some/most/all of them. (Curiously, no word on any other ballots Franken might want counted under those same murky standards that have nothing to do with MN law...)

> Most of the filing was weak - but I think the substantial compliance argument for the absentee ballots is reasonable...
>
> Their rational basis review argument completely ignores the actual rational basis - we want to have locally administered elections. *(PJ at The UpTake)*

But then they continue to press for the EX-clusion/DIS-enfranchising of these 133/2 Minneapolis ballots that MEET the state standards and WERE lawfully cast because... well, Eric Kleefeld at Talking Points Memo summed up not only the Reply AND the appeal Brief BUT ALSO the entire Coleman ECC case this way. The ENTIRE effort since January 5 (when the State Canvassing Board ended its work and declared Franken the winner by +225), ALL the 20,000 pages of ECC trial record, ALL the testimony from over 140 witnesses, ALL the 1,900+ exhibits, ALL the Ben Ginsberg bull farting in the Judiciary Building halls... ALL that boils down to THE Coleman position: "COUNT MORE VOTES FOR ME."

WineRev Predicts: The MN Supreme Court reads Kleefeld and rules unanimously for Franken.

Other Takes

Jeff Rosenberg at MNPublius reports a great press release from the MN Democratic Party (DFL) under the headline "Minnesota Republicans decide elections don't matter":

> We may as well not have held an election in 2008. First, former senator Norm Coleman has deprived Minnesotans of their full representation in the United States Senate, refusing to concede that Al Franken got more votes and is entitled to the seat. Now, Coleman's crony Governor Tim Pawlenty has threatened to dispense with the elected Legislature, and run the state's finances in the middle of a historic economic and fiscal crisis using only his executive powers of line-item veto and unallotment. *(MN Plubius)*

Maybe I need to explain how our Republic works. I thought this was fairly common knowledge, but here goes:

The public votes for their representatives, and it is accepted that the election results express the will of the people...

Well, I hope that will hold you through your weekend. As there are developments going down to the oral arguments on June 1 I will post diaries but YOU have spring to get to, so have at it! That's the latest from yust southeast of Lake Wobegon.

Shalom.

All 3 MN Senators
May 19, 2009

Comments: 84   Recs: 191   Tips: 184

As all the news organizations are doing until June 1, ya gotta write about something...

The FORMER and ex-Senator

Yes, that guy, a man who by entering a room can make a used-car salesman's convention become as sincere as Linus' (Great) Pumpkin patch. In a final addendum to Saturday's diary I noted the former/ex/indictable Senator was going to be appearing at a Republican Jews for Gefilte & Lute Fisk fundraiser. (Gefilte fish or lutefisk, topped with either Japanese horse- radish or limburger cheese, would be threatened to be served unless attendees coughed up the dough.) I invited any MN Kossacks who were inclined to exercise their right to free speech to turn up.

Well... some folks did. A representative of the "Make Norm Go Away, Give a Dollar a Day" turned up, complete with video camera. The rep was there to THANK Norm (politicians like to be thanked... a LOT, sort of like Major Frank Burns in his fantasy episode at the MASH 4077th when he not only gets to put Hawkeye on trial for mutiny but also is the hero of the operating room. Chaos and disaster all around a glowing Frank and a nurse pauses in her weariness to gasp, "Thank you doctor." "For what?" Burns replies. "Just for being you.")

The rep was there to THANK Norm for being Norm, for being the raison d'etre for over $92,000 being raised for progressive causes. Couldn't have done it without you, Norm. Thanks.

Chris Steller also reports on some speculation as to what's coming next from the Coleman side:

> One of the more interesting aspects of the reply brief that Coleman filed at the Minnesota Supreme Court Friday is what it didn't say. As the Politico observes, the former senator had nothing to say in response to a major point that Democratic rival Al Franken made in his brief: that the high court should direct Gov. Tim Pawlenty to issue an election certificate as soon as the state's judiciary is done with Coleman's appeal.
>
> That silence could mean Coleman is ready to bow out if he loses his current appeal (wrong, says a staffer). Or, Coleman could be readying a request for an injunction from the U.S. Supreme Court to prevent Pawlenty from issuing Franken the certificate he would need to take Coleman's old seat in the Senate. *(MN Independent)*

The Senator-Elect Future is So Close
I Can Taste It Senator

The Senator-to-Be was doing some party-building this weekend. Franken got himself elected (YAY! Happy dance!) as a delegate to the DFL (MN alphabet soup for "Democratic-Farmer-Labor" party; i.e. the good gals (which also includes men/guys as a figure of speech) citywide convention. He got to make a speech endorsing Minneapolis mayor R.T. Rybak for reelection. (A name like that sounds like a cousin of a Steven Segal action movie. Might boost the local economy...hmmm.)

Franken was both gracious and funny.

The gracious:

> "I want to thank all of you. When you win an election by 312 votes, there's not a lot of effort that goes to waste," Al Franken told Minneapolis Democrats Saturday. "We ran a very efficient campaign." *(MN Independent)*

The funny:

> "A lot of people here have been asking me, "What do I call you?" And the answer to that is: Al. There is only one person in the state who will have to call me senator and that, of course, is [his wife] Franni. *(MN Independent)*

The CURRENT Senator

Kevin Diaz of the *Star Tribune* had a nice backgrounder on what the current Senator from MN is up to these days. For the life of me I can't find the story on the ST website but I have the bugger here in front of me on the couch just past the 4th bag of Cheetos.

She and her staff are working insanely hard:

> "After inheriting 400 constituent cases from Republican Coleman, whose office closed in early February, the first-term Democrat says she has seen a doubling of requests from ordinary Minnesotans on everything from veteran's benefits to overseas adoptions and lost Social Security checks." *(Star Tribune)*

The side benefit for Senator K is the focus is giving the lie to the Reichving bleatings that float around the internet tubes and sewers of the state like "well, she's not doing anything" and "she always WAS lazy" and other bilgewater like that.

"An Internet search on "Minnesota's only senator" now yields more than 9 million hits." Yowser!

She has been effortlessly tap-dancing through the political stuff by holding a consistent position on the Coleman-Franken duel:

> "I've said what I thought. That is that Norm has the right to his appeal to the MN Supreme Court, but that MN has a right to 2 Senators." *(Star Tribune)*

What helping has been her sense of humor (maybe to keep from crying or go screaming into, say, John Cornyn's face and grab that worthless suntanned armadillo husk by the neck and shove him butt-first onto the nearest cactus).

> "She misses few chances to tell audiences that she is both MN's "junior senator and senior senator", noting that the arrangement makes for a lot less friction.
>
> She's a frequent guest on MSNBC's Rachel Maddow show where she was introduced as: "the entire Senate delegation from Minnesota." *(Star Tribune)*

It is wearing on her, and the pressure gets high some times. A recent Medicare funding bill as part of the economic stimulus meant $300 million to MN, and it passed by 2 votes. The jr./sr./present Senator breathed a sigh of relief at that close call. She HAS asked for extra staff but at least one senator has objected (anonymously) so under Senate rules it's a no-go. (Your nominations HERE for which rancid turkey it might be.)

"For now Klobuchar says she has decided to to press the staffing issue. The recount might be resolved soon – or not.

If all else fails, she jokes, "maybe I'll faint on the floor (of the Senate.) I really haven't figured out what I'm going to do."

OK, hope that will hold you as we grind toward June 1. That's the semi-latest from yust southeast of Lake Wobegon.

Shalom.

Some Things
May 21, 2009

Comments: 97   *Recs:* 167   *Tips:* 170

Things the People Think

For those reporters who haven't forgotten, or for those who have fallen into the doghouse with their editors, the MN Senate Recount still counts as news... under the fold on page C19, alongside "Woman Bitten by Jackalope; Rabies treatments begun." But news! by gum. It's like having the ghost of George Carlin come out and do stand-up while pretending to read news items. (*"On-Duty Criminal Shot by Off-Duty Cop"* or *"The Food & Drug Administration announced today that saliva causes stomach cancer...however only when consumed in small quantities over a long period of time."*)

Lets start with...the People. Particularly the People of MN, who had 90+ degrees in the Twin Cities the last 2 days while also "enjoying" enough snow at Lutsen two weeks ago to close the golf course. Really.

According to Rachel Stassen-Berger at the *St. Paul Pioneer Press*, Rasmussen has polled the good snowed-on-in-May, un-golfed and yet sweating people of MN and found 63% think Franken will (finally) be declared the winner while only a "Cheney-ian" 15% come out of their home bunkers and think Coleman will. That 4-1 grip on reality is a good sign.

54% think Norm should concede...NOW, without waiting for the MN Supreme Court decision, while 41% disagree. As Coleman got 42% of the vote in November he has his supporters with him. As 42% (Franken) and 15%(Barkley) voted AGAINST Coleman (=57%), well, they are still agin' him.

AND, to drag another interested (if despised) politician into the equation, 67% (a damned hefty number) think Governor Pawlenty should sign a certificate of election for Franken if the MN Supreme Court rules in his favor. Only a "Bush-esque" 25% say otherwise, so still better than 5:2.

Things Pawlenty

Tim Kaine, head of the Democratic National Committee, wrote an open letter to fellow Tim-ster the Gov urging him to sign off on Franken's election once the MN courts are done. Governor Tim is in his annual "Democrats are Scum of the Earth" mode and he is vetoing everything that smells vaguely Democratic (like emergency health services in the state; Gov. Tim? This winter people are going to DIE because they can't get treated by overworked ER personnel. It will be YOUR fault, yours and the MN Taxpayer's League nutzoids who should have all the street snow in their communities plowed and dumped on their front lawns...fume!) I don't think Kaine got very far, but every little bit of pressure helps.

Things Klobuchar

AND...after my Tuesday diary in this series that took a leaf from the Sunday *Star Tribune* and had a story on Senator Amy Klobuchar (D-MN), Cynthia Dizikes of the MN Post thought writing about Senator Amy Klobuchar might be a neat idea. Covers a lot of the same ground, obviously, but with an added bonus. Two Very Prominent Minnesotans think Klobuchar is doing a tremendously good job:

> Former Republican Sen. Norm Coleman agrees. "I have always appreciated the efforts of Senator Klobuchar to reach across the aisle to meet the needs of Minnesotans," Coleman told MinnPost via email Tuesday. "I also appreciate that she has respected my desire to enfranchise more than 4,400 Minnesotans who have not had their voices heard or had their votes counted in spite of the additional burdens on her and her office." *(Star Tribune)*

Yeah, the usual crap-tacular tag line in the back half, but still... Norm? You *almost* had a sincere moment there. And as George Burns pointed out in Hollywood, "The hardest thing in this business is sincerity. Once you learn to fake that, you've got it made." But keep working on it Norm.

> Democrat Al Franken also lauded Klobuchar's efforts. "No one is better prepared to do double duty than Amy Klobuchar," Franken told Minnpost via email on Tuesday. "Amy is one of the hardest workers I have ever met, and Minnesotans know that she's been working overtime for them for the last five months." *(Star Tribune)*

Nice and subtle, Al. Just a little reminder how LONG it's been.

OK, not much as you can see but here in MN we go into Mary Tyler Moore mode: "We can take a nothing day, and suddenly make it all seem worthwhile..." So your WineRev will be tossing his doff (DOFF!) hat in the air as he heads to the late shift at the wine shop. Thats the semi-latest from yust southeast of Lake Wobegon.

Shalom.

Meet the MN Supremes
May 27, 2009

Comments: 117   Recs: 192   Tips: 185

Meet the MN Supremes (Again, for the First Time)

Who ARE these people who would read over 19,000 pages of trial transcripts from the Election Contest Court (ECC), consider over 1,800 exhibits and review the testimony of over 140 witnesses? What sort of people would also read through (with footnotes; this is for all the marbles) Coleman's Appeal Brief (60+ pages, reduced from the 146 in the original Crayola), Franken's Respondent's Brief (50+ pages, with attached HoloDisc that allows a 3-D re-creation of any instant of the Recount from the close of polls on Nov. 4 until today) and Coleman's Reply to Respondent (just under 30 pages and maybe the best work his legal team has done; it rises to the level of lousy)?

Chief Justice Eric Magnuson and Associate Justice G. Barry Anderson were on the State Canvassing Board ruling on challenged ballots and Recount issues. They have quite properly recused themselves from any further involvement in the process, since it would amount to a judge reviewing and appealing their own work.

That leaves 5 other justices. In MN when a vacancy occurs on the Supreme Court the governor appoints a new justice. (I don't know if this is subject to MN Senate confirmation like at the federal level. I suspect someone here will let us know.) The appointment is subject to approval by the voters at the next general election (even-numbered years, unless the appointment occurs less than 1 year before such an election; then the appointee gets an extra 2 years before facing the electorate) and approval is for 6-year terms. An appointee CAN be defeated in the election and replaced by the winner of that vote (apparently rather common before 1950; rather rare since then.)

Alan Page, 63; BA Notre Dame '67, JD U Minn. School of Law '78. (Got his JD while employed full time by the NFL.) Asst. Attorney General, State of MN 1985-1993. Trading off his name recognition and work in the AG office, defeated a governor appointee and was elected directly in 1992. When Sen. Paul Wellstone was killed in 2002 Page was briefly mentioned as his possible replacement (the MN Democrats eventually settled on Walter Mondale).

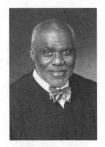

Alan Page

Paul Anderson, 62, BA Macalester Collge '65, JD U. Minn. Law '68. Private practice 71-92. Chief Judge MN Court of Appeals, '92-94. Appointed in '94 (Gov. Carlson R- Normal).

Anderson was reelected in 2008 (when some Senate race was going on) with 70%+ of the vote. His opposition was Tim Tingelstad who was trying to get on the MN Supreme Court as a "mission from God" (and NOT in the Blues Brothers' sense either. Think Michele Bachmann sense... or not. That hurts. I mean, Michele Bachmann and "sense" don't belong in the same sentence.)

Back in December, Anderson was the Justice who climbed on Roger Magnuson of Team Coleman in the opening 30 seconds of the opening argument.

Paul Anderson

Magnuson came in with a caution to the Court to avoid becoming another Florida. Anderson snapped off, "This is NOT Florida"... just to establish some turf and pin back Magnuson's ears. Magnuson has not been seen or heard from since that hearing.

Helen Meyer, about 55, BSW, U. Minn, '76, JD William Mitchell College of Law, '82. Founded her own law firm twice (in Al Franken's old suburb of St. Louis Park). A fair bit of arbitration and mediation work. Served on professional boards for trial lawyers and obviously knows her way around a courtroom. Served for 3 years as Gov. Ventura's chief Judicial appointment advisor. Appointed by Ventura (Independently Independent) in '02, going directly from head of a law firm to Justice (with no prior time on the bench.)

She was born in St. Joseph, Minnesota and raised on a Stearns County dairy farm, one of seven children.

Helen Meyer

Lorie Skjerven Gildea, about 49, BA '83, U. Minn.-Morris; JD, magna cum laude, Order of Coif, Georgetown Univ. '86. Private practice 86-93; Univ. Minn.General Counsel '93-'04; Hennepin County Judge '04-'06. Appointed '06 (Pawlenty R-Miser).

Born in Plummer, MN (pop. 400; 40% Norwegian)... (My sense is the Order of Coif is NOT a special award for hairstyling, hung on the wall at Inga Ingabritsen's Salon and Nail Emporium...) while at U of M led lawsuit v. basketball coach Clem Haskins and recovered $800K for University... white-collar crime cases in her judgeship... 2008 was her first time facing election; was confirmed by voters with about 55% of the vote.

Lorie Skjerven Gildea

Christopher Dietzen, 61, BA '69 and Law degree '73 both Gonzaga Univ. Private practice '73-'04 in Washington state & Minnesota; Judge, MN Court of Appeals '04-'08. Appointed to Supreme Court in late '07 (Pawlenty, R- Piker).

Since Dietzen was appointed late in 2007 he will face voters for the first time in 2010... Was Pawlenty's campaign lawyer in 2002: campaign was accused of running an improper TV ad; so found, fined $100,000, and spending-limit reduced by $500,000... served as Pawlenty's Judicial appointment advisor (parallel to Meyer's work for Ventura) prior to appointment...

Christopher Dietzen

Politics and Money

As the whole Coleman v. Franken case moved out of the ECC and toward the MNSC in late April, a number of stories surfaced regarding the politics of the Justices. In particular Justice Dietzen was pinned down as having made (gasp!) contributions to (gasp!) Republicans, in particular Norm Coleman, and so shouldn't he recuse himself like Magnuson and Anderson?

One of the newest justices, Christopher Dietzen, is facing calls from left-leaning bloggers to step back, too. That's because he was a Coleman donor prior to joining the bench, including $500 in contributions to his Senate fund. *($250 in 2001 and another $250 in 2004.)*

> Dietzen is not alone in making donations in his pre-judge days:
>
> Lorie Gildea gave to Coleman's 1998 gubernatorial campaign and Helen Meyer cut checks to Democrats years ago, including Wellstone *(and perennial Democratic candidate Mike Ciresi).*
>
> None of the justices would comment on their donations or their status in the case, a court spokesman said. *(Minnesota Public Radio)*

In the next few days it's likely the whole matter will resurface. While I understand the worry I can't share it. By all accounts the amounts are small. Tons of people on Daily Kos making a LOT less money have made contributions larger than $250 to a candidate. Also the contributions are old in the scheme of things. And by all accounts there is no evidence of any other political support (door-knocking, being the campaign lawyer for Barkley, Miami rioting for Brooks Bros. Inc.) For me it would be a lot more worrisome if, say, Alan Page had contributed the legal maximum to Al Franken and given a dozen rally speeches for him and called Norm Coleman "the pyorrhea on the teeth of the Minnesota body politic."

Then too if there was some skullduggery afoot (CAN *skull*duggery involve a foot? Seems anatomically challenging.) we might have expected to see it before now. There have been several instances of Coleman (and one of Franken) going to the MNSC during the Recount for relief, for a ruling, for an order or injunction. With one exception the Supremes have turned Norm down 5-0 every time. If bias was going to express itself you'd think at least and occasional 4-1 or 3-2 would have shown up by now.

(Franken's motion for a Certificate of Election apart from the governor's office issuing one was also turned down 5-0. The one non-unanimous call was the Dec. 18th, 3-2 decision [Meyer, Gildea, Dietzen v. Page, Anderson] that set up the "both sides agree on disputed, Pile 5 absentee ballots in order for them to count" cantankery. It made for a tedious mess but it is very hard to make a case the process favored Coleman... or Franken.)

But good on Senate Guru and Eric Kleefeld from TPM for raising up the matter. This is just the kind of vigilance the press needs to do and every citizen should exercise toward their public servants.

I am disturbed (but you knew that already) that this issue comes up at all. To me it is a symptom of politicization creeping into places it should not be. While so many here at Kos are of the politically vital, I'm grateful for pet diaries, recipes, and tributes to, say, John Denver. There is a LOT in life apart from politics and to me it is unsettling that the justice system might be coming under the political storm. (After the outrage of *Bush v. Gore*, the judicial tragedy inflicted upon Gov. Siegelman, the US Attorney manipulation, and the insult to justice that IS Alberto Gonzales, I completely understand where this is coming from.)

But I don't think the answer is rooting for judges to rule "our way." (And not for a moment am I saying Senate Guru or Kleefeld are calling for this, to be clear.) Much more disturbing is the assault on the justice system in general, verbally ("that's just what some judge says"), contemptuously ("if Obama appoints her then she has to be a liberal, activist, empathetic..."), and even physically.

Folks, to me this attitude puts us on the road to the Weimar Republic stuff and we do NOT want to go there. The Southern Poverty Law Center reports a LOT of the Reichwingers buying guns. To me the answer is NOT to likewise arm the Left (given the availability of guns in this country I think this may have already happened.)

In the late 1920s German gangs from the left & right engaged in huge street battles, mostly with fist and clubs, but with gunfire too. Prisoners were taken by both sides (and then exchanged after negotiations). The police made tons of arrests but then both sides packed the courtrooms to intimidate the judicial system into letting many/most of them go or with slap on the wrist penalties. Both sides had an interest in toppling the rule of law so they could be lawless against the other side.

We are NOT there and we should NOT go there.

Far better for democracy we should back the courts and police (you know, drive the Faux Noise gang crazy by using George Wallace's old slogan, "Law and Order"). Not so much cheering when a ruling upholds "the good side" but when justice is served. I'd wholeheartedly support judges who say not "Baliff, clear the courtroom!" but "Baliff, have the deputies arrest everyone in the courtroom visitor's gallery." Then contempt of court up to 21 days: choice of 21 days solitary or 21 days in a group cell with your most-feared ethnic group.

A few rounds like that and even the reptile brains would get the message.

OK. We all wait for the 1st to arrive. If anything breaks (like Norm's nerve: [sobbing] *"I concede, I concede! Mitch McConnell kissed me on the mouth and made me do all these horrible things, He threatened to send me to John Cornyn's ranch with Larry Craig, some jumper cables, a dentist's drill and a, a goat..."*) I'll let you know, but for now that's the latest from yust southeast of Lake Wobegon.

Shalom.

June 2009

Oral Arguments 9:00 a.m. CDT
June 1, 2009

Comments: 151   Recs: 290   Tips: 272

Franken wins by +312 votes.

The MN Supreme Court has also had a chance to examine 19,000 pages of trial record, over 1,800 exhibits, and testimony of over 140 witnesses. TODAY enough with paper...let's talk.

Orals

(Minnesotans feel like they've been at the dentist for 7 months... without novocaine)

This morning is Der Tag. 9:00 a.m. CDT Team Coleman and Team Franken face off with oral arguments for 1 hour in front of the MN Supreme Court (MNSC).

The Star-Tribune ran a front-page, above-the-inserted-fold story in the Sunday edition on today's events. Nice publicity. They offered up a backgrounder on each of the 5 members of the MNSC and the issues at stake. BUT YOU already knew all this because the Internet/Cheetos-dusted/pajama-wearing/lib'rul bloggers who aren't real writers had the story up... 5 days ago!

(Hey, reporter Pat Doyle? Skimming the internet for story ideas? Nyuk, nyuk!)

Still, Pat did have up a few nuggets and one FLAT-out wrongness. The error is he reports Franken has named (true) and hired (false) staff for his soon-to-be Senate office. Uh, Pat? Al has indeed NAMED a couple of folks to begin assembling a staff but he has NO MONEY to pay them. By the Noah of Webster, Pat, "hired" means to "PAY for labor" so please, spare us the Reichving talking point of Franken's "presumption."

Setting and Format

If you are watching today, the setting will look familiar: Room 300 of the MN Judiciary Building. The room is actually the home of the MN Supreme Court but they generously gave up their space for the Election Contest Court trial. *(Cool fact of Room 300: Over the door are carved the words "Where Law ends, tyranny begins"--- a sober thought looking back over the last 8 years to a certain 5-4 decision regarding Florida ballots...).*

The format is Coleman will open for up to 25 minutes. **Joe Friedberg** will present.

Then Franken's side will have 25 minutes to respond. **Marc Elias** will do the honors for Al.

Then (as the appellant carrying the burden of proof) Coleman gets up to a 10-minute rebuttal.

No particular factual evidence will be presented (although it may be mentioned in passing; factual issues are the provenance of the ECC. Appeals are on law.) The Justices will sit in their semicircle, the attorney will step up to the podium and dare to say a few words, and then the Justices pick up their gavels and begin playing judicial "Whack-a-Mole." (In regular Whack-a-Mole you have one mallet and the moles keep popping up from everywhere singing "I'm Alright" and giving you the Bill Murray finger. In Judicial Whack-A-Mole there are 5 mallet/gavels and one lawyer/mole. Any of the justices can (and often does) break in and say, "Well, counselor, what about...?" or "Does the plaintiff really expect this court to...?")

I really think Joe Friedberg for Team Coleman will be at a disadvantage here. His sonorous (or is that "snore-ous"? So hard to stay awake with Joe to tell) delivery and deliberate style, his lifetime of trying to get to a threshold of "reasonable doubt", and his admittedly folksy charm, will not serve him well in a high-profile case heavy on documents, election-law minutiae, and a civil-law standard of "preponderance of evidence."

OTOH Team Franken's Marc Elias was BORN for this kind of setting, will relish the intellectual repartee, can swing from detail to big picture (and probably from Latin to Sanskrit via the original Old Norse of the original draft of Minnesota's election laws) with delight, and give the justices solid grounds to side with his argument by citing reasons from the Magna Carta through the US Constitution right down to the serinakaker or syltkaker recipe for recount workers in Wanamingo.

Things to Watch For

Friedberg will likely use the phrase often: "The Election Contest Court erred when they..." He's not calling the ECC incompetent or dumb. This is sort of lawyer's boilerplate on appeal. To take your case to a higher court you HAVE to frame it in terms of "The prior court made the following errors or mistakes when they did/did not do..." No disrespect or slamming here, just par for the course.

As Doyle wrote in his front pager:

> Court experts will watch to see whether the justices direct more skeptical questions to either Coleman's or Franken's team. But such questioning could merely reflect a devil's advocate approach, in which judges interrogate the very side they are leaning toward. *(Star Tribune)*

Sort of a "I'm leaning your way; talk me out of it or show me how you'd handle this/that objection." So cheer if you like if, say, Justice Dietzen nails Friedberg on something Joe can't answer, but keep your salt shaker handy. It may mean less than it appears.

While Coleman mentioned both the Minneapolis 133 and the "duplicate/double-counted ballots" in his brief, I'll be rather surprised if either get mentioned. The Mpls 133 (where 133 voters in question showed up to voted, signed in to vote, and according to the voting-machine tapes voted, and then whose ballots were misplaced/lost by city election officials; the 133 broke for Franken net by +46) is SO dead that in 500 years archaeologists excavating under 20 meters of concrete will find the bones of Jimmy Hoffa before they find any evidence of these votes being anything other than already counted and settled.

The Coleman Team did not offer facts, testimony or evidence of the alleged/supposed/possible/theoretical/made-up duplicate ballots that might possibly/maybe/perhaps/coulda/sorta/mighta been counted along with their original ballots in the Recount. Well, there was election Judge Pamela Howell, the "strike her testimony"/ so stricken/ "I'm sorry it will never happen again or my name isn't Tony Trimble" reinstate Ms. Howell's testimony/tamper with the witness/"I renew my motion to strike this witness' testimony AND HER CLAIM"/ ordered stricken/"Fine me, sanction me if you must but please reenter this woman's testimony"/ So sanctioned, so $7500 fined Mr. Trimble/so reinstated with limits," THAT election judge and THAT claim. Well, that's about as likely to gain traction with the MN Supreme Court as an Icelander marrying a Finn (known in MN as "kinky"; rare, rare.)

Equal Protection.

Did the counties apply different standards to the counting of absentee ballots? Enough to make a difference? Coleman/Friedberg will argue yes. Elias for Franken will argue that the differences were NOT discriminatory and they did NOT invalidate the election. (Elias has already pointed out VA requires a driver's license or state equivalent to vote; MN does not...(can substitute a recent utility bill, or have a neighbor vouch for you)... yet no one has ever argued either state's votes are invalid.)

The ECC decision from April 23 spent 25 of its 58 pages addressing equal protection and shooting down every Coleman angle and argument. Watch Elias cite this often during his turn at bat.

Outcomes

Likely: MN Supreme Court will thank both sides for their arguments, take everything "under advisement" and adjourn. Then we wait, although maybe only a few days. (Court has been swift---2-3 days-- on earlier motions; but then this is an appeal.)

I think it was first Terrible Tom or Allen03 who raised a possibility the Court could issue a ruling quite quickly (days) and issue its **opinion** rather later (months). Is that possible? How common is it? If so, does any lawyer here think this possible? Likely?

In My dreams #1: Court thanks both sides for their arguments and announces, "Court is in recess"... rather than adjourned... until 1:00pm." They all tramp back in and find in Franken's favor 5-0, agree with Franken's brief and order Governor Pawlenty to issue a Certificate of Election or face a contempt-of-court charge.

In my dreams #2: Grace Kelly at MN Progressive Project asks "Who would enforce dream #1?"

> "...would Ramsey County Attorney Susan Gaertner enforce the contempt charge, with Sheriff Fletcher as the possible arresting officer?...Interestingly, Gaertner is running for governor herself and might therefore allow a fully press covered arrest of Governor Pawlenty." *(MN Progressive Project)*

But two can play at this game!

> "...if the directive is seen as originating with the MN Supreme Court, then would the Minnesota Attorney General Lori Swanson enforce the contempt charge, with local police forces from either Eagan or St Paul as the possible arresting officers?... Although currently undeclared, Minnesota Attorney General Lori Swanson has been frequently mentioned as a possible candidate for governor." *(MN Progressive Project)*

Grace actually called up and asked each office.

Funny Pages

Grace wasn't finished this weekend. She got wind of the Tea Party Patriots rallying for Norm Coleman. You MN teabaggers can sign up for a Capitol lawn rally to "get it right, Minnesota" by reelecting Norm Coleman Senator. Turn up the heat on the Supreme Court! Sign up if you're coming TODAY from 3pm to 6pm in St. Paul on the Capitol lawn.

And 3...3 people have said they are coming, with 1 more "maybe." 3! WOW!

OK, I've got the early shift at the shop and limited access to the Internet there, so you'll have to let me know how it goes. Fill in your comments and help write the latest from yust southeast of Lake Wobegon.

Shalom.

Coleman's Smoking Ruin
June 2, 2009

Comments: 259   Recs: 507   Tips: 548

The MN Supreme Court heard oral arguments yesterday morning and has now had the case with all its glory almost 24 hours. I think the earliest we might get a ruling is 48 hours but I doubt it (would LOVE to be surprised!).

Opening Round: Coleman's Appeal

The room was familiar and yet not, with lawyers' tables facing each other instead of the Bench, tons of evidence 3-ring binders and easels missing. 5 judges rather than 3. No witnesses.

A lot less clutter in the room... except for all the equipment everyone brought for this final round: Whack-a-Mole mallet/gavels, lightsabers, light quarterstaffs (those 2-ended jobbers the Supreme Court justices get issued when they are seated to the high bench), football and hockey equipment, biathalon rifles, and several "violin cases" with cute Valentine's hearts stuck on them here and there.

Joe Friedberg for Coleman (who was there for the oral argument) stepped up to the podium battling a bout of laryngitis from the past few days. Having gaveled Court to order it took Justice Alan Page about 2 minutes to unleash on Friedberg. Joe was coming with the same tired argument about absentee ballots being "substantially compliant" with the law rather than "strictly compliant." Page swung his Light Quarterstaff (LQS) three minutes in: "What exactly do you mean by substantiality?" While Joe parried decently he kept getting forced back by the next question and the next. About 9 minutes in his lightsaber sagged enough that he said flat out: "There was no election fraud. There was no voter fraud."

Now take THAT to the bank, progressives! THE man, the Coleman legal champion charged with making the best possible case for the greatest set of teeth the US Senate has seen since a State of the Union Address from Jimmy Carter, as an officer of the Court THIS man has said, "There was no fraud" in the MN senate election. And you know what that means: All of the Hannitys, OReillys, Slowbaughs, Glen Beck-Back Mountains, Pawlentys, and various mouth-breathing, amphibian-brained, walleye suckers in MN who have been going around slobbering "fraud... abuse... ballots in trunks... fake ballots... manufactured ballots from ACORN on George Soros-watermarked stationery" all of them and all the stuff they keep say can just. Shut. UP.

Because Joe Freidberg says so, that's who and that's why. This guy, who could REALLY use a little voter fraud, who could use a ballot or 2 from a car trunk, who could leverage a phony ballot into something big, says he can't... because these things DO NOT EXIST. So tell them just. shut. up.

Back to our regularly scheduled whatever this is:

Justice Christopher Dietzen has been under the gun from some progressives since he made contributions to Republicans including Coleman. (Norm should give a refund.) Dietzen came out from under that gun, cracked open one of those "violin cases" marked Valentine's Day, Chicago and opened up like Jean-Luc Picard in "First Contact" ("With the safety protocols off, even a holographic bullet can kill").

> "I've never seen an offer of proof like this," said Dietzen, complaining that the offers didn't actually identify specific potential witnesses or what their presumed evidence would have been been -- only continued arguments that "a substantial number" of ballots exist. Dietzen added that "the rules of evidence, the rules of civil procedure apply. Now why is this offer of proof not inadequate, in that we don't have admissible evidence that can show whether you've met your burden?"
> *(Eric Kleefeld at TPM)*

The guy thought to be maybe most on your side is asking about how inadequate your offer of proof is? Sounds like Norm's case can't be cured of its inadequacy by 50 kilos of Viagra.

Norway was heard from in the form of Justice Gildea. Friedberg was arguing the ECC prevented Coleman from entering evidence. Justice Lori eschewed (!) her LightQuarterStaff and surprised everyone by snapping on the chin strap of her helmet, picking up her stick, and popping over the bench/boards. She met Friedberg on a long glide at center ice with a hip check that will be replayed on "Hockey Night in Canada" for years.

> Once, Justice Lori Skjerven Gildea sharply rebuked Friedberg when he tried to explain that the election contest panel had prevented Coleman from presenting certain evidence during the trial
>
> Gildea: "Where did the contest court so rule?"
>
> Friedberg: "It ruled right from the beginning, your honor, and we answered it by submitting in an offer of proof ..."
>
> Gildea: "Pardon me for interrupting, but when I say where, I mean where. Page citation in the record." *(Jay Weiner at MinnPost)*

The cameras didn't catch it but after that as Gildea circled back to the Bench past the Franken table, Marc Elias was seen holding down David Lillehaug's hands so "Lills" wouldn't stand up and give "Skjerves" a fist bump congrats for the hit.

While the kids were good, leave it to one of the vets to show how to scold a lawyer in style.

> Friedberg said they've gathered plenty of evidence from the two-dozen counties they did call -- that counties used a varying standard, and that substantial compliance should be enough to let these ballots in, as opposed to a strict compliance

standard used by the trial court. "We've made our case," he said forcefully. "You can't make it any better than that!"

Justice Anderson shot back. "I still have problems with your saying we're a substantial compliance state," Anderson said. "And as loud as you speak on this issue there's language I don't think you can overcome." *(Eric Kleefeld at TPM)*

"And as loud as you speak..."!? WHOA! Anderson trotted back to the huddle and asked Page, "Is that how you play defensive line?" Page nodded. "Now you're gettin' it."

Live reaction to the proceedings yesterday from the Kossacks:

DK   Friedberg is really getting grilled! They haven't let him finish one thought without interruption! *(msirt)*

DK   This is amazing! Friedberg's shouting now. Damn this is entertaining. *(middlewest)*

DK   Oh, now Friedberg is telling the judge that he's WRONG. That will sit well with them... *(Fiddlegirl)*

DK   You nailed the Lutheran inner life! But since I grew up with the "Wisconsin" brand, I was spared the lutefisk. *(Fiddlegirl)*

Round II: Team Franken

Marc Elias was almost caught off guard by his first question. Justice Page suddenly channeled Yoda for a meta-query of the Force: "Decide the US Senate this will, so why here are we?"

(To be fair, it was heard by some in the courtroom as:

Page: "If the U.S. Senate will ultimately decide this, why are we all here?" *(quoted at The UpTake)*

Elias agreed but that since Coleman had appealed, Franken was going to do his best to respect the judiciary process. Indeed Elias had a much friendlier reception from the Court. A few minutes in Justice Gildea asked:

Talk about a friendly question. "Forget the legal niceties. He didn't prove his case, did he?" *(Shlif at The UpTake)*

Now how could Marc disagree with the premise of THAT question?

Gildea then asked whether she was properly summarizing Elias' argument: "It was his [Coleman's] burden to prove it. He didn't prove it, he can't stand up here now and speculate." Elias agreed that this is indeed his argument. *(The UpTake)*

Once again Elias was MOST agreeable.

Justice Anderson showed he could do meta too by walking around the Universe, engage in chaos theory, and even bring in Intelligent Design, while Elias had to rein in the good Justice by reminding him Coleman has to show the votes AS EVIDENCE and he ain't got the votes.

Anderson: "We're talking here about the universe of Minnesota absentee ballots ... You say there is some intelligent design mandated by statute. There is not chaos. It is order ... There may be some and you can see some aberrant star systems or galaxies ... What Mr. Coleman is focusing on is, 'Look at this aberrant galaxy ... This is proof that the universe is chaos.' The fact is they've shown me that. They've shown there's some chaos in this universe ... Tell me why [it matters that we] can't see the whole universe, but they've shown us enough?"

> Because Elias said, Coleman can't speculate, can't suggest there has been an "amalgam" of problems. The errors statewide have been "garden variety," not widespread or fraudulent. Coleman, he said, has to show them the votes, and there aren't enough out there to overcome Franken's lead, even though Coleman is seeking as many as 4,400 votes to be counted. *(Eric Black at MinnPost)*

More live reaction yesterday from Kossack the new:

DK

> Franken's Lawyer is great. He has an answer for everything. Very prepared, and very brief and to the point. He's really driving the train on this. *(the new)*

Round III: Coleman's Rebuttal

Having been refreshed by Elias' reloading of their photon torpedoes, the Court swung back with all phasers firing on Friedberg's mercifully final 10 minutes.

> Justice Meyer was bothered by a statement in Coleman's brief that said the "overwhelming majority" of Minnesota's counties used "substantial compliance" (rather than "strict compliance") standards in assessing absentee ballot envelopes. Where's the evidence? she asked. *(MinnPost)*

How many did you contact (let alone actually put on the stand to testify)? she asked. 26 out of 87. Yeah right. Odd version of "majority."

The whole rebuttal was like that, glimpsed in this sequence from the UpTake's comment string:

> Judge [Anderson to Friedberg] quoting Franken's lawyer as part of his question. Wow again! (Shlif at The UpTake)

> WOW: Friedberg just said, "We don't have to prove it, just likely prove it MIGHT happen"?????? Really??? *(lostboyjim at The UpTake)*

> "I suspect the other side would say..." "Their argument would be.." I love this. The judges are clearly supporting Franken here. *(Shlif at The UpTake)*

> BS! They DO have to show some proof, not show that it's possible there might be proof! *(LEK at The UpTake)*

Summary: Coleman is toast.

So writes Eric Black at MinnPost:.

So writes Jay Weiner at MinnPost.

So writes Markos at DailyKos.

So writes Ned Foley of Ohio State Law School.

So writes Rick Hasen of LA Loyola Law school.

Only the maybe-30 people who showed up for the Tea Party rally on the Capitol Lawn didn't think so. *(They were busy surrounding Grace Kelly from MN Progressive Project.)*

How soon? Not soon enough of course but I think the Court will rule by Kossack Clem Yeobright's prediction of June 33rd. One expert said on the UpTake radio show last night the Court has shown some trend to hand down a decision on Tuesdays, having informed the principals in a case the prior Friday... but we'll see.

OK, now you have Tuesday reading material. I've got the VERY late shift today (start at noon, go to 10) so I'll blog with you for a while in comments. That's about the latest from yust southeast of Lake Wobegon.

Shalom.

Waiting in the Fallout Shelter
June 4, 2009

Comments: 112   Recs: 188   Tips: 192

The Legal Beagles

To round up what legal types have been saying about the Monday orals, there has been something of a contrast of "before" and "after." Going into orals (which took a month, and still sounds to me like a trip to the dentist without benefit of painkillers) there was a fair bit of talk about "equal protection." This was keying off of Coleman's Brief (and Franken's Response, as well as the Election Contest Court Decision – which spent 25 of its 58 pages dealing with "EP") and perhaps his best legal argument: When the 87 MN counties received absentee ballots from almost 300,000 voters, did they handle those votes "equally"? Accept them to be counted or reject them on a consistent basis (particularly as to the 4 reasons or tests an absentee ballot has to meet)?

Everybody agrees there was some variation and that likely some ballots were accepted in Pelican Rapids that might have been turned down in Spring Grove. What Coleman had to prove (there's that really pesky word again; not just "assert," "claim," "presume," "argue," or "fart off to the press about," but PROVE) was that

- the variations were wider than the law allows/assumes
- the variations were systematic across the state
- the variations were either biased by design ("the addresses on these absentee ballots are all from Pretentious Acres on Lake Ain'tWeRich, so dump 'em") or by outcome ("gee, its a coincidence all the naturalized voters from Somalia in this apartment house voting absentee were rejected; unfortunate, but a coincidence")
- the variations were so numerous they could swing the outcome of the election

which would mean the election failed to provide equal protection (EP) to all voters and to candidate Coleman, was unfair and unconstitutional. It was a tall order.

Team Coleman didn't come close.

Instead of approaching the Constitutional level virtually all the oral questions were about something much more basic: e-v-i-d-e-n-c-e ("find out what it means to me!" Sing it Aretha!)

What it seemed to mean to the Court is that Coleman didn't have much, or enough, or any with strength. The Court can actually IGNORE the Constitutional stuff and base their ruling on (as Team Franken argued) meeting the burden of proof.

As Eric Black put it.

> The Justices didn't show that much interest in what is presumed to be Coleman's biggest and best argument: That variations in the treatment of absentee ballots across county lines constitute a violation of the U.S. Constitution's Equal Protection Clause. Their interest seemed closer to the ground and to state law and specifically on whether the Three Judge election contest court correctly concluded that Minnesota is a state that requires strict compliance with all the requirements of the law governing absentee voting. And they asked no question that implied any of them thought the trial court got it wrong. *(MinnPost)*

Professor Ned Foley of "The" Ohio State University Law School was in agreement:

> "This momentous case may end up with a rather anticlimactic ruling that Coleman loses not because his legal arguments lacked merit, or even that the ballots he wanted counted weren't voted for him in a large enough ratio, but instead because he simply failed to take the evidentiary steps necessary to show which specific ballots were wrongly treated by local election officials." *(Election Law @ Moritz)*

Kossack ABowers 13 weighed in with a devastating point at the end of a massive comment string from Tuesday:

DK

[Team]Franken noted that the Contest Court examined all absentee ballots entered by Coleman and found that only about 650+ met the requirement that the voter be registered! They then allowed about 370 to be opened and counted as these ballots also met other requirements.

This left less than 300 ballots from registered voters that were NOT counted. So even if ALL other requirements - voter signature, witness, etc were ignored, there still were not enough ballots to overcome Franken's lead of 312 ballots. And that is assuming every single one of the 300 unopened ballots was a vote for Coleman - which clearly was NOT so. In fact a majority were probably for Franken.

Even Coleman never argued that a ballot from a person not registered to vote should count. So even if the "substantial compliance" was used, he still cannot get enough votes to overturn the result. *(ABowers13)*

Norm? You want 4,400 ballots considered as e-v-i-d-e-n-c-e, you gotta bring 4,400 ballots into court. You bring in 650, all you get is 650. That is all the ECC considered in their findings of fact. And that looks like all the MN Supreme Court is going to consider as well.

Things Pawlenty

As everyone political has likely heard by now our esteemed governor Tim Pawlenty announced he will NOT run for a 3rd term in 2010. Since it is up to the governor's office to issue a Certificate of Election in race for US Senator he is on the spot.

So far he has been saying (and quite correctly and fairly in my view) that he will not issue such a certificate until the election process has played out. Team Franken even went to the MN Supreme Court to try to pry a Certificate from him apart from the whole "ECC & Appeal" procedure and were turned down (5-0) in early February.

But there is talk about Tim running for higher office. (He was apparently on John McCain's final and very short list for Veep before Senator Magoo opted for Caribou Barbie – which led to the St. Paul spectacle (as one Kossack brilliantly summarized it) at the Rethug National Convention when she gave her acceptance speech it was "Gidget addresses the Reichstag." Pawlenty was seen shaking his head lamenting, "That could have been me" as cheers of "ein folk, ein reich, ein fuhrer-ette" filled the hall.) He has often been careful to say he will wait for "the court process" to play out without telling whether he means JUST the State courts or ALSO the federal courts.

He's still at it.

Appearing on Faux Noise from high atop the Joseph Goebbels Studio, T-Paw said: "You know, Neil, if the Minnesota Supreme Court says, 'You sign the certificate' — and there's not an appeal or some other contrary direction from a federal court — you know, that's my duty."

OTOH he then swings over on a jungle vine to Andrea Mitchell's MSNBC ("MainStreamNothingBut-Crap") show and says:

Pawlenty: Yea, we're anxious to get it resolved but I can't sign the certificate until the State court process is complete, we don't know who the winner is, but as soon as that process is complete and they give direction as to signing the certificate, I'm going to sign it, there's not going to be any undue delay or tactics like that so we'll follow the direction of the court. *(quoted at MN Progressive Project)*

(I don't know which interview came first so the sequence here may be reversed, but he said both of these.)

Other Quarters heard from (or Not)

Rachel Stassen Berger of the St. Paul Pioneer Press had the nerve to look up what a certain Republican "national leader" (not Limbaugh) had to say, then and now.

"Big Bad John" Cornyn of Texas a couple months back weighed in:

"This is about making sure every legal vote is counted, this isn't just about Norm Coleman. This is about protecting the rights of voters," said National Republican Senatorial Committee Chairman John Cornyn (R-Texas). "It's to my mind a very

> noble endeavor and one in which, frankly, I admire his perseverance, I support getting it right, and if that includes a federal lawsuit, then so be it..."
>
> Around the same time he told Politico that the fight could take "years" and threatened World War III if Democrats tried to seat Franken before federal appeals were through. *(Politico)*

Now? Not so much.

> The head of the Senate GOP's campaign committee said Wednesday that he would not press Republican Norm Coleman to mount an appeal in the federal court system if the Minnesota Supreme Court rules that Democrat Al Franken won their Senate race.
>
> "I think it's entirely up to him," said John Cornyn, chairman of the National Republican Senatorial Committee. *(Pioneer Press)*

And out on the delusional wing of the Republican party these days... MN Democrats Exposed (the name says it all) is a North Country Whack site for all things aquavit-induced. THE oral argument that will settle THE MN senate race was Monday. All sorts of media outlets covered it, wrote about it, put up pix and video, commented on it on DailyKos. But as of this morning, 3 full days after, MN Democrats Exposed has said...

*

* * *(sound of crickets leaving town)*

...utter silence. Way to keep all 7 of your followers informed, guys.

And for more delusion (and which way is delusion-er is hard to say on this one) with Pawlenty announcing he is not running, all sorts of people in all three parties are climbing into the governor's race or being mentioned. One prominent, well-known Republican being mentioned who has high statewide recognition is... (I kid you not)... Norm Coleman.

Yup. Although when confronted with this delusion a Coleman media hack answered with his own delusion:

> Republican Norm Coleman's spokesman answered the 'would the ex-Senator run for governor in 2010' question with the line:
>
> "I'm still not willing to entertain the possibility of us losing," the Senate race, Tom Erickson said.
>
> Not a bad reminder to those pushing Coleman's name for 2010 – he's still in the midst of a 2008 race. *(Rachel Stassen-Berger at Pioneer Press, emphasis mine - WR)*

."..still not willing to entertain..." Hooo boy! Lets all just walk quietly away. Oh, and Tom? Those guys coming all dressed in white? Carrying the butterfly net? Yeah, Tom. Take it easy. They are here to HELP you. Really. (WineRev tiptoes out of diary softly.)

OK I hope that will hold you until the MN Supremes lay down the law in a way so heavy the wind blows Al Franken right into the US Senate. That's some of the latest from yust southeast of Lake Wobegon.

Shalom.

"Dear MN Supreme Court"
June 17, 2009

Comments: 166   Recs: 362   Tips: 395

Franken wins by +312 votes.

The MN Supreme Court heard oral arguments on Monday, June 1 so today is about 382 hours into "The Wait." We are also more than 225 freakin' days since the ELECTION (not that anyone's counting).

From: The Minnesota Affairs Desk, WineRev

Date: June, Freaking 17th, 2009

To: The Minnesota Supreme Court

Dear Alan, Paul, Helen, Laurie and Christopher (and hello to Eric and G. Barry),

Thank you for all your hard work this last judicial term. I mean look, just here in May you heard several criminal appeals (eg. State of MN vs. Jackson, and vs. Cauz-Ramirez, and vs. Lessley). Also you heard Fleeger vs. Wyeth Pharmaceuticals and a hairy bank case against a mortgage company and the United States Government itself. You had to hear the MN Voters Alliance suit against the city of Minneapolis and Secretary of State Mark Ritchie over Instant Runoff Voting. Your oral argument calendar stretched to June 10 (for a case involving a zoning variance and the MN Dept. of Natural Resources.)

And after hearing all these you have to write and issue opinions about them and your website says you have a regular method for doing this:

> Minnesota Supreme Court opinions are issued every Thursday and are available to the public at 10:00 a.m. CST/CDT.
>
> On Monday of each week, the Supreme Court mails a notice that informs counsel, pro se parties, and court personnel associated with a case that an opinion will be released the following Thursday. Opinions are available online or by visiting the Clerk of Appellate Courts, 305 Minnesota Judicial Center, 25 Rev. Dr. Martin Luther King Jr. Blvd., St. Paul, after the Thursday release time. Copies of the opinions are mailed to involved parties on Thursdays.
>
> In certain time-sensitive cases, the Supreme Court may issue opinions or orders on a business day other than Thursday. In these instances, involved parties will be contacted just prior to the special release. *(MN Courts website)*

And you know, A-P-H-L&C, I really get (more than you know) it's been a bear of a year with this Senate thing hanging over every one.

But can I ask all of you for something? Could tomorrow be a decision/opinion day for Coleman v. Franken? I want to speak in favor of public mental health because people are really starting to lose it. There's nothing to write about or talk about. Its like we are all living in Mr. Bean's Holiday, the Carson Clay Production/Film/Script/Leading Actor/Director. Everything about this case is leaving us feeling "like a cop with a broken heart": "Nothing, nothing, nothing, nothing..."

Look, MN Independent had to report Norm & Al were on the same plane the other day from MN to DC (Al in coach – with the People, man! Dig it!; Norm in first class – with the economic royalists/up-grade fanatics/involuntarily bumped from earlier flights). I mean, MN-Indy reported this as NEWS for cryin' out loud.

Chris Stoller over there, once a coming reporter, has been reduced to comparing the Coleman-Franken log jam to Ahmadinejad and Moussavi in Iran! Can you see the pain of this good reporter cracking under the strain?

Joe Kimball over at MinnPost is having to reprint Politco columns that declare Coleman doesn't stand a chance in the court case before you. I mean, he doesn't, but Joe is reduced to stating not just the obvious ("the sun rises in the East") but the stunningly obvious ("Dick Cheney should be on trial for treason") when he has to print stuff like that.

Joe's friend at MinnPost, David Brauer of Braublog, has been forced to write articles about media covering the Coleman-Franken struggle rather than the struggle itself. Granted, it's a gentle, strong and praise-worthy piece on the upstart UpTake video that many have come to love, but still, I really think David would like to write fini to the case itself.

Eric, Joe Bodell and Grace Kelly have been putting up a brave front with stories about US Senators quietly quitting on Norm and what governor Pawlenty will do with a Certificate of Election after he unfolds it as a paper airplane, but they haven't been able to bring themselves to write anything for over a week:

Yes, yes, I know not everyone is hurting. Michael Brodkorb, the founder and webmeister of Minnesota Democrats Exposed, is blithely careening along the right side/seig heil shoulder of MN politics. He STILL hasn't put up anything about the Coleman-Franken oral arguments in front of you from June 1. Rachel Stassen-Berger of the Pioneer Press called him on his stunt of filing a suit to get a count of absentee ballots (whether or not these ballots are legal or not).

But he DID find time to get himself elected the #2 gaulieter of the MN Republican Party. Yeah, really! A blogger parlaying his blogginess into a real job.

So look you 5 (who are on our mind), people are really cracking under the strain. (Brodkorb was pre-cracked, so he doesn't really count.) It would mean a lot to the mental health and general karma of the entire state of Minnesota if you 5 could deliver yourselves of a decision...and maybe tomorrow?

Once again, thanks for all you do for so many.

Your BFF (ask your teen),

WineRev

PS. No pressure. Just think of ME out on this ledge... no biggie... teetering here while reporting the latest from yust southeast of Lake Wobegon.

Shalom.

Curia Eleison
June 24, 2009

The MN Supreme Court heard oral arguments in Coleman v. Franken on June 1 at 9:00 a.m. So since that ended around 10 a.m. it's been about 540 hours....and we're still waiting.

In the mid 1980s the rock group Mister Mister took music in an orthodox direction. No, not toward stringed orchestras or symphonic composition, but REALLY orthodox as in Greek Orthodox.

Of all things, for a very dance-able chorus they reached into the ancient Church east of the Adriatic for a prayer: Kyrie Eleison.

Kyrie: "Lord/Master/or simply sir, mister" and

Eleison: "To show/have mercy": as used in the liturgy (of both Eastern and Western Christianity) "have mercy upon us".

(Aorist, plural and reflexive I believe, but my Greek has gone rusty, and it's early. Subject to better conjugation...which sounds like fun...)

So WineRev joined millions of others in the mid-80s dancing to a prayer under a mirrored ball and with a fog machine.

Kyrie Eleison (Lord have mercy)
Down the road that I must travel
Kyrie Eleison
Through the darkness of the night....

Last week my open letter to the MN Supreme Court touched off a lot of hoping and yearning, but no results, since we are all here reading THIS diary. It amounted to reeling in your bobber and finding the fish have eaten all your bait off the hook. There were bobs and whisper-soft tugs, but no strike. (*High pitched whizzing:* "Get behind me, chief, and pour that dipper-full onto the reel! Hooper! Watch him now! He's taking a hell of a lot of line!" Quint to Brodie and Hooper: Jaws)

I mean, I like how Eric Black writes for Minn Post, but even he is reduced to writing columns about off-beat lawsuits from Minnesota TV stations and getting philosophical. It's good, but it doesn't fry up in the pan over the campfire, yanno?

We are stuck with stories that continue to follow the decay of Team Norm. Not only did PR guy Luke Friedrich leave a while back, so did PR guy Mark Drake about a month ago. Then the Coleman communications director (more PR) LeRoy ("I'm not Norm but he stole my last name") Coleman joined the Republican National Committee in media affairs. (You have all noticed how sizzling Republican National PR is these days.)

NOW the RNC has dipped into the Norm well again and hired away...Cullen Sheehan! Really! Norm's campaign director (whoa!) and co-plaintiff in *Coleman & Sheehan v. Franken*, the Iowa wonder (and on these boards people have wondered if he's STILL from Iowa, as in resident, as in ineligible to cast that MN absentee ballot that he cast). (That was one hell of a sentence; good thing I don't have to diagram it.)

I mean if all these people keep LEAVING the FORMER Senator's organization, why should anyone think he's suddenly going to be calling them back?

And speaking of Republican decay, I give you John Cornyn of Texas, a senator who represents decay, fully-decayed half-life (now no-life?) at the national level. Good old Cactus Breath is still blabbering about backing Norm's alleged/possible/demented "appeal to federal courts". But the spines on his attitude sound as soggy as wilted sagebrush, not the fire-breathing "World War III" guy from this spring.

Sooo...in order to put an end to this thrashing around, these legal maneuvers that amount to no more than stripping the milfoil infestation from the boat propeller, WineRev turns from letter writing to the MN Supremes to song writing. Maybe I can charm them to a decision? Or scare them, with "Kyrie" lyrics like this, re-written to the "Curia" (medieval Latin for "court"):

> *The Ballots cast in November snow*
> *Absentees came in the mail*
> *Lost, recounted, challenged ballots grow*
> *Coleman's lead begins to fail...*
> *December's gone and Ritchie makes the call*
> *Canvass Board votes five to nil*
> *Franken leads and Coleman plays the stall*
> *Contest Court for time to kill*
>
> *CHORUS:*
> *Curia Eleison, Down the road that we have travelled*
> *Curia Eleison, Through the mighty boring stuff*
> *Curia Eleison, Will you save us from our boredom?*
> *Curia Eleison, Can't you see we've had enough?*
>
> *Lillehaug, Elias, Hamilton*
> *Tony, Joe and Ginz you've heard*
> *Autumn, winter, spring and summer run*
> *This case deserves your final Word!*

Rehearsals start on the Capitol front lawn by the Judiciary building just as soon as we can get 42 semis and a Stimulus Package crew of 811 people to start setting up speakers and a platform. Sound checks ("Check one, check 2, check, check") will be 24/7 until the amps can be heard on Lake Minnetonka, 20 miles away. And then, O august members of the MN Supreme Court, we start vocal rehearsals from the "Can't Carry a Tune in a Bucket" brigade of singers (Roseanne Barr division).

Take all the time you need. This diary has yust been a public service/friend of the Curia briefing from yust southeast of Lake Wobegon.

Shalom.

July 2009

Friday on Franken Tuesday
July 1, 2009

Comments: 212   Recs: 511   Tips: 494

(Best enjoyed out in a gravelly, monotoned flat voice)

This is the city, St. Paul, Minnesota. According to the last United States Census not sold out to ACORN, over 282,000 people live and work here. St. Paul's suburbs, small towns and villages all get along peacefully – except for Lake Elmo, which is attempting a hostile takeover of Woodbury and Maplewood because they hate names that include the word "wood."

The citizens elect leaders from among themselves to represent them, whether in the state capitol building with 4 golden horses that opened in 1905, or in Washington DC. When elections go sideways, I go to work.

I carry a blog.

(Music: Dum, du, dum, dum, DUMMMMMMmmmmm)

The story you're about to read is true. The names have been inserted to provoke the ridiculous.

It was Tuesday, June 30. It was cool in St. Paul with a 20% chance of rain. We were working Judicial Watch out of Kos division. The boss is Captain Barrett. My partner's Pep Streebek. My name's WineRev. At 1:13pm the captain called us in his office.

"Boys, the Senate Operation is breaking with a Decision. Go down to Judiciary and check it out."

I nodded, took a drag on my cigarette, and crushed it out. That drag felt good heading for Judiciary.

"Oh, and Wine?"

"Yeah, Captain?"

"Watch out for an old football player named Page. Don't talk football with him."

"Why not, Captain?"

"Let's just say we want to stay on the right side of a judge."

I flashed a quick grin and we left. Streebek requisitioned the Judiciary squad's 1989 Yugo, a 4-door sedan, , the cutting edge of late 20th century Serbo-Croatian automotive technology. He gunned the 55 horses through 1300 ccs displacement and we sped at the 25 mile per hour limit 3 blocks to the address. While I read 32 typed pages of the ruling, Streebek used voice command on his iPhone (still keeping a safe driving 2 hands on the wheel) to put up what he called a "link", even though he's missing a few himself.

> Ignorant commentary at MSNBC - of course, White House correspondent asserts Franken ahead by only "a few dozen" at the point case was sent to Minnesota Supreme Court. Where do they get their information? did no one send Mike McIntee's documentary to MSNBC? I guess their prettyboy thought he didn't need to know the facts. @ 1:17; MSNBC corrects 1:46 *(worth at The UpTake)*

> The decision is "per curiam" – a designation that it is the opinion of the court, but anonymously. This designation is often used to dispose of a case, and in my mind carries a rather dismissive tone. *(Headlight at The UpTake)*

I used the passenger's side visor mirror made of shiny-side gum wrappers (a luxury upgrade for the Yugo) to check the four-in-hand knot on my navy blue solid tie. I decided it looked sharp and within regulations against my starched, white, button down 60/40 cotton & poly Arrow shirt I'd bought last week on clearance at TJ Maxx.

Outside the courtroom a woman in black robes sobbed hysterically. We recognized Justice Helen Meyer.

(Quavering, ragged voice) "Lost. 133 in Minneapolis," she managed to gasp out. "They said, "Ignore machine tapes. Ignore voter sign-in logs. Ignore the math..." she doubled over shaking.

I flashed my blog. "I'm WineRev. Ma'am, could you give us just the facts?"

She straightened up, her face blank as a Borg drone:

> We addressed a similar situation in Moon v. Harris, (1913). In the 1912 race for registrar of deeds of Beltrami County, the county canvassing board declared Harris the winner over Moon by five votes... But in the recount, the ballots from two of the 67 precincts in the county could not be found. We ruled that the official returns for the two missing precincts should be used in lieu of the missing ballots: "The official returns are evidence of the votes cast. The presumption is that they correctly state the result of an accurate count of the ballots."
>
> Coleman articulates no compelling reason why that same principle should not apply here. *(Decision, page 31)*

Streebeck & I exchanged glances. We realized Justice Meyer's hysteria was not based in sorrow or pain, but laughter. We made notes, Streebeck on his PDA, me on a good old-fashioned, flip-over pocket notebook with a yellow, No. 2 Ticonderoga American pencil. We made our way to another black-robed woman who we saw was Justice Lorie Gildea, waving around her signature 150mm cigarette in her famous black & silver 12inch holder.

The opening line of "Satin Doll" floated through my head, and, as I looked over at Streebek, certain twisted dialogue from the Cheech & Chong marijuana 8-track we'd just heard playing in the Yugo came to mind.

"Sergeant WineRev," she said, blowing a cloud in my direction, "how good of you to come."

I coughed, "Yes ma'am. Did you rule on the double counting of duplicate ballots?"

"Nothing to rule on, doll. No facts, no evidence it happened."

"Yes, ma'am. Good facts. Did you have anything to say about equal protection?"

"We did, Wine, baby, but talk to Alan, Paul and Dietzie about it," she said, pointing. We pointed too. "Wine-y? I know you're working but give me a call soon after hours, will you?" She flashed an evocative smile as Streebeck gave me an inquiring look. I nodded to Gildea but gave Streebeck a growl and muttered, "None of your business" as we pushed through various St. Paul and surrounding community citizens to the remaining Justices.

As we drew near we heard Page saying to Anderson & Dietzen, "Nickel go green dog weak. Paul, stunt left with a mean Joe Greene on the center, strong no-go dog, deke 17... Dietze, 52 monster with a twist right."

Professor Larry Jacobs of the University of Minnesota spoke to a Minneapolis *Star-Tribune* reporter:

> "Kaboom! This is kind of the exclamation point after the 7 month battle...It's an across-the-board rejection of the Coleman legal challenges." *(Star Tribune)*

For our investigation, a member of the Fourth Estate, reporter Eric Black of the Minnesota Post, provided a translation:

> But as far as throwing out the election result, or changing the count after the vote, or counting thousands more ballots that failed to meet the statutory standards, the Supremes said Coleman was nowhere near meeting his burden of proving that these disparities constituted either due process or equal protection violations. *(MinnPost)*

"What's next, Black?" I said to the intrepid columnist.

"Next is 3:00 p.m. over at the Coleman back yard. He's holding a presser and the betting among the media crowd is a possible concession."

At that moment my walkie-talkie sounded. The captain ordered us to head over to the Coleman back yard on the double. We left in a hurry.

(2 minute block of commercials: a car salesman in loud pants, a louder jacket, screaming at you to "Buy today". Next, a DoubleMint gum commercial featuring a pair of twin teens so wholesome that Wil Wheaton from Star Trek and Diane Chambers from Cheers come off as a chain & leather biker and his lady. A double shot of Billy Mays hawking Oxi-Clean and the PBA 10-X, and how to order a set of Ginzu knives.)

We were informed on the way over that the address had been the scene of egg-related vandalism a couple months prior, marking the area as a tough neighborhood. Upon arrival, we observed approximately 30 members of the Fourth Estate entering the back yard except for one group being stopped. The man doing the stopping identified himself as Coleman's assistant Erickson. He said we were on private property and he would decide which journalists would be admitted.

> Coleman staffer Tom Erickson is telling us we can't film their presser cuz we're not real news. We have Capitol creds. He says our pass is homemade. *(Mike McIntee at The UpTake)*

As much as we support the First Amendment of the Constitution guaranteeing freedom of the press, we were forced to agree with Erickson and advised McIntee, reporter Noah Kunin, and reporter Grace Kelly with the MN Progressive Project they would have to move away. Kunin contacted his headquarters for suggestions. A British accented, female voice (using "garden" in place of "yard") advised:

> Noah needs a trampoline in next door's garden. *(Mrs B at The UpTake)*

Despite her dancer's name, Grace Kelly acted more like the spunky Lois Lane of the *Daily Planet* ("a great metropolitan newspaper"). Grace went around to the Coleman back yard neighbors on the next street and worked from there.

But a Badger state blogger provided the real ingenuity. Wisconsin, a major dairy state producing wholesome, fresh milk, cheese curds for all ages, and, for those of responsible legal age in their jurisdictions, tasty beer, also produced this line from the home of the Packers.

> Noah can tape his iPhone to a broom handle and broadcast it over the hedge, or fence or whatever 'screen of secrecy' he has... StickCam® *(Joe in GB at The UpTake)*

Finally McIntee caught the eye of KARE-TV producer Tom Lindner who allowed the UpTake to use the Channel 11 video feed of Coleman's concession speech (best moments were opening & closing):

> The Supreme Court of Minnesota has spoken and I respect its decision and will abide by the result. It's time for Minnesota to come together under the leaders it has chosen and move forward. I join all Minnesotans in congratulating our newest United States Senator – Al Franken.
>
> ...we all should take a moment to thank Amy Klobuchar and her staff. They have done a great job of carrying the burden of two Senators these last six months. She is an extraordinary public servant. *(Norm Coleman quoted at The UpTake)*

Back in the Yugo, word came from HQ Governor Pawlenty would sign the Certificate of Election and later in the evening sent it on to Secretary of State Ritchie for his signature as well. We headed over to Minneapolis for the Franken statement. Streebeck took I-94, part of the national network of interstate highways connecting Minnesota with the rest of America. The Yugo's horsepower strained to meet the national speed limit of 55mph, but with the auxiliary set of bicycle pedals that sprang up from the floor at 32 mph, I was personally able to provide extra power and speed. As we arrived Streebeck tossed another link (and I don't mean sausage, mister) out the window that was caught by *Minnesota Independent* reporter Chris Steller.

The crowd of about 150 press types and ordinary, wholesome citizens were noisy but otherwise well-mannered at the Senator-elect's public acceptance. Mr. Franken announced he had had a gracious phone call in advance from Mr. Coleman.. The new Senator also announced he had spoken with Senate Majority leader Harry Reid.

> "I go to Washington DC not to be the 60th Democratic senator; I'm going to be the second senator from the state of Minnesota." *(quoted at Star Tribune)*

Even the editorial board of the *Star-Tribune* ("once a fine metropolitan newspaper") approved. They

> ...supported Coleman's bid for a second term. But we admire much about Franken's values and his desire for public service...We wish him well as he sets out to earn the trust of all of the people of Minnesota. *(Star Tribune)*

During questions, the junior Senator noted he would be on 4 Senate committees: Judiciary (so he will be in on the hearings for Justice Sotomayor, as well as the prosecution of all sorts of lying liars from the last 8 years), and Health, Education, Labor and Pensions (HELP) – the one squarely on the spot in the health care overhaul. He will also serve on the committee on Aging and, as he put it, "one that I asked for" Indian Affairs.

The crowd dispersed, offering the Frankens, and even us, salutations and jollifications. Streebeck and I called in our location as we settled in for a well-deserved dinner break of chili dogs.

I picked up my 8 pound SCR-536, "Donald Hings" Motorola walkie-talkie, warmed up the vacuum tubes and called in to HQ. Capt. told us "well done" and that we were authorized for an extra 20 minutes. I thanked him and lit up a Lucky Strike downwind of Streebeck, who has an allergic condition...

(Voiceover: On November 4th, election was held in and for the state of Minnesota, with a swearing in to follow. ~~In 238 days to today + six more 'til Monday~~ In a moment, the results of that swearing in.)

> *BBzzrt – Network Trouble, Please Stand By... The conclusion of this episode, complete with swearing in and the final chapter of this saga will be posted at a later date (probably Monday after it happens.)*

Sincerely,

Anders Dahlstrom,

station manager of Channel 1, YUST, southeast of Lake Wobegon.

Shalom...from Badge 714

(Steady drumroll. Brawny, sweaty forearm gripping steel rod pressed against stone wall. Other arm swings short mallet, "clang"...*(harder)* "CLANG")

A
Mark
VII
Limited
Production

STATE of MINNESOTA

EXECUTIVE DEPARTMENT

TIM PAWLENTY
GOVERNOR

Certificate of Election for Six-Year Term

To the President of the Senate of the United States:

This is to certify that on the fourth day of November, 2008, Al Franken was duly chosen by the qualified electors of the State of Minnesota a Senator from said State to represent said State in the Senate of the United States for the term of six years, beginning on the 3rd day of January, 2009.

Witness: His excellency our governor Tim Pawlenty, and our seal hereto affixed at Saint Paul, Minnesota this 30th day of June, in the year of our Lord 2009.

By the governor:

TIM PAWLENTY
Governor

MARK RITCHIE
Secretary of State

Hats Off, Patriots!
July 8, 2009

Comments: 204   Recs: 359   Tips: 352

(Cue music: "Fanfare for the Common Man" –Aaron Copeland)

After 245 days, flanked by former Vice President Mondale and Senior Senator Amy Klobuchar, on Tuesday, July 7 at 12:16pm EDT Alan Stuart Franken stood in the well of the United States Senate and raised his right hand. It took Vice President Joseph Biden about 28 seconds to recite the words of the oath of office. Al Franken, his hand on a Bible that once belonged to his mentor Paul Wellstone, responded simply, "I do." He was the 39th woman or man from Minnesota to do so since Henry Rice and James Shields first so swore in 1858.

Despite some efforts from the ushers in the visitor galleries, applause rose and continued most of three minutes as Senators pressed forward for handshakes and embraces. Senator Leahy gave Senator Franken a pen, holding it up first to say a few words about it.

There was no blood. Vice President Joe Biden's personal wealth did not spike in exchange for this swearing-in. The previous seat-holder, Norm Coleman, was not dead, not in exile, not an outlaw, but merely one of 4 million Minnesotans now represented in the Senate by Klobuchar and Franken.

> **DK**
>
> I was most struck by your putting this in perspective.
>
> As one who has worked on elections in some 15 other countries over the last two decades, in Africa and elsewhere, I can gladly testify that the American experience remains a model which millions of voters around the world aspire to emulate. And it's a model which hundreds, even thousands of foreign politicians aspire to overthrow, as they overthrow their own constitutions (viz. Niger, Madagascar, Iran, Honduras, et al.).
>
> I have used the Minnesota example – the close election, the recount, the trial, the SC ruling – as examples when speaking with local officials, voters and civil society activists – and I based my comments on the day-by-day, blow-by-blow reporting of WineRev (and, to a lesser extent due to connectivity issues, to TheUptake).
>
> So for the contribution you have made to my efforts to spread democracy in this corner of Africa, I doff (DOFF!!) my hat to you, sir. *(stevenwag)*

> **DK**
>
> The good men do dies with them... but not WineRev. For we now know these diaries have had an impact, however small, in other nations, nudging the world a little closer to solving our disputes with ballots, not bullets. *(blue aardvark)*

All 5 negatives in the last paragraph are possible thanks to statesmen and arguers over the Constitution like James Madison, George Mason and Roger Sherman. They are possible thanks to defenders of the Constitution like John Marshall, Abraham Lincoln, and Barbara Jordan. They are possible thanks to extenders of Constitutional liberties like Susan Anthony, Thaddeus Stevens and Thurgood Marshall.

As drama this moment rated hardly more than a C-Span re-run, and yet that is its tempered glory. The day was a shot in the gut to those who urge might makes right. The swearing-in was a gauntlet slapped to the face of those moved by the aristocratic impulse ("Some born to rule, others born to serve" – oddly never said by those serving. Ponder again Aristotle's question from 2,500 years ago: "Is aristocratic behavior how aristocrats behave, or behavior that preserves aristocracy?")

It was in miniature what happened January 20th, when one man moved out, and another man moved in, to public housing at 1600 Pennsylvania Avenue, with a 4 year lease (option to apply for one renewal.) Millions came for that one and millions more watched from around the globe. For the earliest arriving, most-senior Senator of the class of 2010, the ceremony yesterday was small, short and sweet, with dignity and a raft of smiles. But it warrants some jollification.

To Senator Franken: Hurrah! Huzzah! Whoooohoooo!

(WineRev stands and tosses (TOSSES!) *hat!)*

(Hat lands among others: a white day bonnet embroidered on one edge: "Abby Adams", a grey kepi, a John Deere cap, a three-corner job, a ladies' round skimmer with the inside liner marked "R. Parks", a blue kepi, a GI steel helmet, a black stovepipe. WineRev fetches back his own.)

This series, now a book, has been an accident. I set out to post a few diaries about a little footnote to Election 2008 – a recount in the MN Senate race – and add a little local color...but things got a little out of hand.

157 diaries out of hand. 300,000 words out of hand.

Now I had help getting out of hand: the 1963 MN legislature and their Recount law. Secretary of State Mark Ritchie and his staff. 87 county auditors. Over 30,000 poll workers in 4,131 precincts. Hundreds of Coleman and 2,000 Franken recount monitors and ballot challengers.

I had help getting out of hand: lawyers local and lawyers from Seattle to DC. Law professors from L.A. Loyola to Duke via Ohio State. 5 canvassing board members and 8 judges--good women and men, tried, tested and found equal to every lawyer, law and precedent in the room.

I had help getting out of hand: Jimmy Olson and Lois Lane wannabes, Woodward and Bernstein look-alikes from the UpTake to the (MN (distributive axiom) Post, Independent, Progressive Project and Publius.) They all came across like Clark Kent AFTER visiting the phone booth and made the yo-yos at the Star Tribune and the rapscallions at the Wall Street Journal look like hungover Mortimer Snerds.

And then there were YOU! You! with the 18,000 comments at DailyKos and the UpTake live blog, cranking out almost half a million (!) words! You! with words of insight, law, humor, explanation. You! blew coffee on your monitors, corrected spelling, recoiled appropriately from both lutefisk and Ben Ginsberg, pondered 17 below zero, translated from geek to English so we all understood the Coleman credit card security breech, laughed at lawyers and their light sabers.

So this has been a community effort. I have been the catalyst but you! have been the engaged citizenry, the informed estate, the wisdom of crowds, the body politic and the audience of activists in the Great Orange Hall that Kos Built. Your personal support came through, whether hed pots, legal counsel, Hebrew pun translation, or lessons in writing Yoda. Your good wishes, your reading and caring about a tedious and exasperating exercise of democracy – well for all that:

(WineRev stands and doffs (DOFFS!) *hat to the Kossacks!)*

The argument is settled, the contest decided. I will continue to hang around these boards, putting up diaries, cracking wise in comments, laughing, fuming or shedding a tear by turns. There will come other causes that need to be winerevved. The "morons" still bleat, the "ass"inine still haunt the RNC, the proto-fascists still spew their jingoistic mirages. Mock-moral plastic patriots still win headlines from Bachmannlandia to Wasilla to Argentina. All these will feel the lash of my keyboard.

> *My thanks too, for remembering (and reminding us) that all politics is local. For keeping it in perspective. For making us laugh when tears or rage threatened. And for always-always-always bringing to the fore that HOW we got here is just as important as getting here. The saga of this process is -- as you point out -- a microcosm of the "great experiment" in democracy. That it was clean, open, fair, and ultimately correct is the real win for all of us. (rincewind)*

But on this topic, the struggle for the senate seat of Minnesota, I hope you will let me hang up my hat.

Kossacks *(en masse, firmly):* No.

WineRev: Just this race. Just this hat.

Kossacks: No.

(WineRev looks sidelong at Kossacks)

WineRev: You'd do it for Randolph Scott.

Kossacks *(gasping, rising to feet, all uncover heads):* Randolph Scott??! *(Orchestral music; 6 part harmony with descant; sung)* Randolph Scott!

Markos: Okay, WineRev. Just this race. Just this hat.

DK

As he rides his tan palomino off into the sunset, a burnt orange sunbeam glimmering off his Gucci saddlebags, we wave a fond farewell to WineRev. His diaries kept us informed, entertained, and hopeful in the vast wasteland of Rovian politics that still lingers 9 months after the call to change. We salute you with this Laurel. . . and Hardy handshake. We the citizens of Rock Ridge, will never forget you. *(dditt)*

DK

Congratulations, sir. You have fought the good fight; you have finished the race; your hat is well hung. *(blue aardvark)*

Thank you for all your help and kindness. Until I write you next, good afternoon, good evening and good night, from yust southeast of Lake Wobegon.

Shalom.

The Final Word: Mighty Coleman Has Struck Out!

by Terrible Tom, originally posted at DailyKos

The outlook wasn't brilliant for the Thugville slate that day,
McCain struck out and Palin popped a bunt to Tina Fey.
And then, when Dole imploded and Sununu came up lame,
A sickly silence fell upon the patrons of their game.

   In unison, the Dittoheads blamed Acorn for the mess
   While others held out for a hope that sprung within their breasts:
   They thought, "If only Coleman can hold on to his small lead,
   We can filibuster every day; it's forty-one we need!"

Yet Chambliss was in trouble and with Wicker in a slump –
The two of them are morans and they sound like Forest Gump;
The feckless faithful who remained were looking mighty glum
For there seemed but little chance of Coleman batting forty-one.

   But Musgrove soon walked Wicker who was glad to take his base;
   Then Chambliss finally beat a pickle, barely saving face.
   And when the dust had settled and they saw what had occurred,
   There was Saxby standing safe at first and Wicker huggin' third.

Then out from Minnesota there arose a lusty yell,
"The people here have spoken and the Dems can go to hell."
And Lo! the librul New York Times picked up this shameless screed:
Norm Coleman, mighty Coleman, called for Franken to concede.

   There was ease in Coleman's manner as he calmly made his speech,
   Delivered with a Brooklyn pride through Hall-of-Famer teeth.
   Responding to the cheers, he said, "So there! I have prevailed";
   No stranger in the crowd could doubt 'twas Franken who had failed.

The nation's eyes were on him as he claimed his victory;
"The winning score's been tallied and there's been no trickery;
A gentleman would spare the cost of counting once again
So Al, resume your day job as a crass comedian."

   But it seems there was a curve ball hung in Minnesota law,
   that applied to any contest that was so close to a draw.
   The umpire had no choice in this: A replay must be done
   to make the call conclusively on which side really won.

   And then in extra innings, Coleman's grin turned to a pout
   When Franken filled the bases in the tenth with no one out.
   Before the count reached three and two, Norm went to court instead.
   "You have got to call a rainout." "Strike one," the umpire said.

"Fraud," cried a dozen Freepers, and the echo answered "Fraud."
It was time to make a brilliant move – the faithful all were awed –
When Coleman clenched his dentures in a gesture all could see,
And he waved-in 'Righty' Ginsberg, just acquired from D.C.

   While tossing sliders to the press, Ol' Ginsberg clearly shone;
   He chattered on for ten long weeks and so the game went on;
   But Friedberg's knuckleballs went wild—inside and wide they flew –
   Until at last the guy was gassed. The umpires said, "Strike two."

From the bleachers of the beltway, all the Thugville fans got loud
And Harry Reid was speechless; he could not control the crowd.
"Kill them; kill the umpires!" shouted Cornyn, Kyl and Steele;
And it's likely they'd have killed them if it weren't for this appeal.

   The sneer is gone from Coleman's lip; his chin is soaked with foam.
   And Ginsberg pounds the podium before he heads for home.
   And now five umpires heard his pitch, and now the five have ruled
   As Franken rounds the bases since not one of them was fooled.

Oh, somewhere in this favored land the sky is shining bright;
A tax cut takes effect somewhere, and somewhere soldiers fight.
And somewhere gays are cowering, and somewhere bigots shout;
But there is no joy in Thugville—mighty Coleman has Struck Out.

Appendix A
Timeline of Events

Date	Major Events	Difference
11/4/2008	Election Day	Coleman +775
11/5/2008	**Coleman** claims win, says he would "step back" from a recount if he were trailing. **Franken** says we'll "have to wait a little longer" to find out who won.	Coleman +447 (*SoS later reports difference of +443*)
11/12/2008	Secretary of State Ritchie names **State Canvassing Board**: **Eric Magnuson**, Chief Justice, **MN Supreme Court** **G. Barry Anderson**, Assoc Justice **MN Supreme Court** **Kathleen Gearin**, Asst Chief Judge, Ramsey Co. **Edward Cleary**, Asst. Chief Judge, Ramsey Co. **Mark Ritchie, SoS**, MN, Chief Elections Officer	Coleman +206
11/13/2008	**Franken** campaign files suit over 461 absentee ballots rejected in Hennepin & Ramsey Counties . **WineRev** posts diary #1.	Coleman +206
11/15/2008	**Jay Leno** states "Minnesota" is an old Indian word for "Florida."	Coleman +206
11/16/2008	Attorneys noted for both campaigns: **Coleman** - **Fritz Knaak & Tony Trimble** **Franken** - **David Lillehaug & Marc Elias**	Coleman +206
11/17/2008	**Franken** campaign files brief with **SoS Ritchie** asking rejected absentee ballots be included in certified vote totals. **AG Lorie Swanson** rules those ballots "are not cast in an election"; request denied. **SoS Ritchie** releases final list of 107 recount location sites.	Coleman +206
11/18/2008	**State Canvassing Board**'s first meeting; **SoS Ritchie** officially announces Recount. **Franken** legal team files brief to **SCB** asking the Board to reconsider including the rejected ballots in the recount. First mentions of *lefse* and *lutefisk*.	Coleman +215
11/19/2008	Recount officially starts. **Franken** briefs **Harry Reid** on recount and receives update on upcoming legislation. Ramsey Co rules in favor of **Franken** re access to names of absentee voters . First appearance of **Joe Mansky**, election director.	Coleman +174
11/20/2008	Ballots challenged today: **Franken** 374, **Coleman** 360 Ballot marked via write-in for **"Lizard People"** (and **Franken**) **Coleman** challenges.	Coleman +129
11/21/2008	61% of ballots recounted. First **WineRev** Patriotic moment. **Mark Ritchie** called a Communist. First notice challenged ballots can be Unchallenged.	Coleman +115
11/22/2008	Woman recounter in Dakota Co. caught putting 26 Franklin ballots in 25-count ballot piles. She had done this at least 6 times. No word on consequences.	Coleman +167
11/23/2008	St. Paul Saints baseball team announces May, 2009 game will feature a "Re" Count figurine giveaway, with **Coleman**'s face on one side and **Franken**'s face on the other	Coleman +167
11/24/2008	Joe the Plumber inks a book deal; **WineRev** goes ballistic. Mower Co. auditor scolds **Franken** representative for making challenges; **The UpTake** citizen journalism group breaks story, rides to rescue. **Franken** campaign states **Coleman**'s margin is under 100 votes. First note of 1865 (!) court case Taylor v. Taylor on MN election law.	Coleman +172

11/25/2008	61 uncounted ballots discovered in Becker County.	Coleman +238
11/26/2008	**State Canvassing Board** meets to question both campaigns. **Franken** campaign has obtained 6,400 names and addresses of rejected absentee voters from 66 of the 87 counties. Board sides with **Coleman**: SCB does not have jurisdiction over rejected absentee ballots, but county boards do.	Coleman +238
11/27/2008	Folks crank up **Arlo Guthrie**'s "Alice's Restaurant" and eat lots of turkey. UT slams A&M 49-9.	Coleman +238
11/30/2008	**Coleman** campaign manager **Cullen Sheehan** is "stunned, STUNNED!" **Franken** team has read US Constitution that **US Senate** can determine its own members.	Coleman +238
12/1/2008	**Elias** notes as many as 700 ballots from the original count may be missing. **SoS** office e-mails all 87 counties asking them to re-sort Rejected Absentee ballots into 4 "piles" (reason for rejection under law) and a "5th pile" for those rejected for other reasons, including by mistake.	Coleman +344
12/2/2008	The count changes again.	Coleman +303
12/5/2008	Minneapolis recount does not turn up missing 133 ballots but does turn up an uncounted 20 overseas/military ballots. **Franken** side calls for a "forensic search" of church where voting was held. **Coleman** side calls this "raiding the church."	Coleman +192
12/8/2008	Minneapolis suspends search for missing 133 ballots. Will use original machine counts and voter sign-in logs to count.	Coleman +192
12/9/2008	**SoS** will award the withdrawn challenges to candidates before the **State Canvassing Board** meets Dec. 16.	Coleman +192
12/10/2008	**Elias** requests that the "5th pile" (rejected ballots that don't meet one of the 4 statutory reasons for rejection) be counted. **Coleman** side argues missing Mpls 133 ballots should not be included	Coleman +192
12/11/2008	**Franken** campaign sends 62 affidavits to the **State Canvassing Board** of voters who voted absentee and were informed their vote was not counted. **Attorney General** states the scope of the recount is limited to the "determination of the number of votes validly cast." The queston before the Board is to determine if the votes were cast.	Coleman +192
12/12/2008	**State Canvassing Board** (5-0) includes missing 133 Minneapolis ballots in Recount. Net gain to **Franken** +46. Only challenged and rejected absentee ballots remain to be counted. Board releases AG opinion on "5th pile" ballots: count them if both sides agree. **WineRev**'s diary placed on **DailyKos** FrontPage.	Coleman +188
12/14/2008	**WineRev** gives a 10% chance of a Certificate of Election being issued by Dec 19th.	
12/15/2008	**Coleman**'s files for TRO with the **MN Supreme Court** to halt counting of rejected absentee ballots that have been un-rejected. Hennepin Co. is opening & counting "5th pile" ballots as valid; sending adjusted totals to **SoS**.	Coleman +188
12/16/2008	**State Canvassing Board** publicly rules on 206 of **Franken**'s 436 challenged ballots. No final list of **Coleman** challenges, may add MORE. Board NOT pleased. First time: **Coleman** raises possible 137 precincts where original and duplicate ballots may have been double-counted; **Franken** counters this is changing rules. **Franken** files suit in Olmsted Co.: election officials accepted 27 absentee ballots but mistakenly put them in the rejection pile.	Coleman +188
12/17/2008	**MN Supreme Court** hears oral arguments on TRO request, NFL Films style. Board has considered 415 **Franken** challenges; 93% completed.	Coleman +188

12/18/2008	Board reviews 642 challenges including 1 where voter added to **Franken**'s name: **Franken***stin*. (Challenge denied, 3-2). **MN Supreme Court** denies the **Coleman** TRO by a 5-0 vote; denies request to stop sorting rejected absentee ballots into 5 piles, 5-0. By 3-2 decision orders County Election Boards to decide "5th pile" ballots open and count them *with agreement of BOTH campaigns*. **Coleman** files **MNSC** motion over "double counted" ballots.	Coleman +5
12/20/2008	Norwegian extroverts defined	Franken +41
12/21/2008	**Franken** camp states after withdrawn challenges are added back into vote totals they will lead by 35-50 votes. **WineRev** sings with the choir (in -20 degree windchill)	Franken +41
12/22/2008	Hennepin County Canvassing Board files brief with the **MNSC** denying facts **Coleman** is using in suit	Franken +48
12/23/2008	*Pioneer Press* notes **Ben Ginsberg** has been advising the **Coleman** recount legal team since late November. **Ginsberg**: legal advisor to the 2004 Swift Boaters; central role in the 2000 Florida recount. **Ritchie** sets goal of Jan. 6 to certify a winner. **WineRev** rants. **MNSC** hear oral arguments re: possible "double-counted" ballots.	Franken +47
12/24/2008	**MN Supreme Court** agrees to request for extension to Jan 4th by **SoS Ritchie** and AG **Swanson**: all "5th pile" ballots will be sent to the **SoS**' office unopened for counting Jan 4th. **MN Supreme Court** denies (5-0) **Coleman**'s request for a TRO to prevent certification of results. Denies (5-0) jurisdiction over "double-counted" ballots BUT directs **Coleman** to "**Election Contest Court**" (First time ECC) to settle this.	Franken +47
12/27/2008	**WineRev** sees **SoS** office at Wimbeldon.	Franken +47
12/29/2008	**SoS Ritchie** notes 1,346 ballots have been noted as improperly rejected absentee ballots. **Franken** agrees to count these; **Coleman** wants to count some of them AND add 654 legally barred ballots. First appearance of **Franken** attorney **Kevin Hamilton.**	Franken +47
12/30/2008	Cameras for meeting turned on by **UpTake** technicians. MN GOP accuses Board of liberal bias for allowing. Anoka Co. talks between camps re: rejected absentee ballots break down. County auditor **Rachel Smith** sends all home after 8 minutes of bickering.	Franken +50
12/31/2008	**Coleman**'s files with the **MN Supreme Court** to get their list of 654 ballots included in the 5th pile ballot. **The UpTake** tells off the MN GOP. First appearance of *Horse Dentures*.	Franken +50
1/2/2009	Rejected absentee ballots to be counted stand at 953; remaining 393 are in limbo because 1 of the 3 parties objected.	Franken +49
1/3/2009	Sen. **Coleman**'s term officially expires at 11:00am CST. 954 improperly rejected absentee ballots opened by **SoS Ritchie**'s office; **Franken** nets +176. 20,000 people worldwide watch count on **the UpTake** on-line.	Franken +225
1/5/2009	**MN Supreme Court** (5-0) rejects **Coleman**'s request to include 654 additional rejected ballots. Board certifies count: **Franken** 1,212,431; **Coleman**, 1,212,206 *Wall Street Journal* editorial calls **Franken**'s victory "illegitimate;" **WineRev** flings (FLINGS!) hat at WSJ. **Coleman** will contest the election and Recount results; states he won the election and now must prove it in court.	Franken +225
1/6/2009	Election contest filed by **Coleman**. **Judge Cleary** of SCB writes open letter denouncing WSJ editorial.	Franken +225

1/7/2009	The UpTake notes **Coleman** is trying to add 654 rejected absentee ballots, BUT on Nov 10th, **Coleman**'s team blog stated **Franken**'s attempt to count rejected absentee ballots was "stuffing the ballot box."	Franken +225
	A Roseau Co. felony sex offender w/o voting rights voted for **Coleman**: *Strib*, Rightwing Blog Powerline denounces WSJ editorial.	
1/8/2009	Chief Justice **Magnuson** recuses self from naming 3-judge **Election Contest Court (ECC)** and gives task to sr. Assoc. Justice **Alan Page**.	Franken +225
	Illinois House votes to impeach Governor **Rod Blagojevich**.	
1/9/2009	**Coleman** subpoenas Blue Earth, Stearns, and Ramsey counties for absentee ballot applications and election day registration applications; due January 14th.	Franken +225
1/12/2009	The cost for complying with the document requests will be borne entirely by the **Coleman** team.	Franken +225
	Justice **Alan Page** names 3-judge panel for the Election Contest: **Elizabeth Hayden** (Presiding); **Denise Reilly**, and **Kurt Marben**.	
	Franken sends letter to **SoS Ritchie** and **Gov Pawlenty** requesting a Certificate of Election; both declined.	
	Franken files answering brief for Election Contest.	
	MN Democratic Party (DFL) files a formal complaint with the **Federal Elections Commission** re **Coleman**'s fund raising efforts.	
1/13/2009	**Franken** files with the **MN Supreme Court** asking **Pawlenty** and **Ritchie** produce a Certificate of Election.	Franken +225
	64 of the 400 absentee voters whose votes had not been counted file affidavits with the **MN Supreme Court**. Led by attorney **Nauen**; First appearance of "Nauen64."	
1/14/2009	**MN Supreme Court** schedules Feb. 5 for oral arguments on **Franken**'s request for Certificate of Election.	Franken +225
	Coleman proposes ECC trial calendar w/action beginning Feb. 9.	
1/15/2009	ECC will start Jan 21, and open with **Franken**'s Motion to Dismiss.	Franken +225
	Franken proposes ECC trial calendar opening Jan. 26 & ending Feb. 13.	
	US Senate allows **Coleman**'s former Senate staff access to his office to archive files and send constituent cases to office to **Sen Klobuchar**'s office.	
1/16/2009	**MN Supreme Court** combines all 64 individual suits on absentee ballots into one suit, (Nauen64) and refers the suit to the ECC.	Franken +225
	Attorney **Joe Friedberg** added to **Coleman** legal team.	
1/19/2009	**Coleman** team wants to include all 12,000 rejected absentee ballots, regardless of whether they had been correctly rejected or not.	Franken +225
	Coleman's new attorney, **Friedberg**, quoted: he "Would do anything for Norm, except vote for him."	
	MN media outlets petition ECC to permit cameras for proceedings. Both camps agree .	
1/20/2009	**Bush**'s term ends at noon EST.	Franken +225
	Identity of trial experts disclosed .	
	First mention of "universe of ballots."	
1/21/2009	First full day of the Restoration of Constitutional Democracy.	Franken +225
	ECC hears **Franken**'s Motion to Dismiss.	
	21 motions and briefs connected to summary judgment filed **Coleman** proposes all 12,000 rejected absentee ballots be brought before ECC.	
1/22/2009	ECC denies **Franken** Motion to Dismiss.	Franken +225
	ECC denies **Coleman** proposal to examine all 12,000 rejected absentee ballots.	
	ECC issues 75 page Order for Trial Rules.	
	Coleman proposes 86 "inspectors" examine absentee ballots & voter rolls.	
	Coleman takes job as lobbyist for Republican Jewish Coalition.	

1/23/2009	Court hears motions for summary judgment, followed by a pre-trial status conference. ECC denies **Coleman** motion for 86 inspectors.	Franken +225
1/26/2009	ECC trial starts; **Coleman** team sloppy handling of evidence immediately apparent.	Franken +225
1/28/2009	**Coleman** side moves to strike its first 2 days of trial; granted. Re-starts case.	Franken +225
1/29/2009	Illinois Senate unanimously votes to remove Governor **Rod Blagojevich** from office.	Franken +225
1/30/2009	**Coleman** moves to bar **Franken** side from using **Coleman** legal team statements against them in court. Denied. **Coleman** campaign claims upsurge of absentee MN voters looking to join **Coleman** case and/or make donations to his effort was so great it crashed their computers. Claims proven false in hours. **WineRev** goes to Florida to visit mother.	Franken +225
1/31/2009	"Nauen64" group of voters reduced to "Nauen61."	Franken +225
2/1/2009	**WineRev** rants (with a sword) against CNN's **Alex Castellanos**.	Franken +225
2/4/2009	ECC rules **Coleman** "universe" of possible rejected absentee ballots is limited to 4,797. Rules 392 "Pile 5" Improperly rejected absentee ballots WILL be counted.	Franken +225
2/5/2009	Texas lawsuit alleging **Nasser Kazeminy** illegally funneled $75K to **Coleman** is delayed for 60 days . **MN Supreme Court** hears **Franken** Motion for Certificate of Election apart from ECC process.	Franken +225
2/6/2009	**Coleman** declares, "God wants me to serve."	Franken +225
2/7/2009	Secretary of State **Mark Ritchie** gives keynote address at the National Association of Secretaries of State meeting in Washington, DC.	Franken +225
2/9/2009	**WineRev** opens a magnum of "Chateau du Rant, '09" against the **Coleman** team.	Franken +225
2/10/2009	ECC rules on 10 motions, declares 174 **Coleman** ballots inadmissibll late, so shrinks **Coleman** ballots from 4,797 to 4,623. ECC rules 24 of 61 **Nauen** ballots to be counted (**Franken** +24). ECC orders both sides to submit arguments by 2/11/2009 on whether 19 categories of absentee ballots are legal.	Franken +249
2/11/2009	ECC receives written arguments from both sides on the 19 categories.	Franken +249
2/12/2009	**Abraham Lincoln**'s 200th birthday **Charles Darwin**'s 200th birthday ECC hears oral arguments regarding the 19 categories.	Franken +249
2/13/2009	Friday the 13th **Coleman** lawyer **James Langdon** says to ECC **Judge Reilly**, "I see you are not buying this, are you?" ECC rules 12 of 19 categories are out ("The Friday the 13th Ruling"). **Coleman** universe of disputed ballots reduced to approximately 3,300.	Franken +249
2/14/2009	~~Valentine's Day~~ "Talk Like a Gangster Day"	Franken +249
2/16/2009	Presidents Day ECC holds "Motions Day" – a dud. **WineRev** predicts EC will last four more weeks; notes lawyer jokes.	Franken +249
2/17/2009	ECC rules **Franken** may expand his universe of 771 ballots but must file by February 20th.	Franken +249
2/18/2009	ECC rejects **Coleman**'s plea to reconsider the Friday the 13th ruling on the 19 categories. **Ben Ginsberg** files pro hac vice motion to appear as an attorney for **Coleman**. **The Uptake** holds a Meet-n-Greet at Groveland Tap in St. Paul.	Franken +249

2/19/2009	WineRev is interviewed by **Mike McIntee** of **The Uptake** on Minneapolis radio station KTNF.	Franken +249
	Ben Ginsberg is admitted as "pro hac vice" attorney to the case for Coleman.	
	Kossacks begin to call for publication of **WineRev**'s MN-Sen diaries.	
2/20/2009	**Coleman** team attempts to renege on earlier "stipulation with prejudice" re: absentee ballots.	Franken +249
	Franken team files written response and calls for *sanctions* against **Coleman** attorneys. **ECC** hears oral arguments this afternoon.	
	Deadline for **Franken** universe expansion moved to February 21st.	
2/21/2009	**Franken** team defines Universe de **Franken** of ballots at 1,585.	Franken +249
2/22/2009	**George Washington**'s Birthday	Franken +249
2/23/2009	19 of 37 rejected Nauen voters file motion to have their votes counted **Coleman** team announces their universe has shrunk to about 2,000 ballots.	Franken +249
	ECC orders 12 ballots opened later and included in the vote total.	
2/24/2009	Estonian Independence Day	~~Franken +249~~
	Kossack **Clem Yeobright** predicts **Franken** will be sworn in June 33rd.	Franken +261 *(Maybe)*
	ECC denies **Coleman** request to renege on "stipulation w/ preudice" but does not impose sanctions as requested by **Franken**.	
	ECC denies **Coleman** motion to treat all 10,962 rejected absentee ballots as a class action suit.	
2/25/2009	**Nauen** files petition with the **MN Supreme Court** for 30 more voters to have their votes counted.	Franken +249
	Franken attorney **Lillehaug** mores to strike testimony of **Coleman** witness Pamela Howell because violation of discovery rules. Granted.	
	Apology. Team **Coleman** almost tampers with witness. Renewed motion to strike. Granted.	
	WineRev describes all as a curling match.	
2/26/2009	**ECC** vacates order striking Howell's testimony.	Franken +249
	ECC orders absentee ballots of unregistered voters to be opened to see if a registration card is in the sealed envelope (AKA "Pile 3A ballots").	
	Ben Ginsberg withdraws as attorney for Coleman but continues as spokesman.	
	ECC grants **Franken** motion to prevent **Coleman** from gathering evidence from county election officials by email rather than having them testify in person.	
2/27/2009	**ECC** suspends **Howell**'s testimony when revealed there were additional discovery violations.	Franken +249
	Coleman team moves to re-examine all 286,000 absentee ballots statewide. Submit proposal to do this mathematically/statistically rather than one-by-one.	
	WineRev diary goes *Casablanca.*	
3/2/2009	**Howell** completes testimony **Coleman** "provisionally" rests case **ECC** rules 3 of 24 previously admitted Nauen ballots thrown out for registration issues (**Franken** -3).	Franken +246
	ECC sanctions **Coleman** attorney **Tony Trimble** $7,500 for discovery violations.	
3/3/2009	**Franken** opens case in **ECC** trial; calls 24 witnesses.	Franken +246
	Franken attorneys send letter to **ECC** arguing down **Coleman** proposal to re-examine 286,000 absentee ballots.	
3/4/2009	**ECC** rejects **Coleman** attempt to add additional evidence to the record and officially rests the **Coleman** case.	Franken +246

3/5/2009	Franken files motion to dismiss some or all claims made in **Coleman** case; contends **Coleman** has only proved 9 (!) ballots need to be recounted.	Franken +246
	Coleman files motion in **MN Supreme Court** to intervene in the **Nauen 30** case.	
3/6/2009	**Coleman** files response to **Franken**'s motion to dismiss, ECC hears orals on motion.	Franken +246
	MN Supreme Court denies (5-0) **Franken**'s request for an election certificate stating, "...a certificate of election cannot be issued until the *state* courts have finally decided on an election contest pending..."	
	Franken attorney **Lillehaug** says **Coleman** case is "Big Boat, No Walleye," coining an instant "old saying."	
3/8/2009	**WineRev** delivers rant against *StarTrib*'s **Pat Doyle**.	Franken +246
3/9/2009	**MN Supreme Court** deny **Nauen 30** petition to be heard by **ECC**.	Franken +246
3/10/2009	Last **Franken** witnesses delayed by snowstorm.	Franken +246
	State hockey tournament opens.	
3/11/2009	**Franken** case rests.	Franken +246
	Nauen61 final arguments heard (26 voters left in group).	
	Coleman campaign leaves credit card info of donators unsecured on Internet; denies wrong-doing, notifies 4,000 card holders to close accounts; blames those who exposed problem.	
	First day of **Coleman** Rebuttal.	
3/12/2009	**WineRev** writes diary #100.	Franken +246
	Coleman continues rebuttal.	
3/13/2009	ECC closing arguments: **Friedberg** for **Coleman**, **Hamilton** for **Franken**.	Franken +246
3/14/2009	**WineRev** grades lawyers & ECC .	Franken +246
3/17/2009	St. Patrick's Day	Franken +246
	Both sides due to submit Proposed Findings of Facts.	
3/20/2009	**Coleman** attorney **Joe Friedberg** on KFAN radio interview concedes **Franken** leads and will likely win **ECC** case.	Franken +246
3/26/2009	UpTake Meet & Greet Event to pass time waiting for **ECC** decision.	Franken +246
3/30/2009	NY-20 special election ends with Recount needed. Both camps look to **Coleman** v. **Franken** for guidance & inspiration.	Franken +246
3/31/2009	ECC: 32 page ruling ordering 400 absentee ballots collected from counties and brought to **SoS** office by April 6. If they all pass legal muster, opened and counted April 7.	Franken +246
	WineRev writes up ruling as biathlon event.	
4/1/2009	**National Republican Congressional Committee** puts out letter to fund **Tedisco**'s recount effort vs. **Murphy** in NY-20, claiming **Franken** and Democrats are "stealing the Senate election in Minneosta."	Franken +246
	"**WineRevving**" becomes a verb.	
4/2/2009	**NY Supreme Court** issues injunction to impound all voting machines in NY-20 until all absentee ballots are received.	Franken +246
4/7/2009	ECC rules several rejected absentee ballots defective. 353 ballots opened and counted by **SoS** Election Director Gary Poser; **Franken** 198, **Coleman** 111, Other 42.	Franken +312
4/12/2009	ECC orders final **Nauen24** dismissed.	Franken +312
4/13/2009	ECC issues 68-page Finding of Fact: **Coleman** did not make the case.	Franken +312
	Conclusions of Law: Supports **Franken** and 25 pages on why Equal Protection arguments fail. Election was clean and fair. MN should be proud. **Franken** wins by 312 votes and deserves Certificate of Election.	
	Coleman can appeal to **MN Supreme Court** within 10 days.	
4/16/2009	Public opinion polls show over 60% of Minnesotans want **Coleman** to concede.	Franken +312
4/17/2009	"Pull a **Coleman**" (vb. To delay conceding in a hopeless cause) goes national on *Larry King Live*.	Franken +312

4/20/2009	**Coleman** formally files Appeal to **MN Supreme Court**; ECC erred in its decision mostly on grounds of equal protection.	Franken +312
4/23/2009	**Franken** team sends **Coleman** side bill via affidavit for $16,000 for attorney costs for the 3 days of the **Pamela Howell** fiasco.	Franken +312

4/24/2009	MN Supreme Court sets appeal calendar:
	
	  Coleman Brief due April 30
	
	   Franken Response May 11
	
	  Coleman's Reply to Response May 15
	
	  Oral arguments June 1
	
	In NY-20, **Jim Tedisco** concedes to **Scott Murphy**.
		Franken +312

4/26/2009	MN Poll: 64% of Minnesotans want **Coleman** to quit.	Franken +312
4/29/2009	Senator **Arlen Specter** (PA) leaves Republican Party to join Democratic Party.	Franken +312
4/30/2009	**Coleman** files Appeal Brief: 62 pages.	Franken +312
5/6/2009	**WineRev** goes off on neo-Democrat **Arlen Specter** for saying MN Recount has been unjust to Norm **Coleman**. He then leaves for Florida to visit **Mama WineRev**.	Franken +312
5/11/2009	**Franken** files Respondent's Brief: 50+ pages dismantling Appeal Brief. Closes by asking Court to not only find for **Franken** but direct Governor to issue Certificate of Election upon decision. Former MN Governor **Jesse Ventura** calls **Dick Cheney** a coward on *Larry King Live*.	Franken +312
5/12/2009	**WineRev** returns from Florida	Franken +312
5/13/2009	**Coleman** files Reply to **Franken**: 33 pages.	Franken +312
5/17/2009	Norwegian Independence Day	Franken +312
5/20/2009	*St. Paul Pioneer Press* poll: 63% polled think **Franken** will be seated as Senator. 54% want **Coleman** to concede without waiting for **Supreme Court**.	Franken +312
5/21/2009	Al Franken's Birthday	Franken +312
6/1/2009	Oral arguments, MN Supreme Court, Coleman v. Franken. **Friedberg** for **Coleman**, **Elias** for **Franken**. **Friedberg** admits there was no election fraud and no voter fraud. Justices' questioning skeptical of **Coleman**'s evidence (lacking) and hence need for Constitutional issue of equal protection.	Franken +312
6/17/2009	**WineRev** writes open letter to **Supreme Court** asking for decision for sake of mental health.	Franken +312
6/30/2009	**MN Supreme Court** rules 5-0 in favor of **Franken** **Coleman** concedes. **Governor Tim Pawlenty** and **Secretary of State Mark Ritchie** sign Certificate of Election.	Franken +312
7/7/2009	Al **Franken** is sworn in as the junior senator from the State of Minnesota by **Vice President Joe Biden**.	

Appendix B
List of Sources

Alberta Lea Tribune	albertleatribune.com
Center for Independent Media	publicintegrity.org
Duluth News Tribune	duluthnewstribune.com
Election Law @ Moritz	moritzlaw.osu.edu/electionlaw/index.php
FiveThirtyEight	fivethirtyeight.com
Huffington Post	huffingtonpost.com
Mankato Free Press	mankatofreepress.com
Media Matters for America	mediamatters.org
Minn Post	minnpost.com
Minneapolis Star Tribune	startribune.com
Minnesota Independent	minnesotaindependent.com
Minnesota Judicial Branch	mncourts.gov
Minnesota Public Radio	minnesota.publicradio.org
Minnesota Secretary of State	sos.state.mn.us
MN Blue	mnblue.com
MN Democrats Exposed	minnesotademocratsexposed.com
MN Plubius	mnplubius.com
MN Progressive Project	mnprogressiveproject.com
New York Times	nytimes.com
Newsmax	newsmax.com
Politico	politico.com
Power Line	powerlineblog.com
Roll Call	rollcall.com
St. Cloud Times	sctimes.com
St. Paul Pioneer Press	twincities.com
Talking Points Memo	talkingpointsmemo.com
The Hill	thehill.com
The Timberjay Newspapers	timberjay.com
The UpTake	theuptake.org
Think Progress	thinkprogress.org

Photo Credits

Front Cover: Minnesota Independent; Franken for Senate, http://blog.alfranken.com/content/media

Page ii: http://millcreek.com/shop/images/planterg.jpg

Pages 1-2, 117, 165, 364-365, 383: Minnesota Judicial Branch

Page 233: Kayakbiker, Minneapolis, Minnesota

Page 287: Franken for Senate, http://blog.alfranken.com/content/media

Page 358: Paul Demko, Minnesota Independent

Page 361: Franken for Senate, http://blog.alfranken.com/content/media

Page 381: Chris Steller, Minnesota Independent

Page 384: Noah Kunin, The UpTake

Back Cover: Author self-portrai